796.522 Wolf

 W9-ASX-026

796.522 Wolf

Praise for *High Summits*

"Great things are done when men and mountains meet," wrote English poet William Blake in 1808. A goodly share of those great things are annotated in Fred Wolfe's labor of love of mountains. *High Summits* is a monumental effort, in which Wolfe covers an expanding universe of major moments of mountaineering history, seasoned by a rucksack full of fascinating miscellanea about the explorers and their sometimes curious ways."

> Dr. Thomas Hornbein
> First ascent of Mount Everest's
>   West Ridge in 1963
> Author of *Everest, The West Ridge*
> 2011 Inductee to the American Alpine Club's
> Hall of Mountaineering Excellence

"Wolfe has opened the door on a vast and intriguing history of international mountaineering and has done it well."

> Robert Craig
> Founder of Colorado's Keystone Center
> Past President of the American Alpine Club
> Member of the 1953 American
>   K2 Expedition
> 2010 Inductee to the American Alpine Club's
> Hall of Mountaineering Excellence

"Fred Wolfe has given mountaineers, mountaineering aficionados, and mountain historians both an invaluable reference and a fascinating compendium of mountaineering activities. Included are not only well-known ascents of major peaks, but a unique and useful chronology of mountaineering miscellanea. A rare achievement."

> John Evans
> First ascents of Antarctica's
> Mounts Vinson and Tyree

"Fred Wolfe has created the ultimate reference for climbers, for those who love the mountains, for history buffs, and for anyone with a curiosity about climbing, mountaineering and the events surrounding these adventures. The changes associated with mountaineering are all here: clothing, equipment, techniques, routes, new innovations, as well as important medical discoveries from the beginning of time. Researching and collating these facts must have been as arduous and thrilling as climbing an 8,000 meter peak successfully. What an achievement!"

> Dr. Benjamin Honigman
> Medical Director of the Altitude Medicine
> Clinic, University of Colorado Hospital

"In *High Summits*, Fred Wolfe has scaled his own 8,000 meter peak. Tenaciously combing through detailed information, moving forward and upward through the vast accumulation of multiple ascents over time, Fred has produced a magnum opus for the mountaineering world. Truly a herculean effort, *High Summits* is an authoritative guide to first ascents of all kinds and to the rich history of one of the world's most precious resources—it's high peaks and alpine terrain."

Tony Lewis
Executive Director
Donnell-Kay foundation
Denver, Colorado

"Fred Wolfe has assembled and organized a mountaineering reference book like no other. He has gone beyond merely listing events on a timeline. He puts them into context and brings life to them with added bits of history. In addition to the history, Fred has included a huge number of maps and spreadsheets. This book is a keeper."

Gary Neptune
Neptune Mountaineering and Ski Museum
Boulder, Colorado

"Mountaineers and writers are driven by passion and persistence and Fred Wolfe's remarkable history of mountaineering, *High Summits*, has been driven by a passion for mountaineering and the persistence to spend years collecting the information for this amazing reference book. Not only is it a remarkable collection of valuable information, but it is fascinating reading. Every page contains a jewel of history that the reader did not know—a name, a climb, a date, perhaps a memory. This book should be beside every climber's reading chair. It will be in constant use."

Dr. Bruce Paton
Former Chairman-Board of Trustees,
Colorado Outward Bound School
and President of the Wilderness Medical Society

"*High Summits* is the result of Fred Wolfe's interest and enthusiasm for mountaineering coupled with meticulous research and record keeping. This unique book is extremely readable and serves as a very useful reference book. *High Summits* is an invaluable addition to the library of every climber."

Dick Pownall
Grand Teton mountain guide and member of
the 1963 American Mount Everest Expedition

HIGH SUMMITS

370 Famous Peak First Ascents

and Other Significant Events
in Mountaineering History

FREDERICK L. WOLFE

Hugo House

HIGH SUMMITS: 370 Famous Peak First Ascents and Other Significant Events in Mountaineering History
By Frederick L. Wolfe

©2013 Frederick L. Wolfe

All rights reserved.

No portion of this book may be reproduced mechanically, electronically, or by any other means, including photocopying, without written permission of the publisher. It is illegal to copy this book, post it to a website, or distribute it by any other meanswithout permission from the publisher.

ISBN: 978-1936449-42-2

Library of Congress Control Number: 2013946278

Cover Design/Interior Layout: NZ Graphics. www.NZGraphics.com
Illustrations: Richard E. Wolfe

Published by

Hugo House Publishers, Ltd.
Englewood, Colorado
Austin, Texas
(877) 700-0616
www.HugoHousePublishers.com

For more information, visit www.high-summits.com

Publisher's Cataloging-in-Publication Data

Wolfe, Frederick L.
    High summits : 370 famous peak first ascents and other significant events in mountaineering history / Frederick L. Wolfe.
        p. cm.
    ISBN: 978-1-936449-42-2 (pbk.)
    ISBN: 978-1-936449-35-4 (hardcover)
    Includes bibliographical references and index.
    1. Mountaineering—History. 2. Mountaineering—Equipment and supplies. 3. Adventure and adventurers.
I. Title.
GV199.89 .W65 2013
796.522—dc23   2013946278

First Edition

Printed in the United States of America

This book is dedicated to my father Lawrence C. Wolfe
who first introduced me to the world of mountaineering
and to my wife Nancy who understood my love of the
mountains and gave me the time to pursue my dreams.

And to my son Ian and my daughter Katie for sharing
climbs past and for hills yet to come.

Given in memory of
Robert Cain

CONTENTS

APPENDICES

INDEXES

LIST OF MAPS

ACKNOWLEDGMENTS

I have climbed with many different people over the past fifty years. Many of these climbers have become good friends and have joined me on various types of ascents. Several of these climbers are professional mountain guides who have taught me many of my mountaineering skills. To all of these climbing partners, I want to say thank you for sharing the mountains with me. You have all had some influence on the writing of *High Summits*.

I began to research this book more than thirty years ago. I have had the good fortune to meet and talk with many well-known international mountaineers about their experiences in the mountains. My conversations with these climbers have been very useful in the crafting of this book. I owe a special word of thanks to six mountaineers who reviewed an early book manuscript and offered many valuable comments, corrections, and suggestions as to content and organization. These six climbers are: Walter Borneman, Dr. Ben Honigman, Dr. Tom Hornbein, Tony Lewis, Gary Neptune, and Phil Powers. These same climbers were joined later by well-known mountaineers Bob Craig, John Evans, Dr. Bruce Paton, and Dick Pownall in reviewing the final manuscript. I am indebted to all of you for helping me think through many of the organizational ideas and referenced events in this book.

I want to particularly thank John Evans for sharing with me his personal climbing journals for Antarctica and Mount Logan. I also want to thank Walt Borneman for the many hours we spent together talking about the book-publishing process. Walt has authored several very successful history and climbing books. My thanks go to Australian mountaineer and well-known Antarctica climber, explorer, and author Damien Gildea for carefully reviewing my chapter on Antarctica. Damien verified all of my noted climbs and events, offered me several important suggestions, and assisted me in obtaining two beautiful photos of Antarctica peaks. I would like to thank climbers Jed Brown and Camilo Rada for allowing me to us their photos of Antarctica peaks. Also I would like to thank Phil Powers for allowing me to use his photographs of K2 and Gasherbrums I and II.

To my editor and publisher, Dr. Patricia Ross of Hugo House Publishers, thank you for your faith in me and your constant support, encouragement, and many book design ideas. And thank you to Robert Topp of the Hermitage Bookshop in Denver for introducing me to Dr. Patricia Ross. Patricia and Nick Zelinger of NZ Graphics could not have been more enthusiastic and helpful with the entire publishing process. You helped me smooth out the rough edges of my manuscript.

I would also like to thank the American Alpine Club for allowing me unlimited access to their unique book and photographic archives and to the Bradford Washburn American Mountaineering Museum. Special thanks to Beth Heller, Gary Landeck, Bridget Burke, Chris Case, and Nina Johnson for your assistance and encouragement. I am also grateful to Mike Chessler of Chessler Books in Evergreen, Colorado, for sharing his knowledge of mountaineering history around the world with me over many years.

Additionally, a very special thank you to Swiss mountain guide David Fasel for sharing his knowledge of the Swiss and French Alps with my son Ian and me as he guided us up Monte Rosa, the Riffelhorn, the Breithorn, the Matterhorn, the Aiguille du Midi, and Mont Blanc. We will always remember those fantastic climbs with you.

My brother Rich contributed all of the magnificent pen and ink drawings that are displayed on each chapter heading. Thank you for your interest in my book. We have shared many climbs over the years.

I am especially grateful to Denise Camacho for her virtually faultless typing and re-typing of the book manuscript. Your suggestions, patience, and bright smile will never be forgotten. Chandra Wheeler also assisted me with last-minute additions and corrections to the final manuscript. Thank you.

Most of all, I must thank my wife Nancy for her encouragement, support, and patience with my book project. I have been truly fortunate to have her as my business partner and soul mate. I am certain we will continue to share many more alpine walks together.

AUTHOR'S NOTE

Mountains have been a part of my life since I was ten years old. The year was 1957 and my father had just presented me with a first edition copy of Maurice Herzog's best-selling book *Annapurna*. He encouraged me to read this remarkable account of the 1950 French mountaineering expedition to the Nepal Himalaya that climbed the first 8,000 meter peak in the world—Annapurna (26,545 feet/8,091 meters). At first, I just read the captions below each black-and-white photograph and examined the climbing route maps. Then I began to read this 316-page story and became completely involved with each member of this French climbing team, their route-finding frustrations, the final climb to the summit by Herzog and Louis Lachenal and their rescue on the epic descent. I have read *Annapurna* several more times over the years. In 2003, I finally met Maurice Herzog (then age 84) at a mountaineering celebration in San Francisco, California. Herzog's Annapurna climb will forever represent one of the most important events in the history of mountaineering.

Mountaineering history has always fascinated me. *High Summits* is the result of many years of research into this rich and interesting area of literature. The yearly references I have made to a particular first ascent or mountaineering event were obtained from expedition accounts, biographies and autobiographies, climbing journals and diaries, mountaineering museums, magazine and newspaper articles, films, documentaries, newsletters, and interviews. The first ascents and climbing events described in *High Summits* focus primarily on alpine-style climbing, big-wall climbing, and expeditionary mountaineering. Few, if any events, relate to those specialized areas of climbing known as bouldering, sport climbing, competitive ice climbing or traditional cragging. Nor have I included any events relating to general camping or caving. In the interest of accuracy, nearly every reference to the first ascents and mountaineering events in *High Summits* has been obtained from at least two different sources.

"I have always been thrilled with any chance to explore the world's mountains. The quiet crunch of new-fallen snow, a quick slip of hobnailed boots on the rock, our perseverance through wind and blizzard, the priceless camaraderie of trusted friends, and the solitude of high places ignited my senses, yet also provided opportunities for both reflection and achievement that soothed my soul. Through my photography, I was able to capture a taste of these moments and share this passion with others, expanding their knowledge and helping inspire others to join your and my small community of climbers."

Bradford Washburn
American mountaineer, explorer, photographer, and cartographer
(1910 – 2007)

INTRODUCTION

High Summits is a reference book on mountaineering history. The climbs and events included in this book have been organized by world continent and by the specific date and/or year in which they occurred. *High Summits* is aimed to interest both the mountain-lover of whatever age and the experienced climber. I hope that the mountain ascents that I have included in this book revive recollections of pleasure and satisfaction as well as to suggest the possibility of future climbs to the mountain traveler.

Climbers have always been attracted to the challenge of climbing "up." To reach the topmost snow or rock summit of a mountain—that has nearly always been the goal or objective of the mountain climber. People have been climbing mountains for over 2,500 years. Geographers have determined that 29.3 percent of the earth's surface is land. Three percent of this land is located above 6,000 feet or 1,800 meters and 1percent is located above 11,800 feet or 3,600 meters. Man originally viewed mountains as barriers to be crossed (via passes) for invasion or commerce. Mountain summits were known as the homes of local deities and to reach a high summit was to tempt instant death. Due to their closer proximity to the heavens, mountains have always inspired mankind and were considered ideal locations for shrines, monasteries, and hermitages. High mountain environments in Europe were where hunters could find chamois (a goat-like antelope) and various mineral crystals that were used for medicinal purposes. Due to their mountain knowledge, many of these chamois and crystal hunters eventually became paid mountain guides for tourist hikers and climbers.

Early mountain climbs in the European Alps (mid 1700s) frequently had a scientific purpose— measuring summit elevations and temperatures, studying glacial formations and movements, collecting botanical specimens, etc.—to justify the physical effort. In the mid 1800s, wealth, increased leisure time, and improved transportation allowed men and women (primarily British) to visit high mountain areas in the European Alps so as to enjoy the alpine scenery and nature. Lower elevation hiking soon led to higher ridge climbing which eventually resulted in the "conquest" of a mountain summit and, in many cases, a first ascent.

The first successful, documented (recorded) attainment of the top of a mountain is known as a "first ascent." Mountaineers have always been inspired by committing to the uncertainty of a first ascent. To be the first to reach a mountain's summit or to climb a new route up a narrow ridge or a steep face has been a creative achievement and a worthy goal for mountaineers. As legendary American rock climber Royal Robbins once said, "The lure of the first is strong."

There are hundreds of peaks between 6,000 meters (19,686 feet) and 7,000 meters (22,967 feet) in the Himalayan mountain range of Asia awaiting their first ascent. There are also countless possible first ascents yet to be made in the European Alps, the South American Andes, and the mountains of Alaska. These first ascents are primarily located on steep unclimbed ridges and faces. Every year experienced mountaineers from many different countries study photographs, climbing records and journals and topographic maps in search of an unclimbed summit, mountain ridge or steep face that could represent a first ascent for them. Even to "put up a new line" (new climbing route) on a rock or ice face or a steep ridge without ever reaching the mountain's summit has become the goal for some experienced rock and ice climbers.

Although all of the first ascents that I have selected for this book were significant in their particular year, there are those specific first ascents that have continued to fascinate serious climbers, armchair mountaineers, and the general public over many years. For example: Mount Everest (1953), K2 (1954), Annapurna (1950), the Eiger north face (1938), the Matterhorn (1865), Mont Blanc (1786), El Capitan—Nose route (1958), Half Dome—Northwest face (1957), etc.

High Summits identifies many of the important first ascents that have occurred on all seven world continents. Each one of the book's seven chapters is devoted to a particular world continent. I have tried to identify the earliest recorded peak first ascent on these continents. In addition to these first ascents of unclimbed mountain summits, I have also noted other types of first ascents that have been accomplished by climbers. For example:

- First ascent: In winter conditions
- First ascent: By a new climbing route
- First ascent: Solo (climbing alone)
- First ascent: Free (ascent that uses climbing hardware for protection only)
- First ascent: By nationality
- First ascent: By ethnicity
- First ascent: With a specific physical disability
- First ascent: Without using mountain guides
- First ascent: Using a specific climbing style
- First ascent/descent: On skis
- First ascent: Without using supplemental oxygen

Mountaineering, hiking, and trekking have become very popular physical activities in many countries. The Swiss Alpine Club (founded in 1863) had a membership of over 110,000 in 2006, and the German Alpine Club's membership is over 930,000. On the continent of Asia, there are approximately 635 named peaks between 6,000 to 6,999 meters (19,686 to 22,963 feet), 253 named peaks between 7,000 to 7,999 meters (22,967 to 26,244 feet), and 22 named peaks over 8,000 meters (26,248 feet). In the Andes Mountains of South America, there are 84 peaks over 6,000 meters (19,686 feet). In the United States, there are 114 mountains that exceed 14,000 feet (4,267 meters) and the European Alps include 82 named peaks over 4,000 meters (13,124 feet). Mountaineers have made the first ascent on many of these peaks. The most prominent peaks have had numerous first ascents by different routes in different seasons. Mount Everest on the Nepal/Tibet border, for example, has at least eighteen different named climbing routes to its 29,035 foot (8,849 meters) summit. As of 2011, over 5,600 ascents of Mount Everest have been made by over 3,000 different climbers from over 60 nations.

Over 2,800 mountaineering events are included in *High Summits* including 502 specific references on the evolution of mountaineering equipment and clothing and the development of a wide range of climbing techniques. These mountaineering events describe significant climbs/traverses/enchainments, unique climbing records and accomplishments, mountaineers celebratory events, major climbing accidents and rescues, famous and interesting personalities, climbing organizations, and sacred mountains. The names of over 750 mountaineers from many different countries are included in *High Summits*. These climbers participated in over 370 famous peak first ascents and over 600 other types of first ascents. I have always admired and been fascinated with the courage, vision, determination, and endurance of these climbers.

Collectively, the climbing events included in *High Summits* tell the story of how mountaineering was born, evolved, and matured into the physical activity that millions of people enjoy today around the world. I have not attempted to compile a 100 percent complete list of all first ascents in all of the world's mountain ranges. I have, however, noted those important first ascents in each of the major mountain ranges of all seven continents. There are certain mountain ranges in foreign countries that I could not find any historical climbing information in the English language. In some cases, I have discovered discrepancies in specific dates, summit elevations, climbing routes, and spellings of peak names and place names. I have tried to research, verify, and correct this difference in information. In all cases, I have used the most commonly accepted names, dates, and elevations. My sincere apology for any information that still may not be 100 percent correct.

Classic mountaineering books that I used in my research are listed in the Selected Bibliography section at the end of each chapter for those who want to delve deeper into any particular expedition account, climbing personality, or mountaineering event. The appendices includes mountaineering information for many countries, world summit altitude records for both men and women, a description of seventeen unique mountain summit collections, and my personal list of the ten most significant events in mountaineering history.

"The true mountaineer is a wanderer, and by a wanderer I do not mean a man who expends his whole time in traveling to and from in the mountains on the exact tracks of his predecessors...but I mean a man who loves to be where no human being has been before, who delights in gripping rocks that have previously never felt the touch of human fingers, or in hewing his way up ice-filled gullies whose grim shadows have been sacred to the mists and avalanches since 'Earth rose out of chaos.' In other words, the true mountaineer is the man who attempts new ascents. Equally, whether he succeeds or fails, he delights in the fun and jollity of the struggle."

1895
Albert Frederick Mummery
British mountaineer
(1855 – 1895)

"The mountains are a world of their own.
They are not so much a part of this planet as
an independent kingdom, unique and mysterious,
where, to adventure forth, all that is needed is the will
and the love."

1963
Gaston Rebuffat
French mountaineer and guide
(1921 – 1985)

ONE

AFRICA

Snow on the Equator

Years 1841 to 2011

"Mountain climbing is the supreme occasion of physical enjoyment. Even so, the days when the condition of every member of the party are all perfect and working perfectly in accord can come but rarely. But when they do come, for their duration the delight of rhythmic movement dominates all our consciousness."

1905
Geoffrey Winthrop Young
British mountaineer
(1876 – 1958)

AFRICA

Hot deserts, dense jungles, endless grasslands, and high mountain glaciers all describe the wide range of climatic regions of Africa. This continent of fifty-three independent countries includes twenty-two mountains that are over 15,000 feet (4,572 meters) high and ten mountains that exceed 16,000 feet (4,876 meters). Sixteen different mountain ranges are located in Africa but only three mountain areas have any significant mountaineering importance. These areas are:

1. Mount Kenya in Kenya: 17,058 ft./5,199 m.
2. Mount Kilimanjaro in Tanzania: 19,341 ft./5,895 m.
3. Mount Stanley in Uganda and the Democratic Republic of the Congo: 16,763 ft./5,109 m.

The history of mountaineering in Africa began with the names Abruzzi, Brocherel, Mackinder, Meyer, Ollier, Purtscheller, Shipton, and Tilman. These early mountaineers explored and eventually first climbed Mounts Kilimanjaro and Kenya, and Margherita Peak on Mount Stanley as well as many other lesser peaks. Three-and-a-half miles above the equator lies the summit of Mount Kilimanjaro—"the roof of Africa." Thousands of hopeful climbers journey to Africa each year and make their attempt to reach this high summit, one of the so-called Seven Summits. Approximately half of these climbers are successful. Kilimanjaro has two climbing seasons. The dry season is composed of seven months (January, February, June, July, August, September, and October) and represents the most favorable climbing period. The rainy season (March, April, May, November, and December) is less favorable and often more cloudy. Glacial retreat on Kilimanjaro and other African peaks is a fact but there is still "snow on the equator" for climbers to enjoy.

Mount Kenya in Kenya provides many interesting and challenging rock and ice climbing routes to its twin summits. Margherita Peak on the Mount Stanley massif is more difficult to access than Kenya or Kilimanjaro but does provide the mountaineer with an excellent snow and ice experience.

Ten Highest Peaks in Africa

1.	Mount Kilimanjaro	Tanzania	19,341 ft./5,895 m.
2.	Mount Kenya* – Batian	Kenya	17,058 ft./5,199 m.
3.	Mount Kenya – Nelion	Kenya	17,022 ft./5,188 m.
4.	Mawenzi Peak – Hans Meyer Peak	Tanzania	16,893 ft./5,149 m.
5.	Mount Stanley – Margherita	Uganda	16,763 ft./5,109 m.
6.	Mount Stanley – Alexandra	Uganda	16,704 ft./5,091 m.
7.	Mount Speke	Uganda	16,064 ft./4,896 m.
8.	Mount Baker	Uganda	15,893 ft./4,844 m.
9.	Mount Emin	Congo	15,742 ft./4,798 m.
10.	Mount Gessi	Uganda	15,470 ft./4,715 m.

*Mount Kenya includes five sub-peaks that all exceed 16,000 ft. (4,876 m.): Point Lenana, Point Pigott, Dutton Peak, Point John, and Point Melhuish.

This chapter identifies twenty-four (24) first ascents of previously unclimbed peaks in nine African countries. I have also identified twenty (20) other types of first ascents primarily on Mounts Kenya, Kilimanjaro, and Stanley. In addition to noting these first ascents, I have included forty other mountaineering-related events that occurred in Africa.

▲ Highest Mountain: Mount Kilimanjaro – 19,341 ft./5,895 m.
Location: Tanzania
First Ascent Date: October 6, 1889
Expedition: German

Africa Timeline

1841: PEAK FIRST ASCENT *RAS DASHAN*

French military officers Pierre V.A. Ferret and Joseph G. Galinier made the first recorded ascent of Ethiopia's highest peak Ras Dashan (15,158 ft./4,620 m.). There is no evidence of earlier ascents by local people. This mountain is located in the far northern part of Ethiopia near the city of Gonder in the Semien mountains. There are five peaks above 13,000 feet (3,962 meters) in this mountain range.

1848:

May 11. German missionary Johannes Rebmann (1820 – 1876) was the first European to see Mount Kilimanjaro (19,340 ft./5,895 m.) in Tanzania. Many people, however, did not believe him because they thought it was not possible that snow could be found this close to the equator. Kilimanjaro is the tallest free-standing mountain in the world—15,100 ft./4,603 m. base to summit.

1849:

December 3. German missionary Dr. Johann Ludwig Krapf (1810 – 1881) was the first European to see the Mount Kenya (17,058 ft./5,199 m.) mountain group in Kenya from 100 miles away. Krapf was a colleague of fellow missionary Johannes Rebmann who first saw Mount Kilimanjaro in 1848.

1861: PEAK FIRST ASCENT *CAMEROON*

Gustav Mann and Richard F. Burton (1821 – 1890) made the first ascent of Mount Cameroon (13,354 ft./4,070 m.), the highest mountain (volcano) in Cameroon. Burton was an English explorer, writer, diplomat, and soldier who spoke 29 languages. The native name for this mountain is Mongo ma Noemi which means "Mountain of Greatness." Mount Cameroon is located just west of the city of Douala near the Gulf of Guinea in the Atlantic Ocean.

1876:

British explorer Henry Morton Stanley (1841 – 1904) made the first documented sighting of the Ruwenzori mountains in Uganda by a European. Ruwenzori in the Bantu language means "hill of rains." The local natives described these mountains as "covered in salt" due to the snow.

1887:

In the November issue of England's *Alpine Journal*, an article declared that Mount Kilimanjaro (19,340 ft./5,895 m.) in Tanzania had been first ascended by Dr. Hans Meyer (1858 – 1929) of Leipzig, Germany. This claim was not true. Meyer actually reached 17,880 ft./5,450 m. above the saddle between Kilimanjaro and Mawenzi in August. Meyer later clarified the journal's article. This was one of the highest elevations any European had ever reached.

1889: PEAK FIRST ASCENT *KILIMANJARO* [7▲]

October 6. Geographer Dr. Hans Heinrich Josef Meyer (1858 – 1929) of Leipzig, Germany and Austrian mountain guide Ludwig Purtscheller (1849 – 1900) made the first ascent of Mount Kilimanjaro (19,340 ft./5,895 m.) in Tanzania. Yohannes Kinyala Lauwo (1871 – 1996), a local Chagga guide, was also with Meyer and Purtscheller. An eight-man Somali bodyguard and sixty-two porters completed this climbing expedition. Purtscheller was considered to be the best ice climber of his day having built his reputation on many first ascents in the Alps. He used a pair of climbing irons (early crampons) while Meyer climbed in hobnailed boots. They took 11 hours from their high camp to the crater rim. Upon reaching the summit, they erected a German flag and named the mountain "Kaiser Wilhelm's Peak." This summit point was re-named in 1961.

On October 15, Meyer and Purtscheller attempted to make the first ascent of Purtscheller Peak (17,191 ft./5,240 m.), one of the seven pinnacle peaks of Mawenzi immediately to the east of Kilimanjaro. Due to altitude illness, they were only able to climb a subsidiary peak now known as Klute Peak (16,720 ft./5,096 m.). In the Swahili language, Kilimanjaro means "shining mountain." Lauwo went on to guide climbers up Kilimanjaro for seventy more years and died in 1996 at age 125.

1893:

Scottish geologist Dr. John W. Gregory and his porters made the first recorded attempt to climb Mount Kenya (17,058 ft./5,199 m.) in Kenya. They reached the glacial zone at a point just below Point Lenana (16,355 ft./4,985 m.). Gregory's porters quit climbing because they were afraid of snow. Gregory was the first European to reach these glaciers.

1899: PEAK FIRST ASCENT *KENYA*

September 12. British explorer Sir Halford Mackinder (1861 – 1947) and his two Italian mountain guides Cesar Ollier and Joseph Brocherel (from Courmayeur, Italy) made the first ascent of Mount Kenya's Batian summit (17,058 ft./5,199 m.) in Kenya via the southeast face and the Diamond Glacier. C.B. Hausburg, E.H. Saunders (plant collector), and C.F. Camburn (Taxidermist) were also members of this expedition. Mackinder also had 66 Swahili porters and two tall Masai local guides with him.

This ascent was Mackinder's third attempt to climb Batian during the same expedition. He named the Batian summit after a Masai witch doctor named Mbatiang and the Nelion summit (17,022 feet/5,188 meters) after Mbatiang's brother Neilieng.

1899: Equipment – Food: First ascent of Mount Kenya

(17,058 ft./5,199 m.) in Kenya. This was the second time* that expedition food was specifically measured out and pre-packed for a climbing expedition. Forty tin-lined boxes, each weighing twenty-five pounds, contained a day's complete rations for six (6) men. Two boxes per man load were carried in to the mountain.

See Europe – 1879.

[7▲] One of the world's Seven Summits.

1903: PEAK FIRST ASCENT *KARISIMBI*

Berthelmy made the first ascent of Karisimbi (14,784 ft./4,506 m.), the highest peak in Rwanda. This inactive volcano is the highest of eight volcanos in the Virunga region of Ruanda and the Democratic Republic of Congo. Each of these volcanos is over 10,000 feet (3,048 meters).

1905:

November. The first true mountaineers visited the Ruwenzori mountains of Uganda. British mountaineers Douglas William Freshfield (1845 – 1934), Arnold Louis Mumm (1859 – 1927), and Zermatt (Switzerland) guide Moritz Inderbinnen (1856 – 1926)* reached the snowline but were stopped by heavy rainfall. The Ruwenzori mountains contain twenty-six peaks over 14,000 feet (4,267 meters) and nine named peaks over 16,000 feet (4,876 meters).

1906: PEAK FIRST ASCENT *MARGHERITA, ALEXANDRA, SPEKE, BAKER, EMIN, GESSI, LUIGI DI SAVOIA*

June – July. Italian mountaineer Duke of the Abruzzi (Luigi Amadeo Giuseppe, 1873 – 1933) led a major climbing expedition to the Ruwenzori ("Mountains of the Moon") Massif in Uganda and the Democratic Republic of the Congo. Italian mountaineer/photographer Vittorio Sella (1859 – 1943) and mountain guides Joseph Brocherel, Cesar Ollier, and Joseph Petigax and six scientists accompanied the Duke. It is interesting to note that guides Brocherel and Ollier were also with Halford Mackinder on the first ascent of Mount Kenya's Batian summit in 1899. Twenty-one previous expeditions had failed to make any first ascents in this mountain range. The Duke of the Abruzzi's party made a total of fifteen first ascents of peaks over 15,000 feet. Here are the seven most prominent summits:

   – Margherita Peak third highest peak
     in Africa on Mount Stanley (June 18)†   : 16,763 ft./5,109 m.
   – Alexandra Peak on Mount Stanley   : 16,704 ft./5,091 m.
   – Mount Speke (Vittorio Emanuele Peak)   : 16,064 ft./4,896 m.
   – Mount Baker (Edward Peak) (July 2)   : 15,893 ft./4,844 m.
   – Mount Emin   : 15,742 ft./4,798 m.
   – Mount Gessi   : 15,470 ft./4,715 m.
   – Mount Luigi di Savoia   : 15,178 ft./4,626 m.

1909: FIRST ASCENT

July. The first ascent of the Marangu Route on Mount Kilimanjaro (19,342 ft./5,895 m.) in Tanzania was made by surveyor M. Lange and his assistant Weigele. This route is now considered to be the normal or tourist route up Kili. It is known as the "Coca-cola route" because climbers buy Coke cans along the route. About 90% of the "Kili" climbers follow it. This was the second overall ascent of Mount Kilimanjaro.

---

* Uncle of famous Matterhorn guide Ulrich Inderbinen (1900 – 2004)

† Named for journalist and explorer Sir Henry Morton Stanley (1841 – 1904)

1912: PEAK FIRST ASCENT *HANS MEYER*

July 29. German mountaineers Edward Oehler and Fritz Klute (1885 – 1952, glaciologist) made the first ascent of Hans Meyer Peak (16,893 ft./5,149 m.), the highest pinnacle peak of Mawenzi which is located approximately 6 ½ miles southeast of Mount Kilimanjaro in Tanzania. The Mawenzi Massif includes ten lower sub-peaks.

1923: PEAK FIRST ASCENT *JEBEL TOUBKAL*

June 12. The highest summit in North Africa and in the High Atlas Mountains of Morocco was finally located in 1922 – Jebel Toubkal (13,665 ft./4,165 m.). French mountaineers V. Berger, M. Dolbeau, and the Marquis De Segonzac made the first ascent. There are thirteen peaks over 11,500 feet (3,505 meters) in the High Atlas mountains.

1926:

Pastor Richard Reusch, a missionary for the Lutheran Church and a longtime resident of Marangu, completed the first of his forty separate ascents of Kilimanjaro.

1927: FIRST ASCENT

July 28. British climber Sheila MacDonald became the first woman to climb Hans Meyer Peak (16,893 ft./5,149 m.) on Mawenzi in Tanzania. William West and Otho Brown accompanied MacDonald to the summit. On July 31st, MacDonald became the first woman to climb Mount Kilimanjaro (Uhuru Point) (19,341 ft./5,895 m.) in Tanzania.

1927: PEAK FIRST ASCENT *MIKENO*

August. Pere Van Hoef, a local settler, and one native companion made the first ascent of Mikeno (14,725 ft./4,488 m.), a volcano in the Virungas mountains of Rwanda. Mikeno is the second highest mountain in Rwanda.

1929: PEAK FIRST ASCENT *KENYA*

January 3. British mountaineers Eric Shipton (1907 – 1977) and Percy Wyn Harris (1903 – 1979) made the first ascent of Mount Kenya's Nelion summit (17,022 ft./5,188 m.) in Kenya via the southeast face. They also made the second ascent of the Batian summit (17,058 ft./5,199 m.) of Mount Kenya on the same day. Prior to reaching the two summits of Mount Kenya, Shipton and Harris made the first ascents of two sub-peaks: Point Dutton—16,025 ft./4,884 m. and Point Peter—15,605 ft./4,756 m.

1929: PEAK FIRST ASCENT: *POINT JOHN*

December 18. Eric Shipton and Pat Russell made the first ascent of Point John (16,021 ft./4,883 m.), a satellite peak of Mount Kenya.

1929:

The Mountain Club of East Africa was founded in Moshi, Tanzania. It eventually became the Kilimanjaro Mountain Club.

1930: PEAK FIRST ASCENT *POINT PIGGOTT, SENDEYO, MIDGET*

August 1. British mountaineers Bill Tilman (1898 – 1977) and Eric Shipton (1907 – 1977) made the first traverse of the twin summits of Mount Kenya (Batian: 17,058 ft./5,199 m. and Nelion: 17,022 ft./5,188 m.) in Kenya. They also made the first ascents of the following sub-peaks of Mount Kenya:

Point Piggott	16,264 ft./4,957 m.	August 6
Sendeyo Peak	15,434 ft./4,704 m.	August 5
Midget Peak	15,421 ft./4,700 m.	August 9

1933:

March 18. The Duke of the Abruzzi (1873 – 1933) died at age 60 in Somalia, Africa, of an undisclosed illness. He was buried there. Luigi Amadeo Giuseppe was the grandson of King Victor Emmanuel II of Italy. He led many large and well-organized mountaineering expeditions. He went to Alaska in 1897, the Arctic in 1899, Africa in 1906, and the Karakoram Range in 1909.

1933:

British mountaineer H.W. "Bill" Tilman (1898 – 1977) made a solo ascent of Mount Kilimanjaro (19,342 ft./5,895 m.) in Tanzania. Tilman bivouaced close to the summit at an elevation above 19,000 ft./5,791 m.

1938: PEAK FIRST ASCENT *PURTSCHELLER*

January 9. E. Eisenmann and R. Hildebrand first reached the summit of Purtscheller Peak (16,799 ft./5,120 m.) on the Mawenzi Massif. Purtscheller is the third highest Mawenzi peak.

1938: FIRST ASCENT

January 12. The Decken Glacier route to the summit of Kilimanjaro was first climbed by E. Eisenmann and T. Schnackig.

1938: FIRST ASCENT

February. A party of four mountaineers reached the Nelion Summit (17,022 ft./5,188 m.) of Mount Kenya in Kenya. Included in this group was Miss C. Carrol, the first woman to reach the Nelion summit along with Mtu Mathara, the first African to summit.

1938: FIRST ASCENT

Ms. Una Cameron became the first woman to reach Mount Kenya's Batian Summit (17,058 ft./5,199 m.).

1943:

Italian foreign service officer Felice Benuzzi (1910 – 1988) was placed in a prisoner-of-war (P.O.W.) camp in Kenya in 1941. In 1943, Benuzzi and two fellow Italian prisoners from P.O.W. Camp 354 in Nanyuki, Kenya decided to temporarily escape and climb nearby Mount Kenya (17,058 ft./5,199 m.).

Over a period of many months, they secretly made all of their climbing clothing and equipment (two ice axes and crampons) and saved various food items. Warm jackets were made from blankets. Boots were re-stitched studding the soles with nails. A picture label from a meat-ration can served as their map. Their rope was seventy feet of sisal cord. Barbed wire was fashioned into crampons. Stolen hammer heads were re-worked and fitted to steel-tipped hardwood shafts for their ice axes. They made their escape on January 24,1944, summited a sub-peak of Mount Kenya called Point Lenana (16,355 ft./4,985 m.) on February 6th and returned to their P.O.W. camp on February 10th. They were then sentenced to 28 days in solitary confinement but served only seven days. Benuzzi completed his book entitled *No Picnic On Mount Kenya* in July of 1946 in P.O.W. Camp 336 in Gilgil, Kenya. This book, however, was not published until 1953.

1946:

April to June. Belgium Congo/Rwanda. Canadian-born mountaineer Earl Denman became the first white man to climb all eight of the high peaks (all volcanoes) in the Virunga Mountains (Ruwenzori Range). These peaks are:

1.	Karasimbi	14,784 ft.	4,506 m.
2.	Mikeno	14,725 ft.	4,488 m.
3.	Muhavura	13,550 ft.	4,130 m.
4.	Vishoke	12,370 ft.	3,770 m.
5.	Sabinio	12,150 ft.	3,703 m.
6.	Mgahinga	11,400 ft.	3,475 m.
7.	Nyiragongo	11,385 ft.	3,470 m.
8.	Nyamlagira	10,046 ft.	3,062 m.

1946:

The Mountain Club of Uganda was founded. This club was responsible for developing the Bujuku-Mubuku hut system which was begun in 1948 with the Bujuku Hut (13,048 ft./3,977 m.) just east of Margherita Peak on Mount Stanley.

1949:

The Mountain Club of Kenya was established.

1950:

February 20. American mountaineer Bill Hackett (1918 – 1999) and a local climber named Daudi reached Kibo, the summit point of Mount Kilimanjaro (19,342 ft./5,895 m.) in Tanzania. Hackett became the first American to climb Kilimanjaro and first climber to reach the highest summit on three continents:

1947	Mount McKinley	20,320 ft./6,193 m.	North America
1949	Aconcagua	22,834 ft./6,959 m.	South America
1950	Kilimanjaro	19,344 ft./5,895 m.	Africa

1950:

British mountaineer Arthur Firmin completed his fifth ascent of Mount Kenya (Batian Summit: 17,058 ft./5,199 m.) between 1943 and 1950. Firmin climbed every known route on Mount Kenya except the west face.

1954: FIRST ASCENT

British mountaineer June Slinger became the first woman to reach the summit of Margherita (16,763 ft./5,109 m.), the highest peak on Mount Stanley in Uganda. R.F. Davies and I. Keith were with Slinger.

1955: FIRST ASCENT

January 7. Mountaineers Robert Caukwell and Gerald Rose made the first ascent of the icy west face of Batian on Mount Kenya (17,058 ft./5,199 m.).

1957: FIRST ASCENT

September 20 to 25. A. Nelson, H.J. Cooke, and D.N. Goodall made the first recorded traverse of Mount Kilimanjaro's (19,342 ft./5,895 m.) main three peaks in Tanzania. This traverse spanned that mountain area from the Machame Route to the Marangu Route including the ascents of Shira Peak (13,140 ft./4,005 m.), Kibo (19,341 ft./5,895 m.), and Mawenzi (16,891 ft./5,148 m.). This climb also made the first ascent of the Heim Glacier on Kilimanjaro.

1959:

October. The first climbing guidebook to Mount Kilimanjaro and Mount Kenya was published. Ian Reid-Editor.

1960:

American mountaineer J. Graham became the first person to summit all six prominent African peaks over 16,000 feet (4,877 m.). These peaks are:

Mount Kilimanjaro	19,341 ft./5,895 m.
Mount Kenya – Batian	17,058 ft./5,199 m.
– Nelion	17,022 ft./5,188 m.
Mount Stanley – Margherita	16,763 ft./5,109 m.
– Alexandra	16,704 ft./5,091 m.
Mount Speke	16,064 ft./4,896 m.

1960: FIRST ASCENT

Italian mountaineer Piero Ghiglione (1883 –   ) celebrated his 77th birthday by making the first ascent of the west face of Punta Alexandra (16,704 ft./5,091 m.) in the Ruwenzori Group (Democratic Republic of the Congo). Italian climbers Carlo Mauri (1930 – 1982) and Bruno Ferrario were with Ghiglione.

1961:

December 9. Mount Kibo, the highest point on Mount Kilimanjaro (19,341 ft./5,895 m.) in Tanzania, was re-named Uhuru Peak (Swahili for "Freedom") when Tanzania gained its independence from Great Britain.

1970:

February. Mountaineer Ian Howell erected the Howell Hut on the summit of Mount Kenya's Nelion (17,022 ft./5,188 m.) in Kenya. Five loads of construction materials were parachuted onto the Lewis Glacier for this construction project. Howell then backpacked these materials up Nelion thirteen times solo to build this mountain hut which measured six feet by six-and-a-half feet square with an average height of three feet. This hut held four climbers.

1973: FIRST ASCENT

October 4 and 5. British mountaineer Phil Snyder and local Park Ranger Thumbi Mathenge made the first ascent of the Diamond Couloir on Mount Kenya (17,058 ft./5,199 m.) in Kenya. This 1,000 foot/305 meter steep ice chute on the mountain's south-west flank was once considered one of the most classic ice climbs in the world. Due to glacial retreat, however, this ice route now rarely forms. The first ascent of the upper headwall of the Diamond Couloir was accomplished in January of 1975 by American climbers Yvon Chouinard and Michael Covington.

1974:

Mountain Travel began leading regular treks up Mount Kilimanjaro (19,341 ft./5,895 m.) in Tanzania.

1975:

Rusty Baillie and Barry Cliffs climbed both Mount Kilimanjaro (19,341 ft./5,895 m.) and Mount Kenya (17,058 ft./5,199 m.) in 23 hours including a 400 mile/667 kilometer drive in between climbs.

1977: FIRST ASCENT

Hillary Collins became the first woman to climb the Diamond Couloir on Mount Kenya (17,058 ft./5,199 m.).

1978: FIRST ASCENT

January 31. Mountaineers Reinhold Messner (1944 –   ) and Konrad Renzler made the first ascent of Mount Kilimanjaro's (19,341 ft./5,895 m.) Breach Wall Direct Route (15,093 ft./4,600 m.) in Tanzania. Messner and Renzler accomplished this difficult route in 12 hours. The normal climbing time is two days. They used no ice axes or ice screws. This route, however, has now been closed by the Kilimanjaro National Park Authority. On January 4, 2006 three American climbers on this route were killed by a sudden rockfall.

1980: FIRST ASCENT

January. Ms. S. Morris and Ms. L. Wayburn made the first ascent of Mount Kenya's Batian summit (17,058 ft./5,199 m.) by an all-female rope team.

1982: FIRST ASCENT

American climber Galen Rowell (1940 – 2002) made the first one-day ascent of Mount Kilimanjaro in Tanzania.

1983:

July 21. American mountaineers Scott Fischer (1955 – 1996) and Wes Krause made the first American ascent of the Breach Wall Direct Route on Mount Kilimanjaro (19,341 ft./5,895 m.) in Tanzania. This was the second overall ascent. Reinhold Messner and K. Renzler made the first ascent in 1978.

1985:

British mountaineer Ian Howell had now climbed Mount Kenya (17,058 ft./5,199 m.) more than 160 times. Kenya.

1987:

American woman mountaineer Lorraine Bonney (1922 –   ) bicycled around Mount Kenya (17,058 ft./5,199 m.) in Kenya and then climbed both Mount Kenya and Kilimanjaro (19,341 ft./5,895 m.) in Tanzania. Bonney was 65 years old.

1990:

After observing the Ruwenzori glaciers for twenty years (1970 – 1990), Austrian researchers determined that these glaciers had retreated 39.4 feet/12 meters per year or a total of 788 feet/240 meters.

1991:

Independent trekking was banned on Mount Kilimanjaro (19,342 ft./5,895 m.). All trekkers must now follow one of the established paths and use a licensed guide and a team of porters.

Here are the four most popular climbing routes on Mount Kilimanjaro:*

1. Marangu Route (Marangu Gate to summit)
    • 26 hours of climbing over four days
    • Trailhead to summit: 13,105 ft./3,994 m. of elevation gain.

2. Machame Route (Machame Gate to summit)
    • 38 hours of climbing over five days
    • Trailhead to summit: 13,440 ft./4,096 m. of elevation gain.

---

* There are, however, at least 21 known routes to the summit.

3. Rongai Route (Naremoru Gate to summit)
   • 22 hours of climbing over four days
   • Trailhead to summit: 12,943 ft./3,945 m. of elevation gain

4. Umbwe Route (Umbwe Gate to summit)
   • 18 hours of climbing over three days
   • Trailhead to summit: 14,748 ft./4,495 m. of elevation gain

1994: FIRST ASCENT

January 10. American climber Joshua Stewart (1983 –   ) from Fairburn, Georgia became the youngest person (age 11) to climb Mount Kilimanjaro (19,341 ft./5,895 m.) in Tanzania. He climbed with his father Michael Stewart, a professional mountain guide and one native guide, K.C. Mtui. They climbed the Machame-Mweka Route.

1997:

Mount Kilimanjaro (19,341 ft./5,895 m.) in Tanzania is both the highest free-standing mountain in the world and the highest mountain that can be climbed by a tourist (no climbing experience is required). In 1997, 18,327 people attempted to climb "Kili." Approximately 50 % of these climbers reached the summit. People attempting to climb Mount Kilimanjaro generate more foreign currency than any other business in Tanzania.

1997:

American blind mountaineer Erik Weihenmayer (1968 –   ) reached the summit of Kilimanjaro (19,341 ft./5,895 m.) in Tanzania. This was Weihenmayer's second continental summit (1995: Mount McKinley in Alaska). While on Kilimanjaro, he married Ellie Reeve at the 13,000 foot (3,962 meters) elevation. He completed his quest to climb all Seven Summits in 2008.

2000:

Less than one square mile of ice remained on Mount Kilimanjaro (19,341 ft./5,895 m.) in Tanzania, Africa. This represented 18% of that ice that was mapped in 1912.

2001:

Italian climber Bruno Brunod made the fastest verified ascent time of Mount Kilimanjaro—5 hours 38 minutes 40 seconds. Brunod reached Uhuru Peak from the Marangu Gate.

2002:

Native mountain guide Jacob summited Mount Kilimanjaro (19,341 ft./5,895 m.) in Tanzania for the 241st time.

2003: FIRST ASCENT

February. Climber Warren Macdonald (1965 –   ) summited Mount Kilimanjaro (19,341 ft./5,895 m.) in Tanzania. Macdonald was the first double, above-the-knee amputee to summit Kilimanjaro. He lost his lower legs in a hiking accident in April of 1997 on Hinchinbrook Island, Australia.

2004:

December 26. Local mountain guide Simon Mtuy made the fastest ascent/descent of Mount Kilimanjaro (19,341 ft./5,895 m.)—8 hours 27 minutes.

2004:

American climber Karl Haupt (1925 –   ) became the oldest person at age 79 to reach the summit of Kilimanjaro.

2005: FIRST ASCENT

September 20. Kenyan Douglas Sidialo became the first blind African to summit Mount Kilimanjaro (19,341 ft./5,895 m.) in Tanzania. He reached the summit with American blind climber Erik Weihenmayer (his second ascent) and three other blind climbers. These five climbers were:

> Douglas Sidialo – Kenya
> Erik Weihenmayer – United States
> Carl Kroonenberg – United States
> Andy Holzer – Austria
> Koichiro Kobayashi – Japan

2006:

January 31 – February 12. Benny Bach, Cam Burns, and Charlie French plus twelve porters and one park ranger made a traverse of the Ruwenzori Range (central portion) in Uganda. This traverse included the ascents of Mount Speke (16,064 ft./4,896 m.), Mount Stanley (16,763 ft./5,109 m.), and Mount Baker (15,893 ft./4,844 m.).

2006:

June 10 to 25. An event called "In The Footsteps Of The Duke" was held in Kampala, Uganda to celebrate the 100th anniversary of the first ascent of Mount Stanley by the Duke of the Abruzzi (1873 – 1933). An Italian expedition team reached the summits of Margherita Peak (16,763 ft./5,109 m.) and Alexandra Peak (16,704 ft./5,091 m.) on June 18th.

2006:

August. American climbers Charley Mace (1968 –   ), Hans Florine (1964 –   ), and Erik Weihenmayer (blind) reached the twin summits of Mount Kenya (Batian: 17,058 ft./5,199 m. and Nelion: 17,022 ft./5,188 m.) via the north face.

2007

Over 90% of those climbers attempting to climb Mount Kilimanjaro in Tanzania used the Marangu Route (a.k.a. Coca-Cola Route). This is the only route with huts (vs. tents) for climbers.

2008: FIRST ASCENT

August 27 to 31. Slovak mountaineers Dusan Beranek and Richard Nyeki climbed a new route up the east face of Tsaranoro Be in Madagascar (a large island just off the southeast coast of Africa). They named this new route Old Master (2,625 ft./800 m.).

2008: FIRST ASCENT

American climber Keats Boyd (2001 –) became the youngest person at age 7 to reach the summit of Kilimanjaro.

2009:

Climbing Mount Kilimanjaro in Tanzania:
- Approximately 30,000 people attempt this climb every year.
  18,000 reach the summit or 60% and 12,000 fail to summit or 40%.

- 8 to 9 climbers die each year from either a heart attack or Acute Mountain Sickness.

2009:

June. Well-known American blind mountaineer Erik Weihenmayer (1968 –) and his climbing team guided eight blind students from the Foundation for Blind Children (Phoenix, Arizona) up Mount Kilimanjaro (19,341 ft./5,895 m.) in Tanzania. This climbing expedition raised funds to donate Braille typewriters, canes, and magnifiers to the Mwereni Integrated School for the Blind in Moshi, Tanzania.

2009:

February. Legendary Nepalese Mount Everest mountaineer Lakpa Rita Sherpa (1966 –) reached the summits of Mount Elbrus (18,510 ft./5,642 m.) in Europe and Mount Kosciuszko (7,310 ft./2,228 m.) in Australia on his way to becoming the first Sherpa to climb the Seven Summits. He completed this unique climbing goal when he summited Mount Kilimanjaro (19,341 ft./5,895 m.) in Africa in 2009.

2010: PEAK FIRST ASCENTS *CITADEL, WINE BOTTLE, ARCH OF BASHIKELE*

November. American climbers Jimmy Chin, Tim Kemple, Alex Honnold, Renan Ozturk, James Pearson (British) and Mark Synnott made three first ascents of sandstone towers in the Ennedi Desert area of eastern Chad. These three towers are: The Citadel—200 ft./61 m., The Wine Bottle—300 ft./91 m., and The Arch of Bashikele—200 ft./61 m.

2011:

No significant mountaineering events could be identified.

"Mountaineering is a pursuit in which the deepest motives
behind it are a longing for adventure, a love of nature,
and a sentiment that can only be called mystical.
The traditional mountaineer matches himself against
the forces of nature, and does not seek to vie with
other men in the sort of competition that
requires regulations and rewards."

Charles F. Meade
British mountaineer
(1881–1975)

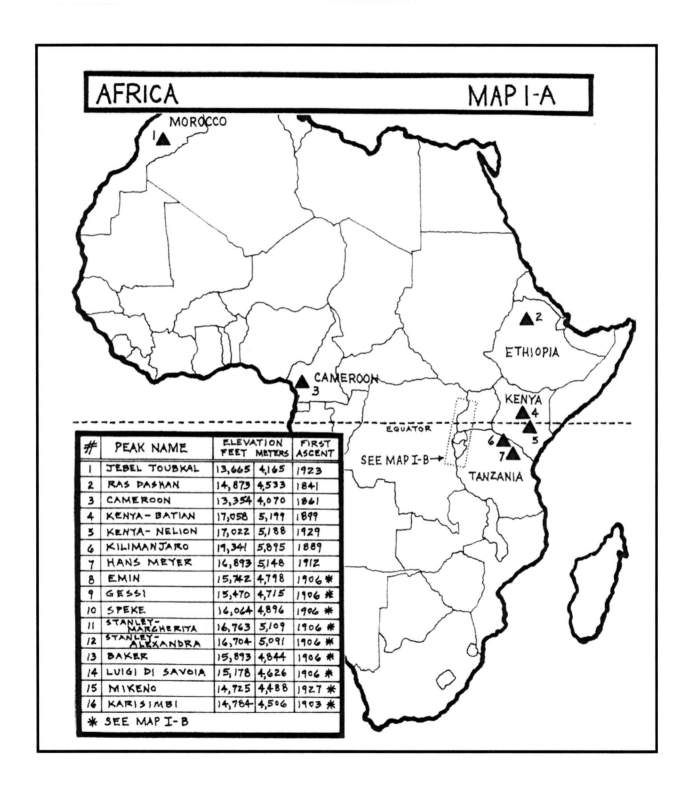

AFRICA   MAP I-A

MOROCCO
1 ▲

▲2
ETHIOPIA

▲ CAMEROON
3

KENYA
▲4
EQUATOR   ▲5
SEE MAP I-B→   6▲
7▲
TANZANIA

#	PEAK NAME	ELEVATION FEET	METERS	FIRST ASCENT
1	JEBEL TOUBKAL	13,665	4,165	1923
2	RAS DASHAN	14,873	4,533	1841
3	CAMEROON	13,354	4,070	1861
4	KENYA – BATIAN	17,058	5,199	1899
5	KENYA – NELION	17,022	5,188	1929
6	KILIMANJARO	19,341	5,895	1889
7	HANS MEYER	16,893	5,148	1912
8	EMIN	15,742	4,798	1906 ✳
9	GESSI	15,470	4,715	1906 ✳
10	SPEKE	16,064	4,896	1906 ✳
11	STANLEY-MARGHERITA	16,763	5,109	1906 ✳
12	STANLEY-ALEXANDRA	16,704	5,091	1906 ✳
13	BAKER	15,893	4,844	1906 ✳
14	LUIGI DI SAVOIA	15,178	4,626	1906 ✳
15	MIKENO	14,725	4,488	1927 ✳
16	KARISIMBI	14,784	4,506	1903 ✳

✳ SEE MAP I-B

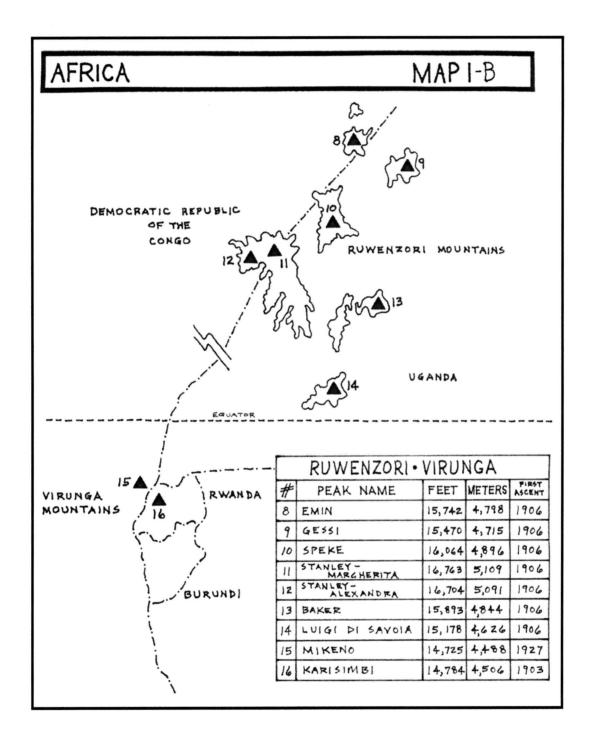

AFRICA   MAP I-B

DEMOCRATIC REPUBLIC
OF THE
CONGO

RUWENZORI MOUNTAINS

UGANDA

EQUATOR

VIRUNGA
MOUNTAINS

RWANDA

BURUNDI

RUWENZORI · VIRUNGA				
#	PEAK NAME	FEET	METERS	FIRST ASCENT
8	EMIN	15,742	4,798	1906
9	GESSI	15,470	4,715	1906
10	SPEKE	16,064	4,896	1906
11	STANLEY-MARGHERITA	16,763	5,109	1906
12	STANLEY-ALEXANDRA	16,704	5,091	1906
13	BAKER	15,893	4,844	1906
14	LUIGI DI SAVOIA	15,178	4,626	1906
15	MIKENO	14,725	4,488	1927
16	KARISIMBI	14,784	4,506	1903

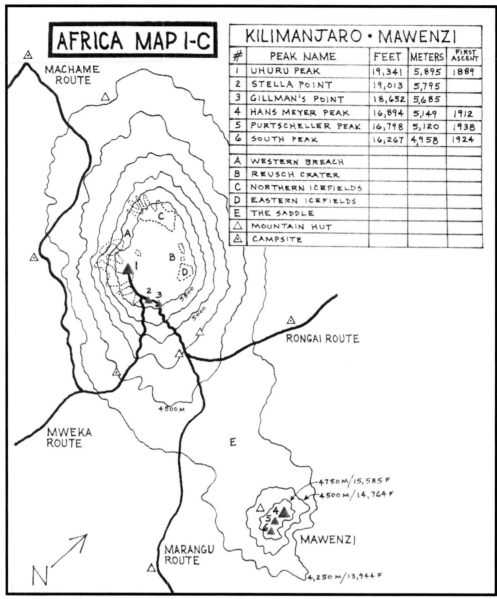

AFRICA MAP I-C

KILIMANJARO · MAWENZI				
#	PEAK NAME	FEET	METERS	FIRST ASCENT
1	UHURU PEAK	19,341	5,895	1889
2	STELLA POINT	19,013	5,795	
3	GILLMAN'S POINT	18,652	5,685	
4	HANS MEYER PEAK	16,894	5,149	1912
5	PURTSCHELLER PEAK	16,798	5,120	1938
6	SOUTH PEAK	16,267	4,958	1924
A	WESTERN BREACH			
B	REUSCH CRATER			
C	NORTHERN ICEFIELDS			
D	EASTERN ICEFIELDS			
E	THE SADDLE			
△	MOUNTAIN HUT			
△	CAMPSITE			

MACHAME ROUTE

RONGAI ROUTE

MWEKA ROUTE

4500M

E

4750M/15,585 F
4500M/14,764 F

5
4
6
MAWENZI

4,250 M/13,944 F

N

MARANGU ROUTE

Mount Kilimanjaro
Tanzania
19,341 ft./5,895 m.

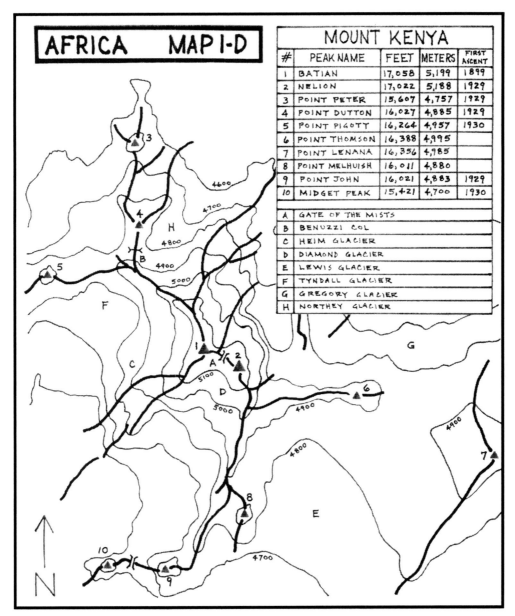

AFRICA   MAP I-D

MOUNT KENYA

#	PEAK NAME	FEET	METERS	FIRST ASCENT
1	BATIAN	17,058	5,199	1899
2	NELION	17,022	5,188	1929
3	POINT PETER	15,607	4,757	1929
4	POINT DUTTON	16,027	4,885	1929
5	POINT PIGOTT	16,264	4,957	1930
6	POINT THOMSON	16,388	4,995	
7	POINT LENANA	16,356	4,985	
8	POINT MELHUISH	16,011	4,880	
9	POINT JOHN	16,021	4,883	1929
10	MIDGET PEAK	15,421	4,700	1930

A	GATE OF THE MISTS
B	BENUZZI COL
C	HEIM GLACIER
D	DIAMOND GLACIER
E	LEWIS GLACIER
F	TYNDALL GLACIER
G	GREGORY GLACIER
H	NORTHEY GLACIER

Mount Kenya
Kenya
17,058 ft./5,199 m.

AFRICA: The 25 Highest Peaks

RANK and PEAK NAME	ELEVATION FEET•METERS	LOCATION	FIRST ASCENT DATE	EXPEDITION	SUMMIT CLIMBERS
1 Mount Kilimanjaro	19,341•5,895	Tanzania	10-6-1889	German	H. Meyer L. Purtscheller
2 Mount Kenya-Batian	17,058•5,199	Kenya	9-1899	British	H.J. Mackinder C. Ollier J. Brocherel
3 Mount Kenya-Nelion	17,022•5,188	Kenya	1-1929	British	E. Shipton P. Wyn Harris
4 Hans Meyer Pk.	16,893•5,149	Tanzania	7-29-1912	German	F. Klute E. Oelher
5 Margherita Pk. of Mount Stanley	16,763•5,109	Uganda-Zaire	6-18-1906	Italian	Duke of the Abruzzi J. Petigaxr C. Ollier J. Brocherel
6 Alexandra Pk. of Mount Stanley	16,704•5,091	Uganda-Zaire	1926		G.N. Humphreys and party
7 Pt. Lenana	16,356•4,985	Kenya	1943	Italian	Felice Benuzzi
8 Pt. Pigott	16,267•4,958	Kenya	8-1930	British	H.W. Tilman E. Shipton
9 Mount Speke	16,064•4,896	Uganda-Zaire	6-23-1906	Italian	Duke of the Abruzzi J. Petigax C. Ollier J. Brocherel
10 Dutton Peak	16,028•4,885	Kenya	8-1930	British	H.W. Tilman E. Shipton
11 Mount Baker	15,893•4,844	Uganda-Zaire	6-10-1906	Italian	Duke of the Abruzzi J. Petigax C. Ollier J. Brocherel

AFRICA: The 25 Highest Peaks (continued)

RANK and PEAK NAME	ELEVATION FEET·METERS	LOCATION	FIRST ASCENT DATE	EXPEDITION	SUMMIT CLIMBERS
12 Mount Emin	15,742·4,798	Uganda-Zaire	6-28-1906	Italian	Duke of the Abruzzi J. Petigax L. Petigax C. Ollier
13 Point Peter	15,608·4,757	Kenya	8-1930	British	H.W. Tilman E. Shipton
14 Mount Gessi	15,470·4,715	Uganda-Zaire	6-16-1906	Italian	Duke of the Abruzzi J. Petigax C. Ollier
15 Tereri	15,467·4,714	Kenya			
16 Sendeyo	15,434·4,704	Kenya	8-1930	British	H.W. Tilman E. Shipton
17 Midget	15,421·4,700	Kenya	8-1930	British	H.W. Tilman E. Shipton
18 Mount Luigi di Savoia	15,178·4,626	Uganda-Zaire	7-4-1906	Italian	Vittorio Sella J. Brocherel Botta
19 Wollaston Pk.	15,178·4,626	Rwanda-Zaire	1906	British	A.F.R. Wollaston H.B. Woosnam
20 Ras Dashan	15,158·4,620	Ethiopia	1841	French	Ferret Galinier
21 Mount Selki	14,771·4,502	Ethiopia			Berthelmy
22 Humphrey's Pk.	15,020·4,578	Uganda-Zaire			
23 Meru	14,978·4,565	Tanzania	1910		Jaeger
24 Mount Buahit	14,797·4,510	Ethiopia			
25 Karisimbi	14,784·4,506	Rwanda	1903		

Selected Bibliography — Africa

Of the numerous books, journals, newspaper and magazine articles, and internet sites that have been used in the research for this book, the author is particularly indebted to the following sources:

Allan, Iain. *Guide to Mount Kenya and Kilimanjaro*. The Mountain Club of Kenya, 1991.

American Alpine Club Journals. *American Alpine Club*, 1902 to 2008 (various years).

Anderson, Robert Mads. SUMMITS – *Climbing the Seven Summits Solo*. Clarkson Potter Publishers, 1995.

Ardito, Stefano. *History of the Great Mountaineering Adventures*. The Mountaineers, 2000.

Ardito, Stefano. *Tales of Mountaineering*. White Star Publishers, 2000.

Barnes, Malcolm. *The Mountain World 1955*. George Allen & Unwin Ltd., 1955.

Bass, Dick. Wells, Frank. Ridgeway, Rick. *Seven Summits*. Warner Books, 1986.

Beazley, Mitchell. *World Mountaineering – The World's Great Mountains by the World's Great Mountaineers*. Octopus Publishing Group, 1998.

Benuzzi, Felice. *No Picnic on Mount Kenya*. E.P. Dutton & Company, 1953.

Bonington, Chris. Heroic Climbs – *A Celebration of World Mountaineering*. The Mountaineers, 1994.

Bueler, William. Mountains of the World – A Handbook for Climbers and Hikers. The Mountaineers, 1970.

Burns, Cameron M. *Kilimanjaro & East Africa – A Climbing and Trekking Guide*. The Mountaineers Books, 2006.

Cleare, John. *Mountains*. Crown Publishers, Inc., 1975.

Douglas, John Scott. *Summits of Adventure*. Dodd, Mead & Company, 1954.

Frison – Roche, Roger. Jouty, Sylvain. *A History of Mountain Climbing*. Flammarion, 1996.

Heckmair, Anderl. *My Life – Eiger North Face, Grandes Jorasses, & Other Adventures*. The Mountaineers, 2002.

Heckmair, Anderl. *My Life as a Mountaineer*. Victor Gollancz Ltd., 1975.

Kelsey, Michael R. *Climber's and Hiker's Guide to the World's Mountains & Volcanoes*. Kelsey Publishing, 2001.

Lawe, Dr. Ferdinand C. *The Story of Mountains*. Doubleday & Company, 1950.

Le Bon, Leo. Where Mountains Live – Twelve Great Treks of the World. An Aperture Book, 1987.

Mackinder, H.J. *The First Ascent of Mount Kenya*. Ohio University Press, 1991.

Magazine Article

Travel Africa. Kilimanjaro – The Complete Guide.

A Place At High Table. Edition 33. Winter 2005/6

McNamee, Gregory. *The Mountain World – A Literary Journey*. Sierra Club Books, 2000.

Megarry, Jacquetta. *Explore Mount Kilimanjaro – Marangu, Machame and Rongai Routes*. Rucksak Readers, 2005.

Milne, Malcom. *The Book of Modern Mountaineering*. G.P. Putnam's Sons, 1968.

Moushabeck, Michel. *Kilimanjaro – A Photographic Journey to the Roof of Africa*. Interlink Books, 2009.

Pluth, David. *Uganda Rwenzori – A Range of Images*. Little Wolf Press, 1996.

Poindexter, Joseph. *To The Summit – Fifty Mountains That Lure, Inspire, and Challenge*. Black Dog & Leventhal Publishers, 1998.

Pyatt, Edward. *Mountains & Mountaineering – Facts & Feats*. Guinness Superlatives Limited, 1980.

Reuther, David. Thorn, John. (editors). *The Armchair Mountaineer*. Charles Scribner's Sons, 1984.

Ridgeway, Rick. *The Shadow of Kilimanjaro – On Foot across East Africa*. Henry Holt and Company, 1998.

Robson, Peter. *Mountains of Kenya.* East African Publishing House, 1969.

Salkeld, Audrey. *Kilimanjaro – To the Roof of Africa.* National Geographic, 2002.

Sedeen, Margaret. *Mountain Worlds.* The National Geographic Society, 1988.

Shipton, Eric. *That Untraveled World.* Charles Scribner's Sons, 1969.

Shulman, Neville. On Top Of Africa – *The Climbing of Kilimanjaro and Mount Kenya.* Element, 1995.

Spectorsky, A.C. *The Book of the Mountains.* Appleton – Century – Crofts, 1955.

Styles, Showell. *On Top of the World – An Illustrated History of Mountain Climbing.* The MacMillan Company, 1967.

Tilman, H.W. *The Seven Mountain – Travel Books.* Diadem Books Ltd., 1983.

Ullman, James Ramsey. *The Age of Mountaineering.* J.B. Lippincott Company, 1954.

Unsworth, Walt. *Encyclopaedia of Mountaineering.* Hodder & Stoughton, 1992.

Venables, Stephen. *Voices from the Mountains – 40 True-Life Stories of Unforgettable Adventure, Drama, and Human Endurance.* Reader's Digest, 2006.

Venables, Stephen. *First Ascent – Pioneering Mountain Climbs.* Firefly Books, 2008.

Wielochowski, A.L., *Ruwenzori Map and Guide.* A.L. Wielochowski, 1989.

TWO

ANTARCTICA

High Peaks Above the Great White Open

Years 1905 to 2011

"Difficult and dangerous as it may sometimes be,
there is a purity and simplicity inherent in climbing.
I think the reason mountaineering has become popular
in recent years is that climbing feeds an emotional need:
a climb has a beginning, a middle, and an end. It has a
clear purpose – getting to the summit and dealing with
the intricacies of the route and the sense of exposure – and
it has a clear outcome – you reach the summit or you do not.
It is not vague or uncertain or equivocal, like so much of
modern life. And it is more than just a physical challenge;
it is an intellectual and emotional challenge as well.
You reach a high point not just topographically
but emotionally. Nothing epitomizes the idea of
accomplishment and the satisfaction one gets from
it better than climbing to the top of a mountain."

1999
Jochen Hemmleb
German Mount Everest Historian
(1973 –   )

ANTARCTICA

Antarctica represents ten percent of the world's land mass and includes approximately 86 peaks over 10,000 feet (3,048 meters) above sea level. Seven of these mountains exceed 15,000 feet (4,572 meters) and fourteen are over 14,000 feet (4,267 meters) high. Mount Vinson (16,050 ft./4,892 m.) is the highest mountain in Antarctica. The mountain range containing Mount Vinson was discovered in 1957 by United States navy pilots. Of the seven highest continental summits ("Seven Summits"), Mount Vinson was the last to be climbed (1966).

Antarctica's polar plateau lies mostly between 2,000 to 4,000 meters (6,562 feet to 13,124 feet). The South Pole is located at 2,800 meters or 9,187 feet. Surrounding the South Pole are approximately twenty-five named mountain ranges. The Ellsworth Mountains in West Antarctica contains the five highest summits. Although several high summits were reached prior to the late 1960s (1908, 1938, 1958), it was in December of 1966 and January of 1967 that the four highest summits were first climbed. Well-known American mountaineer Nick Clinch (1930 –) led an American Alpine Club expedition to Antarctica that first climbed Mount Vinson, Mount Tyree (15,919 ft./4,852 m.), Mount Shinn (15,289 ft./4,660 m.), and Mount Gardner (15,004 ft./4,573 m.). The normal climbing season in Antarctica is during the months of November, December, and January when there is nearly 24 hours of daylight.

The single most complete chronology of mountaineering first ascents in Antarctica was published by Australian climber, writer, and Antarctica researcher Damien Gildea (1969 –) in 1998. *The Antarctic Mountaineering Chronology* identified over 850 first ascents of Antarctic peaks (not including high points* or nunataks**) from 1902 to 1998. Sixty of these first ascents were on peaks over 3,000 meters (9,843 feet) in elevation and twenty-one ascents were over 4,000 meters (13,124 feet). Between 2001 and 2008, Gildea accomplished many ascents in Antarctica including the first ascent of Mount Anderson (13,594 ft./4,143 m.) in 2007. The Gildea Glacier on the south side of the Mount Vinson is named for him.

There has been a dramatic increase in mountaineering in Antarctica since 1983 when Mount Vinson was climbed (sixth overall ascent) by American mountaineers Dick Bass (1929 –) and Rick Ridgeway (1949 –). Bass was on his quest to become the first person to climb all Seven Summits in the world which he completed in 1985. Mount Vinson was the fifth summit of the Seven Summits for Dick Bass.

I have selected twenty-three (23) peak first ascents of mountains in Antarctica, eighteen (18) first ascents, and twenty-eight (28) other mountaineering events for this chapter.

Ten Highest Peaks in Antarctica

1.	Mount Vinson	16,050 ft./4,892 m.***
2.	Mount Tyree	15,919 ft./4,852 m.****
3.	Mount Shinn	15,289 ft./4,660 m.****

Ten Highest Peaks in Antarctica (continued)

---

* High Point: A high point of land, snow, or ice in non-mountainous terrain.
** Nunatak: An isolated hill, knob, ridge, or peak of bedrock projecting prominently above the surface of a glacier and completely surrounded by glacial ice.

4.	Mount Gardner	15,004 ft./4,573 m.****
5.	Mount Kirkpatrick	14,856 ft./4,528 m.****
6.	Mount Branscomb	14,830 ft./4,520 m. ****
7.	Mount Epperly	14,791 ft./4,508 m.****
8.	Peak 4500	14,764 ft./4,500 m.****
9.	Mount Elizabeth	14,698 ft./4,480 m.****
10.	Mount Rutford	14,689 ft./4,477 m.****

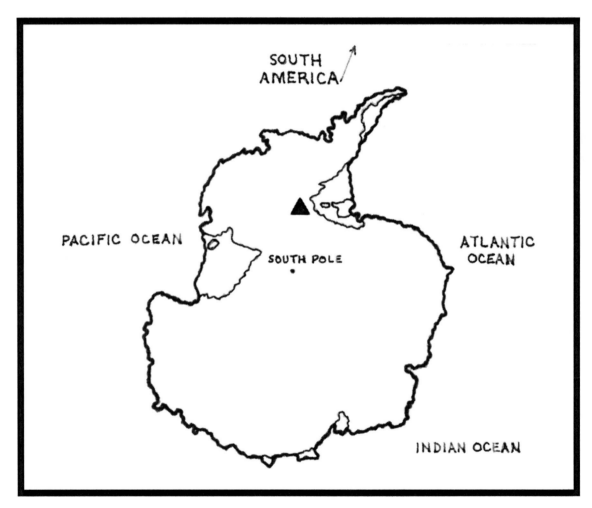

▲ Highest Mountain: Mount Vinson – 16,050 ft./4,892 m.
First Ascent Date: December 18, 1966
Expedition: American

*** Elevation recalculated in 2001. The Vinson Massif includes five named sub-peaks over 15,000 feet (4,572 meters).
**** Elevations re-calculated in 2006.

Antarctica Timeline

1905: PEAK FIRST ASCENT *SAVOIA*

February 7. Two members of French explorer Jean-Baptiste Charcot's expedition to Antarctica (1904 to 1907) made the first ascent of Savoia Peak (4,643 ft./1,415 m.). This was the first major peak to be climbed on Antarctica's Peninsula. Pierre Dayné and Jacques Jabet reached the summit. Dayné (Italian) was the first professional mountain guide to be employed in Antarctica.

1908: PEAK FIRST ASCENT *EREBUS*

March 10. The first major peak in Antarctica to be climbed was Mount Erebus (12,451 feet/3,795 meters) on Ross Island. This was also the first winter ascent of any major Antarctic mountain. Five members of Ernest Shackleton's expedition made this first ascent from the mountain's west side in five days. Jameson Adams, Edgar Davis, Alistair Forbes MacKay, Eric Marshall, and Douglas Mawson all reached the summit. Erebus is a volcano that last erupted in 1947 and it is the most southerly volcano in the world. "Erebus" was the name of one of the two ships that Sir James Clark Ross sailed near Antarctica in 1841. The second ascent of Mount Erebus occurred in 1912

1935:

November 23. American Antarctic explorer and pilot Lincoln Ellsworth (1880 – 1951) discovered the Ellsworth Mountains and more specifically the Sentinel Range during his trans-Antarctic flight from Dundee Island to the Ross Ice Shelf. Ellsworth made four expeditions to Antarctica from 1933 to 1939. The Sentinel Range contains the four highest peaks in Antarctica.

1957:

The highest summit in Antarctica was first identified by U.S. Navy pilots and then named for Georgia U.S. Congressman Carl Vinson (1883 – 1981) who supported Antarctica research and exploration. This peak was named Mount Vinson.

1958: PEAK FIRST ASCENT *HUGGINS*

January 27. New Zealand mountaineers F.R. Brooke and B. Gunn made the first ascent of Mount Huggins (12,254 ft./3,735 m.) in the Royal Society Range. Their high camp was established at the 8,000 foot elevation. The ascent from this camp to the summit took eight hours. They were members of the Trans-Antarctica Expedition that was led by New Zealand's most famous mountaineer Sir Edmund Hillary (1919 – 2008). This peak was named for Sir William Huggins (1824 – 1910) — President of the Royal Society from 1900 to 1905.

1962: PEAK FIRST ASCENT *FRIDTJOF NANSEN*

January. W. Herbert of England, V. McGregor, P. Otway, and K. Pain (all three from New Zealand) made the first ascent of Mount Fridtjof Nansen (13,353 ft./4,070 m.) in the Queen Maud Mountains.

1962: PEAK FIRST ASCENT *SCOTT*

November 20. Three members of the Falkland Islands Dependency Survey team made the first ascent of Mount Scott (2,887 ft./880 m.) via its east ridge. This peak is one of the most photographed peaks on Antarctica's Peninsula. Edward Grimshaw, Peter Kimber, and Bob Lewis all reached the summit.

1964: PEAK FIRST ASCENT *JACKSON*

Scottish mountaineer John Cunningham (1927 – 1980) and several other members of Scotland's Creagh Dhu Mountaineering Club made the first ascent of Mount Jackson (10,447 ft./3,184 m.)—the highest peak on the Antarctic Peninsula.

1966/1967:

December/January. The American Antarctic Mountaineering Expedition was led by Nicholas B. Clinch (1930 –   ). This expedition made the first ascents of six peaks in the Ellsworth Mountains including the highest peak in Antarctica—Mount Vinson (788 miles from the South Pole). The American Alpine Club was one of the primary organizations that sponsored this expedition. These six first ascents were:

> [7]▲ **1. PEAK FIRST ASCENT *MOUNT VINSON*** (16,050 ft./4,892 m.)
> December 18: Barry Corbet, John Evans, Bill Long, and Pete Schoening
> December 19: Eiichi Fukushima, Charley Hollister, and Brian Marts
> December 20: Nick Clinch, Dick Wahlstrom, and Sam Silverstein
>
> Excerpts from John Evans' Mount Vinson climbing journal:
>
> Camp I. Sunday. December 18 (1966)
>
> *"The day of the first ascent of Mount Vinson!*
>
> *For some reason I was unable to sleep again last night and was quite happy to get up and moving at 6. Felt very sick until about 7 or so and abstained from breakfast. Roped up with Corbett and left at 8:15 following Long and Schoening. Alternated leading with the other rope to suit Barry's filming. The view to the north across Shinn was particularly spectacular. I felt good until we reached rock about 500 feet below the summit. Here the altitude got me and I was a real drag on the rope.*
>
> *Long took a level sight with his Brunton and declared ours was the highest point. I sighted with Hollister's Brunton and at first thought another peak a couple miles farther was higher, but fortunately I was in error and soon convinced myself we were on the highest point in the range."*

---

7 One of the world's Seven Summits.

Base camp. Tuesday. December 20 (1966)

"Message from climbing team to USARP* at McMurdo:

Mount Vinson climbed by all members of American Antarctic Mountaineering Expedition. We hope to climb Mount Shinn when weather clears. All members OK and morale good."

2. PEAK FIRST ASCENT *MOUNT SHINN* (15,289 ft./4,660 m.)
December 21: Barry Corbet, Charley Hollister, Sam Silverstein, and Dick Wahlstrom
December 22: Bill Long and Pete Schoening
December 24: Nick Clinch, John Evans, Eiichi Fukushima, and Brian Marts
December 31: John Evans and Brian Marts

3. PEAK FIRST ASCENT *MOUNT GARDNER* (15,004 ft./4,573 m.)
January 2: Barry Corbet, Nick Clinch, Charley Hollister, and Eiichi Fukushima
January 7: Bill Long, Pete Schoening, Sam Silverstein, and Dick Wahlstrom

4. PEAK FIRST ASCENT *MOUNT TYREE* (15,919 ft./4,852 m.)
January 5: Barry Corbet and John Evans. This climbing team had to first climb Mount Gardner in order to traverse over to Mount Tyree.

Excerpt from John Evans' Mount Vinson climbing journal about the first ascent of Mount Tyree:

Base camp. Sunday. January 8 (1967)

"Barry belayed from a knife-blade at the top of the 11th pitch of the summit block, and when I finished the next lead I could see that the summit was only 60 feet away on easy snow. Barry led to the crest and I joined him, delighted to find we had happily come out precisely on the highest point of the long summit crest. The rocky prong at the north end of the crest was only about 30 feet away and a few feet below us; the summit was the culmination of 3 snowy ridges.

We summited just at 6 p.m. and I tried to raise Camp II without success. After a minute or so Barry took the radio and heard Dick Wahlstrom asking where we were. Barry's reply will not soon be forgotton; 'Look on the summit, you lunkheads!' Wahlstrom verified our position with binoculars and replied: 'Good. Now we can go back to bed.'"

---

* United States Antarctic Research Program

5. PEAK FIRST ASCENT *MOUNT LONG GABLES* (13,488 ft./4,111 m.)

January 12: Eiichi Fukushima, Bill Long, Brian Marts, and Pete Schoening

6. PEAK FIRST ASCENT *MOUNT OSTENSO* (13,403 ft./4,085 m.)

January 12: John Evans, Charley Hollister, Sam Silverstein, and Dick Wahlstrom

1967: PEAK FIRST ASCENT *ANDRUS*

November 14. American mountaineers Robert Maigetter and Gary Neptune (1946 –) made the first ascent of Mount Andrus (9,770 ft./2,978 m.) in Marie Byrd Land. Andrus is an extinct shield volcano with a three-mile wide summit caldera.

1968: Equipment – Deadman Anchor

This anchor is a metal plate or fluke (various sizes) that has a hole in it for a rope or wire cable to be attached. Other holes allow for snow/ice to freeze through the fluke and hold it firmly in place. This anchor was originally designed for tethering dogs in the ice of Antarctica. Mountaineers came to adopt the deadman as a reliable one-direction snow anchor.

1979:

December 22. Members of a United States scientific party made the second expedition ascent of Mount Vinson (summit elevation at this time was 16,864 ft./5,140 m.). They recalculated the summit elevation and adjusted it downwards to 4,897 meters or 16,067 feet.

1979:

An Air New Zealand sightseeing flight carrying 257 passengers and crew crashed into Mount Erebus (12, 450 feet/3,795 meters) killing all on board. This high volcanic peak is located on Ross Island in McMurdo Sound. Famous New Zealand mountaineer Sir Edmund Hillary (1919 – 2008) was to have been a passenger on this flight but changed his schedule just before this flight took off.

1983: FIRST ASCENT

November 30. British mountaineer Chris Bonington (1934 –) made the fifth ascent of Mount Vinson (16,050 ft./4,892 m.) followed shortly thereafter by American climbers Dick Bass (1929 –) and Rick Ridgeway (1949 –). Japanese mountaineers Tae Maeda and Yuichiro Miura joined American climbers Steve Marts and Frank Wells (1932 – 1994) in making the seventh overall ascent. Bass and Wells were on their quest to become the first climbers to reach all Seven Summits in the world.

1985: FIRST ASCENT

June 7. British mountaineer Roger Mear made the first winter ascent (solo) of Mount Erebus (12,451 ft./3,795 m.) on the Ross Ice Shelf. This was the first winter ascent of any Antarctica peak. The temperature on the summit was -76°F.

1985:

November 19. An American – Canadian mountaineering team climbed Mount Vinson. Canadian Pat Morrow became the second person to climb all Seven Summits. Morrow and M. Williams became the first to ski down Mount Vinson.

1985: PEAK FIRST ASCENT *MARKHAM*

December 5. American climbers D. Egerton and E. Stump and Australian climber R. Korsch made the first ascent of Mount Markham (14,272 ft./4,350 m.) in the Queen Elizabeth Range. This climbing party used both a helicopter and a snowmobile to reach their higher camps. This peak was named for English geographer, polar explorer and former president of the Royal Geographical Society (1863 to 1888) Sir Clements Markham (1830 – 1916). Markham organized the National Antarctic Expedition of 1901 – 04 (British).

1985:

British-Canadian pilot Giles Kershaw (1956 – 1997) began his flight service transporting mountaineers from South America to Antarctica to climb Mount Vinson (16,050 ft./4,892 m.). Kershaw was tragically killed in March of 1990 when his kit-built gyro-copter crashed on the Antarctic Peninsula. He was 41 years old.

1988: PEAK FIRST ASCENT *MINTO*

February 18. Australian mountaineers Jonathan Chester, Lyle Closs, Lincoln Hall, Chris Hilton, Greg Mortimer, and Glenn Singleman made the first ascent of Mount Minto (13,665 ft./4,165 m.) in the Admiralty Mountains. This is the highest peak in North Victoria Land. All six climbers reached the summit via the World Park Ridge (south ridge).

1988: FIRST ASCENT

December 9. Dr. Lisa Densmore from the Yukon Territory of Canada became the first woman to climb Mount Vinson (16,050 ft./4,892 m.) in the Sentinel Range of the Ellsworth Mountains.

1988:

December 12. Alaskan mountaineer Vern Tejas (1953 –) made the first solo climb of Mount Vinson (16,050 ft./4,892 m.) in Antarctica's Ellsworth Mountains. Tejas completed this roundtrip (base camp-summit-base camp) climb in 14 hours.

1988:

American professional mountain guides Phil Ershler (1951 –) and Vern Tejas (1953 –) began guiding clients up Mount Vinson (16,050 ft./4,892 m.).

1989: FIRST ASCENT

November. American climber Terry "Mugs" Stump (1949 – 1992) made the first solo ascents of Mounts Gardner (15,004 ft./4,573 m.) and Tyree (15,919 ft./4,852 m.) in the Sentinel Range of the

Ellsworth Mountains. This was the second overall ascent of Mount Gardner (southwest face)—23 years after the first ascent in 1966.

1989: FIRST ASCENT

November. New Zealand mountaineer Rob Hall (1961 – 1996) made the first solo ascent of Mount Shinn (15,289 ft./4,660 m.) in the Sentinel Range. This was the eighth overall ascent.

1989: FIRST ASCENT

November. The first alpine style ascent of Mount Vinson (16,050 ft./4,892 m.) was made by two New Zealand climbers (P. Fitzgerald and R. Hall) and two American climbers and brothers (E. Stump and T. Stump).

1990:

March 5. British-Canadian pilot Giles Kershaw (1949-1990) was killed when his kit-built gyrocopter crashed on the Jones Ice Shelf of the Antarctic Peninsula. He was buried on Antarctica's Blailock Island. Kershaw began his flight service from South America to Antarctica in 1985.

1990:

December 12. New Zealand mountaineers Rob Hall (1961 – 1996) and Gary Ball (– 1993) completed their climbing of the world's Seven Summits (the highest summit on each of the world's seven continents) in one seven-month period (May 10 to December 12). Their final summit (the 7th) was Mount Vinson (16,050 ft./4,892 m.).

1991: PEAK FIRST ASCENT *KIRKPATRICK*

January 7. The first ascent of Mount Kirkpatrick (14,856 ft./4,528 m.) in the Queen Alexandra Range was made by American climbers D. Elliot, T. Fleming, and C. Miller.

1991: FIRST ASCENT

January. German mountaineer Rudiger Lang made the first true solo ascent of Mount Vinson (16,050 ft./4,892 m.) via a new route on the west face.

1992: FIRST ASCENT

November 26. American mountaineer Robert Anderson solo climbed two new routes on Mount Vinson: the south face (Sunshine Wall) and the west-southwest ridge (Rolex Ridge).

1992: PEAK FIRST ASCENT *CRADDOCK*

December 14. Four climbers from the United States (C. Anker, C. Duval, J. Smith, and P. Teten) made the first ascent of Mount Craddock (14,331 ft./4,368 m.) in the Sentinel Range of the Ellsworth Mountains. Anker and Smith reached the summit. Their summit route followed the west spur.

1994: PEAK FIRST ASCENT *ULVETANNA*

February 2. Norwegian mountaineers Robert Caspersen, Ivar Tollefson, and Sjur Nesheim made the first ascent of the 9,617 ft./2,931 m. granite spire known as Ulvetanna (northwest face) in Queen Maud Land via the northwest face. This Norwegian expedition of 13 members climbed 36 peaks in the Fenriskjeften Massif.

1994: PEAK FIRST ASCENT *EPPERLY*

December 1. Swiss climber Erhard Loretan (1959 – 2011) made the first ascent (solo) of Mount Epperly (14,791 ft./4,508 m.) in the Sentinel Range via a couloir on the southwest face.

1994: PEAK FIRST ASCENT *VAUGHAN*

December 16. American Norman Vaughan (1905 – 2005) from Salem, Massachusetts made the first ascent of Mount Vaughan (10,302 ft./3,140 m.) in Antarctica just prior to his 89th birthday. He was guided up this peak by Alaskan mountaineering guide Vern Tejas (1953 –   ). Vaughn's wife, Carolyn Muegge-Vaughan, was also with him. This peak was named after Norman Vaughan by Admiral Richard E. Byrd in 1929 when Vaughan accompanied Byrd to explore Antarctica. Norman Vaughan died on December 23, 2005 at age 100.

1997: PEAK FIRST ASCENT *RAKEKNIVEN*

January 3. An American expedition made the first ascent of Rakekniven ("The Razor," 7,759 ft./2,365 m.) in Queen Maud Land. Conrad Anker (1962 –   ), Mike Graber, Jon Krakauer (1954 –   ), Alex Lowe (1958 – 1999), Rick Ridgeway (1949 –   ), and Gordon Wiltsie (1952 –   ) all reached the summit. They named their route the Snow Petrel Wall. Approximately 2,000 ft./610 m. of Rakekniven is located above the icecap while 5,700 ft./1,737 m. lies below the ice. This American team also climbed three other Antarctica peaks: Kubus Mountain (9,793 ft./2,985 m.), Trollslottet (8,980 ft./2,737 m.), and Kyrkjeskipet Peak (10,115 ft./3,083 m.).

1998:

Over 400 ascents of Mount Vinson (16,050 ft./4,892 m.) had been accomplished by the end of this year (1966 to 1998). Many of these ascents were by those climbers seeking to complete the world's Seven Summits.

2001: FIRST ASCENT

January. An American expedition used a Global Positioning System unit (Trimble Model 4800) to remeasure the summit elevation of Mount Vinson. This GPS unit was placed on the summit for twenty minutes. The previously accepted elevation of 4,897 meters (16,067 feet) was corrected to 4,900.3 meters (16,077 feet). This measurement was obtained in -35°F temperatures. The members of this scientific expedition were: Conrad Anker, John Armstrong, Liesl Clark, Dave Hahn, Jon Krakauer, Andrew McLean, Rob Raker, and Dan Stone. This expedition also made the first ascent of the east side of Mount Vinson. The current accepted summit elevation for Mount Vinson is 16,050 feet/4,892 meters (see 2005).

2002:

December. Australian mountaineer and Antarctic researcher Damien Gildea (1969 –) and Chilean mountaineer Rodrigo Fica spent seven hours camping on the summit of Mount Shinn. They placed a Trimble 5700 dual-frequency GPS on this summit to determine an accurate summit elevation. The new elevation was 4,660 meters or 15,289 feet. This GPS project was sponsored by the US based Omega Foundation.

2004: FIRST ASCENT

January. British mountaineer Heather Morning made the first female solo ascent of Mount Vinson (16,050 ft./4,892 m.).

2004: FIRST ASCENT

December. American climber Johnny Strange (age 12) became the youngest person to climb Mount Vinson (16,050 ft./4,892 m.) in the Sentinel Range. He was accompanied by his father Brian and American guide Vern Tejas (1953 –).

2005:

January. The US-based Omega Foundation sponsored Damien Gildea, Rodrigo Fica, and Camilo Rada to summit Mount Vinson, pitch their tent on the summit, and determine a revised GPS elevation. They accomplished these objectives and produced a new summit elevation: 4,892 meters or 16,050 feet.

2005:

Five sub-peaks of Mount Vinson were officially named for members of the 1966 first ascent expedition. These sub-peaks are: Clinch Peak (15,883 ft./4,841 m.), Corbett Peak (15,821 ft./4,822 m.), Schoening Peak (15,562 ft./4,743 m.), Silverstein Peak (15,716 ft./4,790 m.) and Wahlstrom Peak (15,388 ft./4,690 m.). Two lower peaks near Mount Vinson were named for John Evans and Bill Long, members of the team that first climbed Vinson in 1966.

2005/2006:

140 mountaineers reached the summit of Mount Vinson (16,050 ft./4,892 m.) only four climbers were unsuccessful during this climbing season.

2006:

August 18. The United States Geological Survey Advisory Committee on Antarctic Names officially approved the name "Mount Vinson" as the highest summit of the Mount Vinson.

2006:

November.

2006: FIRST ASCENT

December 9. American mountaineer Jed Brown made a solo first ascent of Mount Rutford (14,689 ft./4,477 m.) in the Craddock Massif south of the Mount Vinson. Brown climbed the 6,500 foot/1,981 meter west face.

2006:

Four members of the 1966 first ascent of Mount Vinson met at the Vinson base camp to celebrate the 40th anniversary of this climb. Eiichi Fukushima, John Evans (1938 –   ), Sam Silverstein, and Brian Marts were present.

2006:

The Omega Foundation of Australia recalculated the summit elevations of the following peaks in Antarctica:

1.	Mount Vinson	16,050 ft.	4,892 m.
2.	Mount Tyree	15,919 ft.	4,852 m.
3.	Mount Shinn	15,289 ft.	4,660 m.
4.	Mount Craddock	15,256 ft.	4,650 m.
5.	Mount Gardner	15,050 ft.	4,587 m.
6.	Mount Kirkpatrick	14,856 ft.	4,528 m.
7.	Mount Elizabeth	14,699 ft.	4,480 m.
8.	Mount Rutford	14,689 ft.	4,477 m.
9.	Peak 4360	14,305 ft	4,360 m.
10.	Mount Epperly	14,302 ft.	4,359 m.

2006: FIRST ASCENT

A Norwegian expedition made the first ascent of Ulvetanna's (9,712 ft./2,960 m.) north face in Queen Maud Land. Robert Caspersen, Ivar Tollefsen, Stein-Ivar Gravdal, and Trond Hilde climbed this rock peak in sixteen-days capsule style (21 pitches, 3,149 ft./960 m. route).

2007: PEAK FIRST ASCENT *ANDERSON*

January 8 and 9. Australian climber Damien Gildea (1969 –   ) and American climber Jed Brown made the first ascent of Mount Anderson (13,594 ft./4,143 m.) in the Sentinel Range. This 5,000 ft./1,524 m. vertical route took 13 hours to climb. Mount Anderson is located 30 miles/50 kilometers north of Mount Vinson.

2007: FIRST ASCENT

December 28. Camilo Rada and Damien Gildea (1969 –   ) climbed a new route (6,890 ft./2,100 m.) on the south face of Mount Epperly (14,791 ft./4,508 m.) in the Sentinel Range. This was the third overall ascent of   Epperly. This ascent required 20 hours of continuous climbing.

2007:

As of this year's climbing season, Mount Vinson has had a total of 1,090 ascents with 157 ascents (including 19 women) in the 2007 – 08 season. American climber and guide Dave Hahn (1962 –) had reached this summit 25 times.

2008:

January 21. Tomiyasu Ishikawa (1936 –) became the oldest Japanese mountaineer (age 71) to climb all Seven Summits when he reached the summit of Mount Vinson (16,050 ft./4,892 m.).

2008: FIRST ASCENT

January. Maria Paz Ibarra and Jarmila Tyrril established a new route on the west face of Mount Vinson (16,050 ft./4,892 m.). Named the Chilean-Slovak Route, this 1,500 meter (4,921 feet) mixed route was the first new route on Vinson to be climbed by an all-women team.

2008:

December. 2008 was the busiest year ever for climbing activity on Mount Vinson (16,050 ft./4,892 m.). The summit was reached by 190 mountaineers. As of this month, an estimated 1,147 climbers had reached Mount Vinson's summit (1966 to 2008).

2008: FIRST ASCENT

Austrian climber Chris Stangl made a solo direct first ascent of Mount Shinn's (15,289 ft./4,660 m.) south face.

2009:

January 19. American mountaineer and professional guide Dave Hahn (1962 –) reached the summit of Mount Vinson (16,050 feet/4,892 meters) for the 27th time.

2009: FIRST ASCENT

January. French mountaineers Mathieu Cortial and Lional Daudet made the first ascent of the northwest ridge of Mount Parry (8,268 ft./2,520 m.) on Brabant Island just off the coast of the Antarctic Peninsula.

2009:

Approximately 190 climbers reached the summit of Mount Vinson this year bringing the total number of summit climbers to over 1,330.

2010:

January 22. American teenager Johnny Collinson (1992 –) became the youngest person to climb all Seven Summits when he reached the summit of Mount Vinson (16,050 ft./4,892 m.). At age seventeen, Collinson climbed all Seven Summits in 367 days. His climbing partner was Willie Benegas.

2010: PEAK FIRST ASCENT *INVERLEITH*

December 14. British mountaineers Derek Buckle, Mike Flethcher, Stu Gallagher, Richard MacIntyre, Olly Metherell, Dave Wynne-Jones, and Phil Wickens (leader) made the first ascent of Mount Inverleith (6,686 ft./2,038 m.) on the Antarctic Peninsula via the east face and north ridge. This is one of the highest Antarctic Peninsula peaks.

2011: FIRST ASCENT

January 13. British mountaineers Gordon Clark, Simon Hall, Rajiv Joshi, and James Lancashire made the first complete ascent of Mount Branscomb's (14,830 ft./4,520 m.) north ridge. This peak is located near the west face of Mount Vinson in the Ellsworth mountains.

2011:

December 25. American mountaineer Jordan Romero (1996 –   ) became the youngest person (age 15) to climb the Seven Summits when he reached the summit of Mount Vinson (16,050 ft./4,892 m.) in Antarctica. His father and step-mother were with him on this ascent. In 1996, Romero climbed Kilimanjaro at age 10—his first of the Seven Summits. In 2009, at age 13, he summited Mount Everest—the youngest climber to reach this summit. The previous record for the youngest age was 16 which was briefly held by British climber George Atkinson who completed all seven climbs in May of 2011.

2011:

Mount Elizabeth (14,698 ft./4,480 m.) remains the highest unclimbed peak in Antarctica. It is the ninth highest peak and is located in the Victoria Land region.

"So if you cannot understand that there is something in man which responds to the challenge of this mountain and goes out to meet it, that the struggle is the struggle of life itself upward and forever upward, then you won't see why we go. What we get from this adventure is just sheer joy. And joy is, after all, the end of life.
We do not live to eat and make money.
We eat and make money to enjoy life."

George Leigh Mallory
British mountaineer
(1886 – 1924)

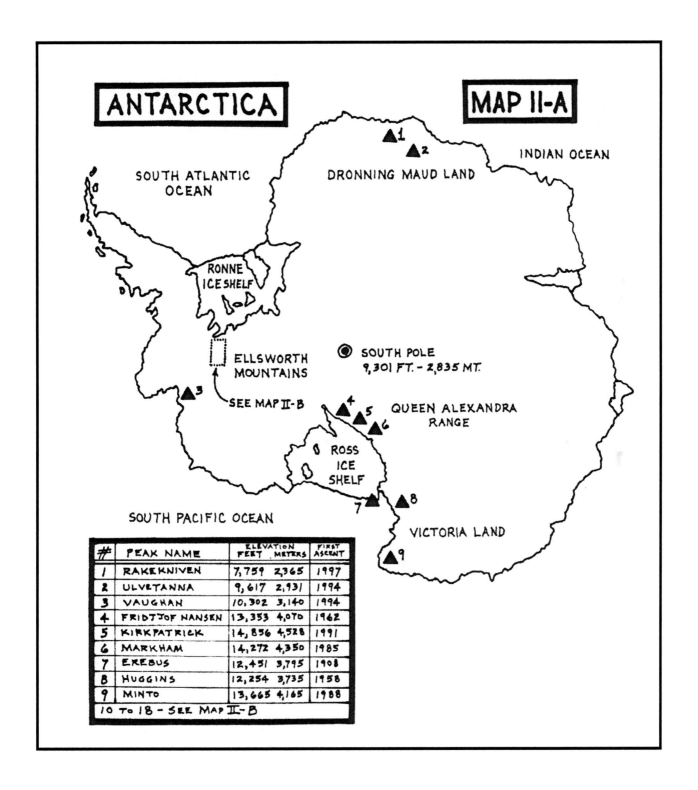

ANTARCTICA

MAP II-A

INDIAN OCEAN

SOUTH ATLANTIC OCEAN

DRONNING MAUD LAND

RONNE ICE SHELF

ELLSWORTH MOUNTAINS

SEE MAP II-B

SOUTH POLE
9,301 FT. – 2,835 MT.

QUEEN ALEXANDRA RANGE

ROSS ICE SHELF

SOUTH PACIFIC OCEAN

VICTORIA LAND

#	PEAK NAME	ELEVATION FEET	METERS	FIRST ASCENT
1	RAKEKNIVEN	7,759	2,365	1997
2	ULVETANNA	9,617	2,931	1994
3	VAUGHAN	10,302	3,140	1994
4	FRIDTJOF NANSEN	13,353	4,070	1962
5	KIRKPATRICK	14,856	4,528	1991
6	MARKHAM	14,272	4,350	1985
7	EREBUS	12,451	3,795	1908
8	HUGGINS	12,254	3,735	1958
9	MINTO	13,665	4,165	1988
10 TO 18 – SEE MAP II-B				

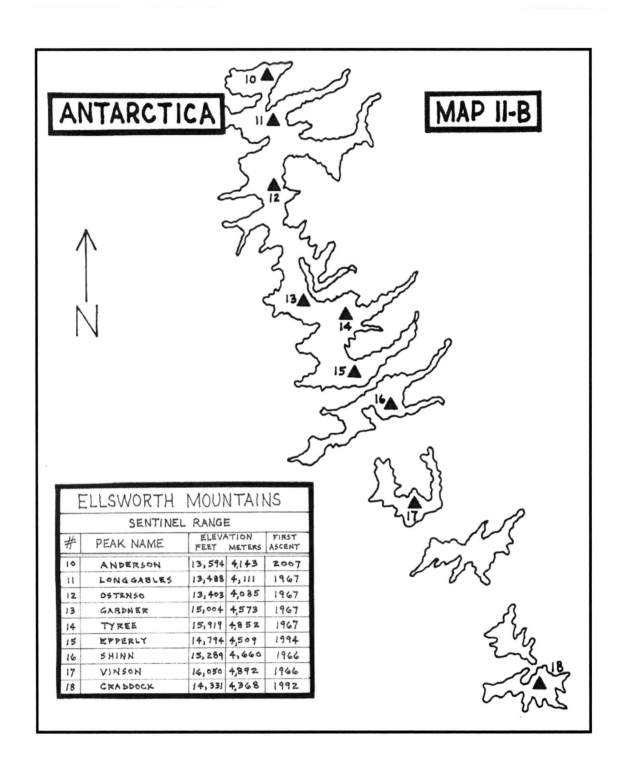

ANTARCTICA   MAP II-B

N

ELLSWORTH MOUNTAINS			
SENTINEL RANGE			
#	PEAK NAME	ELEVATION FEET METERS	FIRST ASCENT
10	ANDERSON	13,594	4,143	2007
11	LONG GABLES	13,488	4,111	1967
12	OSTENSO	13,403	4,085	1967
13	GARDNER	15,004	4,573	1967
14	TYREE	15,919	4,852	1967
15	EPPERLY	14,794	4,509	1994
16	SHINN	15,289	4,660	1966
17	VINSON	16,050	4,892	1966
18	CRADDOCK	14,331	4,368	1992

Left to right: Mounts Shinn (far left), Tyree, and Gardner.
Photo by Camilo Rada

The Sentinel Range from the northeast. Left to right: Mounts Vinson, Shinn, Tyree, Gardner, and Giovinetto.
Photo by Jed Brown

ANTARCTICA: The 25 Highest Peaks

RANK and PEAK NAME	ELEVATION FEET·METERS	LOCATION	FIRST ASCENT DATE	EXPEDITION	SUMMIT CLIMBERS
1 Mount Vinson	16,050·4,892	Ellsworth Mountains	Dec. 18, 1966	American	Barry Corbet John Evans Bill Long Pete Schoening
			Dec. 19, 1966	American	Eiichi Fukushima Charley Hollister Brian Marts
			Dec. 20, 1966	American	Nick Clinch Dick Wahlstrom Sam Silverstein
2 Mount Tyree	15,919·4,852	Ellsworth Mountains	Jan. 6, 1967	American	Barry Corbet John Evans
3 Mount Shinn	15,289·4,660	Ellsworth Mountains	Dec. 21,1966	American	Barry Corbet Charley Hollister Sam Silverstein Dick Wahlstrom
			Dec. 22, 1966	American	Bill Long Pete Schoening
			Dec. 24, 1966	American	Nick Clinch John Evans Eiichi Fukushima Brian Marts
4 Mount Gardner	15,004·4,573	Ellsworth Mountains	Dec. 31,1966	American	John Evans Brian Marts
			Jan. 2, 1967	American	Barry Corbet Nick Clinch Charley Hollister Eiichi Fukushima
5 Mount Kirkpatrick	14,856·4,528	Queen Alex. Range	Jan. 7, 1991	American	D. Elliot T. Fleming C. Miller

ANTARCTICA: The 25 Highest Peaks (continued)

RANK and PEAK NAME	ELEVATION FEET·METERS	LOCATION	FIRST ASCENT DATE	EXPEDITION	SUMMIT CLIMBERS
6 Mount Branscomb	14,830·4,520				
7 Mount Epperly	14,791·4,508	Ellsworth Mountains	Dec. 1, 1994	Swiss	Erhard Loretan
8 Peak 4500*	14,764·4,500	Sentinel Range			
9 Mount Elizabeth	14,698·4,480	Victoria Ld.	Unclimbed as of 2011		
10 Mount Rutford	14,689·4,477	Sentinel Range	Dec. 2006	American	Jed Brown
11 Mount Craddock	14,331·4,368	Sentinel Rg.	Dec. 14, 1992	American	C. Anker C. Duval J. Smith P. Teten
12 Mount Markham	14,272·4,350	Victoria Ld.	Dec. 5, 1985	American/Australian	D. Egerton E. Stump R. Korsch
13 Mount Bell	14,118·4,303	Unclimbed as of 2010			
14 Mount Mackeller	14,076·4,290	Victoria Ld.	Unclimbed as of 2010		
15 Mount Sidley	14,059·4,285	Marie Byrd Land	Jan. 1990	New Zealand	Bill Atkinson
16 Mount Kaplan	13,878·4,230	Victoria Land	Unclimbed as of 2010		
17 Mount Minto	13,665·4,165	Admiralty Range	1988	Australian	Jonathan Chester Lyle Closs Lincoln Hall Chris Hilton Greg Mortmer Glenn Singleman

*a.k.a. "Peak of Kindness" or Peak Loretan"

ANTARCTICA: The 25 Highest Peaks (continued)

RANK and PEAK NAME	ELEVATION FEET·METERS	LOCATION	FIRST ASCENT DATE	EXPEDITION	SUMMIT CLIMBERS
18 Mount Miller	13,669·4,160	Queen Elizabeth Range	Unclimbed as of 2010		John Evans Charley Hollister Sam Silverstein Dick Wahlstrom
19 Mount Anderson	13,596·4,144	Sentinel Range	Jan. 8 and 9, 2007	Australian/ American	Damien Gildea Jed Brown
20 Mount Bentley	13,573·4,137		Dec. 1995	Finland	P. Degerman V. Gustafsson
21 Mount Dickerson	13,518·4,120	Unclimbed as of 2010			
22 Mount Long Gables	13,488·4,111	Sentinel Range	Jan. 12, 1967	American	E. Fukushima B. Long B. Marts P. Schoening
23 Flat Top	13,403·4,085	Unclimbed as of 2010			
24 Mount Ostenso	13,403·4,085	Ellsworth Mountains	Jan. 12, 1967	American	John Evans Charley Hollister Sam Silverstein Dick Wahlstrom
25 Mount Wade	13,403·4,085	Unclimbed as of 2010			

Selected Bibliography — Antarctica

Of the numerous books, journals, newspaper and magazine articles, and internet sites that have been used in the research for this book, the author is particularly indebted to the following sources:

American Alpine Club Journals. American Alpine Club, 1902 to 2010 (Various years).

Anderson, Robert Mads. *SUMMITS – Climbing the Seven Summits Solo.* Clarkson Potter Publishers, 1995.

Ardito, Stefano. *History of the Great Mountaineering Adventures.* The Mountaineers, 2000.

Ardito, Stefano. *Tales of Mountaineering.* White Star Publishers, 2000.

Barnes, Malcolm. *The Mountain World 1960/61.* George Allen & Unwin Ltd., 1961.

Barnes, Malcom. *The Mountain World 1962/63.* George Allen and Unwin Ltd., 1964.

Bass, Dick. Wells, Frank. Ridgeway, Rick. *Seven Summits.* Warner Books, 1986.

Beazley, Mitchell. *World Mountaineering – The World's Great Mountains By The World's Great Mountaineers.* Octopus Publishing Group, 1998.

Bonington, Chris. Quest For Adventure – *21 Stories of the Men and Women Who Challenged Oceans, Mountains, Deserts, Snow and Space.* Clarkson N. Potter, Inc., 1981.

Bonington, Chris. Heroic Climbs – *A Celebration of World Mountaineering.* The Mountaineers, 1994.

Cleare, John. *Mountains.* Crown Publishers, Inc., 1975.

Dyson, James L. *The World of Ice.* Alfred A. Knopf, 1962.

Frison-Roche, Roger. Jouty, Sylvain. *A History of Mountain Climbing.* Flammarion, 1996.

Fuchs, Sir Vivian. Hillary, Sir Edmund. *The Crossing of Antarctica – The Commonwealth Trans-Antarctic Expedition 1955 – 1958.* Little, Brown and Company, 1958.

Gildea, Damien. *The Antarctic Mountaineering Chronology.* Damien Gildea, 1998.

Gildea, Damien. *Mountaineering in Antarctica – Climbing in the Frozen South.* Editions Nevicata, 2010.

Hillary, Sir Edmund. *Nothing Venture, Nothing Win.* Coward, McCann & Geoghegan, Inc., 1975.

Hillary, Sir Edmund. *View From The Summit.* Doubleday, 1999.

Hillary, Sir Edmund. *No Latitude For Error.* Hodder & Stoughton, 1961.

Kurz, Marcel. *The Mountain World 1954.* George Allen & Unwin Ltd., 1954.

Messner, Reinhold. *Antarctica – Both Heaven and Hell.* The Mountaineers, 1991.

Milne, Malcolm. *The Book of Modern Mountaineering.* G.P. Putnam's Sons, 1968.

Neider, Charles – Editor. *Antarctica.* Dorset Press, 1972.

Poindexter, Joseph. *To The Summit – Fifty Mountains That Lure, Inspire and Challenge.* Black Dog & Leventhal Publishers, 1998.

Pyatt, Edward. *Mountains & Mountaineering – Facts & Feats.* Guinness Superlatives Limited, 1980.

Salkeld, Audrey – General Editor. *World Mountaineering – The World's Great Mountains By The World's Great Mountaineers.* Mitchell Beazley, 1998.

Sedeen, Margaret. *Mountain Worlds.* The National Geographic Society, 1988.

Spectorsky, A.C. *The Book of the Mountains.* Appleton – Century – Crofts, 1955.

Ullman, James Ramsey. *The Age of Mountaineering.* J.B. Lippincott Company, 1954.

Unsworth, Walt. *Encyclopedia of Mountaineering.* Hodder & Stoughton, 1992.

Vaughan, Norman D. *My Life of Adventure.* Stackpole Books, 1995.

Venables, Stephen. *Voices From The Mountains – 40 True-Life Stories of Unforgettable Adventure, Drama and Human Endurance.* Reader's Digest, 2006.

Venables, Stephen. *First Ascent – Pioneering Mountain Climbs.* Firefly Books, 2008.

Weber, Alan S. *Because It's There – A Celebration of Mountaineering, From 200 B.C. To Today.* Taylor Trade Publishing, 2003.

THREE

ASIA

The Highest Summits Are Reached

Years 633 to 2011

"The man who sets out for a climb from a well-equipped, well-provisioned and comfortable camp or bivouac is more likely to succeed than the man who does not concern himself with creature comforts. It is a fallacy to suppose that cold, discomfort and ill-provisioning conduce to success in mountaineering or exploration by increasing the hardihood of the mountaineer or explorer; on the contrary, they lower both the physical and mental vitality. The highest mountains in the world will not be climbed until it is realized that the equipping and the provisioning of an expedition is a fine art deserving of expert attention and advice."

1940
Frank Smythe
British mountaineer
(1900 – 1949)

ASIA

Asia is the world's largest continent. It contains one-third of the earth's total land area. The highest mountains in the world are located in Asia which therefore has been called "The Roof of the World." This continent of fifty independent countries has over one hundred separate mountain ranges that lure mountain climbers to their high summits every year. However, only fifteen of these countries have a peak exceeding 15,000 feet (4,572 meters) within their borders. Mountaineering activity has generally been concentrated in only ten Asian countries. These countries are:

Country	Mountain Range	Highest Peak	Feet	Meters
Georgia	Caucasus	Kazbek	16,541	5,041
India	Himalayas	Nanda Devi	25,644	7,816
Indonesia: Papua	Maoke	Carstenzs Pyr.	16,023	4,885
Japan	Japanese Alps	Fujiyama	12,389	3,776
Kazakhstan	Tien Shan	Khan Tengri	22,998	7,009
Kyrgyzstan	Tien Shan	Pik Pobeda	24,405	7,434
Nepal	Himalayas	Everest	29,035	8,849
Pakistan	Karakoram	K2	28,253	8,611
Tajikistan	Pamir	Pik Kommunizma	24,590	7,495
Tibet	Himalayas	Everest	29,035	8,849

There are fourteen separate mountains in the world that exceed 8,000 meters (26,248 feet) in elevation above sea level. All of these mountains are located in Asia. Mount Everest on the Nepal – Tibet border is the world's highest peak and the most well-known peak of the fourteen 8,000 meter mountains. Hundreds of books and films have been produced in many different languages about Mount Everest and its climbing history. This mountain continues to represent perhaps the ultimate challenge for serious mountaineers.

Most of the 8,000 meter high summits are located in the Greater Himalayan Range that stretches for approximately 1,500 miles (2,500 kilometers) from Bhutan on the east to northern India on the west. This mountain range has many sub-ranges and varies in width from 100 to 150 miles (166 to 250 kilometers). The name "Himalaya" represents the combination of two Sanskrit words: "hima" meaning "snow" and "laya" meaning "abode" (or home). Therefore, "Himalaya" translates to "the abode of snow." Ten of the fourteen 8,000 meter peaks are located in the Himalayas of Nepal, northeastern Pakistan, and Tibet. The remaining four 8,000 meter summits are part of the Karakoram Range on the Pakistan-China border. "Karakoram" is a Turkish word meaning "black earth" or "black gravel." All fourteen 8,000 meter peaks were first climbed during the fifteen year period from 1950 to 1964. The following two charts summarize these fourteen 8,000 meter peaks by elevation and first ascent dates.

14 Highest Mountains By Elevation

Peak Name	Location	Feet	Meters
1. Mount Everest	Nepal/Tibet	29,035	8,849
2. K2	China/ Pakistan	28,253	8,611
3. Kangchenjunga	Nepal/Sikkim	28,171	8,586
4. Lhotse	Nepal/Tibet	27,940	8,516
5. Makalu	Nepal/Tibet	27,764	8,462
6. Cho Oyu	Nepal/Tibet	26,906	8,201
7. Dhaulagiri	Nepal	26,796	8,167
8. Manaslu	Nepal	26,760	8,156
9. Nanga Parbat	Pakistan	26,658	8,125
10. Annapurna	Nepal	26,546	8,091
11. Gasherbrum I	China/Pakistan	26,471	8,068
12. Broad Peak	China/Pakistan	26,402	8,047
13. Gasherbrum II	China/Pakistan	26,363	8,035
14. Shishapangma	Tibet	26,291	8,013

14 Highest Mountains By First Ascent Date

Date	Peak Name	Feet/Meters	Expedition
June 3, 1950	Annapurna	26,546/8,091	French
May 29, 1953	Mt. Everest	29,028/8,847	British
July 3, 1953	Nanga Parbat	26,658/8,125	German/Austrian
July 31, 1954	K2	28,253/8,611	Italian
October 19, 1954	Cho Oyu	26,906/8,201	Austrian
May 15, 1955	Makalu	27,764/8,462	French
May 25, 1955	Kangchenjunga	28,171/8,586	British
May 9, 1956	Manaslu	26,760/8,156	Japanese
May 18, 1956	Lhotse	27,940/8,516	Swiss
July 7, 1956	Gasherbrum II	26,363/8,035	Austrian
June 9, 1957	Broad Peak	26,402/8,047	Austrian
July 5, 1958	Gasherbrum I	26,471/8,068	American
May 13, 1960	Dhaulagiri	26,796/8,167	Swiss
May 2, 1964	Shishapangma	26,291/8,013	Chinese

Mountaineering activity began in the Himalayas in the early 1800s. In 1818, two Englishmen—Gerard and Lloyd—reached just over 19,000 feet (5,791 meters) on a peak named Leo Pargyal (22,280 feet/6,791 meters) in the Himachal Pradesh Himalaya of northern India. The highest summit reached to date (excluding higher summits in the South American Andes mountains by earlier civilizations) was Mount Shilla (20,050 feet/6,111 meters) in 1860. An unnamed surveyor's assistant carried a wooden pole to this summit to establish a survey field station. Mount Shilla is also located in the Himachal Pradesh Himalaya. .

The most significant early first ascents included Pioneer Peak (22,600 feet/6,888 meters) in the Karakoram Range in 1892 by British mountaineer William Martin Conway's party. Pioneer Peak is a sub-peak of Baltoro Kangri (23,990 feet/7,312 meters) and was the highest summit reached in the world as of 1892 (recorded ascent). In 1899, American mountaineer and explorer William H. Workman and his wife Fanny B. Workman reached the summit of Mount Koser Gunge (20,997 feet/6,400 meters) which is also located in the Karakoram Range of northern Pakistan.

Two significant summits were first reached in the early 1900s: Pyramid Peak (23,392 feet/7,129 meters) in the Karakoram Range in 1902 and Trisul (23,361 feet/7,120 meters) in the Garhwal Himalaya of India in 1907. These first ascents were soon followed by the ascents of Pik Lenin (23,407 feet/7,134 meters) in the Pamir Range of Tajikistan in 1928, Kamet (25,447 feet/7,756 meters) in the Garhwal Himalaya of northern India in 1931, and Minya Konka (24,892 feet/7,587 meters) in China in 1932.

The first British mountaineering expedition to Mount Everest occurred in 1921. Over the next thirty-two years, eight more British and two Swiss expeditions attempted to climb Mount Everest culminating in its first ascent by the British in 1953.

The Himalayas of Bhutan, India, Nepal, and Tibet as well as other Asian mountain ranges include hundreds of other significant peaks that do not reach the magical 8,000 meter elevation. There are over four-hundred peaks in the Himalayas whose summits reach between 7,000 to 7,999 meters (22,967 to 26,245 feet) and there are sixty-four peaks in the Karakoram Range that exceed 23,000 feet (7,010 meters). Many of these peaks remain unclimbed and some peaks in Nepal and China will never be climbed due to local religious beliefs. Nepal and India have also specifically designated certain peaks between 5,600 and 6,650 meters (18,374 to 21,818 feet) as "trekking peaks" which can be more easily climbed and with less expense and regulation than the higher and more difficult peaks.

This chapter identifies seventy-five (75) peak first ascents, one hundred and two (102) first ascents, and three hundred and fifty (350) other mountaineering events that occurred on mountains throughout Asia.

▲ Highest Mountain: Mount Everest—29,035 ft./8,849 m.
Location: Nepal – Tibet Border
First Ascent Date: May 29, 1953
Expedition: British

Asia Timeline

633: PEAK FIRST ASCENT *FUJISAN*

The first ascent of Mount Fujisan (12,389 ft./3,776 m.) in Japan (the highest mountain in Japan) was by a Japanese monk named Enno Shokaku. This was the first recorded climb of a snowcapped peak (actually a volcano—last eruption in 1707) in the world. There are six mountain paths each with ten pilgrim shelters leading to the summit. The average ascent takes approximately six hours. Mt. Fuji is the biggest of the 86 active volcanoes in Japan and is the most frequently climbed mountain in the world—200,000 people climb Mt. Fuji during the months of July and August. The elevation gain from Fuji's south side is 11,000 feet/3,353 m. and from the north side 9,000 feet/2,743 meters. Japan contains 15 peaks over 3,000 meters (9,843 ft.). Most of these mountains are dormant volcanoes.

636: PEAK FIRST ASCENT *MUSUR*

Well-known Chinese Buddhist explorer Xuan Zang (602 – 664) traveled from China to India over the Pamir mountain range to obtain Buddhist scriptures from India. During this journey from 627 to 645, Zang climbed Mount Lingshan (19,686 ft./6,000 m.) which is now known as Mount Musur in the Tengri Range of the Tien Shan Mountains of western China. Zang had to cut (or chop) steps in the snow and ice of this mountain but with what tool it is not known. Some consider Xuan Zang "to be the first high-altitude climber in the history of the world."

760: Equipment – Boot Nailing

Chinese poet Li Bai (701 – 762) mentions in one of his poems that a climber named Xie Lingyun (385 – 433) wore special wooden shoes that had soles with removable studs. The material (wood or metal) of these studs was not identified. These studs could be removed either from the front sole when ascending mountains or from the rear sole when descending mountains.

This is the earliest record of climbing footwear in Chinese history (*Footprints On The Peaks*, 1995).

800:

The Tibetan name "Chomolungma" was given to the high peak we now know as Mount Everest (29,035 ft./8,849 m.) by the inhabitants of the Rongbuk Valley in southern Tibet (and just north of Mount Everest). The name "Chomolungma" is translated as "Mother Goddess of the World" or "Mother Goddess of the Wind."

905: PEAK FIRST ASCENT DAMAVAND

Iran's highest mountain (or dormant volcano) is known as Damavand (18,606 ft./5,671 m.). It is located in the Alborz Mountains approximately sixty miles northeast of Teheran. Damavand's first ascent is credited to Abu Dolaf Kazraji in 905. However, there are records that credit Sir W. Taylor Thompson with this first ascent in 1836. There are sixteen climbing routes to the summit.

1558:

The Japanese government issued an order that prohibited women from making the ascent of Mount Fujisan (12,389 ft./3,776 m.).

1623:

Dutch explorer Jan Carstensz (a.k.a Jan Carstenszoon) discovered the snow peaks of Irian Jaya (Papua, New Guinea).

1624:

The first Europeans to cross the Himalayas were Portuguese missionary Antonio de Andrade (1580 – 1634), head of the Jesuit mission to the Mogul Court, and his small party. They trekked over the remote, high Mana pass (18,400 ft./5,608 m.) between India and Tibet. Perplexed to find themselves very short of breath, Andrade recorded: "According to the natives, many people die on account of the noxious vapours that rise. It is fact that people in good health are suddenly taken ill and die within a quarter of an hour." This is one of the earliest written accounts of altitude sickness. Andrade explored the western part of the Himalayan range disguised as a Hindu pilgrim.

1707:

The first ascent of Mount Ararat (16,860 ft./5,137 m.) was made by French botanist Joseph Pitton de Tournefort (1656 – 1708). Ararat is the highest mountain in Turkey. This ascent, however, has been questioned. The recognized first ascent occurred in 1829.

1788: PEAK FIRST ASCENT *KLIUCHEVSKAYA*

A Russian mining engineer named Daniil Gauss and two companions made the first ascent of the volcano named Kliuchevskaya (15,585 ft./4,750 m.) on the Silberian Peninsula (Russia). The Kliuchevskaya Group includes twelve volcanoes within a thirty-mile area.

1802:

The great height of the Himalayan peak Dhaulagiri (26,795 ft./8,167 m., 7th highest mountain in the world) was first recognized by Robert Colebrooks, Surveyor-General of Bengal. The name Dhaulagiri in Tibetan is translated as "the rock that stands alone." The Swiss first climbed Dhaulagiri in May of 1960.

1808:

The name "Kurrakooram" appeared on a map drawn by a Lt. MacCartney. The name "Karakoram" (a mountain range in Pakistan) was derived from this name meaning "black earth" or "black gravel."

1809:

Lt. W.S. Webb made observations on the position and height of the Himalayan peak known as Dhaulagiri from four different survey stations. Webb calculated its height at 26,862 ft./8,187 m. causing disbelief among geographers in the west who still believed that Chimborazo (Ecuador) in the South American Andes mountains was the highest mountain in the world at 20,577 ft./6,272 m.

1820:

The Himalayan Mountains were at last acknowledged to be loftier than the South American Andes. The peak of Nanda Devi (25,644 ft./7,816 m.), known then as "A2" and measured at 25,479 ft./7,766 m., was then thought to be the highest mountain in the world. Nanda Devi (in northern India) retained this distinction for twenty-five years.

1822: Book

Hodgson and Herbert published the book entitled *Latitudes, Longitudes and Elevations of Principal Peaks and Stations in the Survey*. This survey listed 46 Himalayan peaks in the Garhwal-Kumaon region. The three highest peaks were numbered A1, A2, and A3. A2 at 25,644 ft./7,816 m. proved to be the highest of the three peaks. This peak was known locally as Nanda Devi, the highest peak in India.

1829: PEAK FIRST ASCENT *ARARAT*

October 9. German mountaineer Dr. Friedrich Parrot (1792 – 1841) and Khachatur Abovian (1809 – 1848) made the first recorded ascent of Mount Ararat (16,854 ft./5,137 m.), the highest mountain in Turkey. This was their third attempt from the northeast side. Ararat is located approximately ten miles west of the Iranian border. The first American ascent of Ararat was on July 4, 1891 by Thomas G. Allen, Jr. and William L. Sachtleben.

1845:

The Great Trigonometrical Survey (of India) first identified Dhaulagiri (26,794 ft./8,167 m. – Peak 42) in Central Nepal and then Kangchenjunga (28,169 ft./8,586 m. – Peak 8) on the Nepal-Sikkim border as the world's highest peaks. This survey fixed the location of 79 high Himalayan peaks. Peak H was soon renamed Peak XV. In 1856, Peak XV's altitude was set at 29,002 ft./8,839 m. This peak was later renamed Mount Everest after Sir George Everest (1790 – 1866) who served as the Surveyor General of India from 1830 to 1843.

1847:

Surveyor Andrew Scott Waugh (1810 – 1878), who joined the India survey team in 1832, identified a new mountain as the world's highest and reopened the debate about the height of the Himalayas. Waugh's new peak was Kangchenjunga (actually the third highest in the world at 28,169 ft./8,586 m.). In November, Waugh sighted a distant peak from Tiger Hill above Darjeeling, India. He called this high peak "Gamma" which in 1852 became known as "Peak XV" (Mount Everest).

1848:

Surveyor Richard Strachey (1817 – 1908) first discovered the great Himalayan peak named Kamet (25,447 ft./7,756 m.) from a hill-station survey point 100 miles away in India. Kamet was known to Tibetans as Kangmen meaning "huge grandmother of the sacred snowchain." Strachey calculated Kamet's height at 7,756 meters. It is located in India west of Nepal.

1848:

British botanist Sir Joseph Hooker (1817 – 1911) made a nearly complete circuit of the Kangchenjunga (28,169 ft./8,586 m.) range in Nepal-Sikkim. Hooker was the first European to explore the Kangchenjunga region. Viewed from the northeast, he called Kangchenjunga "Liklo," a name that he heard from the Lepcha porters that accompanied him. Hooker also made the first written description of the peak now known as Mount Everest when he first saw it from the lower slopes of Kangchenjunga: "There was no continuous snowy chain; indeed the Himalayas seemed suddenly to decline into black and ragged peaks, 'til in the north west they rose again in a white mountain mass of stupendous elevation." In 1849, Hooker reached 22,700 ft./6,919 m. on the flanks of Kangchenjunga (28,171 ft./8,586 m.) in Nepal.

1850:

The triangulation of the Mount Everest region in Nepal from various survey stations on the Plains of India was completed. Two years later (1852), after all calculations had been worked out, the peak that was soon to be named Mount Everest was found to be the highest in the world.

1852:

Bengali survey clerk Radhanath Sikhdar (1813 – 1870) told India's Surveyor General Sir Andrew Waugh (1810 – 1878) that he had just discovered the highest mountain in the world. Measured at 29,002 ft./8,839 m., this mountain was designated as Peak XV. This peak would soon be renamed Mount Everest. Survey station observations from six stations on the plains of India calculated this peak's elevation. These stations were about 108 miles (180 kilometers) from the mountain. Summit elevations by future measurements reported varying heights: 29,141 feet, 29,028 feet, and 29,035 feet.

1854:

Three Munich, Germany brothers (Adolf: 1928 – 1857, Hermann: 1826 – 1882, and Robert: 1833 – 1885 Schlagintweit) were the first explorer/mountaineers in the Himalayas that had any experience and knowledge of snow mountaineering techniques (gained in the Alps). They reached 22,500 ft./6,858 m. on Abi Gamin (24,132 ft./7,355 m.), a subsidiary peak of Kamet in the central Himalayas and spent ten consecutive nights on this peak in camps ranging from 16,642 ft./5,060 m. to 19,326 ft./5,800 m. The Swiss finally reached the summit of Abi Gamin in 1950.

1856:

Map maker Lt. Thomas George Montgomerie (1830 – 1878) with the British Royal Engineers discovered the second highest mountain in the world—K2 (28,253 ft./8,611 m.)—as he was conducting a survey of India. "K" stood for Karakoram and "2" for the second peak in the range to be identified. K1 is now known as Masherbrum (25,611 ft./7,821 m.). K3 is now known as Broad Peak (26,402 ft./8,047 m.). Montgomerie logged peaks K1 through K32 in the Karakoram Range.

1856:

After seven years of verifying the elevation calculations (1850 to 1856) for Peak XV's height, the elevation of 29,002 ft./8,839 m. was officially accepted. The name "Everest" was formally placed on a map of Nepal following many years of surveying.

1860:

September 15. Sir Rutherford Alcock (1809 – 1897), British Minister to Japan, became the first foreigner to climb Mount Fujiyama (12,389 ft./3,776 m.) in Japan. He climbed from Fuji's base to the summit in twelve hours over two days.

1861:

Henry Haversham Godwin-Austen (1834 – 1923) became the first Westerner to travel up the Baltoro Glacier in Pakistan and see the giant peaks up close (K2, Broad Peak, the Gasherbrum Group, etc.) He made the first 1:500,000 scale map of the Karakoram region. This region contains thirty-six summits that exceed 24,000 feet (7,300 meters). Godwin-Austen is regarded as the first mountaineer in the Karakoram.

1862 to 1864: PEAK FIRST ASCENTS *E57, E58, E61*

Surveyor William Henry Johnson (1829 – 1878) was an assistant to T.G. Montgomerie of the Kashmir Survey. Johnson first climbed these three peaks on his journey to Khutan:

> E57 – 21,757 ft./6,631 m.
> E58 – 21,971 ft./6,696 m.
> E61 – 23,890 ft./7,281 m.*

By 1862, Johnson had located nine survey stations on summits above 20,000 feet (6,096 m.).

*This summit claim has been denied. As of 1968, this peak had remained unclimbed. This is the only peak other than K2 that still retains its letter and number as assigned to it by the Survey of India.

1865:

Sir Andrew Waugh (1810 – 1878), the Surveyor General of India, recommended that his predecessor, Sir George Everest, have the honor of having the world's highest mountain named after him. Sir George Everest died in 1866 at age 76 without ever seeing the mountain that is named for him. Everest was the Surveyor-General of India from 1830 to 1843.

1867: FIRST ASCENT

Lady Fanny Parkes (British) became the first non-Japanese woman to climb Mount Fujisan (12,389 ft./3,776 m.) in Japan. She was the wife of Sir Harry Parkes (1828 – 1885), British ambassador to Japan (1865 to 1883).

1871:

Russian geographer Alexei Pavlovich Fedchenko (1844 – 1873) discovered the second highest peak in the Pamir Range which is now known as Pik Lenin (23,407 ft./7,134 m.). The highest peak in the Pamir Range is Pik Communism (24,591 ft./7,495 m.). These peaks are located in Tajikistan.

1878:

French physiologist Paul Bert (1833 – 1886) made the original suggestion that Mount Everest (29,002 ft./8,839 m.—accepted elevation at that time) could be climbed by the respiration of super-oxygenated air.

1879:

The Széchewyi Expedition first sighted the high peak now known as Minya Konka in the southeast Tibetan Highlands and calculated its elevation at 24,934 feet or 7,600 meters. The accepted elevation for this high peak is 24,900 feet or 7,589 meters.

1883: PEAK FIRST ASCENT *FORKED*

Spring. British mountaineer William Woodman Graham (1859 – 1932) was the second pure climber to visit the Himalaya. With his Swiss guide Joseph Imboden (from St. Niklaus), Graham visited Sikkim and explored the southern approaches to Kangchenjunga (28,171 ft./8,586 m.). Graham made the first ascent of Forked Peak (20,340 ft./6,199 m.), but was unsuccessful on Kabru (24,256 ft./7,393 m.) and Dunagiri (23,184 ft./7,066 m.). The lightweight equipment achievement of this small-scale expedition was well ahead of its time.

1885:

British mountaineer and author Clinton Dent (1850 – 1912) first predicted that Mount Everest (29,002 ft./8,839 m.—accepted elevation at that time) in Nepal could be climbed. Dent wrote an article in the English magazine *Nineteenth Century* (October, 1892) entitled "Can Mount Everest be Climbed?" He wrote about the difficulty of supplying camps and the logistics of the venture, yet remained optimistic that the human spirit could place a person on the summit.

1886: PEAK FIRST ASCENT P*AEKTU-SAN*

British explorer and mountaineer Lt. Francis Younghusband (1863 – 1942) made the first ascent of Paektu-san (9,003 ft./2,744 m.), North Korea's highest peak. This volcanic peak is located on the North Korea – China border.

1887:

British mountaineer Lt. Francis Younghusband (1863 – 1942) and his loyal guide Wali were the first people to see the peak K2 (28,253 ft./8,611 m.) and the Gasherbrum Mountain group in Pakistan from the north. Younghusband's comment upon seeing K2: "A peak of appalling height." He also made a daring crossing of the Great Karakoram range via the 19,000 foot/5,790 meter Muztagh pass.

1888: PEAK FIRST ASCENT *LOW'S*

March 3. British mountaineer J. Whitehead made the first true ascent of Low's Peak (13,436 ft./4,095 m.), the highest summit of Mount Kinabalu in Borneo. Whitehead was the first westerner to climb Kinabalu, the highest mountain in southeast Asia.

1891:

British soldier Charles Granville Bruce (1866 – 1939) persuaded British mountaineer William Martin Conway (1856 – 1937) to attach Parbir Thapa and three other Gurkhas from his regiment to the 1892 Karakoram expedition. This action thus began the history of native participation (Gurkhas, Bhotias, Sherpas, Hunzas, etc.) in Himalayan mountaineering.

1892: PEAK FIRST ASCENT *PIONEER*

British mountaineer, explorer, and art critic William Martin Conway (1856 – 1937) led the first major climbing expedition to the Karakoram region of the Himalayas. Conway was accompanied by a young Lt. Charles Bruce, Roudebush, McCormick, Eckenstein, Matthias Zurbriggen (Swiss Guide), and his Gurkha porters. This expedition was the first to be funded by the Royal Geographical Society in London. Conway and his party made the first ascent of Pioneer Peak (22,600 ft./6,888 m.), the highest summit reached to date and a new altitude record as well. They also made fifteen other first ascents of peaks over 16,000 feet (4,876 m.). They explored and mapped the Baltoro Glacier area. Conway named the junction of the Godwin Austen and Upper Baltoro glaciers "Concordia" which is located at 15,000 ft./4,572 m. Conway was also the person who named Gasherbrum I (26,471 ft./8,068 m.) "Hidden Peak," Broad Peak, and Pioneer Peak. According to some accounts, Conway was the first climber to use crampons in the Himalayas. At the conclusion of this expedition, Conway wrote *Climbing in the Himalayas* considered by many to be the first modern expedition book.

1894:

British mountaineer Edward Whymper (1840 – 1911) referred to Mount Everest in the Himalayas as the "Third Pole."

1894:

Famous Swedish explorer/mountaineer Sven Anders Hedin (1865 – 1952) made four attempts to climb Muztagata (24,757 ft./7,546 m.) in the Kunlun Range of Western China. All four attempts failed. Hedin's highest altitude reached was 20,600 ft./6,279 m. Muztagata means "Father of the Ice Mountains." Its first ascent was in 1981.

1894:

The Reverend Walter Weston (1860 – 1940) made the first full traverse of the Japanese Alps north to south (island of Honshu) with friends H.J. Hamilton from Nagoya, Japan and Uraguchi Bunji from Kobe, Japan. This traverse ended with an ascent of the ancient volcano Ontake ("the August Peak"), elevation 10,063 ft./3,067 m. There are twenty-six peaks in the Japanese Alps that exceed 3,000 meters (9,843 feet).

1895: PEAK FIRST ASCENT *DIAMIRAI*

British mountaineer Albert Frederick Mummery (1855 – 1895) led John Norman Collie (1859 – 1942), Geoffrey Hastings (1860 – 1941), and Lt. Charles G. Bruce (1866 – 1939) on the first serious attempt to climb an 8,000 meter (26,248 feet) peak. Their objective was to climb Nanga Parbat (26,660 ft./8,125 m.) in the Himalayas. Prior to attempting Nanga Parbat, Collie and Mummery made on August 11 the first ascent of Diamirai Peak (19,000 ft./5,791 m.). On August 24, Mummery and two Gurkha porters (Raghabir Thapa and Goman Singh) disappeared at nearly 15,000 ft./4,572 m. while ascending the Diamir Valley. They have never been found. Thapa and Singh were the first two Nepalese to die on a Himalayan expedition. The next expedition to attempt climbing Nanga Parbat was in 1932. Mummery will always be remembered for his first ascents of the Dent du Requin, Grand Charmoz, the Grépon, Teufelsgrat, Zmutt Ridge on the Matterhorn and the Furggen Ridge on the Matterhorn. Mount Mummery (10,919 ft./3,328 m.) in the Canadian Rockies is named for A.F. Mummery.

1896: Book

The Reverend Walter Weston (1860 – 1940) authored the book entitled *Mountaineering and Exploring in the Japanese Alps*. Weston (1860 – 1940) was an English clergyman, missionary, and mountaineer who first traveled to Japan in 1888. He became the Chaplain in Kobe, Japan from 1889 to 1895. He was one of the founders of the Japanese Alpine Club in 1905. Some British climbers have referred to Weston as "the father of mountaineering in Japan."

1899:

September 5 to October 24 British explorer/mountaineer Douglas William Freshfield (1845 – 1934) began a seven-week circumnavigation of Kangchenjunga (28,169 ft./8,586 m.) in eastern Nepal to map this uncharted country. This was the first tour of this area by Europeans. With Freshfield were Professor Edmund J. Garwood (Geologist and Cartographer), Italian mountaineer/photographer Vittorio Sella (1859 – 1943), Erminio Sella, Erminio Botta, Angelo Maquignaz (Guide), and Rinzin Namgyal. They began and ended their journey in Darjeeling, India (September – October). At 20,000 feet/6,096 meters, Vittorio Sella made some of the highest photographs ever taken anywhere in the world.

1899: PEAK FIRST ASCENTS *SIEGFRIED HORN, BULLOCK WORKMAN, KOSER GUNGE*

American mountaineers/explorers Fanny Bullock Workman (1859 – 1925) and her retired surgeon husband William Hunter Workman (1847 – 1937) organized the first of their seven exploratory expeditions to the Karakoram range of the Himalayas (1899 to 1912). They explored the Biafo Glacier and Fanny made three first ascents for women in the Karakorum:

Siegfried Horn	18,600 ft./5,669 m.
M. Bullock Workman	19,450 ft./5,928 m.
M. Koser Gunge	20,997 ft./6,400 m.

1899: Equipment – Tents

British mountaineer Douglas W. Freshfield (1845 – 1934) used Whymper Tents on his tour of Kangchenjunga (28,169 ft./8,586 m.) in Sikkim and Nepal. These tents were nearly rainproof, had sewn-in floors and were strongly constructed. They were designed by and named for famous British mountaineer Edward Whymper (1840 – 1911).

1902:

American explorer and mountaineer Dr. William Hunter Workman (1847 – 1937) established a new altitude record for climbing by reaching the summit of Pyramid Peak (23,392 ft./7,129 m.) in Baltistan (Karakoram Range).

1902:

British mountaineer Oscar Eckenstein (1859 – 1921) led the first serious, fully-equipped attempt to climb K2 (28,253 ft./8,611 m.) in Pakistan's Karakoram Range. K2 was known locally by different names that varied in each small area village (i.e. Chogori, Dapsang, and Lamba Pahar). This six-man international expedition established five camps on the mountain that was approached via the Baltoro Glacier. In addition to Eckenstein (British), the other climbers were G. Knowles (British), Aleister Crowley (British), H. Pfanni (Austrian), V. Wessley (Austrian), and J. Jacot-Guillarmod (Swiss). They reached 21,655 ft./6,600 m. on the East Ridge before being stopped by heavy snow.

1902: Technique – Ski Mountaineering

During the first serious attempt to climb K2 (28,253 feet/8,611 meters) in the Karakoram Range of Pakistan, skis were used for the first time as part of a mountaineering expedition. This was also the first time skis were used above 5,000 meters (16,405 feet).

1903:

J. Claude White, a young military officer, took the first photograph of Mount Everest from 94 miles/157 kilometers away in Khamba Dzong, Tibet. The east face of Everest can be clearly seen in this photograph.

1905:

August. British mountaineer Aleister Crowley (1875 – 1947) led the first serious attempt to climb Kangchenjunga (28,171 ft./8,586 m.) in the Sikkim Himalaya. In addition to Crowley, the other climbers were Alexis A. Pache (Swiss), Charles A. Reymond (Swiss), R. De Righi (Italian), and Dr. J. Jacot-Guillarmod (Swiss). Their attempt ended when six climbers fell in an avalanche at 21,400 ft./6,522 m. resulting in four deaths (Pache and three porters).

1905:

The Japanese Alpine Club was founded with the support and encouragement of English clergyman Walter Weston (1860 – 1940) and Usui Kojima. Its membership in 2005 was approximately 6,000. This club was originally called Nihon Hakubutsu Doushikai (Japanese Natural History Club).

1905: Technique – Remedy For Snow Blindness

British mountaineer Thomas G. Longstaff (1875 – 1964) recommended the use of gelatin capsules of castor oil for the relief of snow blindness. A drop of oil between the eyelids provided immediate relief.

1906:

American woman mountaineer Fanny Bullock Workman (1850 – 1925) established a new climbing altitude record for women when she reached 22,737 ft./6,930 m. on Pinnacle Peak (22,810 ft./6,952 m.) in the Himalayas near Kangchenjunga. Unfortunately, she was not able to reach the actual summit. Italian mountain guide Cyprien Savoye was with Workman. This new altitude record would last until 1934.

1907:

May. Scottish mountaineer Dr. Alexander M. Kellas (1868 – 1921) hired Swiss mountain guides to accompany him for his first exploration in Sikkim but this experiment failed. He preferred the guidance of the Sherpas who came with him as local porters. This was the earliest recorded reference to Sherpas in mountaineering literature. Kellas and his party reached the Simvu Saddle (16,300 ft./5,882 m.) near Kangchenjunga for the first time.

1907: PEAK FIRST ASCENT *TRISUL*

June 12. British mountaineer Thomas George Longstaff (1875 – 1964) and Swiss guides Alexis and Henri Brocherel and a porter named Kabir made the first ascent of Trisul (23,361 ft./7,120 m.) in the Garhwal Himlaya of India. They climbed from 17,450 ft./5,319 m. to 23,361 ft./7,120 m. in ten hours with no ill effects. British mountaineers Charles Granville Bruce (1866 – 1939) and Arnold Louis Mumm (1859 – 1927) were also members of this expedition. This was the first summit over 7,000 meters (22,967 feet) to be reached. Trisul (the Trident for the triple-headed summit) would remain the highest summit reached until 1930. Longstaff and his two guides climbed the final 6,000 feet/1,829 meters (ascent and descent) in one day. Mumm took several oxygen cartridges with him on this expedition—the first time oxygen was used on a high-altitude expedition. British Captain P.R. Oliver and one local Garhwali made the second ascent of Trisul in 1933.

1907:

October 21. Norwegian explorers and mountaineers Carl Wilhelm Rubenson (1885 – 1960) and Monrad-Aas arrived in Darjeeling, India. On October 5, they began their journey to climb Kabru (24,002 ft./7,315 m.) in the Sikkim Himalaya. They established two camps on the mountain (Camp II at 19,500 ft./5,943 m. was the highest point in mountaineering history to which porters had carried substantial loads). They came within 100 ft./31 m. of reaching the summit on October 21 after spending twelve days above 20,000 feet/6,096 meters.

1907:

British mountaineers Dr. Thomas G. Longstaff (1875 – 1964), Charles G. Bruce (1866 – 1939), and Arnold L. Mumm (1859 – 1927) along with Swiss guides Alexis and Henri Brocherel explored the area around the peak named Kamet (25,447 ft./7,756 m.) and eventually reached 20,178 ft./6,150 m. on its slopes. Kamet received eight expeditions between 1907 and 1914. British mountaineer Charles F. Meade (1881 – 1975) reached the high point in 1912 at 23,492 ft./7,160 m., guided by Pierre Blanc. Kamet was eventually climbed in 1931.

1907:

Swedish explorer Sven Hedin (1865 – 1952) became the first westerner to circumambulate (33 miles/55 kilometers) Mount Kailas (22,028 ft./6,714 m.) in western Tibet (China). The high point of this trek is the Dolma La Pass (18,600 ft./5,669 m.).

1907: Equipment – Supplemental Oxygen

The first recorded use of supplemental oxygen (encapsulated) for mountaineering occurred during the Himalayan ascent of Trisul (23,361 ft./7,120 m.). British climber A.L. Mumm (1859 – 1927) brought several small oxygen cartridges with him.

1909:

Italian mountaineer the Duke of the Abruzzi (1873 – 1933) led an expedition to climb K2 (28,253 ft./8,611 m.) in the Karakoram Range of Pakistan. Expedition members included naval Lt. Marchese Federico Negrotto (topographer), Dr. Filippo de Filippi (medical), Vittorio Sella (photographer), Mr. Barnes (English – logistics), three Courmayeur, Italy guides (Giuseppe Petigax, Alessio Brocherel, and Enrico Brocherel), and four porters from the Alps. Abandoning their K2 attempt at 21,871 feet/6,666 meters on the southeast ridge (to be known as the Abruzzi Spur), they retreated and then attempted to climb Chogolisa or Bride Peak (25,110 ft./7,653 m.). On this peak, they were able to reach 24,601 feet/7,498 meters which represented a new climbing altitude record that would remain until the 1922 British Mount Everest Expedition. This Italian expedition spent 37 days over 5,000 meters (16,405 feet). Four land features near K2 are named for members of this expedition: Filippi Glacier, Negrotto Col, Saudia Glacier, and Sella Pass. K2 was known to the local people as "Chogori" meaning "great mountain."

1909:

Well-known Italian mountaineer and photographer Vittorio Sella (1859 – 1943) took his famous photograph "Panorama of the Baltoro Glacier." To take this photo, Sella's porters carried his heavy Ross and Company camera to 17,330 feet/5,282 meters. Sella made over 800 photographic images on this expedition on 30 x 40 centimeter glass plates.

1909: Technique – Use of Nepalese Porters

Italian mountaineer the Duke of the Abruzzi (1873 – 1933) led an expedition to K2 (28,251 feet/8,611 meters) in the Karakoram Range of Pakistan. This expedition was the first to discover and use Nepalese hill people (known as Sherpas) to carry expedition loads to higher altitudes.*

1909: Technique – Expedition Camps

Italian mountaineer the Duke of the Abruzzi (1873 – 1933) led an Italian expedition to K2 (28,251 feet/8,611 meters) in the Karakoram Range of Pakistan. This expedition eventually reached an altitude of 24,571 feet/7,489 meters on nearby Chogolisa—a new altitude record. In addition to discovering the eventual climbing route up K2 (the Abruzzi Ridge), this expedition also established the technique of locating a series of well-supplied camps at ever increasing altitudes up the mountain.

1910: PEAK FIRST ASCENT *PAUHUNRI*

British mountaineer Dr. Alexander M. Kellas (1868 – 1921) and two Sherpas made ten first ascents over 6,000 meters/19,686 feet in the Sikkim Himalaya including Pauhunri (23,180 ft./7,065 m.).

1912:

British mountaineer Charles Francis Meade (1881–1975) was forced to endure an open bivouac at 23,420 ft./7,138 m. on Kamet (25,447 ft./7,756 m.) in the Himalayas. This was the highest bivouac to date in the world.

1912:

British climber and explorer Alexander Frederick Richmond (A.F.R.) Wollaston (1875 – 1930) made the first attempt to climb the snow peaks of Irian Jaya (New Guinea). He reached to within 500 feet of Carstensz Pyramid's (16,023 ft./4,883 m.) summit.

1913: FIRST ASCENT

Japan's Mount Fujisan (12,389 ft./3,776 m.) was first climbed on skis. A Japanese student also made the fastest ascent of Mount Fuji in order to win a $300.00 prize. He climbed the Gotemba Trail (9,000 vertical feet/2,743 meters) in two hours thirty-eight minutes.

---

* This chapter contains numerous references to the mountain people of eastern Nepal known as the "Sherpas." The name Sherpa is derived from "Shar" meaning "east" and "pa" meaning "people." For over 600 years, Sherpas have migrated to Nepal from eastern Tibet. The Solu-Khumbu region of Nepal (south of Mount Everest) contains approximately 3,500 Sherpa people with the village of Namche Bazaar being the largest settlement. An additional 30,000 Sherpas live in the Solu, Langtang, Helambu, and Rolwaling valleys. A distinction needs to be made between the word "sherpa" with a lowercase "s" and the name "Sherpa" with a capital "S." Since 1921, mountaineering expeditions to Nepal and Tibet have employed Sherpas as load carriers on both approach treks to base camps and as high-altitude load carriers to mountain locations above base camps. Eventually, experienced Sherpas were promoted to the status of full-time expedition climbers. The Sherpa people are known for their unique genetic system that allows them to adapt to high altitudes. The term "sherpa," however, is frequently applied in our culture to anything or anybody that helps people carry things.

When speaking specifically about the Sherpa people or about a particular Sherpa person, then the "S" is capitalized. According to custom, a Sherpa (or Sherpani for females) will sign his name by first using the day of the week he was born on. For example: Dawa – Monday, Mingma – Tuesday, Lhakpa – Wednesday, Phurbu – Thursday, Pasang – Friday, Pemba – Saturday, and Nima – Sunday. The word "Sherpa" then follows this first name: Dawa Sherpa, Mingma Sherpa, etc.

1914:

Tenzing Norgay (1914 – 1986) was born in the Tibetan village of Tsa-chu or Tshechu (14,500 ft./4,419 m.) just north of the 8,000 meter peak Makalu. Tsa-chu means "hot springs." He was the 11th of 13 children (7 sons, 6 daughters). Tenzing's mother Kinzom was 44 years old when Tenzing was born. The family relocated to the Nepalese village of Thame in the Solu Khumbu region when Tenzing was a young boy. At birth, Tenzing was named Namgyal Wandi. Later, he was renamed Tenzing ("supporter of religion") Norgay ("wealthy") by religious leader Dzatrul Rimpoche. Tenzing was 39 years old when he and New Zealand mountaineer Edmund Hillary first reached the summit of Mount Everest (29,035 ft./8,849 m.) in 1953. Tenzing died in 1986 at age 72.

1916:

The original construction of the Tengboche monastery (12,688 ft./3,867 m.) in the Solu-Khumbu region (just south of Mount Everest) of Nepal was begun and took three years to complete. Approximately forty Buddhist monks now live and study at this monastery. Many mountaineers visit this site on their trek to Mount Everest from the south.

1919:

The first trail to the summit of the Taiwanese peak known as Mount Yushan (12,966 ft./3,952 m.) was officially opened. Yushan is the highest peak in northeast Asia. It is 577 feet/176 meters higher that Mount Fuji in Japan.

1920:

British mountaineer and scientist Alexander M. Kellas (1868 – 1921) wrote an unpublished manuscript entitled: "A Consideration Of The Possibility Of Climbing Mount Everest." In the manuscript (published in 2001), he predicted the maximum climbing rate near the summit as being 300 to 350 feet per hour without oxygen. He also concluded that Mount Everest (29,035 ft./8,849 m.) could be ascended without the help of bottled oxygen. This type of ascent was actually first accomplished in 1978 by Reinhold Messner and Peter Habeler.

1920:

London, England. A joint-meeting of the Alpine Club and the Royal Geographical Society was held to discuss the feasibility of climbing Mount Everest. At this meeting, British explorer Francis Edward Younghusband (1863 – 1942) said: "We refuse to admit that the highest mountain in the world cannot be scaled. The man who first stands on the summit of Mount Everest will have raised the spirit of countless others for generations to come, and given men a firmer nerve for scaling every other mountain."

1920:

British diplomat Sir Charles Bell (1870 – 1945), a personal friend of the Dalai Lama, visited Lhasa, Tibet and obtained permission from the Tibetan government for a British mountaineering expedition to approach Mount Everest (29,035 ft./8,849 m.) through their country. The Dalai Lama of Tibet handed to Bell an important document (unsigned) that read: "To the west of the Five Treasures of Great Snow

Mount in the jurisdiction of White Grass Fort near Inner Rock Valley monastery is the district called 'The Southern Country where birds are kept.'" This note and the official passport that came with it represented the first permission ever given to Europeans to climb the world's highest peak— Chomolungma, Goddess Mother of the World: Mount Everest. In the Spring of 1921, the first British Mount Everest expedition was led by Lt. Col. Charles Kenneth Howard-Bury (1883 – 1963). Over the next 33 years, 8 major expeditions would journey to Everest before it was finally climbed in 1953.

1921:

The first British expedition to Mount Everest (29,035 ft./8,849 m.) on the Nepal – Tibet border was led by 38-year-old Lt. Col. Charles Kenneth Howard-Bury (1883 – 1963). The four members of the climbing team were: 56-year-old Scottish mountaineer Harold Raeburn (1865 – 1926), 53-year-old Scottish climber Dr. Alexander M. Kellas (1868 – 1921), 35-year-old English climber George Leigh Mallory (1886 – 1924), and 33-year-old English climber George Ingle Finch (1888 – 1970) who was eventually replaced by English climber Guy H. Bullock (1887 – 1956). E.O. Wheeler was the expedition's surveyor. The expedition assembled in Darjeeling, India in early May and departed for Lhasa, Tibet on May 18 and 19 in two groups. Dr. Kellas died of a heart attack (age 53) on June 5 while coming over a 17,000 ft./5,181 m. pass on the approach march—Mount Everest's first fatality. Kellas may have been the first scientist to study the effects of altitude on the human body. He made eight expeditions to the Himalayas from 1907 to 1921. In 1911, Kellas made ten first ascents in the Himalayas of peaks over 20,000 feet/6,095 meters. George Mallory and Guy Bullock became the first western mountaineers to see the massive east or Kangshung face of Mount Everest. Mallory promptly rejected this face as too dangerous to climb. The climbing team came upon mysterious footprints in the snow at 21,000 ft./6,400 m. which the native porters claimed were made by "a wild man of the snows." Bullock, Mallory, and Wheeler along with three Sherpas were the first to reach the North Col (23,183 ft./7,066 m.) of Mount Everest on September 24th. This was the highest that man had ever camped. On July 18, Mallory and Bullock first reached the Lho La (19,000 ft./5,791 m.) pass and were the first mountaineers to view the long, deep valley on Everest's south side that Mallory named the "western cwm" (cwm is a Welsh spelling of the word "combe" meaning: a narrow valley or deep hollow especially one enclosed on all but one side—Random House Dictionary of the English Language, 2nd edition, 1987). This 1921 expedition eventually reached a maximum altitude of 23,183 feet/7,066 meters (North Col).

This 1921 British Mount Everest expedition accomplished two important goals: 1. discovering a feasible climbing route as far as the northeast shoulder (27,500 ft./8,382 m.) and 2. surveying over 12,000 square miles/20,000 square kilometers of the Everest region. Mr. Marcel Kurz (1887 – 1967) of Switzerland was ruled out as an expedition member because he was not British. Kurz was one of the most distinguished mountain cartographers in Europe.

1921:

The name "Lhotse" (meaning "south peak") was given to the peak immediately south of Mount Everest by the 1921 British Mount Everest expedition. This expedition also discovered the correct name for peak T. 45 or M. 1—Cho Oyu. "Cho" means deity or demon and "Yu" means turquoise.

1921: Equipment – Cameras

The Kodak vest-pocket autographic camera was first introduced. This small camera was made between 1921 and 1926. It had two speeds (1/25 and 1/50 of a second). Its 1921 cost was $21.00 ($250.00 in 2004 dollars). Its developed photos measured 2 ¼" x 3 ¼." British mountaineer George Leigh Mallory (1886 – 1924) carried this small collapsible camera on his final day (June 8, 1924) on Mount Everest. Mallory disappeared (until 1999) along with this camera.

1921: Equipment – Batteries

The first use of batteries on a mountaineering expedition in severe conditions was on Mount Everest (29,035 ft./8,849 m.) in Nepal. Electric (battery-powered) flashlights or "torches" were used by the 1921 British Mount Everest Expedition. One of these flashlights was discovered in 1933 at the site of Camp VI (27,400 ft./8,351 m.) of the 1924 British Mount Everest Expedition.

1921 and 1922: Equipment – Sleeping Bags

British Mount Everest Expeditions. Eiderdown sleeping bags were used. Each bag accommodated two climbers for added warmth. These sleeping bags were made air-tight and damp-proof with a coating of Duroprene. Each bag weighed less than five pounds.

1922:

The 1922 British Mount Everest Expedition was led by Charles Granville Bruce (1866 – 1939). This expedition was composed of 13 British, 50 Nepalese, 100 Tibetans, and 300 yaks. The primary climbing team members were George Leigh Mallory (1886 – 1924, the only member of the 1921 expedition to return), Edward "Teddy" Norton (1884 – 1954, grandson of Alpine pioneer Sir Alfred Wills), Howard Somervell (1890 – 1975), George Ingle Finch (1888 – 1970), Henry Morshead (1882 – 1931), and Geoffrey Bruce (1896 – 1972). The 8,000 meter (26,248 feet) barrier was passed for the first time on May 20 when Mallory, Norton, and Somervell reached 26,985 feet/8,225 meters on the north face without using supplemental oxygen (called "English air" by the Tibentan Porters). Using their oxygen apparatus (10 oxygen sets were taken to Everest in 1922 but only 3 sets eventually worked), George Finch and Geoffrey Bruce attained an altitude of 27,318 feet/8,326 meters on May 27. Lance-Corporal Tejbir Bura Gurkha became the first high-altitude porter to carry a load to above 8,000 meters (26,248 feet). No crampons were used on this expedition. On the descent to Camp IV, Morshead slipped and fell pulling Norton off of his feet. They, in turn, pulled Somervell off. Mallory, last on the rope, instinctively thrust his axe into the snow, wrapping the climbing rope around his axe and saving the group from a long fall down the north face. On June 7th, a huge avalanche engulfed a climbing party as they ascended the steep snow slopes leading up to the North Col (23,183 ft./7,066 m.). Seven Sherpas died in this avalanche.

1922: FIRST ASCENT

Japanese mountaineer Yuko Maki (1894 – 1989) made the first winter ascent of Yari-gatake (10,433 ft./3,180 m.) in Japan. In 1956, Maki was the leader of the Japanese expedition that made the first ascent of Manaslu (26,760 ft./8,156 m.) in Nepal.

1922: Clothing – Down-Filled Parka

British Mount Everest Expedition. The first known use of a down-filled jacket or duvet (French for a down-filled quilt or comforter). British mountaineer George Ingle Finch (1888 – 1970) made for himself a rudimentary knee-length duvet jacket from thin balloon material and filled the various quilted panels with eiderdown (breast feathers from the female Eider duck). No other member of the 1921, 1922, or 1924 British Mount Everest expeditions had windproof or adequate clothing for the cold conditions. Finch, therefore, was the first climber to take down-filled clothing to the Himalaya. The British climbing community considered Finch's down jackets too radical.

1922: Equipment – Supplemental Oxygen

British Mount Everest Expedition. Supplemental (bottled) oxygen was first used on Mount Everest. Its use was limited and the apparatus was clumsy. Comprised of four steel cylinders, tubes, valves, and a mask, the total apparatus weighed fifteen kilograms or thirty-three pounds. Each steel cylinder was filled with 240 liters of compressed oxygen and would last for approximately two hours. Tibetan porters called this bottled oxygen "English air."

1922: Technique – Sleeping Oxygen

British Mount Everest Expedition. Team member George Ingle Finch (1888 – 1970) was the first mountaineer to use an oxygen apparatus while sleeping at high altitudes. Finch eventually reached 27,318 feet/8,326 meters on the north face of Mount Everest (29,035 feet/8,849 meters) in Tibet.

1923: Equipment – Tents

British mountaineer George Leigh Mallory (1886 – 1924) demanded a better tent design for expeditions to Mount Everest (29,035 ft./8,849 m.) in Nepal – Tibet. A tunnel (sleeve) entrance replaced the tent flap entrance on the Meade Tent.

1924:

June 3. 1924 British Mount Everest Expedition. This was the first time that Nepalese Sherpas had climbed above 8,000 meters (24,248 feet). These Sherpas, now living in Darjeeling, India were Narbu Yishé, Llakpa Chédé, and Semchumbi. They reached Camp VI at 26,700 ft./8,138 m. on the north ridge. The title "Tiger" was first used on this expedition to designate those fifteen porters who climbed high on Everest and performed exceptionally well.

1924:

June 4. The 1924 British Mount Everest Expedition was led by General Charles Granville Bruce (1866 – 1939). Bruce became ill and Lt. Col. Edward Felix Norton (1884 – 1954) was then appointed the new expedition leader. Norton and his partner Howard Somervell (1890 – 1975) ascended the upper north face of Mount Everest (29,035 ft./8,849 m.). Somervell became ill with mountain sickness and turned back. Norton, without using supplemental oxygen, climbed to within 874 feet/266 meters of the summit (then calculated to be 29,002 feet/8,839 meters). Suddenly realizing that he was going snow blind, he turned to descend. He had no rope, crampons, or down jacket. British mountaineer Frank S. Smythe (1900 – 1949) ,matched this altitude (28,128 ft./8,573 m.) record in 1933. This altitude record would remain until the 1952 Swiss Expedition to Mount Everest).

1924:

June 8. 1924 British Mount Everest Expedition. British mountaineers George Leigh Mallory (1886 – 1924) and his young climbing partner Andrew "Sandy" Irvine (1902 – 1924) disappeared into the clouds on the northeast ridge of Mount Everest near the First Step at around 27,724 feet/8,450 meters. They were last seen at 12:50 p.m. to be climbing up at the time by Noel Odell who was approximately 2,100 ft./640 m. away from them at an altitude of 25,920 feet/7,900 meters. They were never seen again. Mallory's well-preserved body, however, was finally discovered in 1999 on the north face. Irvine remains missing. Mount Mallory (10,729 ft./3,270 m.) in the Canadian Rockies is named for Mallory.

> *"Now they'll (Mallory and Irvine) never grow old and I am*
> *very sure they would not change places with any one of us."*
>
> 1924
> Tom Longstaff
> (1875 – 1964)
> British mountaineer and
> explorer upon learning of
> the disappearance of
> Mallory and Irvine

1924:

October 17. A memorial service for British mountaineers George Mallory (1886 – 1924) and Andrew "Sandy" Irvine (1902 – 1924) was held at St. Paul's Cathedral in London. Mallory and Irvine disappeared and died on Mount Everest on June 8, 1924. This memorial service represented the only time that British mountaineers had been honored at St. Paul's.

1924:

Pope Pius XI (Italian mountaineer Achille Ratti, 1857 – 1939) was in the early years of his reign as Pope (1922 – 1939). He blessed the 1924 British Mount Everest Expedition with these words: "May God, who dwells on the heights, bless your expedition." Expedition members sent the Pope a rock from the highest elevation they reached. This rock was mounted on a plaque with all the expedition member's names engraved. This plaque was placed inside a mahogany case which Ratti kept on his Vatican desk.

1924:

1924 British Mount Everest Expedition. This expedition named the "first" (28,110 ft./8,567 m.) and "second" (28,280 ft./8,619 m.) rock step features on the north ridge.

1924:

The 1924 British Mount Everest Expedition proved that with proper acclimatization and a high level of fitness, it was possible to climb higher without using supplemental oxygen than had been previously thought. Edward F. Norton (1884 – 1954) climbed to 28,128 ft./8,573 m. on the upper north face without using supplemental oxygen.

1924: Clothing – Windproof Parkas

The 1924 British Everest Expedition wore parkas made of a breathable/windproof fabric called "Burberry." Thomas Burberry (1835 – 1926) was a Hampshire, England outfitter that began making hunting and shooting clothing in 1865.

1924: Equipment – Crampons

Although the 1924 British Everest expedition took eight-point crampons with them, Mallory and Irvine chose not to use them.

1926:

British explorer Hugh Ruttledge (1884 – 1961) and his wife became the first Europeans to walk completely around the sacred Tibetan peak known as Mount Kailas (22,028 feet/6,714 m.). This peak is also known as Kangchen Rimpoche meaning "Precious Ice Mountain." The Ruttledge trek took four days.

1928:

February 17. The Himalayan Club was founded by the British in New Delhi,India with branch offices in Bombay, Calcutta, and Darjeeling, India. The Mountain Club of India became the Himalayan Club. This new club was composed of leading geographers, soldiers, and senior civil servants. It encouraged and assisted Himalayan travel and exploration. The initial meeting of the Himalayan Club was at British Army Headquarters in Delhi, India. Kenneth Mason (1887 – 1976) was a leading figure in the establishment of this Club.

1928: PEAK FIRST ASCENT *LENIN*

September 25. German mountaineer Willi Rickmer Rickmers (1873 – 1965) led a Soviet-German expedition to the first ascent of Pik Lenin (23,407 ft./7,134 m.) in the Pamir Range on the border of Tajikistan and Kyrgyzstan. Originally named Mount Kaufmann, this high peak was renamed Lenin Peak in 1928 and renamed again in 2006 Avicenna Peak. The official name in Kyrgyzstan remains Lenin Peak. It is the second highest peak in the Pamirs (Pik Communism is first at 24,591 ft./7,495 m.). Eugen Allwein (1900 – 1982), Karl Wien (1906 – 1937), and Erwin Schneider (1906 – 1987) reached the summit via the northeast ridge. This was the first mountaineering expedition into the Pamir Range.

1929:

May 27. American mountaineer Edgar Francis Farmer (New Rochelle, New York) made a solo attempt to climb Kangchenjunga (28,171 ft./8,586 m.) on the Nepal/Sikkim border. He recruited four porters in Darjeeling, India and climbed up the Yalung Glacier to the southwestern base of the mountain. He disappeared on May 27 at approximately 21,900 feet/6,675 meters while climbing towards the Talung Saddle. Farmer was the first American killed in the Himalayas.

1929:

A German party led by Paul Bauer (1896 – 1990) made the first serious mountaineering expedition to the Himalayas. They attempted to climb Kangchenjunga (28,171 ft./8,586 m.) in the Nepal – Sikkim border. All of these climbers were members of the Akademischer Alpenverein of Munich, Germany. Climbing the northeast spur and north ridge, mountaineers Eugen Allwein and Karl von Kraus reached 24,280 ft./7,400 m. before retreating due to heavy snows and bad weather.

1929:

Austrian mountaineer and geologist Erwin Schneider (1906 – 1987) made the following ascents in the Pamir mountains of Kyrgyzstan and Tajikistan:

15 peaks in the 17,000 foot/5,181 meter range

8 peaks in the 20,000 foot/6,096 meter range

Mount Kaufmann—23,407 ft./7,134 m. (known as Pic Lenin prior to 1971).

1929: Technique – Shaft Boring

September. German mountaineer Paul Bauer (1896 – 1990) led an expedition to Kangchenjunga (28,171 feet/8,586 meters) in Nepal. This expedition first used the technique of boring shafts (tunnels) through snow and ice towers and cornices on a ridge if they could not climb them by cutting steps. In one ridge location, a 25 foot/8 meter tunnel was bored through a ridge crest (two days work). High winds and six feet of fresh snow halted this expedition at 24,450 feet/7,452 meters.

1930: PEAK FIRST ASCENT *JONGSONG*

Swiss mountaineer Gunter Oscar Dyhrenfurth (1886 – 1975) led a four-nation (Swiss, Austrian, German, and British) climbing party on an attempt to climb Kangchenjunga (28,171 ft./8,586 m.) on the Nepal – Sikkim border. The attempt failed at 20,800 ft./6,340 m. This team (Schneider and Hoerlin) did, however, make the first ascent of Jongsong Peak (24,344 ft./7,420 m.) on June 3 near the Nepal – Sikkim border. This was the highest mountain climbed to date. This height record, however, lasted for just over one year. Kamet (25,447 ft./7,756 m.) was climbed in 1931. Other team members included: Frank S. Smythe, G. Wood-Johnson, Marcel Kurz, and Sherpas Lewa and Tsering Norbu.

1930:

Botanist Joseph Rock (1884 – 1962) claimed that the height of Minya Konka in China was 30,250 feet (9,220 m.). Rock sent a cable message to the National Geographic Society in the United States with this new altitude. Minya Konka's actual elevation is 24,934 feet (7,589 m.) which was calculated by an American team in 1932.

1931: PEAK FIRST ASCENT *KAMET*

June 21. British mountaineer Frank S. Smythe (1900 – 1949) led an expedition to the Garhwal Himalaya of India that made the first ascent of Kamet (25, 447 ft./7,756 m.). This was the highest mountain climbed to date. Other expedition members were E.B. Beaumann, Robert L. Holdsworth, Raymond Greene, E. St. J. Birnie, Eric Shipton, and eight Sherpas. On June 21st, Smythe, Shipton, Holdsworth, and Lewa Sherpa reached the summit. This was the first first ascent of any major peak by a Sherpa. On June 23rd, Greene, Birnie, and Kesar Singh Sherpa also reached the summit. This was the first of over 60 Himalayan peaks over 25,000 feet/7,620 meters to be climbed. More climbing attempts (10) were made on Kamet before it was climbed than any other Himalayan peak. After the Kamet ascent, members of this expedition made eleven other first ascents in the Badrinath Range and crossed three virgin passes. The second ascent of Kamet occurred on July 6, 1955—24 years after the first ascent.

1931: PEAK FIRST ASCENT *KHAN TENGRI*

September 5. A Soviet expedition led by M. Pogrebetsky made the first ascent of Khan Tengri (23,000 ft./7,010 m.) by a route from the south and west ridge. This is the second highest peak in the Tien Shan Range on the border of Kazakhstan and Kyrgyzstan. Khan Tengri is one of five 7,000 meter peaks that comprise the Snow Leopard climbing award. Tien Shan means "heavenly mountains."

1931:

Nepalese Ang Tharkay Sherpa (1910 – 1965) joined his first mountaineering expedition—a German expedition to Kangchenjunga (28,169 ft./8,585 m.). He then joined expeditions to:

Mount Everest	1933, 1935, 1936, 1938, 1951, 1965
Nanda Devi	1934
Kabru	1935
Karakoram	1937, 1939
Annapurna	1950
Nun Kun	1953

1931: Equipment – Crampons

On the first ascent of Kamet (25,447 ft./7,756 m.) in the Himalaya, leader Frank S. Smythe (1900 – 1949) used an eight-point crampon which is now on display in the Alpine Museum in Zermatt, Switzerland.

1931: Equipment – Sleeping Air Mattress

German expedition to Kangchenjunga (28,169 ft./8,586 m.) in Nepal-Sikkim. Air mattresses known as "Li-Lo's" were used as insulation. These mattresses measured 3½ feet long by two feet wide. All expedition members felt these air mattresses were too short to be effective.

1932: PEAK FIRST ASCENT *MINYA KONKA*

October 28. An American expedition composed of Richard Burdsall (1895 – 1953), Arthur Emmons (1910 – 1962), Terris Moore (1908 – 1994), and Jack Young made the first ascent of Minya Konka (24,892 ft./7,587 m.), the highest peak in China (Szechwan Province). Burdsall and Moore reached the summit via the northwest ridge. Emmons lost all of his toes to frostbite on this climb. This was the highest complete ascent ever achieved by American climbers and the second highest summit reached in the world to date. Minya Konka is now known as Gongga Shan. A higher summit for American climbers would be achieved 26 years later in 1958 with the first ascent of Hidden Peak or Gasherbrum I (26,471 ft./8,068 m.) in the Himalayas.

1932:

German mountaineer Willi Merkl (1900 – 1934) led a German-American expedition to make the second attempt to climb Nanga Parbat (26,658 ft./8,125 m.) in the Punjab Himalaya. This expedition included six Germans and three Americans (Rand Herron, Elizabeth Knowlton, and Fritz Wiessner). It had been 37 years since the first serious climbing attempt in 1895 by British mountaineer Albert F. Mummery's party. Bad weather forced a retreat of Merkl's party after reaching nearly 7,000 meters (22,967 feet) on the northeast (Rakhiot) face.

1932: Equipment – Sleeping Bags

First ascent of Minya Konka in China by an American expedition. Some of the sleeping bags were specially equipped with zippers (Woods Arctic Eiderdown Bags).

1932: Technique – Route Marking

October. A small American mountaineering expedition made the first ascent of the Chinese peak known as Minya Konka (24,790 ft./7,556 m.). Willow sticks were used to mark the climbing route. These sticks or wands were placed in the snow at intervals of 100 feet/30 meters (or approximately 50 per mile). This placement interval frequently depended upon how many climbers were tied into a single rope.

1933:

April 3. The first photographs of the unknown southern (Nepalese) side of Mount Everest (29,035 ft./8,849 m.) were taken during an aerial survey. The Houston-Westland Expedition to Mount Everest produced these photographs which clarified topographical information. Two bi-planes were used—a Westland PV3 and a Westland Wallace. These airplanes were based 500 kilometers/300miles north of Calcutta, India and flew 100 feet above Everest's summit. The pilots were Lt. David McIntyre and Sir Douglas Douglas-Hamilton.

1933:

The 1933 British Mount Everest expedition (B.M.E.E.) was led by Hugh Ruttledge (1884 – 1961). The climbing team was composed of Frank S. Smythe (1900 – 1949), Percy Wyn Harris (1903 – 1979),

Lawrence Wager (1904 – 1965), Eric Shipton (1907 – 1977), C.G. Crawford (1890 – 1959), J.L. Longland, R. Greene, and S. MacLean. Frank Smythe eventually reached 28,126 ft./8,573 m. below the north ridge in the Great (Norton) Couloir. He took 3 hours to climb his last 600 feet/183 meters. This was the first expedition to carry a radio on Mount Everest and the first expedition to bring rock pitons to this mountain. In addition, a telephone line was laid between camps 3 and 4 to improve communications. Camp 4 was located on the North Col at 23,183 ft./7,066 m. Sirdar (head Sherpa) Nursang acquired a Tibetan mastiff dog to help guard the expedition supplies. Named "Police-ie" this dog reached 22,500 feet/6,858 meters on the north side of Mount Everest.

1933:

B.M.E.E. May 30. British mountaineers Percy Wyn Harris (1903 – 1979) and Lawrence "Bill" Wager (1904 – 1965) found an old ice axe lying on rock slabs 60 feet below the crest of the northeast ridge of Mount Everest and approximately 200 yards (600 feet) east of the First Step (28,110 ft./8,567 m.) rock feature. This axe was stamped with its maker's name: Willisch of Täsch (Täsch is a village in the Zermatt Valley of Switzerland). Due to particular markings on the wooden shaft, this axe has now been determined to have belonged to Andrew "Sandy" Irvine (1902 – 1924) who disappeared with George Leigh Mallory (1886 – 1924) on June 8, 1924.

1933: PEAK FIRST ASCENT *STALIN*

September 3. Russian mountaineer Yevgeniy Abalakov (1907 – 1948) made the first ascent (solo) of Mount Stalin (24,591 ft./7,495 m.) in the Pamir mountains of Tajikistan. Abalakov erected a tablet on the summit recording the elevation and naming the peak Stalin. This peak was previously known as Mount Garmo and then renamed Pik Communism in 1962. It was renamed again in 1998 Ismoil Somoni Peak.

1933: Clothing – Climbing Suits

British Mount Everest Expedition. Windproof suits of Grenfell cloth were used for the first time. British mountaineer Frank Smythe (1900 – 1949) wore the following clothing at the Camp Six high camp: Shetland (wool) vest, a thick flannel shirt, a heavy camel-hair sweater, 6 light Shetland pullovers, two pair of long Shetland pants, a pair of flannel trousers, and over all a silk-lined "grenfell" windproof suit. A Shetland balaclava and another helmet of "grenfell" cloth protected his head and his feet were encased in four pairs of Shetland wool socks and stockings.

1933: Equipment – Boots

Each mountaineer on the British Mount Everest Expedition was equipped with:
1. A trekking boot for the approach march into base camp.
2. A sheepskin-lined boot for in-camp comfort.
3. A high-altitude boot designed by Robert Lawrie of London, England. These boots were designed to prevent frostbite by being lined with felt and having a layer of asbestos placed between the outer leather sole and the inner sole. The outer boot edges were nailed with "clinker" nails.

1933: Equipment – Radios

Radio communications between camps in the Himalayas was experimented with for the first time on the British Mount Everest expedition.

1933: Equipment – Tents

The British Mount Everest expedition was the first to use the comparatively warm and comfortable double-walled Arctic Tent. This igloo-shaped frame tent was covered with a material called Jacqua. This tent had two mica windows, 1 ventilating cowl, a sewn-in floor, and accommodated six men. This tent design enabled climbers to endure violent storms. This same expedition also used a version of the old Whymper Tent that allowed climbers to stand-up inside. It was made of Grenfell cloth fabric.

1934:

April – May. Britisher Maurice Wilson (1898 – 1934) was the first person to attempt climbing an 8,000 meter (26,248 feet) peak solo. Wilson, known as the "Mad Yorkshireman" flew a fabric-winged 1925 Gypsy Moth airplane he named "Ever Wrest" from England to Cairo (Egypt) to Tehran (Iran) to India. He began this journey on May 21, 1934. He sold this airplane for 500 upon arriving in India. Disguising himself as a Buddhist monk, he hired three Sherpa porters in March of 1934 and trekked 300 miles/500 kilometers to the Tibetan Plateau. On April 14, Wilson arrived at the foot of Mount Everest's (29,035 ft./8,849 m.) north side. His plan was to summit Mount Everest on April 21st, his birthday. He eventually reached a height of 22,700 ft./6,919 m. below the North Col (23,183 ft./7,066 m.) of Everest. Wilson's climbing boots were made with insulated cork running the entire length from heel to toe. On or about May 31, Wilson died in his high camp (age 36). British mountaineers Eric Shipton (1907 – 1977) and Charles Warren discovered Wilson's body in 1935 curled up next to his shredded tent on the East Rongbuk Glacier. They buried Wilson's remains in a glacial crevasse. His remains, however, have continually resurfaced over the years (1959, 1975, 1985, 1989, and 1999).

1934:

July 7. Mountaineer Willi Merkl (1900 – 1934) led the second German expedition to attempt climbing Nanga Parbat (26,658 ft./8,125 m.) in the Punjab Himalaya of Pakistan. Nanga Parbat is the ninth highest peak in the world. Merkl was considered by many to be the finest German mountaineer between the two world wars. In addition to Merkl, there were eleven other German climbers, thirty-five Sherpas, and two hundred porters. The climbing team selected the Rakhiot Glacier route. Alfred Drexel (– 1934) died of high altitude pulmonary edema in the early days of this expedition. Peter Aschenbrenner (1902 – 1998) and Erwin Schneider (1906 – 1987) reached approximately 25,900 feet (7,894 m.) on July 6th but were forced to return to their camp due to worsening weather. On July 7th, they and fourteen others were trapped by a terrible snowstorm (eight feet of snow in six days) at 24,540 feet (7,479 m.). During their retreat down the mountain, a sudden avalanche buried Merkl, Willo Welzenbach, Uli Wieland and six Sherpas. This was the worst mountaineering disaster since 1870. The last survivor of this avalanche to reach safety was Ang Tsering Sherpa who was awarded the German Red Cross medal for his courage and gallantry. As a result of this expedition, Sherpa and Tibetan porters began to believe that they could actually climb rather than just carry loads. In 1938, German mountaineer Fritz Bechtold returned to Nanga Parbat to recover the bodies of Willi Merkl and his porter. He then gave them a proper burial on the peak.

1934:

German mountaineer Willo Welzenbach (1900 – 1934) died in a storm on Nanga Parbat (26,658 ft./8,125 m.) in the Punjab Himalayas. Welzenbach's climbing career spanned fourteen years and included 940 ascents—72 peaks were over 4,000 meters (13,124 ft.) and 50 were first ascents. In 1925, Welzenbach climbed 149 separate peaks.

1935: PEAK FIRST ASCENT *KABRU NORTH*

November 18. British mountaineer Conrad Reginald Cooke (1901 – 1996) made the first ascent (solo) of Kabru North (24,256 ft./7,393 m.) in the eastern Nepal Himalaya. This ascent would remain the highest solo climb until 1953. This was the first 7,000 meter (22,967 ft.) post-monsoon ascent in the Himalayas. An 1883 Kabru first ascent was claimed by W.W. Graham with guides Emil Boss and Ulrich Kaufmann. This 1883 ascent, however, was never confirmed.

1935:

This year saw the fifth British Mount Everest expedition (1921, 1922, 1924, and 1933). British mountaineer Eric Shipton (1907 – 1977) led this reconnaissance expedition. The other climbers were Edwin Kempson, Charles Warren (physician), Dan Bryant (New Zealand), Edmond Wigram, H.W. "Bill" Tilman, Michael Spender (photographer) and Karma Paul (interpreter). The highest point reached was 24,000 feet/7,315 meters. A young Tenzing Norgay (21) was recruited to this expedition (his first) along with 14 other Sherpas from Darjeeling, India. Norgay (1914 – 1986) was Charles Warren's personal Sherpa and was able to reach the North Col (23,186 feet/7,067 meters).

1935: PEAK FIRST ASCENT *KHARTAPHU*

After their withdrawal from Mount Everest, the British climbing team went on to climb 26 other peaks over 20,000 feet/6,096 meters in the next six weeks. Shipton, Kempson, and Warren climbed Khartaphu (23,640 ft./7,205 m.). More peaks over 20,000 feet were climbed by this one expedition than had been ascended worldwide before this date. They also explored three branches of the Rongbuk Glacier and contributed a significant amount of information to cartographic surveys.

1935: Equipment – Ropeway

During the approach march-in to Mount Everest, the British climbing team utilized a mechanical ropeway to transport expedition equipment to Kalimpong, India.

1936:

May. The first French expedition to the Himalayas was led by Henry de Segogne (1901 – 1979). Segogne and nine other climbers attempted to climb Gasherbrum I or Hidden Peak (26,471 ft./8,068 m.). After establishing five camps and reaching 22,400 ft./6,827 m., they were stopped by deep snow.

1936: PEAK FIRST ASCENT *NANDA DEVI*

August 29. After seven attempts (1883, 1905, 1907, 1926, 1927, 1932, and 1934) to reach the Nanda Devi Sanctuary before 1936, an American – British expedition led by H.W. "Bill" Tilman (1898 – 1977) made the first ascent of Nanda Devi (25,644 ft./7,816 m.) in northern India (the highest peak in India). On this date, Tilman and Noel E. Odell (1890 – 1987) reached the summit of Nanda Devi ("The Blessed Goddess") via the South Ridge. No crampons or pitons were used on this ascent. This summit height record would last for 14 years until Annapurna (26,545 ft./8,091 m.) was first climbed in 1950 by the French. Other expedition climbers included Charles Houston (American), T. Graham Brown (British), H. Adams Carter (American), Arthur Emmons (American), W.F. Loomis (American), and Peter Lloyd (British). Nanda Devi was considered to be a holy mountain. As a result of this expedition, Dr. Charlie Houston (1913 – 2009) began researching the effects of altitude on the human body.

1936: PEAK FIRST ASCENT *NGGA PULU*

A Dutch party led by Dr. A.H. Colijn made the first ascent of Ngga Pulu (15,946 ft./4,860 m.) in Irian Jaya—New Guinea. This peak is near Carstensz Pyramid (16,024 ft./4,884 m.) which they explored but did not summit. Ngga Pulu has also been spelled "Ngga Posloe."

1936: Equipment – Boots

Felt-lined climbing boots were used by some mountaineers in the Nepal Himalaya. The large size accommodated three pair of socks.

1936: Equipment – First Aid Kits

Himalayas. A typical first-aid kit included a tube of Anti-Lux for sunburn protection, sticking plaster for bone breaks and sprains, and an envelope of aspirin.

1936: Equipment – Radios

Lightweight radio sets were used for the first time by Frank Smythe (1900 – 1949) and High Ruttledge (1884 – 1961) on the British Mount Everest Expedition.

1936: Equipment – Sleeping Air Mattresses

First ascent of Nanda Devi (25,645 ft./7,816 m.) in the Himalayas by a British team. This was one of the first expeditions to the Himalayas to experiment with air mattresses for sleeping on snow rather than the usual rubber mats (½" thick, 3' x 4' in size). Punctures to these air mattresses were numerous. A French expedition to Gasherbrum I (26,471 ft./8,068 m.) in the Karakoram mountains used pneumatic compressed air sleeping mattresses that weighed 13 oz. each.

1936: Equipment – Windlass

The French expedition to Gasherbrum I or Hidden Peak (26,471 ft./8,068 m.) in the Karakoram Range used a duraluminum windlass between Camps I and II. A windlass is a mechanical device that is used to move heavy weights. This expedition used a lightweight windlass that was easily dismantled for transport. The haul distance was approximately 750 feet/229 meters.

1937: PEAK FIRST ASCENT *CHOMOLHARI*

May 21. British mountaineers Frederick Spencer Chapman (1907 – 1971), Charles Crawford, and Pasang Dawa Sherpa made the first ascent of the Tibetan peak Chomolhari (23,997 ft./7,314 m.) located on the Tibet-Bhutan border via the southeast spur. Chomolhari lies 150 miles east of Mount Everest and is the most sacred mountain in Bhutan. Chapman and Dawa reached the summit and then both took a bad, long fall on the descent (neither was injured). Chomolhari when translated means "Goddess of the Holy Mountain." The second ascent of Chomolhari occurred on April 23, 1971.

1937:

October. India granted the first permit to climb K2 to an American expedition.

1938:

July. An American mountaineering expedition was led by Dr. Charles Houston (1913 – 2009) to climb K2 (28,253 ft./8,611 m.) in the Karakoram Range of Pakistan ($9,000.00 budget). Paul Petzoldt (1908 – 1999) first instructed the expedition's Sherpas on how to belay and how to rappel. William P. House (1913 – 1997) successfully climbed in 2 ½ hours without a rope an 80-foot/24-meter rock chimney at 21,600 feet/6,583 meters that was the key to opening the climbing route above. This difficult chimney is now known as House's Chimney. Petzoldt and Dr. Charles Houston eventually reached 25,985 ft./7,920 m. on July 21 before turning back due to their lack of matches to light their stove to melt water. On July 22, Petzoldt climbed to 26,000 feet/7,924 meters alone before turning back. Other expedition members included Robert Bates (1911 – 2007), Richard Burdsall (1895 – 1953), and Captain Norman R. Streatfield (British). The primary achievement of this expedition was their finding a safe ascent route up the southeast ridge which they named the "Abruzzi" Ridge after the Duke of the Abruzzi (1873 – 1933). This expedition lasted for 90 days.

1938:

British mountaineer H.W. "Bill" Tilman (1898 – 1977) also used the name "Tiger" for those Sherpas who performed well at high-altitudes. The "Tiger" designation became official on the 1938 British Mount Everest Expedition that was led by Tilman. Tiger Medals were awarded in 1939 to all of those Sherpas who reached Camp VI on Everest. The Tiger designation began to disappear in the 1960s.

1938: :

The Himalayan Club in India began giving each porter on a mountaineering expedition to the Himalayas a book in a thick leather pouch. On each expedition, the climbing leader wrote a chit or note in this book about the performance and attitude of the porter. This was the first register (similar to the Führerbüch that guides in the Alps began using in the 1850s) for high-altitude porters. In each book, the Secretary of the Himalayan Club entered a short record of the porter's service prior to 1938.

1938:

British mountaineer H.W. "Bill" Tilman (1898 – 1977) led the seventh British Mount Everest expedition (B.M.E.E.). On the first summit attempt, Frank Smythe (1900 – 1949) and Eric Shipton (1907 – 1977) reached 27,400 feet/8,351 meters without using supplemental oxygen. On the second attempt, Tilman and Peter Lloyd also reached 27,400 feet/8,351 meters with Lloyd using bottled oxygen. This expedition produced the first undisputed evidence that the use of supplemental oxygen increased the climbing rate at high altitudes. This small expedition cost about 3,000 and it was the last expedition to Mount Everest from the Tibetan (north) side until 1960.

1939: PEAK FIRST ASCENT *TENT*

May 29. A Swiss – German expedition made the first ascent of Tent Peak (24,165 ft./7,365 m.) on the Indian – Nepalese border. Ernst Grob, Ludwig Schmaderer, and Herbert Paider reached the summit. This peak is also known as Kirat Chuli.

1939:

An American expedition attempted to climb K2 (28,253 ft./8,611 m.) in the Karakoram Mountains of Pakistan. This was the fourth expedition to attempt climbing K2 (1902, 1909, 1938). Fritz Wiessner (1900 – 1988), and Pasang Dawa Lama Sherpa reached 27, 450 ft./8,366 m. on July 19 (without using supplemental oxygen) before retreating because Pasang accidentally lost two pairs of crampons and he refused to climb at night. Wiessner wore a wool coat at 27,000 feet/8,229 meters. Faithful Sherpas Pasang Kikuli, Kitar, and Phinsoo were lost in a snowstorm attempting to rescue sick climber Dudley Wolfe (1896 – 1939) at Camp VII (24,700 ft./7,528 m.). Wolfe became the second American fatality in the Himalayas on July 31st and K2 had claimed its first four victims. This expedition marked two turning points in Sherpa mountaineering history: 1) This was the first time that a Sherpa was a member of the summit team for a great Himalayan peak (Pasang Dawa Lama), and 2) Pasang Kikuli and Tsering changed everyone's idea of what a Sherpa was capable of doing at high altitudes. They climbed from Base Camp to Camp VI in one day—a vertical gain of 6,800 feet or 2,072 meters. This was the strongest single day ascent to date by a climber on an 8,000 meter peak. This expedition cost $17,500. Dudley Wolfe's remains were discovered on the Godwin-Austen Glacier at the base of K2 in 2002. The remains of the three Sherpas were found in 1995.

1939:

Austrian mountaineer Heinrich Harrer (1912 – 2006) was invited to be a team member of the 1939 German Nanga Parbat Expedition. Harrer, in 1938, made the first ascent of the Eiger's north face in Switzerland. After arriving in India on April 30th and accomplishing a reconnaissance of a climbing route up the Diamir Face of Nanga Parbat, Harrer and his German companions were arrested on September 3rd and sent to a British internment camp in Dehra Dun, India. After escaping in April of 1944 (his fifth escape attempt), Harrer and Peter Aufschnaiter (1899 – 1973) made their way to Lhasa, Tibet. This 1,500-mile walk took 21 months. They climbed 62 mountain passes. Harrer eventually became the personal tutor for the fourteen-year-old Dalai Lama and Aufschnaiter assisted the local Tibetians in developing water storage projects. When the Chinese attacked Tibet in October of 1950, Harrer fled Lhasa. He returned to India and then back to Austria. In 1953, Harrer wrote of his Tibet experience in his book entitled *Seven Years in Tibet.*

1940 to 1944:

The outbreak of World War II caused many mountaineering expeditions to the Himalayas to cancel their climbs. British mountaineers did, however, manage to make two first ascents in the Himalayas of northern India (1941 and 1944). British climbers also attempted to summit three other peaks.

1940, 1941, and 1942:

The British sought permission to organize climbing expeditions to Mount Everest during each of these years. These requests, however, had no future in light of the events of World War II.

1945:

September 15. The Korean Alpine Club was founded in Seoul, Korea. Song Suk-ha was elected the first president. This climbing club currently has twelve branch offices for its 4,000 members.

1945:

M.F. Milne and Arthur R. Hinks (1873 – 1945) of the Royal Geographic Society made the first map of both the Nepalese and Tibetan sides of Mount Everest (29,035 ft./8,849 m.).

1947:

March – April. Canadian-born poverty-stricken electrical engineer Earl Denman attempted to solo climb Mount Everest (29,035 ft./8,849 m.) on the Nepal – Tibet border. He recruited Sherpas Tenzing Norgay (1914 – 1986) and Ang Dawa in Darjeeling, India and agreed to pay them 5 rupees each in advance. Denman did not have official permission to enter Tibet so as to approach Mount Everest from the north side. It took this small group of three climbers seventeen days to trek from Darjeeling to the Rongbuk Glacier on Everest's north side. They spent the next twenty days trying to reach the North Col (23,183 ft./7,066 m.) of Everest before retreating. Denman reached 22,000 ft./6,705 m. This group then safely returned to Darjeeling on April 28th (five week roundtrip). Denman returned in 1948 for a second attempt but again with no permission. He was persuaded not to proceed. In 1953, Tenzing wore Denman's balaclava (head covering) to the summit of Mount Everest.

1947: PEAK FIRST ASCENTS *KEDARNATH, SATOPANTH*

July and August. A Swiss party made the first post-war foreign mountaineering expedition to the Himalaya. Led by André Roch (1906 – 2002), this expedition made the first ascents of Kedarnath Peak (22,770 ft./6,940 m.) and Satopanth Peak (23,420 ft./7,138 m.). These are the highest of the Bhagirathi Peaks near Shivling. This was Sherpa Tenzing Norgay's (1914 – 1986) first expedition as sirdar (lead Sherpa) and Kedarnath was the first mountain summited by Tenzing.

1949:

As of this year, the highest peaks in the world that had been climbed were:

1936	Nanda Devi	25,644 ft./7,816 m.
1931	Kamet	25,447 ft./7,756 m.
1932	Minya Konka	24,791 ft./7,556 m.

1930	Jongsong Peak	24,550 ft./7,483 m.
1930	Mana Peak	23,860 ft./7,272 m.
1928	Pik Lenin	23,407 ft./7,134 m.
1910	Pauhunri	23,387 ft./7,128 m.
1907	Trisul	23,360 ft./7,120 m.

All of these peaks are located in or near the Himalayas.

*1950: PEAK FIRST ASCENT *ANNAPURNA*

June 3. A French expedition led by Maurice Herzog (1919 – 2012) made the first ascent of Annapurna (26,546 ft./8,091 m.) in Nepal. Herzog and Louis Lachenal (1921 – 1955) reached the summit of the tenth highest mountain in the world and the first 8,000 meter peak to be climbed. They climbed unroped up the north face. Herzog lost all of his fingers and toes to frostbite and Lachenal lost all of his toes. Herzog was carried out from base camp in a wicker basket on the back of expedition porters. The Himalayan Golden Age was said to have begun with this ascent and would extend over the next fifteen years (until 1964) when all of the fourteen 8,000 meter peaks were finally climbed. Annapurna ("Goddess of the Harvests") was the only 8,000 meter peak to be climbed on its first attempt. Other members of this French expedition were Lionel Terray (1921 – 1965), Gaston Rebuffat (1921 – 1985), Jean Couzy (1923 – 1958), Marcel Schatz, Jacques Oudot, and Francois de Noyelle. No supplemental oxygen was used. Maurice Herzog wrote his book *Annapurna* from his hospital bed in 1950. He dictated the book's text to others because he had no fingers left to hold a pen. This book was published in 1951 in French and in 1952 in English. The last paragraph in this book reads as follows: "Annapurna, to which we had gone empty-handed, was a treasure on which we should live for the rest of our days. With this realization we turn the page: A new life begins. There are other Annapurnas in the lives of men." From 1958 to 1963, Maurice Herzog became the French Minister of Youth and Sport. He was also elected mayor of the village of Chamonix-Mont Blanc. In 1970, Herzog was appointed a member of the International Olympic Committee and served until 1995.

1950: PEAK FIRST ASCENT *TIRICH MIR*

July 21 and 22. A Norwegian expedition made the first ascent of Tirich Mir (25,283 ft./7,706 m.) in the Hindu Kush Mountains of Afghanistan, China, Kyrgyzstan, and Pakistan. Tirich Mir is located in Pakistan. The expedition members were Per Kuernberg, Arne Naess, Henry Berg, and British mountaineer Tony Streather (all reached the summit). Streather became the first Englishman to summit a 25,000 foot peak since Odell and Tilman summited Nanda Devi (25,645 ft./7,816 m.) in 1936. In 1964, the Norwegians also made the first ascent of Tirich Mir East (25,236 ft./7,692 m.) on July 25.

1950:

November. The first party of westerners to visit the Nepalese side (south side) of Mount Everest was an Anglo-American group (Houston-Tilman Everest Reconnaissance Expedition) that included H.W.

* 1 of the 14 peaks in the world over 8,000 meters (26,248 feet).

"Bill" Tilman (1898 – 1977), Oscar Houston (1883 – 1966), Dr. Charles S. Houston (1913 – 2009), Elizabeth Cowles (1902 – 1974), and Anderson Bakewell (a Jesuit priest). His Highness the Maharajah Mohan Shumshere Jung Bahadur Rana gave his approval for this group to visit the region just south of Mount Everest known as the Solu Khumbu. It took 16 days for this group to trek from the Indian border to Namche Bazaar. They arrived there on November 14. Upon arriving in the Sherpa's primary village— Namche Bazaar (11,300 ft./3,444 m.)—this group found approximately 30 white-washed, two-story homes with low-pitched shingle (stone) roofs. By 2001, Namche Bazaar included over 350 Sherpa homes. On November 17, Tilman and Charles Houston became the first people to climb Kala Pattar (18,600 ft./5,669 m.) to reach a vantage point to view the Western Cwm of Mount Everest. They actually reached 17,890 feet on Kala Pattar because Houston was not acclimatized. They were also the first westerners to set foot on the Khumbu Glacier. Tilman and Charles Houston both suffered severe headaches on their climb up Kala Pattar. Houston later believed they had experienced some level of high-altitude cerebral edema at the time but this medical term was not known in 1950.

1950:

Nepal opened its borders providing sudden access to ten peaks over 8,000 meters (26,248 feet). This was a very significant event in the history of mountaineering.

1950: Technique – Siege Climbing

1950 to 1965. This fifteen year period has been called the Himalayan Golden Age. All of the world's fourteen 8,000 meter (26,248 feet) peaks had been successfully climbed during this period using the "siege" approach. Multiple, well-supplied camps, many high-altitude climbing Sherpas, fixed ropes, numerous porters, and up-to-date equipment, clothing, food, etc. characterized the climbing expeditions during this period. Using the siege style approach, no attempt was made to reach the summit until all climbers and supplies were in their proper camp locations.

1951:

British mountaineer Eric Shipton (1907 – 1977) and New Zealand mountaineer Edmund Hillary (1919 – 2008) climbed the north flank of Pumori (23,507 ft./7,165 m.) up to about 20,000 feet and became the first men to see and realize a possible climbing route through the Khumbu Icefall, up the Western Cwm, and then up the Lhotse face to the South Col (25,950 ft./7,909 m.) of Mount Everest (29,035 ft./8,849 m.).

1951:

Himalayan Club Secretary Jill Henderson first developed a basic form of expedition insurance for Sherpas and their families in the event of an disabling mountaineering accident or death.

1951:

A small French expedition to Nanda Devi (25,644 ft./7,816 m.) in the Himalayas of northern India attempted a traverse of the two main summits (25,644 ft. and 24,400 ft.). After reaching the main summit, Roger Duplat (32) and Gilbert Vignes (25) accidentally fell through a cornice on their traverse to the second summit and disappeared. This was probably the first expedition to the Himalayas with the objective of doing an "interesting" route on a previously climbed major peak. One of the Sherpas on this expedition, Tenzing Norgay (1914 – 1986), summited Nanda Devi East (24,400 ft./7,437 m.) while searching for Duplat and Vignes. This ascent would represent the second highest summit for Tenzing after Mount Everest (1953).

1952:

Spring. The Swiss Mount Everest Expedition was led by Dr. Edouard Wyss-Dunant (1897 – 1983). The climbing team included Rene Dittert, André Roch (1906 – 2002), Raymond Lambert (1914 – 1997), and Tenzing Norgay Sherpa (1914 – 1986) who was on his fifth expedition to Everest. On May 28, Lambert and Norgay left their high camp (27,560 ft./8,400 m.) on Everest's southeast ridge at 6:00 a.m. and climbed to 27,910 ft./8,507 m. just below the South Summit (28,700 feet/8,747 m.). Strong winds, faulty oxygen equipment, and dehydration forced them to retreat 1,118 feet/341 meters from the summit. Swiss mountaineer Jean-Jacques Asper climbed down and up the sixteen-foot-wide final crevasse of the Khumbu Icefall to become the first person to actually enter the Western Cwm of Mount Everest. This was the first Mount Everest expedition to reach the South Col (25,890 ft./7,891 m.). This expedition also named the rock buttress on the Lhotse Face the "Eperson des Genevois" or Geneva Spur and renamed the Western Cwm the "Valley of Silence" (the Western Cwm remains as the official geographical name). Expedition leader Wyss-Dunant coined the phrase "death zone" for those altitudes above 7,500 meters (24,607 feet). He believed that even with supplemental oxygen, bodily functions rapidly deteriorated. In December of 1952, the King of Nepal awarded Tenzing Norgay Sherpa the Nepal Pratap Bardhak Medal for his achievements on Mount Everest.

1952:

Fall. The Swiss returned to Mount Everest once again. On November 20, Reiss, Lambert, and Sherpa Tenzing Norgay reached 26,600 feet/8,107 meters just above the South Col but were forced to turn back due to high winds and cold temperatures. The expedition leader was Dr. Gabriel Chevalley. Mingma Dorje Sherpa died when an ice sliver pierced his lung. He was the first climber to die on Everest since Maurice Wilson in 1934. Tenzing Norgay was appointed a full member of the climbing team—the first Sherpa to achieve this distinction.

1952: Book

November 24. French mountaineer Maurice Herzog (1919 – 2012) dictated the writing of *Annapurna – Heroic Conquest of the Highest Mountain—26,493 ft.—Ever Climbed By Man* from his hospital bed in 1950 as he was undergoing ten operations for the amputation of his fingers and toes following his successful first ascent of Annapurna (26,545 ft./8,091 m.) on June 3, 1950. *National Geographic Adventure* called *Annapurna* "the most influential mountaineering book of all time." Eventually *Annapurna* was translated into forty different languages and has sold over twenty million copies making it one of the best-selling mountaineering books of all time. Herzog was decorated with the Grand Cross in France's Legion of Honor in 2011 (France's highest civilian honor).

1952: Equipment – Ropes

Plymouth Goldline ropes were first used in the Himalayas on an expedition to Cho Oyu (26,906 ft./8,201 m.) led by British mountaineer Eric Shipton (1907 – 1977). This is the sixth highest mountain in the world and is located on the Nepal – Tibet border west of Mount Everest.

1953:

The eighth British Mount Everest Expedition (B.M.E.E.) was led by John Hunt (1910 – 1999). On May 26th, the first summit team of British mountaineers—Tom Bourdillon (1924 – 1956) and Robert C. Evans (1912 – 1996)—left their South Col camp at 7:30 a.m. and first reached the South Summit (28,720 ft./8,753 m.) of Mount Everest at 1:10 p.m. This was higher than anyone had ever climbed. Due to Evans' faulty oxygen set, they were forced to return to their South Col camp. The second summit team of Hillary and Norgay would now make their summit attempt. If a third attempt was necessary, this would be led by Wilfrid Noyce (1918 – 1962). If the Swiss had succeeded in 1952, the British may have chosen Kangchenjunga for its first ascent. Including the two Swiss Mount Everest expeditions of 1952, this was the eleventh mountaineering expedition to Everest.

* [7]▲1953: PEAK FIRST ASCENT *EVEREST*

May 29. The British Mount Everest Expedition (B.M.E.E.) was led by John Hunt (1910 – 1999). On May 29th at 11:30 a.m. , New Zealand mountaineer Edmund Hillary (1919 – 2008) and Tenzing Norgay Sherpa (1914 – 1986) reached the summit of Mount Everest (29,035 ft./8,849 m.) via the southeast ridge after leaving their high camp at 27,620 feet/8,418 meters. This was the highest campsite in history. They both used open-circuit oxygen sets (4 litres per minute). This oxygen apparatus was far in advance of the 1952 Swiss Everest oxygen sets. This was the most important factor leading to this successful ascent. The other reasons for success were: 1. Favorable weather conditions, 2. Swiss pioneering the South Col Route, and 3. The superb leadership of John Hunt. This was the eleventh expedition to Mount Everest (1921, 1922, 1924, 1933, 1935, 1936, 1938, 1951, 1952 – 2, and 1953). There were also three solo attempts (1934, 1947, and 1951). Hillary summited eleven Himalayan peaks from 1951 to 1961, all above 6,000 m./19,686 ft.

1953: B.M.E.E.

June 1. The London *Times* correspondent that was assigned to the expedition sent the following coded message from the Mount Everest base camp back to London: "Snow conditions bad (code for Everest climbed). Advanced base camp abandoned (Hillary) yesterday (May 29th). Awaiting improvement (Tenzing). All well (nobody killed or injured)." This coded message was published in the *Times* on the morning of June 2nd—Coronation Day in England.

1953: B.M.E.E.

Sherpa Tenzing Norgay (1914 – 1986) wore to the summit of Mount Everest the red scarf that Swiss mountaineer Raymond Lambert (1914 – 1997) gave him in 1952, the balaclava that Maurice Wilson

---

* 1 of 14 peaks in the world over 8,000 meters (26,248 feet)
[7] ▲ One of the world's Seven Summits

gave him in 1934, and the socks that his wife Ang Lahmu knitted for him. This was Tenzing's seventh expedition to Mount Everest (1934, 1935, 1936, 1938, 1952 – 2, 1953) and his fourth British expedition.

> *"…on a mountain I can put away all other thoughts—of the*
> *world, the problems of living, even of home and family—and*
> *think of nothing, care for nothing, except what lies ahead.*
> *There is base camp and in the days to come only one thing,*
> *of all things, mattered to me. And that was Everest. To*
> *climb Everest."*

> 1955
> Tenzing Norgay
> (1914 – 1986)
> Nepalese Sherpa
> mountaineer reflecting
> on his 1953 first ascent
> of Mount Everest.

1953: B.M.E.E.

Queen Elizabeth II officially bestowed knighthood on Mount Everest summiter Edmund Hillary (1919 – 2008) and later to expedition leader John Hunt (1910 – 1999). Hillary's knighthood occurred while he was still on the mountain. In 1995, Hillary was also named a Knight of the Order of the Garter by Queen Elizabeth II.

1953: B.M.E.E.

England presented Tenzing Norgay Sherpa (1914 – 1986) with the George Medal, Britain's second highest civilian award for bravery after the George Cross. Nepal presented the Nepal Tara (Star of Nepal) to Tenzing, the highest decoration that a non-royal Nepalese can receive. In the United States, Tenzing received the National Geographic Society's Hubbard Medal and he was made an Honorary Member of the American Alpine Club. American author James Ramsey Ullman (1908 – 1971) in his biography of Tenzing entitled *Tiger Of The Snows* (1955) called Tenzing "the first humbly born Asian in all of history to attain world stature and world renown."

All of the Sherpas of the 1953 British Mount Everest Expedition received the Queen's Coronation Medal and their Tiger Badge from the Himalayan Club.

* 1953: PEAK FIRST ASCENT *NANGA PARBAT*

July 3. Austrian mountaineer Hermann Buhl (1924 – 1957) made the first ascent (solo) of Nanga Parbat (26,658 ft./8,125 m.) in the Punjab Himalaya via the Rakhiot Face and the Silbersattel. Buhl left his high camp at 22,639 ft./6,900 m. and climbed the final 1,200 m./3,937 ft. alone which took seventeen hours (without using supplemental oxygen). He reached the summit at 7:00 p.m. Just prior to leaving

---

* 1 of 14 peaks in the world over 8,000 meters (26,248 feet)

the summit at 9:00 p.m., Buhl decided to leave his ice axe with the Austrian flag as proof of his climb. Buhl's axe was found on the summit in 1999. Beginning his descent in the dark, he was forced to bivouac 450 feet/137 meters below the summit. Standing up all night for seven hours on a snow ledge, Buhl took Pervitin (a stimulant drug) tablets to stay awake and ward off frostbite. This was the highest open-air bivouac to date. Hermann Buhl was part of an Austrian – German expedition (Willy Merkl Memorial Expedition) led by Dr. Karl M. Herrligkoffer (1917 – 1991). Buhl's climbing partner, Otto Kempter, had to stop climbing 3,000 ft./914 meters below the summit. Buhl continued on alone to the top. This was the first and only solo ascent of an 8,000 meter peak. Buhl did suffer some frostbite resulting in the loss of one big toe and part of a second toe. Up until 1953, Nanga Parbat had claimed the lives of fourteen climbers and seventeen porters for a total of 31 deaths over a period of fifty-eight years (1895 to 1953). Nanga Parbat is the Urdu name for "naked mountain."

1953:

American mountaineer and physician Dr. Charles Houston (1913 – 2009) led the third American Karakoram Expedition to K2 (28,253 ft./8,611 m.). The climbing team included Robert Bates (42), George Bell (27), Robert Craig (28), Dee Molenaar (34), Pete Schoening (26), British climber Tony Streather (27), and Art Gilkey (27). The first summit team was to be Craig and Bell with the second summit team of Gilkey and Schoening. Gilkey developed thrombophlebitis (blood-clot formation) in his left leg at Camp VIII (25,592 ft./7,800 m.) which forced the expedition to immediately retreat in order to get Gilkey down and hopefully save his life. While carefully lowering Gilkey down a steep snow/ice slope on August 10th at about 24,800 ft./7,559 m., George Bell accidentally slipped and fell dragging his rope partner Tony Streather down. Their rope became entangled in the Bates-Houston rope which caused them to fall. Both ropes (four climbers) then pulled across Molenaar's rope. Now five men were falling out of control with no chance at self-arresting. The sixth and last man, Pete Schoening, planted his wood-shafted ice axe behind a frozen rock and stopped this group fall just short of a sheer cliff. These five climbers fell between 150 to 300 feet before being stopped. All of the fallen climbers were badly injured. Bob Craig was the only climber not involved in this accident. The descent to base camp after the accident took five days. Schoening performed the most famous ice axe belay in mountaineering history (he saved five lives). Climbers have called this the Miracle Belay. Art Gilkey disappeared on the snow/ice slope on August 10th forever, probably due to an avalanche. A British expedition to K2 in 1993 found Art Gilkey's remains on the Godwin-Austen Glacier. Schoening's K2 ice axe is now on display in the Bradford Washburn American Mountaineering Museum in Golden, Colorado. This expedition coined the name "The Savage Mountain" for K2.

> *"I knew, we all knew, that no one could be carried, lowered,*
> *or dragged down the Black Pyramid (K2), over the dreadful*
> *loose rock to Camp V, down House's Chimney. My mind's*
> *eye flew over the whole route. There was no hope, absolutely*
> *none. Art (Gilkey) was crippled. He would not recover*

enough to walk down. We could not carry him down…but we could try, and we must."

1955
Dr. Charlie Houston
(1913 – 2009)
American mountaineer
reflecting on the 1953
American expedition to K2
and the attempted rescue
of Art Gilkey.

1953: Book

British expedition leader John Hunt (1910 – 1999) raced to complete *The Ascent of Everest* (expedition account book) in 30 days in the Shropshire Village of Llanfair Waterdine in England. This book was in bookshops by November and sold for 25 shillings. 639,000 copies were eventually sold. The American edition was titled *The Conquest of Everest* (1954).

1953: Clothing – Windproof Climbing Suit

British Mount Everest expedition. Hooded, windproof suits were designed by the Polar Research Institute of Cambridge, England. This new windproof material was woven from cotton and nylon threads and lined with nylon. Each suit weighed 3 ¾ pounds. This new material was called "Wyncol."

1953: Equipment – Boots

The S.A.T.R.A. (Shoe and Allied Trades Research Association) boot was specifically designed for the successful British Mount Everest Expedition. This special high-altitude boot was called a "tropal" and combined an inner vapor barrier, mesh insoles, and an integrated rubber outer gaitor. Five layers (total thickness of one inch) of unwoven kapok fibers (a natural hollow fiber) provided the insulation. The S.A.T.R.A. boot soles were made of an airy, micro-cellular rubber. Each pair weighed 4 pounds 4 ounces. 33 pairs were made to measure for all the British climbers and the high-altitude Sherpas. This boot was widely used until the development of the Kolflach plastic climbing boot in 1978.

1953: Equipment – Supplemental Oxygen

British Mount Everest Expedition. The open-circuit oxygen model was used. Two cylinders of oxygen were carried. This set weighed 28 ½ pounds. A closed-circuit model was also used which contained one oxygen bottle and one canister and weighed thirty-five pounds.

1953: Equipment – Packs

British Mount Everest Expedition. Pack frames were made of lightweight aluminum. Each pack frame weighed less than one pound. These frames came from the British Army.

1953: Equipment – Sleeping Bags

British Mount Everest expedition. The climbing team used nylon-covered sleeping bags. The inner and outer bags were both filled with eiderdown. Each bag weighed 9 pounds.

1953: Equipment – Tent

British Mount Everest expedition. The favorite tent was the two-man Meade Tent. A new cotton-nylon weave material was used that could withstand winds of 100 miles per hour.

1953: Technique – Food Preparation

British Mount Everest Expedition. Food rations were divided into march-in rations, base camp rations, and assault rations. These food rations were then packed in numbered boxes. The standard daily ration pack for two men at a high camp included rolled oats, milk powder, sugar, jam, sweet biscuits, a mint bar, cheese, boiled sweets, salt, cocoa, tea, soup, and lemonade powder. This ration pack weighed four pounds. This expedition used vacuum-packed beverage boxes. Each box supplied powdered milk, tea, coffee, and cocoa for twenty-eight men for one day.

1953: Technique – Sleeping Oxygen

British Mount Everest Expedition. British mountaineer Peter Lloyd conceived the idea of using supplemental oxygen as an aid to sleeping. Oxygen warmed the body and reduced headaches at high altitudes. Lloyd recommended an oxygen flow rate of two liters per minute.

* 1954: PEAK FIRST ASCENT *K2*

July 31. An Italian expedition led by Dr. Ardito Desio (1897 – 2001) made the first ascent of K2 (28,253 ft./8,611 m.) or Chogori as it is locally known in the Karakoram Range of Pakistan. Desio, a professor of geology, had previously led eleven scientific and mountaineering expeditions abroad. This was the sixth expedition to K2. Italian mountaineers Achille Compagnoni (1914 – 2009) and Lino Lacedelli (1925 – 2009) reached the summit at 6:00 p.m. via the Abruzzi Ridge. Their supplemental oxygen ran out shortly before they summited. Other expedition members included Cirillo Floreanini (30), Gino Soldá (47), Erich Abram (32), Walter Bonatti (24), Pino Gallotti (36), Ugo Angelino (31), Ubaldo Rey (31), Sergio Viotto (26), and Mario Puchoz (36—died on June 21 at Camp II from either pneumonia or high-altitude pulmonary oedema). The circumstances surrounding July 30th and 31st high on K2 near the expedition's Camp IX have been very controversial over the years since 1954. Until recently, these circumstances have never been accurately revealed. In 2006, Lino Lacedelli (age 81) and Giovanni Cenacchi wrote the book entitled *K2 – The Price of Conquest*. This book reveals the truth about the ascent of the world's second highest peak. This ascent was also the longest recorded climb of an 8,000 meter peak—70 days of continuous action. Desio and his two cameramen made the first aerial photographs of K2 just prior to the climb. The second ascent of K2 was in 1977 by a Japanese expedition.

---

* 1 of 14 peaks in the world over 8,000 meters (26,248 feet)

* 1954: PEAK FIRST ASCENT *CHO OYU*

October 19. An Austrian expedition led by Dr. Herbert Tichy (1912 – 1987) made the first ascent of Cho Oyu (26,906 ft./8,201 m.) on the Nepal – Tibet border in the Himalayas. This was to be the smallest expedition (3 Europeans and 7 Sherpas) to climb an 8,000 meter peak. Three climbers reached the summit: Tichy, Sepp Jöchler, and Pasang Dawa Lama Sherpa. They did not use supplemental oxygen on this climb of the east face. Cho Oyu is located 19 miles west of Mount Everest. As an 8,000 meter peak, Cho Oyu can claim four important mountaineering firsts:

1. First 8,000 meter peak climbed during the post-monsoon season.
2. First 8,000 meter peak to be climbed in the winter via a new route. (Polish. February 12, 1984).
3. First 8,000 meter peak to be climbed in the winter alpine-style (Czechoslovakians. 1985).
4. First 8,000 meter peak solo ascent by a woman—Marianne Chapuisat (Swiss. 1993).

1954: PEAK FIRST ASCENT *CHOMO LONZO*

October 30. The south summit (the highest) of Chomo Lonzo (25,559 ft./7,790 m.) in the Kangshung Valley of Nepal was first climbed by French mountaineers Lionel Terray (1921 – 1965) and Jean Couzy (1923 – 1958) via the west and south ridges. They used supplemental oxygen. This was an unauthorized ascent.

1954:

November 4. India's Prime Minister Pandit Nehru (1889 – 1964) officially opened the Himalayan Mountaineering Institute (H.M.I.) in Darjeeling, India. Nehru had asked Mount Everest summiter Tenzing Norgay (1914 – 1986) to establish this institute saying to Tenzing: "I want you to produce a thousand Tenzings." Tenzing Norgay was appointed the first Director of Field Training—a position he held until 1976. Field training operated in the Koktan Region near Kang Peak. Two hundred thousand people a year now visit the Himalayan Mountaineering Institute and its museum. The Swiss Foundation initially donated 25 sets of crampons, 25 ice axes, etc. to the H.M.I.

1954:

The second summit team for K2 in 1954 was Italian mountaineer Walter Bonatti (1930 – 2011) and Balti climber Mahdi. In support of Compagnoni and Lacedelli, they were forced to spend the highest bivouac to date at 26,500 ft./8,077 m. It is interesting to note that Mahdi was also the high-altitude porter who carried Austrian mountaineer Hermann Buhl (1924 – 1957) down from Nanga Parbat (first ascent in 1953) with frost-bitten feet.

1954:

B.L. Gulatee of the Survey of India fixed the height of Mount Everest at 8,847 meters or 29,028 feet. This accepted elevation would remain until 1999 when the summit elevation was increased to 8,849 meters or 29,035 feet.

---

* 1 of 14 peaks in the world over 8,000 meters (26,248 feet)

1954: Technique – Windlass

First ascent of K2 (28,251 ft./8,611 m.) in the Karakoram Range in Pakistan by an Italian expedition led by Ardito Desio (1897 – 2001). Hand-operated windlasses (a type of winch) were used to transport equipment up the lower slopes.

* 1955: PEAK FIRST ASCENT *MAKALU*

May 15. The fifth highest mountain in the world, Makalu (27,764 ft./8,462 m.), was first climbed by a French expedition. Led by Jean Franco, three different teams reached the summit. Jean Couzy (1923 – 1958) and Lionel Terray (1921 – 1965) summited first on May 15. Franco, Guido Magnone, and Sirdar Gyaltsen Norbu Sherpa summited on May 16 followed on May 17 by Jean Bouvier, Serge Coupe, Pierre Leroux, and André Vialatte. All three teams climbed the northwest ridge and used supplemental oxygen. This was the first time that an entire expedition had summited an 8,000 meter peak. This expedition was blessed with extremely good weather during the approach trek and the ascent periods. Makalu is located approximately twelve miles southeast of Mount Everest.

* 1955: PEAK FIRST ASCENT *KANGCHENJUNGA*

May 25. A British expedition led by Dr. Robert C. Evans (1912 – 1996) made the first ascent of Kangchenjunga (28,171 ft./8,586 m.), the third highest mountain (five separate summits) in the world. There had been eleven previous climbing attempts and eight deaths prior to 1955. Located on the Nepal – Sikkim border (46 miles from Darjeeling), Kangchenjunga's ("Five Treasure Houses in the Snow") summit is considered to be sacred and is, therefore, traditionally left untrodden. George Band (1929 – 2011) and Joe Brown (1930 –) first reached the summit on May 25 via the southwest face. They were the first true British mountaineers to reach an 8,000 meter summit. Norman Hardie (1924 –) and Tony Streather repeated this climb the next day. All four of these climbers stopped five feet below the summit out of respect. Supplemental oxygen was used both for climbing and sleeping. This expedition cost 13,652 and was totally funded by the Mount Everest Foundation. Other expedition members included: Dr. John Clegg, John Jackson, Neil Mather, and Tom McKinnon. One death occurred on this expedition. On May 26, Pemba Dorje Sherpa died from cerebral thrombosis. Kangchenjunga was not climbed again until 1977 (Indian Army Expedition).

1955: PEAK FIRST ASCENT *GYALGEN*

May. The first women's expedition to the Himalayas made the first ascent of Gyalgen Peak (22,002 ft./6,706 m.) in the Jugal Himal of Nepal. Monica Jackson and Betty Stark reached the summit. These climbers were members of the Ladies Scottish Climbing Club. Evelyn Camrass was the third member of this expedition.

1955:

August 15. Future Professor of Chinese Sports History Zhou Zheng (1929 –) and his companions ascended October Peak (22,245 ft./6,780 m.) in the former U.S.S.R. This ascent established the first official national altitude record for mountaineering by Chinese climbers.

---

* 1 of 14 peaks in the world over 8,000 meters (26,248 feet)

1955: PEAK FIRST ASCENTS *LOBUCHE, LANGCHA, KANTEGA IV*

American mountaineer Norman Dyhrenfurth (1919 –) led the International Himalayan Expedition to Lhotse (27,940 ft./8,516 m.) in Nepal. American climber Fred Beckey (1923 –) established a world high-altitude ski record when he skied up Mount Everest's Western Cwm to an altitude of 7,000 meters (22,967 feet). Although this international team did not summit Lhotse, they did achieve three first ascents in the Solu Khumbu area: south summit of Lobuche (16,175 ft./4,930 m.), Langcha (20,660 ft./6,297 m.) and Kantega IV (22,311 ft./6,800 m.). Beckey was included in all of these first ascents. Langcha was the first Nepalese peak to be climbed by Americans. This was the first expedition to the Everest area to include American climbers: Fred Beckey (1923 –), George Bell (1926 – 2000), and Richard McGowan (1933 – 2007).

1955: Technique – Sleeping Oxygen

The technique of using supplemental oxygen while sleeping was systematically applied to all members of the French expedition to Makalu (27,764 feet/8,462 meters). Leader Jean Franco advocated sleeping with oxygen in addition to climbing with it. His climbers used ½ liter per minute for sleeping.

* 1956: PEAK FIRST ASCENT *MANASLU*

May 9. The first ascent of Manaslu (26,760 ft./8,156 m.) in Nepal was made by a Japanese expedition under the leadership of Yuko Maki (1894 – 1989). This was the fourth attempt by the Japanese to climb Manaslu. Toshio Imanishi and Gyaltsen Norbu Sherpa reached the summit of this peak, the eighth highest mountain in the world. Two days later on May 11, M. Higeta and K. Kato made the second ascent. Norbu became the first man to reach the summit of two 8,000 meter peaks (Makalu – 1955). The name "Manaslu" comes from the Sanskrit word "manasa" meaning "soul."

* 1956: PEAK FIRST ASCENT *LHOTSE*

May 18. A Swiss expedition led by Albert Eggler made the first ascent of Lhotse (27,940 ft./8,516 m.) on the Nepal – Tibet border. Lhotse ("South Peak" in the Tibetan language) is the fourth highest mountain in the world. Ernst Reiss and Fritz Luchsinger (1921 – 1983) reached the summit. This was the first 8,000-meter peak climbed by the Swiss. They did use supplemental oxygen. This same expedition also made the second ascent of Mount Everest (29,035 ft./8,849 m.) when Jürg Marmet, Ernst Schmied, Hans-Rudolf von Gunten, and Adolf Reist summited on May 23 and 24. This expedition used 12-point crampons for the first time in the Himalayas. The second ascent of Lhotse occurred in 1977.

* 1956: PEAK FIRST ASCENT *GASHERBRUM II*

July 7. An Austrian expedition led by Fritz Moravec (1922 – 1997) made the first ascent of Gasherbrum II (26,363 ft./8,035 m.) in the Karakoram Range of Pakistan. Moravec, Sepp Larch, and H. Willenpart reached the summit of this peak, the thirteenth highest mountain in the world via the east ridge. Supplemental oxygen was not used.

---

* 1 of 14 peaks in the world over 8,000 meters (26,248 feet)

1956: PEAK FIRST ASCENT *POBEDA*

August 30. Eleven Soviet mountaineers made the first ascent of Pik Pobeda (Victory Peak 24,407 ft./7,439 m.) in the Tien Shan mountain range on the China/Kyrgyzstan border. Russian mountaineer Vitaly Mikhailovich Abalakov (1906 – 1986) reached the summit. This peak was discovered in 1937 and first attempted in 1938. The Kyrgyz name for this peak is Jengish Chokosu which means "Victory Peak."

* 1957: PEAK FIRST ASCENT *BROAD*

June 9. A small Austrian expedition (Austrian Alpenverein Karakoram Expedition) led by Marcus Schmuck (1925 – 2005) made the first ascent of Broad Peak (26,402 ft./8,047 m.) in the Karakoram Range of Pakistan. This peak was originally known as "K3." Schmuck and Fritz Wintersteller (1927 –) reached the summit first followed a few hours later by Kurt Diemberger (1932 –). On his descent, Diemberger rejoined Hermann Buhl (1924 – 1957) on his way up to the summit. Diemberger turned around and accompanied Buhl to the summit. Buhl became the first mountaineer to make the first ascents of two 8,000 meter peaks (Nanga Parbat in 1953 and Broad Peak in 1957). This climbing group of four did not use supplemental oxygen or porters and they climbed Broad Peak alpine style. This was the first and only 8,000 meter peak to be first climbed alpine-style. This was also the first time that an entire team reached the summit of an 8,000 meter peak on the same day.

1957:

June 13. The first Chinese mountaineering expedition comprised of 100 percent Chinese climbers made the ascent (not the first ascent) of Minya Konka (24,791 ft./7,556 m.), the highest peak in the Hengduan Range of eastern Tibet. This ascent, unfortunately, experienced one fatality on the ascent. Climber Ding Xingyou became the first death in Chinese mountaineering history. Three other climbers—Shi Xiu, Guo Decun, and Peng Zhongmu—disappeared on the descent in a storm for a total of four deaths.

1957: PEAK FIRST ASCENT *SKIL BRUM*

June 19. After the Broad Peak first ascent, expedition members Marcus Schmuck and Fritz Wintersteller proceeded to make the first ascent of nearby Skil Brum (24,148 ft./7,360 m.). On June 27, the other two expedition members, Hermann Buhl (1924 – 1957) and Kurt Diemberger (1932 –), decided to attempt climbing Chogolisa (25,157 ft./7,668 m.). Due to its constant white snow cover, Chogolisa is also known as "Bride Peak." Buhl and Diemberger had no permission to make this ascent. Due to low visibility, the two climbers were forced to turn around on a ridge and begin an unroped descent. Buhl accidentally broke through a cornice at 23,600 ft./7,193 m. and disappeared forever.

1958:

April 8. The Chinese Mountaineering Association was founded in Beijing. This association became a formal member of the International Mountaineering and Climbing Federation in October of 1985.

---

* 1 of 14 peaks in the world over 8,000 meters (26,248 feet)

1958:

May 15. The Indian Mountaineering Foundation was established in New Delhi, India by the government of India. Its goal was to encourage mountaineering expeditions to the Himalayas.

1958: PEAK FIRST ASCENT *RAKAPOSHI*

June 21. The British – Pakistan Forces Expedition made the first ascent of Rakaposhi (25,551 ft./7,788 m.) in the Himalayas. This mountain is located 60 miles/100 kilometers north of the city of Gilgit. In the local language, Rakaposhi means "Snow Covered." Mike Banks (1922 –) and Tom Patey (1932 – 1970) reached the summit via the southwest ridge. This was the fourth expedition to attempt Rakaposhi.

* 1958: PEAK FIRST ASCENT *GASHERBRUM I*

July 5. The American Karakoram Expedition made the first ascent of Gasherbrum I or Hidden Peak (26,471 ft./8,068 m.) in the Karakoram Range of Pakistan via the southeast arête. The expedition leader was Nick Clinch (1930 –). Peter Schoening (1927 – 2004) and Andrew Kauffman (1920 – 2003) reached the summit at 3:00 p.m. and spent one hour there in -20°F temperatures. This was the highest first ascent by American mountaineers and the first time that American mountaineers used supplemental oxygen. Other expedition members included Robert Swift, Tom McCormack, Tom Nevison, Dick Irwin, Gil Roberts, Mohd Akram, Captain N.A. Soofi, and Tas Rizvi. Gasherbrum I is the eleventh highest mountain in the world. Clinch wrote the expedition book *A Walk In The Sky* in 1959. However, this book was not published until 1982.

1958: PEAK FIRST ASCENT *GASHERBRUM IV*

August 6. An Italian Alpine Club expedition, led by well-known mountaineer Riccardo Cassin (1909 – 2009), made the first ascent of Gasherbrum IV (26,023 ft./7,932 m.) in the Karakoram Range of Pakistan via the east ridge. Walter Bonatti (1930 – 2011) and Carlo Mauri (1930 – 1982) reached the summit via the northeast ridge. Gasherbrum IV is the highest 7,000 meter independent peak in the world. The previous five expeditions to this peak were defeated.

1959:

October 2. French woman mountaineer Claude Kogan (1919 – 1959) led an all-women's expedition (Expedition Feminine au Nepal) to an 8,000 meter (26,248 ft.) peak. They attempted to climb Cho Oyu (26,906 ft./8,201 m.) on the Nepal Tibet border. Kogan, Claudine van der Stratten, and Ang Norbu Sherpa disappeared in a blizzard avalanche near their Camp IV at 24,300 ft./7,406 m. on their way to the summit. Other expedition members included Jeanne Franco, Countess Dorothea Gravina, Margaret Darvall, Eileen Healey, and Loulou Boulaz. This was the first Himalayan expedition to include Sherpanis (Sherpa women). Three Sherpanis (2 daughters and one niece of famous Sherpa Tenzing Norgay) were members of this expedition.

---

* 1 of 14 peaks in the world over 8,000 meters (26,248 feet)

* 1960: PEAK FIRST ASCENT *DHAULAGIRI*

May 13. A Swiss expedition led by Max Eiselin made the first ascent of Dhaulagiri (26,796 ft./8,167 m.) in Nepal (the 7th highest mountain in the world). This was the sixth attempt to climb Dhaulagiri. Five climbers reached the summit: Kurt Diemberger, P. Diener, Nima Dorje, Nawang Dorje, and E. Forrer. The Swiss had made many attempts on Dhaulagiri. This was the first expedition to be directly supported by an airplane (that eventually crashed on the mountain). This Pilatus PC-6 airplane landed gear and climbers on a glacier at 16,500 feet and 18,700 feet. Dhaulagiri in the Tibetan language means "the rock that stands alone."

1960: FIRST ASCENT

May 25. This Chinese expedition to Everest was led by Shih Chan-Chun. This was the first ascent of Mount Everest (29,035 ft./8,849 m.) from the North Col (23,183 ft./7,066 m.). It took three hours to climb the Second Step rock feature (28,479 ft./8,680 m.) on the northeast ridge. The three mountaineers who reached the summit at 4:20 a.m. (in the dark) were Wang Fuzhou (25), Gongbu (27), and Qu Yin-Hua (25) who lost all of his toes and six fingers to frostbite. Gongbu, the strongest climber of the three, led the way to the summit. Liu Lianman was also with these three climbers. Liu conceived the idea of creating a human ladder in order to climb the Second Step. Qu Yin-Hua climbed up in his stocking feet from Liu's shoulders. Liu stopped climbing at 28,545 feet/8,700 meters and waited for the three others to return from the summit. The expedition brought 214 Chinese and Tibetan climbers to the mountain. A plaster bust of chairman Mao Tse-Tung was left in the summit snows. This ascent marked the beginning of the "golden age of mountaineering" in China. This expedition also found the body of Maurice Wilson (died in 1934) lying on the glacier above the site of old Camp III. This body was once again buried in a glacier crevasse.

1960: PEAK FIRST ASCENT *MASHERBRUM*

July 6. The American – Pakistani expedition, led by Nick Clinch (1930 –), made the first ascent of Masherbrum (25,660 ft./7,821 m.) in the Karakoram range of Pakistan after three previous attempts by other climbing groups. The climbing leader was George Bell (1926 – 2000). Bell and Willi Unsoeld (1926 – 1979) first reached the summit and two days later (July 8) Nick Clinch and Capt. Jawed Akhtar Khan followed. This was the second highest first ascent by American mountaineers after the first ascent of Gasherbrum I or Hidden Peak (26,471 ft./8,068 m.) in 1958. Nick Clinch also led that expedition. This was the first time that a Pakistani had reached the summit of a major peak. Dr. Tom Hornbein (1930 –) and Dick Emerson (1926 – 1982) were also members of this expedition.

1960: PEAK FIRST ASCENT *NOSHAQ*

August 17. The highest peak in Afghanistan was first climbed by a Japanese expedition. Noshaq or Nowshak's (24,581 ft./7,492 m.) summit was reached by Goro Iwatsubo and Toshiaki Sakai via the south ridge. By 1988, Japan had made 80 first ascents in the Himalayas. When translated Noshaq means "higher than the eagle flies."

---

* 1 of 14 peaks in the world over 8,000 meters (26,248 feet)

1960: PEAK FIRST ASCENT *TRIVOR*

August 17. The Anglo-American Karakoram expedition made the first ascent of Trivor (25,370 ft./7,732 m.) in the Himalayas of Pakistan. British mountaineer Wilfrid Noyce (1918 – 1962) and American mountaineer Jack Sadler reached the summit after a 14-hour climb from their highest camp.

1960:

The Himalayan Scientific and Mountaineering Expedition was led by New Zealand mountaineer Sir Edmund Hillary (1919 – 2008) and British physician Dr. Griffith Pugh. This was the first expedition to spend the winter in the Himalaya. Twenty-one scientists, mountaineers, and other specialists spent part of nine months in the pre-fabricated and insulated Silver Hut at 18,765 feet/5,719 meters on the Mingbo Glacier below Ama Dablam (22,494 ft./6,856 m.). Extensive glacial research and studies on the physiologic effects of altitude on cardiovascular and respiratory systems were conducted from December of 1960 through March of 1961.

1960: Technique – Air Support

May. A Swiss expedition made the first ascent of Dhaulagiri (26,796 feet/8,167 meters) in the Nepal Himalaya. This climbing team used a six-seat Pilatus-Porter PC6 nicknamed the "Yeti" to land supplies at 16,000 feet/4,877 meters. This airplane reached the Northeast Col of Dhaulagiri (18,700 feet/5,700 meters) before eventually crashing at 16,733 feet/5,100 meters. Ernst Saxer (pilot) and Emil Wick (co-pilot and engineer) were not injured.

1960: Technique – Barefoot Climbing

May 25. A Chinese expedition made the first ascent of Mount Everest's (29,035 feet/8,849 meters) northeast ridge. Upon reaching a steep rock formation on the ridge (now known as the Second Step, 28,192 ft./8,593 m.), the three mountaineers struggled until Qu Yinhua took off his crampons and boots and then climbed in his wool socks onto the shoulders of Liu Lianman to gain the needed height that allowed him to climb to the top of this rock step. Yinhua then pulled his partners up and they successfully reached the summit at 4:20 a.m. on May 25.

1961: PEAK FIRST ASCENT *AMA DABLAM*

March 13. Ama Dablam (22,494 ft./6,856 m.) in Nepal was first climbed by Barry Bishop (1932 – 1994), Mike Gill, Michael Ward (1925 – 2005), and Wally Romanes. This ascent was accomplished without first obtaining official permission of the Nepalese government which caused expedition leader Sir Edmund Hillary (1919 – 2008) to be fined 800 rupees. The ascent route was via the southwest ridge.

1961: PEAK FIRST ASCENT *NUPTSE*

May 16. A British expedition led by Joe Walmsley made the first ascent of Nuptse ("West Peak," 25,850 ft./7,879 m.) just west of Mount Everest (29,035 ft./8,849 m.) in Nepal. The first team to reach the summit was Dennis Davis and Tashi Sherpa. The second summit team was composed of Chris Bonington (1934 –), Les Brown, Jim Swallow, and Ang Pemba Sherpa (May 17). The ascent route was the south central ridge.

1961:

June 12. New Zealand mountaineer and Mount Everest first ascender Sir Edmund Hillary (1919 – 2008) established The Himalayan Trust Foundation (originally named The Sherpa Trust). Hillary's first project was to build a school in the Sherpa village of Khumjung (12,467 ft./3,800 m.) in the Solu Khumbu region of Nepal. The World Book Encyclopedia organization donated $7,000.00 for this school project. This new three-room school for 58 students officially opened on June 12th. By 1985, this school had 341 students in ten grades. Ang Rita Sherpa (1953 –) was in the first class to graduate from the Khumjung School. He would eventually achieve ten Mount Everest summits. By the year 2000, The Himalayan Trust Foundation had built 30 schools, 2 hospitals, 12 medical clinics, 12 fresh water pipelines, and 3 mountain airfields.

> Hillary: *"What will happen to you all (Sherpas) in the future?"*
>
> Urkein: *"In the mountains, we are as strong as you—maybe stronger—but our children lack education. Our children have eyes but they cannot see. What we need more than anything is a school in Khumjung village."*
>
> 1960 – October.
> Sirday Urkein's reply to
> Ed Hillary's question.

1961:

June 17. Chinese women mountaineers Panduo and Xirao accompanied by Wu Zongyue and Chen San reached the summit of Kongur Tiubie (24,919 ft./7,595 m.) in the Kun Lun Range of western China. This ascent established a new height record for Chinese women. A Chinese/Soviet Union team made the first ascent in 1956.

1962: PEAK FIRST ASCENT *CARSTENSZ PYRAMID*

February 13. Austrian Heinrich Harrer (1912 – 2006) and New Zealand mountain guide Phillip Temple made the first ascent of Carstensz Pyramid (16,024 ft./4,884 m.) in Irian Jaya – New Guinea. Bert Huizenga (Dutch government official) and Russell Kippax (Austrian physician) were also members of this climbing team. After this first ascent, Harrer and Temple went on to climb many of the other summits (31 first ascents) surrounding the Carstensz Pyramid. This is the highest island peak in the world. It is also known as Puncak Jaya.

1962: PEAK FIRST ASCENT *JANNU*

April 27. A French expedition led by well-known mountaineer Lionel Terray (1921 – 1965) made the first ascent of Jannu (25,295 ft./7,710 m.) in the eastern Nepal Himalaya near Kangchenjunga. This ascent (via the south ridge) was considered to be the most extreme big climb in the world at that time. The first summit team was René Desmaison, Paul Keller, Robert Paragot, and Gyalysen Sherpa. On April 28, André Bertrand, Jean Bouvier, Paul Leroux, Yves Pollet-Villard, Jean Ravier, Lionel Terray, and Wangdi Sherpa also reached the summit. The second ascent of Jannu was not until 1983.

1962: PEAK FIRST ASCENT PUMORI

May 16. A Swiss-German expedition made the first ascent of Pumori (23,442 ft./7,145 m.) just west of Mount Everest in Nepal. G. Lenser, V. Hurlemann, and H. Rutzel reached the summit via the northeast ridge. This peak was named in 1921 by British mountaineer George Leigh Mallory (1886 – 1924) after his daughter Clare. Pumori means "honorable daughter."

1962: Clothing – Underwear

String net underwear (tops and bottoms) were widely used by mountaineers. Even though this underwear was made of cotton, it was effective over a wide temperature range.

1962: Equipment – Belaying Device

Distinguished Russian mountaineer Vitaly Abalakov (1906 – 1986) first fabricated a cam device for belaying safety.

1963:

March 23. The American Mount Everest Expedition (A.M.E.E.). American mountaineer John Edgar "Jake" Breitenbach (1935 – 1963) was suddenly killed in the Khumbu Icefall of Mount Everest when a collapsing wall of ice buried him. Climbers Dick Pownall (1928 –) and Ang Pema Sherpa were on Breitenbach's rope but escaped serious injury. Breitenbach became the first climber to die in the Khumbu Icefall. Since 1963, at least 18 other climbers have lost their lives in this icefall that can flow downhill at approximately three feet (one meter) per day. The remains of Jake Breitenbach were found in 1969 at the foot of the Khumbu Icefall by a Japanese expedition. Mount Breitenbach (12,145 ft./3,702 m.) in Idaho's Lost River Range is named for Jake Breitenbach.

1963: FIRST ASCENT

May 1. A.M.E.E. This expedition was led by Norman Dyhrenfurth (1919 –) and had a budget of just over $400,000. Six climbers reached the summit (29,035 ft./8,849 m.) from two different routes. Jim Whittaker (1929 –) and Nwang Gombu Sherpa (1931 – 2011) summited on May 1st at 1:00 p.m. via the southeast ridge. Three weeks later Lute Jerstad (1937 – 1998) and Barry Bishop (1932 – 1994) also reached the summit by the southeast ridge. On this same day, May 22, Dr. Tom Hornbein (1930 –) and William "Willi" Unsoeld (1926 – 1979) pioneered a new climbing route up the West Ridge of Mount Everest (29,035 ft./8,849 m.) and arrived on the summit at 6:15 p.m. Their final camp was located at 27,200 ft./8,290 m. Barry Corbet, Al Auten, Dick Emerson, and five Sherpas supported Hornbein and Unsoeld on the West Ridge. They were the 11th and 12th mountaineers to reach the summit. In their effort to complete the first traverse of Everest, they began their descent of the southeast ridge in the dark. They accidentally stumbled upon the exhausted bodies of Jerstad and Bishop who were making their descent of this same southeast ridge. These four climbers were forced to bivouac on this ridge at approximately 28,200 feet/8,600 meters until daylight allowed them to continue their descent to the South Col camp. Unsoeld and Bishop would suffer severe frostbite to their toes and undergo amputations. Two teams of four Sherpas each carried Unsoeld and Bishop on their backs in 400-yard relays for

20 miles until Unsoeld, Bishop, and Jerstad could be flown by helicopter to Kathmandu hospitals. Other expedition members included: Allen C. Auten (36), James Barry Corbet (26), Dr. David L. Dingman (26), Daniel E. Doody (29), Richard M. Emerson (38), James T. Lester (35), Maynard M. Miller (41), Richard Pownall (35), Barry W. Prather (23), Dr. Gilbert Roberts (28), Lt. Colonel James O.M. Roberts (45), William E. Siri (44), and James Ramsey Ullman (55).

1963:

British Defense Attache to Nepal Lt. Colonel James O.M. "Jimmy" Roberts (1918 – 1997) began creating a plan to develop a trekking company in Nepal. This plan would eventually establish Mountain Travel as the first trekking company in the world. In March of 1965, Roberts conducted his first commercial trek. He guided three American women to the Tengboche Monastery at 12,700 ft./3,871 m. for $450.00 each. This 150-mile/250-kilometer roundtrip trek took 35 days.

1963: Equipment – Boots

The climbing team for the successful American Mount Everest Expedition wore the Dolomite Reindeer Boot as their high-altitude boot. This boot had a reindeer fur knee-length upper, a foot area lined with felt, a shallow cleated rubber sole, and was sized large enough to accept two or three pairs of heavy woolen socks. This boot was made by an Italian shoe factory for this American expedition.

1963: Equipment – Overboots

American Mount Everest expedition. The high-altitude climbing team wore nylon, lace-up overboots that reached almost to the knees.

1963: Equipment – Tents

A total of 52 tents were taken on the American Mount Everest Expedition. Of this total, 42 tents were of the Draw-Tite design invented by Robert L. Blanchard. These were the first tents to be supported by an exterior pole system. This system was comprised of aluminum wands. Four different Draw-Tite tent sizes were used. 42 Draw-Tite Tents:

>   2 – 12' x 12' – base camp tents
>   6 – 10' x 10' – base camp tents
>   10 – 2-man – double-walled for added warmth
>   24 – 4-man – double-walled for added warmth (most durable)
> These tents could easily be erected in high winds.

1963: Equipment – Winches

April 16 to May 13. American Mount Everest expedition. Three winches were used (two motor-driven and one hand operated) to haul oxygen bottles and supplies up 2,000 feet/610 meters of 30° slopes from the Western Cwm to the West Ridge of Mount Everest. Three pairs of skis were lashed together to create a ski-sled. The motor winches could lift (haul) 500 pounds of dead weight at eight feet per minute. These winches experienced many mechanical problems.

1964: PEAK FIRST ASCENT *GYACHUNG KANG*

April 10. A Japanese expedition led by Kazuyoshi Kohara made the first ascent of Gyachung Kang (25,989 ft./7,921 m.) on the Nepal-Tibet border immediately east of Cho Oyu (26,906 ft./8,201 m.). Yukihiko Kato, Kiyoto Sakaizawa, and Pasang Phutar Sherpa first reached the summit. On April 11, K. Machida and K. Yasuhida also reached the summit. Many people regard Gyachung Kang as the highest non-8,000 meter peak in the world (79 meters short of 8,000 meters).

* 1964: PEAK FIRST ASCENT *SHISHAPANGMA*

May 2. A Chinese expedition of 200 mountaineers led by Hsu Ching made the first ascent of Shisha-pangma (26,291 ft./8,013 m.) in Tibet (China). This is the only 8,000 meter peak located entirely in China (80 miles northwest of Mt. Everest) and was the last of the fourteen 8,000 meter peaks to be climbed. Ten mountaineers took 4 ½ hours to climb the final 1,023 feet/312 meters to the summit. These climbers were: Xu Jing, Wu Zongyue, Sodnam Doje, Cheng Tianliang, Zhang Junyan, Mima Zaxi, Doje, Chen San, Yundeng, and Zhou Zheng. The name Shishapangma when translated means "The Crest Above The Grassy Plain." The second ascent of Shishapangma (also known as Gosainthan) occurred 16 years later in 1980 by a German team.

1964:

The ascent of Shishapangma in 1964 ended the first ascent quest of the world's fourteen 8,000 meter peaks. Here is the final first ascent summary:

Rank	Year	Date	Peak Name	Feet	Meters	Expedition
10th	1950	June 3	Annapurna	26,546	8,091	French
1st	1953	May 29	Mount Everest	29,035	8,849	British
9th	1953	July 3	NangaParbat	26,658	8,125	Ger/Aust
2nd	1954	July 31	K2	28,253	8,611	Italian
6th	1954	October 19	Cho Oyu	26,906	8,201	Austrian
5th	1955	May 15	Makalu	27,764	8,462	French
3rd	1955	May 25	Kangchenjunga	28,171	8,586	British
8th	1956	May 9	Manaslu	26,760	8,156	Japanese
4th	1956	May 18	Lhotse	27,940	8,516	Swiss
13th	1956	July 7	Gasherbrum II	26,363	8,035	Austrian
12th	1957	June 9	Broad Peak	26,402	8,047	Austrian
11th	1958	July 4	Gasherbrum I	26,471	8,068	American
7th	1960	May 13	Dhaulagiri	26,796	8,167	Swiss
14th	1964	May 2	Shisha Pangma	26,291	8,013	Chinese

1964:

The mountainside airstrip at Lukla, Nepal (9,300 ft./2,835 m.) was first constructed by Sir Edmund Hillary (1919 – 2008) of New Zealand and anthropologist Jim Fisher. This 1,000 foot/305 meter long

---

* 1 of 14 peaks in the world over 8,000 meters (26,248 feet)

earthen airstrip cost approximately $2,000.00 and was later lengthened. This landing strip was built in order to transport building materials quickly into the Khumbu region for the construction of a hospital in the village of Khunde (12,599 ft./3,840 m.) and a school in the village of Khumjung (12,402 ft./3,780 m.) in 1966. Originally built by 110 Sherpa men and women working for four months, this dirt and stone airstrip was finally paved in May of 2001.

1965: FIRST ASCENT

May 20. The first successful Indian expedition to Mount Everest (29,035 ft./8,849 m.) was led by Captain Manmohan Singh Kohli (1931 –). The summit was reached four times within one week by nine mountaineers. Nwang Gombu Sherpa (1931 – 2011) became the first person to climb Mount Everest twice (1963 and 1965). Seven of the summit climbers had been students of Tenzing Norgay Sherpa (1914 – 1986) at the Himalayan Mountaineering Institute in Darjeeling, India. The nine summit climbers were A.S. Cheema, Nawang Gombu, Sonam Gyatso, Sonam Wangyal, C.P. Vohra, Ang Kami, H.C.S. Rawat, Phu Dorje, and H.P.S. Ahluwalia.

1965: PEAK FIRST ASCENT *GANGAPURNA*

May. A German expedition made the first ascent of Gangapurna (24,457 ft./7,454 m.) in the Anna-purna Himal of Nepal. G. Hauser, L. Greissl, H. Kellensperger, E. Reismuller, Ang Temba Sherpa, and Phu Dorje Sherpa reached the summit. This was the last major Himalayan climb prior to Nepal banning mountaineering expeditions.

1968:

American journalist-correspondent Elizabeth Hawley (1923 –) began collecting and reporting Nepalese mountaineering news on a regular basis. "Miss Hawley" lives full-time in Kathmandu, Nepal. She became known as the "Official Chronicler of Himalayan Climbing." In addition to working with the Reuters News Agency, Hawley also submitted expedition information to the American Alpine Journal, the Himalayan Journal (India), Alp (Italy), Climber (United Kingdom), Die Alpin (Switzerland), Vertical (France), and Yama-Kei (Japan). She first arrived in Kathmandu in 1959.

1969:

Spring. The Nepalese government lifted the restrictions on climbing expeditions.

1969:

April 29. An American expedition attempted to climb Dhaulagiri (26,796 ft./8,167 m.) in the Nepal Himalaya. On this date, a huge avalanche suddenly hit the climbing team sweeping seven climbers (five Americans and two Sherpas) down the mountain. One American, Louis Reichardt (1943 –), survived. This was the most deadly accident to American mountaineers in the Himalaya. Those five American climbers killed were:

Boyd N. Everett, Jr.   1933 – 1969
Paul A. Gerhard   1943 – 1969

John V. Hoeman	1936 – 1969
William B. Ross	1938 – 1969
David Seidman	1946 – 1969

1969: Clothing – Synthetic Pile

A British expedition to the South Face of Annapurna was the first expedition to use synthetic-pile clothing.

1970:

May 6. Japanese ski mountaineer Yuichiro Miura (1932 –) made a filmed ski descent from the South Col (26,000 ft./7,924 m.) of Mount Everest down into the Western Cwm. He began skiing and reached 100 m.p.h. before opening his parachute brake and then fell and tumbled 1,320 ft./402 m. His backpack parachutes stopped him just short of several large crevasses. He survived uninjured. Miura summited Mount Everest in 2003 at the age of 70 and again in 2008 at age 75.

1970:

May 11. The Japanese Southwest Face Expedition to Mount Everest was led by Saburo Matsukata. On this date, T. Matsuura and Naomi Uemura reached the summit. On May 12, K. Hirabayashi and Chotare Sherpa also summited. This was the first Japanese ascent of Mount Everest. Woman mountaineer Setuko Watanable became the first woman to reach the South Col, a new height record for women.

1970: FIRST ASCENT

May 27. The British Annapurna South Face Expedition was led by Chris Bonington (1934 –). This expedition made the first ascent of the 11,480 ft./3,499 m. high south face of Annapurna (26,546 ft./8,091 m.) in Nepal. This was the first really big Himalayan wall climb of significant technical difficulty. Don Whillans (1933 – 1985) and Dougal Haston (1940 – 1977) reached the summit. Whillans wore no socks in his climbing boots to the summit as he believed they (the socks) constricted blood flow. American climber Tom Frost (1940 –) nearly reached the summit climbing solo. Other members of this expedition included Ian Clough (killed on the descent in an avalanche), Nick Escourt, Martin Boysen, Mike Thompson, and Dave Lambert.

1970: FIRST ASCENT

June 27. Tyrolean mountaineers (and brothers) Reinhold Messner (1944 –) and Günter Messner (1946 – 1970) reached the summit of Nanga Parbat (26,658 ft./8,125 m.) via the Rupal Face (14,763 ft./4,500 m.) in the Punjab Himalaya of Pakistan. This was the third ascent of Nanga Parbat. The Rupal Face (13,500 ft./4,114 m.) is the highest rock and ice face in the world. Günter became separated from Reinhold on the descent (they carried no rope) down the Diamir Face and was probably killed in an avalanche. The remains of Günter were discovered in 2005. This ascent was the first of Reinhold's fourteen 8,000 meter peak summits. Due to frostbite, Messner had seven toes and three fingertips amputated. This was the eighth German expedition to Nanga Parbat (1932, 1934, 1937, 1938, 1939, 1953, 1962, and 1970). Siegi Low Memorial Expedition.

1970:

Dr. Anatoly Ouchinnikov (1927 –), a Russian mountaineer, earned the Order of the Snow Leopard in the former Soviet Union by climbing all five Soviet 7,000 meter peaks:

1. Peak of Communism   24,591 ft./7,495 m.
2. Peak Pobeda   24,407 ft./7,439 m.
3. Peak of Lenin   23,407 ft./7,134 m.
4. Peak of Eugenia Korzheneuskaya   23,312 ft./7,105 m.
5. Khan Tengri   23,000 ft./7,010 m.

1970: Equipment – Tents

The much-improved Whillans Box was used for the first time in the Himalayas on the 1970 British South Face of Annapurna Expedition. This storm proof, metal-framed, heavy (72 pounds) box tent (4' x 6 ½') was erected on a structured platform. All sections were bolted together and covered with canvas. Manufactured by Karrimor (British), the Whillans Box could be slotted into a steep snow slope.

1970: Technique – Ascending Fixed Ropes

Mechanical rope ascenders known as Jumars (brand name) were used to climb fixed ropes in the Himalayas of Nepal for the first time. British Annapurna expedition.

1971: PEAK FIRST ASCENT *KUNYANG CHHISH*

August 26. Polish mountaineer Andrzej Zawada (1928 – 2000) led the first ascent of Kunyang Chhish (25,762 ft./7,852 m.) in the Karakoram mountains of the Himalayan Range. Zygmunt A. Heinrich, Jan Stryczynski, Ryszard Szafirski, and Zawada all reached the summit. Over the next twenty-five years (1971 to 1996), Polish mountaineers organized fifty-eight separate climbing expeditions to the Himalayas that accomplished nineteen peak first ascents, thirty-seven first ascents, and ten winter first ascents. Polish mountaineers became well-known for their courage, strength, endurance, and willingness to suffer extreme weather and temperature conditions.

1971:

The 1971 International Himalayan Expedition to Mount Everest was led by American mountaineer Norman G. Dyhrenfurth (1919 –). Thirty climbers from thirteen nations were represented on this expedition. In support were forty high-altitude Sherpa climbers and 830 porters. The various climbing teams attempted both the direct west ridge and the southwest face of Everest. This expedition witnessed many disputes as a result of personality clashes and over-inflated national interests as well as bad weather and sickness. The summit was never reached. British mountaineers Dougal Haston (1940 – 1977) and Don Whillans (1933 – 1985) did, however, reach 27,396 ft./8,350 m. before a lack of supplies forced their retreat. On April 18th, Indian mountaineer Harsh Bahuguna (1939 – 1971) died in a snowstorm on the west ridge (the 28th climber to die on Mount Everest). He was brought down the mountain and cremated at Gorak Shep. One of the climbers was a woman—Yvette Vaucher (1929 –) from France.

1972: FIRST ASCENT

April 25. South Tyrol mountaineer Reinhold Messner (1944 –) made the first solo first ascent of Manaslu (26,783 ft./8,163 m.) in Nepal. Messner was a member of an Austrian expedition led by Wolfgang Nairz.

1972:

The following four peaks in the Pamir and Tien Shan Ranges were climbed in 1972 by Soviet mountaineers:

1. Pik Kommunizma (24,591 ft./7,495 m.)—193 climbers including 9 women.
2. Pik Pobeda (24,407 ft./7,439 m.)—18 climbers including 2 women.
3. Pik Lenin (23,407 ft./7,134 m.)—23 climbers including 3 women.
4. Pik Eugenia Korzheneuskaya (23,312 ft./7,105 m.)—65 climbers including 10 women.

1972:

The Kingdom of Bhutan (just east of Nepal and Sikkim) officially opened its borders to climbers and tourists. However, in 1983, the King prohibited all mountain climbing in his country after several foreign expeditions attempted to climb Jitchu Drake (22,290 ft./6,794 m.) and angered the local population.

1973: FIRST ASCENT

February 13. Noshaq (24,581 ft./7,492 m.), the highest peak in Afghanistan, was the first 7,000 meter (22,967 feet) peak in the Himalayas to be climbed in the winter. A Polish expedition led by Andrzej Zawada (1928 – 2000) made this ascent. Zawada and Tadeusz Piotrowski (1940 – 1986) reached the summit just before midnight. Noshaq was first climbed in 1960 by a Japanese expedition. Polish mountaineers went on to climb many peaks in the Afghan Hindu Kush mountain range.

1973: FIRST ASCENT

May 12. An American expedition to Dhaulagiri (26,796 ft./8,167 m.) in Nepal was led by James Morrissey. John Roskelley (1948 –), Louis Reichardt (1943 –), and Nawang Samden reached the summit via the northeast ridge. Roskelley and Reichardt were the first Americans to climb Dhaulagiri.

1973: FIRST ASCENT

October 26. A Japanese expedition led by M. Yuasa made the first post-monsoon ascent of Mount Everest (29,035 ft./8,849 m.) in Nepal. H. Ishiguro and Y. Kato reached the summit via the southeast ridge route. This expedition was composed of 48 mountaineers. This was the first successful post-monsoon expedition to Mount Everest.

1973:

November 1. The Nepal Mountaineering Association was established. Its first President was Kumar Khadga Bikram Shah (1973 to 1983).

1973:

The Himalayan Rescue Association was established in Nepal by physicians John Dickenson, Peter Hackett (1947 –), and David Shlim. Its objective was to reduce casualties in the Himalayas.

1974: FIRST ASCENT

July 13 to August 16. The Sports Federation of the Soviet Union organized a twelve-nation international mountaineering festival. 160 climbers from western countries and 60 climbers from eastern Europe and the Soviet Union participated in this festival in the Pamir mountains. The United States was represented by 19 climbers led by Pete Schoening (1927 – 2004). American climber Molly Higgins became the first American to summit Peak Lenin (23,407 ft./7,134 m.). Nearly 200 climbers attempted Peak Lenin with about 50 percent succeeding. On August 7, eight Soviet women mountaineers led by Elvira Shataeyava died from altitude sickness and exposure just below the summit of Peak Lenin. They were the first all-female team to summit this peak. This was one of the worst tragedies in mountaineering history. A total of fifteen mountaineers died during this international climbing festival.

1974:

December 25. A Polish expedition led by Andrzej Zawada (1928 – 2000) was the first expedition to attempt the climbing of an 8,000 meter peak in the winter. This expedition climbed the northwest face of Lhotse (27,940 ft./8,516 m.) from the Western Cwm of Mount Everest. Zawada and A. Heinrich were able to reach 27,068 ft./8,250 m. on Christmas day before being forced to retreat by high winds and cold temperatures. Zawada became the first person to climb above 8,000 meters in the winter. A new variation of Himalayan climbing was born with this expedition—winter ascents.

1974:

The Alpine Club of Pakistan was founded.

1974:

Pakistan re-opened its Karakoram Range to foreign visitors (climbers) after having been closed for fifteen years due to border disputes with China and India. India re-opened the Nanda Devi region to climbing.

1975: FIRST ASCENT

May 16. A Japanese all-female Mount Everest expedition placed the first woman on the summit. Junko Tabei (1939 –), a Tokyo mother, music teacher, and scientific journalist and Ang Tschering Sherpa reached the summit on May 16 via the southeast ridge. Tabei was also the first woman to surpass the 8,000 meter (26,248 ft.) barrier. This achievement occurred 25 years after a man accomplished this goal (Maurice Herzog and Louis Lachenal on Annapurna, June 3, 1950). This all-female Japanese expedition was led by Eiko Hisano and also included M. Manita, F. Nasa, Y. Watanabe, S. Kitamura, M. Naganuma, S. Fujiwara, T. Hirashima, Y. Mihara, R. Shioura, F. Arayama, S. Naka, Y. Taneia, and Dr. M. Sakaguchl. The expedition was sponsored by the Tokyo women's mountaineering club.

1975: FIRST ASCENT

May 27. A Chinese expedition made the second ascent of Mount Everest's northeast ridge (first ascent also by the Chinese in 1960). A climbing team of 8 Tibetans and 1 Chinese were led by Mr. Shi Zhanchun. A Tibetan housewife and mother of three children Phanthog (37) reached the summit in a group of nine mountaineers 11 days after Junko Tabei, the first woman to summit Mt. Everest. She became the first woman to summit via the northeast ridge and the second woman to summit Mount Everest overall. In 1959, Phanthog was selected by the Chinese government to be one of the first Tibetan women to be trained as mountaineers. There were 36 women on the 1975 Mount Everest expedition. It is interesting to note that the year 1975 had been officially designated the "International Year Of The Woman" by the United Nations. This Chinese expedition did use supplemental oxygen.

1975: PEAK FIRST ASCENT *CHOGOLISA*

August 2. An Austrian expedition made the first ascent of Chogolisa (25,148 ft./7,665 m.) in the Karakoram Range of Pakistan. Fred Pressl and Gustav Ammerer reached the summit first via the west ridge. On August 4, Alois Furtner and Hilmar Sturm also reached the summit.

1975: FIRST ASCENT

August 10. Tyrolean mountaineer Reinhold Messner (1944 –) and Austrian mountaineer Peter Habeler (1942 –) made the second ascent of Gasherbrum I or Hidden Peak (26,471 ft./8,068 m.) in the Karakoram range of Pakistan. This ascent via the northwest face represented a major break-through in Himalayan climbing because Messner and Habeler made this climb in alpine style in five days roundtrip (no fixed ropes, no supplemental oxygen, no porters or high-altitude Sherpas, and no intermediate camps). They did not even carry a climbing rope. Messner, with this ascent, became the first mountaineer to stand on three 8,000 meter summits.

1975: PEAK FIRST ASCENT *GASHERBRUM III*

August 11. The Polish Women's Karakoram Expedition reached the summits of Gasherbrum II (26,363 ft./8,035 m.) and Gasherbrum III (26, 090 ft./7,952 m.) in the Karakoram Range of Pakistan. Alison Chadwick-Onyszkiewicz, Janusz Onyszkiewicz, Wanda Rutkiewicz (1943 – 1992), and Krzysztof Zdzitowiecki reached both summits. Alison Chadwick-Onyszkiewicz set foot on the summit first thereby making Gasherbrum III the highest mountain to be first climbed by a woman. This expedition also made three ascents of Gasherbrum II by three separate routes in thirteen days. Halina Kruger and Anna Okopinska became the first all-female rope team to reach the summit of an 8,000 meter peak—Gasherbrum II.

1975: FIRST ASCENT

September 24. The Southwest Face of Mount Everest (29,035 ft./8,849 m.) was first climbed by a British expedition led by Chris Bonington (1934 –). Doug Scott (1941 –) and Dougal Haston (1940 – 1977) reached the summit but were then forced to make an open bivouac (shallow snow cave) near the South Summit at 28,700 ft./8,747 m. without any tent, sleeping bags, food, sleep, or supplemental oxygen.

This was the highest bivouac in the history of mountaineering. Doug Scott became the first Englishman to reach the summit of Mount Everest (Sir Edmund Hillary was a New Zealander). Two days later, Peter Boardman (1950 – 1982) and Pertemba Sherpa also reached the summit. Mick Burke was believed to have reached the summit by himself after Boardman and Pertemba but then vanished.

1975:

A Chinese Mount Everest expedition installed an aluminum ladder on the 100 foot/30 meter high rock feature known as the Second Step (28,192 ft./8,593 m.) on Everest's northeast ridge. The crux (most difficult section) of the Second Step is a 16 foot/5 meter perpendicular rock slab. American mountaineer Conrad Anker (1963 –) free-climbed the Second Step in 1999 and rated it initially at 5.8 (1999) and later at 5.10 (2007).

1975:

Chinese mountaineer Wang Hongbao took a short walk from the Chinese expedition's Camp VI on Mount Everest's north face and came across the body of "Engleese Engleese" (now considered to be the body of Andrew Irvine of the 1924 British Mount Everest Expedition) at 8,100 meters (26,576 feet). Hongbao later related his experience to Japanese climber Ryoten Hasegawa in 1979. Shortly thereafter, Hongbao was killed in an avalanche. Irvine's body has never been found.

1975: Equipment – Tents

Scottish mountaineer Hamish MacInnes (1931 –) invented the "Superbox" which was an improved version of the Whillan's Box. This 4' x 6 ½' box-tent was first used on the 1975 British expedition to the southwest face of Mount Everest. Each of these box-tents weighed 66 pounds and had a special floor of plastic honey-comb sandwiched between plywood and bulletproof tarpaulins. Camp IV on the Southwest Face of Mount Everest had five of these box-tents.

1975: Technique – Alpine Style Climbing

Alpine style climbing (no fixed ropes, no chain of camps, no reconnaissance of route, no porters, all equipment and food trimmed to the minimum, and one continuous push) was first applied to an 8,000 meter peak by Austrian mountaineer Peter Habeler (1942 –) and South Tyrol mountaineer Reinhold Messner (1944 –). This three-day ascent and two-day descent of Gasherbrum I or Hidden Peak (26,470 feet/8,060 meters) in the Karakoram Range of Pakistan was accomplished without using supplemental oxygen. This Himalayan style of climbing has also been called "super alpine climbing."

1976: FIRST ASCENT

September 1. The Indo-American Nanda Devi Expedition was led by Willi Unsoeld (1926 – 1979) and H. Adams Carter (1914 – 1995). John Roskelley, Jim States, and Louis Reichardt reached the summit of Nanda Devi via a new route on the northwest face and north ridge. This was the fifth overall ascent of Nanda Devi (25,645 ft./7,816 m.). On September 8, Willi Unsoeld's 22 year old daughter Devi (named after this peak) became sick from the altitude and an abdominal illness and died in Willi's arms at Camp

IV (24,000 ft./7,315 m.). Other expedition members included Peter Lev, Elliot Fisher, John Evans, Andy Harvard, and Marty Hoey. "Nanda" in Sanskrit means "Joy" and "Devi" means "Goddess."

1976:

October 8. The 1976 American Bicentennial Everest Expedition was led by Phil Trimble (38). Dr. Chris Chandler (1948 – 1985) and Robert Cormack reached the summit via the southeast ridge of Mount Everest (29,035 ft./8,849 m.). Eleven climbers, thirty Sherpas, and a six-man television crew from CBS Sports comprised this expedition.

1976: FIRST ASCENT

October 15. The true start of climbing extremely difficult routes in the Himalayas began when British mountaineers Peter Boardman (1950 – 1982) and Joe Tasker (1948 – 1982) made the first ascent of the 8,000 foot/2,438 meter West Face of Changabang (22,252 ft./6,782 m.) in the Garhwal Himalaya of northern India.

1976:

Tenzing Norgay Sherpa (first ascent of Mount Everest in 1953) retired at age 62 as Field Director of the Himalayan Mountaineering Institute (Darjeeling, India) after 22 years (1954 to 1976). Tenzing (1914 – 1986) died in 1986 at age 72. Nawang Gombu Sherpa (1931 – 2011) was appointed to this position.

1976: FIRST ASCENT

Japanese mountaineers Yoshinori Hasegawa and Kazushige Takami completed a first traverse between the east (24,272 ft./7,398 m.) and main (25,645 ft./7,816 m.) summits of Nanda Devi. This Japanese expedition included 21 total climbers.

1977: PEAK FIRST ASCENT *OGRE*

July 13. A small British expedition reached the west summit of the Ogre (23,902 ft./7,285 m.) which is also known as Biantha Brakk (first ascent). Chris Bonington (1934 –) and Doug Scott (1941 –) climbed this tower (main summit) of steep ice and rock in the Karakoram Range of Pakistan via the west ridge. During the descent from just below the summit, Scott broke both of his ankles while rappelling during a pendulum. For the next eight days he lowered himself off the mountain and then hauled himself along the Biantha Brakk Glacier moraines to a reunion with his team. Bonington broke several ribs in a fall after Scott's fall. The other expedition members were Mo Anthoine, Clive Rowland, Nick Escourt, and Paul (Tut) Braithwaite. On July 12, Anthoine and Rowlands reached the slightly lower west summit.

1977: Equipment – High Altitude Pressure Chamber

American Dr. Peter Hackett (1947 –) and Hamish MacInnes (1931 –) of Scotland designed and produced the world's first high-pressure chamber for the treatment of Acute Mountain Sickness (AMS). This development took place at the medical aid facility of the Himalayan Rescue Association at Pheriche, Nepal.

1978: FIRST ASCENT

May 8. The summit of Mount Everest (29,035 ft./8,849 m.) was reached for the first time by mountaineers without using supplemental oxygen. Reinhold Messner (1944 –) and Peter Habeler (1942 –) made this historic ascent that several noted climbers believe to be the true first ascent. They were able to climb at the rate of 100 meters/328 feet per hour. After reaching the summit at 1:00p.m., Messner and Habeler stayed there for fifteen minutes before beginning their descent. Habeler took only one hour from the summit to the South Col by glissading wherever possible. During this descent, Habeler lost his ice axe and snow goggles and twisted his ankle. Messner imagined himself on the summit as "nothing more than a single, narrow, gasping lung." Habeler and Messner called their ascent "Everest by fair means." They climbed unroped.

> *"To be able to grasp Everest's towering height, I have to*
> *climb it free of technology's tricks. Only then will I know*
> *what it is up there that really goes through and fills a man,*
> *what new dimensions open up to him, and whether he can*
> *gain there a new kind of rapport with the universe."*
>
> 1978
> Reinhold Messner
> Austrian mountaineer
> (1944 –)

1978: FIRST ASCENT

August 9. Tyrolean climber Reinhold Messner (1944 –) solo climbed Nanga Parbat (26,658 ft./8,125 m.) in Pakistan via the Diamir Face. This was the first complete solo ascent (base camp to summit to base camp) of an 8,000 meter peak. This was Messner's second ascent of Nanga Parbat (the first was in 1970).

1978: FIRST ASCENT

September 7. An American expedition led by Jim Whittaker (1929 –) placed four climbers on the summit of K2 (28,253 ft./8,611 m.) in the Karakoram Range of Pakistan. Jim Wickwire (1940 –) and Louis Reichardt (1943 –) reached the summit on September 6 with Reichardt becoming the first climber to summit K2 without using supplemental oxygen. Rick Ridgeway (1949 –) and John Roskelley (1948 –) reached the summit on September 7. Wickwire began his descent late and was forced to endure an open bivouac at 8,500 meters/27,889 feet without a bivy sack or down parka (he did wear down pants). This bivouac caused him to suffer from frostbite, pneumonia, pleurisy, and lung clots. He did recover. These were the third and fourth overall ascents of K2.

1978: FIRST ASCENT

October 15. American mountaineer Arlene Blum (1945 –) led the American Women's Himalayan Expedition—the first all-female team (except for male Sherpas) to climb Annapurna I (26,545 ft./8,091 m.) in Nepal and the first American ascent of Annapurna. Ten women spent 43 days on the mountain making this historical ascent. This expedition was organized, financed, and carried out by only women. Irene Miller (42), Vera Komarkova (36), Chewang Rinjing Sherpa, and Mingma Tsering Sherpa reached the summit. Alison Chadwick-Onyszkiewicz (37) and Vera Watson (45) died on their ascent attempt. Other expedition members included Joan Firey (50), Piro Kramer (41), Margi Rushmore (21), Annie Whitehouse (22), and Liz Klobuslcky (34). This was the fifth expedition to reach Annapurna's summit.

1978: FIRST ASCENT

October 16. Polish mountaineer Wanda Rutkiewicz (1943 – 1992) became the first Polish woman and the first European woman to climb Mount Everest (29,035 ft./8,849 m.) in Nepal. This was her first 8,000 meter peak and the third ascent by a woman. Coincidentally, Wanda's summit day was the same day Poland's Karol Cardinal Wojtyla was elected as Pope John Paul II in Rome, Italy. She later met the Pope on his visit to Poland.

1978:

The Nepalese government identified eighteen peaks between 18,331 feet (5,587 meters) and 21,832 feet (6,654 meters) as "trekking peaks" for climbers. Permits to climb these peaks were easily obtainable at a low cost.

1979: PEAK FIRST ASCENT *GAURISHANKAR*

May 8. An American expedition made the first ascent of Gaurishankar (23,439 ft./7,144 m.) in the Rolwaling Himalaya on the Nepal – Tibet border. John Roskelley (1948 –) and Pertemba Dorje Sherpa reached the summit of this peak via the west face. This was the last major unclimbed summit in the Nepal Himalaya.

1979: FIRST ASCENT

May 13. A 31-member Polish expedition led by Tone Skarja made the first true (complete) ascent of the West Ridge of Mount Everest (29,035 ft./8,849 m.) in Nepal. Five climbers reached the summit: two on May 13 (Andrej Stremfelj and Nejc Zaplotnik) and three on May 15.

1979: FIRST ASCENT

American mountaineer Jeff Lowe (1950 –) made a solo first ascent of the 4,500 ft./1,372 m. south face of Ama Dablam (22,494 ft./6,856 m.) in Nepal. This climb represented the first time a major new technical climbing route was soloed in the Himalaya.

1979:

During a Sino-Japanese Reconnaissance Expedition to the north side of Mount Everest (29,035 ft./8,849 m.), climbing leader Ryoten Hasegawa was approached by Chinese high-altitude porter Wang Hongbao with his story of finding an "English dead" in 1975 at 26,600 ft./8,100 m. on Everest's north face. Hongbao told Hasegawa this old body had a hole in one cheek and was dressed in old-fashioned clothing. Unfortunately, Wang Hongbao died in an avalanche the next day before he could elaborate on his story. The Chinese government discredited Hongbao and denied this whole "English dead" finding.

1979: FIRST ASCENT

Ang Phu Sherpa became the second man to climb Mount Everest twice and the first mountaineer to climb Everest by two different routes (Southeast Ridge in 1978 and the West Ridge in 1979).

1979:

A German expedition to Mount Everest placed all of its members on the summit and became the shortest expedition to Everest on record: 32 days base camp to summit to base camp.

1980: FIRST ASCENT

February 17. An expedition of Polish mountaineers led by Andrzej Zawada (1928 – 2000) made the first winter ascent of an 8,000 meter (26,248 feet) peak—Mount Everest. Leszek Cichy (1950 –) and Krzysztof Wielicki (1951 –) reached the summit (29,035 ft./8,849 m.) from the South Col. They experienced temperatures of -50°F. From 1980 to 2005, Polish mountaineers first climbed seven 8,000 meter peaks in the winter.

1980:

March 27 to May 7. An American ski mountaineering team made the first complete ski traverse of the Karakoram Range of northern Pakistan in winter. Galen Rowell (1940 – 2002), Dan Ansay, Ned Gillette (1944 – 1997), and Kim Schmitz made this 285-mile, six-week traverse each carrying 120 pounds (60 pounds in a backpack and 60 pounds in a sled). They reached altitudes up to 22,500 ft./6,858 m. They linked-up the Siachen, Baltoro, Biafo, and Hispar glaciers.

1980: FIRST ASCENT

May 10. A Japanese Alpine Club team led by Eizaburo Nishiberi became the first foreign expedition to climb Mount Everest (29,035 ft./8,849 m.) from the northern side (via the Japanese Couloir). Tsuneo Shigehiro and Takashi Ozaki reached the summit. One climbing member—Yasuo Kato—was the first person to climb Mount Everest from both the north (Tibet) and south (Nepal) sides. He was the first non-Sherpa mountaineer to accomplish this feat and the first foreigner to climb Mount Everest from the north. Unfortunately, Kato died on Mount Everest in 1982 after making his third ascent.

1980: FIRST ASCENT

July 21. An American expedition climbed Muztagata (24,757 ft./7,546 m.) on skis in the Chinese Pamir Range and then made the highest recorded ski descent. This was also the first American expedition permitted to climb in China since the 1932 ascent of Minya Konka. The expedition members were Ned Gillette (1944 – 1997), Galen Rowell (1940 – 2002), Jan Reynolds (1956 –), Dick Dorworth (1939 –), Cameron Bangs (1937 –), Jo Sanders (1949 –) and Liason Officer Chu Ying Hua. Rowell, Reynolds, and Gillette reached the summit and made the historic ski descent.

1980: FIRST ASCENT

August 2 and 3. American climbers Geoffrey Tabin (1956 –), Robert Shapiro, and Samuel Moses made the first ascent of the north face direct route on Carstensz Pyramid (16,024 ft./4,884 m.) in Irian Jaya – New Guinea. On August 5, Tabin and Shapiro climbed Ngga Pulu (15,946 ft./4,860 m.) and Sunday Peak (15,887 ft./4,842 m.).

1980: FIRST ASCENT

August 20. Tyrolean mountaineer Reinhold Messner (1944 –) made the first solo ascent of Mount Everest (29,035 ft./8,849 m.) without using supplemental oxygen via the North Face and the Great Couloir. He was the second non-Sherpa to climb Mount Everest by two different routes. After paying the Chinese a $50,000.00 climbing fee, Messner climbed a new route (the 8th route) up Everest in three days completely unsupported and carrying only a 33-pound pack (small tent, extra clothing, sleeping pad, food, stove, and fuel), a camera and an ice axe. He reached the summit at 3:00 p.m. and then made a 20-hour descent. Many mountaineers regard this ascent as the greatest climb in the history of mountaineering.

> *"It was only when I reached the foot of the mountain and the ordeal was over when I no longer had to worry about falling, or dying of exhaustion, or freezing to death, that I collapsed. I no longer had to grope forwards in the mist; no longer summon my whole will to take another step forward—and with that, all will left me."*
>
> 1980
> Reinhold Messner
> South Tyrol mountaineer
> after his solo ascent of
> Mount Everest.
> (1944 –)

1980: Clothing – Underwear

Patagonia introduced polypropylene undergarments in several weights. These clothes wicked (transported) moisture away from the body.

1981: FIRST ASCENT

April 30. Japanese mountaineer Junko Tabei (1939 –) made the first ascent of Shishapangma (26,399 ft./8,046 m.) in Tibet by a woman.

1981: FIRST ASCENT

September 19. The highest peak in India, Nanda Devi (25,644 ft./7,816 m.) was first climbed by an all-female team. R. Sharma, H. Bishr, and C. Aitwal reached the summit.

1981:

October. The American Medical Research Expedition was led by Dr. John West. From a research standpoint, this expedition discovered new information about the condition known as H.V.R. or Human Hypoxic Ventilatory Response. H.V.R. is the volume of air that moves into and out of the human lungs. From a mountaineering standpoint, this expedition placed five climbers on Mount Everest's summit (29,035 feet/8,849 meters). Dr. Peter Hackett (1947 –) became the eleventh American to summit and the 111th climber to summit overall. Hackett was also the first person to reach the summit solo from the South Col. Christopher Kopczynski, Christopher Pizzo, Sundare Sherpa, and Young Tenzing Sherpa also reached the summit.

1981 – 82:

Winter. Well-known American climber and ski mountaineer Ned Gillette (1944 – 1997) and five friends made a 300-mile/500-kilometer circumnavigation of Mount Everest. Their average altitude was 20,000 ft./6,096 m. This journey also included the first winter ascent of Pumori (23,442 ft./7,145 m.) in Nepal.

1982: FIRST ASCENT

August 14. A Japanese mountaineering team made the first ascent of K2's (28,253 ft./8,611 m.) North Ridge in China. Expedition leaders Isao Shinkai and Masatsugo Konishi placed three climbers on K2's summit: Nade Sakashita, Hiroshi Yoshino, and Yukihiro Yanagisawa (who fell and died on the descent).

1982: FIRST ASCENT

October 5. The Canadian Everest Expedition was led by W. March. Laurie Skreslet, (1949 –) became the first Canadian to summit Mount Everest (29,035 ft./8,849 m.) in Nepal. This expedition experienced four deaths (3 Sherpas and cameraman Blair Griffiths) in the Khumbu Icefall and the loss of six other climbers (they decided to leave the expedition and return home). Skreslet, Sundare Sherpa, and Lapka Dorje Sherpa reached the summit first followed by Pat Morrow, Pema Dorje Sherpa and Lakpa Tsering Sherpa on October 7.

1982:

October 15. The Union Internationale des Associations D' Alpinisme (U.I.A.A.) General Assembly adopted the "Declaration of Kathmandu," which addressed the mountaineer's responsibilities and conservation ethics.

1982:

Swiss ski mountaineer Sylvain Saudan (1936 –) made the first ski descent of an 8,000 meter peak— Gasherbrum I, a.k.a. Hidden Peak (26,471 ft./8,068 m.).

1982:

South Tyrol mountaineer Reinhold Messner (1944 –) climbed three 8,000 meter peaks this year: Kangchenjunga (28,171 ft./8,586 m.), Gasherbrum II (26,363 ft./8,035 m.), and Broad Peak (26,402 ft./8,047 m.).

1983: FIRST ASCENT

May 7. Larry Nielson became the first American to climb Mount Everest (29,035 ft./8,849 m.) without using supplemental oxygen. Nielson was a member of the American South Col Expedition which was led by West German Gerhard Lenser. With Nielson on the summit were Peter Jamieson, David Breashers, Ang Rita Sherpa, and Gerald Road. On May 14, Gary Neptune, Jim States, and Lhakpa Dorje Sherpa also summited.

1983: FIRST ASCENT

June 30. Two young Polish women mountaineers—Anna Czerwinska and Krystyna Palmowska—climbed Broad Peak (26,401 ft./8,047 m.) alpine style in one continuous ascent. They used no porters, no high-altitude Sherpas, no fixed lines, and no supplemental oxygen. This was the first wholly female ascent of an 8,000 meter peak.

1983: FIRST ASCENT

September 30. Mountaineer Glenn Porzak (1948 –) became the first American to reach the summit of Shishapangma (26,291 ft./8,013 m.) in Tibet. This is the 14th highest mountain in the world. Porzak went on to climb three more 8,000 meter peaks (Makalu – 1987, Everest – 1990, and Cho Oyu – 2005). With Porzak on the summit were Michael Browning and Chris Pizzo.

1983: FIRST ASCENT

October 8. An American expedition (American Kangshung Face Expedition) made its second attempt to climb the Kangshung (east) Face of Mount Everest (29,035 ft./8,849 m.) in Tibet. This post-monsoon expedition, led by James Morrissey (1936 –), placed Louis Reichardt (1945 –), Carlos Buhler (1954 –), and Kim Momb (1956 – 1986) on the summit first. One day later on October 9, Jay Cassell (1948 –), Dan Reid (1943 –), and George Lowe (1944 –) also summited. This climb represented the 10th route to the summit.

1983:

The small country of Bhutan opened its mountains to foreign mountaineering expeditions (commercial only). Only the peak of Jitchu Drake (22,281 ft./6,791 m.) in the Jomolhari Group in western Bhutan was available for mountaineering.

1983: Equipment – Winches

American Kangshung Face (East face of Mount Everest) Expedition. A winch-driven aerial cableway was utilized to lift supplies 4,000 feet/1,219 m. up the Lowe Buttress. This proved to be too long a distance. Two shorter hauling systems were therefore established on the steepest sections of this rock buttress.

1984: FIRST ASCENT

June 27. French mountaineer Liliane Barrard (1948 – 1986) became the first woman to reach the summit of Nanga Parbat (26,661 ft./8,126 m.) in Pakistan. Barrard also reached the summit of K2 in 1986 but died on the descent. A Korean team found her body one month later at approximately 17,500 feet.

1984: FIRST ASCENT

July 14. Polish mountaineer Krzysztof Wielicki (1950 –) became the first person to solo climb an 8,000 meter peak in a single day—Broad Peak (26,401 ft./8,047 m.). He reached the summit in 17 hours after leaving his base camp (4,950 meters). His roundtrip time was 22 hours and 10 minutes.

1984: FIRST ASCENT

October 20. An American expedition led by Lou Whittaker (1929 –) climbed the upper north face of Mount Everest (29,035 ft./8,849 m.) in Tibet. Using supplemental oxygen, Phil Erschler (1951 –) climbed to the summit solo from 27,500 feet/8,382 m. after John Roskelley (1948 –) turned around (he was not using supplemental oxygen). This was the 12th route to the summit. Ershler became the first American to climb Mount Everest from the north (Tibetan) side.

1984:

The summit of Lobuche (20,076 ft./6,119 m.) in Nepal was reached by thirteen women from different ethnic groups in Nepal. This was a landmark expedition in the history of Nepalese women in mountaineering.

1984: FIRST ASCENT

A Swiss mountaineering team made the first traverse of the Annapurna Massif. Erhard Loretan (1959 – 2011) and Norbert Joos (1960 –) climbing in alpine-style reached the east (26,281 ft./8,010 m.), central (26,041 ft./7,937 m.) and main (26,547 ft./8,091 m.) summits of Annapurna.

1984: FIRST ASCENT

Polish mountaineers Woytek Kurtyka (1947 –) and Jerzy Kukuczka (1948 – 1989) completed a traverse over the three summits of Broad Peak (24,220 ft./7,382 m.—26,300 ft./8,016 m.—26,401 ft./8,047 m.) in Pakistan. This traverse took 4 ½ days.

1985: FIRST ASCENT

January 21. Polish mountaineer Jerzy Kukuczka (1948 – 1989) made the first winter ascent of Dhaulagiri (26,795 ft./8,167 m.) in Nepal. He died in 1989 while attempting an alpine-style ascent of Lhotse's South Face.

1985:

April 21. Well-known British expedition leader and mountaineer Christian Bonington (1934 –) finally reached the summit of Mount Everest (29,035 ft./8,849 m.) after leading three expeditions to the mountain (1972, 1975, and 1982). Norwegian mountaineers Bjorn Myrer-Lund and Odd Eliasson along with Dawa Buru Sherpa, Pertemba Sherpa, and Ang Lhakpa Sherpa were with Bonington on the summit. Bonington had previously reached the summits of Annapurna II (1960), Nuptse (1961), Brammah (1973), Changabang (1974), and the Ogre (1977).

1985:

April 30. The dawn of guided climbs on the fourteen 8,000 meter peaks began.

American mountaineers Dick Bass (1929 –) and Frank Wells (1932 – 1994) hired American mountaineer and film-maker David Breashears (1956 –) to guide them up Mount Everest. Breashers, Bass, and Ang Phurba Sherpa reached the summit on April 30th. Bass, at age 55, became the oldest climber to reach the summit of Mount Everest to date. He also was the first person to climb the highest peak of each of the seven continents of the world—the Seven Summits. It took Bass five years to accomplish this goal (1981 to 1985). Breashears became the first American to summit Mount Everest (29,035 ft./8,849 m.) twice (May 7, 1983 and April 30, 1985).

1985: FIRST ASCENT

July. David Breashears, William Garner, and Randall Starrett became the first foreigners to climb Pik Pobeda (24,407 ft./7,439 m.) in the Tien Shan mountains of Tibet. Twelve Soviet mountaineers were with these three foreign mountaineers. The ascent was via the west ridge. Pik Pobeda means "Peak of Victory." With this ascent, Garner and Starrett became the first non-Soviet climbers to earn the Order of the Snow Leopard Award which is presented to those mountaineers who reach the summits of five 7,000 meter peaks in the former Soviet Union. See Appendix III. Pik Pobeda is the world's most northerly peak over 7,000 meters (22,967 feet).

1985: FIRST ASCENT

A Japanese-Chinese expedition made the first ascent of Gurla Mandhata (25,356 ft./7,728 m.) in the Tibet Himalaya. British mountaineer Thomas George Longstaff (1875 – 1964) and his two Swiss guides attempted to climb this peak in 1905 but were caught in a 3,280 foot/1,000 meter avalanche (they all survived).

1986: FIRST ASCENT

January 11. Polish mountaineers Jerzy Kukuczka (1948 – 1989) and Krzysztof Wielicki (1950 –) made the first winter ascent of Kangchenjunga (28,171 ft./8,586 m.) in Nepal. This was Kukuczka's tenth 8,000 meter peak ascent.

1986:

May 9. Well-known Nepalese mountaineer Tenzing Norgay Sherpa (1914 – 1986) died at his home Ghang La in Darjeeling, India at age 72 from a lung infection. Norgay and Sir Edmund Hillary (New Zealand) first climbed Mount Everest (29,035 ft./8,849 m.) in Nepal on May 29, 1953. Tenzing was the first to realize the value of reaching Everest's summit—honor, fame, Sherpa prestige, even wealth. Tenzing's birth name was Namgyal Wangdi.

1986: FIRST ASCENT

May 20. Canadian mountaineer Sharon Wood (1957 –) reached the summit of Mount Everest (29,035 ft./8,849 m.) in Nepal becoming the first North American woman to reach this goal. She and Canadian climber Dwayne Congdon summited via the West Ridge.

1986: FIRST ASCENT

June 23. Polish mountaineer Wanda Rutkiewicz (1943 – 1992) became the first woman to summit K2 (28,253 ft./8,611 m.) in the Karakoram Range of Pakistan. She climbed the Abruzzi Spur and did not use supplemental oxygen. Climbing with Rutkiewicz were Michael Parmentier and Maurice and Liliane Barrard. The Barrard's disappeared on the descent at 25,500 feet/7,772 m.

1986:

July 5. Polish mountaineer Josef Rakowcaj became the first person to summit K2 (28,253 ft./8,611 m.) twice (July 31, 1983 and July 5, 1986).

1986:

June 21 to August 10. Thirteen mountaineers from seven different countries died on K2 (28,253 ft./8,611 m.)on the Pakistan – China border. The causes of these deaths included avalanches, disappearance, falls, rockfall, exhaustion, and high altitude pulmonary edema (H.A.P.E.). Those climbers who died included:

Name	Country	Cause of Death
John Smolich (1951 – 1986)	United States	Avalanche
Alan Pennington (1952 – 1986)	United States	Avalanche
*Maurice Barrard (1941 – 1986)	France	Disappeared
*Lilliane Barrard (1948 – 1986)	France	Disappeared
*Tadeusz Piotrowski (1940 – 1986)	Poland	Fall
Renato Casarotto (1948 – 1986)	Italy	Fall
*Wojciech Wroz (1942 – 1986)	Poland	Fall
Muhammed Ali (– 1986)	Pakistan	Rockfall
*Julie Tullis (1939 – 1986)	England	H.A.P.E.
*Alan Rouse (1951 – 1986)	England	Exhaustion
Hannes Wieser (– 1986)	Austria	Exhaustion
*Alfred Imitzer (– 1986)	Austria	Exhaustion
Dobroslawa-Miodowicz Wolf (1953 – 1986)	Poland	Exhaustion

*Reached K2's summit

1986: FIRST ASCENT

August 30. Swiss mountaineers Jean Troillet (1948 –) and Erhard Loretan (1959 – 2011) climbed the 8,200 ft./2,500 m. north face of Mount Everest (29,035 ft./8,849 m.) via the Hornbein Couloir Direct in 40 ½ hours. They established no intermediate camps, used no supplemental oxygen, and carried no ropes. They climbed at night when the snow and ice were frozen and rested during the warm daylight hours. After spending 1 ½ hours on the summit in perfect weather, they descended in a fast 3 ½ hours by glissading. Their route is now known as the Super Couloir.

1986:

August – September. An American research expedition made the first systematic search for British mountaineers George Mallory (1886 – 1924) and Andrew Irvine (1902 – 1924) who disappeared on June 8, 1924 while climbing the northeast ridge of Mount Everest (29,035 ft./8,849 m.) in Tibet. This search for Mallory and Irvine and a camera Mallory was thought to be carrying was led by American mountaineers Andrew Harvard and David Breashears (1956 –). Bad weather and a Sherpa's death prevented the expedition from reaching the defined search area on Everest's north face.

1986:

Austrian mountaineer Kurt Diemberger (1932 –) reached the summit of K2 (28,253 ft./8,611 m.) in Pakistan at age 54. This was his sixth 8,000 meter summit (Broad Peak – 1957, Dhaulagiri – 1960, Mount Everest – 1978, Makalu – 1978, Gasherbrum II – 1979, and K2 – 1986). Unfortunately, his climbing partner on K2, British mountaineer Julie Tullis (1939 – 1986), died on their descent on August 7. No other climber would reach K2's summit until 1992.

1986:

Polish mountaineer Jerzy Kukuczka (1948 – 1989) reached the summits of three 8,000 meter peaks in one year. These climbs were: Kangchenjunga (January 11th), K2- south face (July 6th), and Manaslu (November 10th). After climbing all fourteen 8,000 meter peaks in just under eight years, Kukuczka died on the south face of Lhotse in 1989 when his rope broke.

1986:

Tyrolean mountaineer Reinhold Messner (1944 –) first completed the climbing of all fourteen 8,000 meter peaks in the world. Messner spent seventeen years (1970 to 1986) pursuing this goal and he reached all fourteen summits without using supplemental oxygen. In total, he was a member of 31 expeditions to 8,000 meter peaks. Here is a summary of Messner's fourteen climbs:

1.	1970 – Nanga Parbat	June 27	26,658 ft./8,125 m.
2.	1972 – Manaslu	April 25	26,760 ft./8,156 m.
3.	1975 – Gasherbrum I	August 10	26,471 ft./8,068 m.
4.	1978 – Mount Everest	May 8	29,035 ft./8,849 m.
5.	1979 – K2	July 12	28,253 ft./8,611 m.
6.	1981 – Shishapangma	May 28	26,291 ft./8,013 m.
7.	1982 – Kangchenjunga	May 6	28,171 ft./8,586 m.
8.	1982 – Gasherbrum II	July 24	26,363 ft./8,035 m.
9.	1982 – Broad Peak	August 2	26,402 ft./8,047 m.
10.	1983 – Cho Oyu	May 5	26,906 ft./8,201 m.
11.	1985 – Annapurna	April 24	26,546 ft./8,091 m.
12.	1985 – Dhaulagiri	May 15	26,796 ft./8,167 m.
13.	1986 – Makalu	September 16	27,764 ft./8,462 m.
14.	1986 – Lhotse	October 16	27,940 ft./8,516 m.

Messner went on to complete several other remarkable adventures including the first:
1. 1990: Crossing 1,550 miles/2,583 kilometers of Antarctica on foot by ski and sledge.
2. 1992: Traverse of the Taklimakan Desert in northwest China (124 miles/207 kilometers).
3. 1993: Trek across 1,243 miles/2,072 kilometers of Greenland (south to north) solo by foot.

Reinhold Messner is regarded by many as the greatest mountaineer in history. While climbing, he never placed an expansion bolt, never wore an oxygen mask, and never used a satellite telephone.

1986: Technique – Night Climbing

Himalayan mountaineers Erhardt Loretan (1959 – 2011) and Jean Troillet (1948 –) climbed the north face of Mount Everest (29,035 feet/8,849 meters) at night. They were the first Himalayan climbers to employ the "night naked" climbing strategy. This involved resting in the warmth of the daylight and then climbing light and fast at night when snow conditions were more favorable. They did not carry any sleeping bags, a tent, or a stove.

1987:

September 19. Polish mountaineer Jerzy Kukuczka (1948 – 1989) became the second climber (Reinhold Messner was the first in 1986) to reach the summits of all fourteen 8,000 meter peaks in the world. His final peak was Shishapangma. Kukuczka accomplished this climbing feat in nine years (1979 to 1987) versus the seventeen years it took Messner (1970 to 1986). On 12 of these 14 peaks, Kukuczka completed either a new route or did the first winter ascent. Ironically, he was killed on Lhotse (27,941 ft./8,516 m.) in 1989 which was his first 8,000 meter summit (October 4, 1979).

1987: FIRST ASCENT

American mountaineer Kitty Calhoun (1960 –) led an expedition to Dhaulagiri (26,796 ft./8,167 m.) in Nepal. She made the first American female ascent. Colin Grisson and John Culberson were with Calhoun on this climb of the northeast ridge. Dhaulagiri (7th highest in world) was first climbed in 1960 by a Swiss expedition.

1987: Equipment – High-Altitude Pressure Chambers

An early prototype of the Gamow bag was tested on Makalu (27,826 ft./8,481 m.) in the Nepal Himalaya.

1988: FIRST ASCENT

May 3. Carlos Buhler (1956 –) became the first American to climb Kanchenjunga (28,171 ft./8,586 m.) in Nepal. With Buhler were Austrian Peter Habeler (1942 –) and Spaniard Martin Zabalet (1950 –). The first American attempt on Kangchenjunga was in 1929.

1988: FIRST ASCENT

May 5. A three-nation (China, Japan, and Nepal) expedition achieved a double traverse of Mount Everest (29,035 ft./8,849 m.). The fourteen member North Team placed three climbers (Cering Doje,

Lhakba, and Yamato) on Everest's summit on May 5 at 12:44 p.m. This group then descended the southeast ridge. The fourteen member South Team placed two climbers (Da Cering and Phurba) on the summit on the same day at 3:43 p.m. These two climbers then descended the northeast ridge. A total of twelve climbers reached the summit. The first live telecast to millions of viewers was made from the summit.

1988: FIRST ASCENT

May 12. An American expedition finally climbed the 11,000 foot/3,353 meter Kangshung (east) face of Mount Everest (29,035 ft./8,849 m.). This expedition was led by Robert Anderson. Only Stephen Venables (1954 –) was able to reach the summit after struggling for 16 ½ hours from the South Col. He was then forced to bivouac at 28,000 ft./8,534 m. on his descent. Venables became the first British mountaineer to summit Mount Everest without using supplemental oxygen. Robert Anderson and Ed Webster (1956 –) both reached the South Summit (28,710 ft./8,750 m.). Paul Teare was forced to turn back from illness after nearly reaching the South Col.

1988: FIRST ASCENT

September 29. Stacey Allison (30) became the first American woman and the seventh woman overall to climb Mount Everest (29,035 ft./8,849 m.) in Nepal. Pasang Gyalzen Sherpa was with Allison on the summit. Peggy Luce (29), climbing three days behind Allison, became the second American woman and 8th overall to summit Mount Everest. American mountaineer Geoff Tabin (32) was with Luce on October 2.

1988:

October. American mountaineer, explorer, photographer, and cartographer Bradford Washburn (1910 – 2007) presented the first copy of his new Mount Everest map to His Majesty the King of Nepal. This detailed topographical map was published by the National Geographical Society and circulated to its 10.6 million members. Eleven million copies were printed worldwide.

1988: FIRST ASCENT

December 31. Polish mountaineer Krzysztof Wielicki (1950 –) made the first winter ascent of Lhotse (27,940 ft./8,516 m.) in Nepal.

1988: PEAK FIRST ASCENT *JITCHU DRAKE*

A small British expedition made the first ascent of Jitchu Drake (22,278 ft./6,790 m.) in Bhutan. Doug Scott, Victor Saunders, and Sharu Prabhu reached the summit. Shortly after this expedition, mountaineering became banned in Bhutan. British mountaineer Doug Scott (1941 –) had thus far participated in 28 expeditions to high mountains in Asia and reached the summits of 25 peaks of which half were first ascents and all were climbed by new routes.

1988: FIRST ASCENT

New Zealand mountaineer Lydia Bradley (1962 –) became the first woman to summit Mount Everest (29,035 ft./8,849 m.) without using supplemental oxygen.

1989:

January 19. An electrical malfunction started a fire which destroyed the Tengboche monastery (12,688 ft./ 3,867 m.) in the Solu-Khumbu region (just south of Mount Everest) of Nepal. The new gompa (or village monastery) was consecrated on September 17, 1993. This new construction cost $160,000 USD. This money was raised mostly by Sir Edmund Hillary's Himalayan Trust.

1989:

April 9 to May 3. A Soviet expedition led by Eduard Myslovski to Kangchenjunga (28,171 ft./8,586 m.) included 27 Soviet mountaineers and one Nepalese Sherpa. This group made a total of 85 ascents of the four main summits of Kangchenjunga (all above 8,400 meters/27,560 feet). This was the first traverse of all four summits in both directions.

1989: FIRST ASCENT

May. Russian mountaineer Anatoli Boukreev (1957 – 1999) made a solo traverse of the four 8,000 meter summits of Kangchenjunga (28,171 ft./8,586 m.) in Nepal. These four summits are:

Main	28,171 ft./8,586 m.
West	27,905 ft./8,505 m.
Central	27,829 ft./8,482 m.
South	27,869 ft./8,494 m.

1989:

American mountaineer and ophthalmologist Dr. Geoffrey Tabin (1956 –) became the fourth climber in the world to complete the climbing of the Seven Summits. In 1994, Tabin established the Himalayan Cataract Project. By 2005, this organization had cured nearly 75,000 eye cataract cases in the remote villages of Nepal, India, Bhutan, and Pakistan. Tabin summited Mount Everest in 1988.

1989: Book

Britisher Jill Neate (1934 –), author of *High Asia* (1989), compiled a comprehensive list of the world's highest peaks (over 7,000 meters or 22,967 feet) and first ascents from 1907 to 1988. 21 countries took part in these 280 peak first ascents. These countries were:

Japan	80 First ascents
Austria	34 First ascents
Great Britain	31 First ascents
Germany	25 First ascents
Italy	14 First ascents

Poland	14 First ascents
France	12 First ascents
India	10 First ascents
Switzerland	9 First ascents
United States	7 First ascents
Russia	7 First ascents
Czechoslovakia	6 First ascents
Nepal	6 First ascents
Spain	5 First ascents
China	5 First ascents
New Zealand	4 First ascents
South Korea	4 First ascents
Tibet	2 First ascents
Holland	2 First ascents
Norway	2 First ascents
Pakistan	1 First ascent
	280

1990:

May 7. The 1990 Mount Everest International Peace Climb was led by well-known American mountaineer Jim Whittaker (1929 –). Climbers from the United States, Russia, Tibet (China), Kazakhstan, and the Ukraine participated. Twenty-three climbers from three countries reached the summit. Each ascent team had one climber from the United States, Russia, and China. On May 7, two Americans (Robert Link and Steve Gall), two Russians (Sergel and Ekaterina Ivanova—first Russian woman to summit Everest), and two Chinese (Tibetans Gyal Bu and Da Qimi) reached the summit. Five ascents were made without using supplemental oxygen. For the first time, garbage was carried down Mount Everest from the South Col (26,000 ft./7,924 m.). This effort started the environmental expedition movement on Everest.

1990:

May 10. The American Everest-Lhotse Expedition was led by Glenn Porzak (1948 –). Porzak, Pete Athans, Mike Browning, Dana Coffield, Brent Manning, Ang Jambu, Dawa Nuru, and Nima Tashi reached the summit at 7:15 a.m. via the southeast ridge. On May 13, Wally Berg (1955 –) and Scott Fischer (1956 – 1996) made the first American ascent of Lhotse (27,941 ft./8,516 m.). Lhotse, the fourth highest peak in the world, is located immediately south of Mount Everest. Lhotse means "south peak." Other expedition members included Dr. Charles Jones, Ron Crater, and Andrew Lakes. Glenn Porzak became the only sitting President of an alpine organization (American Alpine Club) to climb the world's highest peak.

1990: FIRST ASCENT

May 10. New Zealand mountaineers Peter Hillary (his fourth attempt), Gary Ball, and Rob Hall reached the summit of Mount Everest (29,035 ft./8,849 m.) in Nepal. Using a satellite radio link, Peter Hillary called his famous father Sir Edmund Hillary (Mount Everest first ascent in 1953) in New Zealand from the summit. This was the first time a previous summiters' son had also reached Everest's summit.

1990: FIRST ASCENT

May 11. Australian mountaineer Tim Macartney-Snape made the first absolutely pure ascent of Mount Everest (29,035 ft./8,849 m.). He began his climb on February 5 by standing in the waters of the Bay of Bengal and then walking the 620 miles/1,033 kilometers to Everest's Nepal base camp (17,800 ft./5,425 m.) in three months. He solo-climbed Mount Everest via the southeast ridge without using supplemental oxygen. His journey to Mount Everest also involved a two-mile swim across the Ganges River.

1990:

May 14. American mountaineer Mark Udall (1951 –) made a solo ascent (southwest face) of Kangchenjunga (28,171 ft./8,586 m.) in Nepal from 27,500 ft. to the summit. This was the third American ascent of the third highest peak in the world. The co-leaders of this expedition were Rob Gustke and Bill Roos. Expedition members included John Bercaw, Jeff Brinck, George Gardner, Frank Coffey, Craig Miller, and Gunnar Paulsen. Udall was elected to the United States Senate from Colorado in 2008.

1990:

July 13. The worst single accident in mountaineering history took place on Peak Lenin (23,406 ft./7,134 m.) in Kyrgyzstan. A serac fall triggered a huge avalanche at 5,300 meters (17,389 feet) which then swept away one complete campsite killing 43 climbers.

1990:

Polish mountaineer Andrej Stremfelj (1956 –) and his wife Marija became the first married couple to summit Mount Everest. They climbed the South Col route.

1990:

American mountaineer Kitty Calhoun (1960 –) reached the summit of Makalu (27,764 ft./8,462 m.) on the Nepal – Tibet border. She climbed the West Pillar route and became the first female to climb two 8,000 meter peaks. In 1987, Calhoun climbed Dhaulagiri (26,796 ft./8,167 m.) via its northeast ridge—the first ascent by an American woman.

1991: FIRST ASCENT

May 8. Lobsang Sherpa conceived the first all-Sherpa expedition to Mount Everest (29,035 ft./8,849 m.) in Nepal. American Mount Everest summiter Pete Athans (1957 –) led the fund-raising effort for this expedition and then acted in a support role for these Sherpa climbers once on the mountain. Sonam

Dendu Sherpa (30), Ang Temba Sherpa (25), Apa Sherpa, and Athans reached the summit via the southeast ridge.

1991:

October. Polish mountaineer Wanda Rutkiewicz (1943 – 1992) summited Annapurna (26,546 ft./8,091 m.) in Nepal, her eighth 8,000 meter peak.

1991: FIRST ASCENT

French mountaineers Pierre Beghin (1951 – 1992) and Christophe Profit (1961 –) made the first ascent of K2's northwest ridge.

1991:

In Kathmandu, Nepal, this year was known as the "Russian Year in the Himalayas." Soviet mountaineers climbed the:

South face of Lhotse	27,940 ft./8,516 m.
South face of Annapurna	26,546 ft./8,091 m.
South face of Manaslu	26,758 ft./8,156 m.
East ridge of Cho Oyu	26,906 ft./8,201 m.
West wall of Dhaulagiri	26,796 ft./8,167 m.

1992:

May 12. Polish woman mountaineer Wanda Rutkiewicz (1943 – 1992) died at 27,232 ft./8,300 m. while attempting (her third attempt) to climb Kangchenjunga (28,171 ft./8,586 m.) in Nepal. She had already climbed eight 8,000 meter peaks. Many climbers considered Rutkiewicz to be the best female Himalayan climber ever. The following is a summary of her 8,000 meter ascents:

1. 1978 – Mount Everest
2. 1985 – Nanga Parbat. Leader. First all-women ascent.
3. 1986 – K2. First women to summit.
4. 1987 – Shishapangma
5. 1989 – Gasherbrum II
6. 1990 – Gasherbrum I (Hidden Peak)
7. 1991 – Cho Oyu. Solo.
   – Annapurna. Solo. First summit by women.
8. 1992 – Kangchenjunga. Died on ascent.

1992: PEAK FIRST ASCENT *NAMCHA BARWA*

October 30. A joint Sino – Japanese expedition made the first ascent of Namcha Barwa (25,533 ft./7,782 m.), the world's highest unclimbed peak and separate mountain. This high peak is located in China approximately 250 miles directly east of Lhasa, Tibet. Eleven of the twelve expedition members reached the summit including Japanese climbers J. Tsuneo, Shigehiro, and C. Sangju.

1992:

Japanese mountaineer Junko Tabei (1939 –) became the first woman to climb all Seven Summits (highest peak on each of the world's seven continents).

1992:

Ed Viesturs (1959 –) became the first American mountaineer to climb the three highest peaks in the world: Mt. Everest (1990), K2 (1992), and Kangchenjunga (1989).

1993: FIRST ASCENT

April 22. Pasang Lhamu Sherpa reached the summit of Mount Everest (29,035 ft./8,849 m.) on her fourth attempt to become the first Sherpa woman (Sherpani) to do so. Unfortunately, she died on the descent just below the South Summit. Her body was taken back to Kathmandu, Nepal where she became a heroine for modern Nepal. She was awarded the Nepal Tara Medal.

1993: FIRST ASCENT

May 17. Rebecca Stephens (1961 –) became the first British woman to climb Mt. Everest. She also became in 1994 the first English-speaking woman in the world to climb the Seven Summits.

1993: FIRST ASCENT

May 27. Mountaineer Dawson Stelfox (1958 –) made the first Irish ascent of Mount Everest (29,035 ft./8,849 m.) and the first British ascent of Everest from the north (Tibetan) side. Stelfox had dual nationality (Irish and British). He eventually established the Irish Himalayan Trust.

1993: FIRST ASCENT

July 7. American mountaineer Phil Powers (1961 –) and Canadian mountaineers Dan Culver and Jim Haberl reached the summit of K2 (28,253 ft./8,611 m.) on the Pakistan – China border. Culver (died in a fall on the descent) and Haberl became the first Canadians to summit K2. Powers was appointed the Executive Director of the American Alpine Club in 2005.

1993: FIRST ASCENT

Finnish mountaineer Veikka Gustafsson (1968 –) became the first climber from Finland to reach the summit of Mount Everest (29,035 ft./8,849 m.) in Nepal.

1993: FIRST ASCENT

The Indian Mountaineering Foundation sent an all-women team to Mount Everest (29,035 ft./8,849 m.). Led by Bachendri Pal, this expedition placed 18 mountaineers (7 Indian women and 11 Nepalese Sherpas) on the summit.

1993:

Russian mountaineer Anatoli Boukreev (1958 – 1997) over the past 13 years (1981 – 1993) had made thirty ascents of 7,000 meter (22,967 feet) peaks and over two-hundred ascents of peaks in the

5,000 meter to 6,000 meter range. All of these ascents occurred in the Tien Shan, Pamir, and Caucasus mountains.

1993:

New Zealand mountaineers Rob Hall (1961 – 1996) and wife Jan Arnold (physician) became the third husband-and-wife team to summit Mount Everest (29,035 ft./8,849 m.).

1994:

May 9, 1994 to July 15, 1995. American Himalayan mountaineer Ed Viesturs (1959 –) reached the summits of six of the world's fourteen highest peaks in a span of 20 months.

1994	Mount Everest. May 8.	29,035 ft./8,849 m.
	(Viestur's third ascent)	
	Lhotse. May 16	27,940 ft./8,516 m.
	Cho Oyu. October 6	26,906 ft./8,201 m.
1995	Makalu. May 18	27,764 ft./8,462 m.
	Gasherbrum II. July 4	26,363 ft./8,035 m.
	Gasherbrum I. July 15	26,471 ft./8,068 m.

After 1995, Viesturs now had climbed eight of the fourteen 8,000 meter peaks, all without using supplemental oxygen. He now decided to try to climb all fourteen 8,000 meter peaks naming this quest "Endeavor 8,000."

1994:

New Zealand mountaineer Rob Hall (1961 – 1996) became the first Westerner to summit Mount Everest (29,035 ft./8,849 m.) four times. After failing to reach the summit in 1995, Hall unfortunately died on his next Everest summit attempt in 1996. Hall did complete in 1994 the so-called "Himalayan Trilogy" by climbing Mount Everest, K2 (28,253 ft./8,611 m.), and Lhotse (27,940 ft./8,516 m.) in the span of two months.

1994:

American mountaineer Brent Bishop (1966 –), son of Barry Bishop (1932 – 1994, Mount Everest summit in 1963), created the incentive to clean-up the South Col (26,000 ft./7,924 m.) of Mount Everest (29,035 ft./8,849 m.) in Nepal. After proposing a $6.00 per item incentive to the Sherpas, 600 empty oxygen bottles were brought down the mountain to base camp (17,800 ft./5,425 m.). These bottles were then flown to the United States and sold to raise funds for additional clean-up efforts. The Sherpas also brought down 4,000 kilograms/8,800 pounds of other garbage.

A sad note to Brent Bishop's Mount Everest summit and his environmental efforts was the accidental death of his father Barry Bishop (1932 – 1994) in an automobile accident in the United States four months after Brent reached the summit of Mount Everest.

1995:

May 10. Swiss mountaineer Erhard Loretan (1959 – 2011) became the third person to climb all fourteen 8,000 meter peaks in the world (1982 to 1995). His final peak was Kangchenjunga (28,171 ft./8,586 m.).

1995: FIRST ASCENT

May 11. British woman mountaineer Alison Hargreaves (1962 – 1995) solo climbed Mount Everest (29,035 ft./8,849 m.) in Nepal without using supplemental oxygen or Sherpa support (1st woman). Hargreaves died a few months later on August 13th after reaching the summit of K2.

1995:

May 14. George Leigh Mallory III reached the summit of Mount Everest (29,035 ft./8,849 m.) via the north side in Tibet. This was the same climbing route that his grandfather George Leigh Mallory (1886 – 1924) was attempting to climb in 1924 with the third British expedition to Mount Everest. After reaching the summit, Mallory III said: "A moment infused with the deepest meaning swept over me. I placed a photograph of my grandparents in the summit snow, knowing my grandfather would have been proud of me." By the end of June (1995), 125 men and 5 women had climbed the 'Mallory Route.'

1995:

Babu Chiri Sherpa (1965 – 2001) climbed Mount Everest (29,035 ft./8,849 m.) twice in the span of 14 days. Eventually he climbed Everest ten times. In 2001, he accidentally fell into a crevasse near Camp II (south side) on Everest and died.

1995:

Mexican mountaineer Carlos Carsolio (1962 –) became the first person to climb four 8,000 meter peaks in one year. These peaks were:

April 29	Annapurna	26,546 ft./8,091 m.
May 15	Dhaulagiri	26,796 ft./8,167 m.
July 4	Gasherbrum II	26,363 ft./8,035 m.
July 15	Gasherbrum I	26,471 ft./8,068 m.

1995: Equipment – Boots

British mountaineer Alison Hargreaves (1962 – 1995) used battery-heated double plastic mountaineering boots to ward off frostbite on Mount Everest. She also wore battery-heated socks.

1995: Technique – Fixed Ropes

By the mid 1990s, fixed ropes nearly to the summits became the normal practice on 8,000 meter (26,248 feet) peaks.

1996:

May 10 and 11. Eleven climbers from three different expeditions died in a terrible storm high on Mount Everest (29,035 ft./8,849 m.) in Nepal and Tibet. On the south (Nepal) side, Scott Fischer (1956

– 1996), Rob Hall (1961 – 1996), Andy Harris, Doug Hansen, and Yasuko Namba died of exhaustion and hypothermia. On the north (Tibet) side, three Indian climbers perished. Russian mountaineer and professional guide Anatoli Boukreev (1958 – 1997) rescued ten American climbers from the storm on the South Col of Mount Everest. Boukreev was later presented with the American Alpine Club's David Sowles Award for his courage and valor. An additional four climbers would die on Everest during this climbing season bringing the total to twelve deaths.

1996:

May 12. Nepalese army helicopter pilot Lt. Col. Mandan Khatri Chhetri ("K.C.") airlifted injured American (Dallas, Texas, pathologist) climber Seaborne Beckwith ("Beck") Weathers (1946 –) and injured Taiwanese climber "Makalu" Gau from the 20,000 foot/6,096 m. Camp I site in the Western Cwm of Mount Everest. This was the highest recorded helicopter landing in Himalayan history.

1996:

May 12. Mexican mountaineer Carlos Carsolio (1962 –) became the fourth person (and the youngest at 33) to climb all fourteen 8,000 meter peaks in the world. He began in 1985 with an ascent of Nanga Parbat (26,658 ft./8,125 m.) in Pakistan and finished by summiting Manaslu (26,760 ft./8,156 m.) in 1996.

1996:

May. American mountaineer and filmmaker David Breashears (1956 –) led an IMAX expedition to Mount Everest (29,035 ft./8,849 m.). Following the tragic storm of May 10th, five IMAX team climbers reached the summit including Jamling Tenzing Norgay (1966 –), son of Tenzing Norgay and the ninth member of the Norgay clan to reach the summit, Araceli Segura (26—first Spanish woman to summit Mt. Everest), and Ed Viesturs (his fourth ascent of Mount Everest). Breashear's film generated approximately $68 million during its first year.

1996:

August 22. American mountaineer Andy Evans reached the summit of Pik Pobeda (24,407 ft./7,439 m.) in the Tien Shan range of Kazakhstan. Evans had now climbed all five 7,000 meter peaks in the former Soviet Union and earned the Order of the Snow Leopard Award (See Appendix III).

1996:

September 1. Polish mountaineer Krzysztof Wielicki (1950 –) became the fifth person to climb all fourteen 8,000 meter (26,248 ft.) peaks in the world. He began his quest in 1980 and finished on September 1, 1996 by summiting Nanga Parbat (26,658 ft./8,125 m.) in Pakistan.

1996:

Darjeeling, India. A statue of Tenzing Norgay Sherpa (1914 – 1986) was unveiled at the Himalayan Mountaineering Institute where Norgay had served as Field Director from 1954 to 1976. New Zealand mountaineers Sir Edmund Hillary (1919 – 2008) who first summited Mount Everest with Tenzing Norgay in 1953 and well-known Indian mountaineer Captain M.S. Kohli were present at this unveiling.

1996:

Swedish mountaineer Göran Kropp (1966 – 2002) rode his bicycle unsupported from Sweden to Nepal (7,000 miles/11,667 kilometers), trekked to the Mount Everest base camp (his backpack weighed 143 pounds), solo climbed Everest without using supplemental oxygen, and then bicycled back to Sweden—a 14,310 mile/23,850 kilometer roundtrip journey. In October of 2002, Kropp was killed in a rock climbing accident near Seattle, Washington.

1996:

Following the May 10th disaster on Mount Everest, a total of nine books and five documentaries were produced about this tragic storm and its consequences.

1996: FIRST ASCENT

French mountaineer Chantal Mauduit (1964 – 1998) became the first woman to reach the summit of Lhotse (27,940 ft./8,516 m.) in Nepal. She made a solo ascent. Mauduit died in her tent on Dhaulagiri (26,796 ft./8,167 m.) in 1998. Ang Tshering Sherpa was with Mauduit and also died. Maudit had reached the summits of six 8,000 meter peaks prior to her death.

1997:

May 23. The grandson of Tenzing Norgay Sherpa (1914 – 1986), Tashi Tenzing (1964 –), summited Mount Everest (29,035 ft./8,849 m.) and carried a six-inch bronze statue of Budda to the summit as a message of peace to the world. In addition to Tashi Tenzing, nine other members of the Norgay clan had also summited Everest.

1997:

Russian mountaineer Anatoli Boukreev (1958 – 1997) climbed four 8,000 meter peaks in one 80-day period:

April 26	Mt. Everest
May 26	Lhotse
July 7	Broad Peak
July 14	Gasherbrum II

On December 25, 1997, Boukreev died in an avalanche on Annapurna in Nepal. He was 39 years old.

1997:

August. American mountaineer Greg Mortenson (1958 –) completed and opened the first of many schools he would build for girls in northern Pakistan. This first school in the village of Korphe cost $12,000.00 (USD) to build. His organization is called the Central Asia Institute (C.A.I.). Mortenson wrote of his experiences in Pakistan in the book Three Cups of Tea (2006). By September of 2007, the

C.A.I. had built 61 private girl's schools (primary and middle school levels) in the Karakoram Mountains of northern Pakistan and 3 private schools in Afghanistan.

1997: FIRST ASCENT

American mountaineer Christine Boskoff (1967 – 2006) became the first North American woman to climb Lhotse (27,940 ft./8,516 m.) in Nepal. She eventually reached the summits of six 8,000 meter peaks. She disappeared while climbing in China in 2006.

1997:

From 1978 to 1997, 71 percent of those mountaineers that summited K2 did not use supplemental oxygen.

1997: FIRST ASCENT

Charlie Mace (1968 –) made the first American ascent of Manaslu (26,760 ft./8,156 m.) in Nepal.

1997: Book

American mountaineer and author Jon Krakauer (1954 –) published his book entitled *Into Thin Air – A Personal Account of the Mount Everest Disaster*. This book is a detailed account of the 1996 tragedy on Mount Everest. It is considered to be one of the best-selling mountaineering books of all time.

1998: FIRST ASCENT

May 18. British mountaineer Ginette Harrison (1958 – 1999) became the first woman to climb Kangchenjunga (28,171 ft./8,586 m.) in Nepal. She reached the actual summit ignoring local religious beliefs. This was the last 8,000 meter peak unclimbed by a woman. Harrison died in an avalanche on Dhaulagiri (26,796 ft./8,167 m.) in Nepal in 1999. On May 22, 1999, Harrison became the first British woman to climb Makalu (27,764 ft./8,462 m.).

1998:

May 20. The Everest Environmental Expedition (EEE '98) was led by American Robert Hoffman with Pasquale V. Scaturro of Colorado serving as climbing leader. After ten members reached the summit of Mount Everest (29,035 ft./8,849 m.) the expedition then proceeded to remove 229 empty oxygen bottles, 216 empty gas canisters, 520 abandoned batteries, and 2,840 pounds/1,291 kilograms of other garbage from the mountain.

1998: FIRST ASCENT

May 27. American mountaineer Tom Whittaker (1948 –) reached the summit of Mount Everest (29,035 ft./8,849 m.) in Nepal thereby becoming the first disabled climber to summit Everest. Whittaker lost the lower part of his right leg in a car accident in 1979. His two previous Everest summit attempts (1989 and 1995) failed. Four Nepalese Sherpas accompanied Whittaker to the summit along with a cameraman for television.

1998:

American mountaineer Wally Berg (1955 –) installed the world's highest global positioning satellite station on the South Col (25,889 ft./7,891 m.) of Mount Everest. Berg then made his fourth ascent of Mount Everest and American climber Ed Viesturs (1959 –) reached the summit for his fifth ascent.

1999:

April 22. American mountaineer Ed Viesturs (1959 –) and Swedish mountaineer Veikka Gustafsson (1968 –) became the first climbers to ascend two separate 8,000 meter peaks within 30 days. On April 22, they summited Manaslu (26,760 ft./8,156 m.) in Nepal followed twelve days later by reaching the summit of Dhaulagiri (26,796 ft./8,167 m.) in Nepal, 75 miles/125 kilometers southeast of Manaslu. They climbed Dhaulagiri in a single push of three days.

1999:

May 1. The well-preserved body of British mountaineer George Leigh Mallory (1886-1924) was accidentally found by American mountaineer Conrad Anker (1963-) below the northeast ridge of Mount Everest (29,035 ft./8,849 m.) in Tibet. Anker and his team were actually searching for Mallory's climbing partner Andrew Irvine (1902-1924). Lying face-down on the rock rubble at approximately 26,760 feet/8,156 meters, Mallory had broken his right leg just above his hobnailed boot, damaged a shoulder, and punctured his skull above his left eye. It is believed that Mallory fell approximately 460 feet/140 meters down the north face before stopping. He was wearing a climbing rope (broken) proving that he and Irvine were roped together when the fall occurred. Irvine has never been found. Mallory and Irvine disappeared on June 8,1924, on their way to the summit of Mount Everest. Anker and his search team found in Mallory's pockets several perfectly preserved letters in their envelopes, a pair of nail scissors, a pocket knife, an altimeter, a pair of sun goggles, a box of matches (still useable), and a burgundy handkerchief with the monogram "GLM" (George Leigh Mallory). Anker's team carefully covered Mallory's body with rocks and agreed not to disclose the actual location on the mountain's face of their discovery. The families of Mallory and Irvine supported the efforts of this search team. Mallory's Vest Pocket Autographic camera was not found on his body.

> *"If you had lived as they lived (Mallory and Irvine), and*
> *died in the heart of nature, would you, yourself, wish for*
> *any better grave than the pure white snow of Everest?"*
>
> 1988
> Captain John B.L. Noel
> British mountaineer
> (1890 – 1989)

1999:

May 5. American mountaineer Pete Athans (1957 –) summited Mount Everest (29,035 ft./8,849 m.) for the 6th time. He was the only Westerner to have this many Everest summits. Eighteen other climbers reached the summit on this day.

1999:

May 5. The Mount Everest Research Expedition, sponsored by the National Geographic Society, recalculated the height of Mount Everest. American mountaineer Pete Athans (1957 –) and Chewang Nima Sherpa placed a Trimble 4800 GPS (Global Positioning System) unit on the summit for several minutes. American mountaineer and cartographer Bradford Washburn (1910 – 2007) analyzed this GPS data and on November 11, 1999 publicly announced in Washington, D.C. a new altitude for Mount Everest—29,035 feet/or 8,849 meters. The previous elevation was 29,028 feet or 8,847 meters. Washburn also announced that Mount Everest was steadily moving northeastward at a rate of 60 millimeters per year.

1999:

May 7 and 8. Babu Chiri Sherpa (1966 – 2001) climbed Mount Everest (29,035 ft./8,849 m.) for the ninth time and remained on the summit for 21 hours without using supplemental oxygen. He erected a small tent and remained in his sleeping bag for the 21 hours. Unfortunately, Babu Chiri fell into a hidden crevasse at the Camp II site (Nepal side) on Everest on April 29, 2001 and was killed. He made 10 ascents of Mount Everest from 1990 to 2000.

1999: FIRST ASCENT

May 29. South African mountaineer Cathy O'Dowd (1969 –) became the first woman to climb Mount Everest (29,035 ft./8,849 m.) from both its south side (Nepal, 1996) and its north side (Tibet, 1999).

1999:

October 5. American mountaineer Alex Lowe (1958 – 1999) and photographer David Bridges (1970 – 1999) were killed in an avalanche on Shishapangma (26,291 ft./8,013 m.) in Tibet. Lowe was an outstanding world mountaineer with five first ascents. Conrad Anker (1963 –) was able to avoid being struck by this avalanche.

1999:

Basque (Spain) mountaineer Juanito Oiarzabel (1956 –) completed the climbing of all fourteen 8,000 meter peaks in the world. He was the sixth climber to accomplish this goal. Annapurna (26,546 ft./8,091 m.) was his final peak.

1999:

Russian mountaineer Denis Urubko (1973 –) climbed all five peaks in the former Soviet Union over 7,000 meters (22,967 feet) in 42 days. He has also made nineteen ascents of 8,000 meter peaks.

1999: Books

Five books were published this year about the mysterious disappearance and deaths of British mountaineers George Leigh Mallory (1886 – 1924) and Andrew Irvine (1902 – 1924) on Mount Everest June 8, 1924. These books are:

1. *George Mallory*, David Robertson
2. *Ghosts Of Everest*, Jochen Hemmleb, Larry A. Johnson, and Eric R. Simonson
3. *Last Climb*, David Breashears and Audrey Salkeld
4. *Lost On Everest*, Peter Firstbrook
5. *The Lost Explorer – Finding Mallory On Mount Everest*, Conrad Anker and David Roberts

2000: FIRST ASCENT

May 5. French climber Jean-Christophe Lafaille (1966 – 2006) solo climbed a direct line route up the northeast face of Manaslu (26,760 ft./8,156 m.) in Nepal.

2000:

May 21. Babu Chiri Sherpa (34) climbed Mount Everest (29,035 ft./8,849 m.) from base camp (17,800 ft./5,425 m.) on the Nepal side to the summit in 16 hours 56 minutes. He climbed mostly at night. The previous record was 20 hours 54 minutes set in 1998 by Kaji Sherpa. This Everest ascent by Babu Chiri was his tenth, all without using supplemental oxygen.

2000: FIRST ASCENT

May 22. Anna Czerwinshka (1949 –) became the oldest woman to summit Mount Everest (29,035 ft./8,849 m.) at the age of 50. She is also the first Polish woman to climb the Seven Summits.

2000: FIRST ASCENT

Pemba Doma (1970 –) became the first Sherpani (Sherpa woman) to summit Mount Everest from Tibet (via the northeast ridge). She also climbed Everest from the Nepal side (via the southeast ridge) in 2002.

2001:

May 1. American mountaineer Ed Viesturs (1959 –) reached the summit of Shishapangma (26,291 ft./8,013 m.) in China, his 12th 8,000 meter peak.

2001:

May 24. American climbers Dave Hahn, Andy Politz, Tap Richards, and Jason Tanguay gave up their Mount Everest summit attempt on the northeast ridge in order to rescue five stricken climbers at 28,300 ft./8,625 m. who would have died. These stricken climbers were American guide Andy Lapkass and his client Jaime Vinals and three Russian climbers.

2001: FIRST ASCENT

May 25. Five unique events occurred on the summit of Mount Everest (29,035 ft./8,849 m.) on this particular day:

1. American mountaineer Erik Weihenmayer (1968 –) became the first blind climber to reach the summit.

2. American climber Dr. Sherman Bull (64) became the oldest person to summit.

3. Sherman Bull and his son Brad became the first father and son team to reach the summit together.

4. 19 climbers from one team reached the summit in a single day—a record.

5. First summiting of Mount Everest filmed in high definition.

2001:

December 25. The Nepalese Government opened 103 new peaks to mountaineers. Several of these peaks exceeded 20,000 feet/6,096 meters and remained unclimbed. 263 peaks in Nepal were now open to mountaineers.

2001:

The Chinese granted permission to a western team to climb Mount Kailas (22,028 ft./6,714 m.) in southwest Tibet in order to insult Tibetans. An international protest forced this expedition to cancel its plans. The Tibetan name for Mount Kailas is Kang Rimpoche which means "Jewel of Snow." One circumnavigation of Kailas (33 miles/52 kilometers) is called a "kora." The completion of one kora brings one closer to nirvana, insures a prosperous life, and increases one's goods. 108 koras means that nirvana has been attained. One kora takes from one to four days to complete. Altitudes along the kora route range from 14,961 feet/4,560 meters to 17,094 feet/5,210 meters.

2002: FIRST ASCENT

May 16. American woman mountaineer Ellen Miller (1959 –) of Vail, Colorado, became the first North American climber to summit Mount Everest (29,035 ft./8,849 m.) from both the north (Tibetan) side (May 23, 2001) and the south (Nepalese) side (May 16, 2002). Only four women had reached Everest's summit twice and two of these were Sherpanis (Sherpa women).

2002:

May 16. Basque mountaineer Alberto Inurrategi (1968 –) became the tenth person to climb all fourteen 8,000 meter peaks. His final summit was Annapurna (26,546 feet/8,091 meters) which he reached with French climber Jean-Christophe Lafaille (1965 – 2006).

2002:

May 16. American mountaineers Phil (1951 –) and Susan (1967 –) Ershler became the first couple to climb the Seven Summits with their ascent of Mount Everest. Danuru Sherpa and Dorjee Sherpa accompanied them to the summit.

2002:

Spring. American journalist and film-maker Jennifer Jordan (1957 –) uncovered the remains of American mountaineer Dudley Wolfe (1896 – 1939) at the base of K2 (28,253 ft./8,611 m.) in Pakistan. Wolfe died at 24,700 ft./7,528 m.) in July of 1939 along with three Sherpas. Wolfe's mitten (his name was on it) plus 30 of his ribs and vertebrae were discovered. These remains had traveled 1.5 miles/2.5 kilometers down the Godwin-Austen Glacier since 1939 (63 years). As of 2002, fifty-two climbers had been killed on K2.

2002:

The world's highest unclimbed peak is now Bhutan's Gangkar Punsum (24,836 ft./7,570 m.). It is located on the border of Bhutan and Tibet. Four expeditions in 1985 and 1986 all failed to reach the summit. In 2003, Bhutan became closed to all mountaineering.

2002:

Mount Everest summit summary:

1921 through 1996 (75 years) 148 deaths	679 climbers reached the summit
1997 through 2002 (5 years) 27 deaths	800+ summit climbers

2002:

Ang Tsering Sherpa (1904 – 2002) died at age 98 in Darjeeling, India. He was the last surviving member of the 1924 British Mount Everest Expedition. His other expeditions included:

1929	Kangchenjunga (British)
1930	Kanchenjunga (German)
1931	Kamet
1933	Mt. Everest (British)
1934	Nanga Parbat (German)
1952	Mt. Everest (Swiss)
1956	Nanda Ghunti *
1964	Abi Gamin

*He summited at age 52: 20,700 ft./6,309 m.

2002:

From 1962 through 2002, mountaineers from the Indo – Tibetan Border Police had reached over 100 Himalayan summits, nearly half of which were first ascents.

2002:

American mountaineer Pete Athans (1957 –) reached the summit of Mount Everest (29,035 ft./8,849 m.) in Nepal for the 7th time.

2003: FIRST ASCENT

May 21. American mountaineers John (55, father) and Jess (20, son) Roskelley reached the summit of Mount Everest (29,035 ft./8,849 m.) via the north ridge. Jess became the youngest American climber to summit to date.

2003: FIRST ASCENT

May 22. Japanese climber Yuichiro Miura (70 years, 222 days old) became the oldest climber to summit Mount Everest (29,035 ft./8,849 m.) in Nepal.

2003: FIRST ASCENT

May 25. Sherpani woman Ming Kipa (15) became the youngest person to summit Mount Everest (29,035 ft./8,849 m.). She climbed the north (Tibet) side with her two sisters, ages 24 and 30.

2003:

May 26. Lhakpa Gelu Sherpa set a new Mount Everest climbing time (base camp to the summit—11,235 feet/3,424 meters) of 10 hours 46 minutes (Nepal side).

2003:

Spring. American high-altitude physician Dr. Luanne Freer founded the Mount Everest Base Camp Clinic with the assistance of the Himalayan Rescue Association. This clinic was located at 17,600 feet/5,364 meters below the Khumbu Icefall. Since 2003, Dr. Freer has treated approximately 700 climbers and trekkers for a variety of high-altitude related illnesses. Known as "Everest ER," this 200 square foot medical tent is staffed by three volunteer physicians and one Sherpa. This medical facility provides mountaineers with two hyperbaric chambers for treating altitude sickness, full-body rewarming bags, an oxygen concentrator, IV fluids, and IKG monitors. Everest ER is supported by climber donations and the Himalayan Rescue Association.

2003:

Summer. American Elizabeth Hawley (1923 –) was presented the Sagarmatha (Nepalese name for Mount Everest) National Award from the Nepal Ministry of Tourism for her contribution in promoting the mountains of Nepal for 43 years (1960 to 2003). She is the official chronicler of Himalayan mountaineering expeditions.

2003:

American woman climber Christine Boskoff (1967 – 2006) had climbed six of the fourteen 8,000 meter peaks to date—more than any other woman alive. Her six 8,000 meter ascents were:

1. 1995 Broad Peak
2. 1996 Cho Oyu
3. 1997 Lhotse
4. 1999 Gasherbrum II

   5. 2000 Mt. Everest

   6. 2003 Shishapangma

Boskoff died while climbing Genyen Peak in China in November of 2006.

2003:

Fourteen climbers reached the summit of Nanga Parbat (26,658 ft./8,125 m.) in Pakistan. From its first ascent in 1953 through 2003, a total of 216 climbers have summited Nanga Parbat.

2003:

As of the end of this year, five women had summited K2 (28,253 ft./8,611 m.) in Pakistan. 3 of these 5 died on their descent of K2 while 90 women had summited Mount Everest. K2's casualty (death) rate is 1 out of 5 climbers, while Mount Everest's rate is 1 out of 12 climbers.

2003:

The Mount Everest First Ascent 50th Anniversary celebration was held in Kathmandu, Nepal. Nepal King Gyanendra awarded Honorary Nepalese Citizenship to Sir Edmund Hillary (84) in recognition of his historic climb (May 29, 1953) and his work helping the Sherpa people of Nepal. 264 climbers reached the summit of Mt. Everest this year.

2004:

February. The Khumbu Climbing School was established in the village of Phortse (12,468 ft./3,800 m.) in the Solu Khumbu region of Nepal. American mountaineer instructors Conrad Anker, Chris Booher, Topher Donahue, and Jon Krakauer focused on ice climbing for the first class of 32 Sherpa students (free admission). This school is funded by the Alex Lowe Charitable Foundation. Jennifer Lowe Anker (Alex's widow) was also a part of this team. Conrad Anker and Jennifer Lowe Anker conceived the idea for this school in the Spring of 2002.

2004:

May 20 and 21. Pemba Dorje Sherpa (27) made an ascent of Mount Everest (29,035 ft./8,849 m.) from the Nepal base camp (17,800 ft./5,425 m.) to the summit in 8 hours 10 minutes. This was his third Everest summit. He only used oxygen above 7,900 meters (25,919 feet). This was a new ascent record. The previous record of 10 hours 46 minutes was established by Lhakpa Gelu Sherpa in 2003.

2004:

May 24. Middlebury College (Middlebury, Vermont) student Britton Keeshan (1982 –) reached the summit of Mount Everest (29,035 ft./8,849 m.) thereby completing the Seven Summits. Keeshan became the youngest climber (22) to accomplish all Seven Summits. The previous age record belonged to 23-year-old Japanese climber Astsushi Yamada. Keeshan's first (of all seven) ascent was Mount McKinley/Denali (20,320 ft./6,193 m.) on July 3, 1999.

2004: FIRST ASCENT

May 28. A Russian expedition to Jannu (25,295 ft./7,710 m.) in the Nepal Himalaya climbed a direct line route (72 vertical pitches) on the north face (10,660 feet/3,250 meters high). This was the most difficult high-altitude wall ever climbed. Dmitry Paulenko, Alexander Ruchkin, Sergey Borisov, Gennady Kirievsky, and Nick Totmianin reached the summit.

2004: FIRST ASCENT

July 24 and 25. American climber Steve House (1970 –) solo climbed the south face (first ascent) of K7 (22,750 ft./6,934 m.) in the Karakoram Range of Pakistan. House only carried a seven-pound pack on this roundtrip (base camp-summit-base camp) climb of 41 hours 45 minutes.

2004:

July 26. Spanish woman mountaineer Edurne Pasabán (1973 –) summited K2 (28,253 ft./8,611 m.) in the Karakoram Range of Pakistan—the sixth woman to do so. As of this year, she had climbed seven 8,000 meter peaks in four years (three 8,000 meter peaks in a period of eight weeks in 2003). She has also summited four of the top five peaks in the world. Of the six women that have stood atop K2, Pasabán is the only one still living. The five deceased women are:

> 1986: Polish – Wanda Rutkiewicz (1943 – 1992). Summited K2. Died on Kangchenjunga in 1992.
>
> French – Liliane Barrard (1948 – 1986). Summited K2 but died on the descent.
>
> British – Julie Tullis (1939 – 1986). Summited K2 but died on the descent.
>
> 1992: French – Chantal Mauduit (1964 – 1998). Summited K2. Died on Dhaulagiri in Nepal in 1998.
>
> 1995: British – Alison Hargreaves (1962 – 1995). Summited K2 but died on the descent.

2004:

December 11. French mountaineer Jean-Christophe Lafaille (1965 – 2006) reached the summit of his 11th 8,000 meter peak—Shishapangma (26,291 ft./8,013 m.) in Tibet. He climbed the south face solo in winter without using supplemental oxygen. Lafaille has Mount Everest, Kangchenjunga, and Makalu yet to climb. This was the first winter ascent of Shishapangma and the only winter ascent of an 8,000 meter peak by a non-Polish mountaineer.

2004:

Lhakpa Sherpani (1973 –) made her fourth ascent of Mount Everest (29,035 ft./8,849 m.)—the most by any woman.

2004:

Mount Everest – 2,251 individual ascents to date (90 ascents by women)
K2 – 238 individual ascents to date (5 ascents by women)
Kangchenjunga – 195 individual ascents to date

2004:

Spanish mountaineer Juanito Oiarzábel (1956 –) had climbed all fourteen 8,000 meter peaks during 21 different expeditions. In 2004, Oiarzábel reached his 29th summit of an 8,000 meter peak. This is the highest number of summit ascents to mountains over 8,000 meters by any mountaineer. Oiarzábel reached his first 8,000 meter summit in 1985. These 29 summits can be divided into Nepal (12), Pakistan (10), and China (7).

2004:

As of this year, Japanese woman mountaineer Junko Tabei (1939 –) had participated in 44 all-women's expeditions all around the world.

2004: FIRST ASCENT

Spanish mountaineer Carlos Soria (65) became the oldest person to reach the summit of K2 (28,253 ft./8,611 m.) in Pakistan.

2005:

April. Japanese woman mountaineer Junko Tabei (1939 –), the first woman to summit Mount Everest (1975), set the goal for herself of climbing the highest peak in every country in the world. As of April, 2005, she had reached the highest summit in 34 countries. Tabei is 66 years old.

2005:

April. South Korean mountaineer Park Young-Seok (1963 – 2011) completed the "True Adventurer's Grand Slam" which is comprised of the following four accomplishments:

1. Reach the North Pole
2. Reach the South Pole
3. Climb the Seven Summits
4. Reach the summits of all fourteen 8,000 meter peaks in the world.

Young-Seok disappeared as he was descending Annapurna (26,546 ft./8,091 m.) on October 23, 2011.

2005:

May 12. American mountaineer Ed Viesturs (1959 –) finally reached (his third attempt) the summit of Annapurna (26,546 ft./8,091 m.) in the Nepal Himalaya thereby completing his climbs of all fourteen 8,000 meter peaks in the world. Viesturs was the 12th person to accomplish this mountaineering feat, the first American mountaineer, and the sixth to climb these 14 peaks without using supplemental oxygen. He was accompanied by Swedish mountaineer Veikka Gustafsson (1968 –) who completed his 10th 8,000 meter peak. Here is a summary of Viestur's fourteen 8,000 meter peak climbs:

Peak Name	Elevation Rank	Date Climbed	Elevation Feet Meters	Location	Summit Partner(s)
1. Kangchenjunga	3rd	May 18, 1989	28,171 8,586	Nepal	Phil Ershler, Craig Van Hoy
2. Mt. Everest	1st	May 8, 1990	29,035 8,849	Nepal/Tibet	Solo
3. K2	2nd	August 16, 1992	28,253 8,611	Pakistan	Scott Fisher, Charley Mace
4. Lhotse	4th	May 16, 1994	27,940 8,516	Nepal/Tibet	Rob Hall
5. Cho Oyu	6th	October 6, 1994	26,906 8,201	Nepal/Tibet	Rob Hall, Jan Hall
6. Makalu	5th	May 18, 1995	27,764 8,462	Nepal/Tibet	Rob Hall, Veikka Gustafsson
7. Gasherbrum II	13th	July 4, 1995	26,363 8,035	Pakistan	Solo
8. Gasherbrum I	11th	July 15, 1995	26,471 8,068	Pakistan	Carlos Carsolio, Krzysztof Wielicki
9. Manaslu	8th	April 22, 1999	26,760 8,156	Nepal	Veikka Gustafsson
10. Dhaulagiri	7th	May 4, 1999	26,796 8,167	Nepal	Veikka Gustafsson
11. Shishapangma	14th	April 30, 2001	26,291 8,013	Tibet	Veikka Gustafsson
12. Nanga Parbat	9th	June 23, 2003	26,658 8,125	Pakistan	Jean-Christophe Lafaille
13. Broad Peak	12th	July 15, 2003	26,402 8,047	Pakistan	Jean-Christophe Lafaille
14. Annapurna	10th	May 12, 2005	26,546 8,091	Nepal	Veikka Gustafsson

Viesturs was a member of thirty Himalayan expeditions to 8,000 meter peaks. He reached twenty 8,000 meter summits and turned back on ten others (Mount Everest– 4, Annapurma– 2, Shishapangma– 1, Broad Peak– 1, Dhaulagiri– 1, and Nanga Parbat– 1).

2005:

May 30. Nepalese couple Pem Dorjee and Moni Mulepati became the first to get married on the summit of Mount Everest—a ten-minute ceremony. There were 45 climbers in the wedding party. Mulepati became the first non-Sherpa Nepali woman to summit Mount Everest.

2005: FIRST ASCENT

September 1 – 8. American mountaineers Vince Anderson (1969 –) and Steve House (1970 –) made a direct new route up the 14,763 ft./4,500 m. Rupal Face of Nanga Parbat (26,658 ft./8,125 m.) in Pakistan. This pure alpine line up this near vertical face took six days with a two-day descent. No supplemental oxygen or fixed ropes were used. Anderson and House carried minimal gear (one sleeping bag and a 1 kilogram/2.2 pound tent). For this ascent, Anderson and House were awarded the 2005 Piolet d' Or ("Golden Pick Axe") award.

2005:

October 20. A French mountaineering team attempting to climb Kang Guru in the Nepal Himalaya experienced a huge avalanche at their base camp location. Seven French climbers and eleven Nepalese were killed (18 total deaths). This was the worst disaster in Nepal Himalaya mountaineering. The previous worst disaster occurred in April of 1972 when ten Nepalese, four Koreans, and one Japanese climber were killed by an avalanche on Manaslu (26,760 ft./8,156 m.) in Nepal. The worst single mountaineering avalanche death toll happened in 1990 on Pik Lenin (23,407 ft./7,134 m.) in the Pamir Range of Russia when 43 climbers in one camp were overwhelmed.

2005:

As of this year, Polish mountaineers had made eight (8) winter ascents of 8,000 meter peaks. These climbers became known as the "Ice Warriors." These eight ascents are:

1980	Mount Everest
1984	Manaslu
1985	Cho Oyu
	Dhaulagiri
1986	Kangchenjunga
1987	Annapurna
1988	Lhotse
2005	Shishapangma

2005:

Mount Everest (29,035 ft./8,849 m.) is the most frequently climbed 8,000 meter peak with Cho Oyu (26,906 ft./8,201 m.) the second most popular. Annapurna (26,546 ft./8,091 m.) is the least climbed of all the 8,000 meter peaks (total of fourteen) and the most deadly (ascents vs. death ratio is the highest).

2005:

After Mount Everest and Cho Oyu, Ama Dablam (22,494 ft./6,856 m.) in Nepal is the third most popular peak for mountaineers. It was first climbed in 1961. To date, Ama Dablam has had 411 expeditions and 1,296 summit climbers.

2006: FIRST ASCENT

May. The following "firsts" were achieved by those who reached the summit of Mount Everest (29,035 ft./8,849 m.) this May:

1. Oldest Climber to summit: Japanese climber Takao Arayama—70 yrs. 7 mons, 13 days. Via north (Tibetan) side. May 16.
2. New Zealander Mark Inglis became the first double amputee to summit. He lost both legs below the knee to frostbite on a previous expedition.
3. Maxim Chaya became the first Lebanese to summit.
4. Leo Oracion became the first Filipino to summit.

2006:

October 18. American mountaineer Kit Deslauriers (1969 –) reached the summit of Mt. Everest (her final seventh summit) and then descended from the summit on skis becoming the first person to ski from all Seven Summits. Her husband Rob (1965 –) was also with her. American photographer Jimmy Chin (1973 –) and guide Dave Hahn (1961 –) completed this team. Deslauriers skied nearly 6,000 vertical feet (1,829 meters) from the summit to base camp which represents approximately half of the total vertical distance (12,000 feet/3,657 meters).

2006:

Australian climber Christopher Harris (15) reached the summit of Mount Everest (29,035 ft./8,849 m.) in Nepal to become the youngest person to complete the climbing of the world's Seven Summits.

2006:

As of this year, well-known mountaineer Reinhold Messner (1944 –) had authored 48 mountaineering books. British mountaineer Chris Bonington (1934) had written eighteen climbing books.

2007:

March. 198 mountaineers had climbed all Seven Summits using either Mount Kosciuszko or Carstensz Pyramid to complete their list. Thirty percent of these mountaineers climbed all eight peaks.

2007:

May 16. Apa Sherpa (1962 –) reached the summit of Mount Everest for the 17th time (15th consecutive summit). He was a member of the SuperSherpas Expedition (all Sherpas). Apa, Lhakpa Gelu Sherpa and four other Sherpas climbed from Camp 2 to the summit in 24 hours non-stop.

2007:

May 17. American mountaineer Samantha Larson (18) became the second youngest foreign climber to reach the summit of Mount Everest. With this summit, Larson completed the Seven Summits. She also became the second youngest person to achieve the Seven Summits.

2007: FIRST ASCENT

May 22. Nepalese woman mountaineer Pemba Doma Sherpani (1970 – 2007) from the village of Namche Bazaar died in a fall while climbing Lhotse (27,940 ft./8,516 m.) in Nepal. She was the first Nepalese woman to climb Mount Everest via the north face. She was also one of six women to have two or more Everest summits.

2007:

June 14. American mountaineer Conrad Anker (1963 –) free-climbed the Second Step (28,280 ft./8,619 m.) rock feature on the northeast ridge of Mount Everest in Tibet. Anker rated this rock climb 5.10 and concluded the George Mallory (1886 – 1924) could not have climbed it in 1924. Anker continued his climb to the summit of Everest with five other Western mountaineers and ten Sherpas. Anker and Leo Houlding were dressed in 1924 vintage climbing clothes as they played the roles of George Mallory (Anker) and Sandy Irvine (Houlding) that disappeared on Everest in 1924. A British film (The Wildest Dream) directed by Anthony Geffen was made of this 2007 ascent.

2007: FIRST ASCENT

October 14 to 23. Russian mountaineers Valery Babanov and Sergey Kofanov made an alpine-style ascent of Jannu's (25,295 feet/7,709 meters) West Pillar in Nepal. This ten-day ascent earned them the

2007 Golden Piton Award for Alpine Climbing by Climbing magazine. This was the first time that a new route in the Himalayas was climbed alpine-style.

2007: FIRST ASCENT

October 28. Slovenian mountaineer Tomaz Humar (1969 – 2009) made a solo ascent of Annapurna's (26,546 ft./8,091 m.) south face in Nepal. As of 2007, 106 climbers had summited Annapurna from a total of 120 different expeditions. To date, 51 climbers have died on Annapurna.

2007:

American mountaineer Dave Hahn (1962 –) reached the summit of Mount Everest for the ninth time—a new record for American-born climbers. Over 530 men and women reached the summit of Mount Everest during this pre-monsoon climbing season. Seven mountaineers died on the mountain. Hahn had also made 245 ascents of Mount Rainier in Washington, 18 ascents of Denali in Alaska, and 25 ascents of Mount Vinson in Antarctica.

2007: FIRST ASCENT

A new age record for Mount Everest summiters was set this year when 71-year-old Katsusuke Yanagisawa (Japanese) reached the summit.

2007: Book

Elizabeth Hawley and Richard Salisbury published *The Himalaya By The Numbers – A Statistical Analysis of Mountaineering in the Nepal Himalaya*. This 162-page book is a detailed analysis of three climbing periods in the Nepal Himalaya:

1950 to 1969	The expedition period
1970 to 1989	The transitional period
1990 to 2006	The commercial period

2008:

March 10. The China-Tibet Mountaineering Association announced its decision to close the north side of Mount Everest to foreign expeditions in order to allow Chinese mountaineers to carry the Olympic torch to the summit on its way to Beijing for the 2008 Summer Olympics. This climbing ban was also applied to Cho Oyu from the north.

Following the Chinese announcement, the Nepalese government followed suit by restricting expeditions to Mount Everest from the south. These expeditions would not be permitted to climb above base camp until after May 10th although this decision was later changed to Camp II in the Western Cwm.

2008: FIRST ASCENT

April 24. Swiss mountaineers Simon Anthamatten (1980 –) and Ueli Steck (1976 –) made the first complete ascent (on the second attempt) of the northwest face of Tengkangpoche (21,326 ft./6,500 m.) in Nepal. They used no fixed ropes or expansion bolts during their two attempts to climb this 2,000 meter face.

2008:

May 21. Apa Sherpa (1961 –) reached the summit of Mount Everest (29,035 ft./8,849 m.) in Nepal for the eighteenth time.

2008:

May 22. Seventy-five mountaineers reached the summit of Mount Everest.

2008:

May 23. American mountaineer and professional guide Dave Hahn (1961 –) summited Mount Everest for the tenth time.

2008:

May 25. Nepalese climber and retired soldier Min Bahadur Sherchan (1932 –) became the oldest person (age 76) to reach the summit of Mount Everest. He climbed the South Col route. Pemba Dorje Sherpa was with Sherchan.

2008: FIRST ASCENT

July 17. Russian mountaineers Viktor Afanasien and Valery Bababov (1964 –) completed two new routes on two 8,000 meter peaks within two weeks. On July 17, they summited Broad Peak (26,402 ft./8,047 m.) via the Central Buttress (alpine style) and then climbed the southwest face/southwest ridge of Gasherbrum I (26,471 ft./8,068 m.) reaching its summit on August 1.

2008:

August 1. The worst mountaineering accident in K2's history occurred high on the peak between Camp IV (25,800 ft./ 7,863 m.) and the summit (28,251 ft./ 8,611 m.). Eleven mountaineers from seven different countries (France – 1 death, Ireland – 1, Nepal – 2, Norway – 1, Pakistan – 2, Serbia – 1, and South Korea – 3) died. These eleven deaths (plus three injured climbers) resulted from avalanches, serac (large block of ice) falls, fixed ropes being torn away, misplaced, or non-existent, high-altitude sickness, and accidental falls. Eighteen climbers did reach the summit on this day.

2008: FIRST ASCENT

October 5. Japanese climbers Kazuya Hiraide and Kei Taniguchi made an alpine style first ascent of the southeast face of Kamet (25,447 ft./7,756 m.) in the Central Garhwal Himalayas of India. This thirteen day (roundtrip) climb is now known as the Samurai Direct.

2008:

Ecuadorian mountaineer Ivan Vallejo (1959 –) became the fourteenth climber to reach the summits of all fourteen 8,000 meter peaks in the world. His 14-peak quest began in 1997 and ended with his Dhaulagiri summit. Vallejo was the seventh climber to accomplish this unique mountaineering feat without using supplemental oxygen.

2009:

February 9. The first winter ascent of Makalu (27,764 ft./8,462 m.) on the Nepal – Tibet border was accomplished by Italian mountaineer Simone Moro (1967 –) and Kazakh mountaineer Denis Urubko (1973 –). Makalu was the final Nepalese 8,000 meter peak to be climbed in the winter. There had been thirteen winter attempts over a twenty-nine year period.

2009:

May 20. American climber E. Dawes Eddy III (1943 –) became the oldest American (66 years old) to summit Mount Everest (29,035 feet/8,849 meters) in Nepal.

2009:

May 21. Apa Sherpa (1961 –) reached the summit of Mount Everest for his 19th ascent.

2009:

Four mountaineers accomplished their goal of climbing all fourteen 8,000 meter peaks in the world. These climbers are:

    1. Ralf Dujmovits (1961 –). German.
        Climbing period: 1990 to 2009.
    2. Veikka Gustafsson (1968 –). Finnish.
        Climbing period: 1993 to 2009.
    3. Andrew Lock (1961 –). Australian.
        Climbing period: 1993 to 2009.
    4. Denis Urubko (1973 –). Kazakhstan.
        Climbing period: 2000 to 2009.

Lock became the 18th mountaineer to reach all fourteen summits. Urubko, Gustafsson, and Lock did not use supplemental oxygen on their fourteen ascents.

2009:

Slovenian mountaineer Tomasz Humar (1969 – 2009) attempted to solo climb Langtang Lirung (23,710 feet/7,227 meters) in the Himalayas. His body was located at the 18,373 foot (5,600 meters) elevation. Humar had achieved over 1,500 ascents including 70 ascents via new climbing routes.

2009:

American mountaineer Ed Viesturs (1959 –) reached the summit of Mount Everest for the seventh time. Viesturs completed his climbing of all fourteen 8,000 meter peaks in the world in 2005.

2009:

Basque Spanish mountaineer Edurne Pasaban (1973 –) reached the summit of Kanchenjunga (28,171 ft./8,586 m.) in Nepal thereby becoming the first woman to summit twelve 8,000 meter peaks.

2009:

Climbing summary for K2 (1954 to 2009):

297 reach summit

78 climbers die on mountain

2010:

April 27. Polish mountaineer Piotr Pustelnik, (1951 –) reached the summit of Annapurna (26,546 feet/8,091 meters) in Nepal. With this summit, he had now climbed all fourteen 8,000 meter peaks in the world. As of this date, twenty men and one woman had achieved this unique mountaineering goal (See Appendix III).

2010:

May 17. Basque Spanish mountaineer Edurne Pasaban (1973 –) became the first woman (and 21st climber overall) to climb all fourteen 8,000 meter peaks in the world. She spent ten years (2001 to 2010) climbing these fourteen mountains.

2010:

May 22. American climber Jordan Romero (1997 –) became the youngest person to reach the summit of Mount Everest (29,035 feet/8,849 meters) in Nepal. Romero, age 13, had now climbed six of the seven summits (highest summit on each of the world's seven continents. Only Mount Vinson (16,050 feet/4,892 meters) in Antarctica remains for him to climb.

2010:

October. American mountaineer and explorer Eric Larsen (1971 –) became the first person to reach the South Pole, North Pole, and the summit of Mount Everest over a 365-day period. Larsen's purpose for accomplishing this goal was to raise public awareness for global warming.

2010:

The China-Tibet Mountaineering Association recently announced its new climbing policy that beginning in the Fall of 2010, Mount Everest climbers from the north side (Tibetan side) must be between the ages of 18 and 60. Nepal also banned climbers under the age of 16 from climbing Mount Everest from the south side.

2010:

A three-person Spanish mountaineering team was rescued at the 23,000 foot (7,010 meters) level on Annapurna (26,545 ft./ 8,091 m.) This was the highest helicopter rescue in history. The helicopter was a Eurocopter AS350 B3 (capacity: 4) which costs approximately $2 million. It has been used in the Himalaya since the late 1990s.

2010:

Mount Everest climbing summary (for 2010):

- 513 total summit climbers (347 climbers from the south/166 from the north)
- 4 reported deaths—all on north side
- 1953 to 2010: Over 5,000 total summit climbers (3,431 different climbers and 1,639 repeat climbers).

2011:

February 4. The first winter ascent of an 8,000-meter peak in the Karakoram Range of the Himalayas was accomplished by a three-man team: American Cory Richards (1981 –), Italian Simone Moro (1967 –), and Kazakh Denis Urubko (1973 –). This team reached the summit of Pakistan's Gasherbrum II (26,363 feet/8,035 meters). A massive avalanche buried all three mountaineers on their descent. Moro, fortunately, was able to dig himself and his two partners out of the avalanche debris.

2011:

April 21. Swiss mountaineer Ueli Steck (1976 –) made a solo ascent of Shishapangma's (26,291 ft./8,013 m.) south face (6,562 ft./2,000 m.) in 10 ½ hours. Steck's roundtrip (base to summit to base) climb took 20 hours. Shishapangma is located in Tibet and is known to Hindus as the sacred peak of Gosainthan. A Chinese climbing party first climbed Shishapangma in 1964.

2011:

May 11. Apa Sherpa (early 1960s –) reached the summit of Mount Everest for the 21st time. Born Lhakpa Tenzing Sherpa in Thame, Nepal, Apa Sherpa began serving as a kitchen boy and porter on mountaineering expeditions in 1985. He summited Mount Everest for his first time in 1990 with a New Zealand expedition on his fourth attempt. Apa Sherpa and his family now reside in Draper, Utah.

2011:

May 14 and 15. American guide Michael Horst reached the summits of Mount Everest (29,035 ft./8,849 m.) and Lhotse (27,940 ft./8,516 m.) on the Nepal – Tibet border. Horst accomplished this double summit climb without descending below the South Col (25,940 ft./7,906 m.) with less than twenty-one hours elapsing between the two summits.

2011:

May 20. Indian mountaineer Arjun Vajpai became the youngest climber to reach the summit of Lhotse (27,940 ft./8,516 m.) on the Nepal – Tibet border: 17 years 11 months 16 days.

2011: FIRST ASCENT

August 18. Kazakh mountaineers Gennady Durov and Denis Urubko (1973 –) forged a new climbing route up the north face (8,202 ft./2,500 m.) of Pik Pobeda (24,407 ft./7,439 m.).

2011:

August 23. Austrian mountaineer Gerlinde Kaltenbrunner (1970 –) became the first woman to climb all fourteen 8,000 meter peaks in the world without using supplemental oxygen when she reached the summit of K2 (28,253 ft./8,611 m.) on the China – Pakistan border. This was her fourth attempt to climb K2. She was the second woman (after Spanish climber Edurne Pasaban in 2010) overall to climb the 8,000 meter summits. Kaltenbrunner was a member of the International 2011 K2 North Pillar Expedition. She reached K2's summit shortly before Kazakhstan climbers Maxut Zhumayev (1977 –) and Vassily Pivtsov (1975 –) summited. K2 was also their final 8,000 meter summit (of all fourteen).

2011: PEAK FIRST ASCENT *SASER KANGRI II EAST*

August 24. Three American mountaineers from the 2001 SKII Joint Indo-American expedition made the first ascent of Saser Kangri II (24,666 ft./ 7,518 m.) via its southwest face. Expedition leader Mark Richey (1958 –), Steve Swenson (1957 –), and Freddie Wilkinson (1979 –) reached the summit. This peak is located in the Eastern Karakoram Mountains of India. Prior to this first ascent, Saser Kangri II was the second-highest unclimbed mountain in the world.

Various members of this same expedition also made the first ascents of four other peaks in this same region:

Tsok Kangri	21,605 ft./ 6,585 m.
Pumo Kangri	20,506 ft./ 6,250 m.
Saser Ling	20,014 ft./ 6,100 m.
Stegosaurus	21,851 ft./ 6,660 m.

The highest unclimbed mountain in the world is Gangkar Punsum (24,837 ft./7,570 m.) in Bhutan. This high peak may remain unclimbed due Bhutan's prohibition to climbing its highest mountains. This policy was begun in 1994.

2011: FIRST ASCENT

October 2. Eleven days after leaving their advanced base camp, American mountaineers Conrad Anker (1963 –), Jimmy Chin, and Renan Ozturk reached the summit of Meru Central (20,703 ft./6,310 m.) in India. Their first ascent route was up the 4,250 foot (1,295 meters) knife-edge of ice and granite known as the Shark's Fin. Over twenty previous attempts had been made of this route. Meru Central was first climbed in 2001.

"Some men appear to derive a strong philosophical
satisfaction from dragging a sledge across miles of
arctic snow, or from mere existence in strange conditions.
Many people have an intangible though profound feeling
for certain types of country, and can be completely content
during any job which takes them into such places.
Presumably such a feeling for mountain country
is the principle reason for climbing."

1943
Eric Shipton
British Mountaineer and Explorer
(1907 – 1977)

Annapurna, Nepal, 26,546 ft./8,091 m.

Fred Wolfe (L) and Rich Wolfe (R) on the summit of Kala Pattar (18,233 ft./5,554 m.)
with Mount Everest (29,035 ft./8,849 m.) above

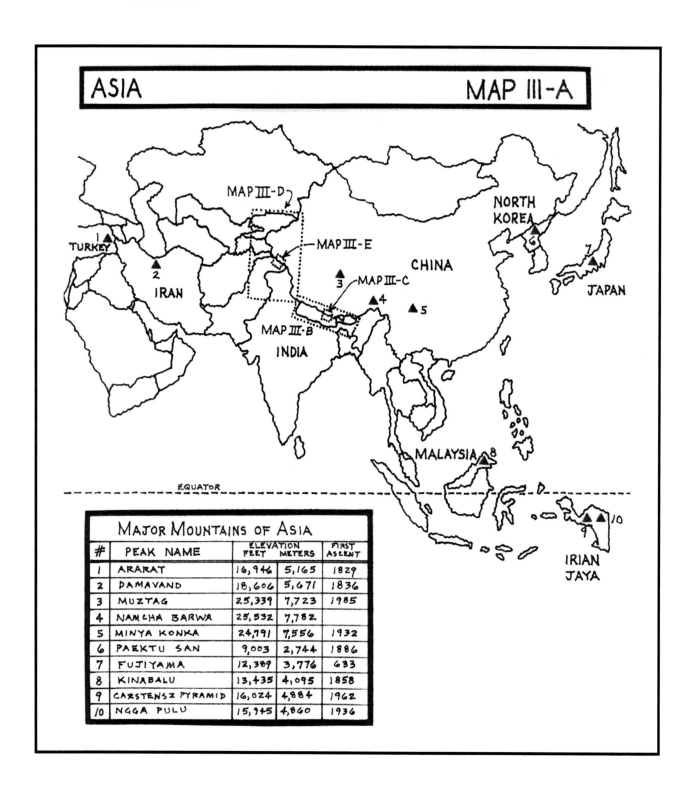

#	PEAK NAME	ELEVATION FEET	METERS	FIRST ASCENT
1	ARARAT	16,946	5,165	1829
2	DAMAVAND	18,606	5,671	1836
3	MUZTAG	25,339	7,723	1985
4	NAMCHA BARWA	25,532	7,782	
5	MINYA KONKA	24,791	7,556	1932
6	PAEKTU SAN	9,003	2,744	1886
7	FUJIYAMA	12,389	3,776	633
8	KINABALU	13,435	4,095	1858
9	CARSTENSZ PYRAMID	16,024	4,884	1962
10	NGGA PULU	15,945	4,860	1936

Makalu, Nepal-Tibet, 27,826 ft./8,481 m

Manaslu, Nepal, 26,760 ft./8,156 m.

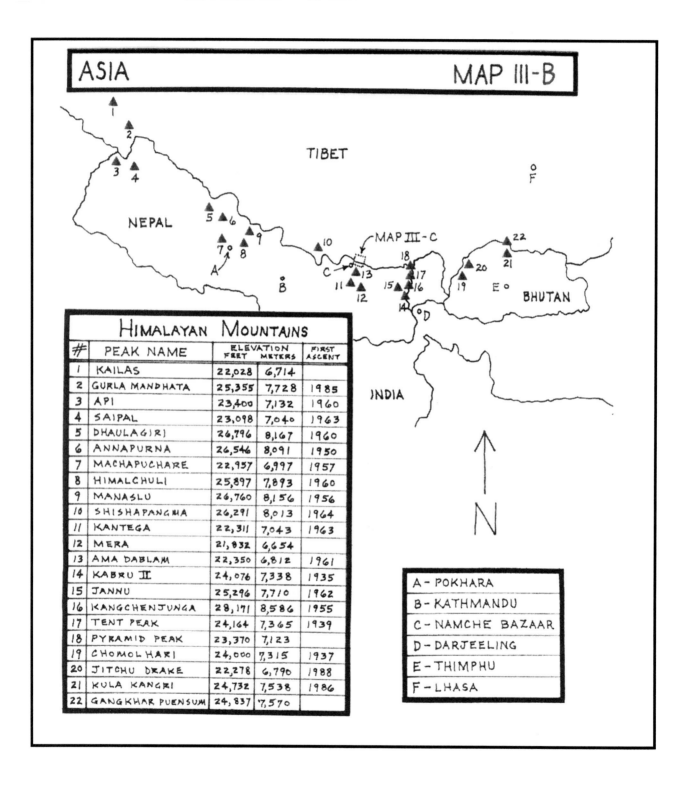

#	PEAK NAME	ELEVATION FEET	METERS	FIRST ASCENT
1	KAILAS	22,028	6,714	
2	GURLA MANDHATA	25,355	7,728	1985
3	API	23,400	7,132	1960
4	SAIPAL	23,098	7,040	1963
5	DHAULAGIRI	26,796	8,167	1960
6	ANNAPURNA	26,546	8,091	1950
7	MACHAPUCHARE	22,957	6,997	1957
8	HIMALCHULI	25,897	7,893	1960
9	MANASLU	26,760	8,156	1956
10	SHISHAPANGMA	26,291	8,013	1964
11	KANTEGA	22,311	7,043	1963
12	MERA	21,832	6,654	
13	AMA DABLAM	22,350	6,812	1961
14	KABRU II	24,076	7,338	1935
15	JANNU	25,296	7,710	1962
16	KANGCHENJUNGA	28,171	8,586	1955
17	TENT PEAK	24,164	7,365	1939
18	PYRAMID PEAK	23,370	7,123	
19	CHOMOLHARI	24,000	7,315	1937
20	JITCHU DRAKE	22,278	6,790	1988
21	KULA KANGRI	24,732	7,538	1986
22	GANGKHAR PUENSUM	24,837	7,570	

A - POKHARA
B - KATHMANDU
C - NAMCHE BAZAAR
D - DARJEELING
E - THIMPHU
F - LHASA

Dhaulagiri, Nepal, 26,796 ft./8,167 m.

Lhotse, Nepal-Tibet
27,940 ft./8,516 m.

Ama Dablam, Nepal, 22,494 ft./6,856 m.

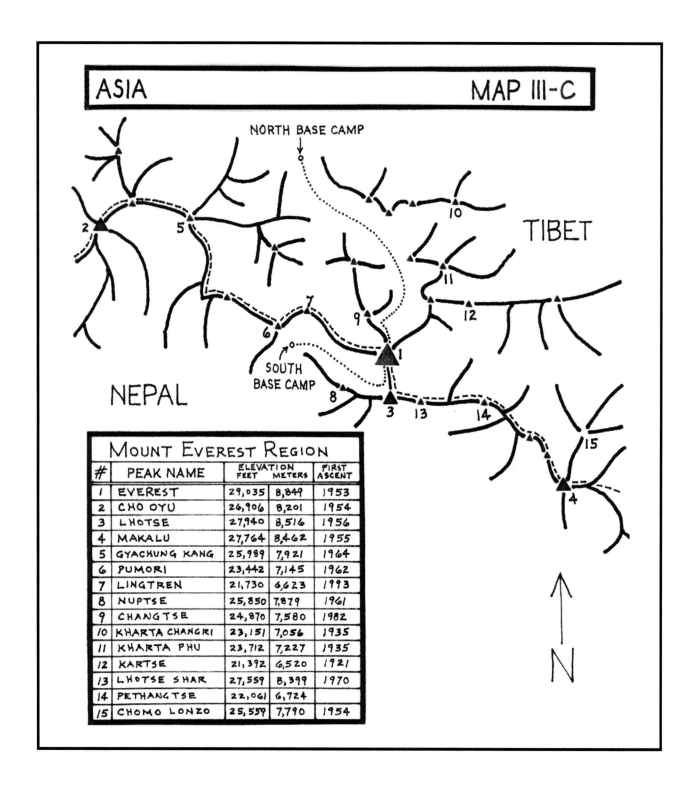

ASIA   MAP III-C

NORTH BASE CAMP

TIBET

NEPAL

SOUTH
BASE CAMP

N

#	PEAK NAME	ELEVATION FEET	METERS	FIRST ASCENT
1	EVEREST	29,035	8,849	1953
2	CHO OYU	26,906	8,201	1954
3	LHOTSE	27,940	8,516	1956
4	MAKALU	27,764	8,462	1955
5	GYACHUNG KANG	25,989	7,921	1964
6	PUMORI	23,442	7,145	1962
7	LINGTREN	21,730	6,623	1993
8	NUPTSE	25,850	7,879	1961
9	CHANGTSE	24,870	7,580	1982
10	KHARTA CHANGRI	23,151	7,056	1935
11	KHARTA PHU	23,712	7,227	1935
12	KARTSE	21,392	6,520	1921
13	LHOTSE SHAR	27,559	8,399	1970
14	PETHANGTSE	22,061	6,724	
15	CHOMO LONZO	25,559	7,790	1954

MOUNT EVEREST REGION

K2. 28,253 ft./8,611 m., Pakistan-China
Photo by Phil Powers

Shishapangma, Tibet, 26,291 ft./8,013 m.

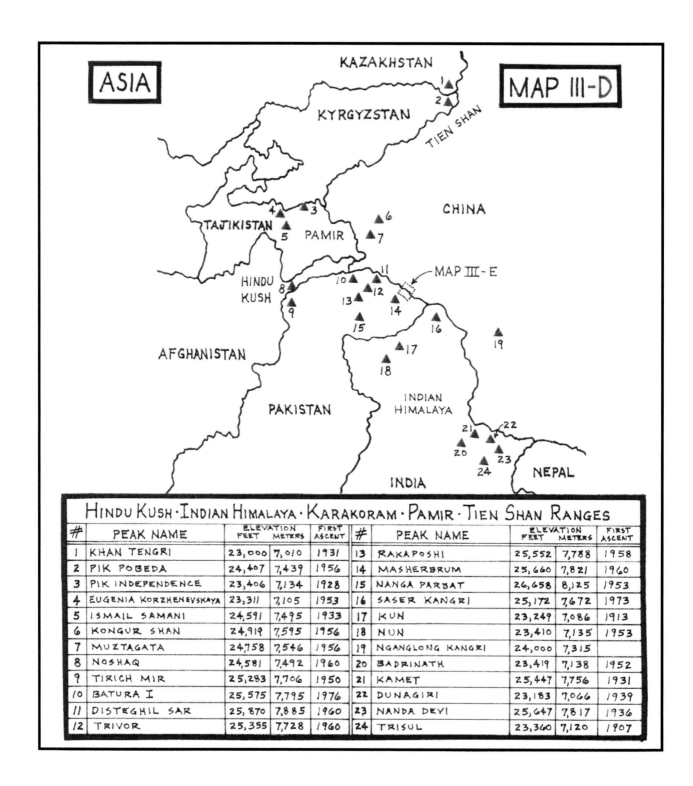

ASIA

MAP III-D

KAZAKHSTAN

KYRGYZSTAN

TIEN SHAN

CHINA

TAJIKISTAN

PAMIR

HINDU KUSH

MAP III-E

AFGHANISTAN

PAKISTAN

INDIAN HIMALAYA

INDIA

NEPAL

Hindu Kush · Indian Himalaya · Karakoram · Pamir · Tien Shan Ranges

#	PEAK NAME	ELEVATION FEET	METERS	FIRST ASCENT	#	PEAK NAME	ELEVATION FEET	METERS	FIRST ASCENT
1	KHAN TENGRI	23,000	7,010	1931	13	RAKAPOSHI	25,552	7,788	1958
2	PIK POBEDA	24,407	7,439	1956	14	MASHERBRUM	25,660	7,821	1960
3	PIK INDEPENDENCE	23,406	7,134	1928	15	NANGA PARBAT	26,658	8,125	1953
4	EUGENIA KORZHENEVSKAYA	23,311	7,105	1953	16	SASER KANGRI	25,172	7,672	1973
5	ISMAIL SAMANI	24,591	7,495	1933	17	KUN	23,249	7,086	1913
6	KONGUR SHAN	24,919	7,595	1956	18	NUN	23,410	7,135	1953
7	MUZTAGATA	24,758	7,546	1956	19	NGANGLONG KANGRI	24,000	7,315	
8	NOSHAQ	24,581	7,492	1960	20	BADRINATH	23,419	7,138	1952
9	TIRICH MIR	25,283	7,706	1950	21	KAMET	25,447	7,756	1931
10	BATURA I	25,575	7,795	1976	22	DUNAGIRI	23,183	7,066	1939
11	DISTEGHIL SAR	25,870	7,885	1960	23	NANDA DEVI	25,647	7,817	1936
12	TRIVOR	25,355	7,728	1960	24	TRISUL	23,360	7,120	1907

Gasherbrum I
a.k.a. Hidden Peak
26,471 ft./8,068 m.
Pakistan-China
Photo by Phil Powers

Gasherbrum II
26,363 ft./8,035 m.
Pakistan-China
Photo by Phil Powers

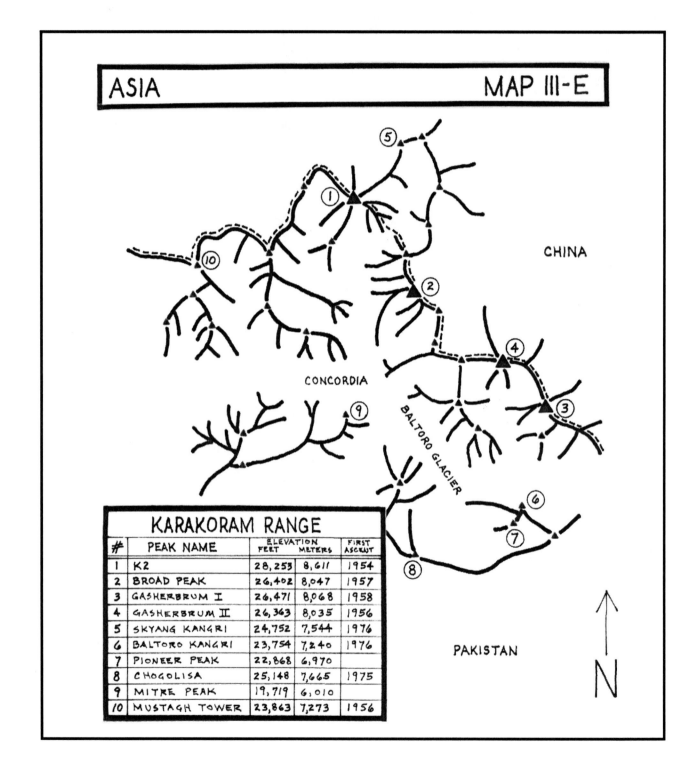

ASIA   MAP III-E

CHINA

CONCORDIA

BALTORO GLACIER

PAKISTAN

N

#	PEAK NAME	ELEVATION FEET	METERS	FIRST ASCENT
1	K2	28,253	8,611	1954
2	BROAD PEAK	26,402	8,047	1957
3	GASHERBRUM I	26,471	8,068	1958
4	GASHERBRUM II	26,363	8,035	1956
5	SKYANG KANGRI	24,752	7,544	1976
6	BALTORO KANGRI	23,754	7,240	1976
7	PIONEER PEAK	22,868	6,970	
8	CHOGOLISA	25,148	7,665	1975
9	MITRE PEAK	19,719	6,010	
10	MUSTAGH TOWER	23,863	7,273	1956

KARAKORAM RANGE

ASIA: The 25 Highest Peaks

RANK and PEAK NAME	ELEVATION FEET•METERS	LOCATION	FIRST ASCENT DATE	EXPEDITION	SUMMIT CLIMBERS
*1 Mt. Everest	29,035•8,849	Nepal-Tibet	May 29, 1953	British	Edmund Hillary Tenzing Norgay
*2 K2	28,253•8,611	China-Pakistan	July 31, 1954	Italian	Ahille Compagnoni Lino Lacedelli
*3 Kangchenjunga	28,171•8,586	Nepal-Sikkim	May 25, 1955	British	George Band Joe Brown
*4 Lhotse	27,941•8,516	Nepal-Tibet	May 18, 1956	Swiss	Fritz Luchsinger Ernst Reiss
5 Kangchenjunga South	27,808•8,476	Nepal-Sikkim			
*6 Makalu	27,767•8,463	Nepal-Tibet	May 15, 1955	French	Jean Couzy Lionel Terray
7 Lhotse Middle	27,659•8,430	Nepal-Tibet	May 22, 2001	Russian	Evgueni Vinogradsky Sergei Timofeev Alexei Bolotov Petr Kuznetov
8 Kangchenjunga West	27,626•8,420	Nepal	May 14, 1973	Japanese	Y. Ageta T. Matsuda
9 Lhotse Shar	27,560•8,400	Nepal-Tibel	May 12, 1970	Austrian	N. Josef R. Walter
*10 Cho Oyu	26,906•8,201	Nepal-Tibet	Oct. 19, 1954	Austrian	J. Jochter Pasang Dawa Lama Herbert Tichy
*11 Dhaulagiri	26,796•8,167	Nepal	May 13, 1960	Swiss	K. Diemberger P. Diener E. Forrer A. Schelbert
*12 Manaslu	26,783•8,163	Nepal	May 9, 1956	Japanese	T. Imanishi Gyaltsen Norbu

*One of the official 8,000 meter peaks.

ASIA: The 25 Highest Peaks (continued)

RANK and PEAK NAME	ELEVATION FEET·METERS	LOCATION	FIRST ASCENT DATE	EXPEDITION	SUMMIT CLIMBERS
*13 Nanga Parbat	26,661·8,126	Pakistan	July 3, 1953	German-Austrian	Hermann Buhl
*14 Annapurna	26,547·8,091	Nepal	June 3, 1950	French	Maurice Herzog Louis Lachenal
*15 Gasherbrum I	26,471·8,068	Pakistan	July 5, 1958	American	Andrew Kaufmann Peter Schoening
16 Annapurna-Northeast I	24,415·8,051	Nepal	1980	German	U. Boning L. Greissl H. Oberrauch
*17 Broad Peak	26,402·8,047	Pakistan	June 9, 1957	Austrian	Hermann Buhl Kurt Diemberger Marcus Schmuck Fritz Wintersteller
*18 Gasherbrum II	26,363·8,035	Pakistan	July 7, 1956	Austrian	S. Larch F. Moravec H. Willenpart
*19 Shishapangma	26,291·8,013	Tibet	May 2, 1964	Chinese	6 Chinese 4 Tibetans
20 Broad Peak Central	26,284·8,011	Pakistan	July 28, 1975	Polish	K. Glazek J. Kulis M. Kesicki A. Sikorski B. Nowaczyk
21 Manaslu Southeast	26,281·8,010	Nepal			
22 Annapurna-Northeast II	26,248·8,000	Nepal			
23 Shishapangma-Northwest	26,245·7,999	Tibet			
24 Manaslu East	26,222·7,992	Nepal			
25 Gyachung Kang	25,989·7,921	Nepal-Tibet	April 10, 1964	Japanese	Y. Kato Pasang Phutar III K. Sakaizawa

*One of the official 8,000 meter peaks.

Selected Bibliography — Asia

Of the numerous books, journals, newspaper and magazine articles, and internet sites that have been used in the research for this book, the author is particularly indebted to the following sources:

Ang Phurba Sherpa. Kunwar, Ramesh Raj. *Nepalese Climbers on Mount Everest.*
Pemba Chhamji Sherpa, 2002.

Anker, Conrad and Roberts, David. *The Lost Explorer – Finding Mallory on Mount Everest.*
Simon & Schuster, 1999.

Ardito, Stefano. *Tales of Mountaineering.* White Star Publishers, 2000.

Ardito, Stefano. *Peaks of Glory – Climbing the World's Highest Mountains.*
Thomasson – Grant, 1993.

Astill, Tony. *Mount Everest – The Reconnaissance 1935: The Forgotten Adventure.* Tony Astill, 2005.

Band, George. *SUMMIT – 150 Years of the Alpine Club.* Collins, 2006.

Band, George. *Everest – 50 Years On Top of the World.* Harper Collins Publishers, 2003.

Barnes, Malcolm. *The Mountain World 1955.* Harper & Brothers Publishers, 1955.

Barnes, Malcolm. *The Mountain World 1956/57.* Harper & Brothers Publishers, 1957.

Barnes, Malcolm. *The Mountain World 1962/63.* George Allen and Unwin Ltd., 1964.

Barnes, Malcolm. *The Mountain World 1964/65.* George Allen and Unwin Ltd., 1966.

Barnes, Malcolm. *The Mountain World 1958/59.* George Allen & Unwin Ltd., 1958.

Bates, Robert H. *The Love of Mountains Is Best – Climbs and Travels from K2 To Kathmandu.*
Peter E. Randall Publisher, 1994.

Bates, Robert H. Burdsall, Richard L. House, William P. Houston, Charles S. Petzoldt, Paul K. Streatfeild, Norman R. *Five Miles High – The Story of an Attack on the Second Highest Mountain in the World by the Members of the First American Karakoram Expedition.* Dodd, Mead & Company, 1939.

Bauer, Paul. *Himalayan Quest – The German Expeditions to Siniolchum and Nanga Parbat.*
Nicholson and Watson Limited, 1938.

Baume, Louis C. *Sivalaya – Explorations of the 8000 – Metre Peaks of the Himalaya.*
The Mountaineers, 1979.

Bayers, Peter L. *Imperial Ascent – Mountaineering, Masculinity, and Empire.*
University Press of Colorado, 2003.

Bechtold, Fritz. *Nanga Parbat Adventure – A Himalayan Expedition.* E.P. Dutton and
Company Inc., 1936.

Bensen, Joe. *Souvenirs From High Places – A History of Mountaineering Photography.*
The Mountaineers, 1998.

Bernbaum, Edwin. *Sacred Mountains of the World.* Sierra Club Books, 1990.

Birkby, Robert. *Mountain Madness – Scott Fischer, Mount Everest & a Life Lived On High.*
Citadel Press, 2008.

Boardman, Peter. *Sacred Summits – A Climber's Year.* The Mountaineers, 1982.

Bonatti, Walter. *The Mountains of My Life.* The Modern Library, 2001.

Bonatti, Walter. *On the Heights.* Rupert Hart-Davis. 1964.

Bonington, Chris. *The Climbers – A History of Mountaineering.* Hodder & Stoughton, 1992.

Bonington, Chris. Clarke, Charles. *Everest – The Unclimbed Ridge.* W.W. Norton & Company, 1983.

Bonington, Chris. *The Everest Years – A Climber's Life.* Hodder & Stoughton, 1986.

Bonington, Chris. *Chris Bonington's EVEREST.* Ragged Mountain Press, 2003.

Bonington, Chris. *Everest – The Hard Way: The First Ascent of the South West Face.*
Hodder & Stoughton, 1976.

Bonington, Chris. *Quest For Adventure – 21 Stories of the Men and Women Who
Challenged Oceans, Mountains, Deserts, Snow and Space.* Clarkson N. Potter, Inc., 1981.

Bonington, Chris. *Mountaineer – Thirty Years of Climbing on the World's Great Peaks.* Sierra Club Books, 1990.

Bonington, Chris. *The Next Horizon.* Victor Gollancz Ltd., 1973.

Bonington, Chris – General Editor. *Heroic Climbs – A Celebration of World Mountaineering.* The Mountaineers, 1994.

Bonington, Chris. Boysen, Martin. Hankinson, Alan. Haston, Dougal. Sandhu, Balwant. Scott, Doug. *Changabang.* Oxford University Press, 1976.

Booth, Pat. *Edmund Hillary – The Life of a Legend.* Moa Beckett, 1993.

Boukreev, Anatoli. DeWalt, G. Weston. *The Climb.* St. Martin's Press, 1997.

Bowley, Graham. *No Way Down – Life and Death on K2.* Harper, 2010.

Breashears, David. Salkeld, Audrey. *Last Climb – The Legendary Everest Expeditions of George Mallory.* National Geographic, 1999.

Breashears, David. *High Exposure – An Enduring Passion for Everest and Unforgiving Places.* Simon & Schuster, 1999.

Brown, Joe. *The Hard Years.* Victor Gollancz Ltd., 1972.

Brown, Rebecca A. *Women on High – Poineers of Mountaineering.* Appalachian Mountain Club Books, 2002.

Bruce, C.G. *The Assualt on Mount Everest 1922.* Longmans, Green & Co., 1923.

Bueler, William. *Mountains of The World – A Handbook for Climbers and Hikers.* The Mountaineers, 1970.

Buhl, Hermann. *Nanga Parbat Pilgrimage – The Lonley Challenge.* The Mountaineers, 1998.

Cameron, Ian. *Mountains of the Gods – The Himalayan and the Mountains of Central Asia.* Facts On File Publications, 1984.

Cameron, Ian. *To The Farthest Ends of the Earth – 150 Years of World Exploration by the Royal Geographical Society.* E.P. Dutton, 1980.

Carter, H. Adams – Editor. *The American Alpine Journal 1964.* Volume 14, Number 1, Issue 38. The American Alpine Club, 1964.

Cassin, Riccardo. *50 Years of Alpinism.* Diadem Books Ltd., 1981.

Child, Greg. *Thin Air – Encounters in the Himalayas.* Gibbs – Smith Publisher, 1988.

Clark, Ronald W. *Men, Myths & Mountains – The Life & Times of Mountaineering.* Thomas Y. Crowell Company, 1976.

Cleare, John. *Distant Mountains – Encounters with the World's Greatest Mountains.* Discovery Channel Books, 1998.

Cliff, Peter. *Ski Mountaineering.* Pacific Search Press, 1987.

Clinch Nicholas. *A Walk in the Sky.* The Mountaineers, 1982.

Collie, Norman. *From the Himalayas to Skye.* Ripping Yarns, 2003.

Conefrey, Mick and Jordan, Tim. *Mountain Men – A History of the Remarkable Climbers and Determined Eccentrics Who First Scaled the World's Most Famous Peaks.* Da Capo Press, 2001.

Conway, William Martin. *Climbing & Exploration in the Karakoram Himalayas.* Indus Publishing company, 2001.

Corbett, Edmund V. *Great True Mountain Stories.* Arco Publications Limited, 1957.

Craig, Robert W. *Storm & Sorrow in the High Pamirs.* Simon and Schuster, 1977.

Curran, Jim. *K2, Triumph and Tragedy.* The Mountaineers, 1987.

Curran, Jim. *High Achiever – The Life and Climbs of Chris Bonington.* The Mountaineers, 1999.

da Silva, Rachel – Editor. *LEADING OUT – Women Climbers Reaching For the Top.* Seal Press, 1992.

Desio, Prof. Ardito. *Ascent of K2 – Second Highest Peak in the World.* Elek Books, 1955.

Diemberger, Kurt. *The Endless Knot – K2, Mountain of Dreams and Destiny.* The Mountaineers, 1990.

Diemberger, Kurt. *Summits & Secrets.* George Allen & Unwin Ltd., 1971.

Diemberger, Kurt. *Spirits of the Air*. The Mountaineers, 1994.

Douglas, Ed. Tenzing – *Hero of Everest. A Biography of Tenzing Norgay*. National Geographic, 2003.

Douglas, John Scott. *Summits of Adventure*. Dodd, Mead & Company, 1954.

Eggler, Albert. T*he Everest – Lhotse Adventure*. George Allen & Unwin Ltd., 1957.

Eiselin, Max. *The Ascent of Dhaulagiri*. Oxford University Press, 1961.

Ershler, Phil and Susan. *Together On Top of the World – The Remarkable Story of the First Couple to Climb the Fabled Seven Summits*. Warner Books, 2007.

Evans, Charles. *Kangchenjunga – The Untrodden Peak*. E.P. Dutton & Co., 1957.

Fanshawe, Andy. Venables, Stephen. *Himalaya Alpine – Style – The Most Challenging Routes on the Highest Peaks*. The Mountaineers, 1996.

Fantin, Mario. Sherpa Himalaya Nepal. The English Book Store, 1974.

Faux, Ronald. *High Ambition – A Biography of Reinhold Messner*. Victor Gollancz Ltd., 1982.

Franco, Jean. *Makalu – A Team Triumphant*. Jonathan Cape, 1957.

Frison-Roche, Roger. Jouty, Sylvain. *A History of Mountain Climbing*. Flammarion, 1996.

Gammelgaard, Lene. *Climbing High – A Woman's Account of Surviving the Everest Tragedy*. Seal Press, 1999.

Gillman, Peter & Leni. *The Wildest Dream – The Biography of George Mallory*. The Mountaineers, 2000.

Gillman, Peter – Editor. *EVEREST – Eighty Years of Triumph and Tragedy*. The Mountaineers, 2000.

Green, Dudley. *Because It's There – The Life of George Mallory*. Tempus, 2005.

Gregory, Alfred. *Alfred Gregory's EVEREST*. Constable, 1993.

Harper, Stephen. *A Fatal Obsession – The Women of Cho Oyu: A Reporting Saga*. Book Guild Publishing, 2007.

Harvard, Andrew. Thompson, Todd. *Mountain of Storms – The American Expeditions to Dhaulagiri.* New York University Press, 1974.

Hattingh, Garth. *CLIMBING – The World's Best Sites.* Rizzoli, 1999.

Heim, Arnold. Gansser, August. *The Throne of the Gods – An Account of the First Swiss Expedition to the Himalayas.* The Macmillan Company, 1939.

Hemmleb, Jochen. Johnson, Larry A., Simonson, Eric R. *Ghosts of Everest – The Search for Mallory & Irvine. The Mountaineers Books, 1999.*

Hemmleb, Jochen. Simonson, Eric R. *Detectives on Everest – The 2001 Mallory & Irvine Research Expedition.* The Mountaineers Books, 2002.

Herrligkoffer, Karl M. *Nanga Parbat.* Elek Books, 1954.

Herzog, Maurice. *ANNAPURNA – Heroic Conquest of the Highest Mountain – 26,493 ft. – Ever Climbed By Man.* E.P. Dutton & Co. Inc., 1953.

Hillary, Sir Edmund. Lowe, George. *East of Everest – An Account of the New Zealand Alpine Club Himalayan Expedition to the Barun Valley in 1954.* E.P. Dutton and Company, 1955.

Hillary, Edmund. *High Adventure.* Hodder and Stoughton, 1955.

Hillary, Sir Edmund. Doig, Desmond. *High in the Thin Cold Air.* Doubleday & Company, Inc., 1962.

Hobson, Alan. *From Everest to Enlightenment – An Adventure of the Soul.* Inner Everests Inc., 1999.

Holzel, Tom and Salkeld, Audrey. *First on Everest – The Mystery of Mallory & Irvine.* Henry Holt and Company, 1986.

Hornbein, Thomas F. *Everest – The West Ridge.* The Sierra Club, 1965.

Houston, Charle S. Bates, Robert H. *K2 – The Savage Mountain.* McGraw – Hill Book Company, Inc. 1954.

Howard-Bury, Charles. Mallory, George Leigh. Keaney, Marian-Editor. *Everest Reconnaissance – The First Expedition of 1921.* Hodder & Stoughton, 1991.

Howard-Bury, Lieut. – *Col. C.K. MOUNT EVEREST – The Reconnaissance, 1921.* Longmans, Green and Co., 1922.

Hunt, John. *The Ascent of Everest*. Hodder & Stoughton, 1953.

Hunt, John. *Life Is Meeting*. Hodder & Stoughton, 1978.

Irving, R.L.G. *Ten Great Mountains*. J.M. Dent & Sons, 1947.

Irving, R.L.G. *A History of British Mountaineering*. B.T. Batsford Ltd., 1955.

Isserman, Maurice. Weaver, Stewart. *Fallen Giants – A History of Himalayan Mountaineering from the Age of Empire to the Age of Extremes*. Yale University Press, 2008.

Izzard, Ralph. *An Innocent on Everest*. E.P. Dutton & Co., 1954.

Johnston, Alexa. *Reaching the Summit – Edmund Hillary's Life of Adventure*. Dorling Kindersley Limited, 2005.

Jordan, Jennifer. *Savage Summit – The Life and Death of the First Women of K2*. Harper, 2005.

Jordan, Jennifer. *The Last Man on the Mountain – The Death of an American Adventurer on K2*. W.W. Norton and Company, 2010.

Kauffman, Andrew J. Putnam, William L. *K2 – The 1939 Tragedy. The Full Story of the Ill-Fated Wiessner Expedition*. The Mountaineers, 1992.

Keay, John. *When Men & Mountains Meet – The Explorers of the Western Himalayas 1820 – 75*. Archon Books, 1982.

King, Tom. *In the Shadow of the Giants – Mountain Ascents, Past and Present*. A.S. Barnes & Company, 1981.

Kodas, Michael. *High Crimes – The Fate of Everest in an Age of Greed*. Hyperion, 2008.

Kohli, Commander M.S. *Nine Atop Everest*. Orient Longmans Limited, 1969.

Krakauer, Jon. *Into Thin Air – A Personal Account of the Mt. Everest Disaster*. Villard, 1997.

Kukuczka, Jerzy. *My Vertical World – Climbing the 8,000-Meter Peaks*. The Mountaineers, 1992.

Kurz, Marcel. *The Mountain World 1953*. Harper & Brothers, 1953.

Kurz, Marcel. *The Mountain World 1954*. George Allen & Unwin Ltd., 1954.

Lacedelli, Lino. Cenacchi, Giovanni. *K2 – The Price of Conquest.* The Mountaineers Books, 2006.

Lane, Dr. Ferdinand C. T*he Story of Mountains.* Doubleday & Company, 1950.

LeBon, Leo. *Where Mountains Live – Twelve Great Treks of the World.* Aperture, 1987.

Lewis, Jon E. – Editor. *The Mammoth Book of EYEWITNESS EVEREST.* Carroll & Graf Publishers, 2003.

Long, John – Editor. *The High Lonesome – Epic Solo Climbing Stories.* Falcon, 1999.

Longstaff, Tom. *This My Voyage.* Charles Scribner's Sons, 1950.

Madge, Tim. *The Last Hero – Bill Tilman: A Biography of the Explorer.* The Mountaineers, 1995.

Maeder, Herbert – Editor. T*he Lure of the Mountains.* Elsevier   Phaidon, 1975.

Mantovani, Roberto. *EVEREST – The History of the Himalayan Giant.* The Mountaineers, 1997.

Maraini, Fosco. *Karakoram – The Ascent of Gasherbrum IV.* The Viking Press, 1961.

Mason, Kenneth. *Abode of Snow – A History of Himalayan Exploration and Mountaineering from Earliest Times to the Ascent of Everest.* Diadem Books, The Mountaineers, 1987.

McCallum, John D. *Everest Diary.* Follett Publishing Company, 1966.

McDonald, Bernadette and Amatt, John – Editors. *Voices from the Summit – The World's Great Mountaineers on the Future of Climbing.* Adventure Press, 2000.

McDonald, Bernadette. *Brotherhood of the Rope – The Biography of Charles Houston.* The Mountaineers Books, 2007.

McNamee, Gregory. *The Mountain World – A Literary Journey.* Sierra Club Books, 2000.

Meade, C.F. *Approach to the Hills.* John Murray, 1940.

Messner, Reinhold. *The Big Walls – From the North Face of the Eiger to the South Face of Dhaulagiri.* The Mountaineers Books, 2001.

Messner, Reinhold. *All 14 Eight-Thousanders.* The Mountaineers, 1999.

Messner, Reinhold. *EVEREST – Expedition to the Ultimate.* Oxford University Press, 1979.

Messner, Reinhold. *The Second Death of George Mallory – The Enigma and Spirit of Mount Everest.* St. Martin's Press, 2001.

Messner, Reinhold. Hofler, Horst. *Hermann Buhl – Climbing Without Compromise.* The Mountaineers Books, 2000.

Milne, Malcolm – Editor. *The Book of Modern Mountaineering.* G.P. Putnam's Sons, 1968.

Murray, W.H. *The Story of Everest 1921 – 1952.* E.P. Dutton & Co. Inc., 1953.

Neale, Jonathan. *Tigers of the Snow – How One Fateful Climb Made the Sherpas Mountaineering Legends.* Thomas Dunne Books, 2002.

Neate, Jill. *High Asia – An Illustrated History of the 7,000 Meter Peaks.* The Mountaineers, 1989.

Noel, Captain John. *The Story of Everest.* Little, Brown and Compnay, 1928.

Noel, Sandra. *Everest Pioneer – The Photographs of Captain John Noel.* Sutton Publishing, 2003.

Norgay, Jamling Tenzing. Coburn, Broughton. *Touching My Father's Soul – A Sherpa's Journey to the Top of Everest.* Harper San Francisco, 2001.

Norton, Lieutenant-Colonel E.F. *The Fight for Everest: 1924.* Longmans, Green & Co., 1925.

Noyce, Wilfrid. *South Col – A Personal Story of the Ascent of Everest.* William Sloane Associates, Inc., 1955.

Ortner, Sherry. *Life and Death on Mount Everest – Sherpas and Himalayan Mountaineering.* Princeton University Press, 1999.

Palin, Michael. *Himalaya.* Weidenfeld & Nicolson, 2004.

Parsons, Mike and Rose, Mary B. *Invisible on Everest – Innovation and the Gear Makers.* Northern Liberties Press, 2003.

Patey, Tom. *One Man's Mountains.* Victor Gollancz Ltd., 1975.

Patterson, Bruce. *Canadians on Everest.* Detselig Enterprises Ltd., 1990.

Perrin, Jim. *The Villain – The Life of Don Whillans.* Hutchinson, 2005.

Petzoldt, Patricia. *On Top of the World – My Adventures with My Mountain-Climbing Husband.* Thomas Y. Crowell, 1953.

Poole, Michael Crawford. *The Love of Mountains.* Crescent Books, 1980.

Pye, David. *George Leigh Mallory – A Memoir* by David Pye. Orchid Press, 2002.

Ramsay, Cynthia Russ. *Sir Edmund Hillary – The People of Everest.* Andrews McMeel Publishing, 2002.

Reinisch, Gertrude. *Wanda Rutkiewicz – A Caravan of Dreams.* Carreg, 2000.

Ridgeway, Rick. *The Last Step – The American Ascent of K2.* The Mountaineers, 1980.

Ridgeway, Rick. *The Boldest Dream – The Story of Twelve Who Climbed Mount Everest.* Harcourt Brace Jovanovich, 1979.

Ringholz, Raye C. *On Belay – The Life of Legendary Mountaineer Paul Petzoldt.* The Mountaineers, 1997.

Roberts, Eric. *Welzenbach's Climbs.* The Mountaineers, 1980.

Roberts, David. *True Summit.* Simon & Schuster, 2000.

Robertson, David. *George Mallory.* Faber and Faber, 1969.

Roper, Robert. *Fatal Mountaineer – The High-Altitude Life and Death of Willi Unsoeld, American Himalayan Legend.* St. Martin's Griffin, 2002.

Roskelley, John. *Nanda Devi – The Tragic Expedition.* Stackpole Books, 1987.

Ruttledge, Hugh. *Attack on Everest.* Robert M. McBride & Company, 1935.

Ruttledge, Hugh. *Everest 1933.* Hodder & Stoughton, 1934.

Ruttledge, Hugh. *EVEREST: The Unfinished Adventure.* Hodder & Stoughton, 1937.

Sale, Richard. *Broad Peak.* Carreg, 2004.

Sale, Richard. Cleare, John. *Climbing the World's 14 Highest Mountains – The History of the 8000-Meter Peaks.* The Mountaineers Books, 2000.

Salkeld, Audrey. *Climbing Everest – Tales of Triumph and Tragedy on the World's Highest Mountain.* National Geographic, 2003.

Salkeld, Audrey. *People in High Places – Approaches to Tibet.* Jonathan Cape, 1991.

Scott, Doug. MacIntyre, Alex. *The Shishapangma Expedition.* The Mountaineers, 1984.

Sedeen, Margaret – Editor. *Mountain Worlds.* The National Geographic, 1988.

Sella, Vittorio. *Summit.* Aperture, 1999.

Shipton, Eric. *Upon That Mountain.* Hodder & Stoughton, 1944.

Shipton, Eric. *The Mount Everest Reconnaissance Expedition 1951.* Hodder and Stoughton, 1952.

Shipton, Eric. *Mountain Conquest.* American Heritage Publishing Co., 1966.

Shipton, Eric. *The Six Mountain – Travel Books.* Diadem Books Ltd., 1985.

Shirakawa, Yoshikazu. *Himalayas.* Harry N. Abrams, Inc., 1976.

Singh, Brigadier Gyan. *Lure of Everest – First Indian Everest Expedition.* The Publications Division, 1961.

Sircar, Joydeep. *Himalayan Handbook.* Rita Sircar, 1979.

Slesser, Malcolm. *With Friends in High Places – An Anatomy of Those Who Take to the Hills.* Mainstream Publishing, 2004.

Smith, J.R. *Everest – The Man and the Mountain.* Whittles Publishing, 1999.

Smythe, F.S. The Kangchenjunga Adventure. Victor Gollancz Ltd., 1930.

Smythe, F.S. *Kamet Conquered.* Hodder & Stoughton, 1947.

Smythe, F.S. *The Spirit of the Hills.* Hodder & Stoughton, 1935.

Smythe, Frank S. *Camp Six.* Adam & Charles Black, 1956.

Snaith, Stanley. *At Grips with Everest.* The Percy Press, 1937.

Somervell, T. Howard. *After Everest – The Experiences of a Mountaineer and Medical Missionary.* Hodder and Stoughton Limited, 1936.

Steele, Peter. Eric Shipton: *Everest & Beyond.* The Mountaineers, 1998.

Stokes, Brummie. *Soldiers and Sherpas – A Taste for Adventure.* Michael Joseph, 1988.

Styles, Showell. *On Top of the World – An Illustrated History of Mountaineering and Mountaineers.* The Macmillan Company, 1967.

Summers, Julie. *Fearless On Everest – The Quest for Sandy Irvine.* Weidenfeld & Nicolson, 2000.

Tenzing. *After Everest – An Autobiography.* George Allen & Unwin Ltd., 1977.

Tenzing, Tashi. *Tenzing Norgay and the Sherpas of Everest.* Ragged Mountain Press, 2001.

Terray, Lionel. *Conquistadors of the Useless – From the Alps to Annapurna.* Victor Gollancz Ltd., 1963.

Terray, Lionel. *The Borders of the Impossible – From the Alps to Annapurna.* Doubleday & Company, 1964.

Tichy, Herbert. *Cho Oyu – By Favour of the Gods.* Methuen & Co. Ltd., 1957.

Tichy, Herbert. *HIMALAYA.* G.P. Putnam's Sons, 1970.

Tilman, H.W. *The Ascent of Nanda Devi.* The Macmillan Company, 1937.

Tilman, H.W. *Mount Everest 1938.* Cambridge University Press, 1948.

Tobias, Michael Charles and Drasdo, Harold – Editors. *The Mountain Spirit.* The Overlook Press, 1979.

Tucker, John. *Kangchenjunga – The Story of an Unprecedented Mountaineering Experience.* Abelard – Schuman Limited, 1955.

Tullis, Julie. *Clouds from Both Sides.* Sierra Club Books, 1987.

Ullman, James Ramsey. *Tiger of the Snows – The Autobiography of Tenzing of Everest.* G.P. Putnam's Sons, 1955.

Ullman, James Ramsey. *Kingdom of Adventure: Everest*. William Sloane Associates, 1947.

Ullman, James Ramsey. *Americans on Everest – The Official Account of the Ascent Led By Norman G. Dyhrenfurth*. J.B. Lippincott Company, 1964.

Ullman, James Ramsey. *Man of Everest – The Autobiography of Tenzing*. The Reprint Society, 1956.

Ullman, James Ramsey. *The Age of Mountaineering*. J.B. Lippincott Company, 1954.

Unsworth, Walt. *Hold the Heights – The Foundations of Mountaineering*. The Mountaineers, 1994.

Unsworth, Walt. *Everest – The Mountaineering History*. Third Edition. The Mountaineers, 2000.

Venables, Stephen. *Lost Mountains – Climbs in the Himalaya – Two Expeditions to Kashmir*. Thunder's Mouth Press, 2001.

Venables, Stephen. *EVEREST – Kangshung Face*. Hodder & Stoughton, 1989.

Venables, Stephen. *EVEREST – Summit of Achievement*. Simon & Schuster, 2003.

Venables, Stephen. *First Ascent – Pioneering Mountain Climbs*. Firefly Books, 2008.

Vermeulen, James P. – Editor. *Mountain Journeys – Stories of Climbers and Their Climbs*. The Overlook Press, 1989.

Viesturs, Ed. Roberts, David. *No Shortcuts to the Top – Climbing the World's 14 Highest Peaks*. Broadway Books, 2006.

Viesturs, Ed. Roberts, David. *K2 – Life and Death on the World's Most Dangerous Mountain*. Broadway Books, 2009.

von Furer-Haimendorf, Christoph. *The Sherpas of Nepal*. University of California Press, 1964.

Ward, Michael – Editor. *The Mountaineer's Companion*. Eyre & Spottiswoode, 1966.

Ward, Michael. *EVEREST – A Thousand Years of Exploration*. The Ernest Press, 2003.

Weathers, Beck. *Left for Dead – My Journey Home from Everest*. Villard, 2000.

Webster, Ed. *Snow in the Kingdom – My Storm Years on Everest*. Mountain Imagery, 2000.

Weihenmayer, Erik. *Touch the Top of the World – A Blind Man's Journey to Climb Farther Than the Eye Can See.* Dutton, 2001.

Wells, Colin. *A Brief History of British Mountaineering.* The Mountain Heritage Trust, 2001.

Whillans, Don and Ormerod, Alick. *Don Whillans – Portrait of a Mountaineer.* Heinemann, 1971.

Willis, Clint. *The Boys of Everest – Chris Bonington and the Tragedy of Climbing's Greatest Generation.* Carroll & Graf Publishers, 2006.

Whittaker, Jim. A *Life on the Edge – Memoirs of Everest and Beyond.* The Mountaineers, 1999.

Whittaker, Lou. Gabbard, Andrea. *Lou Whittaker – Memoirs of a Mountain Guide.* The Mountaineers, 1994.

Wickwire, Jim. Bullitt, Dorothy. *Addicted To Danger – A Memoir about Affirming Life in the Face of Death.* Pocket Books, 1998.

Wielicki, Krzysztof. *Crown of Himalaya – 14 X 8000.* Krakow, 1997.

Willis, Clint – Editor. *Epics on Everest – Stories of Survival from the World's Highest Peak.* Thunder's Mouth Press, 2003.

Younghusband, Sir Francis. *The Everest – The Epic of Great Mount Everest.* Cosmo Publications, 1986.

Zheng, Zhou. Zhenkai, Liu. *Footprints on the Peaks – Mountaineering in China.* Cloudcap, 1995.

FOUR

AUSTRALIA-OCEANIA

The Island Peaks

Years 1794 to 2011

"To those who have struggled with them, the mountains reveal beauties they will not disclose to those who make no effort. That is the reward the mountains give to effort. And it is because they have so much to give and give it so lavishly to those who will wrestle with them that men love the mountains and go back to them again and again… The mountains reserve their choice gifts for those who stand upon their summits."

Sir Francis Younghusband
British mountaineer and explorer
(1863 – 1942)

AUSTRALIA

April 30, 1985. On this date, American mountaineer Dick Bass (1929 –   ) reached the summit of Mount Everest thereby becoming the first person to climb the world's Seven Summits (the highest mountain summit on each of the world's seven continents). On his Seven Summit quest, Bass reached the summit of Mount Kosciusko (7,310 feet/2,228 meters) in December of 1983, the highest mountain in Australia—one of the world's seven continents.

On August 5, 1986, Canadian Patrick Morrow (1952 –   ) reached the summit of Mount Elbrus (18,510 feet/5,641 meters), the highest mountain in Europe and proclaimed that he, not Dick Bass, was the first person to reach all Seven Summits because he had climbed Carstensz Pyramid (16,024 feet/4,884 meters) in western New Guinea (a.k.a. Irian Jaya). Morrow claimed that Carstensz Pyramid was the highest summit in Australasia which included Australia. The Seven Summits debate of Carstensz Pyramid vs. Mount Kosciusko was then begun in the climbing community and it continues even today. Many of those climbers that claim to have climbed all Seven Summits have chosen either Carstensz Pyramid or Mount Kosciusko to complete their list. To eliminate any doubt and receive total credit, there is a growing list of mountaineers that decided to climb both mountains for a total of eight summits. I understand this debate and I have heard both sides of this climbing issue.

Australia is one of the world's seven continents. There are nine mountains in the Snowy Range of the Australian Alps (New South Wales) over 7,000 feet (2,133 meters). The highest of these mountains is Mount Kosciusko (7,317 feet/2,230 meters). Although this gentle mountain does not present any mountaineering challenges (technical climbing or altitude), climbers still pursue its summit because of its Seven Summit status. However, the most well-known mountain in Australia is probably Ayres Rock (2,845 feet/867 meters) which is located in the Northern Territory of Australia southwest of the town named Alice Springs. This is the world's second largest rock monolith and is an Aboriginal sacred site. The first ascent of Ayres Rock was on July 20, 1873 by two climbers named Gosse and Kamram. Since 1985, Ayres Rock has been known as Mount Uluru—an Aboriginal name meaning "island mountain." A rope railing has been installed to assist those who wish to climb the normal route to the top of Uluru.

Many current world atlases and geographical internet sites clearly indicate that Carstensz Pyramid in western New Guinea is actually located in Asia not Australasia. From a geological standpoint (plate tectonics), the western half of New Guinea lies in Asia not Australasia. The dividing line is known as the Java Trench which divides New Guinea into two nations. Carstensz Pyramid then represents the tallest mountain in the world that is located on an island. Some climbers refer to Carstensz Pyramid as the world's "eighth" summit.

Ten Highest Mountains in Australia

1.	Mount Kosciusko	7,317 ft./2,230 m.
2.	Mount Townsend	7,248 ft./2,209 m.
3.	Mount Twynam	7,202 ft./2,195 m.
4.	Rams Head	7,185 ft./2,190 m.
5.	Unnamed peak on Etheridge Ridge	7,152 ft./2,180 m.

Ten Highest Mountains in Australia (continued)

6. Rams Head North   7,143 ft./2,177 m.
7. Alice Rawson Peak   7,087 ft./2,160 m.
8. Unnamed peak southwest of Abbott Peak   7,084 ft./2,159 m.
9. Abbott Peak   7,037 ft./2,145 m.
10. Carruthers Peak   7,037 ft./2,145 m.

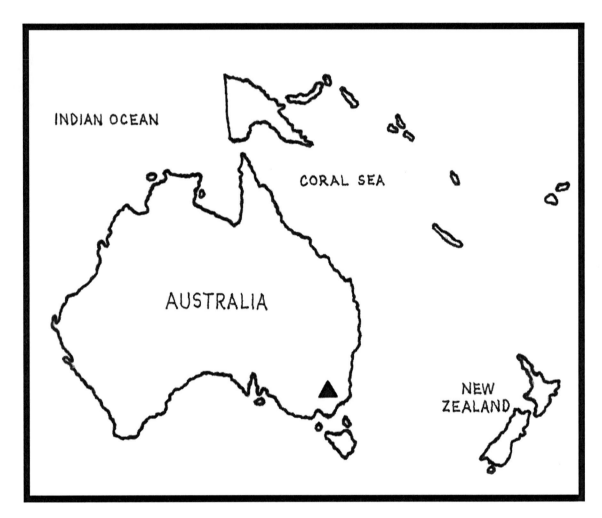

▲ Highest Peak in Australia: Mount Kosciusko – 7,317 ft./2,230 m.
Location: Snowy Mountains in New South Wales
First Ascent Date: 1834
Expedition: Polish

OCEANIA

The vast area to the north and east of Australia is known as Oceania. This geographical term was coined in 1831 by French naval officer and explorer Jules Dumont d'Urville (1790 – 1842) to denote an ethnic and geographical grouping of 25,000 islands east and northeast of Australia. These groupings are known as Melanesia, Micronesia, and Polynesia and include the islands of New Zealand, Hawaii, Fiji, Samoa, Papua New Guinea, etc. Australasia is traditionally included in Oceania. This chapter includes sixteen (16) peak first ascents, nineteen (19) first ascents, and forty-four other mountaineering events in both Australia and Oceania.

Ten Highest Peaks in Oceania

1.	Mount Wilhelm	PapuaNew Guinea	14,793 ft./4,509 m.
2.	Mount Giluwe	Papua New Guinea	14,331 ft./4,368 m.
3.	Mount Herbert	Papua New Guinea	13,999 ft./4,267 m.
4.	Mauna Kea	Hawaii	13,796 ft./4,205 m.
5.	Mauna Loa	Hawaii	13,679 ft./4,169 m.
6.	Mount Victoria	Papua New Guinea	13,364 ft./4,073 m.
7.	Mount Albert Edward	Papua New Guinea	13,091 ft./3,990 m.
8.	Mount Cook	New Zealand	12,311 ft./3,752 m.
9.	The Sugarloaf	Papua New Guinea	12,198 ft./3,718 m.
10.	Mount Michael	Papua New Guinea	1,966 ft./3,647 m.

Australia-Oceania Timeline

1794: PEAK FIRST ASCENT *MAUNA LOA*

February 16. Naturalist Archibald Menzies, Lt. Joseph Baker, and two others made the first ascent of Mauna Loa (13,679 ft./4,169 m.) on the island of Hawaii. Menzies calculated the height of this volcano to within fifty feet of the accepted elevation. The last eruption was on March 24, 1984. Mauna Loa means "long mountain" in the Hawaiian language.

1823: PEAK FIRST ASCENT *MAUNA KEA*

August 26. The first recorded ascent of Mauna Kea (13,796 ft./4,205 m.) on the island of Hawaii was by a missionary party led by Joseph F. Goodrich. Mauna Kea in the Hawaiian language means "white mountain." This extinct volcano is known to be the highest mountain in the world base to summit— 32,796 feet or 9,996 meters. There are eleven summits in Hawaii over 13,000 feet (3,962 meters). However, nine of these eleven are sub-peaks of either Mauna Loa or Mauna Kea.

1834: PEAK FIRST ASCENT *KOSCIUSKO* [7]▲

A Dr. Lhotsky made the first ascent of the peak later to be known as Mount Kosciusko (7,317 ft./2,230 m.), the highest mountain in Australia. A dispute regarding a claimed first ascent of this peak in 1840 by Polish explorer Count Paul Edmond de Strzelecki remains unresolved. Some mountaineers consider Kosciusko, in the Snowy Mountain Range, to be one of the Seven Summits while others believe that Carstencz Pyramid (16,023 ft./4,884 m.) in Papua is the highest peak in Australasia. Kosciusko was a famous Polish-American patriot.

1839: PEAK FIRST ASCENT *EGMONT*

Naturalist Ernst Dieffenbach made the first ascent of Mount Egmont (8,260 ft./2,517 m.) on the north island of New Zealand. As of 1983, Mount Egmont had been the location of 30 recorded deaths. This may be the most popular mountain to climb in New Zealand.

1863:

Sir James Hector (1834 – 1907) became the first person to set foot on the glaciers of New Zealand. Hector was a Scottish geologist, naturalist, and surgeon.

1873: PEAK FIRST ASCENT *AYERS ROCK*

July 20. The first ascent of Ayers Rock (2,845 ft./867 m.) in Australia was made by surveyor William C. Gosse who named this unusual rock for Sir Henry Ayers, Chief Secretary of South Australia in 1873. The second ascent occurred 58 years later in 1931. This 340 meter (1,116 feet) high sandstone rock formation (above ground level) is located in the southern part of the Northern territory. Alice Springs is the largest town near Ayers rock.

---

[7]▲ One of the world's Seven Summits

1882:

March 3. The Reverend William Spotswood Green (1847 – 1919) of Ireland spent a stormy night near the crest of Mount Cook (12,349 ft./3,764 m.) in New Zealand after nearly making the first ascent with guides Ulrich Kaufmann and Emile Boss (both guides from Grindelwald, Switzerland). This climbing party was stopped by a deep crevasse on the ridge twenty minutes (165 ft./50 m.) from the summit. The actual first ascent of Mount Cook occurred in 1894. Some climbers think of Rev. Green as the originator of mountaineering in New Zealand.

1886: PEAK FIRST ASCENT *RUAPEHU*

January 8. James Park, C. Dalin, and W.H. Dunnage made the first ascent of Ruapehu (9,177 ft./2,797 m.), the highest point on New Zealand's North Island. This sacred volcano in Tongariro National Park last erupted in 1950 – 51. Ruapehu is the only mountain on the North Island to have any glaciers (seven).

1888: PEAK FIRST ASCENT *VICTORIA*

Sir William MacGregor's expedition made the first ascent of Mount Victoria (13,364 ft./4,073 m.) in the Owen Stanley Range of Papua New Guinea.

1891:

June 28. The New Zealand Alpine Club was founded in Christchurch, New Zealand by Mr. A.P. Harper, George Mannering, and Marmaduke Dixon. The first meeting was attended by twenty-seven members. Mr. G.E. Mannering became the honorary secretary. This club now has 3,000 members and eleven sections (1 in Australia and 10 in New Zealand).

1891:

The Ball Hut (two rooms) for climbers was constructed at the junction of the Ball and Tasman glaciers below Mount Cook in New Zealand.

1893:

New Zealand climbers Marmaduke Dixon (1828 – 1895) and Tom Fyfe (1870 –)used skis on the Grand Plateau of Mount Cook (12,349 ft./3,764 m.) in New Zealand. This was the first recorded use of skis in New Zealand.

1894: PEAK FIRST ASCENT *COOK*

December 25. Three New Zealand mountaineers—Thomas C. Fyfe – leader (1870 –), George Graham, and Jack Clarke (1875 –) made the first ascent of Mount Cook (12,349 ft./3,764 m.) in New Zealand via the Linda Glacier. They wore hobnailed boots and used a hemp rope. This peak was officially named Mount Cook in 1851 after the great Yorkshire navigator. The Maori name for Mount Cook was "Aoraki" meaning "cloud piercer."

1894: FIRST ASCENT

Late December. Swiss mountain guide Matthias Zurbriggen (1856 – 1917) made the first solo ascent of Mount Cook (12,349 ft./3,764 m.) in New Zealand.

1895: PEAK FIRST ASCENT *TASMAN*

February 6. E.A. Fitzgerald, Matthias Zurbriggen, and Jack Clarke made the first ascent of Mount Tasman (11,475 ft./3,497 m.), the second highest peak in New Zealand via the southwest ridge. Tasman was named after the first European to visit New Zealand—Dutch explorer Abel Tasman. It is located on the South Island just north of Mount Cook.

1895: PEAK FIRST ASCENT *SEFTON*

February 14. E.A. Fitzgerald and Swiss guide Matthias Zurbriggen made the first ascent of Mount Sefton (10,358 ft./3,157 m.) in New Zealand (South Island). On the descent, Zurbriggen placed two large iron spikes to rappel from—the first use of pitons in New Zealand mountaineering.

1895: FIRST ASCENT

March 14. Swiss mountaineering guide Matthias Zurbriggen (1856 – 1917) accomplished a solo first ascent of Mount Cook's (12,349 ft./3,764 m.) east face. He climbed the final 3,850 feet (1,173 meters) solo.

1907: PEAK FIRST ASCENT *LENDENFELD, TORRES, HAAST, DOUGLAS*

February. Mountaineers E. Teichelmann, E. Newton, and A. Graham made four first ascents on the South Island of New Zealand. They climbed:

Mount Lendenfeld	10,450 ft./3,185 m.
Mount Torres	10,345 ft./3,153 m.
Mount Haast	10,296 ft./3,138 m.
Mount Douglas	10,109 ft./3,081 m.

1909: PEAK FIRST ASCENT *ASPIRING*

November 23. New Zealand mountaineers Jack Clarke, Alec Graham, and Bernard Head made the first ascent of Mount Aspiring (9,958 feet/3,035 meters) on the South Island of New Zealand via the west face. This peak is known as "the Matterhorn of the Southern Hemisphere."

1910: FIRST ASCENT

December 3. Australian woman mountaineer Freda du Faur (1882 – 1935) became the first woman to climb Mount Cook (12,349 ft./3,764 m.) in New Zealand. She made this ascent in six hours. Her guides were Peter (1878 – 1961) and Alec Graham (1881 – 1957). They ascended Earles Ridge in six hours.

1913: FIRST ASCENT

January 4. Australian mountaineer Freda du Faur (1882 – 1935) and New Zealand mountaineers Peter Graham and Darby Thompson (– 1914)made the first ascent of the Grand Traverse (3 summits) on New Zealand's Mount Cook (12,349 ft./3,764 m.). This traverse was approximately one mile of hard, exposed ice. They ascended the East Ridge and descended the Zurbriggen Ridge. This same party made the first traverse of Mount Sefton (10,332 ft./3,149 m.) on February 10. Freda du Faur was also the first woman to climb the three highest peaks in New Zealand: Mount Cook, Mount Tasman, and Mount Sefton.

1913:

Canadian mountain guide Conrad Kain (born in Austria, 1883 – 1934) arrived in New Zealand. During his first season in New Zealand (January 7 – March 28), Kain made 48 climbs of which 18 were peak first ascents. On February 22nd, he made the sixteenth overall ascent of Mount Cook.

1914:

British climber Sydney King and his two guides Darby Thompson and Jock Richmond became the first mountaineers to be killed on Mount Cook (12,349 ft./3,764 m.) in New Zealand. They were caught in an avalanche.

1914:

During his second climbing season in New Zealand, Canadian guide Conrad Kain (1883 – 1934) made thirty-three climbs of which nine were peak first ascents. This season for Kain lasted from September 23, 1914 to April 7, 1915.

1915:

Canadian mountain guide Conrad Kain (1883 – 1934) spent a third climbing season in New Zealand (December 6, 1915 to March 14, 1916). He made nineteen climbs of which two were peak first ascents.

1916:

Canadian mountain guide Conrad Kain (1883 – 1934) made a traverse of Mount Cook (12,349 ft./3,764 m.) in New Zealand. His client was Mrs. J. Thomson of Wellington, New Zealand. Kain guided her to fourteen New Zealand summits. This was the seventeenth overall ascent of Mount Cook and may have been Kain's greatest climb in New Zealand. Kain would eventually be credited with 29 first ascents in New Zealand over many climbing seasons.

1919:

July 20. Edmund Perceival Hillary (1919 – 2008) was born in Tuakau, a township 40 miles/20 kilometers from Auckland, New Zealand. Hillary and Tenzing Norgay Sherpa (1914 – 1986) made the first ascent of Mount Everest (29,035 ft./8,849 m.) in 1953.

1919: FIRST ASCENT

New Zealand mountaineer Samuel Turner made the first complete solo ascent of Mount Cook (12,349 ft./3,764 m.) in New Zealand.

1922:

New Zealand mountain guide Peter Graham (1878 – 1961) made 40 new climbing routes in the Mount Cook district including 3 new ridge routes and 2 new traverses on Mount Cook (12,349 ft./3,764 m.). Graham accomplished these new routes during the 1906 to 1922 period.

1923: FIRST ASCENT

August. Frank Milne (1891 – 1933), Head Guide of the Mount Cook Company in New Zealand, made the first winter ascent of Mount Cook (12,349 ft./3,764 m.).

1930:

New Zealand mountaineers J. Pascoe, R.R. Chester, and A.H. Willis traversed eleven unclimbed peaks on New Zealand's South Island in one long day.

1934:

December. G.C.T. Burns and Max Townsend accomplished an eight-pass mountain traverse from Arthur's Pass to Mount Cook.

1935:

Sixteen-year old New Zealand boy Edmund Hillary (1919 – 2008) traveled 150 miles/250 kilometers south of Auckland, New Zealand on a school trip to Mount Ruapehu (9,177 ft./2,797 m.). This volcano is located in Tongariro National Park on the North Island of New Zealand. This was Hillary's first experience on snow in the mountains. The mountaineering seed was planted here that eighteen years later (1953) would culminate with Hillary's first ascent of Mount Everest (29,035 ft./8,849 m.) in Nepal.

1937: FIRST ASCENT

New Zealand mountaineers Lesley "Dan" Bryant and Lud Mahan made the first ascent of the East Ridge of Mount Cook (12,349 ft./3,764 m.) in New Zealand. This 5,578 foot/1,700 meter high ridge took 12 hours to climb.

1938: PEAK FIRST ASCENT *WILHELM*

August 15. Government patrol officer Leigh Vial and two Papuan New Guineans made the first ascent of Mount Wilhelm (14,793 ft./4,508 m.) in Papua New Guinea. This is the most accessible peak to climb in Papua New Guinea and is the highest peak in Oceania.

1938:

New Zealand conservationist, explorer, mountaineer, photographer, and surgeon Dr. Ebenezer Teichelmann (1859 – 1938) died at age 79. After immigrating to New Zealand in 1897, he made twenty-six first ascents in New Zealand and the third ascent of Mount Cook in 1905.

1939:

Edmund Hillary (age 20) took his first long trip to the South Island of New Zealand. He stayed at the Hermitage near the peaks of the Southern Alps. After overhearing several climbers in the lounge talk about their climb of Mount Cook (12,349 ft./3,764 m.), Hillary became particularly excited about this activity and decided at that moment to take up mountaineering and climb something. He soon climbed his first mountain—Mount Oliver (7,500 ft./2,286 m.)—in New Zealand.

"I retreated to a corner of the lounge filled with a sense of futility at the dull, mundane nature of my existence. Those chaps, now, were really getting a bit of excitement out of life. I decided then and there to take up mountaineering. Tomorrow I'd climb something!"

> 1955
> Sir Edmund Hillary (1919 – 2008)
> Quote describing how he got started climbing.

1946:

New Zealand mountaineer Edmund Hillary (1919 – 2008) met New Zealand's foremost climber Harry Ayres (1912 – 1987) who taught Hillary proper ice-craft and made many New Zealand ascents with Hillary. Ayers became the first Ranger of Mount Cook National Park in 1958 and the first Chief Ranger in 1959.

1947:

January. New Zealand mountaineer Edmund P. Hillary (1919 – 2008) made his first ascent of New Zealand's Aoraki or Mount Cook (12,349 ft./3,764 m.) with outstanding New Zealand guide Harry Ayres (1912 – 1987).

1948: FIRST ASCENT

February 6. New Zealand mountaineers Edmund Hillary and Ruth Adams and their two guides Harry Ayres and Mick Sullivan made the first ascent of Mount Cook's south ridge in New Zealand.

1948:

As of this year, there had been 74 ascents of Mount Cook (12,349 ft./3,764 m.) in New Zealand.

1951:

January 28. Mrs. June Ashurst and her New Zealand mountain guide Harry Ayers (1912 – 1987) accomplished a double traverse from Mount Dampier (11,287 ft./3,440 m.) to Mount Hicks (10,443 ft./3,183 m.) in twenty-two hours of climbing. Mount Hicks is also known as St. David's Dome.

1953:

The Mount Cook National Park (173,000 acres) was officially established in New Zealand.

1956:

American mountaineer Bill Hackett (1918 – 1999) reached the summit of Mount Kosciuszko (7,310 ft./2,228 m.) in Australia. This ascent was Hackett's fourth continental summit.

1961: FIRST ASCENT

November. New Zealand mountaineers Don Cowie, Pete Farrell, Lyn Crawford, and Vic Walsh made the first ascent of the East Face (4,922 ft./1,500 m.) of Mount Cook (12,349 ft./3,764 m.) in New Zealand. This long, serious face climb had been attempted numerous times without success.

1963:

New Zealand mountaineer Sir Edmund Hillary (1919 – 2008) and his wife Louise (1930 – 1975) established the non-profit organization named The Himalayan Trust of New Zealand to assist the Sherpa people of Nepal.

1965: FIRST ASCENT

March 10. American climbers John Evans (1938 –   ) and Jeff Foott made the first ascent of Mitre Peak's (5,551 ft./1,692 m.) north face on New Zealand's South Island. This four-day climb of 5,500 vertical feet included a 38-hour bivouac due to over four inches of rain.

1969: Equipment – Wire Nuts

Australian Roland Pauligk (1938 –) produced a series (twelve sizes) of brass wire nuts called "RPs."

1970: FIRST ASCENT

November. New Zealand mountaineers John Glasgow and Peter Glough made the first ascent of the 6,562 foot/2,000 meter Caroline Face of Mount Cook (12,349 ft./3,764 m.). Two days later, fellow mountaineers Graeme Dingle and George Harris repeated the same route. This was the last unclimbed face on Mount Cook. Numerous attempts to climb it had been made and four mountaineers had died trying to climb it.

1971:

New Zealand mountaineers Jill and Graeme Dingle made the first winter traverse of the Southern Alps of New Zealand.

1971:

Well-known New Zealand mountaineer Sir Edmund Hillary (1919 – 2008, Mount Everest first ascent in 1953) made his last major climb at age 52. He completed a grand traverse of Mount Cook (12,349 ft./3,764 m.), New Zealand's highest mountain.

1971: FIRST ASCENT

New Zealand mountaineer Bill Denz (1951 – 1983) at age 20 completed the first solo ascent of Mount Cook's (12,349 ft./3,764 m.) Zurbriggen Ridge followed by the Grand Traverse of Mount Cook.

Denz completed 14 other landmark ascents in the Mount Cook region. Unfortunately, he was killed in 1983 at age 32 in an avalanche on Makalu (27,766 ft./8,463 m.) in the Nepal Himalayas.

1972: FIRST ASCENT

New Zealand mountaineers Rob Rainsbury and John Visser made the first ascent of the Central Spur of the West Face of Mount Elie de Beaumont (10,200 ft./3,109 m.) in the Southern Alps of New Zealand. This ice and snow mountain is the northern most 3,000 meter peak in the Southern Alps. It is the 14th highest peak in New Zealand and was named for French geologist Jean-Baptiste Elie de Beaumont (1798 – 1874).

1973: FIRST ASCENT

New Zealand mountaineer Bill Denz (1951 – 1983) solo climbed the east face of Mount Cook (12,349 ft./3,764 m.) in New Zealand in nine hours.

1973: FIRST ASCENT

New Zealand mountaineer Bill Denz (1951 – 1983) was a member of a team that made the first ascent of the Adelaide Face of Marian Peak (6,897 ft./2,102 m.) in the Darran Mountains of New Zealand's South Island. Denz established twenty new climbing routes in the Darran Mountains.

1973:

American climber Henry Barber (1953 –   ) spent 44 days in Australia climbing in 27 different areas in 6 different states. He climbed 100 rock routes of which 60 were first ascents or first free ascents.

1974:

The New Zealand Mountain Guides Association was established.

1975: FIRST ASCENT

June (winter). New Zealand climbers Bill Denz (1951 – 1983) and Phil Herron (– 1975) made the first winter ascent of the Balfour Face of Mount Tasman (11,484 ft./3,500 m.) in New Zealand. They broke the picks of both their ice axes during this difficult snow and ice climb.

1977:

New Zealand mountaineer Peter Hillary (1954 –   ), son of Sir Edmund Hillary (1919 – 2008), made the first ski descent of Mount Aspiring (9,958 feet/3,035 meters) on the South Island of New Zealand. First climbed in 1910, Mount Aspiring is known as the "Matterhorn of New Zealand."

1977:

New Zealand mountaineers P. Scaife and D. MacNulty traversed the main mountain ridge on the South Island of New Zealand. The reached the summits of 34 peaks (18 over 3,000 meters/9,843 feet). This traverse was from Elie de Beaumont to Harper Saddle.

1977 – 1978:

December to February. New Zealand mountaineers Russell Brice (1952 –   ) and Paddy Freaney first climbed all 31 peaks in New Zealand over 3,000 meters (9,843 feet) in one climbing season.

1979:

To date, 67 ascents have been made of New Zealand's Mount Cook (12,349 ft./3,764 m.) involving 150 climbers. Ten climbers per year would climb Mount Cook in the 1930s.

1982:

New Zealand ski mountaineers made the first ski descent of Mount Cook (12,349 ft./3,764 m.) in New Zealand. They skied from the summit to the Tasman Glacier.

1983: FIRST ASCENT

October. Well-known New Zealand mountaineer Bill Denz (1951 – 1983) died in an avalanche on Makalu (27,826 ft./8,481 m.) in the Himalayas. Denz established many new climbing routes, winter first ascents and solo ascents in the New Zealand Alps (South Island). Many of his first ascents occurred in the Darran Mountains near the south-west coast of New Zealand's South Island. In July of 1983, Denz and Kim Logan made the first winter ascent of the south face of Sabre Peak (7,093 ft./2,162 m.)

1983:

December. American climber Dick Bass (1929 –   ) reached his sixth continental summit of the Seven Summits during the 1983 calendar year. Here is a summary of these six summits:

Dates	Peaks	Elevations
January 21, 1983	Aconcagua – South America	22,841 ft./6,962 m.
July 6, 1983	Mount McKinley – North America	20,320 ft./6,193 m.
September 1, 1983	Mount Kilimanjaro – Africa	19,340 ft./5,895 m.
September 13, 1983	Mount Elbrus – Europe	18,510 ft./5,642 m.
November 30, 1983	Mount Vinson – Antarctica	16,050 ft./4,892 m.
December, 1983	Mount Kosciuszko – Australasia	7,310 ft./2,228 m.

1989:

Well-known New Zealand mountaineer Sir Edmund Hillary (1919 – 2008) married June Mulgrew, the widow of Peter Mulgrew (1927 – 1979), a climbing partner of Hillary's. Hillary's first wife Louise (1930 – 1975) and their daughter Belinda (1959 – 1975) were killed in a plane crash in Nepal in 1975.

1991:

December 14. A huge rock avalanche fell 8,850 feet/2,700 meters down the east face of Mount Cook in New Zealand. Over six million cubic meters of rock fell 3.6 miles/six kilometers down the mountain lowering the summit elevation thirty-nine feet or twelve meters. The pre-avalanche elevation of Mount

Cook (or Aoraki—"Cloud Piercer" in Maori) was 12,350 feet/3,764 meters. The new elevation is 12,311 feet or 3,752 meters.

1992:

New Zealand mountaineers Gary Ball (– 1993) and Rob Hall (1961 – 1996) climbed all Seven Summits during one seven-month period in 1992. Ball died the next year (1993) of pulmonary edema on Dhaulagiri (26,794 ft./8,167 m.) and Hall died on May 10, 1996 high on Mount Everest (29,035 ft./8,849 m.).

1995:

Australian climbers Steve Monks, Simon Mentz, Jane Wilkinson, and Simon Carter made the first free ascent of the Totem Pole (215 ft./65 m.), a sea stack on the coast of Tasmania just south of Australia.

2000:

February 20. As of this date, 52 climbers had completed the world's Seven Summits using Carstensz Pyramid (16,023 ft./4,884 m.) in Irian Jaya as their seventh summit. 45 climbers had completed the Seven Summits using Australia's Mount Kosciusko (7,310 ft./2,228 m.) as their seventh summit.

2002: FIRST ASCENT

September 5. Blind American climber Erik Weihenmayer (1968 –) reached the summit of Mount Kosciusko (7,310 ft./2,228 m.) in Australia to achieve all Seven Summits (highest summit on earth of the world's seven continents).

2005:

March 10. American mountaineer Marshall Ulrich (1952 –) from Colorado climbed Mount Kosciuszko (7,310 ft./2,228 m.) in Australia thus completing his Seven Summits in 2 years, 267 days. He became the 100th climber to reach the Seven Summits and the second oldest (at age 53) seven summiter behind 56-year-old Dick Bass (1929 –) who first climbed all Seven Summits by April 30, 1985.

2006: FIRST ASCENT

September. New Zealand mountaineer Guy McKinnon made the first ascent (solo) of Hochstetter Dome's (9,275 ft./2,827 m.) north face (4,593 ft./1,400 m.) in New Zealand.

2006:

December. New Zealand mountaineers Tim Robinson, Allan Uren, and Julian White climbed the west face of Mount Lendenfeld (10,479 ft./3,194 m.). This peak is located immediately east of Mount Tasman (11,483 ft./3,500 m.) in the New Zealand Alps.

2008:

January 10. Well-known New Zealand mountaineer, explorer, author, statesman, father, and husband Sir Edmund Hillary (1919 – 2008) died at age 88 ½ in Auckland, New Zealand. The New Zealand government held a state funeral for Hillary at the Holy Trinity Cathedral in Auckland on January 21st. Hillary and Tenzing Norgay Sherpa (1914 – 1986) made the first ascent of Mount Everest (29,035 ft./8,849 meters) on the Nepal/Tibet border on May 29, 1953. In addition to his Everest first ascent, Hillary had many other accomplishments including;

1. 1953: Being granted knighthood by Queen Elizabeth II of England.
2. 1957 – 1958: Crossing Antarctica in tracked vehicles and reaching the South Pole.
3. 1961: Established the Himalayan Trust Foundation (HTF) to benefit the Sherpa people of Nepal. By the year 2000, the HTF had built 30 schools, 2 hospitals, 12 medical clinics, 12 fresh-water pipelines, and 3 mountain airfields.
4. 1985: Landing at the North Pole with former American astronaut Neil Armstrong (first man to walk on the moon – 1969). Hillary became the first person to stand at both poles and on the summit of Mount Everest (a.k.a. the "Third Pole").
5. 1985 – 1988: Serving as New Zealand's ambassador to India, Nepal, and Bangladesh.
6. 1954 – 1999: Author of eight books and co-author of five additional books.

2009:

No significant mountaineering events could be identified.

2010:

No significant mountaineering events could be identified.

2011:

August. The South Ridge of Mount Cook (12,311 ft./3,752 m.) was renamed the Hillary Ridge in honor of Sir Edmund Hillary (1919 – 2008). Hillary made the first ascent of Mount Everest in 1953 and was from New Zealand. He first climbed Mount Cook in January of 1948. In February (1948), Hillary, Ruth Adams, guide Harry Ayers (1912 – 1987), and guide Mick Sullivan made the first ascent of Cook's South Ridge to the Low Peak (11,788 ft./3,593 m.).

"To become a good individual climber, we have had to train our limbs and discipline our nerves until movement has become masterful, confident and easy. To become good mountaineers, we have had to educate our judgment by experience, without lessening our spirit of enterprise. In our association with others on a rope, we must contribute, in addition, our share to a common pool of good temper, of unselfishness and of the discretion which deepens resource and makes for a reserve of safety."

Geoffrey Winthrop Young
British mountaineer
(1876 – 1958)

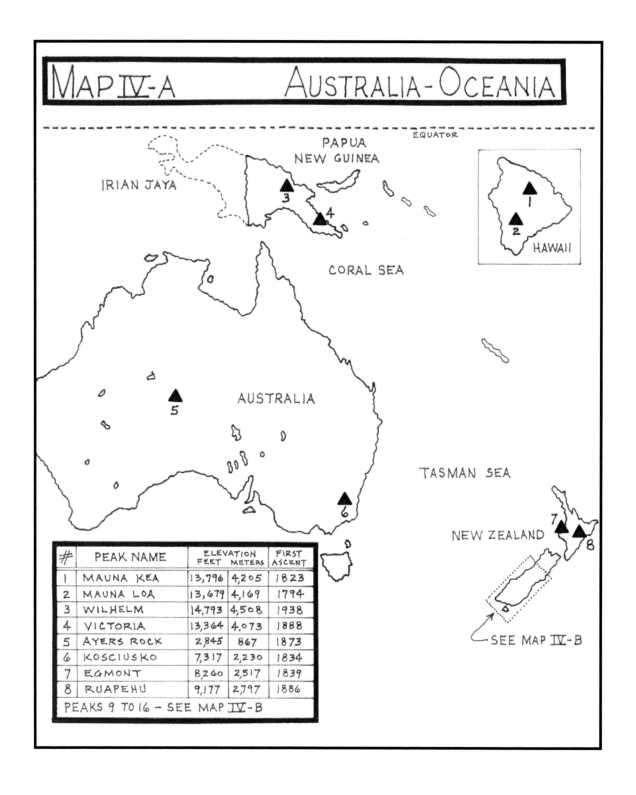

#	PEAK NAME	ELEVATION FEET	METERS	FIRST ASCENT
1	MAUNA KEA	13,796	4,205	1823
2	MAUNA LOA	13,679	4,169	1794
3	WILHELM	14,793	4,508	1938
4	VICTORIA	13,364	4,073	1888
5	AYERS ROCK	2,845	867	1873
6	KOSCIUSKO	7,317	2,230	1834
7	EGMONT	8,260	2,517	1839
8	RUAPEHU	9,177	2,797	1886
PEAKS 9 TO 16 — SEE MAP IV-B				

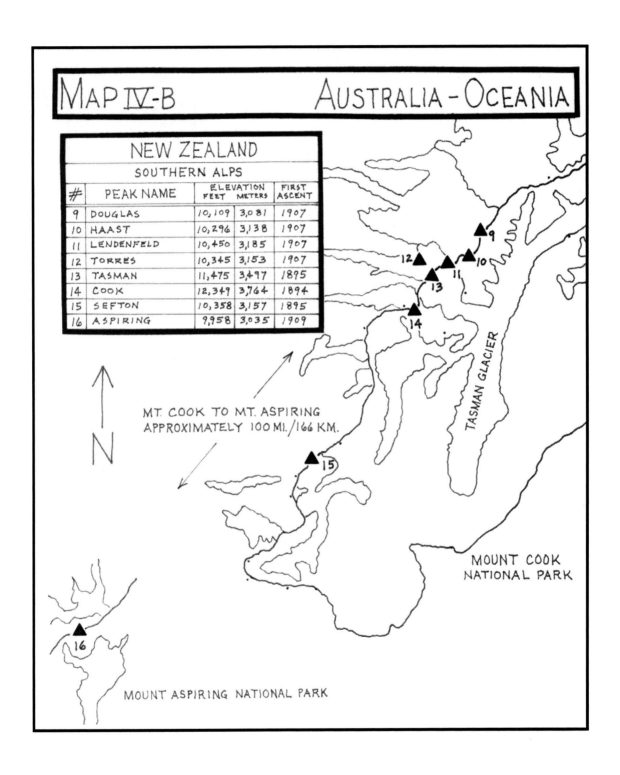

MAP IV-B   AUSTRALIA - OCEANIA

NEW ZEALAND
SOUTHERN ALPS

#	PEAK NAME	ELEVATION FEET	METERS	FIRST ASCENT
9	DOUGLAS	10,109	3,081	1907
10	HAAST	10,296	3,138	1907
11	LENDENFELD	10,450	3,185	1907
12	TORRES	10,345	3,153	1907
13	TASMAN	11,475	3,497	1895
14	COOK	12,349	3,764	1894
15	SEFTON	10,358	3,157	1895
16	ASPIRING	9,958	3,035	1909

N

MT. COOK TO MT. ASPIRING
APPROXIMATELY 100 MI./166 KM.

TASMAN GLACIER

MOUNT COOK
NATIONAL PARK

MOUNT ASPIRING NATIONAL PARK

Mount Cook, New Zealand
12,311 ft./3,752 m.

Mauna Loa, Hawaii
13,679 ft./4,169 m.

AUSTRALIA: The 10 Highest Mountains

Australia

RANK and PEAK NAME	ELEVATION FEET•METERS	LOCATION	FIRST ASCENT DATE	EXPEDITION	SUMMIT CLIMBERS
1 Kosciusko	7,310•2,228	Australia	2-15-1840	Polish	Paul Edmond de Strzelecki
2 Townsend	7,248•2,209	Australia			
3 Twynam	7,202•2,195	Australia			
4 Rams Head	7,185•2,190	Australia			
5 Unnamed Peak – Etheridge Ridge	7,152•2,180	Australia			
6 Rams Head North	7,143•2,177	Australia			
7 Alice Rawson Peak	7,087•2,160	Australia			
8 Unnamed Peak – SW of Abbott Peak	7,084•2,159	Australia			
9 Abbott Peak	7,037•2,145	Australia			
10 Carruthers Pk.	7,037•2,145	Australia			

OCEANIA: The 25 Highest Mountains

Oceania

RANK and PEAK NAME	ELEVATION FEET·METERS	LOCATION	FIRST ASCENT DATE	EXPEDITION	SUMMIT CLIMBERS
1 Wilhelm	14,793·4,509	Papua New Guinea	1938		Leigh Vial and two Papuan New Guineans
2 Giluwe	14,331·4,368	Papua New Guinea			
3 Kubor	14,108·4,300	Papua New Guinea	1965		P. Hardie
4 Herbert	14,000·4,267	Papua New Guinea			
5 Mauna Kea	13,796·4,205	Hawaii	1823		Missionary party
6 Mauna Loa	13,679·4,169	Hawaii	1794		Archibald Menzies Lt. Joseph Baker
7 Bangeto	13,475·4,107	Papua New Guinea			
8 Sarawaket	13,455·4,100	Papua New Guinea			
9 Victoria	13,364·4,073	Papua New Guinea	1889		Sir William MacGregor and party
10 Albert Edward	13,101·3,993	Papua New Guinea			
11 Sugarloaf	12,999·3,962	Papua New Guinea			
12 Dima Peaks	12,999·3,962	Papua New Guinea			
13 Scratchley	12,862·3,920	Papua New Guinea			

OCEANIA: The 25 Highest Mountains (continued)

Oceania

RANK and PEAK NAME	ELEVATION FEET·METERS	LOCATION	FIRST ASCENT DATE	EXPEDITION	SUMMIT CLIMBERS
14 Michael	12,501·3,810	Papua New Guinea			
15 Strong	12,356·3,766	Papua New Guinea			
16 Cook	12,316·3,754	New Zealand	12-25-1894	New Zealand	Thomas C. Fyfe George Graham Jack Clarke
17 St. Mary	11,989·3,654	Papua New Guinea			
18 Tasman	11,477·3,498	New Zealand	2-6-1895	New Zealand	E.A. Fitzgerald M. Zurbriggen
19 Dampier	11,287·3,440	New Zealand	3-31-1912	New Zealand	Freda du Faur P. Graham F. Milne
20 Silberhorn	10,758·3,279	New Zealand			
21 Lendenfeld	10,450·3,185	New Zealand	2-6-1907		
22 Hicks	10,443·3,183	New Zealand	1906	New Zealand	H. Newton R. Lowe A. Graham
23 Malte Brun	10,420·3,176	New Zealand	3-7-1894	New Zealand	M. Ross
24 Teichelmann	10,371·3,161	New Zealand	2-11-1929	New Zealand	H.E.L. Porter Miss Gardiner V. Williams
25 Sefton	10,358·3,157	New Zealand	2-14-1895	New Zealand	

Selected Bibliography — Australia-Oceania

Of the numerous books, journals, newspaper and magazine articles, and internet sites that have been used in the research for this book, the author is particularly indebted to the following sources:

Bangs, Richard. *PEAKS – Seeking High Ground across the Continents.* Taylor Publishing Company, 1994.

Bass, Dick. Wells, Frank. Ridgeway, Rick. *Seven Summits.* Warner Books, 1986.

Birkett, Bill – General Editor. *Classic Treks – The 30 Most Spectacular Hikes in the World.* A Bulfinch Press Book, 2000.

Cleare, John. *The World Guide to Mountains and Mountaineering.* Mayflower Books, 1979.

Cleare, John. *Mountains.* Crown Publishers Inc., 1975.

Gilligan, David Scott. *In The Years of the Mountains – Exploring the World's High Ranges in Search of Their Culture, Geology, and Ecology.* Thunder's Mount Press, 2006.

Hardie, Norman. *On My Own Two Feet – The Life of a Mountaineer.* Canterbury University Press, 2006.

Hattingh, Garth. *Extreme Rock & Ice – 25 of the World's Great Climbs.* The Mountaineers Books, 2000.

Hillary, Sir Edmund. *Nothing Venture, Nothing Win.* Coward, McCann & Geoghegan, Inc., 1975.

Julyan, Robert Hixson. *Mountain Names.* The Mountaineers, 1984.

Kain, Conrad. *Where the Clouds Can Go.* Rocky Mountain Books, 2009.

Kelsey, Michael R. *Climber's and Hiker's Guide to the World's Mountains & Volcanoes.* 4th Edition. Kelsey Publishing, 2001.

Logan, Hugh. *The Mount Cook Guidebook.* New Zealand Alpine Club, 1987.

Logan, Hugh. *CLASSIC PEAKS of New Zealand.* Craig Potton Publishing, 2002.

Mahoney, Michael. *Harry Ayres: Mountain Guide.* Whitcoulls Publishers, 1982.

Neate, Jill. *Mountaineering Literature.* Cicerone Press, 1986.

Newby, Eric. *Great Ascents – A Narrative History of Mountaineering.* The Viking Press, 1977.

Pascoe, John. *Unclimbed New Zealand – Alpine Travel in the Canterbury and Westland Ranges, Southern Alps.* George Allen & Unwin Ltd., 1954.

Pyatt, Edward. *Mountains & Mountaineering – Facts & Feats.* Guinness Superlatives Limited, 1980.

Salkeld, Audrey – General Editor. *World Mountaineering – The World's Great Mountains by the World's Great Mountaineers.* Mitchell Beazley, 1998.

Unsworth, Walt. *Encyclopaedia of Mountaineering.* Hodder & Stoughton, 1992.

Venables, Stephen. *Voices from the Mountains – 40 True-Life Stories of Unforgettable Adventure, Drama, and Human Endurance.* Reader's Digest, 2006.

"The Alps were the first place it ever occurred
to men to climb mountains—where not merely
a sport was born, but an idea."

1941
James Ramsey Ullman
American mountaineer and author
(1908 – 1971)

FIVE

EUROPE

The Birth of Mountaineering

450 B.C. to 2011

"The Alps for all their limitations, their sophistication, their spoiling, have some qualities that I have not found in other ranges. It is difficult to describe these qualities exactly, but they are due I fancy to tradition, to the higher culture of the native inhabitants, to the easy friendships made and to the wonderful variety of scenes small enough in scale to be easily appreciated and large enough to be wholly satisfying."

1928
Eric Shipton
British explorer and mountaineer
(1907 – 1977)

EUROPE

The European continent contains thirty-two countries. The highest peak in six of these countries is over 10,000 feet (3,048 meters) and there are forty-one peaks over 14,000 feet (4,267 meters). Sixteen major mountain groups are located in Europe with the Alps being the most famous and well-known range. In 1871, British mountaineer Leslie Stephen (1832 – 1904) first called the Alps "the playground of Europe." Climbers, hikers, and nature lovers could easily access the Alp's deep valleys, extensive glaciers, and high peaks while still being within a day's travel of many alpine villages.

This great chain of jagged peaks and tremendous precipices extends for approximately 620 miles/1,033 kilometers from Slovenia on the east to southeastern France on the west.* At one time, there were over 1,200 glaciers in the Alps. Today, many of these glaciers have either significantly retreated or completely disappeared. There are now eighty-two recognized peaks over 4,000 meters (13,124 feet) in the Alps. Many believe that the history of mountaineering was written in the Alps particularly in that 45-mile (75 kilometers) strip of mountains from Chamonix, France to Zermatt, Switzerland. The "birth of mountaineering" on August 8, 1786 began when the summit of Mont Blanc above Chamonix, France was finally reached. This is the highest summit in the European Alps. Most of the highest peaks in the Alps were first climbed during the twelve years between 1854 and 1865 (the Golden Age of Mountaineering, 180 first ascents). British mountaineers and their Swiss mountain guides were primarily the first to explore and then systematically climb the highest peaks in the Alps. All of the 4,000 meter peaks had been climbed by 1877. The most recognized peak in the world—the Matterhorn—is located in the Pennine Alps of Switzerland.

Although the Alps receive the most recognition as a mountain range in Europe, they are not the highest peaks in Europe. That distinction truly belongs to the Caucasus Mountains of southwestern Russia. The fourteen highest peaks in Europe are located here in the Caucasus Mountains. The west peak of Mount Elbrus (18,510 feet/5,641 meters) is the highest summit in the Caucasus and the highest in Europe. It is one of the so-called Seven Summits. This mountain range on the Russian side of the border with Georgia contains two peaks above 18,000 feet (5,486 meters) and six peaks over 16,000 feet (4,876 meters).

This chapter identifies ninety (90) peak first ascents, two hundred and seven (207) first ascents, and seven hundred and eighty-two (782) other mountaineering events in the mountains of Europe.

---

* There are approximately 370 summits in the Alps that exceed 3,500 meters or 11,483 feet.

Ten Highest Peaks in Europe

1.	Mount Elbrus: West	– Russia	– 18,511 ft./5,642 m.
2.	Mount Elbrus: East	– Russia	– 18,442 ft./5,621 m.
3.	Dych Tau	– Russia	– 17,077 ft./5,205 m.
4.	Shkhara	– Russia/Georgia	– 17,064 ft./5,201 m.
5.	Koshtan Tau	– Russia/Georgia	– 16,903 ft./5,152 m.
6.	Jangi Tau	– Russia/Georgia	– 16,598 ft./5,059 m.
7.	Dzhangi Tau	– Russia/Georgia	– 16,565 ft./5,049 m.
8.	Kazbek	– Russia/Georgia	– 16,559 ft./5,047 m.
9.	Pushkin	– Russia/Georgia	– 16,513 ft./5,033 m.
10.	Katyn Tau	– Russia/Georgia	– 16,356 ft./4,985 m.

Ten Highest Peaks in the Western European Alps

1.	Mont Blanc	– France/Italy	– 15,782 ft./4,810 m.
2.	Mont Blanc de Courmayeur	– Italy	– 15,577 ft./4,748 m.
3.	Monte Rosa: Dufourspitze	– Switzerland	– 15,204 ft./4,634 m.
4.	Monte Rosa: Nordend	– Switzerland/Italy	– 15,121 ft./4,609 m.
5.	Monte Rosa: Zumsteinspitze	– Switzerland/Italy	– 14,971 ft./4,563 m.
6.	Monte Rosa: Signalkuppe	– Switzerland/Italy	– 14,948 ft./4,556 m.
7.	Dom	– Switzerland	– 14,912 ft./4,545 m.
8.	Lyskamm	– Switzerland/Italy	– 14,853 ft./4,527 m.
9.	Weisshorn	– Switzerland	– 14,781 ft./4,505 m.
10.	Taschhorn	– Switzerland	– 14,732 ft./4,490 m.

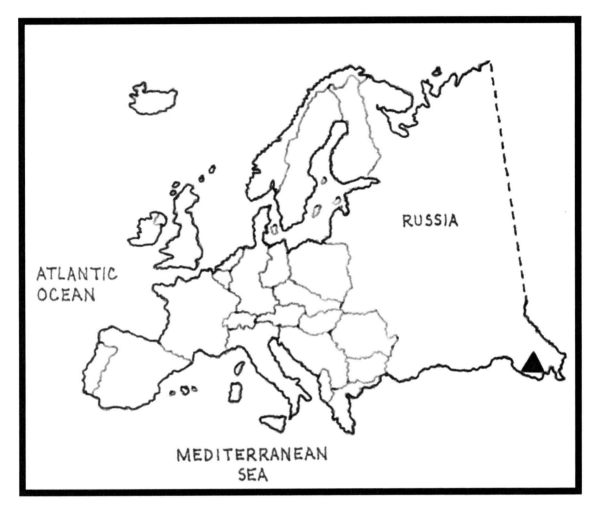

▲ Highest Mountain: Mount Elbrus (West) – 18,511 ft./5,642 m.
Location: Caucasus Range – Russia
First Ascent Date: July 28, 1874
Expedition: British

"For me, it was always fairly simple—the mountains were a
deep source of real happiness. They dispense a lion's share
of sorrow too, but it's the joy that always wins out.
As has been said so often, we climb because we like it.
If someone feels the need to scrutinize the pleasure
it brings further than this, well, that person may
never accept the simplest why of mountaineering."

2013
George Lowe
New Zealand mountaineer
(1924 – 2013)

Europe Timeline

450 B.C.: PEAK FIRST ASCENT ETNA

Greek philosopher, mathematician, explorer, and inventor Empedocles (490 – 430 B.C.) may have made the first ascent of Mount Etna (10,854 ft./3,308 m.) in eastern Sicily. This was the earliest recorded ascent of any peak over 10,000 feet (3,048 m.). Etna is the highest active volcano in Europe.

218 B.C.

Carthaginian General Hannibal (247 – 183 B.C.) took fifteen days to cross the French Alps in late autumn on his journey to attack Rome, Italy. This crossing involved 60,000 foot soldiers (Africans, Celts, and Spaniards), 38 elephants, and 2,000 horses. It is believed that Hannibal crossed the Alps at Mount Genévre at the Col de la Traversette (9,561 feet/2,914 meters) which connects Briancon, France to Sestriere, Italy. Some scholars believe that there are at least five different passes that Hannibal could have crossed. He lost 36,000 soldiers in his crossings of the Pyrenees and the Alps.

181 B.C.: PEAK FIRST ASCENT *HAEMUS*

One of the first recorded accounts of a mountain being climbed occurred when Philip V of Macedon (age 40) ascended Mount Haemus (7,793 ft./2,375 m.) in Thessaly (now known as Botev Peak in the Balkan Mountains of Bulgaria). Philip was the father of Alexander the Great (356 – 323 B.C.). He climbed Mount Haemus (4-day ascent) to gain a better vantage point to understand the topography between the Adriatic and Black Seas. Unfortunately, he reached the summit in thick fog and saw nothing.

B.C.

A.D.

126:

Roman Emperor Hadrian (76 – 138) ascended Mount Etna (10,854 ft./3,308 m.) in Sicily on his return to Rome from Greece. Etna is the highest active volcano in Europe. This may not have been a first ascent.

454:

Saint Patrick (Patron Saint of Ireland) settled a lengthy debate and conceded that MacGillycuddy's Reeks (3,416 ft./1,041 m.) in Ireland's County Kerry was the highest point in Ireland. This mountain is now known as Carrauntoohil.

859:

A hospice for mountain travelers was constructed by Bernard de Mentheon on the summit of the Grand St. Bernard Pass (8,103 ft./2,470 m.) in Switzerland and was significantly rebuilt in about 1059.

Monks lived here for nine centuries. This pass was the only feasible route through the Alps between northern and southern Europe.

1129: Equipment – Alpenstocks

On the Grand St. Bernard Pass (8,108 ft./2,470 m.) in the Pennine Alps between Italy and Switzerland, a party of local men offered to clear a pathway in the deep snow for a group of pilgrims returning to Switzerland from Rome, Italy. These local "guides" were equipped with long (5 to 8 ft.) wooden batons (later called alpenstocks) for support and balance. This may also have been the earliest recorded account of the work of alpine guides. "Alpenstock" is the German word for "Alp Stick" or "Mountain Stick."

1188:

A monk from Christ Church, Canterbury, England—John de Bremble—climbed to the summit of the Grand St. Bernard Pass (8,108 ft./2,470 m.) in Switzerland on his way to Rome and wrote a letter from there expressing his emotions—the joy of mountain climbing.

1211:

An Englishman residing in Provence, France referred to the rock peak Mont Aiguille (6,880 ft./2,097 m.) and its inaccessibility in a published work dedicated to the Emperor Otho the Fourth. Mont Aiguille was first climbed in 1492 by Antoine de Ville and his party (see 1492).

1252:

A Latin land description in Switzerland named a particular mountain the "Egere." The first settlers in this area referred to this same mountain as the "Aigers Geissberg" and later simply as the "Geissberg" which means "Goat Mountain." This peak has been known as the Eiger (13,025 feet/3,970 meters) since the early 1700s. The Eiger was the first mountain in the Swiss Alps to have written proof of possessing a specific name. Its summit is 9,800 feet/2,987 meters above the village of Grindelwald. (See 1858)

1276: PEAK FIRST ASCENT *CANIGOU*

July 4. Peter the III, King of Aragon (1236 – 1285), made a solo first ascent of the Pic Canigou (9,134 ft./2,784 m.) in the eastern Pyrenees (Spain-France border). Legend has it that he threw a stone into the summit lake to set free a large dragon.

1300:

Prior to approximately 1300, man's attention in the mountains concentrated on the mountain passes. Nothing above these passes was of any interest to him. The development of science and the ability to travel allowed men to look up beyond the passes to the high peaks.

1307:

September 17. Six men attempted to climb Mount Pilatus (6,995 ft./2,132 m.) above Lucern, Switzerland without permission. They were jailed for this attempt because a local belief held that Pontius Pilate had drowned in a pond near the summit. Terrible storms would be produced if this pond was disturbed by summit climbers.

1330:

A small mountain village in the French Alps adopted the name "Chamonix" for itself. Founded in 1091, this village's original name was Le Prieure. The mountains above this village were then called "Les Glaciers" and Mont Blanc was known as "Mont Maudit." Chamonix became part of France on March 24, 1860 (from the Kingdon of Sardinia).

1336: PEAK FIRST ASCENT *VENTOUX*

April 26. The first ascent of Mont Ventoux (Windy Mountain, 6,432 ft./1,960 m.) in the south of France (Provence) was accomplished by Italian poet Francesco Petrarch (1304 – 1374) and his younger brother Gerardo. Petrarch's description of this climb is one of the earliest records of mountain climbing. A combination of curiosity and pleasure-seeking caused Petrarch to make this ascent. Upon reaching the summit, however, he was immediately homesick and bored. He returned home for self-analysis and told his friends that his climbing experience was bad. He never climbed another mountain. It took over 500 years for the Alps to regain positive feelings.

1358: PEAK FIRST ASCENT *ROCHEMELON*

September 1. A mountain pilgrim named Bonifacio Rotario (Knight of Asti) made the first ascent of Rochemelon (11,608 ft./3,538 m.) in the Graian Alps near Susa, Italy. Rotario left a bronze plaque (triptych – three panels) on the summit. This was the first known ascent of a 3,000 meter (9,843 ft.) peak in the Alps and the first ascent of an Alpine snow peak. Rochemelon became a pilgrimage destination.

1492: PEAK FIRST ASCENT *AIGUILLE*

June 27. Antoine de Ville (– 1504), Lord of Domp Julien, made the first ascent of Mont Aiguille (6,880 ft./2,097 m.), a rock peak 58 kilometers south of Grenoble, France in the Vercors Mountains. This ascent was ordered by royal command. For many years, this limestone peak was known as "Mons Inascensibilis" or Mount Inaccessible due to its 1,000 foot/305 meter rock walls. Ordered by King Charles VIII to make this climb, De Ville used many artificial aids (wooden pegs, hemp ropes, ladders, chains, and iron claws worn on the hands) to make this ascent which took two days. He built a crude mountain refuge on the summit where he and his fifteen companions stayed for three days. This ascent was not repeated until 1834 (342 years later). The first tourist ascent occurred in 1877 by a Monsieur Rochat. This was the first detailed account of a mountain climb in history.

1500:

The name of the hamlets below the Matterhorn in Switzerland became collectively known as "Zer Matt" meaning "to the meadows." The area name was formerly called Pratoborno ("Meadow Springs"). By 1538, there were 115 families in Zermatt. Zermatt is surrounded by fifteen 4,000 meter peaks.

1511:

Italian painter, sculptor, architect, and musician Leonardo Da Vinci (1452 – 1519) reached the summit of a smaller peak near Monte Rosa (15,204 ft./4,634 m.) in Italy. This ascent was one of the first descriptions of the art of mountain climbing and painting mountains.

1518: PEAK FIRST ASCENT *PILATUS*

Joachim von Watt (1484 – 1551, a.k.a. Joachim Vadian) and three other Swiss scholars made the official first ascent of Mount Pilatus (6,995 ft./2,132 m.) above Lake Lucerne, Switzerland. The Pilatus Railway now takes people to the summit from May to November.

1552: FIRST ASCENT

The first recorded all-women climbing team was Katharina Botsch and Regina Von Brandis. They made the ascent of the Laugenspitze (7,986 ft./2,434 m.) in the Ortler Alps of the Italian Tyrol (northern Italy).

1555:

August 21. Zurich (Switzerland) University professor Conrad Gesner (1516 – 1565) and a friend ascended Mount Pilatus (6,995 ft./2,132 m.) above Lake Lucerne, Switzerland. On the summit, they cast stones into Lake Pilatus proving that no malignant ghost lived there. Gesner has been referred to as the "Forefather of Alpinism." In this same year, Gesner wrote the first book that celebrated the joys of climbing—*On The Admiration Of Mountains*. He vowed to climb one mountain every year of his life.

1574: Book

Swiss naturalist professor Josias Simler (1530 – 1576) is considered to be the "ancient father of mountaineering." He published the book entitled *Descriptio Vallesiae* in 1574. The final chapter of this book was entitled De Alpibus Commentarius (Notes on the Alps). This was the first handbook of mountaineering to be published. In this book, Simler included the first description of crampons, the first major description of the Alps and their relative difficulty, and one of the first mentions of mountain guides.

1574: Clothing – Insulation

Professor Josias Simler of Zurich, Switzerland recommended the placement of paper and parchment beneath clothing to protect the chest area from cold winds.

1574: Equipment – Alpenstocks

One of the first early recorded references to alpenstocks called them "batons" or "staves." These wooden poles varied in length from five to eight feet. An iron point was attached to one end for a more secure grip in snow and ice. Alpenstocks were used for support when ascending or descending snow and ice slopes. When held at each end, they were also used as a handrail for support and balance on ice and snow.

1574: Equipment – Crampons

Professor Josias Simler (1530 – 1576) of Zurich, Switzerland wrote the first climbing guidebook: *Descriptio Vallesiae.* This book included a chapter on climbing techniques. He mentioned the use of three sharp spikes being attached to the feet for traction on ice.

1574: Equipment – Eye Protection

Professor Josias Simler (1530 – 1576) of Zurich, Switzerland proposed the use of a black veil or "objects known as spectacles" to be worn to avoid going blind in bright sunlight on snowfields.

1574: Equipment – Snowshoes

Professor Josias Simler (1530 – 1576) of Zurich, Switzerland wrote his Commentarius de Alpibus. For deep and dangerous snow travel, Simler made reference to a primitive snowshoe as follows: "A lattice-work of cord stretched on a hoop is attached to the foot."

1574: Technique – Glacier Travel

Professor Josias Simler (1530 – 1576) of Zurich, Switzerland published his *Descriptio Vallesiae.* This was the first written record of the early alpine technique of lead mountain guides using a long, iron-tipped wooden staff or pole to poke snow and ice on glaciers in search of crevasses. Simler also first advised wearing dark glasses for eye protection on glaciers and the use of a rope to tie members of a party together when crossing a glacier. He also mentioned in his book the use of sharp spikes fitted to iron shoes that may be worn on ice-covered surfaces (a primitive crampon).

1578:

Bern, Switzerland physician Johannes Stumpf (1500 – 1578) prepared the first detailed maps of the high Alps.

1582: PEAK FIRST ASCENT *TEIDE*

A climber named Sir Edward Scory made the first ascent of Mount Teide (12,192 ft./3,716 m.), the highest peak in Spanish territory. It is located on the Canary Islands off the coast of Africa and is considered to be an active volcano (last eruption in 1909).

1590: Technique – Knots

A Dutch sailor has been credited with inventing the bowline knot which is one of the most important knots to learn for a climber. The name "bowline" first appeared in the English language in 1627. The bowline knot, however, was used much earlier in China to fasten a tether to a trough. This knot is shown in Chinese paintings of the 7th century.

1603:

The earliest known use of the name "Mont Blanc" occurs in a letter written by St. Francois de Sales. This high, snow-capped peak (15,775 ft./4,808 m.) on the border of France and Italy was then known as "Mons Maudite."

1639: PEAK FIRST ASCENT *SNOWDON*

British botanist Thomas Johnson made the first ascent of Mount Snowdon (3,560 ft./1,085 m.) in the Snowdon Group in Wales. Johnson collected and listed twenty different plants on this ascent. Mount Snowdon is the highest point in Wales and its highest summit is known as "Y Wyddfa."

1640:

Italian mathematician and astronomer Gasparo Berti (1600 – 1643) invented the barometer which measured atmospheric pressure. This instrument led to the discovery that higher air is both thinner and lighter than the air at sea level.

1648:

French scientist, philosopher, and mathematician Blaise Pascal (1623 – 1662) carried a barometer up a peak in the Alps to demonstrate that atmospheric pressure decreases with altitude.

1650: Equipment – Pitons

Old English miners and European crystal hunters used a primitive form of a piton called a "stemple" to overcome difficult places on rock. This "stemple" was hammered into a rock crack and then stepped on to gain height.

1673:

Louis XIV's librarian Justel reported to the royal society that a Capuchin monk had found a mountain near Geneva (Switzerland) "Toute de glace et de cristaux" (Wholly made of ice and crystals). This report represented another early glimpse of Mont Blanc (15,775 ft./4,808 m.). The Mont Blanc range contains over 20 peaks above 11,000 feet (3,353 m.).

1678: Equipment – Ropes

Primitive "cord" was first mentioned for climbing techniques on St. Kilda—a group of three islands 40 miles west of the Outer Hebrides Islands off the west coast of Scotland. This cord was used to ascend steep sea cliffs (rising to 1,400 feet/425 meters) to catch sea birds and collect their eggs.

1689:

An early attempt to climb Mont Blanc (15,775 ft./4,808 m.) was made from Courmayeur, Italy. The climbers used primitive crampons and iron hand-claws. The attempt failed.

1689:

One of the earliest mentions of the use of crampons for climbing was made by P.A. Arnod. He noted that his guides used them in an attempt to cross the Col du Géant (11,060 ft./3,371 m.) above Chamonix, France.

1702:

Swiss scholar Johann Jacob Scheuchzer (1672 – 1733) of Zurich began the first of nine journeys (1702 – 1711) through the Alps crossing many passes. He was one of the first mountain travelers to carry and read a barometer, thus determining the height of numerous locations. He then published a four-volume work in 1721 that covered all of Switzerland.

1708:

Monks at the Grand St. Bernard Hospice (Grand St. Bernard pass – 8,101 ft./2,469 m.) began using the Pyrenees Mastiff dog (a crossbreed of the Great Dane and a Newfoundland) to track and rescue mountain travelers trapped in the deep snows. St. Bernard dogs have saved over 2,000 lives since 1708. These dogs then became synonymous with their founding father—St. Bernard.

1710: PEAK FIRST ASCENT *LINARD*

J.C. Zadrell and his party made the first ascent of Piz Linard (11,201 ft./3,414 m.), the highest peak in the Silvretta Alps of Switzerland. Other records indicate that the first ascent of Piz Linard occurred on August 1, 1835 by a geologist named Oswald Heer and his guide Johann Madutz.

1732:

The first major Swiss poet, scientist, and statesman Albrecht von Haller (1708 –1777) of Bern, published his famous book of poems *Die Alpen* which earned him the title of "The Poet of the Alps." This book of poems was about the wonderment and beauties of mountain regions and was inspired by his earliest journey into the Alps in 1728. Thirty authorized editions of this book appeared in Haller's lifetime. He was the uncle of Horace Benedict de Saussure (1740 – 1799).

1741:

June 22. Englishman William Windham (1717 – 1761) led six other Englishmen (Richard Pococke, Benjamin Stillingfleet, Lord Hadington, Aldworth Neville, Mr. Chetwynd, and Robert Price) to Chamonix, France—56 miles southeast of Geneva, Switzerland. They were the first tourists to visit this mountain village and the first to set foot on the Mer de Glace (Sea of Ice) glacier above Chamonix. They actually spent ½ hour walking on the ice itself. They arrived at a location now known as Montenvers (6,303 ft./1,921 m., the name was derived from 'Montagne Verte') This is a small plateau above the Mer De Glace.

1744: PEAK FIRST ASCENT *TITLIS*

Ignatius Herz, Josef Eugen Waser, and two other Engelberg men made the first ascent of the Titlis (10,627 ft./3,239 m.) in Switzerland. Formerly known as the Wendenstock, this was one of the first climbs actually recorded and may have been one of the first ascents of a true snow mountain. The second ascent occurred 50 years later in 1794.

1744 – 1865:

The Swiss climbed more than fifty virgin summits in Switzerland during this 121-year period. Only after 1855 did the English surpass all of their rivals and take the lead in making first ascents.

1754:

The first suggestion that it might be possible to climb Mont Blanc (15,775 ft./4,808 m.) was made by Jacques Barthélémy Michel du Crest (1690 – 1766), a Genevan military engineer, physicist, and cartographer.

1760:

Horace Benedict de Saussure (1740 – 1799), a wealthy Swiss naturalist and geology student (age 20), walked fifty miles from Geneva to Chamonix, France to view Mont Blanc (15,775 ft./4,808 m.) up close. After first seeing Mont Blanc from the summit of the Brévent (8,284 feet/2,525 meters), Saussure began a twenty-five year struggle to climb it. Saussure's guide up the Brévent called the Mont Blanc massif the "montagnes maudites" (the cursed mountains). Pierre Simon, one of the first alpine guides, was selected by Saussure to guide him around Chamonix. Saussure posted notices in every parish of the Chamonix valley offering a cash reward of 20 gold thalers (about $60.00 U.S.) to the first person to successfully climb Mont Blanc. Some historians date the origin of serious mountaineering to this challenge.

1761:

Professor Horace Benedict de Saussure (1740 – 1799) made the first circumnavigation of Mont Blanc (15,775 ft./4,808 m.). This 7 to 10 day trek in France, Italy, and Switzerland (105 miles/175 kilometers) is now a popular tourist excursion. Known as the Tour de Mont Blanc, this trek's highest point is the Col des Fours (8,891 feet/2,710 meters).

1760s:

Marc-Theodore Bourrit (1735 – 1815) of Geneva, Switzerland was the first systematic writer of Alpine books. He is said to have earned the title "Historian of the Alps."

1764: Equipment – Rope

A writer noted that "a rope is the most valuable implement that a man of substance can be possessed of in St. Kilda." (see above 1678 note). St. Kilda ropes were made of cowhide, horse hair, or hempen rope sheathed in cowhide to protect it from abrasion.

1766 to 1785:

Swiss General Pfyffer began the construction of a model or relief map of the Alps. Taking 19 years to complete, this was the earliest accurately triangulated map of the Alps. Pfyffer often worked on the map by moonlight to avoid molestation by the local peasants.

1766:

One of the earliest mentions of the Village of Zermatt, Switzerland occurs in a letter from naturalist Ricou Vaudois to Albrecht Von Haller (1708 – 1777). The village was formerly known as Pratoborno (old Latin name for Zermatt). Ricou collected plants for Haller and stayed with the vicar in Zermatt whose name was Jean-Baptiste Rothärmel. There was no inn in the village at this time. Zermatt means "towards the meadows." A ring of fifteen 4,000 meter (13,124 feet) peaks nearly surrounds Zermatt.

1768:

Walser's map names only three Zermatt mountains:
- Finderlenhorn:
- Matterhorn: 14,692 ft./4,478 m.
- Mettelhorn: 11,175 ft./3,406 m.

1770: PEAK FIRST ASCENT *BUET*

September 20. The De Luc brothers (Jean-Andre, 53 and younger brother Guillaume, 41) and several local chamois hunters made the first ascent of snow-capped Mont Buet (10,158 ft./3,096 m.) near Mont Blanc. This was the first peak to be climbed in the Mont Blanc region and the fourth peak in the Alps to be climbed. They were finally successful on their third attempt (1765, August of 1770). This was the first recorded ascent of a permanent snow peak in French mountaineering. This ascent required them to make the first recorded high-altitude bivouac.

1770: Equipment – Crampons

Snow walkers in Chamonix, France used a simple pair of spiked frames of four points each. Those not having this four-point spiked frame crampon were known to wear thick woolen socks over their shoes for better grip on snow.

1771: PEAK FIRST ASCENT *BEN NEVIS*

August 17. In the process of collecting botanical specimens, Edinburgh (Scotland) botanist James Robertson made the first recorded ascent of Ben Nevis (4,409 ft./1,344 m.). This is the highest peak in Scotland and in the British Isles. It is located at the western end of the Grampian Mountains of the Scottish Highlands. Local inhabitants refer to this mountain as "the Ben" and over 100,000 ascents occur every year. Although the normal hiking route to the summit is called the Pony Track, serious mountaineers are continuously attracted to the 700 meter (2,300 foot) high cliffs of Ben Nevis' north face. Scotland contains nine peaks over 4,000 feet (1,219 meters) in elevation.

1771: Technique – Glissading

Wooden batons (later called alpenstocks) were used to descend mountain snow slopes by glissading. The mountain traveler would lean back on this long (5 to 8 feet in length) wooden baton or staff and slide down the snow slope on his feet. The baton was used as both a speed brake and a steering pole. The term glissading comes from the French word "glisser" meaning "to slide."

1775:

July 13. Four Chamonix, France mountain guides made the first serious attempt to climb Mont Blanc (15,775 ft./4,808 m.) above Chamonix, France. They nearly reached the top of the Dôme du Goûter (14,120 ft./4,304 m.) which is only 1,600 feet or 488 meters below the summit. Thick clouds quickly formed forcing them to descend. The 13,000 foot/3,962 meter altitude barrier in the Alps was first exceeded on this climb. Mont Blanc means "white mountain" in French.

1775:

Marc-Théodore Bourrit (1735 – 1815) completed the tour (circumambulation) of Mont Blanc (15,771 feet/ 4807 meters). Bourrit was the first man to devote his entire life to the study of mountains (now known as Orography). In 1787, Bourrit finally reached the summit of Mont Blanc with a valet and 18 guides. He spent 4 ½ hours on the summit. Mont Blanc was considered to be the highest summit in the Old World. Bourrit published his book *A Relation Of A Journey To The Glaciers, In The Dutchy of Savoy.* This book was quickly translated from French to English by C. and F. Dauy. This was the first book in English to describe the ascent of a glaciated mountain in the Alps.

1778:

August 15. Italian mine inspector Johann Nikolaus Vincent led a large party to explore the upper Grenz Glacier to the west and south of Monte Rosa's Dufourspitze summit (15,204 ft./4,634 m.) in Switzerland. With Vincent were Horace Benedict de Saussure (1740 – 1799), Frederic Parrot, Jean-Joseph Beck, and Joseph Zumstein. This party reached the Col de Lys or Lysjoch (13,619 ft./4,151 m.) west of Monte Rosa. This was one of the first times that an altitude of 4,000 meters (13,124 feet) in the Alps was incontrovertibly surpassed.

1778: PEAK FIRST ASCENT *TRIGLAV*

August 26. First ascent of Triglav (9,396 feet/ 2,864 meters) in the Julian Alps of Slovenia (highest peak in Slovenia). German Doctor L. Willonitzer with a hunter named Rosic and two young miners named M. Kos and L. Korosec reached the summit. Other sources credit the first ascent to B. Hacquet (French) with his guides in 1777.

1778: Equipment – Crampons

August. A climbing party from the Italian side of Monte Rosa (15,205 ft./4,634 m.) searched for the so-called "Happy Valley" between the Lyskamm (14,853 ft./4,527 m.) and Monte Rosa. They provided themselves with primitive crampons called "climbing irons." The reference to "Happy Valley" was actually the Zermatt (Switzerland) valley.

1779: PEAK FIRST ASCENT *VELAN*

August 31. First ascent of Mount Vélan (12,241 feet/3,731 meters) in the Valais Alps of Switzerland. Abbé Laurent-Joseph Murith (1742 – 1816), a priest of the Great St. Bernard Hospice, and two chamois hunters (Moret and Genoud) reached the summit. This was the highest summit in the Alps to have been climbed and was the only ascent by Murith.

1779:

The first mountain hut or refuge for tourists not shepherds (a stone and wood shelter) was erected just below Montenvers (6,303 ft./1,921 meters) beside the Mer De Glace glacier in the French Alps. Englishman Charles Blair contributed four guineas for the cost of this construction. Called Château Blair initially, this mountain hut was also called Blair's Hospital, Blair's Cabin, and Blair's Castle. The interior table was a single stone slab. This small hut remained in use until about 1793.

1783:

Dr. Michel-Gabriel Paccard (1757 – 1827), a Chamonix village physician, made the first of five or six attempts to climb Mont Blanc (15,775 ft./4,808 m.). From the summit of the Brevent (8,281 ft./2,524 m.) across the valley from Mont Blanc, Paccard used a telescope to examine possible climbing routes up Mont Blanc.

1784: PEAK FIRST ASCENT DOME DU GOUTER

September 17. While searching for a climbing route to the summit of Mont Blanc (15,775 ft./4,808 m.), Jean-Marie Couttet and Francois Cuidet made the first ascent of the Dome du Gouter (14,121 ft./4,304 m.). This mountain is actually a shoulder peak of Mont Blanc.

1784: Equipment – Boot Nailing

Chamonix, France. Swiss mountaineer Horace Benedict de Saussure (1740 – 1799) wore strong, thick-soled boots with iron screws with square pyramidal heads to grip on grass and ice.

1786:

June 8. Mountain guide Jacques Balmat (1762 – 1834) attempted to climb Mont Blanc solo. He reached the Dome du Gouter (14,121 ft./4,304 m.). He returned to Chamonix on this date after being forced to bivouac for two consecutive nights on a glacier at 12,800 ft./3,901 m. (Les Grands Mulets). By surviving this bivouac, Balmat put an end to the stubborn superstition that evil spirits would attack anyone spending the night out on a high mountain.

1786: PEAK FIRST ASCENT *MONT BLANC*

August 8. The first ascent of Mont Blanc (15,775 ft./4,808 m.) above Chamonix, France occurred when local physician Dr. Michel-Gabriel Paccard (1757 – 1827) and local chamois hunter Jacques Balmat (1762 – 1834) reached the summit at 6:23 p.m. They had climbed the last 8,000 feet (2,438 meters) in fourteen hours. After taking a few quick measurements (they calculated the summit's elevation as 15,545 ft./4,738 m.), they began their descent at 6:57 p.m. Balmat was considered to be the first professional mountain guide. Many climbers regard this ascent to be the "birth of Alpinism." Paccard and Balmat were forced to wait twenty years before collecting de Saussure's cash prize of 20 gold thalers (about $60.00 U.S.) although Paccard did not want the reward. On their climb of Mont Blanc, Paccard and Balmat used no rope, crampons, or ice axes. They carried and used iron-shod alpenstocks (or batons). Two Chamonix streets are named after them. Paccard was elected Mayor of Chamonix in 1794. Balmat made five more ascents of Mont Blanc. He disappeared on the Mer de Glace in 1834 while searching for gold ore.

1786:

August 16. One week after the first ascent of Mont Blanc (15,775 ft./4,808 m.), the well-known European traveler and British Army officer Mark Beaufoy (1764 – 1827) became the first "tourist" to reach the summit and the first Englishman. Of the first 661 ascents of Mont Blanc, 385 (58 percent) were by Englishmen.

1786: Equipment – Alpenstocks

On the first ascent of Mont Blanc (15,775 ft./4,808 m.) on the French-Italian border, climbers used iron-shod (iron points) wooden batons which were later called alpenstocks.

1786: Clothing – Gloves

During the first ascent of Mont Blanc (15,775 ft./4,808 m.) above Chamonix, France, guide Jacque Balmat (1762 – 1834) used hare-skin gloves he called "mitaines" (mittens).

1786: Equipment – Crampons

English climber and British Army officer Mark Beaufoy (1764 – 1827) climbed Mont Blanc (15,775 ft./4,808 m.) in a party of twelve wearing "cramp-irons" for just the heels of his shoes.

1786: Equipment – Snowshoes

"Snow-rackets" were worn while climbing Mont Blanc in the French Alps.

1786: Technique – Crevasse Crossing

On the first ascent of Mont Blanc (15,775 feet/4,808 meters) above Chamonix, France wooden ladders were carried and used to span crevasses for safe crossings.

1787:

August 13. Horace Benedict de Saussure (1740 – 1799) of Geneva, Switzerland finally reached the summit of Mont Blanc (15,775 ft./4808 m.) on his fourth attempt. A personal servant and 18 guides headed by Jacques Balmat (1762 – 1834) accompanied de Saussure. They spent 4 ½ hours on the summit taking various measurements.

1787: Equipment – Crampons

Chamonix, France. Horace Benedict de Saussure (1740 – 1799) wore a primitive crampon known as a "un crabe." Each foot's metal frame had four sharp spikes.

1788: PEAK FIRST ASCENTS *STOCKGRON, RHEINWALDHORN, OBERALPSTOCK, PIZ URLAUN, PIZ AUL, PIZ SCHARBODEN, PIZ TERRI, AND THE GUFERHORN*

Benedictine monk Father Placious À Spescha (1752 – 1833) from Disentis, Switzerland made his first first ascent in the Swiss Alps at age 36—the Stockgron (11,228 ft./3,422 m.) in the Glarner Alps. His other first ascents from 1788 to 1806 included the Rheinwaldhorn (1789), the Oberalpstock (1792), the Piz Urlaun (1793), the Piz Aul and Piz Scharboden (1801), the Piz Terri (1802), and the Güferhorn (1806). Spescha was regarded by many as the "Father of Mountaineering."

1788:

Horace Benedict de Saussure (1740 – 1799) and his son climbed to the Col du Géant (11,021 ft./3,359 m.) above Chamonix and spent the next sixteen days there making geological and meteorological observations (July 3 to July 19).

1788: Equipment – Tents

Chamonix, France. Horace Benedict de Saussure (1740 – 1799) used a tarpaulin tent made by the Widow Tilliard of Paris, France. It was useful but one had to tolerate the strong canvas odor.

1789:

French geologist Deodat de Gratet, Marquis de Dolomieu (1750 – 1801) visited the northern Italian mountain range now known as the Dolomites. Dolomieu sent samples of carbonate rock to Switzerland for analysis. When these samples were returned to him, he discovered that they had been named after him. The Dolomites contain twenty-one named peaks over 3,000 meters (9,843 feet).

1791:

The Commune of Zermatt (Switzerland) was founded.

1792: PEAK FIRST ASCENT *KLEIN MATTERHORN*

August 13. Geneva, Switzerland naturalist Horace Benedict de Saussure (1740 – 1799), guide Joseph Marie Couttet, Saussure's son, and five other guides made the first ascent of the Klein Matterhorn (12,730 ft./3,880 m.) above Zermatt, Switzerland near Theodule Pass (10,831 ft./3,301 m.). This was the first recorded ascent of a Zermatt mountain. While Saussure was on the Klein Matterhorn, he measured the height of the Matterhorn at 4,501 meters (14,768 feet) which is 76 feet higher than its accepted height of 14,692 feet/4,478 meters. Saussure was also the first visitor to Zermatt to publish what he saw there. The Theodule Pass was named for St. Theodule, the Bishop of Sion from 381 to 391.

1796 to 1815: Equipment – Packs

The two shoulder strap rucksack first appeared during the Napoleonic Wars between France and England/Austria/Russia.

1798: FIRST ASCENT

Snowdon (3,560 feet/1,085 meters) is the highest peak in Wales and the fourth highest in the British Isles. The highest summit point of Snowdon is known as "Yr Wyddfa." An early recorded climb on Snowdon was made in 1798 by the Reverends William Bingley and Peter Williams. They made the first ascent of the Eastern Terrace of Clogwyn du'r Arddu (English translation: the black cliff of the darkness) while searching for alpine plants. Bingley eventually climbed Snowdon by seven different routes. Wales contains fourteen summits over 3,000 feet (914 meters).

1799: PEAK FIRST ASCENT *GROSSGLOCKNER*

July 28. Count Franz Von Salm (1749 – 1822) and his entourage (11 climbers and 19 guides) made the first ascent of the Grossglockner (12,461 ft./3,798 m.). This was the first truly high summit to be reached in the Eastern Alps. It is the highest peak in Austria. There are six peaks in Austria over 12,000 feet (3,657 meters) high and twenty-one peaks over 10,000 feet (3,048 meters). This ascent marked the birth of alpinism in the Austrian Alps.

1799: Technique – Fixed Ropes

The first time that a fixed rope (anchored to the rock by the lead climber and left in place to assist ascending climbers) was used on a climb was on an ascent of the Klein Glockner (12,369 ft./3,770 m.) in Austria.

1800:

A Danish climber, F.A. Eschen, fell into a crevasse on Mont Buet (10,158 ft./3,096 m.) in France and died. He was the first known climber to be killed falling into a crevasse. Mont Buet is the highest summit in the Aiguilles Rouges massif northwest of Chamonix, France. It was first climbed in 1770.

1800:

Geneva, Switzerland. Many believe that the "Birth of Mountaineering" began here in this Swiss city.

1801: PEAK FIRST ASCENT *PUNTA GIORDANI*

Dr. Pietro Giordani (1774 – 1866) from Alagna, Italy made the first serious attempt to climb Monte Rosa (15,204 ft./4,634 m.) on the border of Italy and Switzerland. Climbing solo, Giordani reached a secondary summit of Monte Rosa now known as Punta (point) Giordani (13,275 ft./4,046 m.). This climb was considered an outstanding achievement in the early history of mountaineering. Unfortunately, European politics at this time discouraged anymore climbing for the next sixteen years (until 1817).

1801: PEAK FIRST ASCENT *WATZMANN*

German climber V. Stakig made the first ascent of Mount Watzmann (8,905 ft./2,714 m.) in the Berchtesgaden Alps of southern Germany.

1802: PEAK FIRST ASCENT *SCAFELL PIKE*

August 5. The first recorded rock climb in England occurred when Samuel Taylor Coleridge (1772 – 1834) climbed Scafell Pike (3,209 ft./978 m.) in England's Lake District. This may have been the first ascent of Scafell Pike. Coleridge was a well-known poet, critic, and philosopher. Scafell Pike is the highest mountain in England. Coleridge descended the Broad Stand Route—a steep giant's staircase of rock slabs and sloping ledges. This rock climb began a new period of risk-taking in the mountains. England contains seven peaks over 3,000 feet (914 meters).

1802: PEAK FIRST ASCENT PERDIDO

August 7. Pyrenees Mountain explorer Baron Louis-Fraincois Ramond de Carbonnieres (1755 – 1827) from the Colmar area of France began making visits to the Pyrenees Mountains on the border of France and Spain in 1787. In 1802, he reconnoitered a route to the summit of Monte Perdido (11,007 ft./3,355 m.). On August 7th, Carbonnieres' friend and guide Laurens and a Spanish shepherd named Rondau made the first ascent. Three days later, on August 10th, Carbonnieres and Laurens reached the same summit.

1802: FIRST ASCENT

Baron Dorthesen became the first German to summit Mont Blanc. This was the sixth overall ascent.

1804: PEAK FIRST ASCENT *ORTLER*

September 27. Local chamois hunter Josef Pichler and two companions made the first ascent of the Ortler (12,812 ft./3,905 m.) in northern Italy. The previous five attempts to summit this peak had failed. This is the highest summit of the Southern Limestone Alps in the South Tyrol.

1808:

Well-known Chamonix (France) mountain guide Auguste Balmat (1808 – 1862) was born. He was the great nephew of Jacques Balmat (first ascent of Mont Blanc in 1786). Auguste was employed by Scottish professor James D. Forbes (1809 – 1868) in 1842 and 1843 to study glaciers. He was also with Sir Alfred Wills (1828 – 1912) on Will's famous ascent of the Wetterhorn (12,149 ft./3,703 m.) in 1854. In 1859, Auguste spent twenty hours on Mont Blanc's summit (15,775 ft./4,808 m.) with British mountaineer John Tyndall (1820 – 1893).

1808: FIRST ASCENT

July 14. French woman Marie Paradis (1778 – 1839) made the first ascent of Mont Blanc (15,775 ft./4,808 m.) by a woman. She was apparently "dragged" to the summit by her guides Jacques Balmat, Ferdinand Balmat, Gedeon Balmat, Pierre-Marie Frasserand, and Victor and Michel Tairraz. This was the ninth overall ascent of Mont Blanc. Paradis was the proprietor of a small tea/souvenir shop in Chaumoni (Chamonix), France. Thirty years would pass before the second woman would climb Mont Blanc.

1810:

Dr. George Skene Keith (1819 – 1910) took barometric observations on the major summits of the Cairngorm Mountains in northeastern Scotland. Keith probably made the first ascent of Ben Macdui (4,296 ft./1,309 m.), the second highest peak in the British Isles.

1811: PEAK FIRST ASCENT *JUNGFRAU*

August 3. Johann Rudolph Meyer II, his brother Hieronymus Meyer, and chamois hunters Alois Volker and Joseph Bortis made the first ascent of the Jungfrau's lower summit (13,415 ft./4,089 m.) in the Bernese Alps of Switzerland. They used a rope, but had no ice axes or nailed boots. This was the first Swiss mountain over 4,000 meters (13,124 feet) to be climbed and the third peak (after Mont Blanc and the Dome du Gouter) over 4,000 meters to be climbed in the Alps. The Meyer brothers were ribbon-makers from Aarau, Switzerland. See 1812.

1811: Equipment – Sunscreen

Dark muslin veils were used on the first ascent of the Jungfrau (13,642 ft./4,158 m.) in Switzerland to reduce sun and snow glare.

1811: Equipment – Crampons

"Foot-irons" were worn on the first ascent of the Jungfrau (13,642 ft./4,158 m.) in Switzerland.

1812: PEAK FIRST ASCENT *JUNGFRAU*

September 3. One of the Meyer brothers, Gottlieb Meyer (son of Johann Rudolph Meyer), made the first ascent of the Jungfrau's highest summit (13,642 ft./4,158 m.) above Grindelwald, Switzerland.

1812: FIRST ASCENT

A Scottish climbing party made the first winter ascent of Scottish peak Ben Lomond (3,192 ft./973 m.) in the Grampian mountains. This climbing party cut footsteps in the snow with knives.

1813: PEAK FIRST ASCENT *BREITHORN*

August 13. Henri Maynard, Joseph Marie Couttet, Jean Baptiste Erin, Jean Gras, and Jean-Jacques Erin made the first ascent of the Breithorn (13,665 ft./4,165 m.), a prominent peak above Zermatt, Switzerland via a southwest route (Theodul Pass). The Breithorn ("Broad Mountain") has seven summit points—all over 4,000 meters. The Berner Oberland region of Switzerland also contains a mountain named the Breithorn. This peak is three meters lower than the Zermatt Breithorn.

1817: Technique – Step Cutting

November. On the Mer de Glace Glacier near Chamonix, France, an alpenstock (wooden pole with an iron point at one end) was used for the first time as a device for chopping steps in the ice.

1818: PEAK FIRST ASCENT *AIGUILLE DU MIDI*

August 4. Mountain guide Jean-Michel Balmat led his client, Polish poet Antoni Malczewski (1793 – 1826), up the first ascent of the Aiguille du Midi's (12,605 ft./3,842 m.) north summit above Chamonix, France. This rock needle is located on the Mont Blanc massif. A telepherique (French for "cable care") from Chamonix to its summit was completed in 1955. These cable cars ascend over 9,000 feet (2,743 m.) in two huge bounds.

1818:

British climbers Yeats Brown and Frederick Slade made a failed attempt to climb the Jungfrau (13,642 ft./4,158 m.) in Switzerland. This climb was perhaps the earliest instance of British mountaineering in the high mountains of the Alps. This climb caused a public uproar because Brown and Slade announced their intention of doing this climb simply for fun with no scientific purpose.

1818: Equipment – Ice Axe

Courmayeur, Italy. The Grivel family (Henri Grivel) of blacksmiths began influencing alpinism from their tool factory at the eastern foot of Mont Blanc (15,775 ft./4,808 m.). They modified the common workman's pickaxe into a crude ice-axe.

1819: FIRST ASCENT

July 12. Doctors Jeremiah Van Rensselaer (1793 – 1871) and William Howard (1793 – 1834) with guide Joseph-Marie Couttet made the first American ascent of Mont Blanc (15,775 ft./4,808 m.) above Chamonix, France. This was the 13th overall ascent. This ascent was also the first printed description in America of the ascent of an alpine snow peak. Previous to their Mont Blanc ascent, they had climbed both Mount Etna (10,854 ft./3,308 m.) in Sicily and Mount Vesuvius (4,203 ft./1,281 m.) in Italy.

1820: PEAK FIRST ASCENT *ZUMSTEINSPITZE*

August 1. Italian mountaineer Joseph Zumstein and two friends made the first ascent of the Zumsteinspitze (14,971 ft./4,563 m.) on the Swiss-Italian border. They used no ropes but they did have crampons, alpenstocks, and ladders. This summit is part of the Monte Rosa Massif.

1820:

August 20. A Russian physician named Dr. Joseph Hamel (1788 – 1862, royal court advisor to Russian Emperor Alexander the First) led an ascent of Mont Blanc (15,775 ft./4,808 m.) from Chamonix, France. This group of fifteen climbers including twelve guides was suddenly struck by a huge avalanche at approximately 13,700 feet (4,175 meters) on their ascent. Six of the eleven climbers extricated themselves from the avalanche debris while five others were swept into the Grande Crevasse. Two of the five survived and three were buried—all guides (Balmat, Carrier, and Tairraz). This mountain tragedy became known as the "Affaire Hamel" in mountaineering literature. The remains of the three killed guides were eventually discovered in 1861 at the snout of the Glacier de Bossons—41 years after the avalanche. This was the first great alpine tragedy.

1820: PEAK FIRST ASCENT *ZUGSPITZE*

August 27. K. Naus, Maier, and G. Deutschl made the first ascent of the Zugspitze (9,722 ft./2,963 m.), the highest peak in Germany. The Zugspitze is the only German peak with glaciers. Germany contains three peaks over 9,000 feet (2,743 meters). The Zugspitze is located near the Germany-Austria border southwest of Garmisch-Partenkirchen, Germany.

1820: Technique – Bivouacking

Joseph Zumstein was forced to bivouac in a glacier crevasse high on the slopes of Monte Rosa (15,205 feet/4,634 meters) near the border of Italy and Switzerland. This bivouac was caused by the slow progress of his entire party which preceded him. This was the highest bivouac undertaken at the time. The term "bivouac" is derived from the Swiss word "biwacht" meaning a temporary camp without shelter or protection.

1821:

May 9. Chamonix, France. Local mountain guides founded the Compagne des Guides de Chamonix. This new organization was initially limited to 34 guides. Many former chamois and/or crystal hunters now became mountain guides. Seventy-one separate articles contained a list of the guide's functions and obligations. In 1823, the Sardinian government officially approved this organization. By 1884, 250 mountain guides were registered of which 12 spoke English. This was the world's first guiding trade union.

1823:

Swiss mountaineer and explorer Gottlieb Studer (1804 – 1890) began a 60-year climbing career that included 643 separate expeditions. His first ascent of the Studerhorn (11,936 ft./3,638 m.) bears his name. He was a founder of the Swiss Alpine Club (1863) and the first foreign climber to be elected to an honorary membership in the Alpine Club (British).

1823: Fabric – Macintosh

Charles Macintosh patented his rubber-coated fabric named after himself.

1824: PEAK FIRST ASCENT *TODI*

September 1. Placidus Curschella and August Bisquolm made the first ascent of the Tödi (11,887 ft./3,623 m.) in the Glarner Alps of Switzerland. Tödi means "King of the Little Mountains." Placidus A Spescha (1752 – 1830), the Bénédictine monk from Disentis, took part in this first ascent at age 72 although he did not reach the summit. In 1824, he completed a 36-year period within which he climbed more than thirty peaks.

1828:

The Reverend Charles Hudson (1828 – 1865) was born in England. He was killed on the Matterhorn during its first ascent in July of 1865 (he fell with three others on the descent). In his prime, Hudson could average 80 kilometers (48 miles) per day walking. He made guideless ascents of the Klein Matter-horn (12,740 ft./3,883 m.), the Breithorn (13,665 ft./4,165 m.), and Monte Rosa (15,204 ft./4,634 m.) all in 1855.

1829:

July 22. Russian mountaineer Khillar Khashirov led a Russian scientific expedition to make the first ascent of the east peak (18,442 ft./5,621 m.) of Mount Elbrus in the Caucasus Range of western Russia. This ascent, however, has not been recognized by some Western climbing groups. They believe that the first ascent was in 1868.

1829: PEAK FIRST ASCENT *FINSTERAARHORN*

August 10. Swiss guides Jakob Leuthold (1807 – 1843) and Johann Währen made the first ascent of the Finsteraarhorn (14,026 ft. 4,275 m.) in the Bernese Alps of Switzerland via the north ridge. Their client, Swiss glaciologist Franz Joseph Hugi (1796 – 1855), remained at a point just below the summit. The Finsteraarhorn is the highest peak in the Bernese Alps.

1829:

Italian mountain guide Jean-Antoine Carrel (1829 – 1890) was born in Breuil, Italy below the south face of the Matterhorn (14,692 ft./4,478 m.). He was a stonemason and a soldier (hence his nickname: "Bersagliere"). Carrel was one of the main characters in the Matterhorn ascent (1865) drama. He eventually climbed the Matterhorn with Edward Whymper in 1874 and served as a guide to Whymper in the South American Andes during 1879 and 1880.

1830:

August 26. The Earl of Minto, his son William (16), a friend, and seven guides from Chamonix, France climbed the Breithorn (13,665 ft./4,165 m., not the first ascent) from the Theodul Pass (10,831 ft./3,301 m.) above Zermatt, Switzerland. This was an important climb because all of its members were competent climbers with experience—not tourist climbers being dragged along by the guides. They used blue spectacles, ropes, gaitors, and green veils. Minto thought he was climbing Monte Rosa.

1830:

French mountain guide Michel Croz (1830 – 1865) was born in Le Tour, France. He was the finest Chamonix guide of his generation. His first ascents include: the Écrins (13,455 ft./4,101 m.), Mount Dolent (12,543 ft./3,823 m.), Aiguille de Trelatete (12,894 ft./3,930 m.), Aiguille d' Argentiere (12,796 ft./3,900 m.), Dent Blanche (14,295 ft./4,357 m.), and the Grandes Jorasses (13,806 ft./4,208 m.). Croz was killed on the descent after being part of the Matterhorn's first ascent on July 14, 1865.

1832:

January 14. Professor of Glaciology Franz Joseph Hugi (1796 – 1855) reached the Strahlegg Pass (10,995 ft./3,351 m.) in Switzerland while studying the movement of the Grindelwald Glacier. This was considered to be the first high-altitude expedition in the Alps in winter.

1834: FIRST ASCENT

Count Henri de Tilly became the first Frenchman to climb Mont Blanc (15,775 ft./4,808 m.). He reached the summit with two of his six guides.

1834: PEAK FIRST ASCENT *GERLACHOVSKY*

J. Still and several hunters made the first ascent of Gerlachovsky Stit (8,737 ft./2,663 m.), the highest peak in Czechoslovakia. This peak was once called "Stalin" and is now frequently referred to as "Gerlach."

1834: FIRST ASCENT

Jean Liotard, a local shepherd, made the second ascent (solo) of Mont Aiguille (6,880 ft./2,097 m.) in the Vercor mountains of southeastern France. The first ascent was in 1492 (342 years ago).

1835:

Scottish professor James Forbes (1809 – 1868) began a seven-year study (climbing, traveling, and observing) of glacial movement in the Alps. In 1841, Forbes climbed the Jungfrau (13,642 ft./4,158 m.)

in Switzerland. His glacier study culminated in his ground-breaking work which became known as the "Viscous Theory" which first proposed that glacial ice did not behave like a solid but more like a slowly deforming liquid.

1835:

British woman climber Lucy Walker (1835 – 1916) was born. Her climbing career included 98 summits in the Alps. Only on three occasions did she fail to reach the summit. All of her climbs were done with either her brother Horace (1838 – 1908) or her father Frank (1808 – 1872). Her most frequent guides were Melchior Anderegg (1828 – 1912) or Jakob Anderegg (1827 – 1878) of Meiringen, Switzerland.

1838:

September 3. French woman Henriette D'Angeville (1794 – 1871) was the first woman to feel an intense desire to climb a mountain and then achieve her goal. This was the first ascent of a mountain that was organized by a woman. D'Angeville became the second woman to reach the summit of Mont Blanc (15,775 ft./4,808 m.). She was accompanied by head guide Joseph-Marie Couttet, twenty other guides and six porters. This entire climb took three days. D'Angeville's climbing "costume" weighed 21 pounds. She did, however, wear scotch tweed knickerbockers lined with flannel and fur-lined gloves and bonnet. She later climbed twenty-one different peaks (all first ascents) in the Alps, the last peak at age 69.

1838:

There still remained a law in force prohibiting the climb of Mount Pilatus (6,995 ft./2,132 m.) above Lucern, Switzerland (see Europe – 1307).

1838: Clothing – Knickerbockers

French woman Henriette d'Angeville was the first woman to be shown (in a photo) wearing knickerbockers under her skirt while climbing.

1840:

Mountain guiding was first recognized as a profession in Zermatt, Switzerland and Chamonix, France. The first generation of guides were active during the period of 1840 to 1880.

1840: FIRST ASCENT

Il Marchese Imperiale Di Sant'Angelo, with only one guide, made the first Italian ascent of Mont Blanc (15,775 ft./4,808 m.).

1840: PEAK FIRST ASCENT *MULHACEN*

A climber named Clementi made the first ascent of Mulhacen (11,420 ft./3,482 m.), the highest peak of mainland Spain. Mulhacen is located near the village of Trevelez in southern Spain and is named after Abu L-Hasan Ali—the Muslim King of Granada in the 15th century. There is a local legend that states that this king is buried on Mulhacen's summit which would, therefore, indicate a much earlier first ascent. There are forty-nine named peaks in Spain over 3,000 meters (9,843 feet). Most of these peaks are located in the Pyrenees on the border of Spain and France.

1841: FIRST ASCENT

Scottish mountaineer James David Forbes (1809 – 1868) climbed the Jungfrau (13,642 ft./4,158 m.) in Switzerland thereby becoming the first foreigner to make this ascent. Edouard Desor was with Forbes. This was the fourth overall ascent.

1842: PEAK FIRST ASCENT *PICO DE ANETO*

July 20. Albert de Franqueville, Platon de Tchihatcheff, and guides Argarot, Redonnet, and Ursule made the first ascent of the Pico de Aneto (11,168 ft./3,404 m.) in the Pyrenees Mountains. This is the highest peak in the Pyrenees (France-Spain border). The Spanish name for this peak is Maladetta. There are three named peaks in the Pyrenees over 11,000 feet (3,352 meters) and twenty-six named peaks over 10,000 feet (3,048 meters).

1842: PEAK FIRST ASCENT *RIFFELHORN*

August 8. English naturalist and cartographer James D. Forbes (1809 – 1868), along with English students John Barwell, William and Valentine Smith, made the first recorded ascent of the Riffelhorn (9,607 ft./2,928 m.), a small rock peak in the Pennine Alps just south of Zermatt, Switzerland. The Riffelhorn has always been considered a good training peak for the nearby higher summits of Monte Rosa, the Matterhorn, etc.

1842: PEAK FIRST ASCENT *SIGNALKUPPE*

August 9. G. Farinetti, C. Ferrari, G. Giordani, G. Gnifetti, C. Grober and two porters made the first ascent of the Signalkuppe (a.k.a. Punta Gnifetti to the Italians, 14,948 ft./4,556 m.), one of the Monte Rosa summits on the Swiss-Italian border. It is named for Abbot Giovanni Gnifetti, parish priest of Alagna.

1842: PEAK FIRST ASCENT *STOCKHORN*

August 19. Scottish mountaineer James D. Forbes (1809 – 1868) made the first ascent of the Stockhorn (11,796 ft./3,592 m.) in Switzerland. This was the earliest first ascent of a virgin peak by a British mountaineer. This peak was known as the Wandfluhhorn. With Forbes were Bionaz, Pralong, and Thirraz.

1843: PEAK FIRST ASCENT *WILDHORN*

September. Swiss mountaineer and panorama artist Gottlieb Samuel Studer (1804 – 1890) made the first ascent of the Wildhorn (10,657 ft./3,248 m.) in the Bernese Alps of Switzerland. Studer was one of the founders of the Swiss Alpine Club in 1863. From 1825 to 1885 (60 years), Studer reached 650 summits in Switzerland, France, Spain, and Norway. At age 81, he climbed the Niederhorn (6,398 ft./1,950 m.) in the Bernese Alps of Switzerland.

1844: PEAK FIRST ASCENT *WETTERHORN*

August 31. Swiss guides Melchior Bannholzer and Johann Jaun made the first ascent of the Wetterhorn (12,149 ft./3,703 m.) in Switzerland. This was the only major Swiss mountain to be first climbed by only Swiss guides.

1845: PEAK FIRST ASCENT *MITTELHORN*

July 9. Scottish climber Stanhope Templeman Speer (1823 – 1889)and guides Johann Jaun and K. Abplanalp made the first ascent of the Mittelhorn summit (12,166 ft./3,708 m.), the highest of the Wetterhorn group (three summits) in Switzerland. The other two summits are the Wetterhorn (12,149 ft./3,703 m.) and the Rosenhorn (12,106 ft./3,690 m.). The Wetterhorn mountain group is located immediately east of Grindelwald.

1847:

The Ordinance Survey of Scotland finally established the official height of Ben Nevis at 4,406 feet/1,343 meters eliminating Ben Macdui (4,296 ft./1,309 m.) as the highest peak in Scotland.

1847:

Austrian mountaineer Peter Carl Thurwieser (1789 – 1865), Professor of Oriental Languages at Salzburg, completed his 70th peak ascent in the Austrian Alps including three first ascents (1820 – 1847). He was the first Tyrolean to climb from a purely genuine love of the mountains.

1849:

Englishman John Ruskin (1819 – 1900) became the first tourist to climb Bel Alp—a rocky knoll high above the Rhone River in Switzerland. Ruskin was also the first person to photograph the Matterhorn (14,692 ft./4,478 m.) above Zermatt, Switzerland. He called this first photograph a "sun portrait." Ruskin claimed that this was the first photograph of any Swiss mountain. In addition to being a photographer, Ruskin was also a painter, geologist, philosopher, and poet.

1850: PEAK FIRST ASCENT *PIZ BERNINA*

September 13. Swiss surveyor and mountaineer Dr. Johann Coaz (Swiss Surveyor) and guides Lorenz and Jon Ragut Tscharner made the first ascent of the Piz Bernina (13,284 ft./4,049 m.) above Pontresina, Switzerland. They climbed the east ridge and reached the summit for survey purposes. Coaz also named this peak after the pass. The Piz Bernina is the only 4,000 meter peak in the Eastern Alps. There are four other peaks in the Eastern Alps over 3,900 meters. Coaz made over twenty-five peak first ascents in the Alps.

1850:

The Swiss Academy of Natural Sciences in Zurich, Switzerland recorded the existence of 2,244 Swiss glaciers. By the year 2000 (150 years later), 249 of these glaciers (11 percent) had disappeared.

1850: PEAK FIRST ASCENT *GALDHOPPIGEN*

L. Arnesen, S. Flotten, and S. Sulheim made the first ascent of the Galdhoppigen (8,101 ft./2,469 m.), the highest peak in Norway. This mountain is located in the Jotunheimen region of southern Norway.

1850: Technique – Climbing Rope

(Early to mid-1800s). Mountain guides tied their clients to one another but not to themselves. They held the rope end only in their hands. If a client climber slipped and fell, the guide could release his hold on the rope and not fall with them. Three English tourist climbers and one guide were killed on the Col du Geant in the French Alps in 1864 due to this "roping-up" practice.

1851: FIRST ASCENT

August 13. British showman Albert R. Smith (1816 – 1860) climbed Mont Blanc (15,775 ft./4,808 m.) above Chamonix, France. He was the first member of the Alpine Club to climb Mont Blanc. With Smith were William Edward Sackville-West, E. Philips, and G.C. Floyd. Smith had 18 guides and porters with him and carried ninety-six bottles of wine, cognac, and champagne to the summit. Upon reaching the summit, Smith passed out. In 1852, he produced an elaborate lecture about his Mont Blanc climb which he began presenting to 2,000 London audiences on March 15, 1852. Smith opened his production "The Ascent of Mont Blanc" in Piccadilly's Egyptian Hall in London. This lecture was presented to over 200,000 people during its seven-year run and took in over £30,000. The final performance (the 2,000th) was on July 5, 1858. Smith died of bronchitis in 1860 at age 44.

1852:

By law, each tourist climber of Mont Blanc was required to have four guides.

1852:

Joseph Anton Clemenz (1810 – 1872) opened the Hotel Mont Cervin (14 beds) in Zermatt, Switzerland. "Cervin" is the French name for the Matterhorn. This hotel was expanded to 68 guest beds in 1868. The Monte Rosa Hotel (35 beds) opened in Zermatt in 1855. The early British mountaineers stayed in these two hotels. In 2006, Zermatt contained 117 hotels.

1852: Equipment

Early 1850s. A "graffio" was a five-foot ashen pole with an iron hook at one end that was originally designed for pulling marmots out of their holes. This pole was also used for hauling climbers out of glacier crevasses.

1853:

September 21. Chamonix (France) mountain guides laid the foundation for the first high-altitude refuge or mountain hut. The Grand Mulets Hut was built on Mont Blanc (15,775 ft./4,808 m.) at an elevation of 10,010 ft./3,051 m. Fifty visitors attended the opening day ceremonies including British showman Albert Smith (1816 – 1860). Heavy wires were stretched across the roof of this wooden hut to anchor it in high winds. Mountain huts are known by different names in the following countries in Europe. The approximate number of climbing and hiking huts in these countries is also noted (#).

Austria	*Hütten* (514)	
England	*Hut* (17+)	
France	*Refuge* (4,000)	
Germany	*Hütten* (500+)	
Italy	*Rifugi* (600)	
Norway	*Hytte* (400+)	
Scotland	*Bothy* (30+)	
Slovenia	*Koca* or *Dom* (170)	
Spain	*Refugio* (13)	
Switzerland	*Cabane or Hütte* (153)	

1853:

Well-known mountain guide Christian Klucker (1853 – 1928) was born in Sils in the Engadine Valley of Switzerland. He was one of the greatest alpine guides. Small, thickset, and powerful, Klucker was the leader on over 100 first ascents and accomplished 88 new climbing routes on previously climbed peaks. His best season was in 1890:

Northeast face of the Lyskamm	14,853 ft./4,527 m.
Northeast face of the Piz Roseg	12,917 ft./3,937 m.
Northeast face of the Piz Bernina	13,284 ft./4,049 m.
Northwest face of the Piz Scerscen	13,029 ft./3,971 m.
Traverse of the Wellenkuppe/	12,806 ft./3,903 m.
Obergabelhorn	13,331 ft./4,063 m.

1853: Clothing – Balaclava

To keep their heads and necks warm while climbing, early mountaineers in the Alps wore balaclavas. This soft woolen helmet that covered the full head with an open face area was developed during the Crimean War (Great Britain, France, Turkey, and Sardinia vs. Russia, 1853 – 1856). Balaclavas provided excellent head protection in winter conditions. Balaclavas are now made of silk, nylon, or fleece. The word "balaclava" came from the name of a seaport (Balaklava) on Crimea (now the Ukraine) in the former Soviet Union.

1854: PEAK FIRST ASCENT *STRAHLHORN*

August 15. The three Smyth brothers (James, Christopher, and Edmund) and their two guides Ulrich Lauener and Franz Joseph Andenmatten made the first ascent of the Strahlhorn (13,747 ft./4,190 m.) in the Pennine Alps of Switzerland. This was the first high peak above Zermatt and Saas-Fee to be climbed. The Strahlhorn is part of the three-peak group (Allalinhorn – 4,027 m., Strahlhorn and the Rimpfischhorn – 4,199 m.)

1854:

September 17. The English judge from Grindelwald, Switzerland Sir Alfred Wills (1828 – 1912) climbed the Wetterhorn (Hasli Jungfrau summit point, 12,149 ft./3,703 m.) in Switzerland with four guides. This was actually the peak's fifth or sixth ascent but is regarded as the beginning of modern mountaineering and the beginning of the Golden Age of Mountaineering (1854 – 1865). The name Wetterhorn means "the mountain of weather." The Wetterhorn is comprised of three distinct summits: Mittelhorn (12,166 ft./3,708 m.), Hasli Jungfrau (12,149 ft./3,703 m.), and the Rosenhorn (12,110 ft./3,691 m.). The Hasli Jungfrau summit is commonly known as the Wetterhorn. 180 first ascents in the Alps were made during this eleven-year period. Wills is regarded as the "Father of English Alpinists."

1854:

British mountaineer Horace Walker (1838 – 1908) climbed his first peak—the Vélan (12,353 ft./3,765 m.)—at age 16. His last peak—Pollux (13,426 ft./4,092 m.)—was climbed at age 67 in 1905. Walker's list of ascents occupied six pages in the Alpine Club (British) Register. He accomplished 8 first ascents and numerous 2nd and 3rd ascents. He was the son of mountaineer Frank Walker (1808 – 1872) and the brother of famous woman mountaineer Lucy Walker (1835 – 1916).

1854 – 1865:

The Golden Age of Mountaineering began (this was a British label). Of the 39 alpine peaks over 13,000 feet/3,962 meters climbed during this period (first ascents), British climbers claimed 31. The period began with the ascent (5th) of the Wetterhorn and ended with the ascent (1st) of the Matterhorn. The most notable guides and their significant ascents during this twelve-year period were:

• Christian Almer (1826 – 1898). Grindelwald, Switzerland

1854	Wetterhorn: 12,149 ft./3,703 m. Fifth ascent.
1857	Monch: 13,449 ft./4,099 m. Peak first ascent. (PFA)
1858	Eiger: 13,025 ft./3,970 m. PFA
1862	Fiescherhorn: 13,285 ft./4,049 m. PFA
1864	Barre des Ecrins: 13,459 ft./4,102 m. PFA
1865	Grandes Jorasses – Pointe Whymper: 13,728 ft./4,184 m. PFA
1865	Aiguille Verte: 13,524 ft./4,122 m. PFA
1865	Breithorn – Lauterbrunnen: 12,409 ft./3,782 m. PFA
1865	Silberhorn: 12,123 ft./3,695 m. PFA
1865	Jungfrau: 13,642 ft./4,158 m. First Ascent (FA)

• Jakob Anderegg (1827 – 1878). Meiringen, Switzerland

1864	Lyskamm: 14,853 ft./4,527 m. West Ridge
1864	Balmhorn: 12,169 ft./3,709 m. PFA
1864	Mont Blanc: 15,775 ft./4,808 m. Brenva Route (FA)

• Melchior Anderegg (1828 – 1912). Meiringen, Switzerland

1858	Wildstrubel: 10,640 ft./3,243 m. PFA

1859	Rimpfischhorn: 13,777 ft./4,199 m. PFA
1859	Mont Blanc: 15,775 ft./4,808 m. FA
1860	Alphubel: 13,800 ft./4,206 m. PFA
1860	Blumlisalphorn: 12,021 ft./3,664 m. PFA
1862	Monte Disgrazia: 12,067 ft./3,678 m. PFA
1863	Dent d'Herens: 13,685 ft./4,171 m. PFA
1863	Parrotspitze: 14,541 ft./4,432 m. PFA
1864	Balmhorn: 12,169 ft./3,709 m. PFA
1864	Zinalrothorn: 13,849 ft./4,221 m. PFA

• Franz Andenmatten (1823 – 1883). Almagel, Switzerland

1854	Strahlhorn: 13,747 ft./4,190 m. PFA
1856	Lagginhorn: 13,157 ft./4,010 m. PFA
1858	Nadelhorn: 14,197 ft./4,327 m. PFA

• Auguste Balmat (1808 – 1862). Chamonix, France

1854	Wetterhorn: 12,149 ft./3,703 m. Fifth Ascent
1858	Mont Blanc: 15,775 ft./4,808 m.
1859	Mont Blanc: 15,775 ft./4,808 m. 20 hours on summit
1861	Mont Blanc: 15,775 ft./4,808 m.

• Johann Joseph Bennen (1824 – 1864). Laax, Switzerland

1858	Finsteraarhorn: 14,023 ft./4,274 m.
1859	Aletschhorn: 13,757 ft./4,193 m. PFA
1860	Matterhorn: 14,692 ft./4,478 m. Attempt
1861	Weisshorn: 14,784 ft./4,506 m. PFA
1861	Mont Blanc: 15,775 ft./4,808 m.
1862	Matterhorn: 14,692 ft./4,478 m. Attempt
1863	Aletschhorn: 13,757 ft./4,193 m. FA by a woman
1863	Jungfrau: 13,642 ft./4,158 m. FA by a woman

• Jean-Antoine Carrel (1829 – 1891). Breuil, Italy

1857	Matterhorn: 14,692 ft./4,478 m. Reconnaissance
1861	Matterhorn: 14,692 ft./4,478 m. Attempt
1862	Matterhorn: 14,692 ft./4,478 m. Attempt
1863	Matterhorn: 14,692 ft./4,478 m. Attempt
1865	Matterhorn: 14,692 ft./4,478 m. 2nd ascent

• Michel Croz (1830 – 1865). Tour, France

1860	Grande Casse: 12,648 ft./3,855 m. PFA
1861	Castor: 13,856 ft./4,223 m. PFA
1861	Monte Viso: 12,602 ft./3,841 m. PFA
1863	Grandes Rousses: 11,395 ft./3,473 m. PFA

1864	Barre des Ecrins: 13,459 ft./4,102 m. PFA
1864	Mont Dolent: 12,543 ft./3,823 m. PFA
1864	Aiguille D'Argentiere: 12,796 ft./3,900 m. PFA
1864	Aiguille D'Trelatete: 12,894 ft./3,930 m.
1865	Grand Cornier: 12,999 ft./3,930 m.
1865	Grandes Jorasses-Pointe Whymper: 13,728 ft./4,184 m. PFA
1865	Dent Blanche: 14,295 ft./4,357 m.
1865	Matterhorn: 14,692 ft./4,478 m. PFA. Died on descent.

• Ulrich Lauener (1821 – 1900). Lauterbrunnen, Switz.

1854	Wetterhorn: 12,149 ft./3,703 m. 5th ascent
1855	Monte Rosa-Dufourspitze: 15,204 ft./4,634 m. PFA

1854: FIRST ASCENT

Steinberger made the ascent of the Koenigspitze (12,661 ft./3,859 m.) in the Ortler Alps in Austria. This was the first summit in the Alps reached without using a guide.

1854: Equipment – Alpenstock

All climbers in the Alps carried an alpenstock—a wooden pole at least four feet in length with an iron spike at one end and an axe-head at the opposite end. This is perhaps the first reference to the beginning transition from alpenstock to ice-axe.

1855: PEAK FIRST ASCENT DUFOURSPITZE

August 1. John Birkbeck, Charles Hudson, Christopher C. and James G. Smyth, and Edward Stevenson with guides Ulrich Lauener and Johann and Matthias Zumtaugwald made the first ascent of Monte Rosa's highest summit point—the Dufourspitze (15,204 ft./4,634 m.). The attempts to climb Monte Rosa began in 1847. Formerly known as Höchste Spitze, this point was renamed in 1863 in honor of General Dufour, the Swiss cartographer who published the first accurate Swiss maps. This climbing group ascended the Dufourspitze via the West Ridge. The Monte Rosa Massif contains eleven summits over 4,000 meters (13,124 feet). The Dufourspitze is the highest summit in Switzerland (525 horizontal feet from the Italian border).

1855: FIRST ASCENT

The Reverend Charles Hudson, the Smyth brothers, Charles Ainslie, and Thomas S. Kennedy made the ascent of Mont Blanc (15,775 ft./4,808 m.) for the first time without guides. They climbed the Saint-Gervais route from Chamonix, France. Mountaineers began to recognize that they did not necessarily need a paid mountain guide for all peak ascents. Guideless climbing increased as climbers became more experienced. Those major peaks in the Alps that experienced the first guideless ascents were:

1855 – Mont Blanc

1865 – Finsteraarhorn

1879 – Meije

1881 – Jungfrau

1856: PEAK FIRST ASCENT *AIGUILLE DU MIDI*

August 5. Count Fernand de Bouille's three guides (Jean-Alexander Devouassoud, Ambroise and Jean Simond) from Chamonix, France made the first ascent of the Aiguille du Midi's (12,609 ft./3,843 m.) central summit—the highest of three summits. The slightly lower north summit was the first Chamonix Aiguille (rock needle) to be climbed – 1818.

1856 – 1874:

During these 18 years, British mountaineer Francis Fox Tuckett (1834 – 1913) and his guides reached the summits of 165 peaks (84 were important and 57 were new climbs) and 376 passes in the Alps including the Aletschhorn (13,764 ft./4,195 m.) in 1859, Monte Cristallo (10,552 ft./3,216 m.) in 1864, and the Konligspitze (12,661 ft./3,859 m.) also in 1864.

1856:

A professional mountain guide's organization was founded in Grindelwald, Switzerland—The Grindelwald Corporation. Official certification of Swiss guides occurred in Berne, Switzerland during this year.

1856:

French archaeologist L. Heuzey made what he thought was the first ascent of Mount Olympus (9,571 ft./2,917 m.) in Greece. He actually climbed the peak known as Profitis Ilias (9,551 ft./2,911 m.) near Mount Olympus which was first climbed (Mytikas summit) in 1913. Olympus is located 11 miles/18 km from the Aegean Sea.

1856: Book

British mountaineer Alfred Wills (1828 – 1912) published his book entitled *Wanderings Among the High Alps.* This book is considered to be a classic.

1857:

May 31. Italian mountaineer and future pope Achille Ratti (1857 – 1939) was born in Desio, Italy (20 miles north of Milan). Ratti would become in 1922 (at nearly the age of 65) the 261st pope—Pope Pius XI (1922 – 1939). He was known as "the mountaineer's pope" because of his numerous climbs in the Alps.

1857: PEAK FIRST ASCENT MONCH

August 15. Viennese mountaineer Dr. Siegmund Porges and guides Christian Almer (from Grindelwald), Ulrich and Christian Kaufmann made the first ascent of the Mönch (13,449 ft./4,099 m.) above Grindelwald, Switzerland. This climbing party was forced to bivouac on the mountain before and after reaching the summit.

1857:

September 5. The earliest photograph of American climbers in the Alps was taken at Chamonix, France. The photograph is of George (the first American to climb Mont Blanc twice, 1855 and 1857) and Augustine Heard with their guides. This was George Heard's (1837 – 1875) ninth visit to Chamonix.

1857: PEAK FIRST ASCENT *MONTE PELMO*

September 19th. British mountaineer and future first president of the newly formed Alpine Club (England) John Ball (1818 – 1889) and a local chamois hunter made the first ascent of Monte Pelmo (10,393 ft./3,168 m.). This was the first major Dolomite peak in Italy to be climbed. It is located south of Cortina d'Ampezzo in Northern Italy.

1857: FIRST ASCENT

British mountaineers Kennedy, Mathews, Hardy, and Ellis made the first British ascent of the Finsteraarhorn (14,024 ft./4,274 m.) in Switzerland. It was during this climb that Mathews suggested the formation of an alpine club. On December 22, the first meeting of the Alpine Club (England) was held at the Ashley Hotel in Covent Garden, London, England. This first meeting was attended by twenty members. This was the first mountaineering club in the world and was organized primarily for its members to dine together and exchange mountain information. John Ball (1818 – 1889) was elected President, Thomas Stuart Kennedy (1841 – 1894) Vice-President, and Thomas W. Hinchliff (1825 – 1882) Secretary. The club's membership from 1857 to 1863 consisted of 281 members including:

Barristers	57	Solicitors	23
Clergymen	34	Scientists	5
Schoolmasters	7	Authors	4
Land Aristocracy	15	Artists	4
Architects	2	Librarians	2

* As of 2011, the United Kingdom contained 164 mountaineering and climbing organizations.

1857:

Italian hunters and mountain guides Jean-Antoine Carrel (1829 – 1890), Jean-Jacques Carrel, and Amé Gorret made the first attempt to climb the Matterhorn (14,692 ft./4,478 m.) from Breuil, Italy. They reached the Tête du Lion (12,650 ft./3,856 m.). British mountaineer Marshall Hall made the following comment in the British Alpine Journal in 1849: "As for the giant Matterhorn, it has never entered the mind of man that its ascent was possible." The summit of the Matterhorn was finally reached in 1865. This famous peak is located in the Pennine Alps in a district known as the Valais.

1857: Equipment – Crampons

New president of England's Alpine Club John Ball (1818 – 1889) made the first ascent of the Pelmo (10,394 ft./3,168 m.) from the village of Borca in northern Italy. Ball mentioned in his diary of "screwing-in points to my boots in the hut." This may have been either an early form of crampons or a kind of removable boot nail.

1858: PEAK FIRST ASCENT *EIGER*

August 11. Irish mountaineer Charles Barrington and guides Christian Almer (1826 – 1898) and Peter Bohren made the first ascent of the Eiger (13,025 ft./3,970 m.) in Switzerland via the northwest ridge and west face. They began this climb on August 5th from the village of Grindelwald.

1858: PEAK FIRST ASCENT *DOM*

September 11. Welsh cleric and scholar the Reverend John Llewellyn-Davies and his three Zermatt guides Johann Zumtaugwald, Johann Krönig, and Hieronymus Brantschen made the first ascent of the Dom (14,912 ft./4,545 m.), the highest peak located entirely within Switzerland. They climbed the northwest ridge in one day roundtrip (2:10 a.m. to 4:20 p.m.) from the Village of Randa in the Zermatt valley. This peak was named after Randa surveyor Canon Domherr Berchtold. It is the highest point in the Swiss Alps that can be reached on skis. The Dom's normal climbing route has the greatest vertical ascent of all 4,000 meter peaks in the Alps—3,100 meters or 10,171 feet (from the village of Randa).

1858:

The mountain guides in Zermatt, Switzerland formed their own association.

1858:

Swiss mountain guides Melchior Anderegg (1828 – 1912) and Christian Almer (1826 – 1898) became the first two men to be issued an official guide's badge and a Fuhrerbuch (guide's record-book or leader book in German) by the Guides Society of the Valais. In French, this record book was called a Livret.

1858: Book

The first series of *Peaks, Passes and Glaciers* (five editions) was published by William Longman and the Alpine Club in London. Dublin, Ireland born mountaineer John Ball (1818 – 1889, Alpine Club president) served as the book's editor. This was the British Alpine Club's first publication. The second series of *Peaks, Passes and Glaciers* appeared in 1862. The first volume of the Alpine Club's *Alpine Journal* was published in 1863.

1858: Equipment – Stoves

British mountaineer Francis Fox Tuckett (1834 – 1913) designed one of the earliest portable alcohol stoves and used it on his ascent of the Aletschorn (13,764 ft./4,195 m.) in Switzerland. This stove became known as the Rob Roy and was sold by Silver and Company in London for many years. It was designed to be suspended by a cord in the interior of a tent.

1858: Technique – Frostbite Remedy

British mountaineers Alfred Wills (1828 – 1912) and John Tyndall (1820 – 1893) and their guide Auguste Balmat (1808 – 1862) climbed Mont Blanc (15,775 feet/4,808 meters) above Chamonix, France. Balmat's hands froze and Wills and Tyndall rubbed them with snow until his circulation returned. Balmat's hands were saved.

1858: Technique – Solo Climbing

On August 16, British mountaineer John Tyndall (1820 – 1893) made the first solo ascent of Monte Rosa (15,204 feet/4,634 meters) on the Swiss-Italian border. He made this solo ascent after climbing Monte Rosa on the previous day with guide Ulrich Lauener. Tyndall made this comment regarding solo climbing:

> *"It is an entirely new experience to be alone amid these*
> *scenes of majesty and desolation. The peaks wear a more*
> *solemn aspect, the sun shines with a purer light into the soul,*
> *the blue of heaven is more awful…the feeling of self-reliance*
> *is very sweet, and you contract a closer friendship with the*
> *universe than when you trust to the eye and arm of your guide."*

On the descent from his solo climb, Tyndall accidentally lost (dropped) his ice axe which scared him. As a result of this temporary loss of his axe, he promised himself to never climb solo again.

1859:

An article prepared for the *Gazette Du Valais* suggested that the Matterhorn (14,692 ft./4,478 m.) would never be climbed. It noted that a tunnel to the summit crest would only cost 770,000 Swiss francs.

1859:

British climber, botanist, and explorer Charles Packe (1826 – 1896) began a four-year project (1859 – 1862) to systematically explore the Pyrenees mountains on the France-Spain border. He usually traveled alone with his two Pyrenean sheep dogs. The Pyrenees mountain range is 270 miles long (450 kilometers) and approximately six miles wide at its widest point. There are twenty-six named peaks in the Pyrenees over 10,000 feet (3,048 meters) and three named summits over 11,000 feet (3,352 meters).

1859:

Well-known British rock climber Walter Parry Haskett-Smith was born(1859 – 1946). He was regarded as the "founder of British rock climbing." Haskett-Smith always felt that the climb was more important than reaching the summit. His most famous climb was the first ascent of the striking Napes Needle on Great Gable in the Lake District of England. He climbed this rock route solo without using any ropes.

1859: Book

British mountaineer John Ball (1818 – 1889) served as the editor of the published book entitled *Peaks, Passes and Glaciers.* After three editions, this publication became the *Alpine Journal* of the British Alpine Club in 1863. The *Alpine Journal* continues to be published annually.

1859 – 1885 (27 years):

Climbing with guides resulted in 134 climbing deaths in the Alps. 1886 – 1891 (6 years): Guideless climbing was now widespread. This climbing approach caused 214 climbing deaths in the Alps.

Other recent years with high death rates in the Alps:

1999	93 Deaths
2000	94 Deaths
2001	133 Deaths
2002	102 Deaths

1859: Clothing – Dress Cords

A Mrs. Cole described a woman's climbing outfit in a book titled *A Lady's Tour Round Monte Rosa*. Cole suggests that "small rings should be sewn inside the seams of the dress and a cord passed through them, the ends of which should be knotted together in such a way that the whole dress may be drawn-up at a moment's notice to the required height" for climbing.

1859: Equipment – Snowshoes

Winter. British mountaineer John Tyndall (1820 – 1893) and six others struggled up the snow slopes from Chamonix, France to the Mer de Glace glacier. The guides wore "patters" (patin in French) on their feet which were small wooden planks sixteen inches long and ten inches wide. This was an early type of snowshoe.

1859: Technique – Foot Protection

British mountaineer Leslie Stephen (1832 – 1904) was forced to bivouac on the Aletsch Glacier in Switzerland. He put his feet into his rucksack for protection and warmth.

1860: PEAK FIRST ASCENT *BLUMLISALPHORN*

August 27. British mountaineer Leslie Stephen (1832 – 1904) and American mountaineer James Kent Stone (1840 – 1921) made the first ascent of the Blumlisalphorn (12,021 ft./3,664 m.) in Switzerland. Stone became the first American to climb a virgin peak in the Alps. He was also the first American to climb in more than one region of the Alps and the first American member of England's Alpine Club.

1860: PEAK FIRST ASCENT *GRAN PARADISO*

September 4. British mountaineers John Jermyn Cowell and N. Dundas and guides Michel Payot and Jean Tairraz made the first ascent of the Gran Paradiso (13,324 ft./4,061 m.), the highest summit of the Graian Alps south of Mont Blanc. This is the highest mountain located completely within Italy. Cowell and Payot repeated this ascent the next day in order to enjoy the view. In 1922, the Gran Paradiso National Park was created to protect the area's flora and fauna. This park contains 173,000 acres and includes the peak Gran Paradiso.

1860:

August. British wood engraver Edward Whymper (1840 – 1911) made his first visit to the Swiss Alps at age 20 to prepare wood engravings of alpine scenes for London, England publisher William Longman. Longman needed these illustrations for the second series of Peaks, Passes, and Glaciers. Whymper returned to these Alps again in 1861, 1862, 1863, 1864, and 1865 during which time he made seven attempts to climb the Matterhorn (14, 692 ft./4,478 m.) before finally succeeding on July 14, 1865. In 1860, Whymper climbed his first mountain in Switzerland—the Riffelhorn (9,604 ft./2,927 m.) above Zermatt.

1860:

July. The three Parker brothers (Alfred, Charles, and Sandbach) from England attempted to climb the Matterhorn (14, 692 ft./4,478 m.) from Zermatt, Switzerland without using guides. They reached 10,820 feet/3,298 meters on the east face before retreating due to mist, wind, and time. They tried this climb again in 1861 with the same outcome (they reached 11,520 ft./3,511 m.).

1860: Equipment – Ice Axe

The ice hatchet was replaced by the ice axe. The "piccozza" (Italian for ice axe) was born. "Piolet" in French. "Pickel" in German. "Ice axe" in English. This ice axe came into existence as a cross between the long alpenstock (up to five feet in length) and the mountain guide's short-handled hatchet or long-handled axe. British climber Edward Whymper (1840 – 1911) and his English climbing companions carried ice axes with them on the first ascent of the Matterhorn (14,692 ft./4,478 m.) in July of 1865. Each of these ice axes weighed four pounds.

1860: Technique – Double Roping (On descent)

A mountain guide named Taugwalder insisted on double-roping down the last slope of the Allalinhorn (13,213 ft./4,027 m.) above the Allalin Pass with his British client Leslie Stephen (1832 – 1904). After looping the rope around a boulder or other secure hold, the climber held both strands of the double rope as he lowered himself down the face or slope. At the base of the slope, Taugwalder pulled one rope strand down thereby pulling the entire rope down from its anchor point. This was one of the first uses on record of a double rope for descending.

1860: Technique – Photography

Joseph Tairraz (1827 – 1902) took the first photographs of Mont Blanc (15,775 feet/4,808 meters). He used a wet-plate camera taking 21 x 27 centimeter plates. Tairraz was a member of a famous Chamonix family of guides and mountain photographers.

1861:

July 24. French photographer Auguste Rosalie Bisson (1826 – 1900) reached the summit of Mont Blanc (15,775 ft./4,808 m.) with twenty-five porters carrying his camera equipment. He claimed that this climb represented the first photographically recorded ascent of Mont Blanc. Auguste and his brother Louis Auguste (1814 – 1876) were the official photographers for Napoleon III. Their photographic studio was in Paris.

1861: PEAK FIRST ASCENT *WEISSHORN*

August 19. British mountaineer John Tyndall (1820 – 1893) and guides Johann Josef Bennen (1819 – 1864) and Ulrich Wenger made the first ascent of the Weisshorn (14,804 ft./4,512 m.) in Switzerland via the East Ridge from the Village of Randa (4,613 ft./1,406 m.). This roundtrip ascent/descent was accomplished in a single 19-hour push. Bennen was killed in 1864 in an avalanche. Weisshorn means "white mountain."

1861: PEAK FIRST ASCENT LYSKAMM

August 19. British mountaineers J.F. Hardy, A.C. Ramsey, F. Gibson, T. Rennison, J.A. Hudson, W.E. Hall, C.H. Pilkington, and R.M. Stevenson and guides J.P. Cachet, F. Lochmatter, K. Kerr, S. Zumtaugwald, and P. and J. Perren made the first ascent of the Lyskamm (14,853 ft./4,527 m.) above Zermatt, Switzerland via the Southeast ridge. This peak was formerly named the Silberbast (Silver Saddle—due to its outline). This first ascent climb took 17 hours and 20 minutes from the Riffel above Zermatt.

1861: PEAK FIRST ASCENT *NORDEND*

August 26. British mountaineers Edward and T.F. Buxton, John Jermyn Cowell and guides Michel Payot and Binder made the first ascent of the Nordend (15,122 ft./4,609 m.), the northern summit of Monte Rosa on the Swiss-Italian border. This is the third highest summit in the Alps.

1861:

Summer. Members of the British Alpine Club and their guides hiked and climbed the eighty-mile long Haute Route ("High Level Road") from Zermatt, Switzerland to Chamonix, France. The highest elevation reached on this seven to ten day traverse was the Col de Torrent (9,630 ft./2,935 m.). This route crossed 23 different glaciers. There are now three different Haute Route options:

    1. The Skier's Haute Route (March and April)

    2. The Walkers's Haute Route – This route avoids the glaciers and the
        highest passes.

    3. The Original Haute Route – This route travels mostly on glaciers and
        crosses eleven high mountain passes.

1861: FIRST ASCENT

Twenty-one year old Edward Whymper (1840 – 1911), Reginald Macdonald, and guide Sémiond made the first ascent by a British climber of Mont Pelvoux (12,947 ft./3,946 m.) in the Dauphiné Alps of France. As a result of this ascent, Whymper was elected a member of the British Alpine Club. Mont Pelvoux was first climbed on July 30, 1828.

1861: FIRST ASCENT

The Gouter Ridge route on Mont Blanc was first climbed by British mountaineers Leslie Stephen (1832 – 1904), Francis Fox Tuckett (1834 – 1913), and their Swiss guides Melchior Anderegg (1828 – 1912), Johann Josef Bennen (1824 – 1864) and Peter Perren. This is the most popular climbing route on Mont Blanc. It is commonly known as the "Ordinary Route."

1861: Equipment – Ice Axe

The Simond family of blacksmiths in Chamonix, France, decided to exclusively make mountaineering tools. They were the first blacksmith company to make this total commitment.

1861: Equipment – Sleeping Bags

British mountaineer John Tyndall (1820 – 1893) and his two guides made the first ascent of the Weisshorn (14,804 ft./4,512 m.) in Switzerland. They used primitive sleeping bags made of two rugs that were sewn together.

1861: Equipment – Tents

British climber Edward Whymper (1840 – 1911) designed the first mountain tent. This was the first edition of a tent he would continue to modify. Known as the Alpine Tent, this design would remain popular for the next 72 years (until 1933). His design criteria was as follows: 1) the tent must be portable, and 2) the tent must combine lightness with stability. The base of Whymper's tent measured six feet square. It was designed to accommodate four climbers. One end of this tent had flaps that "opened like a book." The tent fabric (coarse calico) was supported by four ash wood poles each 6 ½ feet long and 1 ¼ inches in diameter. These four poles were shod with iron tips. The tent had a sewn-in floor (Whymper's invention) of ordinary plaid Macintosh and a separate fly of Macintosh for waterproofing. This tent did not perform well in windy conditions which, at times, necessitated taking the tent down and wrapping it around its users. Eventually this tent became known as the Whymper Tent. It weighed 23 pounds without the flysheet and cost 4 guineas. It took three minutes to erect this tent by two people.

In 1893, Whymper again traveled to the French Alps above Chamonix to test a new design modification to his original Alpine Tent (a.k.a. the Whymper Tent).

1861: Technique – Photography

July 25. The Bisson brothers of Paris, France made the first recorded photographic ascent of Mont Blanc and took the first photographs from the summit. Three successful photographs were made with a camera that measured 12 x 18 inches. Twenty-five guides and porters carried all of the Bisson's photography equipment to the summit.

1862: PEAK FIRST ASCENT *DENT BLANCHE*

July 18. British mountaineers T.S. Kennedy (1841 – 1894), William Wigram, C. Wigram, and guides Jean-Baptiste Croz and Johann Krönig made the first ascent of the Dent Blanche (14,292 ft./4,356 m.) west of Zermatt, Switzerland. They began their ascent from Bricolla, Switzerland and climbed the southwest face. The temperature was -20°F on the summit. Dent Blanche means "white fang" in the French language.

1862: PEAK FIRST ASCENT *TASCHHORN*

July 30. The Reverend John Llewellyn-Davies (1826 – 1916) and the Reverend J.W. Hayward and guides Johann and Stephan Zumtaugwald made the first ascent of the Täschhorn (14,732 ft./4,490 m.)

above Zermatt, Switzerland via the northwest face. They began their ascent from the village of Randa. This is the only Zermatt valley mountain that is named for the village below it.

1862:

July. British mountaineer Edward Whymper (1840 – 1911) made his sixth attempt to climb the Matterhorn. He reached 13,460 ft./4,102 m. with Luc Meynet (the Hunchback of Breuil) on the Italian side of the mountain. Whymper made five unsuccessful attempts to climb the Matterhorn from Breuil during this year.

1862:

November 19. The Austrian Alpine Club was founded—the Oesterreichischer Alpen Verein. This was the first European mountain club. Dr. Anton von Ruthner was elected president and the first meeting was held on this date at the Royal Academy of Science in Vienna.

1862: Equipment – Ice Axe

American mountaineer Mr. Hamilton Lockwood (Boston, Massachusetts) made the twenty-sixth ascent of Mont Blanc (French Alps, 15,775 ft./4,808 m.) by an American. Lockwood used a 54" ice axe on the ascent with a demountable head which was held in place by a large screw-knob. Outside of Chamonix, France and Zermatt, Switzerland, ice axes were rare at this time.

1862: Equipment – Sleeping Bag

British climber Edward Whymper (1840 – 1911) and others used a "blanket bag" (sewn up double around the legs) with a piece of elastic riband around the open end.

1862: Equipment

British climber Edward Whymper (1840 – 1911) invented "two little appliances" to aid him in solo climbing:

1. A kind of grappling hook he called the "claw." Made of steel, this claw was five inches long and 1/5" thick. It was attached to a rope which then could be lifted up on the end of an alpenstock or in desperate cases thrown upwards until it fastened itself to a rock. Whymper used this "claw" on his climbs including the Matterhorn (14,692 ft./4,478 m.) in Switzerland.
2. A wrought-iron ring 2 ¼" in diameter and 3/8" thick. A cord was attached to this iron ring which enabled the rope to be pulled away from belay locations when descending with its aid.

1863:

January 28. The Swiss Parliament decided to name the highest peak in the Swiss Alps the Dufour Peak or Dufourspitze (the highest summit of Monte Rosa: 15,204 ft./4,634 m.) in honor of the Surveyor General of Switzerland Guillaume Henri Dufour (1787 – 1875) for his Dufour Map of Switzerland.

1863:

March 6. England's Alpine Club first published the *Alpine Journal,* the world's oldest mountaineering journal. Published by Longmans of London, this journal's first editor was the Reverend Hereford Brooke George (1838 – 1910).

1863:

April 19. The Club Alpin Suisse (Swiss Alpine Club) was founded. Its headquarters were in Zurich. The first meeting was held on this date in Olten with 35 members attending. Dr. Rudolf Théodor Simler (Professor of Geology at Bern) was elected president. By December of 1863, the club had 257 members in eight geographical sections. In 2006, its membership was over 110,000 in 111 sections. The club now maintains 153 mountain huts with 9,500 beds.

1863:

August 9. The Club Alpino Italiano (Italian Alpine Club) was founded in Turin by Quintino Sella (1827 – 1884), Felice Giordano (1825 – 1892), and Bartolomeo Gastaldi (1818 – 1879). As of 1968, this club had over 100,000 members.

1863:

The Swiss Alpine Club built its first climber's hut on the Tödi (11,887 ft./3,623 m.). This was the Grünhorn Hut. The Trift Hut (1864), the Matterhorn Hut (1865), the Mountet Hut (1871), the Weisshorn Hut (1876), and the Boval Hut (1877) followed.

1863: Book

Physiologist, surgeon, and zoologist Dr. Paul Bert (1833 – 1886) began to study altitude physiology. In this year, he published *Barometric Pressure* which concluded that the lack of oxygen caused mountain sickness. Many consider Bert to be the "father of high-altitude physiology."

1863:

British climber/cartographer Anthony Adams-Reilly (1836 – 1885), a friend of Edward Whymper, began his field work on the first reliable map of the Mont Blanc massif on the French-Italian border. Adams-Reilly determined the position of 200 separate points relative to a baseline in the Chamonix Valley. Whymper assisted him. This map was named "The Chain of Mont Blanc" and was published in 1865.

1863: FIRST ASCENTS

Oberland (Switzerland) guide Johann Joseph Brennen (1824 – 1864) led American climbers Mr. and Mrs. Winkworth up both the Aletschhorn (13,764 ft./4,195 m.) and the Jungfrau (13642 ft./4,158 m.) in Switzerland. These two climbs represented the first ascents by a woman.

1863: Book

Irish climber John Ball (1818 – 1889) published the first of three volumes of *The Alpine Guide* – a remarkably comprehensive survey of challenging walks, scrambles, and climbs all over the Alps. This three-volume set represented the first climbing guidebook.

> 1863 – The Western Alps
> 1864 – The Central Alps
> 1868 – The Eastern Alps

1863: Equipment – Ladders

British climber Edward Whymper (1840 – 1911) made another attempt to climb the Matterhorn (14,692 ft./4,478 m.) in Switzerland. Whymper came to the peak with a set of folding (hinged) ladders for climbing steep rock sections. These ladders were designed for lightness and strength.

1863: Equipment – Sleeping Bags

Edward Whymper (1840 – 1911) used his newly designed sleeping bag on his ascent of Monte Viso (12,602 ft./3,841 m.) in the Dauphiné Mountains on the French-Italian border. This sleeping bag used Macintosh material (waterproof) on the underside. The upper-side was of a very dense scarlet blanketing with the trade name of Swanskin. This sleeping bag weighed 8.5 pounds.

1863: Technique – Ice Axe

British mountaineer Sir James Hector (1834 – 1907) may have been the first climber to use the ice axe (instead of an alpenstock) and rope in crevassed terrain in Switzerland.

1863: Technique – Climbing Rope

A rope length of 40 feet/12 meters was considered quite long enough for a party of three climbers. A separate loop of rope was fastened around the waist of each climber. The climbing rope was always kept taut between climbers.

1864: PEAK FIRST ASCENT *MARMOLADA*

September 28. Austrian mountaineer Paul Grohmann (1838 – 1908), Angelo and Augusto Dimai made the first ascent of the Marmolada di Penia (10,965 ft./3,342 m.), the highest peak in the Italian Dolomite mountains. They made this first ascent from the north side. The Dolomites contain eighteen named peaks over 10,000 feet (3,048 meters).

1864:

British mountaineer A.W. (Adolphus Warburton) Moore (1841 – 1887) made six major first ascents of peaks in the Alps, three first pass crossings, and crossed twelve glaciers. Moore's frequent companions on these climbs were Edward Whymper (1840 – 1911) and Horace Walker (1838 – 1908). Moore also made the following ascents in the Alps during his climbing career: Mont Blanc, Eiger, Breche de la Meije, Barre des Ecrins, Rimpfischhorn, Aletschhorn, and the Wetterhorn. Moore died in Monte Carlo, France at age 46.

1864:

As of this year, Swiss mountain guide Peter Perren claimed first ascents of the Alphubel (13,800 ft./4,206 m.), Lyskamm (14,853 ft./4,527 m.), Dent d'Herens (13,685 ft./4,171 m.), and the Grivola (13,022 ft./3,969 m.). He also made the following ascents:

Monte Rosa	: 20 ascents
Breithorn	: 15 ascents
Mont Blanc	: 10 ascents
Jungfrau	: 3 ascents

1864:

Swiss painter Alexander Calame (1810 – 1864) died at age 54. He was regarded as the greatest alpine painter of the 19th century. Calame began his painting in 1830 and painted only mountains. He had only one eye. He painted five versions of Monte Rosa at sunset.

1864:

From 1857 – 1864, eighteen attempts were made to climb the Matterhorn (14,692 ft./4,478 m.). Fifteen of these attempts were made from the Italian (south) side while only three attempts originated from the Swiss (north) side. British mountaineer Edward Whymper (1840 – 1911) was involved in seven of these attempts.

1864: PEAK FIRST ASCENT BALMHORN

British woman mountaineer Lucy Walker (1835 – 1916) became the first woman to take part in a major first ascent- the Balmhorn (12,169 ft./3,709 m.) in Switzerland. This was also the only time in the history of the Alps where a father (Frank Walker), a son (Horace Walker), and a daughter (Lucy) were together for a first ascent. Lucy Walker also made the first ascent of the Eiger (13,025 ft./3,970 m.) by a woman during this year (the fourth overall ascent).

1864:

British mountaineer Rev. Julius Elliott climbed eight peaks in England in eight and a half hours. These peaks (Scafell, Scafell Pike, Great End, Great Gable, Kirkfell, Pillar, Steeple, and Red Pike) required a 15-mile roundtrip.

1864: Equipment – Ropes

September. A special committee of the British Alpine Club (London, England) submitted its report entitled: *Report of the Alpine Club's Special Committee on Ropes*. This committee approved Manilla hemp ropes that would sustain a specific weight falling a specific distance. Manilla hemp fibers are obtained from the leaves of the abach plant. The name "Manilla" refers to the capital of the Philippines where abaca plants are widely found. The initial recommendation of this committee was as follows: "The rope (manila hemp) must be able to withstand one shock of a freefall of seventy-six kilograms (or 167 pounds) from a height of 3.5 meters (or 11.5 feet)." These manila hemp ropes were heavy, possessed no elasticity, and were difficult to manage in wet and/or cold conditions. This testing of ropes led to the setting of the world's first standards for climbing equipment.

The original Alpine Club climbing rope was hawser-laid* manila hemp and was produced by John Buckingham of London who eventually sold his company to Arthur Beale also of London. This rope cost five pence per yard and was identified by a thin red worsted thread woven into the rope's braiding. This rope was known as the Alpine Club Rope. The usual length carried by climbers was eighteen meters or sixty feet although this rope was also produced in lengths of 40, 80, and 100 feet. Hemp ropes were widely used until the early 1950s.

1864: Equipment – Ice Axe

The equipment committee of England's Alpine Club recommended a design specification for ice axe picks. They recommended a curved pick that matched the arc of an ice axe swing. The design of ice axes at this time was determined or strongly influenced by mountain guides in the Alps who often were blacksmiths. Nothing resulted from this Alpine Club recommendation because the guides felt that a curved pick would stick in the ice when cutting steps.

1864: Technique – Ridge Crossing

During the first ascent of the Zinal Rothorn (13,849 feet/4,221 meters) above Zermatt, Switzerland, British mountaineer Leslie Stephen (1832 – 1904) and his guide Melchior Anderegg (1828 – 1912) climbed across steep rock slabs on a ridge by using the "á cheval" technique. This climbing technique involved creeping along a narrow rock ridge with one leg on either side of the sharp ridge. The term "á cheval" is French for "on horseback."

1865: PEAK FIRST ASCENT *POINTE WHYMPER*

June 24. British mountaineer Edward Whymper (1840 – 1911) and guides Michel Croz (1830 – 1865), Christian Almer (1826 – 1898), and Franz Biner made the first ascent of Pointe Whymper (13,728 ft./4,184 m.) on the Grandes Jorasses of the French Alps. This is the second highest summit point of the Grandes Jorasses. This ascent and four other first ascents occurred a few weeks prior to the Matterhorn tragedy. During an 18-day period, this climbing party ascended more than 100,000 feet of peaks and high passes.

1865: PEAK FIRST ASCENT *AIGUILLE VERTE*

June 29. British climber Edward Whymper (1840 – 1911) and guides Christian Almer (1826 – 1898) and Franz Biner made the first ascent of the Aiguille Verte (the Green Needle – 13,524 ft./4,122 m.) on the Mont Blanc massif. This was Whymper's last climb before his first ascent of the Matterhorn on July 14.

---

* A hawser-laid rope consisted of a number of fibers or filaments that were twisted together to make three strands. These strands were then twisted together to make a rope 1 ¼" in circumference.

1865:

July 14. The Matterhorn (14,692 ft./4,478 m.) was finally climbed on the 19th attempt. The first attempt was made in 1857 by J.A. Carrel, J.J. Carrel, and Aimé Gorret on the Lion Ridge. They reached 12,650 ft./3,856 m. Here is a summary of the 19 climbing attempts:

        1857 – 2 attempts
        1858 – 1 attempt
        1860 – 2 attempts
        1861 – 3 attempts
        1862 – 7 attempts
        1863 – 1 attempt
        1865 – 3 attempts – first ascent
        ——
         19

1865: PEAK FIRST ASCENT MATTERHORN

July 14. On his eighth attempt, British mountaineer Edward Whymper (1840 – 1911) finally reached the summit of the Matterhorn (14,692 ft./4,478 m.) with his French guide Michel-Auguste Croz (1830 – 1865) via the Hornli Ridge (4,003 ft./1,220 m.). With Whymper and Croz were British climbers Lord Francis Douglas (1847 – 1865), the Reverend Charles Hudson (1828 – 1865), and Douglas Hadow (1846 – 1865). In addition to guide Michel Croz, Whymper also hired Zermatt guides Peter Taugwalder, Sr. (1820 – 1888) and his son Peter Taugwalder, Jr. (1843 – 1923). Peter Taugwalder ("Old Peter") Sr.'s guide fee for this climb was 200 Swiss francs. This famous peak, the Matterhorn, was known by three names at this time: Matterhorn (English and German), Monte Cervino (Italian), and Mont Cervin (French). It was the last major summit in the Alps to be climbed. The Swiss summit is 43 inches higher and several hundred feet east of the Italian summit. There are now twenty-five named climbing routes to the summit of the Matterhorn.

Whymper and his party reached the summit at 1:40 p.m. and remained there for "one crowded hour of glorious life" according to Whymper. They could see over 100 miles in all directions. He used the white shirt of Croz as a victory flag. Croz, Douglas, Hadow, and Hudson were then killed on the descent when Hadow slipped (his boot heels were fitted with smooth metal plates) and fell pulling the others with him after the rope broke between Douglas and Peter Taugwalder, Sr. These four climbers (Croz, Douglas, Hadow and Hudson) fell 4,000 feet/1,219 meters down the north face to their deaths. Their remains were recovered the next day from the Matterhorn Glacier although nothing was ever found from Lord Francis Douglas except one of his sleeves and one boot.

Over 100 mountains in Africa, Asia, North America, and the Pacific Islands are nicknamed the "Matterhorn" of their particular country or a specific mountain range in that country. Four mountains in the United States are named after the Matterhorn:

        California – Matterhorn Peak 12,264 ft./3,738 m.
        Colorado – Matterhorn Peak 13,590 ft./4,142 m.
        Nevada – Matterhorn 10,838 ft./3,303 m.
        Oregon – Matterhorn Peak 9,826 ft./2,995 m.

1865: FIRST ASCENT

July 14 and 15. British mountaineers William Mathews, Adolphus Warburton ("A.W.") Moore, Frank Walker, Horace Walker, and guides Jakob and Melchior Anderegg made the first ascent of Mont Blanc (15,782 ft./4,810 m.) from the Italian side via the Brenva Spur. A.W. Moore was the first climber to conceive of this route. The four British climbers had alpenstocks but no crampons. The two guides had ice axes but no crampons. This climbing party did use a rope.

1865: FIRST ASCENT

July 17. Italian mountain guides Jean Antoine Carrel (1829 – 1890) and Jean-Baptiste Bich made the first ascent of the Matterhorn (14,692 ft./4,478 m.) from the Italian (south) side. They climbed the Liongrat (Lions Ridge or the Italian Ridge) and then reached the summit via the "Galerie Carrel" and the northwest ridge. Their roundtrip time from Breuil (6,641 ft./2,024 m.) was 56 ½ hours.

1865: FIRST ASCENT

October 2. Ms. Marguerite Claudia "Meta" Brevoort (1825 – 1876) became the first American woman to summit Mont Blanc (15,782 ft./4,810 m.). She climbed primarily with her nephew William Coolidge (25 years her junior). She was 40 and he 15 when her climbing career began. She never married and died at age 51 in her sleep. She was the most accomplished woman climber of her time.

1865 – 1915:

This fifty-year period has been called the "Silver Age of Mountaineering." Climbers began looking for more difficult routes up previously climbed peaks. This period has also been labeled the "Iron Age of Mountaineering" due to the popular use of iron pitons.

1865:

British mountaineer John Tyndall (1820 – 1893) became the first foreigner elected to the Swiss Alpine club.

1865:

The Royal Geographical Society in London, England officially accepted the name "Mount Everest." This recognition occurred one year prior to the death of Sir George Everest (1790 – 1866) at age 76. Sir George pronounced his last name "Eve-rest."

1865:

American mountaineer W.A.B. (William Augustus Brevoort) Coolidge (1850 – 1926) began his first climbing season in the Alps. From 1865 until 1898 (33 years), Coolidge never missed a climbing season. He possibly made more ascents than anyone else—the list of his ascents fills 22 pages in the British Alpine Club Register. He preferred snow and ice routes to rock climbing routes.

1865: FIRST ASCENT

British mountaineer Frederick Morshead made the first solo round-trip ascent of Mont Blanc in a single day from Chamonix.

1865:

Charles Packe (1826 – 1896) and Henry Russell (1834 – 1909) formed the Societe Ramond in the Pyrenees mountains of France-Spain. This organization was the forerunner to the Club Alpin Francais which was established in 1874.

1865: Equipment – Eye Protection

Swiss mountain guide Melchior Anderegg (1828 – 1912) of Zermatt provided his clients with sun veils and snow spectacles in blue, green, or neutral tints.

1865: Equipment – Packs

British climber Edward Whymper (1840 – 1911) on his history—making first ascent of the Matterhorn (14,692 ft./4,478 m.) in Switzerland wore a single shoulder strap hip pack.

1865: Equipment – Rope

There were three different ropes used on the first ascent of the Matterhorn (14,692 ft./4,478 m.) in Switzerland on July 14, 1865. These ropes were:

1. 200 ft./61 m. – Buckingham's Alpine Club White Manilla hemp rope – 12 mm in diameter
2. 150 ft./46 m. – A thicker rope and possibly stronger than the manilLa hemp rope.
3. 250 ft./76 m. – A lighter, weaker sashcord that was used for windows. This sashcord was the rope that broke on the descent allowing four climbers to fall to their deaths.

Edward Whymper also mentions wire rope in his account of the Matterhorn's first ascent.

1866:

September 14. American mountaineer John Wilkinson (1840 – 1891) and his younger brother engaged the services of two Taugwalder guides (from Zermatt, Switzerland) and climbed Mont Blanc (15,775 ft./4,808 m.). This was the first American ascent of Mont Blanc in which Swiss guides were used.

1866:

December 23. British mountaineer A.W. Moore (1841 – 1887) and Horace Walker (1838 – 1908) and guides Melchior Anderegg, Christian Almer, and Peter Bohren initiated the practice of winter mountaineering by crossing the Strahlegg Pass (10,995 ft./3,351 m.) and the Finsteraarhorn and then returning to Grindelwald (Switzerland) on December 24.

1867: PEAK FIRST ASCENT *MONTE CIVETTA*

May 31. British mountaineer and cartographer Francis Fox Tuckett (1834 – 1913) and his guides Melchior Anderegg and Jakob Anderegg made the first ascent of Monte Civetta (10,558 ft./3,218 m.) in the Italian Dolomites. A local hunter named Simeone di Silvestro may have been the primary guide for this party. He claimed that he had made the first ascent in 1855.

1867: FIRST ASCENT

August. British mountaineer Florence Crauford Grove (1838 – 1902) became the first "tourist" to climb the Matterhorn (14, 692 ft./4,478 m.) from Breuil, Italy. His guides were Jean-Antoine Carrel, Salomon Meynet, and Jean-Baptiste Bich. This was the second ascent of the Matterhorn from the Italian side.

1867: Technique – Rappelling

French mountain guide Jean Esteril Charlet (1840 – 1925) is credited with developing the next step in technique for descending a rope. A double rope was taken around one leg and then up and over the opposite shoulder. This body wrap technique was known in French as a "rappel" and in German, Swiss, and Austrian as an "abseil." The English adopted the term "rappel." Charlet climbed partway up the Grand Dru (12,317 feet/3,754 meters) and then rappelled down a double rope (an Edward Whymper innovation). This was regarded as perhaps the first rappel in the Chamonix (France) mountains.

1868: PEAK FIRST ASCENT *POINTE WALKER*

June 29 and 30. British climber Horace Walker (1838 – 1908) and Julien Grange with guides Melchior Anderegg and Johann Jaun made the first ascent of Pointe Walker (13,806 ft./4,208 m.), the highest summit of the Grandes Jorasses in the French Alps (six miles northeast of Mont Blanc). There are five summit points on the Grandes Jorasses—all over 4,000 meters. These summits are:

Point Walker	13,806 ft./4,208 m.	1868 – PFA
Point Whymper	13,728 ft./4,184 m.	1865 – PFA
Point Croz	13,455 ft./4,101 m.	1909 – PFA
Point Marguerite	13,340 ft./4,066 m.	1898 – PFA
Point Helene	13,272 ft./4,045 m.	1898 – PFA

1868: FIRST ASCENT

July 29. British mountaineer John Tyndall (1820 – 1893) and guides Jean-Pierre Maquignaz and brother Jean-Joseph Maquignaz made the first complete traverse of the Matterhorn (14,692 ft./4,478 m.) from Breuil, Italy to Zermatt, Switzerland. This was the seventh overall ascent of the peak. Summit traverses became a new sought-after achievement. Five days later on August 2nd, Tyndall and Jean-Joseph made the same traverse in the opposite direction.

1868: PEAK FIRST ASCENTS KAZBEK, ELBRUS – EAST

July 31. British mountaineer William Douglas Freshfield (1845 – 1934), A.W. Moore (1841 – 1887), and C. Comyns Tucker (1843 –) and French mountain guide Francois Devouassoud (1831 – 1905) made the first ascents of Kazbek (16,541 ft./5,041 m.) and Mount Elbrus (East Peak, 18,442 ft./5,621 m.) in the Caucasus Range of southwestern Russia. This was the first British expedition and the first serious exploration to the Caucasus mountains. Guide Francois Devouassoud was the first alpine guide to travel to a far-distant mountain range. The East Peak of Mount Elbrus was the first high peak in the Caucasus mountain range to be climbed. This range contains thirty peaks over 14,000 feet (4,267 meters). Twelve of these peaks are higher than Mont Blanc (15,775 ft./4,808 m.)

1868: FIRST ASCENT

August 9. German professor Paul Güssfeldt (1840 – 1920) and guides Peter Knubel (1833 – 1919) and Jean Marie Lochmatter (both guides from the village of St. Niklaus down valley from Zermatt) made the first one-day ascent and descent of the Matterhorn (14,692 ft./4,478 m.) from Zermatt (5,300 ft./1,615 m.), Switzerland. Güssfeldt became the first German to climb the Matterhorn.

1868:

The guide's fee for a Matterhorn ascent (from Zermatt) was 100 Swiss francs while a porter's fee for the same climb was 50 francs.

1868: Technique – Fixed Chains and Cables

Thick, metal chains were placed on the Breuil (Italian) side of the Matterhorn (14,692 feet/4,478 meters) as "fixed ropes" on steep, exposed, and difficult sections of rock. Unlike Manilla hemp ropes, these "metal ropes" did not rot away.

1869:

May 9. The Deutscher Alpenverein (German Alpine Club) was founded in Munich, Germany. Architectural historian Gustav von Bezold (1848 – 1934) was elected its first president. The club became the world's largest mountaineering society.

1869: PEAK FIRST ASCENT *SASSOLUNGO*

August 21. Austrian climber Paul Grohmann (1838 – 1908) and his Italian guides Franz Innerkofler and Peter Salcher began the big-wall climbing period in the Alps with their ascent of the 1,148 foot/350 meter south face of the Cima Grande di Lavaredo (9,840 ft./2,999 m.) in the Italian Dolomite mountains. They climbed several steps of 5.4 difficulty. They also made the first ascent of Sassolungo (10,437 ft./3,181 m.) in the Dolomites. From 1862 to 1869, Grohmann made eight peak first ascents in the Dolomites.

1869 – 1876:

The British-born Pigeon sisters (Anna and Ellen) climbed 63 peaks and crossed 72 passes in this seven-year period. They also made the first women's traverse of the Matterhorn from Breuil to Zermatt in 1873. They may have been the first women to use an ice axe in the Alps. Their descent of the Sesia Joch on the southeast face of Monte Rosa (average slope of 62°) was regarded as the first really great feat of climbing by women (1869).

1869:

The first "via ferrata" climbing route was developed over the Studlgrat onto the Grossglockner (12,461 ft./3,798 m.) in Austria. In Italian, via ferrata means "iron ways." These are climbing routes protected with steel cables, steps, ladders, and bridges.

1869: Equipment – Cameras

The Reverend Hereford Brooke George (1838 – 1910), a British mountain photographer, may have been the first climber/photographer to adapt his ice axe as a support (early form of a mono-pod) for his camera.

1870:

All of the main peaks in the Alps were climbed except the Meije (13,068 ft./3,983 m.) in the Dauphiné Alps of southeastern France.

1870:

Englishwoman Katherine Richardson (1854 – 1927) visited Zermatt, Switzerland at age 16 and began her climbing career. She recorded fourteen first ascents by a woman, six pure first ascents and 116 major ascents in the Alps. During one eight-day period in 1882 (28 years old), she climbed the Zinalrothorn (13,849 ft./4,221 m.), the Weisshorn (14,781 ft./4,505 m.), Monte Rosa (15,204 ft./4,634 m.), and the Matterhorn (14,692 ft./4,478 m.). She always wore a skirt while climbing.

1870:

Boulder climbing began in the forests of Fountainbleau approximately 30 miles/50 kilometers southeast of Paris, France. Fountainbleau contains over 1,000 individual sandstone boulders not exceeding 15 meters/49 feet in height. The climbing activity here advanced the technique of friction climbing.

1870: Equipment – Rock Climbing Shoes

The Dolomite mountains in northern Italy were the first mountains where rope-soled shoes were used for rock climbing. These soles could grip the tiniest holds on a rock face.

1870: Technique – Climbing Philosophy

German students developed a distinctive climbing philosophy: Extraordinary self-reliance and self-assurance combined with a degree of fatalism.

1871: FIRST ASCENT

July 22. British woman mountaineer Lucy Walker (1835 – 1916) became the first woman to climb the Matterhorn (14,692 ft./4,478 m.) in Switzerland. Her guide was Melchior Anderegg (plus 4 other guides) and her father, Frank Walker (1808 – 1872), was also with her. This was the nineteenth overall ascent. Frank Walker, at age 65, was the oldest person to reach the summit to date. Lucy Walker wore her favorite old white print dress on this climb. Five days prior to her Matterhorn ascent, she climbed the Weisshorn (14,804 ft./4,512 m.).

1871: FIRST ASCENT

September 4 and 5. Ms. Meta Brevoort (1825 – 1876) and W.A.B. Coolidge (1850 – 1926) and guides Christian Almer, Ulrich Almer, and Nicholas Knubel made the first traverse of the Matterhorn (14,692 ft./4,478 m.) by a woman from Zermatt, Switzerland to Breuil, Italy.

1871: Book

British mountaineer Leslie Stephen (1832 – 1904) published *The Playground of Europe*. This book about climbing in the Alps was considered to be the best-written book on alpine mountaineering to date.

1871: Book

After his 1865 first ascent of the Matterhorn, British mountaineer Edward Whymper (1840 – 1911) began to write *Scrambles Amongst the Alps in the Years 1860 – 69*. This book is considered to be one of the best-selling mountaineering books of all time. It included 115 illustrations drawn mostly by Whymper and five detailed maps indicating the author's climbs and travels in the Alps. He wrote most of the book in Haslemere, England. The publisher eventually produced six editions (1871 – 2, 1880, 1893, 1900, and 1936). There were also three U.S. editions (1871, 1873, and 1899). This was the first book to popularize mountaineering as a worthy craft.

1872: FIRST ASCENT

July 23. Swiss guide Ferdinand Imseng (1845 – 1881) led Richard and William Pendlebury (British), Charles Taylor (British), Gabriel Spechtenhauer (Austrian), and Giovanni Oberto (Italian) on the first ascent of the longest couloir in the Alps on Monte Rosa's (15,204 ft./4,634 m.) east face. This was the first ascent of the 8,200 foot/2,499 meter east face of Monte Rosa. This couloir later became known as the Marinelli Couloir which was named for Damiano Marinelli (– 1881), alpinist and a founding member of the Italian Alpine Club. On August 9, 1881, an avalanche in the couloir killed Marinelli and guides Imseng and Pedranzini. All three bodies were recovered on the Monte Rosa Glacier. The Marinelli Hut was erected in 1885 on the left bank of the couloir at an altitude of 10,150 feet/3,093 meters.

1872: Equipment – Eye Protection

Julbo, a French optical company, began making eyewear for mountain hikers and climbers.

1872: Technique – Bivouacking

The high-mountain bivouac was popularized by American woman mountaineer Meta Brevoort (1825 – 1876) in the Swiss Alps. By camping higher, two peaks could be climbed in a single day.

1872: Technique – Rock Climbing

1872 – 1892: British mountaineer Albert Frederick Mummery (1855 – 1895) revolutionized rock climbing technique. Mummery began to realize the joy and satisfaction of attempting a difficult climb where the chance of success was in question. He was frequently accompanied by mountain guide Alexander Burgener (1846 – 1910).

1873:

June 20. British woman climber Lucy Walker (1835 – 1916) climbed the Titlis (10,627 ft./3,239 m.) in Switzerland—her 80th major alpine ascent.

1873:

Luigi Amedeo Giuseppe Maria Ferdinando Francesco di Savoia was born in Aosta, Italy (1873 – 1933). This famous mountaineer became known as "Il Duca d'Abruzzi" (The Duke of the Abruzzi). He was the grandson of Victor Emmanuel II, King of Italy. He led three important mountaineering expeditions:

      1) 1897 – Mount St. Elias, North America

      2) 1906 – Ruwenzori mountains, Africa

      3) 1909 – K2, Asia

1873:

British mountaineer Frederick Gardiner (1850 – 1919) made his third ascent of the Matterhorn (14,692 ft./4,478 m.). This was the second one-day ascent/descent from Zermatt without requiring a bivouac.

1874: FIRST ASCENT

January 14 and 21. British mountaineers W.A.B. Coolidge (1850 – 1926) and his aunt Meta Brevoort (1825 – 1876) and their guides Christain and Ulrich Almer made the first winter ascents of the Wetterhorn (12,149 ft./3,703 m.) on January 14 and the Jungfrau (13,642 ft./4,158 m.) on January 21.

7▲1874: PEAK FIRST ASCENT *ELBRUS – WEST*

July 28. British mountaineers Horace Walker (1838 – 1908), Frederick Gardiner (1850 – 1919), and Florence Crauford Grove (1838 – 1902) and their Swiss guide Peter Knubel (1833 – 1919) made the first ascent of the west summit (18,511 ft./5,642 m.) of Mount Elbrus in the Caucasus Mountains of western Russia. Russian climber Akhya Sotaev (1788 –) also reached the summit (at age 86) in 1874.

1874:

British mountaineer and first ascender of the Matterhorn (14,692 ft./4,478 m.) in Switzerland Edward Whymper (1840 – 1911) climbed the peak again for his second ascent. His guides were Jean-Antoine Carrel (1829 – 1890), Jean-Baptiste Bich, and Josef-Marie Lochmatter (1837 – 1882). This was the 76th ascent of the famous peak. Whymper returned to this peak to take photographs to illustrate his lecture tours.

1874 – 1912:

Norway. British mountaineer William Cecil Slingsby (1849 – 1929) was credited with making 24 first ascents and new climbing routes on Norwegian peaks over this 38-year period.

---

[7] ▲ One of the world's Seven Summits

1874:

The alpine clubs of Austria (est. 1862) and Germany (est. 1869) were united to form the Deutscher Und Österreichischer Alpenverein. Their combined membership was 18,002. By 1907, its membership was over 70,000 climbers and hikers.

1874:

The Club Alpin Francais (French Alpine Club) was founded by Dr. Millot, Armand-Delille, and Emmanuel Boileau de Castelnau (1857 – 1923). This club admitted women immediately.

1874:

British mountaineer E.R. Whitwell made the first ascent of the Blaitiére (11,556 ft./3,522 m.), the first Chamonix (France) Aiguille ("Needle") to be climbed.

1875: FIRST ASCENT

January 2. Anglo-Austrian mountaineer William Adolf Baillie-Grohman (1851 – 1921) and four guides made the first winter ascent of the Grossglockner (12,461 ft./3,798 m.), the highest mountain in Austria. There are 242 peaks in Austria over 3,000 meters (9,840 feet) in height.

1875: FIRST ASCENT

Henri Cordier, Thomas Middlemore, and John Oakley and guides Jakob Anderegg, Johann Jaun, and Andreas Maurer made the first ascent of the north face of the Aiguille Verte (13,540 ft./4,127 m.) via the Cordier Couloir. This route, highly advanced for this time, would not be repeated until 1924.

1875: Book

Edward Whymper's (1840 – 1911) *Scrambles Amongst The Alps In the Years 1860 – 1869* (1871) was translated into French and became the first mountain book ever read in France.

1875 Onward:

Two major developments occurred in mountaineering: 1. The development of purely sporting mountaineering (and not for scientific purposes), and 2. The continued exploration upon steep rock in the effort to problem solve.

1875: Equipment – Boots

1870s. Special boots were now made for climbing after industrial boots and shooting (hunting) boots proved to be unsatisfactory. Bootmaker James A. Carter (London, England) now made boots that were fitted with a stiffening metal shank. A bellows tongue was added to these boots in the 1890s to keep out moisture and dirt.

1875: Equipment – Ice Axe

The ice axe began to replace the longer alpenstock. Early ice axes were very long (35 ½ in. plus/90 centimeters plus) and heavy. They were designed for chopping hundreds of steps in snow and ice. These ice axes consisted of a head, a shaft, and a ferruled spike.

1875: Technique – Artificial Aid Climbing

The Reverend James Jackson (1796 – 1878) at age 79 and a companion climbed Pillar Rock in England's Lakeland District. They used metal spikes (early pitons) and ropes as artificial aids.

1875: Technique – Ice Axe

1870s. The alpenstock virtually disappeared in Europe with the popularity of the ice axe.

1876: FIRST ASCENT

January 31. Ms. Mary Isabella Straton (1838 – 1918) and guides Jean Estéril Charlet (who Straton later married), Sylvain Couttet, and Michel Balmat (porter) made the first winter ascent of Mont Blanc (15,775 ft./4,808 m.) in the French Alps. Straton's son Robert was also on this climb and became the youngest person to climb Mont Blanc (11 ½ years old). They climbed Mont Blanc via the Grand Mulets and the Bosses Ridge. Charlet was the first guide to join the club Alpin Francais (French Alpine Club).

1876: PEAK FIRST ASCENT STORE SKAGASTOLSTIND

July 21. British mountaineer and "Father of Norwegian Mountaineering" William Cecil Slingsby (1849 – 1929) made the first ascent (solo) of Store Skagastölstind (7,891 ft./2,405 m.), the third highest peak in Norway. This mountain is commonly known as "Storen." With Slingsby on this first ascent were Emmanuel Mohn and guide Knut Lykken. These two climbers stopped their ascent at the lower col (or pass) now known as "Mohn's skar" allowing Slingsby to continue on alone to the summit.

1876: FIRST ASCENT

July 23. British mountaineers A. Cust, A.H. Cawood, and J.B. Colgrove made the first guideless ascent of the Matterhorn (14,692 ft./4,478 m.) in Switzerland. This climb was the first real shock to the belief that professional guides were essential in serious mountaineering.

1876:

The Le Centro Excursionista De Catalunya (Spanish Alpine Club) was founded in Spain.

1876: Technique – Guideless Climbing

A notable change in the art of climbing and exploring mountains was taking place from approximately 1876 to 1890. An increasing number of mountaineers (primarily British) were attempting climbs in the Alps without using mountain guides. British mountaineers Albert F. Mummery (1855 – 1895), Charles Pilkington (1850 – 1918), and his brother Lawrence Pilkington (1855 – 1941) were among the leaders of this guideless climbing trend.

1877: FIRST ASCENT

July 30 and 31. British mountaineer and geologist James Eccles (1838 – 1915) with guides Michel-Clément Payot and Alphonse Payot made the first ascent of the south face of Mont Blanc (15,775 ft./4,808 m.) via the Brouillard and Frêney Glaciers (Peuterey Ridge). This climb was only repeated twice in the next 80 years.

1877: PEAK FIRST ASCENT *MEIJE*

August 16. French mountaineer Henri Emmanuel Boileau de Castelnau (1857 – 1923) and his two guides Pierre (father) and Joseph (son) Gaspard made the first ascent of the Grand Pic de La Meije (13,068 ft./3,983 m.) near the village of La Grave in the Dauphiné region of southeastern France. This summit was finally reached after 17 previous attempts. La Meije was the last of the major alpine peaks to be climbed and is considered by many to be the most difficult. Prior to 1877, Boileau de Castelnau had climbed the Jungfrau, Finsteraarhorn, Matterhorn, Dent Blanche, and Mont Blanc (4 ascents).

1877: FIRST ASCENT

A Frenchman named Rochat made the first tourist ascent of Mont Aiguille (6,880 ft./2,097 m.) in the Vercors mountains south of Grenoble, France. The first ascent of this 1,000 foot/305 meter rock tower occurred in 1492. In 1878, the French Alpine Club installed fixed chains on the more difficult sections.

1877: Fabric – Oilskin

Norwegian sea captain Helly Juell Hansen (1842 – 1914) invented the world's first waterproof fabric ("oilskin") by rubbing linseed oil into canvas cloth. Hansen eventually started his own company that pioneered extreme weather clothing.

1877: Technique – Barefoot Climbing

French mountaineer Henri Emmanuel Boileau de Castelnau (1857 – 1923) and his guide Gaspard made the first ascent of the Grand Pic de La Mieje (13,067 feet/3,983 meters) in southeastern France. They climbed a 65 foot/20 meter pitch near the summit in bare feet for a better grip on small rock holds.

1878: PEAK FIRST ASCENT *GRAND DRU*

September 12. The first ascent of the Aiguille du Grand Dru (12,317 ft./3,754 m.) in the French Alps above Chamonix was made by British mountaineers Clinton Dent (1850 – 1912) and James Walker Hartley (1852 – 1939). This was Dent's 19th attempt to climb this rock peak. Guides Alexander Burgener (1846 – 1910) and Kaspar Mauer were with Dent and Hartley on this ascent up the southeast face.

1878: PEAK FIRST ASCENT *MONT MAUDIT*

September 12. British climbers Henry Seymour Hoare (1849 – 1930) and William Edward Davidson (1853 – 1923) and their Oberland guides Johann Jaun (1843 – 1921) and Johann von Bergen (1836 – ?) made the first ascent of Mont Maudit (14,650 ft./4,465 m.) on the Mont Blanc massif. They climbed the south ridge.

1878:

One of the world's first "via ferrata" climbing routes was created on Mont Aiguille (6,880 ft./2,097 m.) in the French Alps when chains were installed by the Club Alpin Francais (French Alpine Club). These chains aided climbers on steep rock faces. A "via ferrata" is a high mountain route with fixed climbing aids (ladders, bridges, rungs, wire ropes, etc.).

1878:

By this year, 100 Americans had climbed Mont Blanc (15,775 ft./4,808 m.) in the French Alps. The first American ascent was in 1819.

1878: Technique – Rappelling

Strong steel spikes (7" long) were driven into rock cracks in the European Alps to serve as rope anchors for rappels or double rope descents.

1879:

August 14. American climbers William Oxnard Moseley (26 year old Boston physician) and W.E. Craven made the 438th ascent of the Matterhorn (14,692 ft./4,478 m.) in Switzerland. Their guides were Peter Rubi and Christian Inabnit. Unfortunately, on the descent, Moseley (1848 – 1879) insisted on being unroped. He then slipped and fell 2,000 feet becoming the first American fatality on the Matterhorn. The Moseley Slab ("moseley-platte") on the normal Hornli Ridge climbing route is named for him.

1879: PEAK FIRST ASCENT *PETIT DRU*

August 29. Chamonix (France) mountain guides Jean-Esteril Charlet-Straton (1840 – 1925), Prosper Payot, and Frederic Folliguet made the first ascent of the Aiguille du Dru's lower summit known as the Petit Dru (12,248 ft./3,733 m.) via its south face and southwest ridge. Located in the French Alps, this climb was considered a major achievement in the history of mountaineering.

1879: FIRST ASCENT

September 3. British mountaineer Albert Frederick Mummery (1855 – 1895) and guides Alexander Burgener (1846 – 1910), Johann Petrus, and Augustin Gentinetta made the first ascent of the Zmutt Ridge on the Matterhorn (14,692 ft./4,478 m.) in Switzerland. This was the first new route on the Matterhorn in 14 years (since the first ascent in 1865) and this climbing party succeeded on its first attempt.

1879:

Summer. British mountaineers Frederick Gardiner (1850 – 1919), Charles Pilkington (1850 – 1919), and Lawrence Pilkington (1855 – 1941) reached the summit of the Meije (13,067 ft./3,983 m.) in the Dauphine mountains of France. This was one of the first major ascents that was accomplished without guides. This ascent began a new era of guideless climbing in the Alps.

1879: Book

Edward Whymper (1840 – 1911) published the third edition of *Scrambles Amongst The Alps In The Years 1860 to 1869* but titled this abridged version *The Ascent of the Matterhorn.*

1879:

The International Congress of Alpine Clubs met in Geneva, Switzerland. A paper on mountain sickness was presented by Professor Schiess of Bâle (Basel, Switzerland).

1879:

British mountaineer Albert Frederick Mummery (1855 – 1895) began his climbing period of 18 first ascents all with Swiss mountain guide Alexander Burgener (1846 – 1910). From 1879 to 1894, Mummery accomplished all of these first ascents in the Alps and Caucasus mountain ranges.

1879:

Italian mountaineer and pioneer mountain photographer Vittorio Sella (1859 – 1943) began a 16-year period of photographing the entire span of the Alps (1,000 kilometers in length). He used a 40-pound Dallmeyer camera and glass plates each weighing two pounds. Sella exposed over 1,000 plates over the 16 years.

1879: FIRST ASCENT

German mountaineer Karl Blodig (1859 – 1956) climbed the east face of Monte Rosa (15,204 ft./4,634 m.) at age 20 with Swiss guide Christian Ranggetiner. From 1879 (age 20) to 1932 (age 73), Blodig climbed all 76 4,000 meter (13,124 ft.) peaks in the Alps. He died at age 97.

1879:

British woman mountaineer Lucy Walker (1835 – 1916) made her final alpine ascent at age 44. She made a total of 105 different ascents from 1858 (age 19) to 1879. Ninety of these climbs were made with her favorite guide Melchior Anderegg(1828 – 1912). Walker was considered by many to be the first "real" woman mountaineer.

1879: Fabric – Gabardine

Britisher Thomas Burberry (1835 – 1926) obtained a patent for a fabric known as gabardine. Cotton threads were waterproofed before weaving making for the first time a breathable and tolerably water-proof fabric alternate to Macintosh which was a rubber-coated fabric.

1879: Technique – Rappelling

French mountain guides Jean-Esteril Charlet (1840 – 1925) and Frederic Folliguet climbed the north face of the Petit Dru (12,245 feet/3,732 meters) in the French Alps. During the descent, this team used the rappelling technique systematically for the first time to deal with the numerous vertical drops on the face.

1879: Technique – Food Pre-Packaging

British mountaineer Edward Whymper (1840 – 1911) spent several months in England identifying, purchasing, and packaging his food supply in preparation for his 1880 mountaineering expedition to Ecuador. Eventually, Whymper collected over twenty different foods (including beef, ham, mutton, soup, cocoa, tea, sugar, etc.) and medicines (including throat lozenges, zinc sulfate, laxatives, etc.) that were carefully wrapped and sealed in tin cases. These cases were then organized into climbing day packages—one package would provide one day's food and medicine for four climbers. The tin cases were packed in wooden boxes for transport to Ecuador. All of these boxes weighed a total of 2,376 pounds. This was certainly one of the first climbing expeditions to specifically organize and pre-package its food supply.

1880:

September: The Hornli Hutte (hut) was constructed at the base of the Hornligrat (Hornli Ridge) at 10,700 feet/3,261 meters on the Matterhorn (14,692 ft./4,478 m.) in Switzerland. This stone hut was enlarged in 1915 to accommodate 17 climbers. It was then re-built in 1965 to hold 51 climbers. This hut now can accommodate 120 climbers. By 1880, the Swiss Alpine Club had sponsored the construction of 34 mountain huts in various locations in the Alps.

1880: FIRST ASCENT

An American–British blind mountaineer named Sir Francis Joseph Campbell (1832 – 1914) climbed Mont Blanc (15,775 ft./4,808 m.) in the French Alps. He lost his eyesight at age 4. His guide was Christian Almer (1826 – 1898). Almer climbed behind Campbell on the rope. By jerking the rope, Almer could indicate to Campbell the appropriate length of stride. Campbell also climbed the Matterhorn, the Eiger, and the Jungfrau. He was probably the first blind climber to achieve significant ascents. He was affiliated with the Institute for the Blind in Norwood, England. Campbell was knighted in 1909.

1880:

Mountain guides Alexander Burgener (1846 – 1910) and Benedikt Venetz led British mountaineer Albert Frederick Mummery (1855 – 1895) on an attempt to climb the Aiguille du Gèant (13,167 ft./4,013 m.) in the French Alps. At this time, the Aiguille du Gèant was one of the last great unclimbed summits in the western Alps. Reaching an area of blank rock slabs, this trio of climbers left a note attached to a stick that read: "Absolutely impossible by fair means." The Aiguille du Gèant was first climbed on August 14, 1882.

1880 – 1900:

This twenty-year period has been called "The Mummery Era" after British mountaineer Albert Frederick Mummery (1855 – 1895). Mummery developed many improvements to climbing techniques. He was also an early pioneer of climbing in mountain ranges outside of the European Alps.

1880:

British landscape painter and Alpine Club member Elijah Walton (1832 – 1880) died at age 48. He was considered to be one of the finest mountain artists of his time. Walton was one of the first artists to actually climb to mountain high points in order to more effectively interpret mountain scenes.

1880: Technique – Foot Protection

Mountaineers rubbed brandy on their feet to harden the skin. Thick grease was then pressed in through their stockings to reduce friction.

1881: PEAK FIRST *ASCENT GREPON*

August 3. British mountaineer Albert Frederick Mummery (1855 – 1895) and guides Alexander Burgener (1846 – 1910) and Benedikt Venetz made the first ascent of the rock spire called the Grèpon (11,411 ft./3,478 m.) in the French Alps above Chamonix. This ascent of the south summit was accomplished by the fact that this party successfully climbed the famous Mummery Crack, a vertical fissure that was actually led by Venetz. This climb marked the beginning of the modern era of mountain climbing. It also marked a change in attitude: as few people as possible were taken along on climbing expeditions. The days of multiple guides, porters, servants, etc. on a climb were now over. On August 5, Mummery repeated this ascent and then climbed to the higher north summit (11,424 ft./3,482 m.).

1881:

August 4. American Theodore Roosevelt (1858 – 1919, the 26th U.S. President) climbed the Matterhorn (14,692 ft./4,478 m.) after his ascents of the Jungfrau (13,642 ft./4,158 m.) and Pilatus (6,985 ft./2,129 m.), all in Switzerland. Roosevelt climbed the Matterhorn "to show the British that a Yankee could do it too."

1881: Book

British woman mountaineer Elizabeth Le Blond (1861 – 1934) began her outdoor adventures in the Alps where she made significant contributions to winter mountaineering. She authored the book entitled *The High Alps In Winter* (1883), the first book devoted to winter mountaineering.

1881: FIRST ASCENT

Local mountain guide Johann Kederbacher Grill and an Austrian tourist climber named Otto Schuck made the first ascent of the Watzmann's (8,905 ft./2,714 m.) east face (nearly 7,000 ft./2,133 m. high) in the Berchtesgaden Alps in Germany. This is the highest rock wall in the Eastern Alps. 98 climbers have died on this face since its first ascent.

1881: Book

British mountaineer William Martin Conway (1856 – 1937) published the *Zermatt Pocket Book* which was the first real climbing guide. This book identified those villages in which to begin a climb, described the approaches to a particular mountain, and noted the problems of a particular climb.

1882: FIRST ASCENT

March 17 and 18. Italian mountaineer and Alpine photographer Vittorio Sella (1859 – 1943) and his three Carrel guides (Jean Antoine, Luigi and Baptiste) made the first winter ascent and traverse of the Matterhorn (14,692 ft./4,478 m.) from Breuil, Italy to Zermatt, Switzerland. This was a pioneer achievement in winter mountaineering. Sella took many photographs during this traverse with a heavy glass plate camera. The climb from Breuil to the summit took fifteen hours.

1882: PEAK FIRST ASCENT *POINTE SELLA*

July 28. Mountain guide Jean-Joseph Maquignaz (1829 – 1890), his son Daniel and his nephew Battista made the first ascent of the Dent du Geant's lower southwest summit (13,153 ft./4,009 m.) known as Pointe Sella which is located within the Mont Blanc massif. This ascent began the revolution of artificial climbing. They spent four days preparing the ascent route by hammering iron pitons into rock cracks and then hanging fixed ropes. This climbing route was prepared for four members of the Sella family who climbed to the summit the following day. This ascent ended the so-called Silver Age of Mountaineering (1866 – 1882).

1882: PEAK FIRST ASCENT *DENT DU GEANT*

August 14. British mountaineer William Woodman Graham (1859 – 1932) and his Chamonix guides Auguste Cupelin and Alphonse Payot made the first ascent of the Dent du Gèant's highest summit (13,167 ft./4,013 m.) above Courmayeur, Italy near the Grandes Jorasses. Graham led the final rock pitch on this rock peak that is known as Pointe Graham. Dent du Gèant means the "giant's tooth."

1882:

American-British mountaineer W.A.B. (William Augustus Brevoort) Coolidge (1850 – 1926) decided to devote himself exclusively to studying the Alps. Over the next 44 years, he amassed a 15,000 volume mountaineering library. From 1880 to 1889, Coolidge was the Editor of the *Alpine Journal* (England's Alpine Club journal). In 1896, Coolidge moved to Grindelwald, Switzerland.

1882: Equipment – Pitons

Iron-forged pitons were introduced in the Eastern Alps of Europe.

1882: Technique – Photography

June 29. Italian photographer Vittorio Sella (1859 – 1943) made a 360° photographic panorama from the summit of the Matterhorn (14,692 feet/4,478 meters) in Switzerland. Twelve frames comprised this 360° panorama. Sella wrote emphatically about the need to use large-format cameras when photographing mountains.

1882: Technique – Pitons

July. On the first ascent of the Dent du Geant (13,167 feet/4,013 meters) in the French Alps above Chamonix, France, mountain guides Jean-Joseph Maquignaz (1829 – 1890), nephew Battista Maquignaz (son), and son Daniel Maquignaz hammered primitive iron pitons into the rock to ease the difficulty. They then fixed 500 feet/152 meters of rope.

1883: FIRST ASCENT

January 4. British rock climbers T.W. Wall and A.H. Stocker made the first ascent of Lliwedd, an 850-foot (259 meter) cliff just to the east of Snowdon's summit in North Wales. This was the first cliff in the world to have its own guidebook—*The Climbs on Lliwedd* by J.M. Archer Thomson and A.W. Andrews (1909). The Lliwedd ascent took 4 ½ hours.

1883:

October 17. An observatory was erected on the summit of Ben Nevis (4,406 ft./1,343 m.) in Scotland by Mrs. Cameron-Campbell who owned Ben Nevis at this time. Observations were made here from 1883 to 1904.

1883: FIRST ASCENT

Henri Brulle (1854 – 1936) was the first mountaineer to climb the Meije (13,067 ft./3,983 m.) in the Dauphine Alps of southeastern France in a single day.

1883: Technique – Frostbite Remedy

British mountaineer William Martin Conway (1856 – 1937) greased his feet with marmot fat for protection from the cold. He then wrapped his legs with putties (cloth bands).

1884: FIRST ASCENT

January 25 and 26. Italian mountaineer and alpine photographer Vittorio Sella (1859 – 1943) and guides Joseph and Daniele Maquignaz made the first winter ascent of the Dufourspitze summit (15,204 ft./4,634 m.) of Monte Rosa. This ascent required two bivouacs.

1885: FIRST ASCENT

March 2. Italian mountaineer Vittorio Sella (1859 – 1943), British mountaineer Samuel Aitken and guide Jean-Joseph Maquignaz (1829 – 1890) made the first winter ascent of the Gran Paradiso (13,324 ft./4,061 m.), the highest mountain completely located within Italy. On March 22, Sella also made the first winter ascent (from Italy) of the Lyskamm (14,853 ft./4,527 m.) above Zermatt, Switzerland.

1885: PEAK FIRST ASCENT *AIGUILLE BLANCHE DE PEUTEREY*

July 31. Henry Seymour King, Emile Rey (1846 – 1895), Ambros Supersaxo, and Aloys Anthamatten made the first ascent of the Aiguille Blanche de Peuterey (13,492 ft./4,112 m.) in the Mont Blanc massif. The highest summit is known as Pointe Gussfeldt. This Aiguille (needle) was thought to be the hardest and most serious of the 4,000 meter (13,124 ft.) peaks to reach and then escape from. It was also the last major unclimbed peak in the Mont Blanc chain to be climbed.

1885: FIRST ASCENT

August 6. Emil and Otto Zsigmondy and guide Ludwig Purtscheller climbed a new route on the Meije (13,068 ft./3,983 m.) via the eastern arete (July 26). This peak is located in the Dauphine Alps in southeastern France. The two Zsigmondys and Karl Schulz then attempted to climb the Meije's south face. They reached 12,000 ft./3,657 meters. Emil began climbing a chimney and reached an overhang when he fell 2,300 ft./701 m. to the glacier below and died. Emil Zsigmondy (1861 – 1885) made over 100 ascents of peaks over 3,000 meters (9,843 ft.). He used a guide on only six of these ascents.

1885:

English climber and linguist F.H. Bowring (1823 – 1917) completed his 100th climb in the English Lake District at age 62.

1885: Book

British surgeon, author, physiologist, and mountaineer Clinton Thomas Dent (1850 – 1912) published his book entitled *Above the Snow Line*. In this book, Dent made one of the earliest references to the possibility of climbing Mount Everest: "I do not for a moment say that it would be wise to ascend Mount Everest, but I believe most firmly that it is humanly possible to do so; and, further, I feel sure that even in our own time perhaps, the truth of these views will receive material collaboration." Dent died of blood poisoning at age 61.

1885: Equipment – Rope

The Alpine Club Rope (with the identifying red thread) was introduced to the Lake District climbing area of England. This rope was known to some climbers as the "Buckingham rope" after its London, England manufacturer.

1885: Equipment – Crampon

A four-spiked crampon was in use in the Alps.

1886:

June 18. Famous British mountaineer George Leigh Mallory (1886 – 1924) was born in Mobberley, England. Mallory was a lead climber on the 1921, 1922, and 1924 British Mount Everest expeditions. He disappeared with his young climbing partner Andrew Comyn Irvine (1902 – 1924) on June 8, 1924 while climbing the northeast ridge of Mount Everest. Mallory's body was discovered on May 1, 1999 by an American research expedition. Irvine's body remains lost.

1886:

June 27. British rock climber and "Father of British Rock Climbing" Walter Parry Haskett-Smith (1859 – 1946) made the first ascent (solo) of the 70 foot/21 meter high striking thumb of rock in the English Lake District known as the Napes Needle. This is one of the first British rock climbs. Napes Needle is an outlying rock pinnacle of Great Gable (2,950 ft./899 m.). There are now seven different routes to the summit. In April of 1936, Smith climbed the Napes Needle again at age 77.

1887: FIRST ASCENT

January. British woman mountaineer Mrs. Margaret Anne Jackson completed a winter traverse of the Jungfrau (13,642 feet/4,158 m.) in Switzerland. She also completed the first winter ascent of the Lauteraarhorn (13,261 ft./4,042 m.) also in Switzerland. Jackson then published an article on her Lauteraarhorn ascent in the Alpine Journal—the first essay in this journal written by a woman.

1887:

August 2. Frenchman Joseph Vallot (1854 – 1925) returned to Chamonix, France after spending three days on the summit of Mont Blanc (15,775 ft./4,808 m.) making meteorological observations. M. Richard and two guides were with Vallot.

1887: FIRST ASCENT

December 25. Norwegian mountain guide Knud Vole led the first ascent on skis of Galdhopiggen (8,101 ft./2,469 m.), Norway's highest mountain (Jotunheimen Region). Many consider this first ski ascent of a major peak to be the birth of ski mountaineering. Galdo Peak (English name) was first climbed in 1850 by guide Steinar Sulheim, S. Flaatten, and L. Arnesen.

1888: FIRST ASCENT

January 5. Italian mountaineer and Alpine photographer Vittorio Sella (1859 – 1943) and his guides Emile Rey, Giuseppe, Daniele, and Battista Maquignaz completed the first winter traverse of Mont Blanc (15,775 ft./4,808 m.) from Courmayeur, Italy to Chamonix, France. Vittorio's brothers Erminio and Gaudenzio were also a part of this winter traverse.

1888: PEAK FIRST ASCENT *DYCH-TAU*

July 24. British mountaineer Albert Frederick Mummery (1855 – 1895) and guide Heinrich Zurfluh (from Meiringen, Switzerland) made the first ascent of Dych-tau's higher western summit (17,055 ft./5,198 m.) in the Caucasus Mountains of western Russia. They climbed the southwest ridge in 11 hours.

1888: PEAK FIRST ASCENTS *SHKARA, USHBA NORTH, JANGI-TAU*

September 7. British mountaineer John Cockin and guides Ulrich Almer (1849 – 1941) and Christian Roth made the first ascent of the second highest peak—the eastern summit of Shkara (17,064 ft./5,201 m.)—of the Caucasus mountains of western Russia. This was considered to be one of the longest snow and ice ridge climbs in Europe (northeast ridge). On September 28th, they also made the first ascents of Ushba North (15,410 ft./4,697 m.) and Jangi-Tau (16,572 ft./5,051 m.) in the Caucasus. Ushba has been called the "El Cap of the Caucasus" (El Cap for El Capitan in Yosemite National Park, California).

1888: FIRST ASCENT

Miss Katherine Richardson (1854 – 1927) made the first ascent of the north ridge of the Aiguille de Bionnassay (13,291 ft./4,051 m.) in the French Alps with guides Emile Rey and J.B. Bich (both from

Courmayeur, Italy). This climb was the first significant first ascent achieved by a woman in the Mont Blanc range of the French Alps.

1888:

Two British mountaineers, Harry Fox and William Frederick Donkin (1845 – 1888) and their two Swiss guides (Kaspar Streich and Johann Fischer) disappeared near Koshtantau (16,877 ft./5,144 m.) in the Caucasus mountains of western Russia. Their disappearance was probably due to an avalanche. Their bodies have never been found. Donkin died at age 43. He was thought to be the most important mountain photographer of his time. He was a close friend of Vittorio Sella (1859 – 1943), the noted Italian mountaineering photographer.

1889: FIRST ASCENT

July 28. Italian mountaineer and future Pope Achille Ratti (1857 – 1939), Luigi Alberto Grasselli (1847 – 1912), and two guides made the first Italian traverse of Monte Rosa (15,204 ft./4,634 m.) from Macugnaga, Italy to Zermatt, Switzerland. During this three-day traverse, they made the first crossing of the Zumsteinsattel (14,607 ft./4,452 m.). Their ascent of Monte Rosa's east face took 20 ½ hours. Ratti would eventually become Pope Pius XI in 1922.

1889:

Irish politician, scientist, and mountaineer John Ball (1818 – 1889) died. He was the first president of the Alpine club. Ball crossed the main chain of the Alps 48 times by 32 different passes. He made the first ascent of the Pelmo (10,394 ft./3,168 m.) in 1857, the first major Dolomite (northern Italy) peak to be climbed.

1889:

Scottish climber William W. Naismith (1856 – 1935) established the Scottish Mountaineering Club in Glasgow, Scotland. This climbing club currently has over 400 members.

1889:

American mountaineer and future resident of Grindelwald, Switzerland W.A.B. Coolidge (1850 – 1926) completed his 600th climb in the Alps. All of these peaks exceeded 10,000 ft./3,048 m.

1889:

French engineer Alexander Gustave Eiffel (1832 – 1923) completed the two-year construction of the Eiffel Tower in Paris, France. This was the tallest structure (986 feet/300 meters) in the world until 1930. This tower of skeletal iron was climbed for the first time in 1965 by British climber Ian McNaught-Davis (1929 –) and French climber Robert Paragot.

1889:

The C.A.M.P. company was founded by Nicola Codega in Premana, Italy (east of Lake Como in northern Italy). C.A.M.P. is the acronym for Costruzione Articoli Montagna Premana which when translated means "making climbing equipment in Premana." In 1920, C.A.M.P. produced ice axes for Italy's Alpine troops. Now owned and managed by the fourth generation of the Codega family, C.A.M.P. has developed the following major climbing innovations:

1. The first ice-axe with a light alloy shaft.
2. The first U.I.A.A. approved ice-axe.
3. The first modular axe.
4. The first rigid frame crampons.
5. The first crampons with step-in fast-binding system.

1890: FIRST ASCENT

January 7. American mountaineer Charles Walter Mead (1861 – 1895) and his brother-in-law Sir W. Abney made the first winter ascent of the Eiger (13,025 ft./3,970 m.) in Switzerland.

1890:

August 26. Italian mountain guides Jean-Antoine Carrel (1829 – 1890) and Abbè Gorret (1836 – 1907) departed Breuil, Italy to guide Italian mountaineer and musician Leone Sinigaglia (1863 – 1944) up the Italian side of the Matterhorn (14,692 ft./4,478 m.). Due to bad weather, this party was forced to retreat. Carrel collapsed on the descent and died (age 61). He made 53 ascents of the Matterhorn. He was from Valtournanche, Italy.

1890: FIRST ASCENT

Norwegian engineer Olaf Kjelsberg (1857 – 1927) ski-climbed a mountain named Bachtel (3,609 ft./1,100 m.) near Zurich, Switzerland. This may have been the first recorded ski ascent of an alpine peak.

1890:

British mountaineer Frederick Gardiner (1850 – 1919) by this year had climbed 1,200 peaks and passes in the Alps. This was a British record as of this year (1890).

1890: Equipment – Rock Climbing Shoes

British climber Albert Frederick Mummery (1855 – 1895) introduced the use of rubber-soled tennis shoes for difficult rock climbs.

1890: Equipment – Air Mattress

A Mr. Howse (British) designed a Macintosh sleeping sack with the bottom half being capable of inflation, therefore being the first inflatable air mattress for sleeping.

1890: Equipment – Tents

British mountaineer Albert Frederick Mummery (1855 – 1895) introduced his Mummery Tent. This was an easily portable ridge tent made of fine silk. It measured 4' x 6' and slept 2 or 3 climbers. This was the first lightweight mountaineering tent—it weighed 3.5 pounds.

1890: Equipment – Pitons

Some of the first early pitons were the so-called "picture-hook" type. There were two versions: 1) forged pitons and 2) pitons made from a single length of angle iron. The German word for this type of piton was "mauerhaken," which means "wall hook."

1890: Technique – Belaying

Brothers George Dixon Abraham (1872 – 1965) and Ashley Perry Abraham (1876 – 1951) actively climbed in Great Britain. They are credited with inventing an early belaying technique (the shoulder belay) and helped establish rock climbing as a sport in Great Britain.

The word "belay" is a nautical term used in sailing. Sailors used the friction of their ropes around stationary wooden pins to control or "belay" their sails. The word "belay" can be used as a verb ("to protect another climber by minding the rope that person is attached to") or as a noun ("the various stations between climbing pitches that are used to belay from, haul from, jug from and sleep at").

To "belay" a climber means to secure that person by attaching (tying-in) him or her to one end of a rope. The other rope end is attached to another climber or to an object (i.e. rock, piton, etc.) offering stable support or control in the event of a fall.

1891:

September 3. A Dr. Jacottet (Chamonix, France physician) died at 13,895 ft./4,235 m. after reaching the summit of Mont Blanc (15,775 ft./4,808 m.). This was the first recorded case in non-English literature of high altitude pulmonary oedema (the accumulation of fluid in the lungs) caused by altitude sickness although this condition did not have a specific name at this time.

1891:

September. Scottish mountaineer Sir Hugh T. Munro (1856 – 1919) first published the list of those mountains in Scotland that exceeded 3,000 feet/914 meters. He classified these high points as either "tops" or "mountains." Munro, an original member of the Scottish Mountaineering Club, had climbed nearly all of these so-called "Munros." His lists or tables of these high-points (283 summits over 3,000 feet/914 meters and a total of 538 tops in Great Britain and Ireland) were published in the 1891 edition of the Scottish Mountaineering Club Journal. The highest "Munro" was Ben Nevis (4,406 ft./1,343 m.) and the lowest were Ben Vane (3,002 ft./915 m.) and Beinn Teallach (3,002 ft./915 m.).

1891: FIRST ASCENT

December 25. British mountaineer John Norman Collie (1859 – 1942) climbed the Steep Gill route on Scafell (3,160 ft./963 m.). This grade V climb was accomplished in winter conditions and was considered to be the first of its level of difficulty ever achieved (Grade V winter climb).

1891: FIRST ASCENT

Winter. Ski mountaineers Carl Egger and a Dr. Staübli made the first ski ascent of a high peak in the Alps. They ski-climbed Parpan Rothorn (9,794 ft./2,985 m.) above the village of Parpan (near Arosa) in the Churwalden district in eastern Switzerland. Local climbers believe that 1,000 peaks can be seen from this summit.

1891:

The Royal Geographical Society (London, England) sponsored its first major mountaineering venture in the Himalayas—W. M. Conway's Karakoram Expedition. Conway (1856 – 1937) made the first ascent of Crystal Peak (19,400 ft./5,913 m.).

1891:

An engineer named Imfeld drilled a 15 meter (49 foot) deep borehole into the top of Mont Blanc (15,775 ft./4,808 m.) in an effort to find rock. He failed. In June of 1983, a glaciology lab drilled a 16 meter (52 foot) borehole into the summit ice of Mont Blanc without reaching any rock.

1891: Equipment – Rock Climbing Shoes

German rope-soled and wool-soled (felt) boots with canvas uppers called "kletterschuhes" were used in the Alps for climbing on smooth rock (usually limestone).

1891: Technique – Hand Traverse

British climber Ellis Carr (1852 – 1930) took part in the second ascent of the Nose climb on Pillar Rock in England where he is reputed to have invented the hand traverse on the Nose pitch. During this type of traverse, only the hands are gripping the rock. The legs and feet are hanging free or are pushing on the rock below.

1892:

Englishwoman Ms. Lily Briston with British mountaineer Albert Frederick Mummery (1855 – 1895) and several other climbers led the first pitch (one pitch is equal to a rope's length) on the Petit Dru (12,245 ft./3,732 m.) in the French Alps. This was the first serious climbing lead by a woman in the Alps.

1892: FIRST ASCENT

Scientist and inventor Dr. John Hopkinson (1849 – 1898) and his son Bernard made the first ascent of the Northeast Buttress of Ben Nevis (4,406 ft./1,343 m.) in Scotland. This route up the highest peak in Great Britain was considered a fine, powerful climb. This was one of the first recorded rock climbs on the Scottish mainland.

1892: FIRST ASCENT

Winter. An Austrian mountain named Stuhleck (5,847 ft./1,782 m.) became the first alpine mountain to be climbed on skis. This peak is located in the Fischbacher Alps in Styria between Vienna and Graz. Toni Schruf, Max Kleinoscheg, and Walther Wenderich used their Norwegian skis for this climb. Stuhleck is now a popular ski mountain in Austria.

1892:

The rotation system for Chamonix, France mountain guides was finally abandoned. At this time, there were 300 guides on the Chamonix roll. Clients could now use the same guide over and over again.

1892: FIRST ASCENT

British mountaineer Geoffrey Hastings (1860 – 1941) and Albert F. Mummery (1855 – 1895) began a two year period of first ascents:

> First traverse of the Grépon
> (11,424 ft./3,481 m.)
> First ascent of the Requin (11,227 ft./3,422 m.)
> First ascent of the west face of the Aiguille du Plan
> (12,051 ft./3,673 m.).
> First guideless ascent of the Brenva Face of Mont Blanc
> (15,782 ft./4,810 m.)
> Second ascent of the Moine Ridge of the Aiguille Verte
> (13,540 ft./4,127 m.)
> First traverse of the Col Des Courtes.

1892: Equipment – Lanterns

Continental folding lanterns became available. The best folding lantern was the Italian 'Excelsior Mountain Lantern' which was adopted by the Italian Alpine Club.

1892: Equipment – Sleeping Bags

Eiderdown sleeping bags were first used. The soft feathers from the breast of the female Eider duck (a large sea duck) comprise eiderdown. These sleeping bags combined lightweight with warmth. British climber Albert Frederick Mummery (1855 – 1895) was an early user.

1892: Equipment – Stoves

The Primus stove was invented by Swede Franz Lindquist. This portable stove worked by vaporizing paraffin under pressure applied by a heat source. Water could be boiled in three minutes.

1892: Technique – Foot Protection

July. British mountaineers A.F. Mummery (1855 – 1895), Ellis Carr (1852 – 1930), and William Cecil Slingsby (1849 – 1929) bivouacked on the north face of the Aiguille du Plan (12,051 feet/3,673 meters) above Chamonix, France. Carr placed his wet feet inside his rucksack for warmth. This was the second recorded time (in the English-speaking world) that this bivouac technique was used.

1892: Technique – Solo Climbing

British mountaineer Albert Frederick Mummery (1855 – 1895) was a well-known proponent of solo climbing. He was to have said: "The law of survival of the fittest has full and ample chance of eliminating him should he be, in any way, a careless or incapable mountaineer."

1892: Technique – Timing A Climb

Scottish mountaineer Willie Naismith (1856 – 1935) published his climbing time rule (Naismith's Rule) in 1892: "The time allowed for an easy expedition should be an hour for every three miles (4.83 kilometers) on the map, with an additional hour for every 2,000 feet/607 meters of ascent." This rule, however, may not apply to higher mountain elevations.

1893: FIRST ASCENT

February 8. Christoph Iselin and several companions climbed and descended on skis the Schild (7,553 ft./2,302 m.) near Glarus, Switzerland. This may have been one of the first real alpine summits to be climbed on skis.

1893: PEAK FIRST *ASCENT DENT DU REQUIN*

July 25. This rock peak is located in the Mont Blanc Massif in the French Alps. Known as the Shark's Tooth, the Dent du Requin (11,227 ft./3,422 m.) was first climbed by British mountaineers John Norman Collie (1859 – 1942), Geoffrey Hastings (1860 – 1941), Albert Frederick Mummery (1855 – 1895), and William Cecil Slingsby (1849 – 1929). These four climbers were the first British mountaineers to make a guideless ascent of a major unclimbed peak in the Alps.

1893: FIRST ASCENT

August 14 – 17. German mountaineer Paul Güssfeldt (1840 – 1920) and his guides Emile Rey (1846 – 1895), Christian Klucker (1853 – 1928), and Cesar Ollier made the first complete ascent of the Peuterey Ridge to Mont Blanc de Courmayeur (15,578 ft./4,748 m.) and then on to the summit of Mont Blanc (15,782 ft./4,810 m.) with a return descent to Courmayeur, Italy. This 88-hour climb was regarded as Güssfeldt's greatest mountaineering achievement. This was the longest and most difficult ridge ascent in the Alps to date.

1893:

August 18. Queen Margherita (1851 – 1926) of Italy and a large escort climbed the Punta Gnifetti summit (14,942 ft./4,554 m.) of Monte Rosa to dedicate a special altitude research laboratory located at 15,025 ft./4,579 m. She was received on the summit by a committee of the Italian Alpine Club. This laboratory was known as the Capanna Regina Margherita or Margherita Hut. A scientist named Angelo Mosso (Italian physiologist and mountaineer, 1846 – 1910) first studied the effects of high altitude breathing at this laboratory. This is the highest mountain hut in the Alps. This hut was replaced in 1980 by a large, two-story wooden structure covered with sheet copper. Punta Gnifetti is also known as the Signalkuppe.

1893:

A refuge (mountain hut for climbers) was constructed on the Italian side of the Matterhorn at 12,622 feet/3,847 meters. This refuge was named after Rifugio Luigi-Amedeo di Savoia, Prince of Savoy, Duke of the Abruzzi (1873 – 1933).

1893:

The Slovenian Alpine Club was founded.

1893: Technique – Photography

Italian mountaineer and photographer Vittorio Sella (1859 – 1943) began using two Kodak cameras for "instantaneous" and stereoscopic photographs.

1894: FIRST ASCENT

February 5. German ski mountaineer Wilhelm Ritter von Arlt (1853 – 1941) made the first ski ascent of a peak over 3,000 meters (9,843 ft.) when he climbed Rauriser Sonnblick (10,187 ft./3,105 m.) near Salzburg, Austria. Many regard von Arlt as the father of ski mountaineering.

1894: FIRST ASCENT

March 30. British mountaineer John Norman Collie (1859 – 1942), Godfrey Solly, and Joseph Collier made the first ascent of the Tower Ridge on Ben Nevis (4,406 ft./1,343 m.) in Scotland. Collie thought that the Tower Ridge (2,000 ft./610 m. high) resembled the Italian side of the Matterhorn. Collie and Geoffrey Hastings (1860 – 1941) repeated this same climb the next day (March 31).

1894:

August 23. Future British statesman, author, and British Prime Minister Winston Churchill (1874 – 1965) reached the summit of the Dufourspitze (15,204 ft./4,634 m.) on Monte Rosa in Switzerland. His guide was Johann Aufdenblatten.

1894: FIRST ASCENT

British mountaineers John Norman Collie (1859 – 1942), Geoffrey Hastings (1860 – 1941), and Albert F. Mummery (1855 – 1895) made the first guideless ascent of the Old Brenva Route in the Brenva Face of Mont Blanc (15,775 ft./4,808 m.). This climb involved over 5,200 vertical feet (1,585 meters).

1894:

Famous British mountaineer Edward Whymper (1840 – 1911) made his third and final ascent of Mont Blanc (15,782 ft./4,810 m.) at age 54. He became the third climber to spend the night on this summit (1859: John Tyndall, 1887: J. Vallot). This was Whymper's last major mountain climb.

1894:

British mountaineer and explorer William Martin Conway (1856 – 1937) traversed the European Alps from end-to-end with Swiss mountain guide Matthias Zurbriggen (1856–1917). They climbed 21 peaks and crossed 39 passes in this three-month journey that extended from Monte Viso/Col de la Tenda in the west to the Grossglockner (12,458 ft./3,797 m.) in the east (Austria). Conway later became Lord Conway of Allington. He was the last survivor of the heroic age of mountaineering. Conway published his book entitled *The Alps From End To End* in 1895.

1894: Equipment – First Aid Kits

Well-known British physiologist, surgeon, and mountaineer Dr. Thomas Clinton Dent (1850 – 1912) recommended that climbers carry one of two different cases to hold simple remedies for common ailments:

"The Alpine Case" – 8 oz., cost: 21 shillings
"The Mountaineer's Case – 28 oz., cost 25 shillings

1894: Technique – Alpine Distress Signal

British mountaineer Thomas Clinton Dent (1850 – 1912) first proposed the use of an alpine distress signal which was a series of three short shouts, whistles, flashes, etc.

1895: FIRST ASCENT

British mountaineer Sir William E. Davidson (1853 – 1923) made the first traverse of the Wellenkuppe (12,806 ft./3,903 m.)—Obergabelhorn (13,331 ft./4,063 m.) ridge in Switzerland. He also climbed the Riffelhorn (9,604 ft./2,927 m.), a rock peak above Zermatt, Switzerland, 250 times.

1895:

A Slovenian patriotic priest named Jakob Aljaz purchased the summit area of Triglav (9,396 ft./2,864 m.) to ensure that it would remain part of Slovenia forever. Triglav is the highest peak in Slovenia.

1895:

British mountaineer Edward Whymper (1840 – 1911) climbed the Matterhorn (14,692 ft./4,478 m.) for a third and last time at age 55. He made the first ascent on July 14, 1865 at age 25.

1895: FIRST ASCENT

British climber Owen Glynne ("O.G.") Jones (1867 – 1899) made the first traverse of the Taschhorn (14,732 ft./4,490 m.) – Dom (14,911 ft./4,545 m.) ridge in Switzerland. Jones was killed on August 28, 1899 on the west arete of the Dent Blanche in Switzerland when his guide slipped and pulled Jones off his stance.

1895: Book

British mountaineer Albert Frederick ("A.F.") Mummery (1855 – 1895) published his book entitled *My Climbs In The Alps And Caucasus*. This book achieved a prominent position in Alpine literature. Mummery was the first mountaineer to state the ideals of climbing as we know them today. Many consider him the father of modern rock climbing. He disappeared in this year while attempting to climb Nanga Parbat (26,660 ft./8,125 m.) in the Himalayas. Mummery was the first climber to accomplish difficult climbs without using guides. He climbed the Matterhorn (14,692 ft./4,478 m.) seven times by six different routes.

1895: Technique – Top Roping

British rock climber Owen Glynne ("O.G.") Jones (1867 – 1899) used a top-rope for the first time to practice the crux move (the most difficult section of a climb) of the "Very Severe" route Kern Knotts Crack in England's Lake District.

1896: FIRST ASCENT

January 5. German ski pioneer and mountaineer Wilhelm Paulcke (1873 – 1949) and Victor De Beauclair, along with two others made the first ski ascent of a 3,000 meter (9,843 ft.) mountain in Switzerland—the Oberalpstock (10,919 ft./3,328 m.).

1896:

March. American-born British climber and mountaineering historian W.A.B. (William Augustus Brevoort) Coolidge (1850 – 1926) moved from Oxford, England to Grindelwald, Switzerland and remained there for 30 years until his death in 1926. His alpine climbing career included 1,700 separate expeditions that included the first winter ascents of the Jungfrau, the Wetterhorn, and the Schreckhorn and a second ascent of the Meije in the Dauphiné Alps. His personal mountaineering library exceeded 15,000 books which he kept in twelve rooms at his Chalet Montana in Grindelwald. He became known as the "Sage of Grindelwald." Pic Coolidge (12,323 ft./3,756 m.) in southeast France is named for him.

1896:

June 22. Swiss mountain guide Christian Almer (1826 – 1898) at age 70 and his wife Margherita (age 72) climbed the Wetterhorn (12,149 ft./3,703 m.) in Switzerland to celebrate their Golden (50 years) wedding anniversary. They made this 6 hour 20 minute climb from the Gleckstein Hut. This was Margherita's first ascent of a major snow mountain. Also included in this climbing party were 2 porters, 1 photographer, 1 daughter, 2 sons, and 1 friend.

1896:

Apprentice mountain guide Josef Knubel (1881 – 1961) from St. Niklaus in the Zermatt valley of Switzerland climbed the Matterhorn (14,692 ft./4,478 m.), the Dom (14,911 ft./4,545 m.), and Monte Rosa (15,204 ft./4,634 m.) at the age of 15. He made 11 first ascents from 1906 to 1932 and he eventually climbed all of the 4,000 meter (13,124 ft.) peaks in the Alps which at this time numbered 75.

1896: Book

British mountaineer William Douglas Freshfield (1845 – 1934) published his monumental two-volume set of *The Exploration Of The Caucasus*. These books included mountain photography by Italian mountaineer/photographer Vittorio Sella (1859 – 1943). Freshfield made three visits to the Caucasus Range in western Russia traversing the main mountain chain 11 times by 8 different routes.

1896: Book

British climber Owen Glynne ("O.G.") Jones (1867 – 1899) published his book *Rock Climbing In The English Lake District*. In this book, Jones laid out the first system of classification of climbing route difficulty (gradings): Easy, Moderate, Difficult, and Exceptionally Severe. This was the first lavishly illustrated coffee-table type climbing book. Jones collaborated with the two Abraham brothers (George and Ashley) in writing this book.

1896:

Swiss mountaineer Johann Jakob Weilenmann (1819 – 1896) died at age 77. He made 320 peak ascents in the European Alps including the second ascent of Monte Rosa (Dufourspitze) and seven first ascents between 1858 and 1887. On September 11, 1865 Weilenmann made the first ascent of Mont Blanc de Cheilon (12,697 ft./3,870 m.) which is located southeast of Mont Blanc.

1896: Book

British mountaineer Edward Whymper (1840 – 1911) published his guidebook entitled *Chamonix and the Range of Mont Blanc*.

1896: Technique – Crevasse Rescue

Austrian mountaineer Karl Prusik (1896 – 1961) was born in Vienna, Austria. He invented the "prusik knot" in 1922 that proved to be extremely helpful in crevasse rescues on glaciers. Prusik knots will slide up a rope when unweighted but not slide down when holding the climber's weight.

1897:

British mountaineer Geoffrey Winthrop Young (1876 – 1958) made his first visit to the Alps. Young was one of the most important people in British mountaineering. He began his serious climbing in 1905 with Swiss guide Josef Knubel (1881 – 1961). Young made numerous ascents. His last climb was the Zinalrothorn (13,849 ft./4,221 m.) in 1935 at age 59.

1897: Equipment – Pitons

Iron spikes with a ring at the top were in use in the Swiss Alps as an anchor for a double rope descent.

1897: Equipment – Rope

Manilla hemp rope was advertised in Edward Whymper's book *A Guide To Zermatt*: "Specially manufactured for the use of mountaineers by Messrs. Beale & Cloves (successors to Mr. John Buckingham), 194 Shaftesbury Street, London, W.C. which ought to be identified by a red worsted thread woven among the strands."

Manilla hemp ropes were hawser laid ropes. This was an older method of rope construction where the fibers are twisted into 3 or 4 strands which are then twisted into a rope. Manilla hemp ropes twisted badly under a load, kinked more readily, and were heavy.

1897: Technique – Ski Mountaineering

Wilhelm Paulcke (1873 – 1949), Wilhelm Lohmüller, and their companions first used skis in mountaineering to cross the Oberland from Grimsel to Belalp (Switzerland). They climbed (on skis) to 3,780 meters (12,402 feet) on the flanks of the Jungfrau (13,642 feet/4,158 meters).

1898:

Scottish mountaineer Harold Raeburn (1865 – 1926) completed 12 new climbing routes on Ben Nevis (4,406 ft./1,343 m.) in Scotland, the highest mountain in Great Britain. Raeburn was a member of the 1921 British Mount Everest Expedition.

1898:

There were 284 registered mountain guides in Chamonix, France this year. These guides came from many different families in Chamonix. The most popular families were:

Simond	38 Guides
Couttet	28 Guides
Ducroz	19 Guides
Balmat	18 Guides
Payot	16 Guides
Ravanel	16 Guides

In Zermatt, Switzerland, there were 177 registered guides (65 spoke English). The most popular guide families here were:

Biener	14 Guides
Burgener	13 Guides
Perren	10 Guides

1898: FIRST ASCENT

Swiss youth and future mountain guide Edward Feuz, Jr. (1885 – 1981) climbed the Jungfrau (13,642 ft./4,158 m.) to become the youngest person (age 13) to date to reach the summit.

1898:

Well-known Swiss mountain guide Christian Almer (1826 – 1898) died in Grindelwald, Switzerland at age 72. Originally a shepherd and a cheese-maker, Almer continued a Grindelwald tradition of carrying a young fir tree on his climbs to mark the summit. Almer made many ascents in the Alps including his climbing of the Wetterhorn in 1868 and the Meije at age 70 in 1896 and the Wetterhorn again at age 71. Although Almer was only 5 feet 2 inches in height, he was known as being very strong. He was thought to be one of the two or three best guides in the early 1860s. From 1857 to 1884 (28 years), Almer made eighteen first ascents.

1898: FIRST ASCENT

Wilhelm Paulcke (1873 – 1949) made the first solo ascent of the Matterhorn's Hornli Ridge.

1898: Book

After many years of research on the hiking trails around Zermatt, Switzerland, British mountaineer (first ascent of the Matterhorn in 1865) Edward Whymper (1840 – 1911) published his guidebook entitled *The Valley of Zermatt and the Matterhorn.*

1898: Equipment – Sleeping Pad

British climber, engineer, and inventor Oscar Johannes Ludwig Eckenstein (1859 – 1921) used a cork mattress sleeping pad while camping on the Schönbiel Glacier below the Matterhorn's north face.

1898: Technique – Mountain Guiding

Late 1890s: The second generation of mountain guides in the European Alps at last learned how to use and manage ropes, how to use an ice axe instead of an alpenstock, and how to time a climb. The endless procession of guides and porters was now over.

1899:

Switzerland had 368 registered mountain guides.

1899:

Between 1875 and 1899, Austrian guide Ludwig Purtscheller (1849 – 1900) made 75 alpine ascents each year. He made the first ascent of Mount Kilimanjaro (19,341 ft./5,895 m.) in Tanzania (Africa) in 1889.

1899: FIRST ASCENT

German mountaineers Hans Barth and Eduard Pichl made the first traverse of the three Vajolet Towers in the western Dolomite mountains of Italy. These three towers are:

1. Torre Winkler – 9,187 ft./2,800 m. (First Ascent – 1887)
2. Torre Stabeler – 9,203 ft./2,805 m. (First Ascent – 1892)
3. Torre Delago – 9,154 ft./2,790 m. (First Ascent – 1895)

1899: Equipment – Boot Nailing

Late 1800s: Boot screws were designed by British mountaineer Albert Frederick Mummery (1855 – 1895). These were screwed into boot soles to give security when climbing on ice. Crampons eventually replaced these removable screws.

1899: Equipment – Stove

The Alpine Club (England) recommended the Primus stove combined with a set of aluminum pots, pans, and plates as the "best canteen for mountain explorers."

1900: FIRST ASCENT

September 7. Well-known British mountaineer Geoffrey Winthrop Young (1876 – 1958) and his guides Louis and Bendit Theytaz established the first route up the west face of the Weisshorn (14,804 ft./4,512 m.) in Switzerland. This route is known as the Young route.

1900:

December 3. Well-known Matterhorn guide Ulrich Inderbinen (1900 – 2004) was born in Zermatt, Switzerland. He was one of nine children. He first climbed the Matterhorn in 1921 (age 21) and would climb it 370 more times. His final ascent was in 1995 at age 95. In 1996, he was received in Rome by Pope John Paul II. He died in Zermatt on June 10, 2004 at age 103 ½.

1900:

British mountaineers (primarily) now began to climb peaks that were beyond the European Alps.

1900:

Well-known Austrian mountain guide Ludwig Purtscheller (1849 – 1900) died at age 51. He made over 1,700 ascents including 40 peaks over 4,000 meters (13,124 feet). He was most famous for his first ascent in 1889 of the Kibo summit of Mount Kilimanjaro (19,341 ft./5,895 m.) in Tanzania, Africa. He broke his arm in a crevasse fall in 1900 and died six months later.

1900: FIRST ASCENT

British woman mountaineers Elizabeth LeBlond (1861 – 1934) and Lady Evelyn McDonnell made the first "guideless" and "manless" climb of a major peak. They completed a winter traverse of all three summits of the snow-capped Piz Palü (12,835 ft./3,912 m.) on the Swiss – Italian border. This three-summit traverse was first completed on July 22, 1868 by Wachler, Wallner, George, Hans Gross and Christian Gross.

1900:

Famous British mountaineer George Leigh Mallory (1886 – 1924) summited his first major peak in the Alps at age 14. Mallory, Harry Gibson, and Graham Irving climbed the Grand Combin (14,100 ft./4,297 m.) in Switzerland's Pennine Alps. Mallory was the only British mountaineer to participate in all three British Mount Everest expeditions in the 1920s (1921, 1922, and 1924). Mallory disappeared on June 8, 1924 on the northeast ridge of Mount Everest.

1900: Equipment – Tents

A two-man mountaineering tent was developed that measured 3 ft. x 7 ft. This tent was triangular in cross-section. It was named the Meade Tent after British climber Charles Francis Meade (1881 – 1975) who claimed to have no idea why this tent was named for him. A larger version of the Meade Tent was used on Mount Everest in 1921 (British expedition). This thin canvas tent measured 6 feet by 7 feet and was 5 feet in height. It weighed a total of 15 pounds (tent, pegs, and poles).

1900: Technique – Ice Bollards

The descending technique of rappelling off an ice bollard was invented in the Alps at about this time. An ice bollard is a knob carved out of the ice around which the double rappel rope is looped. This rappel anchoring technique was used before ice piton anchors became commonplace.

1901:

September. The Reverend A.E. Robertson became the first person to climb all of the so-called "Munros" (Scottish summits exceeding 3,000 ft./914 m.) in Scotland. There were 283 individual Munro mountains and 538 tops (a top is a summit point on a mountain) recognized at this time.

1901: Technique – Balance On Steep Rock

British engineer, inventor, and climber Oscar Eckenstein (1859 – 1921) advocated the art of balance on steep rock. He was the first person to understand that balance rather than brute strength was the key to rock climbing. This new technique of balance climbing replaced the old "clutch-and-struggle" method. Eckenstein also devised the art of bouldering.

1902: FIRST ASCENT

January 18. Scottish mountaineer C.M. Murray and two local guides made the first winter ascent of the Jungfrau (13,642 ft./4,158 m.) in Switzerland.

1902:

September 24. Valtournanche (Italy) guides carried an iron cross to the Italian summit of the Matterhorn. Priest Abbe A. Carrel then said mass on the summit.

1902:

Swiss mountain guide Aloys Pollinger (1844 – 1910) made his 100th ascent of the Matterhorn (14,692 ft./4,478 m.) in Switzerland.

1902:

Austrian mountaineer Peter Aschenbrenner (1902 – 1998) was born. His fifty-year climbing career included approximately 2,400 summits of which 400 climbs were of 3,000 meter peaks and 67 climbs were of 4,000 meter summits. On three visits to Nanga Parbat in the Himalayas, he reached elevations above 7,000 meters.

1903:

January 16 to 20. Dr. Paul Payot, Alfred Simond (famous French mountain guide), Joseph Ravanel (1869 – 1933), and guide Joseph Couttet became the first people to complete the Haute Route (High Level Route) from Chamonix, France to Zermatt, Switzerland on skis. Their route crossed eleven glaciers. This ski journey now requires seven to eight days to complete. The total distance is approximately 108 miles or 180 kilometers.

1903: FIRST ASCENT

August 12 – 16. German mountaineers Georg Leuchs, Hans Pfann, and Ludwig Distel made the first traverse between the two summits of Ushba (south summit – 15,454 ft./4,710 m., north summit – 15,398 ft./4,693 m.) in the Caucasus Mountains of western Russia. This traverse was an enormous undertaking at the time and required four bivouacs. Ushba's south summit (15,454 ft./4,710 m.) was first climbed on July 26, 1903 by A. Schulze and his German – Swiss party.

1903: FIRST ASCENT

September 6. Mountaineers Etienne Giraud, Joseph Ravanel, and Armand Comte made the first unaided (no fixed ropes or chains) traverse from the Petit Dru (12,248 ft./3,733 m.) to the Grand Dru (12,317 ft./3,754 m.) in the Chamonix Aiguilles (French Alps).

1903:

German mountaineer Willi Rickmer Rickmers (1873 – 1965) brought seventeen people to the Caucasus Mountains in western Russia for seven weeks. They climbed 30 peaks and passes, more than half of which were first ascents and they traversed the two summits of Ushba.

1903: Equipment – Tents

British mountaineer and explorer Thomas George Longstaff (1875 – 1964) led an expedition to the Causasus mountain range in western Russia. Longstaff took a very lightweight silk Mummery Tent (3.5 pounds) that had a sewn-in floor to keep out wind and snow.

1904: FIRST ASCENT

February 25. Ski mountaineers Hugo Mylius, A. Tännler, K. Mauer, and H. Zurfluh made the first ski ascent of Mont Blanc (15,775 ft./4,808 m.) in the French Alps.

1904:

British mountaineer R.L.G. (Robert Lock Graham) Irving (1877 – 1969) led two very active young British climbers up the Dufourspitze (15,204 ft./4,634 m.) on Monte Rosa (Swiss – Italian Border). One of these young climbers was 18-year-old George Leigh Mallory (1886 – 1924). Mallory was a lead climber on the three British Mount Everest expeditions of 1921, 1922, and 1924.

1904: FIRST ASCENT

Mountaineers Gustav Adolf Hasler (1877 – 1952) and guide Fritz Amatter made the first ascent of the 3,000 foot/914 meter northeast face of the Finsteraarhorn (14,024 ft./4,274 m.) in Switzerland. This was the first of the great north faces in the Alps to be climbed.

1904: Book

Italian mountaineer Guido Rey (1861 – 1935) authored the book entitled *The Matterhorn*. This book is the definitive publication on the mountain's early history. Rey (1861 – 1935) made several un-successful attempts to climb the Furggen Ridge of the Matterhorn. With the aid of a rope ladder lowered down to him from near the summit, he was finally able to reach the summit. This ascent, however, was never considered to be a true first ascent.

1904:

Well-known British mountaineer Leslie Stephen (1832 – 1904) died. He made ten first ascents in the Alps including the first ascent of the Zinal Rothorn (13,848 ft./4,221 m.) above Zermatt in 1864. He also made the first traverse of Mont Blanc (15,782 ft./4,810 m.) in 1864. His favorite guide was Melchior Anderegg (1828 – 1912). His classic book *The Playground of Europe* was published in 1871.

1905:

Irish mountaineer Valentine John Eustace Ryan (1883 – 1947) made 25 ascents in the Alps this year.

1905:

French mountain guide Francois Joseph Devouassoud (1831 – 1905) died at age 74. He was one of the first alpine guides to travel to mountain ranges outside of the Alps.

1905: Equipment – Climbing Skins

Early 1900s: Made from the fur of seals, climbing skins were attached to ski bottoms to facilitate climbing up snow slopes. The hairs of seal fur lie in one direction allowing smooth forward motion on skis. However, when skis begin to slide backwards, the seal fur stands-up and grips the snow stopping any reverse motion. Most climbing skins are now made of nylon fibers or mohair. The oldest written description of climbing skins was in 1555 by Norwegian Olaus Magnus.

1905: Equipment – Tents

Englishman Thomas Hiram Holding of Maddox Street in London produced a 13-ounce Japanese silk tent. Support poles and stakes had to be added.

1906: FIRST ASCENT

April 23. Scottish mountaineer Harold Raeburn (1865 – 1926) and Swiss climber Eberhard Phildius made the first ascent of the Green Gully on Ben Nevis (4,406 ft./1,343 m.) in Scotland. This climb was considered to be a classic Grade III/IV ice route.

1906:

April 25. British mountaineer Edward Whymper (1840 – 1911) at the age of 66 married 21-year-old Edith Mary Lewin. This marriage lasted four years and produced one daughter—Ethel (– 1969) who eventually became a fine climber in the Zermatt, Switzerland area. She climbed the Dent du Geant (13,166 ft./4,013 m.) above Chamonix, France in 1933 and reached the summit of Mont Blanc via the Old Brenva Route that same year. Edward Whymper made the first ascent of the Matterhorn on July 14, 1865.

1906: FIRST ASCENT

August 12. Irish mountaineer Valentine John Eustace Ryan (1883 – 1947) and his guides Franz and Joseph Lochmatter joined British mountaineer Geoffrey Winthrop Young (1876 – 1958) and his guide Joseph Knubel (1881 – 1961) in making the first ascent of the southwest face of the Täschhorn (14,732 ft./4,490 m.) in Switzerland. This face was nearly 3,000 feet (914 m.) high and forced these mountaineers to climb ice-covered rock slabs, overhangs, and deep chimneys. This route was not repeated until 1943 (37 years later). Many climbers considered this ascent to be the most difficult climb in the Alps prior to World War I.

1906: FIRST ASCENT
September 1. Hans Pfann made the first solo ascent of the Matterhorn's Zmutt Ridge.

1906: Equipment – Seat Harness
British mountaineer Geoffrey Winthrop Young (1876 – 1958) created a seat harness with leg loops from his rope on the south face of the Taschhorn in Switzerland.

1906: Technique – Bivouacking
August 14. Flynn and Bruederlin made the first unguided ascent of the northeast face (over 3,000 feet/914 meters) of the Finsteraarhorn (14,023 feet/4,274 meters) in the Bernese Alps of Switzerland. They were forced into a bivouac sitting and standing in rope slings inside a rock chimney. This was perhaps the first record in mountaineering history of climbers spending the night in rope slings.

1907:
The Ladies Alpine Club was established in London, England. Ms. Aubrey Le Blond (1861 – 1934) was elected the first president. Prior to her marriage she was known as Elizabeth Hawkins-Whitshed. British climber Lucy Walker (1835 – 1916) was also a founder of this alpine club.

1907: FIRST ASCENT
British mountaineer Geoffrey Winthrop Young (1876 – 1958) and his guide made a multi-day traverse of the five Monte Rosa (15,294 ft./4,634 m.) summits beginning from the Riffelberg, over the five summits, then over the Lyskamm (14,853 ft./4,527 m.) and ending with the summit of Castor (13,872 ft./4,228 m.). They descended from here because the guide was tired of cutting steps in the snow and ice.

1908:
Well-known Austrian mountaineer Paul Grohmann (1838 – 1908) died at age 70. He made eight first ascents in the Italian Dolomites including the Marmolada (10,965 ft./3,342 m.) and Sorapiss (10,516 ft./3,205 m.) in 1864 and Sassolungo (10,437 ft./3,181 m.) and Cima Grande di Lavaredo (9,840 ft./2,999 m.) in 1869. The Dolomites contain approximately eighteen peaks over 10,000 feet (3,048 meters).

1908:
The Norwegian Alpine Club was founded.

1908: Equipment – Crampons
British engineer and climber Oscar Johannes Ludwig Eckenstein (1859 – 1921) invented the ten-point crampon. Each crampon had one joint and weighed 2 ½ pounds. Canvas binding straps held the

iron crampon to the climbing boot. This crampon changed snow and ice climbing forever by reducing or eliminating the need to cut steps. Eckenstein's crampons were made by Henry Grivel of Courmayeur, Italy beginning in 1909. Crampons were also called ice walkers, creepers, and irons.

1908: Technique – Flatfoot Climbing

British mountaineer and inventor Oscar Eckenstein (1859 – 1921) invented the "flatfoot" climbing technique on snow that reduced the need to cut steps with an ice axe. Eckenstein's ten-point crampon facilitated this new climbing technique.

1909: FIRST ASCENT

Geoffrey Winthrop Young (1876 – 1958), American climber Oliver Perry-Smith (1884 – 1969), and guide Josef Knubel (1881 – 1961) made the first ascent of the Weisshorn's (14,804 ft./4,512 m.) south face.

1909: FIRST ASCENT

Scottish mountaineer Harold Raeburn (1865 – 1926) made the first winter ascent of Crowberry Gully on Buachaille Etive Mor (3,353 ft./1,022 m.) in Scotland.

1909:

American woman mountaineer Dora Keen (1871 – 1963) began a two-year climbing period (1909 – 1911) in the Alps during which she climbed:

Mont Blanc	15,782 ft./4,810 m.
Monte Rosa	15,204 ft./4,634 m.
The Weisshorn	14,804 ft./4,512 m.
The Matterhorn	14,692 ft./4,478 m.

1909: Clothing – Hooded Anorak

British mountaineer George Ingle Finch (1888 – 1969) was one of the first climbers to replace a wool jacket with a light, hooded anorak in the Alps.

1909: Equipment – Packs

Bergans designed the first external frame backpack—the Bergans Rucksack—which was used thirty years before any other external design.

1909: Equipment – Rock Climbing Shoes

Italian climbers used "scarpetti" and German climbers used "kletterschuhes" for rock climbing. Both types of footwear were rope-soled.

1909: Equipment – Crampons

Grivel of Courmayeur, Italy produced the world's first modern crampon.

1909: Technique – Step Cutting

Although Eckenstein's ten-point crampons were now in universal use, some "old guard" mountaineers still preferred the laborious technique of step cutting with an ice axe.

1910: FIRST ASCENT

July 18. Italian guides Angelo Dibona (1879 – 1956) and Luigi Rizzi and their clients Guido and Max Mayer made the first ascent of Cima Una's (8,524 ft./2,598 m.) north face in the Italian Dolomites. Dibona developed custom pitons for this 2,600 foot/792 meter ascent.

1910:

Famous Swiss mountain guide Alexander Burgener (1846 – 1910) died at age 64. While climbing up the northeast side of the Monch (13,449 ft./4,099 m.), Burgener and six others were killed in a slab avalanche. He made the following first ascents in the Alps:

1870	Lenzspitze
1871	Portjengrat
1878	Grand Dru
1879	Zmutt Ridge (Matterhorn)
1880	Traverse of the Col Du Lion
	Grands Charmoz
	Charpoua Face of the Aiguille Verte
1881	Grépon
1887	Mont Maudit via the Frontier Ridge
	Taschhorn via the Teufelsgrat

1910:

Eighty percent of the climbing fatalities in the Alps occurred to tourist climbers who were climbing without guides.

1910:

Swiss mountain guide Peter Knubel (1833 – 1919) had climbed the Matterhorn over 100 times.

1910: Fabric – Loden Wool Cloth

Climbing suits in the Swiss Alps were made of loden wool cloth. These suits were warm, somewhat waterproof, and durable.

1910: Equipment – Eye Protection

Swiss Alps. 1. Opticians recommended yellow-lense glacier glasses over blue or black lenses. Blue and black lenses, however, were more widely used. 2. Swiss Alps. Snow goggles were called "lunettes" (French for "glasses"). These goggles were constructed to allow air to circulate next to the eyes.

1910: Equipment – Boot Nailing

In the Swiss Alps, new climbing boots cost 35 francs. These boots were large enough to allow two pair of woolen socks (1 lightweight pair and 1 heavyweight pair). Boot nailing patterns and nail types differed from location to location (Chamonix, France vs. Zermatt, Switzerland).

1910: Equipment – Pitons

Well-known Tyrolean mountain guide Hans Fiechtl (1883 – 1925) from the Munich school of climbing became the first person to design pitons forged as a single piece with an eye hole at one end rather than an attached ring. These pitons were lighter, easier to place, and were convenient to use with the steel karabiners invented (or adapted) by Otto Herzog from Munich. Fiechtl designed a series of pitons ranging in size.

1910: Equipment – Carabiners

Karabiners for climbing were developed from a pear-shaped clip used by Munich, Germany fireman. This clip was adapted for climbing by German climber Otto Herzog (1888 – 1964). Also called "carabiners" (Italy, United States, Great Britain), snap-links, D-rings, and "mousquetons" in France.

1910: Equipment – Ice Axes

January 21. British climber and equipment designer Oscar J.L. Eckenstein (1859 – 1921) created the first functionally short, lightweight ice axe. This axe was 86 centimeters long (34 in.), 2/3 the length of the usual ice axe. Henri Grivel of Courmayeur, Italy produced Oscar Eckenstein's new "short" (86 cm) ice axe.

Three basic ice axe models were available in the Alps: The Chamonix, The Grindelwald, and The Pilkington. Axe shafts were made of ash wood. These axes were intentionally a little heavy for durability and balance.

1910: Equipment – Snowshoes

Snowshoes were also known as "raquettes" (French for snowshoes).

1910: Equipment – Ropes

Manilla hemp ropes ½" in diameter and silk ropes (very light and very expensive) were in use in the Swiss and French Alps. The standard length was 100 feet (30.5 meters) for a climbing party of four.

1910: Technique – Ice Axe

Mountain guides in the Swiss Alps determined that the ice axe should always be carried on the upslope side of the climber and never on the void (downslope) side.

1910: Technique – Pitons

Italian guide Angelo Dibona (1879 – 1956) led Guido and Max Mayer up the north face of the Laliderer in Karwendel, Germany. This may have been one of the first times that pitons were used to protect the leader on an alpine ascent.

1910: Technique – Route Marking

Swiss Alps. By chewing liquorice, prunes, or tobacco, mountain guides would spit (dark colored) to their right side into the snow when ascending. These dark holes were called "guide holes." If guide holes were on your left as you ascended, this meant that another climbing party had descended (holes on their right).

1911: FIRST ASCENT

September 9. Italian mountaineer Mario Piacenza and his guides Jean Joseph Carrel and Joseph Gaspard made the first complete ascent of the Matterhorn's (14,692 ft./4,478 m.) Furggen Ridge in Switzerland. This is the steepest and most difficult ridge on the mountain (3,773 ft./1,150 m. in length).

1911:

September 16. British mountaineer Edward Whymper (1840 – 1911) died in Chamonix, France at age 71. Famous for his first ascent of the Matterhorn (14,692 ft./4,478 m.) in 1865 (at age 25), Whymper arrived in Chamonix on September 9th and soon fell ill. On September 13, he locked himself in his Couttet Hotel room and refused all medical help. He was buried in the Chamonix cemetery.

Whymper made fifteen first ascents in the Alps between 1861 and 1865 including:

Ruinette	1864	12,727 ft.	3,879 m.
Grandes Jorasses	1864	13,806 ft.	4,208 m.
Barre des Ecrins	1864	13,459 ft.	4,102 m.
Mont Dolent	1864	12,543 ft.	3,823 m.
Aiguille de Trelatete	1864	12,894 ft.	3,930 m.
Aiguille d' Argentiere	1864	12,796 ft.	3,900 m.
Aiguille Verte	1865	13,524 ft.	4,122 m.
Matterhorn	1865	14,692 ft.	4,478 m.
Grand Cornier	1865	12,999 ft.	3,962 m.

The Edward Whymper memorial plaque was placed on the Monte Rosa Hotel in Zermatt in 1925.

"I am seventy-two years old and I am finished. Every night, do you understand, I see my comrades of the Matterhorn slipping on their backs, their arms outstretched, one after another, in perfect order at equal distance—Croz, the guide, first, then Hadow, then Hudson, and lastly Douglas. Yes, I shall always see them…"

1911
Edward Whymper
(1840 – 1911)
Whymper's memory of
the 1865 Matterhorn
tragedy six days before
he died.

1911: FIRST ASCENT

August 9. Austrian optician and mountaineer Karl Blodig (1859 – 1956) became the first person to climb all sixty-seven 4,000 meter (13,124 feet) peaks in the European Alps (France, Italy, and Switzerland). His 67th peak over 4,000 meters was Mont Brouillard (4,069 meters/ 13,350 feet) which he climbed on August 9th with G.W. Young, H.O. Jones, and guide Joseph Knubel. Blodig was 52 years old at this time. Immediately after reaching the summit of Mont Brouillard, this climbing team then made the direct first ascent of the Brouillard Ridge to the summit of Mont Blanc (15,775 feet/4,808 meters). Mont Brouillard is part of the Mont Blanc massif in the French Alps. Peak summits over 4,000 meters in the Alps are known as "viertausenders" which in the German language means "a mountain over 4,000 meters." In 1994, the Union Internationale des Associations d' Alpinisme increased this number (67) of 4,000 meter summits by identifying 82 viertausender summits and 46 subsidiary tops over 4,000 meters for a total of 128 summits in the Alps over 4,000 meters in height. This list of 4,000 meter summits, however, varies according to different definitions of eligibility.

1911: FIRST ASCENT

By this year, Austrian mountaineer Paul Preuss (1886 – 1913) had solo climbed over 300 routes in the Alps. He made the first ascent of the Campanile Basso's (9,439 ft./2,877 m.) east face in the Brenta Dolomites of northern Italy in 1911 and solo climbed the west face of the Totenkirchl in the Wilder Kaiser mountains of Germany in 2 ½ hours also in 1911.

1911: Equipment – Crampons

In the Swiss and French Alps, pointed climbing irons were recommended to be only worn by advanced expert climbers.

1911: Technique – Ice Axe

Swiss mountain guide Josef Knubel (1881 – 1961) of St. Niklaus in the Zermatt Valley of Switzerland was the first climber to use the climbing technique known as the "axe cling." The ice axe was hooked into nicks in the rocks above the climber and then used to pull up the climber. Today this technique is called "dry tooling."

1911: Technique – Pendulum

German mountaineer Hans Fiechtl (1883 – 1925) invented the technique of horizontal rappelling known as a "pendulum." This sideways movement technique allowed a climber to swing across a rock face on a rope that is suspended from above.

1911: Technique – Court d' Eschelle

This is a French term meaning "human ladder." It describes a mountaineering technique whereby one climber stands on the shoulders of another climber so as to reach a higher handhold on a rock face. This climbing technique was used on the ascent of the Matterhorn's Furggen Ridge in 1911 by three mountain guides: J. Carrel (first man), J. Gaspard (second man, on carrel's shoulders) and M. Piacenza (third man, on Gaspard's shoulders). This then was a three-climber Court d' Eschelle.

1912: FIRST ASCENT

June 15. Mountaineers Hans Dülfer (1893 – 1915) and Walter Schaarschmidt made the first ascent of the Fleischbank's (7,176 ft./2,187 m.) east face in the Austrian Alps. This was one of the first climbs in which pitons, carabiners, two ropes, and belaying techniques were all used.

1912:

Scottish climbers John and Ian Clarke completed the climbing of all four 4,000 foot (1,219 meters) peaks in Scotland's Cairngorm Mountains in 10 hours 45 minutes (22 total miles with 7,000 feet/2,134 meters of climbing). These four peaks are Ben Macdui (4,296 ft./1,309 m.), Braeriach (4,248 ft./1,295 m.), Cairn Toul (4,241 ft./1,293 m.), and Cairn Gorm (4,084 ft./1,245 m.).

1912:

German mountaineer Hans Dulfer (1892 – 1915) made 155 peak ascents in 1912 and 173 ascents in 1913 in the Alps. In his climbing career, he made fifty first ascents. He was killed in World War I at age 22.

1912:

The Association of British Members of the Swiss Alpine Club completed the construction of the Britannia Hut between the Chessjen and Hohlaub Glaciers above Saas Fee, Switzerland. This 34-bed monument to British-Swiss friendship was expanded in 1929, 1951, and finally in 1996 to 134 beds.

1912: Equipment – Boot Nailing

Geneva, Switzerland jeweler and climber Félix Genecand (1874 – 1957) designed a new type of boot nail and nailing system. He was able to harden the steel edge nails (3 flattened prongs) for the first time by making them in two pieces. Genecand named these boot edge nails "tricouni" after a climbing route near Geneva. Although this tricouni nail would bite into rock, it was problematic on ice pitches. Another type of boot nail was called a "clinker." Made of mild steel, this broad climbing nail was designed to bite into small holes. By the early 1960s, nailed boots had practically disappeared.

1912: Technique – Using Pitons, Carabiners, and Double Ropes In Combination

Austrian mountaineers Hans Dulfer (1892 – 1915) and Walter Schaarschmidt succeeded in climbing the Fleischbank Ost Wand (7,176 feet/2,187 meters) in the Kaisergebirge, Austria. This was the first big climb to combine the use of pitons, carabiners, and a double rope. Dulfer is also credited with inventing the body rappel. He made fifty first ascents in the Alps.

1913: PEAK FIRST ASCENT *AIGUILLE DU PAIN DE SUCRE DU SOREILLER*

June 27. Italian mountain guide and ski instructor Angelo Dibona (1879 – 1956) and his client Guido Mayer made the first ascent of the Aiguille du Pain de Sucre du Soreiller (10,272 ft./3,131 m.) in the French Alps of southeastern France. This granite pinnacle was later re-named Aiguille Dibona in his honor. Dibona made over seventy first ascents in the Italian Dolomite mountains.

1913: PEAK FIRST ASCENT. *OLYMPUS*

August 2. Swiss mountaineers Frederick Boissonnas and Daniel Baud-Bouy and Greek mountaineer Christos Kakalos made the first ascent of Mount Olympus (9,571 ft./2,917 m.) in Greece. They reached the highest summit of Olympus which is known as Mytikas. This peak had experienced many failed attempts.

1913:

Austrian mountaineer Paul Preuss (1886 – 1913) died while solo climbing the north ridge of the Mandlkogel in the Eastern Alps. In his short lifetime (27 years), Preuss climbed 1,200 routes (300 solo climbs, 150 first ascents). He was dedicated to solo climbing. Preuss coined the term "artificial aid."

1913: Film

One of the first mountain films was shown at the West End Cinema in London, England—the ascent of the Matterhorn in Switzerland. This film was produced by F. Burlingham for the British. Burlingham took five mountain guides up the Matterhorn with a 15-kilogram (33 pounds) camera, a 10-kilogram (22 pounds) tripod and 1,500 feet/457 meters of film. His film crew climbed for 19 hours and reached the summit. Burlingham also filmed the ascents of the Jungfrau (13,642 ft./4,158 m.) and Mont Blanc (15,775 ft./4,808 m.).

1913:

Well-known British mountaineer Francis Fox Tuckett (1834 – 1913) died at age 79. Tuckett began climbing in the Alps in 1853 and eventually recorded 269 ascents and 687 pass crossings. The Rifugio Tuckett (mountain hut) in the Italian Dolomite mountains is named for him.

1913:

French painter Gabriel Loppé (1825 – 1913) died at age 88. Loppé was the first artist to specialize in painting ice and snow. His two most famous paintings were: "Glacier of the Gorner and the Matterhorn at Sunset" and "The Black Vein on the Mer de Glace at Chamonix." Both of these paintings measured 4 ft. x 6 ft. Loppé painted from the summit of Mont Blanc (15,775 ft./4,808 m.) eleven times.

1913: Film

German geologist turned film-maker Dr. Arnold Fanck (1889 – 1974) produced his first alpine film. Known as the "father of the alpine film," Fanck produced and directed many films in the 1920s and 1930s. His 1924 film *Mountain of Destiny* was the first feature film to be made on location in the Alps.

1914: FIRST ASCENT

July 28. Ski mountaineers Egger and Miescher made the first ski ascent of Mount Elbrus (18,510 ft./5,642 m.) in the Caucasus Mountains of Western Russia.

1914: FIRST ASCENT

Gritstone-trained climber Siegfried Herford (1891 – 1916) and G.S. Sansom made the first ascent of the Central Buttress on Scafell Pike (3,210 ft./978 m.) in the English Lake District. They climbed a direct line up this face. This was the first climb to be given the climbing grade of 'Hard Very Severe' in Great Britain.

1914: Equipment – Rock Climbing Shoes

Hans Kresz invented a lighter rock climbing shoe that had a felt sole. Called "manchons" (grips), these shoes would remain popular for thirty-three years (to 1947) until the arrival of the hardened rubber lug sole known as the Vibram sole.

1914: Technique – Open Slab Climbing

Rock climbers in England began to change their climbing technique from gully-climbs to open-slab routes.

1915:

Summer. The Mountain War (1915 – 1917) was fought between Italy and Austria in the Dolomite mountains. Climbing routes called "via ferratas" were established to help alpine troops supply their camps. These routes were protected by fixed cables, metal and wooden ladders, suspension bridges, and metal rung steps (called stemples). Via ferrata means "iron ways" in Italian. These routes are now graded according to difficulty. The Via Ferratas are now maintained by a section of the Club Alpino Italiano called the Societa Degli Alpinisti Tridentini.

1915:

Zurich dentist Hans Lauper (1895 – 1936) reached the first of his 18 major first ascents between 1915 and 1932 including the north faces of the Kamm, the Mönch, and the Jungfrau. Lauper and Alfred Zurcher and their guides also climbed the beautiful and difficult route on the east flank of the Eiger (13,025 ft./3,970 m.) which now bears his name—The Lauper Route.

1915: Technique – Knots

Saxon climbers in the Elbsandstein area of Germany made overhand and other knots in rope slings so that this knot could be jammed into rock cracks like a modern wedged nut and the loop then used as a runner.

1916:

British mountaineer Lucy Walker (1835 – 1916) died at age 81. She accomplished 98 separate climbs in the Alps only 3 of which did not reach the summit. Most of her climbs were first ascents by a woman. She climbed nearly all of the major peaks in the Swiss and French Alps. Her most active period was from 1862 to 1871. She was the first woman to climb the Matterhorn (1871).

1916: Technique – Rappelling

Another technique of rappelling steep faces was introduced. Several turns of the rope were wrapped around one ankle. The descending climber then pinched the rope strands between the feet. While holding on tight to the rope strands above, the climber slid down. This was an old circus or school fitness technique.

1917: FIRST ASCENT

June 18. British climber and skier Arnold Lunn (1888 – 1974) and guide Josef Knubel (1881 – 1961) made the first ski ascent of the Dom (14,911 ft./4,545 m.) in Switzerland. The Dom is the highest peak located completely within Switzerland. Lunn was knighted in 1952 for his contributions to the sport of skiing.

1917:

August 8. The construction of the Solvay Hut (13,134 ft./4,003 m.) began on the Hornli Ridge of the Matterhorn above Zermatt, Switzerland. Completed in just five days, this hut measured 16 feet in length, twelve feet in width, and fifteen feet high. This emergency shelter was inaugurated on August 8, 1917. The Solvay Hut was renovated in 1966 and reduced in size. Belgian industrialist Ernst Solvay (1838 – 1922) donated 20,000 Swiss francs to the Swiss Alpine Club to finance the original construction. Solvay climbed the Matterhorn in 1903 at age 65.

1917:

August 31. British mountaineer Geoffrey Winthrop Young's (1876 – 1958) left leg above the knee was severely injured in a World War I explosion (Battle of Monte San Gabriele) and required amputation. He commanded a Quaker ambulance unit. Young recovered and had a special artificial leg made for himself at the Orthopaedic Hospital in Bologna, Italy. His first climb with his new leg was on the Buttresses of Tryfan (England) on Easter Day of 1919. Young's artificial leg had various detachable feet:

> a leather shoe
> a rubber pad
> a ski-ring fitment
> a steel spike for rock climbing with tricouni nails at its base
>> to grip rock and hard ice.

From 1927 to 1935, Young climbed the Riffelhorn, Monte Rosa, the Matterhorn, and the Zinal Rothorn. All of the peaks are located above Zermatt, Switzerland. He continued to climb until 1935.

1917:

Famous Swiss mountain guide Mattias Zurbriggen (1856 – 1917) from Saas Fee succumbed to alcoholism, poverty, and suicide by hanging in Geneva, Switzerland at age 61. He spoke English, French, German, Italian, Spanish, and a little Hindustani. Zurbriggen completed many important ascents including his solo first ascent of Aconcagua (22,834 ft./6,959 m.) in Argentina (South America) in 1897.

1917:

German mountaineer and physician Oskar Schuster (1873 – 1917) died at age 44. He first climbed fifty new routes in the Italian Dolomites and made the first ascent of Ushba's south peak (15,454 ft./4,710 m.) in the Caucasus Range.

1918:

Prominent Swiss alpine landscape painter Ferdinand Hodler (1853 – 1918) died. His most important painting period was 1908 to 1911 when he painted many scenes of the Eiger, Monch, and Jungfrau peaks in Switzerland.

1919: FIRST ASCENT

August 19 and 20. Mountaineers S.L. Courtauld and E.G. Oliver and their guides Adolphe Rey and Adolf Aufdenblatten made the first ascent of the Innominata Ridge of Mont Blanc (15,775 ft./4,808 m.) in the French Alps. This was the first great climb in Europe after World War I.

1919:

The Alpine Club (London) and the Royal Geographical Society (London) met together to establish the Joint Himalayan Committee. It was at this meeting that
British mountaineer and explorer Francis Younghusband (1863 – 1942) made the following comment about climbing Mount Everest: "It must be done…and I think we are all determined that it shall be a British expedition."

1919:

Henri and Joseph Vallot (1854 – 1925) completed a 32-year (1887 – 1919) project of producing a detailed map of the Mont Blanc Massif (18 miles/30 kilometers long and 8 miles/13 kilometers wide) on a scale of 1:20,000. They were pioneers in developing photogrammetry.

1919:

During a bivouac on the Peuterey ridge of Mont Blanc (15,775 ft./4,808 m.), a group of the leading climbers of Chamonix, France decided to form the Groupe de Haute Montagne (G.H.M.). This elite group of mountaineers included Jacques de Lèpiney, Tom de Lèpiney, Paul Chevalier, Henry Bregeault and Philippe Le Bec. It was decided that all G.H.M. members must be capable of leading a severe climb. The G.H.M. represented an off-shoot of the French Alpine Club and promoted guideless climbing.

1919: FIRST ASCENT

British climbers J. Rooke Corbett and Eustace Thomas made the first traverse of all six Welsh 3,000 foot/914 meter peaks in 20 hours.

1919: Equipment – Sleeping Bags

Sleeping bags made of waterproofed silk quilted with eiderdown were used on an ascent of Mont

Blanc (15,775 ft./4,808 m.) in the French Alps. These bags combined lightness with an impressive degree of warmth.

1919: Equipment – Rock Climbing Shoe

British geology professor Noel Odell (1890 – 1987) climbed on the Cornwall Cliffs of southwestern England in tennis shoes called "rubbers." This early rock shoe proved very effective for friction climbing.

1919: Technique – Air Support

Swiss pilot Lt. R. Ackermann made the first glacier landing on the Aletsch Glacier in Switzerland in a DH3 airplane.

1919: Technique – Dry Tooling

British climbers George Leigh Mallory (1886 – 1924), David Pye, Claude Elliot, and Ruth Mallory (George's wife) made the first ascent of Bowling Green Buttress in Wales. They climbed the last few feet with the aid of an ice axe being jammed into a crack in the rock. This ice axe then served as either a handhold or a footstep. This and related techniques are now known as "dry tooling."

1920: FIRST ASCENT

Scottish mountaineers Harold Raeburn (1865 – 1926), Frank Goggs, and W. Mounsey made the first winter ascent of Observatory Ridge on Ben Nevis (4,406 ft./1,343 m.) in Scotland. Raeburn was 55 years old at the time.

1920: Book

Well-known British mountaineer, poet, and educator Geoffrey Winthrop Young (1876 – 1958) published Mountain Craft – a manual of mountaineering instruction. This 300-page book represented an excellent summary of mountain knowledge prior to World War I. Young published seven books (five on mountain climbing) from 1899 to 1953. He is credited with establishing many new climbing routes in the Zermatt area of Switzerland.

1920: Clothing – Linings, Puttees, and Alpine Hats

Wool climbing knickers were lined with the thinnest possible flannel for a more comfortable feel next to the skin. Puttees (or leggings) were generally worn in the Alps. Engadine (Switzerland) mountain guides used a modified half puttee. Soft, felt, wide-brimmed hats, called "Alpine Hats" were worn while climbing.

1920: Equipment – Eye Protection

Tinted spectacles were worn on snow climbs in the Alps. The tint color was called "London smoke." Each climber carried two pairs.

1920: Equipment – Ice Axe

1920s. Alfred Horeschowsky (1895 – 1987) invented the glide ring and wrist loop for the ice axe.

1920: Equipment – Lanterns

The best alpine lantern was the square-folding Italian lantern called the 'Excelsior Lux.' Made of tin, it measured 4" square and 7 ¾" high.

1920: Technique – Alpine Distress Signal

The alpine distress signal that Dent had proposed in 1894 was modified as follows: the signal shall consist of a succession of sounds (or flashes at night) at a rate of six per minute with a one minute interval. The reply rate shall be three sounds per minute with the same interval.

1921:

January 21. British mountaineer and explorer Francis Edward Younghusband (1863 – 1942) presided over the first official meeting of the Mount Everest Committee (MEC). This expedition organizing group was composed of the Alpine Club (3 members) and the Royal Geographical Society (3 members). The MEC organized the 1921, 1922, and 1924 British expeditions to Mount Everest.

1921: FIRST ASCENT

July 23. The north face of the Monch (13,449 ft./4,099 m.) in Switzerland was first climbed by Hans Lauper (1895 – 1936) and Max Liniger. This ascent took fifteen hours.

1921: FIRST ASCENT

September 21. Japanese mountaineer Yuko Maki (1894 – 1989) made the first ascent of the Eiger's true Mittellegi Ridge in Switzerland. Maki's guides were Fritz Amatter, Samuel Brawand, and Fritz Steuri. Amatter had descended this same ridge in 1904. He and Maki climbed this ridge again in 1926. Maki also made the first ascent of Mount Alberta (11,874 ft./3,619 m.) in Canada in 1925 and he led the 1956 Japanese expedition that made the first ascent of Manaslu (26,760 ft./8,156 m.) in Nepal. Maki was the first professional mountaineer in Japan.

1921:

French woman mountaineer Anne Bernard applied to join the 1922 British Mount Everest Expedition. She was refused by the Mount Everest Committee based on gender not nationality. This committee was founded in 1921 and was composed of Alpine Club and Royal Geographical Society members.

1921:

The word "Sherpa" begins appearing frequently in European books due to the first big Mount Everest expedition in 1921 by the British. Coined by the Bhutias people of Tibet, "shar" means "east" and "pa" means "men of." Therefore, "Sherpa" can be translated as "men of the east."

1921:

The Pinnacle Club was founded in England by woman climbers for woman climbers. This was the world's first true national women's climbing club. Its members preferred to climb as all-female ropes and they specialized in severe rock climbing. Mrs. Geoffrey Winthrop Young was elected as the first president.

1921:

British painter Edward T.H. Compton (1849 – 1921) died at age 72. Many considered Compton to be the master of high-mountain painting. In 1919, at age 70, Compton reached the summit of the Grossglockner (12,461 ft./3,798 m.), the highest peak in Austria. He made 300 major ascents in the Alps of which 21 were first ascents.

1921: Equipment – Stove

Primus stoves were modified to operate at high altitudes. Oxford, England. These stoves, however, failed to operate properly above 20,000 feet/6,095 meters on Mount Everest in 1921.

1921: Technique – Air Support

Swiss pilot F. Durafour landed his Caudron G3 biplane (built in 1914) on the Col du Dôme (13,970 ft./4,258 m.) above Chamonix, France—the first glacier landing above 4,000 meters (13,124 feet).

1922:

February 6. Italian mountaineer, scholar, and poet Ambrogio Damiano Achille Ratti (1857 – 1939) was elected Pope Pius XI in Rome, Italy. Ratti was known as "the Mountaineering Pope." He was from Desio, Italy and served as Pope from 1922 to 1939. His active climbing period was from 1885 to 1913.

1922: FIRST ASCENT

Mrs. L.R. Frazeur and Miss Winona Bailey became the first women to climb all four summits of Mount Olympus (9,570 ft./2,917 m.) in Greece.

1922:

British mountaineer Theodore Howard Somervell (1890 – 1975) climbed thirty-two peaks in the Alps. In 1924, Somervell was a member of the British Mount Everest expedition.

1922: Clothing – Insulation

British mountaineer George Ingle Finch (1888 – 1969) made himself a knee-length quilted jacket filled with eiderdown. This was the first known use of eiderdown (the soft breast feathers of the female Eider duck, a large sea duck) as an insulation material.

1922: Equipment – Ice Piton

Herman Angerer invented the first ice piton on the Zillertal peak of Schrammacher (11,208 ft./3,416 m.) in Austria. This ice piton revolutionized the ice climbing technique.

1922: Technique – Crevasse Rescue

Austrian climber Dr. Karl Prusik (1896 – 1961) of Vienna invented the "prusik knot" for self-help in crevasse rescue. This type of knot was adapted from violin string repair. Prusik rope slings served as stirrups to help a climber climb up and out of a glacier crevasse. The climber could ascend a rope by sliding smaller knotted ropes (or nylon web slings) up and by weighting them down prevent themselves from sliding down. Thin cord rope and nylon slings as prusik devices were eventually replaced with a variety of mechanical ascenders (i.e. Jumars).

1923:

June 15. Saint Bernard of Menthon (923 – 1008) was canonized by Pope Pius XI (Italian mountaineer Abate Achille Ratti) and proclaimed the Patron Saint of Mountaineers. His small band of monks in 1049 constructed a building on the Saint Bernard Pass (8,103 ft./2,470 m.) between Switzerland and Italy to feed and shelter mountain travelers. Bernard was born in 923 in Menthon, France.

1923:

July. Scottish mountaineer Rev. R. Burn was the first person to complete the climbing of all Munro peaks and "tops" which totaled 558 summits at this time. A "Munro" is a summit of at least 3,000 feet (914 meters).

1923:

August 12. Austrian mountaineers Alfred Horeschowsky (1895 – 1987) and Franz Piekielo made the first attempt to climb the Matterhorn's north face. Continuous stonefall stopped them at the 4,000 meter (13,124 feet) level. They traversed over to the Solvay Hut (13,134 ft./4,003 m.) on the Hornli Ridge which they then followed to the summit.

1923:

American climber James Waddell Alexander (1888 – 1971, Princeton University Professor of Mathematics) first visited the Swiss Alps and made 22 ascents in the Zermatt-Saas Fee area. He continued to make the following ascents in the Alps in the following years: 25 ascents in 1925, 23 in 1926, 23 in 1927, and 20 in 1928 (age 40).

1923:

Well-known British Himalayan explorer Henry Haversham Godwin-Austen (1834 – 1923) died at age 89. In addition to being an explorer, he was a surveyor, artist, geologist, and mountaineer. Godwin-Austen was the first European to ascend the Baltoro Glacier in the Karakoram Range of Pakistan which he measured and mapped.

1923:

British diplomat and mountaineer Sir William Edward Davidson (1853 – 1923) died at age 70. In addition to making the first ascent of Mont Maudit (14,650 ft./4,465 m.), in 1878, the Aiguille du Tacul (11,300 ft./3,444 m.) in 1880, and the Wellenkuppe (12,805 ft./3,444 m.) – Obergabelhorn (13,330 ft./4,063 m.) traverse in 1895, Davidson also made 250 ascents of the Riffelhorn (9,607 ft./2,928 m.) above Zermatt, Switzerland.

1923: Fabric – Grenfell Cloth

Britisher Sir Wilfred Grenfell received the first bale of Grenfell cloth (windproof gabardine) from Haythornthwaite of Burnley, Lancashire, England. This fabric replaced Burberry as a windproof fabric for high altitude climbing. It weighed 6 ounces per square yard.

1923: Technique – Tension Traverse

A tension traverse was performed for the first time on the north face of the Dent d' Herens (13,684 feet/4,171 meters) in Switzerland by Australian-born scientist and Everest mountaineer George Ingle Finch (1888 – 1970), Guy Forster, and Raymond Peto. This was not the first ascent of this face which occurred two years later in 1925 by Willo Welzenbach (1900 – 1934) and Eugen Allwein. The tension traverse was used to cross a steep, smooth rock wall. The second climber on the rope held the rope in tension as the leader proceeded across the traverse by using sidepulls and friction holds.

1924: FIRST ASCENT

April 20. Ski mountaineers R. von Tscharner and M. Wieland made the first ski traverse of Mont Blanc (15,775 ft./4,808 m.) from Courmayeur, Italy to Chamonix, France.

1924:

June 19. "Mallory Irvine Nove Remainder Alcedo." This was the coded telegram message from British mountaineer E.P. Norton to Arthur Hinks of the Himalayan Committee (London) on the June 8th deaths of George Leigh Mallory and Andrew Irvine on the north ridge of Mount Everest in Tibet. 1924 British Mount Everest Expedition. "Nove" meant that Mallory and Irvine had died. "Alcedo" meant that everyone else was safe.

1924: FIRST ASCENT

July 15. German mountaineers Willo Welzenbach (1900 – 1934) and Fritz Rigele made the first ascent of the northwest face of the Gross Wiesbachhorn (11,694 ft./3,564 m.). This was considered the most difficult ice climb yet accomplished in the eastern Alps. This was also the first climb that used "ice pegs" or ice pitons designed by Rigele.

1924: FIRST ASCENT

August 11 and 12. Roland Rossi and Felix Simon made the first ascent of Monte Pelmo's north face (2,789 ft./850 m.) in the Italian Dolomites. This was the first Grade VI climb in the Dolomites.

1924:

October 17. Two memorial services were held in London in memory of British Mount Everest climbers George Leigh Mallory (1886 – 1924) and Andrew "Sandy" Irvine (1902 – 1924). During the day a service was held in St. Paul's Cathedral. In attendance were his Majesty the King of England, the Prince of Wales, the Duke of Connaught, Prince Arthur, Prime Minister Ramsay MacDonald, former Foreign Secretary Lord Curzon, Lord Mayor of London, and the Mayor of Birkenhead, England (Mallory's birthplace). A Guard of Honor was comprised of the following well-known British mountaineers: General Charles Granville Bruce, Lt. Col. Edward Norton, Dr. Howard Somervell, Professor Noel Odell, Major Guy Bullock, Henry Morshead, Captain John Noel, and Geoffrey Winthrop Young. Also in attendance were Francis Younghusband, Ruth Mallory (George's wife), Rev. Herbert Leigh Mallory (George's father) and Hugh Thackeray Turner (Ruth's father).

An evening memorial service was held at the Royal Albert Hall.

1924: Technique – Ice Climbing

French mountaineers Jacques Lagarde and Henri de Segnone were the first to push the ten-point Oscar Eckenstein crampons to their limit with their climb of the extremely difficult north face of the Aiguille du Plan (12,051 feet/3,673 meters) above Chamonix, France. This ascent involved steep water – ice.

1924: Technique – Ice Piton

July 15. Ice pitons were first used by German mountaineer Willo Welzenbach (1900 – 1934) on an ascent of the Gross Wiesbachhorn (11,694 feet/3,564 meters) in Austria.

1925: FIRST ASCENT

August 7. German mountaineers Emil Solleder (1899 – 1931) and Gustav Lettenbauer free-climbed the 4,000 foot/1,219 meter northwest face ("Wall of Walls") of the Civetta (10,558 ft./3,218 m.) in the eastern Italian Dolomite mountains. They only used 15 pitons for belaying on this 15-hour ascent. This climb was believed to be the most difficult climb in the world at that time and the first route in the Alps to be classified as sixth grade.

1925: FIRST ASCENT

August 10. Bavarian mountaineers Willo Welzenbach (1900 – 1934) and Eugen Allwein (1900 – 1982) made the first ascent of the north face (4,265 ft./1,300 m.) of the Dent d' Herens (13,684 ft./4,171 m.) in Switzerland. This 16-hour climb from the Schonbiel Hut was considered to be the most difficult ice face climb to date.

1925:

German woman mountaineer Eleonore Hasenclever was killed by an avalanche near the Weisshorn (14,804 ft./4,512 m.) summit in Switzerland. She had climbed 150 peaks over 12,000 ft./3,657 m. in the European Alps.

1926: FIRST ASCENT

April. French mountaineers A. Delille and P. Dalloz made the first winter ascent of the Meije (13,067 ft./3,983 m.) in France.

1926:

May 11. American-born British mountaineer William Augustus Brevoort (W.A.B.) Coolidge (1850 – 1926) died at age 76 in Grindelwald, Switzerland. Coolidge left the United States at age 14 and was educated at Oxford University in England. He moved to Grindelwald in 1896 and lived there for the last thirty years of his life. Coolidge made over 1,700 climbs in the Alps of which 900 were important and ten were first ascents. He made 60 ascents with his dog Tschingel. He was the first historian who specialized in the history of mountaineering. His personal mountaineering library of over 26,000 volumes in 4 languages was bequeathed to the Swiss Alpine Club. Coolidge made 230 contributions (articles) to the Alpine Journal, wrote or contributed to 61 books, and contributed 200 articles to the Encyclopedia Britannica. Coolidge became known as the "Magdalen Hedgehog," the "Sage of Grindelwald," and the "Fiery Lamb." Coolidge is credited with making three main mountaineering achievements:

1. He popularized winter mountaineering.
2. He first made use of high bivouacs.
3. He systematically explored the Dauphine mountains of southeastern France.

1926: FIRST ASCENT

September 19. German mountaineers Willo Welzenbach (1900 – 1934) and Karl Wien (1906 – 1937) made the first ascent of the north face (4,593 ft./1,400 m.) of the Grossglockner (12,461 ft./3,798 m.) in Austria. Their climbing route is now known as the Welzenbach Route.

1926:

British mountaineers C.F. Hadfield and W.G. Pape climbed Ben Nevis (4,406 ft./1,343 m.) in Scotland, Scafell Pike (3,192 ft./973 m.) in England, and Snowdon (3,560 ft./1,085 m.) in Wales in a total elapsed time of 22 hours and 56 minutes.

1926: FIRST ASCENT

British female climber Mabel Barber made the first women's ascent of the Central Buttress of Scafell Pike (3,210 ft./978 m.), the highest peak in England. This route was Britain's most challenging rock climb at the time.

1926: Equipment – Rock Climbing Shoes

Rock climbing shoes in the Italian Dolomites were known as "scarpe de gatto" or cat shoes. The soles were comprised of many layers of woolen cloth stitched together.

1926: Equipment – Nuts (or Chocks)

The use of the chock for climbing began in Wales (Great Britain) on a climb of Clogwyn du'r Arddu (600 ft./183 m. high cliff). Climbers carried small rocks which they wedged into cracks on the rock face. Short pieces of rope were looped around these stones to which karabiners were then attached. A railroad was located near this climb and climbers would occasionally find a large metal nut that had fallen off a passing train. This hexagonal nut would also be used as a chock.

1926: Technique – Climb Classification

German mountaineer Willo Welzenbach (1900 – 1934) documented and described the Alpine climbing grade system that involved six rock grades: I. Easy, II. A little difficult, III. Rather difficult, IV. Difficult, V. Very difficult, and VI. Extremely difficult. Welzenbach limited his grading system to dry rock climbs only (no ice or snow).

1927: FIRST ASCENT

August. Miriam O'Brien (1899 – 1976) and Margaret Helburn accomplished two significant climbs in the Chamonix, France aiguilles (rock needles):The ascent of the Grepon (11,424 ft./3,482 m.) via the Mer de Glace face with guide Armand Charlet. They were the first women to do this climb.The ascent of a new route on the northwest face of the Aiguille du Midi (12,605 ft./3,842 m.) with guides Armand Charlet and Alfred Couttet.

1927: FIRST ASCENT

September 1 and 2. British mountaineers Thomas Graham Brown (1882 – 1965) and Frank S. Smythe (1900 – 1949) made the first ascent of the Sentinelle Rouge route on the Brenva Face of Mont Blanc. This ice and rock climb (4,265 ft./1,300 m.) began at the Col Moore and proceeded directly to the summit. The average slope was 47°. Brown and Smythe used no guides. This climb represented the first of three major first ascents that Thomas Graham Brown accomplished on the Brenva Face from 1927 to 1933.

1927:

The Greek Alpine Club was inaugurated on the summit of Mount Olympus (9,570 ft./2,917 m.) in Greece.

1927:

British mountaineer Katherine Richardson (1854 – 1927) died at age 73. She made 116 major ascents in the Alps including six first ascents and fourteen first ascents by a woman (La Meije in 1885).

1927:

Famous Swiss mountain guide Christian Klucker (1853 – 1928) climbed his last peak (a new double traverse of the east arête of Torrione del Ferro) at the age of 74. Kluckner guided clients up Alpine peaks for over fifty years and climbed over 3,000 peaks in the Alps. He was the leader on 34 first ascents, 28 first traverses, 11 new and difficult passes, and completed 65 new routes and route variations.

1927: Equipment – Rock Drill

French mountaineer Laurent Grivel developed the first set of portable tools for placing anchors into rock—the rock drill and the expansion bolt. Grivel first used this tool set on the first ascent of the 200 foot/61 meter rock finger known as Pere Eternal on the north ridge of the Aiguille de la Brenva in the French Alps.

1927: Equipment – Bivouac Sack

August. When British mountaineers Thomas Graham Brown (1882 – 1965) and Frank Smythe (1900 – 1949) were climbing the Brenva Face of Mont Blanc (15,775 ft./4,808 m.) in the French Alps, they used the Zdarsky bivouac sack/tent which was designed and made in Germany. Named after Austrian Matthias Zdarsky (1855 – 1940), a well-known ski pioneer, who introduced this sack and promoted its use to mountaineers as a life-saving piece of equipment. Made of waterproof nylon, this type of bivouac sack allowed two men to sit facing one another and included a small viewing window for weather-watching.

1927: Technique – Chocks

The idea of deliberately placing stones in rock cracks to act as chocks was conceived by British climber Morley Wood during the first ascent of Piggott's Climb on Clogwyn du'r Arddu in Wales. Stones were eventually replaced by steel nuts and other materials.

1928: FIRST ASCENT

July 20. Ivor Richards (1893 – 1979) and Dorothy Pilley (1893 – 1986) and their guides Joseph and Antoine Georges made the first ascent of the north ridge of Dent Blanche (14,295 ft./4,357 m.) in Switzerland. This ascent was considered to be the most difficult first ascent by British climbers during the 1920 – 1930 period.

1928: FIRST ASCENT

August 4. French mountain guides Armand Charlet and Georges Cachat led American mountaineers Miriam O'Brien (1898 – 1976) and Robert Underhill (1889 – 1983) on the first complete traverse of the Aiguilles du Diable in the French Alps. These five pinnacles are located on the southeast ridge of Mont Blanc du Tacul (13,938 ft./4,248 m.). The five pinnacles are: Corne du Diable (13,334 ft./4,064 m.), Pointe Chaubert (13,367 ft./4,074 m.), Mediane (13,442 ft./4,097 m.), Pointe Carmen (13,186 ft./4,019 m.), and l'isolee (13,498 ft./4,114 m.). This entire traverse took nine hours. Many mountaineers at this time believed that this was the most difficult ridge climb in the Alps.

1928: FIRST ASCENT

August 6 and 7. British mountaineer Thomas Graham Brown (1882 – 1965) and Frank S. Smythe (1900 – 1949) made the first ascent of the Major route on the Brenva Face of Mont Blanc. The average slope of this steep ice and rock route (4,265 ft./1,300 m.) is 48°. They did not use any guides. This was the second of three major first ascents on the Brenva (east) face accomplished by Brown.

1928:

Two guides from the Village of Täsch in the Zermatt Valley, Kaspar Mooser and Victor Imboden, made the second serious attempt to climb the Matterhorn's (14,692 ft./4,478 m.) north face. They reached a point 1,650 ft./503 m. above the Matterhorn Glacier before retreating.

1928:

Well-known Swiss mountain guide Christian Klucker (1853 – 1928) died at age 76. He made 44 first ascents and climbed 88 new routes in the Alps. Klucker was from the Engadine region of Switzerland.

1929: FIRST ASCENT

August 17. American woman mountaineer Miriam O'Brien (1898 – 1976) and French woman Alice Damesme made the first manless ascent and traverse of the Grépon (11,424 ft./3,482 m.) above Chamonix, France which was considered a scandalous act in those days. O'Brien was the first female to lead this climb which began the period of all-woman rope teams.

1929: FIRST ASCENT

September 6. American mountaineer Bradford Washburn (1910 – 2007) made the first ascent of the 3,000 foot/914 meter Couturier Couloir on the north face of the Aiguille Verte (13,524 ft./4,122 m.) with guides Georges Charlet (1901 – 1979) and Alfred Couttet (– 1975). This was the boldest climb (6 hours, 20 minutes) to date done in the Chamonix, France area. This first ascent climb was, however, their second choice. They originally planned to make the first ascent of the Walker Spur of the Grandes Jorasses but cancelled this ascent due to excessive rockfall. In the previous two summers Washburn had climbed the Matterhorn, Monte Rosa, Mont Blanc, Les Drus, the Charmoz, and the Grepon.

1929: FIRST ASCENT

Austrian climber Fritz Herrmann made the first solo ascent of the Matterhorn's (14,692 ft./4,478 m.) west face.

1929:

British mountaineer James A. Parker was the first to climb all 311 3,000 foot (914 meters) plus peaks in the British Isles (England – 7, Scotland – 297, Wales – 6, and Ireland – 1).

1929:

British mountaineer John Percy Farrar (1857 – 1929) died at age 72. He made many ascents in the European Alps including the Weisshorn (3 ascents), Schreckhorn (4), Wetterhorn (7), Meije (4), Matterhorn (4), and Mont Blanc (5). In 1893, Farrar made 15 ascents in the Alps.

1929: Equipment – Crampons

Courmayeur, Italy. Mountain guide and equipment manufacturer Laurent Grivel (guide and blacksmith) and British climber/engineer Oscar J.L. Eckenstein (1859 – 1921) introduced the first twelve-point crampon. This new design featured two front-facing points or prongs. This crampon allowed the mountaineer to climb straight up steep snow and ice slopes by kicking in the front two prongs.

1930:

British mountaineer Eustace Thomas (1869 – 1960) became the first Englishman to climb all of the

4,000 meter (13,124 feet) peaks in the Alps. It took Thomas seven years (1924 – 1930) to climb the 83 peaks plus 30 lesser summits (an average of 16 peaks per year for six years).

1930:

Compagnie des Guides of Chamonix, France. The requirement that a Chamonix-based guide must be a native of Chamonix was lifted and the first outsider was admitted. A Chamonix guide, however, must be French-born. In 1994, approximately one-third of the guide members were from outside the 12 mile long Chamonix Valley.

1930: Equipment – Bivouac Sack

European mountaineers used the Zdarsky (Mathius) sleeping bag/bivi sack for those unplanned overnight campsites. Made of lightweight, waterproofed fabric, these rectangular sacks opened down one long side and were designed for the sitting position. Zdarsky (1856 – 1940) was a Czech and also developed the steel ski binding in 1890.

1930: Technique – Long Run-Outs

1930 – 1934. British climber Colin Kirkus (1910 – 1940) and his friends initiated long run-outs on exposed rock faces in England. This was one of the main contributions to English rock climbing. A run-out is defined as a rope length on a pitch where there are no running belays. All early climbs involved long run-outs.

1931: FIRST ASCENT

June. German mountaineers Hans Ertl (1908 – 2000) and Franz Schmid (1905 – 1992) made the first ascent of the Ortler's (12,812 ft./3,905 m.) north face in northern Italy. This 3,937 foot/1,200 meter face is the highest face in the eastern Alps. Schmid made this ascent just a few weeks before he and his brother Anton (Toni) made the first ascent of the Matterhorn's north face in Switzerland.

1931: FIRST ASCENT

July 6 – 10. German mountaineers Willy Merkl (1900 – 1934) and Willo Welzenbach (1900 – 1934) made the first ascent of the North Face (3,600 ft./1,097 m.) of the Aiguille des Grandes Charmoz (11,300 ft./3,444 m.) above Chamonix, France. A storm trapped these two climbers for 60 hours 1,000 meters up this face. The final 100 meters of this five-day climb took 9 hours.

1931: FIRST ASCENT

July 31 – August 1. German mountaineers Franz (1905 – 1992) and Toni Schmid (1910 – 1932) made the first ascent of the Matterhorn's (14,692 ft./4,478 m.) north face (3,600 ft./1,097 m.). They bicycled to Zermatt from Munich (approximately 1,200 miles/2,000 kilometer round trip) with all their climbing gear. They spent 33 hours climbing the face and bivouacked at 13,616 ft./4,150 m.). They carried rock and ice pitons, "clasp-rings" (carabiners), two 130-foot ropes, food, and a rubber sleeping sack. The Matterhorn is located in the Pennine Alps immediately southwest of the village of

Zermatt, Switzerland. The Schmid brothers were awarded Gold Medals at the 1932 Summer Olympic Games in Los Angeles, California for their ascent. During the next thirty-six years (up to 1967), the Matterhorn's north face was climbed 26 more times by 74 mountaineers. The second ascent of this face occurred in July of 1935 by two Munich, Germany, climbers.

1931: FIRST ASCENT

October 15. Italian mountaineers Enzo Benedetti and guides Luigi Carrel and Maurice Bich made the first ascent of the Matterhorn's (14,692 ft./4,478 m.) south face above Breuil, Italy.

1931:

British mountaineer William Martin Conway (1856 – 1937) was named Baron Conway of Allington. He was the first man to be knighted in connection to mountaineering. His primary contribution was his Karakoram map of glaciers which he surveyed.

1931:

The Golden Age of Nordwand (north face) climbing began in the Alps. The six major north faces that were climbed in the 1930s were:

1931	Matterhorn	14,692 ft./4,478 m.	Germans
1933	Cima Grande di Lavaredo	9,840 ft./2,999 m.	Italians
1935	Petit Dru	12,245 ft./3,732 m.	French
1937	Piz Badile	10,853 ft./3,308 m.	Italians
1938	Walker Spur of Grandes Jorasses	13,806 ft./4,208 m.	Italians
1938	Eiger	13,825 ft./3,970 m.	Germans/Austrians

1931:

Chamonix, France guide Joseph Ravanel (1869 – 1931) died at age 62. Ravanel climbed the Grépon (11,424 feet/3,482 meters) 57 times and was one of the first guides to use skis while climbing.

1931: FIRST ASCENT

Women mountaineers were now making first class ascents in the Alps. American climber Miriam O'Brien (1899 – 1976) and French woman Micheline Morin made a complete traverse of the Monch (13,449 ft./4,099 m.) in Switzerland. O'Brien and Jessie Whitehead made a complete traverse of the Alphubel (13,662 ft./4,164 m.) also in Switzerland.

1931: FIRST ASCENT

Italian mountaineer Emilio Comici (1901 – 1940) climbed the 4,000 foot/1,219 meter northwest face of the Civetta (10,558 ft./3,218 m.) in the Italian Dolomites which required 26 pitches of vertical climbing. After making this ascent, Comici said: "I wish some day to make a route and from the summit let fall a drop of water and this is where my route will have gone." The idea of the "direttissima" was then born. Comici inaugurated his direttissima route concept in 1933 when he climbed a direct line up the north face of the Cima Grande di Lavaredo (9,839 ft./2,999 m.). Comici has been given the credit for inventing multi-step aid ladders, hanging bivouacs, and solid belays.

1931: Fabric – Lin-O-Let

Helly Hansen introduced a new fabric called "Lin-O-Let." This was a thin, lightweight, and waterproof lining that was incorporated into outer wear.

1931: Technique – Modern Aid Techniques

Italian mountaineer Emilio Comici (1901 –1940) is credited with inventing many climbing aid techniques including:

> Multi-step aid ladders
>
> Solid belays
>
> Hanging bivouacs
>
> Climbing with a second rope used for hauling up gear.

Comici used these new techniques on his 1931 climbing route up the 1,200 meter (3,937 foot) northwest wall of the Civetta in the Italian Dolomites. His climbing partner was Giulio Benedetti. Their direct route is known as the "Direttissima Italiana."

1931: Technique – Ice Climbing

Italian mountain guide and blacksmith Laurent Grivel modified the ten-point crampon by adding two front prongs pointing directly forward on each crampon. The mountaineer could now climb steep ice and snow by front-pointing straight up the slope eliminating the need to cut steps with an ice axe. This technique became known as the "German method."

1932: FIRST ASCENT

August 12. Miriam O'Brien (1898 – 1976) and Alice Damesme climbed the Matterhorn (14,692 ft./4,478 m.) in Switzerland without using guides via the Hornli Ridge. This was the first all-women ascent of the Matterhorn. O'Brien eventually climbed the Matterhorn three times.

1932: FIRST ASCENT

August 20. Swiss dentist and mountaineer Hans Lauper (1895 – 1936) led the first ascent of the Eiger's (13,025 ft./3,970 m.) northeast ridge above Grindelwald, Switzerland. With Lauper were Alfred Zurcher and guides Josef Knubel (1881 – 1961) and Alexander Graven. This ridge is the rock and snow ridge to the left of the infamous north face. This ascent required 16 hours of climbing. Hans Lauper made 18 first ascents in the Alps from 1915 to 1932, including five north faces (Eiger, Jungfrau, Kamm, Monch, and Stockhorn).

1932:

August. Count Charles Egmond d' Arcis established the Union Internationale des Associations d' Alpinisme (U.I.A.A.) in Geneva, Switzerland. This organization (International Union of Alpinist

Associations) coordinated mountaineering interests between nations world-wide. It also developed minimum equipment standards. 18 countries represented its original members. As of 2003, the U.I.A.A. had 92 member associations in 68 different countries.

1932: FIRST ASCENT

September 18 and 19. Enzo Benedetti, Maurice Bich, Louis Carrel, Lucien Carrel, Antonio Gaspard, and Giuseppe Mazzotti made the first ascent of the Matterhorn's (14,692 ft./4,478 m.) east face (3,300 ft./1,006 m.). One bivouac was required and the last few hundred feet took more than ten hours to climb.

1932:

British mountaineer Edmund Wigram (1911 – 1945) made a 20-hour climbing traverse from Store Skagastolstind (7,890 ft./2,405 m.) to Gjertvasstind (7,717 ft./2,352 m.) in Norway. He crossed six major summits.

1932:

British mountaineer Eustace Thomas (1870 – 1960) completed the climbing (1924 to 1932) of all seventy-three recognized 4,000 meter peaks in the Alps at age 62. His guide on most of these ascents was Valais guide Josef Knubel (1881 – 1961).

1932:

French mountaineer and writer Roger Frison-Roche (1906 – 1999) made the first live radio broadcast from the summit of Mont Blanc (15,782 ft./4,810 m.) for Radio Lyon.

1932: Equipment – Crampons

The newly introduced twelve-point crampon by Laurent Grivel was enthusiastically adopted by both German and Austrian climbers. However, this new crampon was not widely used until after the 1938 first ascent of the Eiger's north face above Grindelwald, Switzerland.

1933:

March 18. The Duke of the Abruzzi (1873 – 1933), Italian mountaineer and expedition leader, died of prostate cancer at age 60. He was born Luigi Amadeo Giuseppe Mario Fernando Francesco Di Savoia-Aosta, Duke of the Abruzzi, Prince of the Ancient House of Savoy, third son of the King of Spain. He led three great mountaineering expeditions: Alaska (1897), Africa (1906), and the Himalayas (1909).

1933: FIRST ASCENT

August 12 – 14. Italian mountaineer Emilio Comici (1901 – 1940) and the Dimai brothers (Angelo and Auguste) made the first ascent of the north face (1,900 ft./579 m.) of the Cima Grande di Lavaredo (9,839 ft./2,999 m.) in the northern Italian Dolomites. This direct climbing route (direttissima) with its 700 foot/220 meter overhang is now known as the Comici Route. Comici used 80 pitons to achieve this two-day climb. At the time, this ascent was considered the most difficult rock climb ever made.

1933: FIRST ASCENT

British mountaineer Thomas Graham Brown (1882 – 1965) became the first climber to make the first ascent of every major route on one significant mountain face. Brown completed his third first ascent on the Brenva (east) Face of Mont Blanc by climbing the Pear Buttress route from the Col Moore directly to the summit of Mont Blanc de Courmayeur (15,578 ft./4,748 m.). Zermatt (Switzerland) guides Alexander Graven and Alfred Aufdenblatten were with Brown. This route contained mixed snow and rock slopes up to 60°. Graham completed the following first ascent routes on Mont Blanc's Brenva Face:

1. 1927 Sentinelle Rouge with Frank Smythe (1900 – 1949)
2. 1928 Route Major also with Frank Smythe
3. 1933 Pear Buttress with Alexander Graven and Alfred Aufdenblatten.

1933: Equipment – Crampon

Grivel introduced the superlight nickel chrome-moly steel crampon.

1934: FIRST ASCENT

January 17. Russian mountaineers A. Gusev and W. Korsun made the first winter ascent of the East Peak of Mount Elbrus (18,442 ft./5,621 m.) in western Russia.

1934:

American mountaineer Paul Petzoldt (1908 – 1999) and New Zealand mountaineer Dan Bryant (1905 – 1957) made a double traverse of the Matterhorn (14,692 ft./4,478 m.) in Switzerland in one long day. (16 hours).

1934:

Over a 150-year period (1784 – 1934), British climbers had made the first ascent of 31 of the highest 50 peaks in Europe (62 percent). The elevations ranged from 13,774 ft./4,198 m. (#50 – Rimpfischhorn) to 18,482 ft./5,633 m. (#1 – Mount Elbrus West).

1934:

British mountaineer Douglas William Freshfield (1845 – 1934) died at age 89. Freshfield was considered to be the greatest all-around alpinist of his period. He climbed regularly for sixty years until 1920 (age 75). After climbing Mont Blanc (15,775 ft./4,808 m.) in 1863 (age 18), Freshfield made ascents in the Caucasus Mountains (western Russia) in 1868, 1887, and 1889 and then explored the Kangchen-junga (28,169 ft./8,585 m.) region of Nepal in 1899. He was President of the Alpine Club in 1893.

1934:

German mountaineer Wilhelm "Willo" Welzenbach (1900 – 1934) died at Camp 7 on Nanga Parbat (26,661 ft./8,125 m.) in Pakistan of exhaustion, illness and starvation. He recorded 946 ascents including 50 first ascents during his short climbing career (1921 – 1934). In the 1920s, Welzenbach adapted extreme rock climbing techniques to ice climbing.

1934:

German mountaineers Kurt and Georg Lowinger and Willy Beck made the first recorded attempt to climb the Eiger's north face in Switzerland. They climbed 2,000 ft./609 m. up this face before being stopped and rescued.

1934: Equipment – Crampons

Austrian ice climbers welded a bar across the hinge of the twelve-point Grivel crampon making a rigid design better suited for hard, steep ice climbs.

1934: Equipment – Pitons

Metal stakes called "stanchions" were driven into the rock to secure metal ladders on the Matterhorn (14,692 ft./4,478 m.) above Zermatt, Switzerland.

1934: Equipment – Rescue Stretcher

In 1933, the Rucksack Club of Manchester, England formed the Joint Stretcher Committee to design a rescue stretcher for specifically carrying injured climbers over rough terrain. By 1934, a preliminary design was approved. This design involved a canvas bed supported by a lightweight aluminum frame which could be quickly dismantled and conveniently carried to a rescue site. This stretcher later became known as the Thomas Stretcher after the well-known British mountaineer Eustace Thomas (1869 – 1960). This rescue stretcher was widely used in the United Kingdom until the early 1970s when the new, improved Bell Stretcher was developed.

1935: FIRST ASCENT

June 29 – 30. German mountaineers Rudolf Peters and Martin Meier made the first ascent of the Grandes Jorasses' (13,806 ft./4,208 m.) north face via the Central Croz Spur. They followed this spur up the middle of the face to the summit of Point Michel Croz (13,474 ft./4,106 m.) which had defeated about 40 previous attempts. French Alps.

1935:

July 19. German climbers Ludwig Leiss and Joseph Schmidbauer made the second ascent of the Matterhorn's (14,692 ft./4,478 m.) north face. Two bivouacs were required. Five days later on July 24, Grindelwald (Switzerland) guide Hermann Steuri and his client Dr. Baur from Saxony climbed the north face from the Hornlihutte (10,700 ft./3,261 m.) and descended back to this same mountain hut in a single day. They only used two pitons on their ascent.

1935: FIRST ASCENT

July 31 – August 1. French mountaineers Pierre Allain (1904 – 2000) and Raymond Leininger made the first ascent of the 2,800 foot/853 meter north face of the Petit Dru (12,248 ft./3,733 m.) in the French Alps above Chamonix, France. This was considered to be the hardest peak in the Alps by the normal route.

1935:

August 25. German mountaineers Max Sedlmayer (1911 – 1935) and Karl Mehringer (1909 – 1935) made the second attempt to climb the 5,900 foot/1,798 meter north face of the Eiger (13,025 ft./3,970 m.) in Switzerland. They reached 10,800 feet/3,292 meters (six days and five nights) on August 25th before freezing to death at a location on the face now known as the Death Bivouac. Sedlmayer and Mehringer were the first deaths of many on the Eiger. Mehringer's body was eventually discovered on the face in 1962 twenty-seven years after his death.

1935: FIRST ASCENT

N. Gusak and a German climbing team made the first winter ascent of the west peak (18,511 ft./5,642 m.) of Mount Elbrus in western Russia.

1930s:

The German Reich encouraged young German climbers called "Nazi Tigers," as they became known, to attempt dangerous ascents like the Eiger's north face. Many of these young, talented climbers died in their attempts. These climbers were also known as "Bergkameraden" (Mountain Warriors).

1935: Equipment – Chest Harness

1930s. Austro-German mountaineer Raimund Schinko was one of the first climbers to use a chest harness (manila hemp rope).

1935: Equipment – Rock Climbing Shoe

French Alpinist Pierre Allain (1904 – 2000) created the first soft-soled climbing shoe for serious rock climbing. He later improved this shoe in 1948. These shoes were known as "PAs" (Allain's initials).

1935: Equipment – Boots

Italian mountaineer Vitale Bramani experienced the loss of six companions on a 1935 climbing expedition. Their lightweight, thin-soled climbing boots (known as "espadrilles") led to frostbite and death from exposure when they were trapped on a mountain in a blizzard. On his return, Bramani began to work on developing a new boot sole that would be effective on both snow and rock. American climbers later developed a harder, more durable rubber for this sole.

1935: Equipment – Bivouac Sack

French mountaineer Pierre Allain (1904 – 2000) designed a bivouac equipment system that he named the "Integrale." This system consisted of: 1) a sleeved waistcoat of quilted down, 2) a short sleeping sack also of quilted down, 3) a half-mattress of rubberized silk, and 4) a rubberized light anorak (pull-over) and sack cover. The total weight of this bivouac system was less than four pounds.

1935: Technique – Friction Climbing

1930s. The French boulder climbing area known as Fontainebleau is located approximately thirty miles/fifty kilometers southeast of Paris. Over 1,000 individual boulders (none exceeding 15 meters/49 feet in height) allowed climbers to develop the friction climbing technique. Some climbers at Fontainebleau used the famous "Pof" to ease many friction problems. A "Pof" was a sticky pine resin clump wrapped in a cloth that the climber tapped against the rock leaving a thin, sticky layer. Friction climbing placed the maximum amount of the shoe sole against the rock surface. Sticky rubber soles have made friction climbing even more effective.

1935: Technique – Friction Climbing

August. French mountaineers Pierre Allain (1904 – 2000) and Raymond Leininger applied the new technique of friction climbing when they made the first ascent of the north face of the Petit Dru (12,245 feet/3,732 meters) above Chamonix, France. This ascent was one of the first sixth degree alpine climbs.

1935: Technique – Ice Axe

Climbers in England's Lake District began using specialized shortened ice picks (short ice axes) when they climbed icy gullies or spin-drifted ridges in the winter. These British mountaineers began to invent a unique style of winter climbing.

1935: Technique – Waist Belays

1930s. Waist belays began to be used by British climbers versus belays directly across rock projections. Manilla hemp ropes were lengthened to 160 feet/49 meters for a party of three climbers instead of the old 80 feet/24 meters for three climbers.

1936:

July 18 – 22. Austrian mountaineers Edi Rainer and Willy Angerer (27) and German mountaineers Anderl Hinterstoisser (23) and Toni Kurz (23) made an attempt to climb the Eiger's (13,025 ft./3,970 m.) north face. All four climbers died on their retreat from the Second Icefield. Switzerland.

1936:

French mountaineers Andre Ledoux and Roger Frison-Roche (1906 – 1999) established the first private school of mountaineering in Chamonix, France.

1936:

Swiss mountaineer Gunter Oskar Dyhrenfurth (1886 – 1975) was awarded an Olympic Gold Medal for mountaineering achievement at the 1936 Olympic Games in Berlin, Germany.

1936: FIRST ASCENT

Swiss woman mountaineer Louise (Loulou) Boulaz (1908 – 1991) became the first woman to climb a major north face in the Alps – the Grand Dru (12,317 ft./3,754 m.). Boulaz was 27 years old at the time.

1936: FIRST ASCENT

German mountaineers Ludwig Schmaderer and Ludwig Wiggerl Vorg (1911 – 1941) made the first ascent of the 7,000 foot (2,133 m.) west face of Ushba North Peak (15,407 ft./4,696 m.) in the Caucasus Mountains. Vorg earned the nickname "The Bivouac King" from his fellow climbers after the Ushba West Face ascent.

1936: Equipment – Ice Axe

Ice axes in Scotland were reduced in length to 31 – 32 inches (80 cm.) and weighed two pounds. They had straight picks which proved to be unwieldy for prolonged, one-handed step-cutting above the head.

1936: Equipment – Rock Climbing Shoes

Rope-soled kletterschuhes were used by Bavarian (German) climbers on a visit to Great Britain. These climbers easily scaled several test-piece rock routes in Wales. These kletterschuhes offered superior performance to the hobnailed boot.

1936: Equipment – Sunscreen

L'Oreal founder Eugene Schueller invented a sunscreen cream.

1937: FIRST ASCENT

July 14 to 16. Italian mountaineers Cassin, Esposito, Ratti, Molteni, and Valsecchi made the first ascent of the 3,000 foot/914 meter northeast face of the Piz Badile (10,853 ft./3,308 m.) in the Bregaglia mountains of Italy – Switzerland. This five-man team was on this face for 52 hours (actual climbing time—34 hours). Molteni collapsed on the summit and died of exhaustion and exposure. Valsecchi died on the descent of exhaustion and hypothermia. The Piz Badile was first climbed in 1867 by W.A.B. Coolidge and his two guides.

1937: FIRST ASCENT

German mountaineer Richard Hechtel (1913 – 2003) made the first solo ascent of Mont Blanc's (15,775 ft./4,808 m.) Peuterey Ridge in the French Alps. This climb took thirty-five hours.

1937: FIRST ASCENT

British mountaineer Robert B. Ferguson became the first amateur to climb the Matterhorn (14,692 ft./4,478 m.) in Switzerland without a guide.

1937: FIRST ASCENT

Russian mountaineers Abalakov (1906 – 1986) and Vasiliev made the first Russian traverse of Ushba (15,453 ft./4,710 m.) in the Caucasus mountains of western Russia.

1937: Equipment – Boots

Italian mountaineer Vitale Bramani developed a new climbing boot sole (with the famous yellow logo) that combined high-traction with abrasion-resistant rubber and a new sole pattern called the "Carrarmato" ("tank tread"). These new soles became known as Vibram (Vitale Bramani) soles. Italian tire manufacturer Leopoldo Pirelli financed the production of the first Vibram soles. These soles are now manufactured in Brazil, China, Italy, and the United States and total more than 34 million soles annually.

1937: Equipment – Boots

Mountaineers Lucien Devies (1910 – 1980) and Giusto Gervasutti (1909 – 1946) made the third ascent of the north face of the Petit Dru (12,248 ft./3,733 m.) above Chamonix, France using Vibram soled boots. This was the first time that Vibram soles were worn on a major ascent. This new sole combined versatility, insulation, and grip.

1938:

February. Well-known Swiss mountaineer Raymond Lambert (1914 – 1997) lost all of his toes to frostbite while making a winter ascent of the Aiguille du Diable (13,498 ft./4,114 m.) in the Alps. Lambert then had special climbing boots made for himself. He and Sherpa Tenzing Norgay (1914 – 1986) reached 28, 210 ft./8,598 m. on Mount Everest in 1952.

1938: FIRST ASCENT

July 20 – 24. Two Austrian mountaineers (Heinrich Harrer and Fritz Kasparek) and two German mountaineers (Ludwig Vörg and Anderl Heckmair) made the first ascent of the Eiger's (13,025 ft./3,970 m.) north face (5,900 ft./1,798 m.) in Switzerland. These four climbers quickly combined to form one strong team. Harrer and Kasparek were on the face for 85 hours while Vorg and Heckmair were climbing for 61 hours. Harrer climbed in nailed boots and Kasparek wore the conventional ten-point crampons while Vörg and Heckmair used the recently introduced twelve-point crampons (the first time these new crampons were used on a major face). Heckmair led every pitch for the entire climb. The Germans referred to the Eiger's north face as the "Mordwand" (murder wall) which was a pun of "Nordwand" (north wall). The first nine climbers to attempt this north face were killed. Many climbers at this time considered this north face to be the "last great problem" in the Alps. By 2008, sixty-five climbers had been killed attempting to climb the Eiger's north face.

Anderl Heckmair (1906 – 2005) and Ludwig Vörg (1911 – 1941) carried the following hardware on their Eiger north face ascent:

> 30 ice pitons
> 20 rock pitons
> 15 carabiners
> 2 ice axes – 1 long and 1 short
> 2 pair crampons (newly developed 12-point design)
> 1 ice hammer

1 piton hammer
2 30-meter (100 foot) ropes
2 thin 30-meter cords

1938: FIRST ASCENT

August 4 – 6. Italian mountaineers Riccardo Cassin (1909 – 2009), Gino Esposito, and Ugo Tizzoni made the first ascent of the north face (3,950 ft./1,204 m.) of the Grandes Jorasses (13,806 ft./4,208 m.) via the Walker Spur. This face is located six miles northeast of Mont Blanc in the French Alps and was the last of the great north faces in the Alps to be climbed. Cassin's team was on this face for 82 hours and used 50 pitons.

1938: Equipment – Sunscreen

Swiss chemistry student Franz Greiter climbed Mount Piz Buin (10,866 ft./3,312 m.) in the Silvretta Range of the Alps on the Swiss-Austrian border. As a result of suffering serious sunburn on this climb, Greiter began his experiments to invent an effective sunscreen. Eight years later (1946), Greiter's product called Gletscher Crème (Glacier Cream) was introduced into the market under the brand name Piz Buin. This sunscreen continues to be sold. By the 1970s, Piz Buin provided sunscreens with ultra-violet filters. This Swiss company (headquarters: Zug, Switzerland) was also the first to introduce the sun protection factor (SPF).

1938: Technique – Twelve-Point Crampons

Austrian climber Anderl Heckmair (1906 – 2005) used the new twelve-point crampon on the first ascent of the 5,900 ft./1,798 m. north face of the Eiger (13,025 ft./3,970 m.) in Switzerland. This was the first major climb for this improved crampon. Step-cutting up steep icefields was now nearly eliminated.

1938: Technique – Ice Climbing

German mountaineer Anderl Heckmair (1906 – 2005) first used a short ice axe with a down-curved pick for ice climbing on the first successful ascent of the north face of the Eiger (13,025 feet/3,970 meters) in Switzerland.

1939:

February 10. Pope Pius XI (Italian Achille Ratti, 1857 – 1939) died in Rome. He was also known as "the mountaineer's pontiff" for his many significant ascents in the Alps from 1885 to 1913. Ratti climbed Monte Rosa in 1889, the Matterhorn in 1889, and Mont Blanc in 1890. He first joined the Club Alpino Italiano in July of 1888.

1939:

Famous Swiss mountain guide Christian Kaufman (1873 – 1939) died at age 66 in Grindelwald, Switzerland. He was particularly famous for his Canadian Rockies ascents. He led British mountaineer James Outram (1864 – 1925) to nine first ascents in 1902 in Canada ranging in elevations from 11,050 ft./3,368 m. to 12,293 ft./3,747 m. and two first ascents in 1903.

1939: FIRST ASCENT

A Slovenian mountaineering team made the first winter ascent of the Triglav (9,394 ft./2,863 m.) the highest peak in Slovenia.

1939: Equipment – Boot Nailing

The five major Italian boot manufacturers each offered between six and twelve different nailing patterns on their climbing boots.

1939: Equipment – Boots

Italian mountaineer Riccardo Cassin (1909 – 2009) made the first ascent of the 2,625 foot/800 meter north face of the Leschaux using Vibram-soled boots.

1939: Equipment – Ice Pitons

Scottish climber Dr. J. H. B. Bell discovered that tubular pitons gripped better in ice. He made these pitons from brass curtain rods, ringing the tops and filing the bottoms to a sharp edge.

1940:

February 10. The Swiss Foundation For Alpine Research was formally established. Dr. Robert Schöpfer was the first president after being the president of the Swiss Alpine Club. This foundation promoted mountain science and exploration.

1940: FIRST ASCENT

July 25 – August 1. Four Russian mountaineers—L. Nadeshdin-Ldr., A. Mazkevitsch, V. Nasharoy, and P. Sysojev—completed the six-peak Shkhelda traverse in the Caucasus Range of southwestern Russia. These six peaks are (west to east):

1. West Peak One	13,872 ft./4,228 m.
2. West Peak Two	14,141 ft./4,310 m.
3. Scientist's Peak	13,780 ft./4,200 m.
4. Pik Aristov	13,875 ft./4,229 m.
5. Central Summit	14,092 ft./4,295 m.
6. East Peak	14,174 ft./4,320 m.

1940:

Mountain guide Arnold Glatthard (1910 – 2002) established Switzerland's first school for Alpine guides. In 1954, Glatthard instructed Tenzing Norgay (1914 – 1986) in mountaineering techniques. Norgay and New Zealand mountaineer Edmund Hillary (1919 – 2008) made the first ascent of Mount Everest in 1953.

1940:

Well-known Italian rock climber Emilio Comici (1901 – 1940) died in a rock climbing accident. Comici made over 200 major first ascents in the Italian Dolomite mountains.

1942:

Famous Swiss alpine landscape painter Albert Gos (1852 – 1942) died at age 90. He is often remembered as "le peintre du cervin" (the painter of the Matterhorn). He first visited the valley of Zermatt in 1874 and returned here frequently (40 different visits). His painting entitled "Le Cervin" now hangs in the lobby of the Zermatterhof Hotel in Zermatt.

1942: FIRST ASCENT

September 22. Italian mountaineer Alfredo Perino and his two guides Luigi Carrel and Giacomo Chiara made the first direct ascent of the Matterhorn's Furggen Ridge. One 300-foot section near the summit took 8 hours to climb. This team reached the summit at 7:30 p.m.

1943:

Famous Italian mountaineer and photographer Vittorio Sella (1859 – 1943) died at age 84 in Biella, Italy (northern Italy) where he was also born. Sella was a member of expeditions to:

Caucasus Mountains	1889, 1890, 1896
St. Elias	1897
Himalayas	1899
Ruwenzori	1906
Karakoram	1909

Sella made the first winter ascents of the Matterhorn (January 1882), Monte Rosa (1884), Lyskamm (1885), and Mont Blanc.

1943:

The standard format for overall climbing route grading was established by the Groupe de Haute Montagne (mountain guide organization) in Chamonix, France. The six categories of grading describe the seriousness of the climbing route based on factors such as route length, objective dangers (i.e. rockfall, avalanches, etc.), and technical difficulty of the hardest pitches. These six categories are:

F	(Facile – Easy)
PD	(Peu Difficile – Fairly Moderate)
AD	(Assez Difficile – Fairly Hard)
D	(Difficile – Hard)
TD	(Tres Difficile – Very Hard)
ED	(Extremement Difficile – Extremely Difficult)

1943: Equipment – Rappelling

French mountaineer and equipment innovator Pierre Allain (1904 – 2000) developed the first descender device for abseiling or rappelling.

1944:

The Zermatt Alpine Association was founded. Its primary goal was to complete the collection of many unique records of the history of climbing made available by the Seiler family of Zermatt and to establish a museum in Zermatt to exhibit them. On December 4, 1995, the Foundation of the Alpine Museum of Zermatt was established. The new Matterhorn Musuem Zermatt was officially opened in December of 2006. It is located beneath the plaza next to the Grand Hotel Zermatterhof.

1944:

The British Mountaineering Council was established to represent all British (England and Wales) climbing clubs. This organization became the basis for training and developing standards. 15,000 climbers received training from 1944 to 1967. British mountaineer Geoffrey Winthrop Young (1876 – 1958) led the movement to organize this council. By 1992, there were over 200 clubs on the council and 2,000 individual members.

1945:

February 18. Operating under the cover of darkness, 700 soldiers from the Colorado-trained Tenth Mountain Division (1st battalion, 86th regiment) of the U.S. Army did an impossible climb—they scaled the 1,700 foot/518 meter cliffs of Riva Ridge in the Italian Appenine Mountains and captured the German army's fortifications in one of the most daring assaults of World War II. This assault cost this Division 192 dead, 730 wounded, and one captured soldier. On May 2, war hostilities ceased in Italy. The Tenth Mountain Division lost a total of 992 mountain troopers with an additional 3,085 wounded. The Tenth was engaged in 114 days of combat against the German army in Italy.

1945: Technique – Hammerless Protection

1940s. The development of hammerless protection originated in Great Britain. British rock climbers carried small rock pebbles that were slotted into rock cracks. A nylon or rope sling was then looped over these pebbles and joined with a carabiner. The climber's rope was then clipped into this carabiner.

1945: Technique – Hand Jam

British climber Peter R.J. Harding is credited with the invention of the modern hand-jam technique in which the hand is wedged into a rock crack to make a handhold. In narrow cracks, the open hand is placed sideways in the crack with the knuckles opposite the fingertips. In wider cracks, the clenched fist is used to create a handhold. Today's climbers wrap their hands and fingers in adhesive tape to reduce rock abrasions when jamming their hands. Well-known British rock climber Joe Brown (1930 –) perfected the hand jam technique. Brown was nicknamed "The Human Spider."

Peter Harding is also credited with inventing the use of thin rope slings for runners.

1946:

Well-known Italian mountaineer and perhaps the finest alpinist of the pre-World War II era, Giusto Gervasutti (1909 – 1946) died at age 37 while climbing Mont Blanc du Tacul (13,938 ft./4,248 m.). Gervasutti made a solo winter ascent of the Matterhorn (14,692 ft./4,478 m.) in 1936 and he climbed the north face of the Grandes Jorasses (13,806 ft./4,208 m.) in 1935.

1946:

Alexander Graven (1898 – 1977) and Alexander Taugwalder became the first Zermatt (Switzerland) guides to climb the Matterhorn's north face.

1947:

July 14 – 16. French mountaineers Lionel Terray (1921 – 1965) and Louis Lachenal (1921 – 1955) made the second ascent of the Eiger's north face above Grindelwald, Switzerland. The first ascent of this 5,900 foot (1,798 meters) vertical face occurred in 1938.

1947:

August 5. Gottfried Jermann and guides Karl Schlunegger and Hans Schlunegger made the first Swiss ascent of the Eiger's north face in Switzerland.

1947: Equipment – Descenders

French climber and climbing equipment designer Pierre Allain (1904 – 2000) produced his first prototype descender in the form of a cross.

1947: Equipment – Rope

European Alps. Plymouth Goldline (nylon) rope was first used. This rope absorbed less water and was more manageable than manilla hemp rope in wet conditions.

1947: Equipment – Carabiners

French climber Pierre Allain (1904 – 2000) marketed the first aluminum carabiners in Europe.

1947: Technique – Barefoot Climbing

August. British woman climber Gwen Goddard Moffat (1924 –) climbed the Innominate Crack on Kern Knotts of Great Gable barefoot. Lake District of England. Moffat also became the first woman to qualify as a climbing and mountaineering guide.

1947: Technique – Direttissima

The climbing concept of the "direttissima" was introduced in Europe by Italian climbers in the years just after World War II. Direct climbing lines (routes) were being forced-up vertical mountain faces in the Alps. Italian climbers defined a direttissima route as "a goccia cadente" which when translated means "a falling drop" of water.

1948:

December 5. Irish mountaineers assembled in Dublin, Ireland and formed the Mountaineering Club. They elected Dr. Robert Lloyd Praeger as their first president.

1948:

Chamonix, France. Four significant changes in the mountain environment were identified:
1. Overcrowding of mountain huts
2. Immense numbers of inexperienced climbers
3. Increase in guiding fees
4. Universal use of vibram soles

1948: Equipment – Boots

Nearly all climbers in the French Alps were using the Vibram sole which required crampons for big snow and ice climbs or on mixed snow and rock climbs. Some expert climbers, however, did not recommend Vibram-soled boots for beginners since their use led to early and continuous use of crampons.

1948: Equipment – Rock Climbing Shoe

The first modern rock climbing shoe was introduced by French climber Pierre Allain (1904 – 2000). Called "PAs" (Allain's initials), these tight-fitting, smooth-soled (rubber compound), blue canvas and suede uppers were designed to maximize friction on rock. They were widely used in the forests of Fontainebleau (30 miles southeast of Paris, France) that contained over 1,000 individual boulders not exceeding fifteen meters (49 feet) in height.

1949: FIRST ASCENT

February 28. French mountaineers Bernard Clos and Marcel Jolly made the first winter ascent of Vignemale's (10,821 ft./3,298 m.) north face (2,625 ft./800 m.) in the Pyrenees of France – Spain.

1949:

A young boy (age 5) from the South Tirol region of northern Italy climbed his first mountain. Reinhold Messner (1944 –) reached the summit the Saas Rigais (9,932 ft./3,027 m.), a rock tower in the Geislerspitzen mountains (western Dolomite Alps). By 1986, Messner (age 42) had become the first person to climb all fourteen 8,000 meter peaks in the world.

1949:

June 27. British mountaineers Frank Smythe (1900 – 1949) contracted cerebral malaria in India and died in England at age 49. Smythe made the first ascents of Jongsong Peak (24,482 ft./7,462 m.) in 1930 and Kamet (25,447 ft./7,756 m.) in 1931. Both of these peaks are located in the Himalayas. Smyth was also a member of the British Mount Everest expeditions in 1933 (he reached 28,126 ft./8,572 m.), 1936, and 1938. He authored 27 books on mountaineering and mountain photography.

1949: Equipment – Chocks

British climber Joe Brown (1930 –) designed the first "chock" for high-angle climbing. This chock was used on the ascent of Cenotaph Corner in England in July of 1949.

1950: FIRST ASCENT

July 26. Austrian mountaineers Erich Waschak and Leo Forstenlechner made the first single-day ascent of the Eiger's (13,025 ft./3,970 m.) north face in Switzerland. This climb took 18 hours (2:00 a.m. – 8:45 p.m.). This was the fourth overall ascent.

1950:

Austrian mountaineers Hermann Buhl (1924 – 1957) and Kuno Rainer made the first complete traverse of the Chamonix (France) Aiguilles (rock needles). These two climbers also made the first winter ascent of the Marmolata's southwest face in the Italian Dolomites.

1950: Technique – Belaying

The commonly used waist belay technique was proven to be dangerous if the weights of the two involved climbers differed widely. Specifically, if the belayer's weight was significantly less than the belayed climber (lead climber) and a slip and fall occurred, it would be very difficult to hold the fallen climber using this belaying technique if the belayer was not properly anchored.

1951:

American ski mountaineer Bil Dunaway (1923 – 2011) and well-known French mountain guide Lionel Terray (1921 – 1965) made the first ski descent of Mont Blanc (15,775 ft./4,808 m.) in the French Alps. This descent represented a major event in the history of extreme skiing.

1951:

British mountaineers Tom Bourdillon (1924 – 1956) and Hamish Nicol climbed the north face of the Aiguille du Dru (12,317 ft./3,754 m.) in the French Alps. This climb represented a major break-through in the European Alps as it was the first major Alpine route to demonstrate that British climbers had at last recovered from the effects of World War II.

1951:

E. Moss climbed all of those peaks in England (377) and in Wales (237) over 2,000 feet (610 meters).

1951: Equipment – Rope

Viking nylon rope was becoming available in Great Britain in four thicknesses: Line weight, half-weight, full-weight, and extra full-weight. This rope was hawser-laid (3 groups of filaments plaited together) and soon became furry and stiff with use.

1951: Technique – Artificial Aid Climbing

July 23. Italian mountaineer Walter Bonatti (1930 – 2011) was the first climber to use the technique of continuous artificial climbing when he ascended the East Face of the Grand Capucin (12,592 ft./3,838 m.) with his partner Luciano Ghigo. They used continuous aid climbing for 1,641 feet/500 meters (160 pitons) on this four-day climb in the French Alps.

1952:

July 26 – 28. The first truly international rope team to climb the north face of the Eiger (13,025 ft./3,970 m.) in Switzerland made the eighth overall ascent. The German – Austrian team of Hermann Buhl (1924 – 1957), Sepp Jochler, Sepp Maag, Otto Maag, Sepp Larch and Karl Winter joined forces with the French team of Gaston Rebuffat (1921 – 1985), Guido Magnone, Jean Bruneau, Paul Habran, and Pierre Leroux.

1952:

Fall. British mountaineer/physician Griffith Pugh (1909 – 1994) reported four main problems to the Joint Himalayan Committee (London, England) that must be solved if the 1953 British expedition to Mount Everest was to be successful. These four problems or concerns were:

1. High altitude
2. Cold temperatures
3. Nutrition
4. Hygiene

1952: FIRST ASCENT

Four French mountaineers made the first ascent of the West Face of the Petit Dru (12,245 ft./3,732 m.) above Chamonix, France. This 3,000 foot/914 meter sheer granite face took seven days to climb in two stages. These climbers were Beradini, Dagory, Laine, and Magnone (leader).

1952: FIRST ASCENT

British climbers Joe Brown (1930 –) and Doug Belshaw were the first to climb the Cenotaph Corner on Dinas Cromlech. This perfect corner climb may be the most famous rock climb in the English Lake District. Brown also climbed six new routes on "Cloggy" in Snowdonia in Wales during the summer of 1952.

1952:

Well-known French mountain guide Gaston Rebuffat (1921 – 1985) became the first climber to ascend all six of the great north faces in the European Alps. These six climbs of Rebuffat were:

1945 Walker Spur on the Grandes Jorasses
   (13,806 ft./4,208 m.)
North face of the Petit Dru
   (12,245 ft./3,732 m.)
Northeast face of the Piz Badile
   (10,853 ft./3,308 m.)
1949 North face of the Matterhorn
   (14,692 ft./4,478 m.)
North face of the Cime Grande di Lavaredo
   (9,840 ft./2,999 m.)

1952 North face of the Eiger
(13,025 ft./3,970 m.)

Gaston Rebuffat died on June 1, 1985, of breast cancer at age 64.

1952: FIRST ASCENT

Austrian mountaineer Hermann Buhl (1924 – 1957) free solo climbed the 850 meter/2,789 foot Cassin route on the northeast face of the Piz Badile (10,853 ft./3,308 m.) in the Italian Dolomites. He climbed this 5.9 graded route in 4 ½ hours, descended the north ridge, and then bicycled back to Innsbruck, Austria. He fell asleep on his bicycle and ended up in the River Inn. He survived and returned to his home.

1952:

Scottish mountaineer/physician Thomas Walton Patey (1932 – 1970) began his climbing career in the Cairngorm Mountains of Scotland. Eventually, Patey climbed seventy new routes in these mountains alone, established fourteen first ascents in Scotland, six first ascents in the European Alps, and made the first ascent of Rakaposhi (25,551 ft./7,788 m.) in the Himalayas in 1958.

1952: Technique – Air Support

July 13. Swiss pilot Hermann Geiger (1914 – 1966) made a landing at the Mutthorn Hut in the Bernese Alps. Known as the "gletscherpilot" (glacier pilot), Geiger was a pioneer of landing light aircraft on glaciers using special landing skis. He made approximately 23,000 glacier landings.

1953:

February 28. Austrian mountaineer Hermann Buhl (1924 – 1957) solo climbed a route on the east face of the Watzmann (8,901 ft./2,713 m.) by moonlight. This is Germany's second highest peak. Buhl considered this a training climb for his upcoming expedition to Nanga Parbat in the Himalayas.

1953: FIRST ASCENT

March 20. Italian climbers Roberto Bignani and Walter Bonatti (1930 – 2011) made the first winter ascent of the Matterhorn's Furggen Ridge (direct). This climb required one bivouac.

1953:

August. Mount Everest summit climber Tenzing Norgay (1914 – 1986) visited London, England and then Switzerland where he climbed the Jungfrau (13,642 ft./4,158 m.) with Swiss mountaineer Raymond Lambert (1914 – 1997).

1953:

British woman climber Gwen Goddard Moffat (1924 –) became the first certified female climbing and mountaineering guide in Great Britain. She was certified by the British Mountaineering Council.

Moffat climbed professionally from 1954 to 1974 in Great Britain, the Swiss and French Alps, and the Dolomites.

1953:

Zermatt (Switzerland) climbers Hermann Biner and Alfons Lerjen made a speed ascent/descent of the Matterhorn (14,692 ft./4,478 m.) in three hours. They climbed the Hornli Ridge.

1953:

The Mount Everest Foundation was established by the Alpine Club and the Royal Geographical Society to encourage exploration in the world's mountain regions. London, England.

1953: FIRST ASCENT

Italian mountaineer Walter Bonatti (1930 – 2011) and Carlo Mauri (1930 – 1982) made the first winter ascent of the Cima Grande di Lavaredo (9,853 ft./3,003 m.) in the Italian Dolomites.

1953: Fabric – Wyncol

A new windproof material called "Wyncol" was developed in England for the 1953 British Mount Everest Expedition. By combining nylon and cotton threads, windproof clothing and tents proved to be very effective.

1953: Clothing – Insulation

Norwegian outdoor clothing manufacturer Helly Hansen developed a new insulation material called "Fibrepile." Worn under waterproof outer garments, Fibrepile was warm, lightweight, and fast-drying.

1953: Equipment – Crampons

Stubai, an Austrian company, developed the Marwa rigid adjustable crampon.

1953: Equipment – Rope

German rope manufacturer Edelrid (founded in 1863), created a new type of climbing rope called "kernmantel." This rope was constructed of two parts: 1) Kern—an inner core of small laid cords, and 2) Mantel—a braided sheath that surrounds and protects the inner core from direct contact with rock. The core accounted for 50 percent of the rope's weight. Edelrid ropes were color-coded which determined the year of manufacture. The first kernmantel ("covered core" in German) rope was called Perlon (the fiber's trade name) which largely replaced the Plymouth Goldline rope.

1954: FIRST ASCENT

British mountaineer Joe Brown (1930 –) and Don Whillans (1933 – 1985) made the first British ascent (third overall ascent) of the West Face of the Petit Dru (12,248 ft./3,733 m.) in the French Alps above Chamonix, France. This ascent took twenty-five hours.

1954:

Scottish climber Frank Williamson made the first traverse of all five of Scotland's 4,000 foot (1,219 meter) summits. This traverse required fifty hours of climbing. These five peaks are: Ben Nevis (4,406 ft./1,343 m.), Ben Macdhui (4,295 ft./1,309 m.), Braeriach (4,249 ft./1,295 m.), Cairn Toul (4,242 ft./1,293 m.), and Cairn Gorm (4,085 ft./1,245 m.).

1955: FIRST ASCENT

August 22. After two unsuccessful attempts, Italian mountaineer Walter Bonatti (1930 – 2011) solo climbed the 3,500 foot/1,067 meter high Southwest Pillar of the Petit Dru (12,248 ft./3,733 m.) in the French Alps. This six-day climb (and five nights alone on the face) was accomplished in terrible weather conditions. Now known as the Bonatti Pillar, this climbing route is considered a classic. British mountaineer Doug Scott (1941 –) once said that this climb was "probably the most important single climbing feat ever to take place in mountaineering." Bonatti hauled a 79-pound/36-kilogram equipment sack up this climb. Many climbers consider this climb to have begun the "modern big wall era" of climbing.

1955:

The telepherique (cable car) from Chamonix to the Aiguille du Midi (12,605 ft./3,842 m.) was completed. This cable car significantly increased the accessibility to the Mont Blanc massif for mountaineers and skiers. This is the world's highest cable car.

1955:

French woman mountaineer Claude Kogan (1919 – 1959) became the first woman to give a talk to members of England's Alpine Club.

1955: Equipment – Ascenders

1950s. The first mechanical ascender was invented by Swiss government bird-banders Adolf Jusi and Walter Marti. Known as a "Jumar" (now a brand name), this cast aluminum handle was equipped with triggers and a toothed-cam. It was developed in order to climb ropes to reach eagle's nests. Prusik knots were still widely used for ascending ropes.

1955: Equipment – Haulsacks

July. Italian climber Walter Bonatti (1930 – 2011) solo climbed the Southwest Pillar of the Dru (12,317 ft./3,754 m.) above Chamonix, France. Bonatti designed a special cylindrical rucksack to hold his equipment, clothing, food, and water. After climbing a pitch (approximately one rope length), Bonatti would then haul this rucksack up to himself. This was the first haulsack. Nearly six feet tall, this haulsack weighed seventy-nine pounds when fully loaded. Bonatti used two ropes: One free rope to haul up his gear bag and a second rope attached to protection (pitons) as he climbed. Arriving at a stance (i.e. ledge) on the face, Bonatti hammered a rappelling piton into a rock crack. He then rappelled back down to his gear bag (haulsack) ledge, removing his ascent protection pitons as he descended. Then he climbed back up his anchored rope and hauled up his gear bag. The process was then repeated.

1955: Technique – Nuts

1950s. A British rock climber in North Wales picked up a hexagonal machine nut that had fallen off a passing train. He threaded this metal nut with a nylon sling and jammed it into a rock crack. Metal wedges of varying sizes were soon being manufactured specifically for rock climbing.

1955: Technique – Solo Climbing

Italian mountaineer Walter Bonatti (1930 – 2011) made a six-day solo ascent of the Southwest Pillar of the Petit Dru (12,248 feet/3,733 meters) in the French Alps. Bonatti reached the summit on August 23 after spending five nights alone on this 3,500 foot/1,067 meter face. This pillar is now known as the Bonatti Pillar. Bonatti used the pendulum technique on a key pitch on his six-day solo climb.

1956:

March 14 – May 18. Italian mountaineer Walter Bonatti (1930 – 2011), Luigi de Matteis, Alfredo Guy, and Lorenzo Longo skied the entire length of the Alps (1,100 miles/1,833 kilometers, 500,000 feet/152,393 meters of ascent and descent, 66 days). They began this ski trek at Monte Canin in the Julian Alps on the east and skied to the Col di Nava in the Maritime Alps on the west in southeastern France.

1956: FIRST ASCENT

July 13. French mountain guide Gaston Rebuffat (1921 – 1985) and his client Maurice Baquet made the first ascent of the southeast face of the south spur of the Aiguille du Midi (12,605 ft./3,842 m.). This vertical 800 foot(244 m.) face took just over two days to climb.

1956:

Mount Elbrus (18,510 ft./5,642 m.) in southwestern Russia was climbed by 400 mountaineers to mark the 400th anniversary of the annexation of Karbardino – Balkaria, the autonomous Soviet Socialist Republic in which Mount Elbrus was located.

1956:

Austrian mountaineer Karl Blodig (1859 – 1956) died at age 97. He was the first person to climb all sixty-five recognized 4,000 meter peaks in the Alps. He was elected an honorary member of the Alpine Club at age 94.

1957: FIRST ASCENT

March 10 – 14. French mountaineers Jean Couzy (1923 – 1958) and Renè Desmaison (1930 – 2007) made the first winter ascent of the west face of the Petit Dru (12,248 ft./3,733 m.) in the French Alps. This was the longest winter expedition of its time.

1957:

August 4 – 8. Two Italian mountaineers (Stefano Longhi and Claudio Corti) and two German mountaineers (Günther Nothdurft and Franz Mayer) attempted to climb the Eiger's (13,025 ft./3,970 m.)

north face in Switzerland. Nothdurft and Mayer disappeared, died, and were eventually found in 1961 frozen at the side of the western snowfield. The famous rescue of Corti involved climber Alfred Hellepart being lowered from the summit 1,000 ft./305 m. down the north face on a steel cable. Strapping Corti to his back, Hellepart was then winched back up to the summit. The body of Stefano Longhi dangled horrifically from the north face until it was finally retreived two years later.

1957:

August 19. The Alpine Club's centennial celebration was held in Zermatt, Switzerland. British mountaineer Sir John Hunt (1910 – 1999) and most of the 1953 British Mount Everest Expedition team arrived in this famous Swiss village. Among the attendees were Noel Odell (1890 – 1987), Sir Arnold Lunn (1888 – 1974), Alfred Zurcher (current Vice President of the Alpine Club), and Edward Whymper's (1840 – 1911) grand daughter. Many Matterhorn guides were also present.

1957:

Italian mountaineer Guiseppe de Francesch (1924 –) completed the climbing of 380 peaks during the five-year period of 1952 – 1957 (an average of 76 peak ascents per year). Nearly all of these peaks were in the Italian Dolomite mountains.

1957: FIRST ASCENT

The first of the big gully climbs on Ben Nevis (4,406 ft./1,343 m.) in Scotland was accomplished by Tom Patey (1932 – 1970), Greame Nicol, and Hamish MacInnes (1930 –). This was the first ascent of Zero Gully (950 ft./290 m.). It took this team five hours to climb this route which was considered a significant breakthrough in British ice climbing. Patey climbed in nailed boots.

1957: Equipment – Ice Axe

The standard ice axe now included a karabiner hole in the metal head at the top of the wood shaft. This hole provided for more effective snow belays. Stubai, an Austrain ice axe maker, may have been the first company to develop this karabiner hole.

1957: Technique – Winches

The first successful rescue from the north face of the Eiger (13,025 feet/3,970 meters) in Switzerland occurred when injured Italian climber Claudio Corti was hauled 1,214 feet/370 meters up the north face (on the back of rescuer Alfred Hellepart) from the exit cracks on a steel cable from a summit winch. Corti had been on the face for nine days.

1957: Technique – Frostbite Remedy

The accepted technique for warding off frostbite was to plunge the affected extremity into hot water and then into snow. This so-called remedy is now avoided.

1958:

July. The Alpine Museum in Zermatt, Switzerland opened to the public. Located just below Zermatt's English Church, this museum displayed the Seiler family's collection of historical mountaineering equipment and clothing including early ski equipment. The cost to build this museum was 70,000 Swiss francs.

1958:

September 6. Well-known British mountaineer and war hero Geoffrey Winthrop Young (1876 – 1958) died at age 82 in England. Young was very influential in establishing alpine climbing ethics. He was a close friend and mentor to George Leigh Mallory (1886 – 1924).

1958: Equipment – Helmets

North face of the Eiger in Switzerland. The climbing party of Hias Noichl, Lothar Brandler, and Herbert Raditschnig used plastic crash helmets while climbing—a first for Eiger climbers.

1958: Equipment – Ice Screws

Arnold Glatthard (1910 – 2002) of Switzerland designed the first ice screw.

1959: FIRST ASCENT

July 21. Mountaineer Arthur Richard of Morzine, France became the first blind Frenchman to summit Mont Blanc (15,775 ft./4,808 m.) in the French Alps.

1959: FIRST ASCENT

July 22. Robin Smith (1938 – 1962) and Gunn Clark made the first British ascent of the Walker Spur on the north face of the Grandes Jorasses (13,806 ft./4,208 m.) in the French Alps. One day later, the second British ascent occurred when Don Whillans, Les Brown, John Streetly, and Hamish MacInnes climbed the same route.

1959: FIRST ASCENT

July 22. Austrian mountaineer Dieter Marchart first climbed the Matterhorn's (14,692 ft./4,478 m.) north face (3,600 ft./1,097 m.) solo in a record five hours.

1959: FIRST ASCENT

Winter. Polish mountain guide Andrzej Zawada (1928 – 2000) made the first complete winter traverse of the Tatra Mountains on the Slovakia-Poland border. This traverse of over 100 peaks took 19 days over a distance of 45 miles (75 kilometers). Zawada gained and lost over 72,000 feet (22,000 meters). The Tatra Mountains contain seventeen peaks over 2,500 meters (8,200 feet). Gerlach (8,710 ft./2,655 m.) is the highest peak in Slovakia while Rysy (8,202 ft./2,500 m.) is the highest peak in Poland. Zawada was the first mountaineer in the world to climb above 8,000 meters (26,248 feet) in the winter (Lhotse – 1974).

1959: Book

After years of research and writing, well-known Austrain mountaineer Heinrich Harrer (1912 – 2006) published his book entitled: *The White Spider – The Story of the North Face of the Eiger.* Harrer was a member of first ascent team of this face in 1938. This book is considered to be one of the best-selling mountaineering books of all time.

1960:

100 woman mountaineers reached the Signalkuppe summit of Monte Rosa (14,948 ft./4,556 m.) above Zermatt, Switzerland as a tribute to recently deceased mountaineers Claude Kogan (1919 – 1959) and Mlle Van der Stratten who died in an avalanche while attempting to climb Cho Oyu (26,906 ft./8,201 m.) in the Himalayas in 1959.

1960:

German-American mountaineer Fritz Wiessner (1900 – 1988) accomplished his life-long dream of climbing all sixty-nine 4,000 meter peaks in the European Alps.

1960:

American mountaineer and photographer Bradford Washburn (1910 – 2007) took his famous Swiss mountain photograph entitled "The East Ridge of the Doldenhorn, Bernese Oberland." This photograph has been celebrated for its dramatic light and form.

1960:

The Union Internationale des Associations d'Alpinism (U.I.A.A.) began to test climbing ropes and the U.I.A.A. safety label for mountaineering equipment was created. By 1982, the Safety Commission had developed standards for ropes, karabiners, helmets, and harnesses.

1961: FIRST ASCENT

March 6 – 12. Austrian mountaineer Walter Almberger (27) and German mountaineers Toni Hiebeler (31), Toni Kinshofer (27), and Anderl Mannhardt (21)—made the first winter ascent of the Eiger's (13,025 ft./3,970 m.) north face in Switzerland. They spent six nights on the face in severe ice conditions. This was the eighteenth overall ascent of this north face. Hiebeler designed a special boot for this winter climb.

1961:

July 11. Two different teams attempted to make the first ascent of the Central Pillar of Frêney on the Mont Blanc Massif. These two teams eventually joined forces. The Italian team was composed of Walter Bonatti, Andrea Oggioni, and Roberto Gallieni. The French team included Robert Guillaume, Pierre Mazeaud, Antoine Vieille, and Pierre Kohlmann. A terrible lightning storm hit the team on the rock face prompting a long and difficult descent down the pillar. Four climbers died of hypothermia and exhaustion (Kohlmann, Guillaume, Vieille, and Oggioni). Bonatti emerged as the leader. This was the worst mountaineering accident in the Alps since the end of World War II.

1961: FIRST ASCENT

August. The British team of Chris Bonington (1934 –), Don Whillans (1933 – 1985), Ian Clough (1937 – 1970), and Polish climber Jan Djuglosz made the first ascent of the Central Pillar of Frêney (French Alps) one month after the Italian – French accident.

1961: FIRST ASCENT

August 29 – 31. British mountaineers Brian Nally and Tom Carruthers made the first British ascent of the Matterhorn's (14,692 ft./4,478 m.) north face in Switzerland. Nally also solo climbed the north face of the Lyskamm (14,853 ft./4,527 m.) which is also located above Zermatt, Switzerland.

1961:

French woman mountaineer Colette Richard (1939 –) summited Mont Blanc du Tacul (13,938 ft./4,248 m.) in the French Alps with her guide Louis Piraly. Richard was blind.

1961:

Italian mountaineer Claudio Barbier solo climbed the five north face routes on the Tre Cime di Lavaredo (9,840 ft./2,999 m.) in the Dolomites (northern Italy) in a single day.

1961: Film

French mountain guide Gaston Rebuffat's (1921 – 1985) mountaineering film *Between Heaven and Earth* received the Grand Prix award of the Italian Alpine Club at the Tenth International Mountain and Exploration Film Festival at Trento, Italy. This film documents Rebuffat's ascents of the Southwest Pillar of the Drus, the Matterhorn, Mont Blanc, the Aiguille du Midi, and the Aiguille Verte. It took Rebuffat eight months (over two summers) to film these five ascents.

1961: Book

Well-known French mountaineer Lionel Terray (1921 – 1965) published his book entitled *Conquistadors of the Useless*. Terray made many important ascents in the European Alps, Alaska, Patagonia, the Andes of South America, and the Himalayas.

1961: Clothing – Insulation

Norwegian Helly Hansen pioneered the use of "pile" in outdoor sports. This type of insulation was highly functional but looked ratty due to its "pilling" appearance. The company Helly Hanson was founded in 1877 in Moss, Norway, by Helly Juell Hansen (1842 – 1914).

1961: Equipment – Ice Screw

The Marwa corkscrew-shaped ice screw was developed and marketed in Austria by Austrian climber Mariner Wastl. This ice screw was made of chrome-vanadium steel and measured 6 ½" long and 5/16" in diameter. It weighed 3 oz. and withstood loads of up to 5,720 pounds.

1961: Equipment – Ice Screw

Stubai, an Austrian company, developed the "corkscrew" ice screw which was lightweight and therefore weak.

1961: Equipment – Nuts

The first manufactured version of the nut was created by Englishman John Brailsford. He made the "Acorn" from a synthetic polymer material which he turned on a lathe. He sold this prototype to Roger Turner Mountain Sports in Nottingham, England.

1961: Technique – Ice Daggers

British mountaineers Brian Nally and Tom Carruthers used ice daggers on their ascent of the Matterhorn's (14,692 feet/4,478 meters) north face in Switzerland. They carried in one hand the pick of their ice axe and in the other hand an ice dagger usually made from a sharpened piton with a short leash of nylon webbing for the hand.

1961: Technique – Ice Hammer

Mountaineers T. Hiebeler, T. Kinshofer, A. Mannhardt, and W. Almberger made the first winter ascent of the Eiger's (13,025 feet/3,970 meters) north face in Switzerland. This team used special ice hammers that were shorter than a normal ice axe and had a hammer-head opposite the pick on the axe's head.

1962: FIRST ASCENT

February 3 and 4. Swiss guides Hilti von Allmen (1935 – 1966) and Paul Etter (1939 –) made the first winter ascent of the Matterhorn's (14,692 ft./4,478 m.) north face above Zermatt, Switzerland in two days. They used corkscrew ice pitons on the 65° face. They endured a fourteen-hour bivouac and arrived on the summit at 3:30 p.m. Their descent to the Solvay Hut was accomplished in a snowstorm. They were immediately followed by two Austrians and three Germans who also made the same climb.

1962: FIRST ASCENT

August 13. Italian mountaineers Renato Daguin and Giovanni Ottin made the first complete ascent of the Matterhorn's (14,692 ft./4,478 m.) west face. This was the last face on the Matterhorn to be completely climbed.

1962: FIRST ASCENT

August 19 – 22. John Harlin (1935 – 1966) became the first American to climb the Eiger's (13,025 ft./3,970 m.) north face in Switzerland (his fifth attempt). Harlin joined German climber Konrad Kirch, Austrians Nikolaus Rafanowitsch and Hans Hauer, and two Swiss climbers. They climbed the original 1938 ascent route. This was the 28th overall ascent of the Eiger's north face.

1962: FIRST ASCENT

August 29 to 31. British mountaineers Chris Bonington (1934 –) and Ian Clough (1937 – 1970) made the first British ascent of the Eiger's (13,025 ft./3,970 m.) north face in Switzerland.

1962: FIRST ASCENT

Gary Hemming (1934 – 1969) and Henry Kendall became the first Americans to climb the Walker Spur of the Grandes Jorasses (13,806 ft./4,208 m.) in the French Alps.

1962: Clothing – Climbing Suits

Early 1960s. One piece windproof climbing suits were developed by British mounineers Don Whillans (1933 – 1985) and Pete Hutchinson.

1962: Equipment – Chocks

British climber Trevor Peck (Leicester, England) filed a patent for wire sling chocks.

1962: Equipment – Crampons

German manufacturer Salewa created the first mass-produced adjustable crampon. "Salewa" is the shortened version of Sattler Lederwaren, a saddle and leather manufacturer in Munich, Germany. This company transitioned to make camera cases, ski poles, crampons, etc.

1962: Equipment – Tents

British climbers Don Whillans (1933 – 1985) and Victor Bray designed and built a prototype tent-box that would eventually evolve into the Whillans Box. Whillans recognized that conventional tents would be useless in the terrible weather conditions of Patagonia (southern tip of South America) and, therefore, designed this sturdy-framed, easy to erect square tent or box. Made of wood and tarpaulin, this pre-fabricated shelter could be assembled on a steep mountain face. Each Whillans Box weighed 250 pounds (114 kilograms) and measured seven feet long, five feet wide, and four feet high.

1963: FIRST ASCENT

January 25 to 30. Italian mountaineers Walter Bonatti (1930 – 2011) and Cosimo Zappelli made the first winter ascent of the Walker Spur on the Grandes Jorasses (13,806 ft./4,208 m.) in the French Alps. This climb required six bivouacs.

1963:

April. Polish mountaineer Jan Mostowski fell 1,600 feet/488 meters to the base of the Eiger's (13,025 ft./3,970 m.) north face in Switzerland. He landed in a snow bank and was not injured.

1963: FIRST ASCENT

July 26. American climbers John Harlin (1935 – 1966), Tom Frost (1940 –), Stuart Fulton, and Gary Hemming (1934 – 1969) made the first ascent of the 1,000 foot/305 meter south face of the Aiguille du Fou (11,486 ft./3,501 m.). This ascent in the French Alps took 25 hours.

1963: FIRST ASCENT

August 2 and 3. Swiss guide Michel Darbellay (1934 –) made the first solo ascent of the Eiger's (13,025 ft./3,970 m.) north face in Switzerland. The actual climb took 18 hours. This was the first significant solo climb of a major mountain face in the modern era. Darbellay followed the original Heckmair route. This was the 41st overall ascent.

1963:

Russian mountaineer Tschokka Zalichanov at age 107 made his 208th ascent of Mount Elbrus (18,481 ft./5,633 m.), the highest peak in the Caucasus mountains of western Russia.

1963: Equipment – Carabiners

French climber and equipment designer Pierre Allain (1904 – 2000) opened his tiny climbing shop in Uriage, France. Allain produced karabiners in twenty-two separate operations totaling three minutes. He produced 30,000 karabiners per year made of lightweight aluminum.

1963: Equipment – Nuts

Yorkshire (England) climber Spud Murphy invented steel nuts called "spuds."

1964: FIRST ASCENT

August 10 to 13. American climbers John Harlin (1935 – 1966) and Royal Robbins (1935 –) made the first direct ascent of the West Face of the Petit Dru (12,248 ft./3,733 m.) in the French Alps.

1964:

September 1 to 3. Dutch woman climber Daisy Voog (1932 –) became the first woman to climb the Eiger's (13,025 ft./3,970 m.) north face in Switzerland. Her climbing partner was electrician Werner Bittner (1938 –). This was the 50th overall ascent.

1964:

Well-known British physiologist, medical doctor, and mountaineer Thomas George Longstaff (1875 – 1964) died in England at age 89. Longstaff made many expeditions to distant mountain ranges including:

> 20 visits to the Alps
>
> 6 visits to the Himalayas
>
> 5 visits to the Arctic
>
> 2 visits to Canada
>
> 1 visit to the Caucasus

1964:

Tyrol (northern Italy) climber Reinhold Messner (1944 –) spent the previous 14 years (1950 – 1964) making approximately 500 separate climbs in the Eastern Alps, primarily in the Dolomites of Italy.

1964: Equipment – Ice Axe

Scottish mountaineer Hamish MacInnes (1931 –) first made ice axes with metal shafts. The blade of his axe (called a MacInnes Axe) was also angled to provide a better anchor in snow.

1964: Equipment – Ice Screw

Fritz Sticht machined a tubular ice screw which was then field-tested by Hermann Huber of Salewa on Mont Blanc.

1965: FIRST ASCENT

February 19 to 22. Italian mountaineer Walter Bonatti (1930 – 2011) solo climbed the Matterhorn's (14,692 ft./4,478 m.) north face in Switzerland. Bonatti chose a direct climbing route (direttissima) for this first winter solo ascent which was accomplished 100 years after the Matterhorn's first ascent in 1865 by Edward Whymper's party. This four-day ascent (94 hours on face) would be Bonatti's last climb of extreme alpinism. The President of Italy awarded Bonatti the Gold Medal for Civil Valour after this ascent.

1965:

July 14. The Swiss Bureau of Commerce officially declared 1965 as "The Year Of The Alps." The focus of the festivities was July 14th—the 100th anniversary of the first ascent of the Matterhorn (14,692 ft./4,478 m.). The village of Zermatt below this famous peak issued two specialty stamps. Village guests included the grandchildren and nephew of Charles Hudson who was a member of the first ascent party but died on the descent, the nephew of Douglas Hadow (also killed on the descent), the nephew and niece of Edward Whymper, and the daughter and granddaughter of Whymper.

> *"There are higher mountains and more difficult mountains; mountains more beautiful and awe-in-spring; but there is only one Matterhorn. There is no mountain in the world of its height and difficulty that has been scaled more often; no mountain to which cling so much hope and disappointment, so much tragedy and joy, so much heroism and so much laughter. Look from Zermatt in Switzerland and you think of Edward Whymper, his triumph and his tragedy; look from Breuil in Italy and you think of Jean Antoine Carrel, the 'Old Soldier'."*

> 1935
> Frank S. Smythe
> British mountaineer
> (1900 – 1949)

1965: FIRST ASCENT

July 14. Swiss mountaineer Yvette Vaucher (1930 –) became the first woman to climb the Matterhorn's north face. She was with her husband Michael Vaucher and guide Othmar Kronig.

1965: FIRST ASCENT

August 13. American climbers John Harlin (1935 – 1966) and Royal Robbins (1935 –) made the first ascent of the west face (3,281 ft./1,000 m.) of the Aiguille de Grand Dru (12,317 ft./3,754 m.) in the French Alps. Their climbing route is now known as the American Direttissima. During this climb, Harlin was hit on his thigh by a falling rock and briefly paralyzed. He completed the ascent.

1965:

September 19. Well-known French mountaineer Lionel Terray (1921 – 1965) and his young climbing partner Marc Martinetti (1940 – 1965) were tragically killed while climbing Mont Gerbier in the Vercors rock-climbing area near Grenoble, France. It was believed that a rockfall caused them to fall 1,000 feet/350 meters —they were still roped together when found. At the time, Terray and Italian mountaineer Walter Bonatti (1930 – 2011) were the most famous climbers in Europe. Terray was buried in a Chamonix cemetery.

1965:

American mountaineer Joel Ellis Fisher (1891 – 1966) completed sixty years of climbing in the Alps. Fisher returned to the Alps every year from 1906 to 1966. He made over 150 major ascents. In 1966, at age 75, he climbed the Riffelhorn (9,617 ft./2,931 m.) above Zermatt, Switzerland.

1965:

Zermatt, Switzerland. Professional mountain guides from Austria, France, Italy, and Switzerland met in this well-known village to establish an international federation of all mountain guide associations. The first by-laws for this new federation were agreed to in 1966. The name of this new association was the Union Internationale des Associations de Guides de Montagnes (UIAGM). This was the French name. The English name is the International Federation of Mountain Guide Associations (IFMGA).

1965: FIRST ASCENT

American climbers George Lowe (1944 –) and British climber Chris Jones made the first American ascent of the Bonatti Pillar on the Petit Dru (12,248 ft./3,733 m.) in the French Alps.

1965:

American climber John Harlin (1935 – 1966) opened the newly-founded International School of Mountaineering at Leysin, Switzerland. British mountaineer Don Whillans (1933 – 1985) was hired as a climbing instructor.

1965: FIRST ASCENT

British climbers Tony Howard (1940 –), John Amatt, and W. Tweedale made the first ascent of Norway's Troll (Trollveggen) Wall (3,300 ft./1,000 m.). Their climbing route is known as the Rimmon Route (3,000 ft./900 m.). This face is believed to be the highest pure rock face in Europe. Four Norwegian climbers (O. Eliassen, O.D. Enersen, L. Pattersen, and J. Tiegland) spent eleven days making the first ascent of the Norwegian Route on the Troll Wall during this same year (4,300 ft./1,300 m.).

1965: Clothing – Underwear

Helly Hansen introduced underwear made of polypropylene known as Lifa. This material moved moisture away from the skin.

1965: Equipment – Chest Harness

Edelrid/Salewa created the first specifically designed chest harness which was initially made of rope.

1965: Equipment – Rock Climbing Shoes

American climber Royal Robbins (1935 –), while working in Switzerland, was asked by the French bootmaker Galibier to develop a specialized lightweight rock climbing boot—the famous blue suede "R-R." This shoe was designed specifically for Yosemite-style rock routes.

1965: Equipment – Seat Harness

British climber Tony Howard designed a leather seat harness with leg loops for use on the first ascent of Norway's Trollryggen (Troll Wall), a 5,250 foot/1,600 meter high rock wall.

1966:

February 23 to March 25. An American – British mountaineering team attempted a direct winter ascent (direttissima) of the Eiger's (13,025 ft./3,970 m.) north face in Switzerland. Americans John Harlin (1935 – 1966) and Layton Kor (1938 – 2013) and Scottish climber Dougal Haston (1940 – 1977) began this new route that is now known as the John Harlin Direct Route. On March 22, John Harlin fell 4,000 feet/ 1,219 meters to his death when his prusiking rope (7mm or about ¼" thick) broke. Kor quit this climb but Haston continued on to the summit with the German team of Siegried Hupfauer, Jorg Lehne, Gunther Strobel, and Roland Votteler. They reached the summit on March 25. Harlin was the 28th climber to die while climbing the Eiger's north face.

1966:

July 9. British climbers Tom Patey (1932 – 1970), Rusty Baille (1940 –), and Chris Bonington (1934 –) made the first ascent of the 443 foot/135 meter sea stack (Orcadian sandstone) known as the "Old Man Of Hoy." This sea stack is located on the Island of Hoy in the Orkney Islands off of the north coast of Scotland. A year later, this ascent was repeated and televised to fifteen million people with three climbing teams:

    1. Chris Bonington and Tom Patey: Original 1966 route
    2. Joe Brown and Ian McNaught-Davis: South Face
    3. Peter Crew and Dougal Haston: Southeast Arete

1966: FIRST ASCENT

September. American climbers Yvon Chouinard (1938 –) and Layton Kor (1938 –) made the first American ascent of a major alpine ice route in the Alps—the 3,000 foot/914 meter north face of Les Courtes (French Alps).

1966:

Two Zermatt, Switzerland guides (Rene Arnold: 1933 – 1980 and Sepp Graven: 1934 –) accomplished a "girdle traverse" of all four ridges of the upper Matterhorn (14,692 ft./4,478 m.) in less than a single day. They went up the Furggengrat, down the Hornligrat, up the Zmuttgrat, and down the Liongrat. A girdle traverse climbs around the mountain without ever reaching the summit.

1966:

The International Federation of Mountain Guide Associations (I.F.M.G.A.) was established.

1966:

Tyrol climber Reinhold Messner (1944 –) and Austrian climber Peter Habeler (1942 –) made their first difficult climb together—the Walker Spur of the Grandes Jorasses (13,806 ft./4,208 m.) in the French Alps.

1966: Equipment – Ice Axe

European ice axes measured 80 to 90 centimeters (31 ½" to 35 ½ in.) in length. They had straight picks that did not hold in ice as well as the curved or drooped picks that were first introduced in 1974.

1966: Equipment – Ice Axe

American climber Yvon Chouinard (1938 –) tested various ice axes on a glacier in the French Alps. With the assistance of Chamonix (France) climbing shop owner Donald Snell, Chouinard convinced the Charlet factory to make a 55 centimeter (21 ½ in.) ice axe with a curved pick for better holding on steep ice climbs.

1966: Technique – Direttissima

American climber John Harlin (1935 – 1966) conceived a "direttissima" route up the Eiger's 5,900 foot/1,798 meter north face in Switzerland. On March 22nd, Harlin fell 4,000 feet/1,219 meters and died during this ascent when a fixed rope broke while he was climbing it. Harlin's direttissima route is now known as the John Harlin Route.

1966: Technique – Ice Climbing

In the European Alps, there were two major ice climbing styles:
> German Style – Alpinists climbed on their toes and the front points of their
> > 12-point crampons.
> French Style – Alpinists climbed with their crampons flat on the ice slope.

1966: Technique – Ice Climbing

American climbers Yvon Chouinard (1938 –) and Layton Kor (1938 – 2013) made the ascent of the north face of Les Courtes (12,652 feet/3,856 meters) in the French Alps. In addition to using the front-pointing technique, Chouinard held an ice dagger in one hand and a short ice axe with a drooped pick (for more secure placement) in the other hand. This "drooped pick" ice axe became available to the public in 1970.

1967: FIRST ASCENT

American climbers Yvon Chouinard (1938 –) and Layton Kor (1938 –) made the first American ascent of the north face of the Les Droites (13,123 ft./4,000 m.) in the Mont Blanc Massif.

1967: FIRST ASCENT

Walter Spitzenstatter and Otti Wiedmann made the first winter ascent of the Vinatzer Route on the south face of the Marmolada (10,968 ft./3,343 m.). This was the most difficult winter climb ever done in the Italian Dolomites.

1967: Technique – Ice Climbing

American ice climbing pioneer Yvon Chouinard (1938 –) used two short ice axes and rigid-platform 12-point crampons for the first time. Chouinard was climbing in California's Sierra Mountains during the winter. This ice climbing technique was later named "piolet traction" by the French.

1968: FIRST ASCENT

August. Dennis D. Eberl and Graham R. Thompson made the first American ascent of the Matterhorn's (14,692 ft./4,478 m.) north face in Switzerland.

1968:

October 8. The Union Internationale des Associations d'Alpinisme (U.I.A.A.) approved the adoption of a Climbing Classification System for 23 member countries. London, England. The six main climbing grades are:

I. Easy
II. Moderate
III. Moderately Difficult
IV. Difficult
V. Very Difficult
VI. Extremely Difficult

1968:

Tyrol mountaineer Reinhold Messner (1944 –) wrote an article entitled "The Murder of the Impossible" for the German magazine Alpinismus. Messner described his fight against bolted (expansion bolts) direttissimas (direct climbing routes) where artificial aids were used to climb the most difficult rock faces.

1968:

Swiss mountaineer Beat H. Perren founded the helicopter rescue service Air Zermatt Ltd. in Zermatt, Switzerland. This mountain rescue service performed 90 missions in its first year. By 1988, over 10,000 rescue operations had been performed. Air Zermatt flew 1,376 rescue missions in 2006. Eight rescue helicopters comprise the Air Zermatt fleet.

1968: Book

British mountaineer Ian Clough (1937 – 1970) published his guidebook entitled *Winter Climbs, Ben Nevis and Glencoe*. This was the first guidebook devoted exclusively to snow and ice climbing. Clough was killed on Annapurna in Nepal in 1970 when an ice avalanche struck him.

1968: Equipment – Helmets

British mountaineers Joe Brown (1930 –) and Mo Anthoine (1939 –) began manufacturing the Joe Brown Safety Helmet in Llanberis, Wales. The German Alpine Club tested sixteen different climbing helmets and rated the Joe Brown Safety Helmet first in every test category.

1968: Equipment – Sleeping Pad

Karrimor (British company) introduced a new waterproof sleeping pad that was called the "karrimat."

1968: Technique – Ice Climbing

Yvon Chouinard (1938 –) learned the "French" technique of ice climbing. On steep ice, the climber would ascend sideways, each cramponed foot being firmly placed parallel to each other and at right angles to the slope's fall line. All crampon points (except the two front-facing prongs) are in full contact with the snow/ice surface.

1968: Technique – Bolting

South Tyrol (northern Italy) mountaineer Reinhold Messner (1944 –) was one of the first climbers to protest the wide use of expansion bolts. He felt that "true climbing" was being eliminated. Earlier climbers Walter Bonatti (1930 – 2011) and Albert Frederick Mummery (1855 – 1895) also were opposed to using "unfair means."

1969: FIRST ASCENT

Tyrolean climber Reinhold Messner (1944 –) solo climbed the north wall of the Les Droites (13,123 ft./4,000 m.) in the French Alps. This was the most formidable ice climb in the Alps at this time. Messner, at age 25, now had fifty first ascents and twenty solo climbs on difficult routes in the Alps.

1969: FIRST ASCENT

Japanese mountaineer Isamu Tatsuno (1948 –) and his partner climbed the Eiger's North Face (5,900 ft./1,798 m.) in Switzerland in 21-hours. Tasuno at age twenty-one became the youngest person to climb this face. He went on to found the Mont-Bell outdoor climbing and equipment company.

1969:

New Zealand mountaineers Murray Jones and Graeme Dingle climbed all six major north faces in the Alps: Matterhorn, Eiger, Grandes Jorasses, Piz Badile, Cima Grande di Lavaredo plus the Bonatti Pillar (1,970 ft./600 m.) of the Dru in the French Alps.

1969:

Well-known British mountaineer Robert Lock Graham (R.L.G.) Irving (1877 – 1969) died at age 92. Irving was a grade school teacher of George Leigh Mallory (1886 – 1924) of Mount Everest fame (1921,1922, and 1924). He authored the following mountain books:

       1933: *La Cime du Mont Blanc*
       1935: *Romance Of Mountaineering*
       1938: *The Mountain Way*
       1939: *The Alps*
       1940: *Ten Great Mountains*
       1955: *A History Of British Mountaineering*

1969: Equipment – Nuts

The first specifically manufactured climbing "nuts" and "rocks" (of plastic or metal) first appeared in continental Europe.

1970:

May 25. Well-known Scottish mountaineer Thomas Walton Patey (1932 – 1970) was accidentally killed while rappelling from the Maiden, a Scottish sea stack off the north coast of Scotland. Patey began climbing in 1949 and made over 70 new climbing routes in the Scottish mountains as well as numerous first ascents in the Alps. He was a member of the two Himalayan expeditions (1956: Muztagh Tower – 23,860 ft./7,272 m. and 1958: Rakaposhi – 25,551 ft./7,788 m.).

1970:

Scottish mountaineers John Cunningham (1927 – 1980) and William Joseph March (1941 – 1990) accomplished the first vertical Scottish ice climb without chopping a ladder of steps with ice axes. This short but absolutely vertical climb was called Chancer on Hell's Lum Crag in the Cairngorm mountains. Cunningham and March wore twelve-point crampons utilizing the front two prongs for climbing.

1970:

The 5,900 foot/1,798 meter north face of the Eiger (13,025 ft./3,970 m.) in Switzerland as of this year had allowed 96 ascents (96 climbers) but caused 39 deaths. Since the first ascent in 1938, twenty new climbing routes have been recorded.

1970: Equipment – Ice Piton

Salewa began marketing a drive-in ice piton that was known as the "Wart Hog."

1970: Equipment – Overboot

The British-based company Karrimor designed a closed-cell neoprene overboot for the British Annapurna Expedition.

1970: Equipment – Seat Harness

British mountaineer Don Whillans (1933 – 1985) designed the first nylon webbing seat harness. Manufactured by the Troll Safety Equipment Company in Great Britain, this seat harness lifted the legs to a sitting position when prusiking and yet offered no restrictions when climbing. A long, repeated fall now became bearable with this type of harness. Whillans designed this seat harness specifically for the 1970 British Annapurna South Face Expedition.

1970: Technique – Ice Climbing

American climbers Yvon Chouinard (1938 –) and Doug Tompkins (1943 –) completed the direct finish to Ravens Gully during the winter (1970 – 71) in Scotland. Many climbers consider this climb to be the start of snow and ice front-pointing and using two ice hand tools.

1971:

September 12. Climbers Peter Siegert and Martin Block were airlifted from the 5,900 foot/1,798 meter north face of the Eiger (13,025 ft./3,970 m.) in Switzerland. This was the first successful helicopter rescue from this face. The helicopter pilot's name was Gunther Amann.

1972: FIRST ASCENT

A Polish women's team made the first all-female ascent of the Eiger's (13,025 ft./3,970 m.) north face in winter. Wanda Rutkiewicz (1943 – 1992), Danuta Gelner, and Stefania Egierszdorff reached the summit via the North Pillar (north buttress).

1972:

Swiss climber Michel Piola (1958 –) began his climbing career at age 14 on a rock crag near Geneva, Switzerland. By the year 2006, Piola (age 34) had recorded 1,300 new climbing routes on peaks in Patagonia, Pakistan, Greenland, Borneo, Turkey, Greece, Morocco, as well as his home Alps. Piola attempted to climb Mount Everest in 1982.

1972: Equipment – Overboots

The British outdoor clothing and equipment company named Berghaus invented the Yeti gaiter/overboot. This sole-less overboot was best known as the first effective overboot system to ensure dry feet under any conditions.

1972: Equipment – Ice Axe

Scottish climber Hamish MacInnes (1930 –) designed the "Terror-dactyl"—a specially shaped ice hammer and axe for climbing steep ice routes.

1973: FIRST ASCENT

January. Walter Cecchinel and Claude Jager made the first ascent of the Drus Couloir in the French Alps. This climb was considered to be the most difficult ice climb in the Alps.

1973:

British mountaineer Joe Tasker (1948 – 1982) and Dick Renshaw climbed five of the six classic north faces in the European Alps. They made a winter ascent of the Eiger's north face in 1975.

1973: Equipment – Tents

Swedes Bo Hilleberg and his wife Renate began designing and manufacturing all-season tents for hikers and mountaineers. Their first tent was named the "Keb." This was the first commercial tent to link an inner tent with a rainfly that were erected simultaneously. Soderkoping, Sweden.

1974:

April 4 to July 24. Scottish mountaineer Hamish Brown (1934 –) traversed all 277 Munros (a "Munro" is a Scottish peak over 3,000 feet/914 meters) in Scotland in a non-stop 112-day journey. He traveled 1,639 miles and gained 449,000 feet of ascent.

1974:

May. Lord Hunt (Sir John Hunt 1910 – 1999) made a motion to admit women to the Alpine Club (founded in 1857). This motion passed by a large majority. The first two women to be elected were Sally Westmacott and Betty Seiffert.

1974:

August 14. Tyrolean climber Reinhold Messner (1944 –) and Austrian climber Peter Habeler (1942 –) made the fastest ascent of the Eiger's (13,025 ft./3,970 m.) north face—10 hours (5:00 a.m. – 3:00 p.m.). They followed the original 1938 route and returned to the mountain's base on the same day.

1974: FIRST ASCENT

August. Chris Kopczynski (1948 –) and John Roskelley (1948 –) made the first all-American ascent of the Eiger's north face in Switzerland.

1974: FIRST ASCENT

Italian mountaineer Renato Casarotto (1948 – 1986) made the first solo winter ascent of the north face of Monte Pelmo (10,394 ft./3,168 m.) in the Italian Dolomites via the Simon-Rossi Route.

1974: Technique – Ice Climbing

French mountaineers Walter Cecchinel and Claude Jager climbed the north couloir of the Petit Dru (12,248 ft./3,733 m.) above Chamonix, France. They used special ice axes and 12-point rigid crampons. This climb represented a conclusive victory for the frontal crampon technique employing the forward two prongs of the crampons and shorter ice axes with angled blades.

1975: FIRST ASCENT

May. French mountaineers Patrick Gabarrou and Jean Marc Boivin made the first ascent of the Super Couloir of Mont Blanc du Tacul in the French Alps. This climb required two days.

1975:

The modern era of marathon mountain linkages or "enchainments" was begun when French mountaineer Nicolas Jaeger successfully climbed the Grand Pillar d'Angle and the Central Pillar of Frêney.

1975: FIRST ASCENT

British climbers Dick Renshaw and Joe Tasker (1948 – 1982) made the first British winter ascent of the 5,900 ft./1,798 m. north face of the Eiger (13,025 ft./3,970 m.) in Switzerland (six days).

1975:

Well-known Swiss geologist and mountaineer Professor Gunter Oskar Dyhrenfurth (1886 – 1975) died at age 89. He reached the summit of over 700 peaks in the Alps and Tatra Mountains (border of Poland and the Czech Republic). He was also awarded a Gold Medal at the 1936 Olympics for mountaineering.

1975:

Well-known French mountain guide Armand Charlet (1900 – 1975) died at age 75. Charlet was a native of Argentiere, a small village just north of Chamonix. He made over 100 ascents of the Aiguille Verte (13,524 ft./4,122 m.) near Mont Blanc in the French Alps. Aiguille Verte was first climbed in 1865.

1975: Equipment – Rock Climbing Shoes

1970s. Smooth-soled rock climbing shoes became the standard footwear: PAs (named after French designer Pierre Allain), RDs (after René Desmaison), and later EBs (after Edouard Bordeneaux).

1975: Equipment – Ice Pick

The French company Simond was the first to market a reverse-curve ice pick. This type of ice pick was easier to remove from water-ice placements.

1976:

British mountaineers Nick Colton and Alex MacIntyre (1954 – 1982) climbed the north face couloir of the Grandes Jorasses (13,806 ft./4,208 m.) in the French Alps. This was perhaps the first of the modern extreme ice routes on alpine terrain.

1976: Fabric – Gore-Tex

The British outdoor clothing company Berghaus was the first British company to experiment with the new Gore-Tex fabric. It was heralded as the "miracle fabric" just as nylon was in the 1930s.

1976: Equipment – Anklets

East German rock climbers were known to wear thick leather anklets to protect their ankles in crack climbs. In addition to the fact that specific rock climbing boots were not available to these climbers, the cost of these boots could not be afforded under the economic conditions for East Germans at this time.

1977:

March 28. Well-known British mountaineer and explorer Eric E. Shipton (1907 – 1977) died at age 70 in Wiltshire, England. His ashes were scattered on the Fonthill Lakes in Dorset. In his first expedition in 1931, Shipton was one of four climbers to reach the summit of Kamet (25,447 ft./7,756 m.) in the Garhwal Himalaya. From 1933 to 1964, he went on sixteen additional expeditions acting as the leader on most of them. Shipton went to Mount Everest in 1933, 1935,1936, 1938, and 1951 and was selected as the original leader of the successful 1953 expedition (he later re-signed prior to the expedition leaving England). He was also a member and/or leader of six expeditions to Patagonia (southern tip of South America) from 1958 to 1964. Shipton authored eight books.

1977:

Winter of 1977 – 78: Italian-born French mountaineer Ivan Ghirardini (1953 –)climbed the three north faces of the Grandes Jorasses (13,806 ft./4,208 m.), the Matterhorn (14,692 ft./4,478 m.), and the Eiger (13,025 ft./3,970 m.) solo in five days.

1977:

The five European countries that had the greatest number of professional mountain guides in 1977 were:

Switzerland	722
France	677
Austria	511
Italy	460
Germany	140

1977: FIRST ASCENT

American mountaineer Tobin Sorenson (1955 – 1980) solo climbed the north face of the Matterhorn (14,692 ft./4,478 m.) in 8 ½ hours. Three years later on October 5, 1980, Sorenson died while attempting to solo climb the north face of Mount Alberta (11,874 ft./3,619 m.) in Canada.

1977: Technique – Free Climbing

French alpinist Jean-Claude Droyer free-climbed the Bonatti Route on the Grand Capucin (12,592 feet/3,838 meters) in the French Alps using only nine points of aid for rest.

1978: FIRST ASCENT

A Polish climbing team made the first ascent of the Matterhorn's (14,692 ft./4,478 m.) north face by an all-female team. Led by Wanda Rutkiewicz (1943 – 1992), this team included Anna Czerwinska

(1949 –), Krystyna Palmowska (1948 –), and Irena Kesa (1954 –). Kesa became sick on the ascent and was airlifted by helicopter from the summit along with Palmowska. Rutkiewicz and Czerwinska were also airlifted from the summit due to bad weather and time.

1978:

Well-known British explorer, mountaineer, and sailor Harold William Tilman (1898 – 1978) died at age 80 when he disappeared in the south Atlantic Ocean while sailing his boat Mischief. Author of fourteen books, Tilman made the first ascent of Nanda Devi in 1936.

1978:

Swiss mountaineer and professor of chemistry Jean Juge (1908 – 1978) became the oldest person to have climbed the north faces of the Eiger (1975 – age 67) and the Matterhorn (1978 – age 70) in Switzerland. Unfortunately, Juge died during the descent of the Hornli Ridge on the Matterhorn.

1978:

A team of French mountaineers from the group Militaire de Haute Montagne made the second winter ascent of the Harlin direct route on the Eiger's north face above Grindelwald, Switzerland.

1979: FIRST ASCENT

February 25 to March 4. Japanese mountaineer Tuneo Hasegawa made the first winter solo ascent of the Walker Spur on the Grandes Jorasses (13,806 ft./4,206 m.) in the French Alps.

1979:

Austrian mountaineer Heinz Mariacher (1956 –) climbed six new routes on the Marmolada (10,968 feet/3,343 meters) in the Italian Dolomites. Each one of these routes was between 2,000 and 3,000 feet in height.

1979:

Well-known French mountaineer (Annapurna first ascent in 1950) and politician Maurice Herzog (1919 – 2012) invited Wanda Rutkiewicz (1943 – 1992), Junko Tabei (1939 –), and Phantog (Tibetan woman mountaineer) to Chamonix, France to feature them in a film about Himalayan woman climbers.

1979:

French mountain guide George Charlet (1901 – 1979) died. He made 80 first ascents in the European Alps including the north face of the Verte (13,540 ft./4,127 m.). Charlet climbed the Aiguille de Verte thirty times including ten new routes.

1979:

French mountain guide and ski mountaineer Jean-Pierre Bernard skied from Chamonix, France to Zermatt, Switzerland via the Haute Route in 24 hours.

1980:

Ms. Martine Rolland became the first fully certified female Alpine mountain guide in Chamonix, France.

1980: FIRST ASCENT

Italian mountaineer Marco Bernardi (1958 –) made the first solo ascent of the east face of the Grandes Jorasses (13,806 ft./4,208 m.) in the French Alps. One day ascent.

1981: FIRST ASCENT

July. Michel Piola and Pierre-Alain Steiner made the first direct ascent of the Zmutt Nose on the northwest face of the Matterhorn (14,692 ft./4,478 m.) in Switzerland. This 3,900 ft./1,200 m. route includes what many climbers regard as the greatest rock overhang in the western Alps.

1981: Equipment – Ice Axe

The Grivel Company of Courmayeur, Italy produced its first modular ice axe heads.

1981: Technique – Free Climbing

Swiss climbers Wiestlibach and Schenkel climbed the west face of the Petit Dru (12,245 feet/3,732 meters) in the French Alps without using any hammers and pitons—a first for the Petit Dru.

1982: FIRST ASCENT

August 24. Seven Italian mountaineers, one British mountaineer, and guides Victorio Chiado, Fikret Gurbuz, and Ahmet Gurbuz made the first foreign ascent of Mount Ararat (16,945 ft./5,165 m.) in Turkey since 1969.

1982:

The Boardman-Tasker Prize For Mountain Literature was established by Joe Tasker's (1948 – 1982) mother as a way to remember her son and Peter Boardman (1950 – 1982). They disappeared on the northeast ridge of Mount Everest on May 17, 1982. This prize has become a prestigious award that is presented annually in London, England.

1982: FIRST ASCENT

French mountaineer Christophe Profit (1961 –) solo climbed the American Direct Route on the Aiguille du Dru (12,317 ft./3,754 m.) in 3 hours and 10 minutes. French Alps.

1982: Equipment – Rock Climbing Shoe

The Spanish footwear manufacturer Boreal introduced a rock shoe with a new sticky rubber compound sole. This shoe made a significant difference on the hardest rock routes where tiny holds and friction moves were critical to success.

1983:

July 27. Austrian mountaineer Thomas Bubendorfer (1962 –) climbed the classic 1938 route on the Eiger's (13,025 ft./3,970 m.) north face in 4 hours 50 minutes in Switzerland. This climbing record would stand for twenty years.

1983:

The Alpine Club Library (London, England) began to develop the Himalayan Index—a computerized database of peak ascents or attempts in the Himalayan, Karakoram, Hindu Kush, and China. As of 2006, over 6,000 ascents and attempts on 2,800 peaks over 6,000 meters (19,686 feet) were included in this database.

1983: FIRST ASCENT

British mountaineer Andy Parkin (1955 –) accomplished the first alpine-style solo winter ascent of the Walker Spur on the Grandes Jorasses (13,806 ft./4,208 m.) north face in the French Alps.

1984: FIRST ASCENT

British woman Alison Hargreaves (1962 – 1995) climbed the Matterhorn's (14,692 ft./4,478 m.) north face solo—a first by a British woman.

1984:

381 people had completed the climbing of all 3,000 foot (914 meter) plus peaks in Scotland—283 separate mountains and 543 tops (main summits and secondary summits). These 3,000 foot peaks are known as the "Munros."

1984: Equipment – Packs

The German company known as Deuter was founded by Hans Deuter in 1898. In 1984, Deuter developed the original ventilated backpack system known as AIRCOMFORT. This new ventilation system revolutionized the backpack market worldwide.

1985: FIRST ASCENT

March. Renato Casarotto (– 1986) made the first winter solo ascent of the east face of the Grandes Jorasses (13,806 ft./4,208 m.) in the French Alps.

1985:

May 31. One of the greatest of the French mountain guides, Gaston Rebuffat (1921 – 1985) died of breast cancer at age 64. Rebuffat made many difficult north face climbs in the Alps and was a member of the successful 1950 French Annapurna expedition. He was also a very successful writer (20 mountaineering books), filmmaker, and photographer. Rebuffat has been credited with first coining the expression "The Brotherhood of the Rope." Rebuffat was the first guide to lead clients up all six great north faces of the Alps. He made over 1,200 climbs that were rated as "difficult" including over 1,000 first ascents.

1985:

September 11. Italian mountain guide Marco Barmasse (1949 –) completed a fifteen-hour solo traverse of all four Matterhorn (14,692 ft./4,478 m.) ridges. Barmasse first climbed the Furggen Ridge, then descended the Hornli Ridge, then up the Zmutt Ridge, and finally down the Lion Ridge.

1985:

Over a five-year period (1985 – 1990), the remains of a human body emerged from the Theodul Glacier above Zermatt, Switzerland. Bone fragments, leather footwear, pieces of a silk shirt, a dagger, numerous coins, and 200 pieces of silver were recovered. It was determined that this body dated from approximately 1595.

1986:

February 14 to March 2. Swiss mountaineers Andre Georges and Erhard Loretan (1959 – 2011) completed a winter traverse of 38 summits (30 over 4,000 meters/13,124 feet) from Grachen to Zinal in Switzerland.

1986:

Ms. Nea Morin (1906 – 1986), regarded by some as the greatest British female mountaineer between World Wars I and II, died at age 80. She climbed from 1927 to 1959 and made 24 major ascents of which 21 were by the first female climber.

1986:

Swiss mountaineer Christophe Profit (1961 –) solo climbed the three north faces of the Eiger, Matterhorn, and Grandes Jorasses in less than 24 hours. He completed these same three climbs in the winter of 1987 in a total climbing time of 40 hours.

1986:

Well-known mountaineer and expedition leader Chris Bonington (1934 –) was awarded the Commander of the Order of the British Empire (CBE).

1986: Equipment – Ice Axe

The Grivel Company of Courmayeur, Italy created the "Rambo" ice axe with its curved, ergonomic shaft.

1987:

February 21. Well-known British mountaineer Noel Odell (1890 – 1987) died at age 96 in his chair at breakfast. Odell made the first ascent of Nanda Devi (25,644 ft./7,816 m.) in 1936 with Bill Tilman (1898 – 1977) and was a member of the 1924 British Mount Everest Expedition. He was the last person to see George Mallory (1886 – 1924) and Andrew Irvine (1902 – 1924) alive on Everest before they disappeared while climbing the northeast ridge (June 8, 1924).

1987:

March 11 and 12. French mountaineer Christophe Profit (1961 –) made solo winter ascents of the three north faces of the Grandes Jorasses (Croz Spur- France), Matterhorn (Schmid Route), and Eiger (Heckmair Route) in 42 hours. He used a helicopter to travel from face-to-face. The Matterhorn and Eiger are located in Switzerland.

1987:

Well-known Italian mountaineer Riccardo Cassin (1909 – 2009) at age 78 climbed the Piz Badile (10,853 ft./3,308 m.) in the Italian Dolomites twice in one week.

1987:

Biella, Italy. The Mountain Wilderness (MW) organization was founded by several well-known mountaineers including Chris Bonington (1934 –) and Kurt Diemberger. MW was established to protect the mountain environment.

1988: FIRST ASCENT

July. Alison Hargreaves (1962 – 1995) made the first ascent by a British woman of the Eiger's (13,025 ft./3,970 m.) north face (5,900 ft./1,798 m.) at age 26.

1988:

May 13 to September 19. British mountaineers Paul MacKrill and John Rowlands were the first climbers to attempt one continuous traverse of all 82 4,000 meter peaks in the Alps. They began this journey on May 13th by climbing the Piz Bernina (13,284 ft./4,049 m.) south of St. Moritz. Their goal was to reach the Barre des Ecrins (13,459 ft./4,102 m.) in southeastern France in three months. On September 19th, MacKrill by himself reached the summit of the Grand Combin (14,100 ft./4,297 m.) in southwestern Switzerland thereby becoming the first climber to achieve one continuous journey over all Swiss 4,000 meter peaks.

1989:

January. Well-known Swiss mountaineer Erhard Loretan (1959 – 2011) and Andre Georges climbed thirteen north faces in thirteen days in the Bernese Oberland of Switzerland. All of these north faces were located between the Eiger and the Doldenhorn. Loretan was the third person to climb all fourteen 8,000 meter peaks in the world (1982 – 1995). Unfortunately, he died in a fall while climbing the Grunhorn in Switzerland in 2011.

1989:

April 3. Austrian mountaineer Wastl Mariner (1909 – 1989)—the "Father of Mountain Rescue"—died at age 80 in Innsbruck, Austria. Mariner was instrumental in the founding of the International Commission for Alpine Rescue. He made thirty-eight first ascents and climbed 3,603 peaks including all of the 5,000 meter peaks in Africa.

1989:

British climber Andy Parkin (1955 –) was badly injured while guiding a client up the Riffelhorn (9,604 ft./2,927 m.) above Zermatt, Switzerland. Unable to continue his climbing, Parkin became a mountain artist and with the assistance of French sculptor Phillipe Vouillemoz created a massive work of art on the Mer de Glace (glacier) above Chamonix, France. This artistic creation was made from garbage left behind by climbers and skiers. Parkin created this sculpture to draw attention to the impact of climbing and skiing on the fragile mountain environment. Glacial movement eventually destroyed this massive work of art. Parkin has lived in Chamonix, France since 1983.

1990:

July 14. Zermatt mountain guide Ulrich Inderbinen (1900 – 2004) made his 371st and final ascent of the Matterhorn (14,692 ft./4,478 m.) above Zermatt, Switzerland at age 90. He was the oldest active mountain guide in the world.

1990:

July 20. French mountaineer and athlete Pierre-Andre Gobet made a round-trip climb of Mont Blanc (15,775 ft./4,808 m.) in France in 5 hours, 10 minutes, and 14 seconds. His ascent from Chamonix took 3 hours 38 minutes. His descent took 1 hour 32 minutes.

1990: FIRST ASCENT

January 14 and 15. Slovenian climber Slavko Sveticic (1958 –) made the first winter ascent (solo) of the John Harlin Route on the Eiger (13,025 ft./3,970 m.) in Switzerland. This ascent took 26 hours.

1990:

As of this year, just over 600 people had climbed all 283 Munros in Scotland. A Munro is a Scottish peak that exceeds 3,000 feet (914 meters). This group of peaks are named for Sir Hugh T. Munro (1856 – 1919) who first systematically recorded them in 1891.

1990: FIRST ASCENT

American climber Lynn Hill (1961 –) made the first female ascent of Masse Critique in Cimai, France. This was also the first 5.14 graded ascent by a woman.

1990:

Geneva, Switzerland mountain guide Stephane Schaffter (1953 –) skied from the summit of Mont Blanc (15,775 ft./4,808 m.) to the summit of Monte Rosa (15,204 ft./4,634 m.) in 36 hours. He made one rest stop at the Valsorey Hut for a meal, a shower, and a 20-minute sleep. The direct line distance between these two summits is approximately 38 miles.

1990:

Well-known alpine film director, mountain guide, and ski instructor Luis Trenker (1892 – 1990) died at age 98. Trenker made many mountain films on climbing, mountain warfare, and skiing including *The White Hell of Piz Palu* (1928) and *The Mountain Calls* (1937).

1991: FIRST ASCENT

June 25 to July 4. The first major high-altitude route in the Alps to be forced by a woman was the work of French climber Catherine Destivelle (1960 –) on the West Face of the Petit Dru (12,248 ft./3,733 m.) in the French Alps in nine days (solo). Destivelle used a six-pound lightweight titanium portaledge on this climb to cook and sleep on.

1991:

September 19. German climbers Erika and Helmut Simon (Nuremberg, Germany) made the ascent of the Finailspitze (11,536 ft./3,516 m.) in the Otztal Alps on the Italian – Austrian border. On their descent, they discovered the remains of a human body preserved in the glacial ice. This discovery was located just inside the Italian territory (South Tyrol) at an elevation of 10,532 ft./3,210 m. on the Similaun Glacier. This dead man was lying face down on a rock. He was 153 centimeters long (60 inches). A careful recovery of this man began on September 23. He was wearing a protective fur coat, a bearskin hat, and wore grass-lined leather boots. He carried a bow-stave made of yew, a crude ice-axe with a copper blade, and a knife with a stone blade. After a detailed analysis, it was determined that this iceman, nicknamed "Otzi" by Viennese reporter Karl Wendl, died during the early Iron Age and therefore was between 5,200 and 5,300 years old. A more detailed analysis of this iceman revealed that he was killed by an arrow in the back which severed an artery causing him to bleed to death. "Otzi" was eventually removed and relocated to the South Tyrol Museum of Archaeology in Bolzano, Italy.

1991: FIRST ASCENT

American mountaineer Jeff Lowe (1949 –) made the first solo winter ascent of the Eiger's (13,025 ft./3,970 m.) north face (5,900 ft./1,798 m.). His route is named Metanoia.

1991:

The Piolet d'Or ("Golden Ice Axe") award was established by France's Groupe de Haute Montagne (Chamonix) and Montagnes magazine to recognize the year's most outstanding achievement in world alpinism as determined by a jury of climbers. Here is a summary of Piolet d' Or recipients from 1991 to 2011:

Piolet d' Or Recipients

Year	Nationality	Climbers	Peak Elevation	Location Route
1991	Slovenian	Marko Prezelj Andrej Stremgelj	Kangchenjunga South Summit 27,810 ft./8,476 m.	Nepal South Pillar

Year	Nationality	Climbers	Peak Elevation	Location Route
1992		Michel Piola Vincent Sprungli	Torre South	Patagonia Del Paine East Face
1993	French	French Alpine Club	Pamir Mountains	Tajikistan/ Kyrgyzstan Multiple Ascents
1994	French English	Francois Marsigny Andy Parkin	Cerro Torre 10,263 ft./3,128 m.	Patagonia Esperance Col
1995	German	Heli Neswabba Andrea Orgler Arthur Wutsher	Mount Bradley	Alaska South Face
1996		Vanja Furlan Tomaz Humar	Ama Dablam 22,494 ft./6,856 m.	Nepal East Face
1997	Russian	Serget Efimov Et Al	Makalu 27,826 ft./8,481 m.	Nepal West Face
1998	Australian New Zealand	Andrew Lindblade Athol Whimp	Thalay Sagar 22,652 ft./6,904 m.	India North Face
1999		Lionel Daudet Sebastian Foissac	Burkett Needle 8,500 ft./2,590 m.	Alaska SE Face
2000		Thomas Huber Iwan Wolf	Shivling 21,467 ft./6,543 m.	India N. Pillar
2001	Russian	Valery Babanov	Meru Central 21,198 ft./6,461 m.	Nepal Solo Climb
2002	British	Mick Fowler Paul Ramsden	Siguniang 25,506 ft./6,250 m.	China N. Face
2003	Russian	Valery Babanov Yuri Koshelenko	Nuptse 25,850 ft./7,879 m.	Nepal S. Face

Year	Nationality	Climbers	Peak Elevation	Location Route
2003	Russian	Valery Babanov Yuri Koshelenko	Nuptse 25,850 ft./7,879 m.	Nepal S. Face
2004	Russian	Alexander Odintsov Et Al	Jannu 25,295 ft./7,710 m.	Nepal N. Face
2005	American	Vince Anderson Steve House	Nanga Parbat 26,661 ft./8,126 m.	Pakistan Rupal Face
2006	Slovenian	Boris Lorencic Marko Prezelj	Chomolhari 23,997 ft./7,314 m.	Bhutan NW Pillar
2007	Award Cancelled			
2008	Swiss	Ueli Steck Simon Anthamatten	Tengkampoche 21,326 ft./6,500 m.	Nepal N. Face
	Japanese	Kazuya Hiraide Kei Taniguchi	Kamet 25,447 ft./7,756 m.	India SW Face
	Japanese	Fumitaka Ichimura Yusuke Sato Kazuki Amano	Kalanka 22,740 ft./6,931 m.	India N. Face
2009	Kazakh	Denis Urubko Boris Dedeshko	Cho Oyu 26,906 ft./8,201 m.	Nepal SE Face
	American Scottish	Jed Brown Kyle Dempster Bruce Normand	Xuelian West	China
2010		Reinhold Messner	Lifetime Achievement Award	
2011	Japanese	Yasushi Okada Katsutaka Yokoyama	Mount Logan 19,550 ft./5,958 m.	Canada SE Face
	Belgium American British	Sean Villanueva Nicolas Favresse Olivier Favresse Ben Ditto Bob Shepton		Greenland Big Walls

1991:

4,000 climbers were guided to the summit of Mont Blanc (15,775 ft./4,808 m.) above Chamonix, France while 35,000 people made the circumnavigation of Mont Blanc in France, Italy, and Switzerland. This ten-day trek (96 miles/160 kilometers) is called the Tour du Mont Blanc.

1992: FIRST ASCENT

March 9. French climber Catherine Destivelle (1960 –) began her attempt at 5:30 a.m. to be the first woman to solo the classic 1938 ascent route on the north face of the Eiger (13,025 ft./3,970 m.) in winter conditions (Switzerland). She reached the Exit Cracks at 7:00 p.m. by headlamp. She arrived on the summit at 10:30 p.m.. The total climb (5,900 ft./1,798 m.) was accomplished in a rapid 17 hours. This climb also represented the first female winter ascent.

1992:

July 6. Well-known Austrian mountaineer Heinrich Harrer (1912 – 2006) opened his personal expedition museum in Hüttenberg, Austria. His close friend, the 14th Dalai Lama, was present to officially open this museum on Harrer's 80th birthday. Harrer made the first ascents of the Eiger's north face (1938) and Carstensz Pyramid (1962) in West New Guinea. His museum includes exhibits from his 4,500 expeditions around the world.

1992:

July 19. Austrian climber Hans Kammerlander (1956 –) and his partner Diego Wellig (1961 –) climbed the Matterhorn (14,692 ft./4,478 m.) four times in 23½ hours for a total gain and loss of 27,889 feet/8,500 meters. Their climbing sequence was:

    1. Up the Zmutt Ridge
       Down the Hornli Ridge
    2. Up the Furggen Ridge
       Down the Lion Ridge
    3. Up the Lion Ridge
       Down the Hornli Ridge
    4. Up the Hornli Ridge
       Down the Hornli Ridge

1993:

June 23 to August 13. Scottish mountaineers Martin Moran and Simon Jenkins made the second continuous traverse of all of the 4,000 meter (13,124 feet) peaks in the Alps—75 summits including a 33 hour traverse of the Mont Blanc summits in 52 days. Fifty of the seventy-five peaks were considered to be major mountains.

1993:

The first "via ferrata" climbing route in Switzerland was opened on the south face of the Gadmerflue (8,334 ft./2,540 m.). This route is called the Talli Via Ferrata and is approximately one kilometer in length. In Italian, "via ferrata" means "iron ways." These are climbing routes that are protected by steel cables, steps, ladders, and bridges.

1993:

British mountaineer Alison Hargreaves (1962 – 1995) became a professional mountaineer at age 31 and set a goal for herself of climbing the six major north faces in the Alps during one climbing season in a combined time of less than 24 hours. She was the first person to solo all six north faces. Here is a summary of her north face climbs:

1st:	The Shroud on the Grandes Jorasses	2 hr. 15 min.
2nd:	The North Face of the Matterhorn	6 hr. 30 min.
3rd:	The North Face of the Eiger	5 hr. 30 min.
4th:	Cima Grande de Lavaredo	3 hr. 30 min.
5th:	Aiguille du Dru	4 hr.
6th:	Northeast Face of the Piz Badile	2 hr.
		23 hr. 45 min.

Hargreaves claimed to have accomplished this six-face climb in 23 hours and 45 minutes over a period of a few weeks. She was also the first female to make solo ascents of the Petit Dru, the Cima Grande, and the Matterhorn.

1993:

Switzerland contains 27 certified mountain climbing schools that belong to the Swiss Association of Mountain Climbing Schools.

1993:

The Swiss Alpine Club owned and managed 150 mountain huts.

1993: FIRST ASCENT

French mountaineer Catherine Destivelle (1960 –) made the first winter solo ascent by a woman of the Walker Spur (3,609 ft./1,100 m.) on the Grandes Jorasses (13,806 ft./4,208 m.) in the French Alps.

1994:

March 13. French climbers Erik Decamp (1954 –) and Catherine Destivelle (1960 –) made a dual winter solo ascent of the Matterhorn's (14,692 ft./4,478 m.) north face. Climbing independently, Decamp followed the 1931 Schmid Route (3,300 ft./1,000 m.) while Destivelle climbed the 1965 Bonatti Route (also 3,300 ft./1,000 m.). This was only the second ascent of Walter Bonatti's 1965 winter ascent. Decamp and Destivelle took 3 days to climb their routes which required three bivouacs (including a summit bivouac).

1994:

The Union Internationale des Associations d' Alpinisme (U.I.A.A.) recognized 21 new summits to add to the official list of 4,000 meter (13,124 feet) peaks in the European Alps. There are now eighty-two 4,000 meter peaks on the new list. The highest peak is Mont Blanc (15,775 ft./4,808 m.) and the lowest is Dome de Neige (Barre des Ecrins) at 13,173 ft./4,015 m.

1994:

Polish woman mountaineer Wanda Rutkiewicz (1943 – 1992) was posthumously awarded the King Albert Mountain Award for her contributions to feminine mountaineering and exploration for more than a quarter of a century. Rutkiewicz died near the summit of Kangchenjunga (28,171 ft./8,586 m.) in 1992.

1994:

Lord John Hunt (1910 – 1999) and American mountaineer, explorer, photographer, and cartographer Bradford Washburn (1910 – 2007) received the first King Albert Gold Medals for Outstanding Achievement in the Mountain World. Geneva, Switzerland.

1995:

April 4 to 19. French mountaineer Jean-Christophe Lafaille (1966 – 2006) enchained ten alpine faces solo. He called this enchainment the "Grand Voyage." Lafaille traveled 140 kilometers/84 miles by skis and climbed up and down a total of 65,620 ft./20,000 m. in fifteen days. These ten faces are:

1.	Northeast face of the Eiger	13,025 ft./3,970 m.
2.	North face of the Monch	13,449 ft./4,099 m.
3.	North face of the Aletschorn	13,754 ft./4,192 m.
4.	North face of the Nesthorn	12,540 ft./3,822 m.
5.	East face of Monte Rosa	15,204 ft./4,634 m.
6.	Schmid route on the Matterhorn	14,692 ft./4,478 m.
7.	North face of the Breithorn	13,665 ft./4,165 m.
8.	North face of Mont Blanc de Cheilon	12,698 ft./3,870 m.
9.	North couloir of Aiguille Verte	13,524 ft./4,122 m.
10.	North face of the Grandes Jorasses	13,806 ft./4,208 m.

Lafaille disappeared on Makalu (27,767 ft./8,463 m.) in the Himalayas on or about January 27, 2006.

1995:

June 9. New Zealand mountaineer Edmund Hillary (1919 – 2008) was recognized and welcomed into the Knights of the Garter by Queen Elizabeth of England at the age of 76. London, England.

1995:

December 3. Swiss mountain guide Ulrich Inderbinen (1900 – 2004) of Zermatt turned 95 years old. He was the oldest mountain guide in the world. Inderbinen first climbed the Matterhorn (14,692 ft./4,478 m.) in 1921 and went on to climb this same peak 370 more times. He guided two female climbers up the Allalinhorn (13,211 ft./4,027 m.) above Zermatt this year. In July of 1995, Inderbinen made more than twelve ascents of the Breithorn (13,662 ft./4,164 m.) and the Allalinhorn. He died on June 10, 2004 at age 103 ½.

1995:

Since 1865 (130 years ago), there have been over 500 deaths on the Matterhorn (14,692 ft./4,478 m.).

1996:

British mountaineer, expedition leader, author, and photographer Christian Bonington (1934 –) was awarded knighthood in London, England by Prince Charles at Buckingham Palace. Sir Christian J.S. Bonington.

1996:

Mountaineer Alexander Ruchkin (1963 –) made a solo winter ascent of the north face of the Grandes Jorasses (13,806 ft./4,208 m.) on the Mont Blanc Massif above Chamonix, France.

1996:

By this year, more than 2,000 people had died on Mont Blanc (15,775 ft./4,808 m.) on the French – Italian border making this peak the deadliest mountain on Earth.

1997: FIRST ASCENT

October 5. Italian mountaineer Benedetto Salaroli (1925 –) became the oldest person (at 72) to climb the Eiger's north face (5,900 ft./1,798 m.) in Switzerland. His two guides were Ueli Buhler and Kobi Reichen.

1998:

August 16. The Priut Hut (or Priut 11 Hut) on Mount Elbrus in southwestern Russia burned down due to a gas cooker fire. Originally built in 1929, this hut was located at 13,649 ft./4,160 m.

1998:

British adventurer David Hempleman-Adams (1956 –) became the first person to complete The Explorers Grand Slam Challenge. To complete this global test, one must reach both the North and South poles and climb all Seven Summits.

1998:

November 8. Well-known British mountaineer and leader of the successful 1953 British Mount Everest Expedition Sir John Hunt (1910 – 1998) died at age 88. Born Henry Cecil John Hunt, he became Lord Llanfair-Waterdine. Hunt's father, also a mountaineer, had climbed with Edward Whymper of Matterhorn fame (1865).

1999:

American mountaineer, explorer, photographer, and cartographer Bradford Washburn (1910 – 2007) and his wife Barbara (1914 –) were honored in Milan, Italy as two of the 100 most distinguished mountaineers of the last 100 years. Brad Washburn was one of the greatest mountain photographers of all time.

2000:

Twenty-five percent of the entire glacial cover had disappeared in the European Alps from 1980 to 2000. The period of 1850 to 1980 (130 years) saw a 50 percent decline in glacial cover.

2000:

Dutch mountaineer Ronald Naar (1955 –) had climbed over 550 peaks in the European Alps since 1968 (32 years). Naar also has been a member of forty expeditions to other mountains in the world.

2000:

Well-known British mountaineer Mike Banks (1922 –) climbed the Old Man of Hoy, a red sandstone Scottish sea stack, at the age of seventy-seven. This 449 foot/137 meter sea stack is located on the island of Hoy in the Orkney Islands off the north coast of Scotland. Banks became the oldest person to climb the Old Man of Hoy which was first climbed in 1966 (3 day climb) by British mountaineers Chris Bonington, Rusty Baillie, and Tom Patey. Banks made the first ascent of Rakaposhi in the Himalayas in 1958.

2000: Book

Fergus Fleming (1959 –) authored a wonderful book about the history of climbing in the Alps. *Killing Dragons – The Conquest of the Alps* is considered to be one of the best-selling mountaineering books of all time.

2001:

February. French climber Patrick Berhault (1957 – 2004) and friends traversed the entire length of the Alps on foot from Slovenia to the French Mediterranean climbing 22 big alpine walls along the way. August of 2000 to February of 2001.

2001:

Céüse, France. After 30 failed attempts, American rock climber Chris Sharma (1981 –) completed the 120 foot/37 meter route known as Realization to become the first and only climber to complete a climb rated 5.15.

2001: Book

British mountaineer Simon Yates (1963 –) published his book entitled *The Flame of Adventure* which is an autobiographical narrative describing Yate's climbing adventures around the world. This book is considered to be one of the best-selling mountaineering books of all time.

2001:

151 climbing parties were assisted by the Mont Blanc (15,775 ft./4,808 m.) High-Mountain Rescue Squad. Thirty percent of the climbers attempting Mont Blanc are injured in some way (i.e. altitude sickness, frostbite, etc.). The success rate (summit reached) of those climbers using guides was 50 percent, those not using guides 33 percent.

2002: FIRST ASCENT

February 21. A Russian expedition made the first ascent of the north face of Trollryggen Peak (5,735 ft./1,748 m.) in the Romspal region of Norway. Oleg Khvostenko led five climbers up this 3,740 foot/1,140 meter high face.

2002:

July and August. Slovenian mountaineer Andrej Stremfelj (1956 –) climbed 30 different routes on 27 different faces in the Slovenian Alps in 40 days.

2002:

September 6. Innsbruck, Austria. 100 mountaineers from many nations met at the Conference On The Future Of Mountain Sports. Their goal was "to create an ethical code (The Mountain Code) to assist climbers as well as the people, cultures, and environments associated with climbing." This code of ethics, principles, and values was distributed to 89 alpine clubs in 67 countries and was published in the American Alpine Journal in 2003. The final adoption of "The Mountain Code" by the U.I.A.A. General Assembly has been scheduled for 2008.

2002:

November 19. Author, climber, and skier Andre Roch (1906 – 2002) died at age 96 in Geneva, Switzerland. Roch was part of the team that made the second ascent of Mount Logan (19,550 ft./5,958 meters) in Canada in 1950. He also made the first ascent of Dunagiri (23,183 ft./7,066 m.) in the Garhwal Himalaya of northern India on July 5, 1939. Roch cut the first ski runs at Aspen, Colorado in 1937 and was a member of the 1952 Swiss Mount Everest Expedition. He climbed 13 different routes up Mont Blanc.

2002: FIRST ASCENT

American blind mountaineer Erik Weihenmayer (1968 –) completed his Seven Summit quest by climbing Mount Elbrus (18,481 ft./5,633 m.) in western Russia and Mount Kosciuszko (7,310 ft./2,228 m.) in Australia. His previous Seven Summit climbs were: Denali (1995) in Alaska, Mount Kilimanjaro (1997) in Tanzania, Aconcagua (1999) in Argentina, Mount Vinson (2001) in Antarctica, and Mount Everest (2001) in Nepal.

2002: Book

The Beckoning Silence by British mountaineer Joe Simpson (1960 –) tells the story about the 1936 attempt to climb the Eiger's north face in Switzerland. It is among the best-selling mountaineering books of all time.

2002:

Swiss guide Richard Andenmatten (1942 –) retired from climbing the Matterhorn (14,692 ft./4,478 m.) in Switzerland after more than 820 ascents. He is a fourth-generation Zermatt guide.

2002:

The Konkordia Hut (9,351 ft./2,850 m.) on the Aletsch Glacier in Switzerland celebrated its 125th anniversary (1877 – 2002). Originally built with 20 beds, this Swiss Alpine Club hut now can accommodate 180 climbers. The final 100 meters (328 feet) to this hut must be climbed via a metal ladder.

2002:

Expert surveyors re-measured the summit elevation of Mont Blanc on the French – Italian border. The revised elevation is 4,810.40 meters or 15,782.92 feet. The summit thickness of Mont Blanc, however, varies according to snow and ice accumulation.

2003:

February. French mountaineers Patrick Berhault (1957 – 2004) and Phillippe Magnin (1964 –) climbed 16 different routes over 19 days on the Italian side of Mont Blanc (15,775 ft./4,808 m.).

2003:

Mid July. Several massive rock towers collapsed on the Matterhorn's (14,692 ft./4,478 m.) Hornli Ridge stranding over 70 climbers and guides. The mountain was temporarily closed to climbing for one week while all of the climbers were air-lifted to safety. An unusually long dry spell and rapid warming caused these rock falls. An average of 15 climbers are killed each year on the Matterhorn in Switzerland.

2003:

Mid August. Mont Blanc (15,775 ft./4,808 m.), on the border of France and Italy, was closed to climbing for the first time in its 217-year climbing history due to falling rocks. Other serious rock slides occurred on the Walker Spur of the Grandes Jorasses and on the Bonatti Pillar of the Petit Dru. These rock slides were apparently caused by the loss of permafrost due to changes in the climate (i.e. global warming).

2003: FIRST ASCENT

Sue Nott (1969 – 2006) became the first American woman to climb both the Eiger's (13,025 ft./3,970 m.) north face in Switzerland and the Croz Spur on the Grandes Jorasses (13,806 ft./4,208 m.) in France in winter.

2003:

Mountaineers Claude-Alain Gailland and Sébastian Gay planned a traverse of the Valais Alps in Switzerland beginning June 1. This Traverse would cover 384 miles/640 kilometers and cross 330 summits (18 of the 61 4,000 meter peaks). They actually completed 2/3 of this distance (253 miles/422 kilometers) and climbed 250 summits before a rockfall broke Gailland's hand.

2004:

March 1 to April 28. French mountaineers Patrick Bérhault (1957 – 2004) and Philippe Magnin (1964 –) completed the climbing of 67 peaks in the Alps over 4,000 meters (13,124 ft.) in 60 days. Bérhault died on April 29 during the descent of the Täschhorn (14,732 ft./4,490 m.) in Switzerland, their final peak. Their original goal was to climb 82 4,000 meter peaks (recognized by the U.I.A.A.) in 82 days.

2004:

June 10. Famous Matterhorn (14,692 ft./4,478 m.) guide Ulrich Inderbinen (1900 – 2004) died in his sleep in Zermatt, Switzerland at age 103 ½. Inderbinen climbed the Matterhorn 371 times (his first ascent was in 1921) and guided his last client up this peak at age 94. He was buried in the Parish Church cemetery where he joined many other Zermatt mountaineers who lost their lives on the Matterhorn. Zermatt also dedicated a public fountain to Inderbinen.

2004:

July 29. Swiss mountaineers Stephan Siegrist (1972 –) and Ueli Steck (1976 –) completed the enchainment of three alpine north face climbs in 25 hours: the Eiger (13,025 ft./3,970 m.), the Monch (13,449 ft./4,099 m.), and the Jungfrau (13,642 ft./4,158 m.). They began this 3-face climb at midnight on July 29th and finished at 1:00 a.m. on the 30th.

2004:

There were approximately 2,250 professional mountain guides in France at this time—1,500 belonged to an organized guide group ("compagnie") and 750 were independent.

2004: Equipment – Crampons

Stubai developed the Stubai Ultralight Crampon that weighed one pound five ounces per pair and cost $100.00. This model represented the new breed of hardened aluminum alloy crampon.

2004: Equipment – Ice Axe/Trekking Pole

Petzl Charlet introduced the Snowscopic—a telescoping ice axe/trekking pole combination. It extended from 65 centimeters (25 ½ inches) to 105 centimeters (41 ¼ inches) and had a carbide tip. Stubai also made a similar combination axe pole that some mountaineers used in the mid 1980s.

2005:

February 1. Famous German mountaineer Anderl Heckmair (1906 – 2005) died atage 98. At age 31 (1938), Heckmair was a member of the four climbers who first climbed the Eiger's (13,025 ft./3,970 m.) north face in Switzerland. He and fellow German Wiggerl Vörg used the recently developed 12-point crampon on this 1938 first ascent.

2005:

April 2. Pope John Paul II (1920 – 2005) died at age 85. Born Karol Jozef Wojtyla in Wadowice, Poland, he had a lifelong love of mountains. He hiked and skied frequently as a young man. He was elected Pope in 1978 and served for 27 years. In June of 2005, a 7,900 foot/2,408 meter peak on the Gran Sasso Massif in the Apennine mountains of central Italy was renamed John Paul II Peak. This peak was formerly called the Gendarme.

2005:

Summer. The organization known as the Alpine Convention officially unveiled the 3,100 mile/5,167 kilometer Via Alpina, Europe's first long-distance hiking trail in the Alps. This specifically signed trail linked together some of Europe's most famous trail routes. A Frenchman named Noël Lebel conceived the Via Alpina in the year 2000. This trekking path was funded by the European Union and the eight countries this trail is located in (Slovenia, Austria, Italy, Germany, Liechtenstein, Switzerland, France, and Monaco).

2005:

September 25. American mountaineer John Harlin III (1956 –), son of John Harlin (1935 – 1966) who was killed on the north face of the Eiger (13,025 ft./3,970 m.) in Switzerland in 1966, climbed this same face with German climbers Daniela and Robert Jasper (3-day ascent). This climb was filmed by MacGillivray Freeman Films as a part of the 2007 IMAX film entitled "The Alps."

2005:

As of this year, Switzerland had developed 32 "via ferrata" climbing routes. These are rock climbing routes that are protected (for the climber's safety) with steel cables, steps, ladders, and bridges.

2005:

British mountaineer Annabelle Bond (1969 –) climbed the Seven Summits in 360 days—a new women's record and the fourth fastest overall time.

2005: Equipment – Ice Tool

The Grivel Company of Courmayeur, Italy introduced the "Grivel Monster." This ice tool is made of chromoly spring steel and has a range of gripping positions. The pick has many teeth angled in different directions.

2005: Equipment – Overboots

Insulated overboots that were fitted for step-in crampons were introduced. These overboots were specifically made for high-altitude cold climbs where protection for preventing frostbite is critical.

2006:

January 7. Famous Austrian mountaineer Heinrich Harrer (1912 – 2006) died at age 93. Harrer was a member of the four-man team (2 Austrians and 2 Germans) that made the first ascent of the Eiger's

(13,025 ft./3,970 m.) north face in 1938. He also spent many years in Tibet as the personal tutor to the Dalai Lama resulting in his very successful book *Seven Years In Tibet* (1953).

2006:

March 14. Swiss climber Ueli Steck (1976 –) solo climbed the Bonatti Route on the Matterhorn's north face in 25 hours. As of this year, there were over twenty-five varied climbing routes to the Matterhorn's summit (14,692 ft./4,478 m.).

2006:

September. Kazakh mountaineer Denis Urubko (1973 –) set a new speed climbing record on Mount Elbrus (18,511 ft./5,642 m.) in the Caucasus Range of Georgia. Urubko climbed from base camp to the summit in just under four hours.

2006:

December. The new Matterhorn Museum/Zermatlantis opened in Zermatt, Switzerland. This underground museum replaced the older Alpine Museum which first opened in 1958 in Zermatt. Museum visitors now can walk through a village of fourteen houses that each represent a particular theme in Zermatt's history. This new museum also includes the Matterhorn Room and the Research Laboratory for archaeologists. The Matterhorn Museum/Zermatlantis is located between the Grand Hotel Zermatterhof and the Church Square.

2006:

British woman mountaineer Brede Arkless (1939 – 2006) died at age 67. She was the first British woman to qualify as an international mountain guide. Arkless climbed in Snowdonia (Wales), the Alps, New Zealand (she guided 22 ascents of Mount Cook), and the Himalayas where she reached 28,000 ft./8,534 m. on Mount Everest in the year 2000.

2006:

World-famous Italian mountaineer Reinhold Messner (1944 –) opened his centrepiece museum of his five mountain museums. Known as the Messner Mountain Museum (MMM), this restored castle is located near Bolzano, Italy and contains a 200-seat rock theatre, museum headquarters and administrative offices for Messner's five different museums. The four satellite mountain museums are:

1. MMM at Juval (opened in 1995)
2. MMM Dolomites (opened in 2002)
3. MMM Ortles (opened in 2004)
4. MMM Ripa (opened in 2011)

Each museum focuses on a different mountain theme.

2006:

As of this year, 55 climbers have died while attempting to climb the Eiger's north face in Switzerland.

2006:

Slovenian ski mountaineer Davo Karnicar (1963 –) became the first person to climb and then ski down all Seven Summits.

2006:

During the past thirty-five years (1971 – 2006), Slovenian mountaineer Andrej Stremfelj (1956 –) had completed over 1,500 climbing routes in the Alps, Himalayas, etc.

2006: Equipment – Crampons

For steep ice climbing, crampons could now be bolted directly onto the boot. For vertical waterfall ice climbing, specific crampons with 14 or more points (prongs) per boot were now available.

2007:

December 27, 2006 to April 7, 2007. Slovenian mountaineer Miha Valic (1978 –) climbed 82 peaks over 4,000 meters (13,124 feet) in the Alps in 102 days. Valic was the first climber to accomplish this goal in the winter. He was joined by fifteen different climbing partners. He climbed the first 74 peaks in 74 days.

2007:

February 21. Swiss mountaineer Ueli Steck (1976 –) made the ascent of the Eiger's north face in 3 hours and 41 minutes. On February 13, 2008, Steck climbed this same 5,900 ft./1,800 m. face in 2 hours 47 minutes.

2007:

July 13. Top free American solo climber Michael Reardon (1970 – 2007) was suddenly swept away and killed by a huge wave while climbing the Irish sea cliff Rinn na Droilan off the southwest coast of Ireland.

2007:

September 6. Zermatt (Switzerland) guides Simon Anthamatten (1983 –) and Michael Lerjen (1985 –) made the fastest roundtrip climb of the Matterhorn—2 hours, 33 minutes from the Hornlihutte (10,700 ft./3,261 m.) to the summit (14,692 ft./4,478 m.) and back down to the Hornlihutte (1:40 ascent, :53 descent).

2007:

September 28. Famous French mountain guide and international mountaineer Rene Desmaison (1930 – 2007) died at age 77. He made over 1,000 peak ascents including 114 first ascents in the Alps, Andes, and Himalayas. Among his most notable ascents are these:

1956: Winter ascent of the west face of the Drus in the French Alps with French climber Jean Couzy (1923 – 1958).

1962: First ascent of Jannu (25,296 ft./7,710 m.) in the Himalayas.

1963: Desmaison's second winter ascent of the Walker Spur on the Grandes Jorasses in the French Alps with Jacques Batkin.

1967: First winter ascent of the Central Pillar of Freney on Mont Blanc.

1972: First solo ascent of the Peuterey Ridge on Mont Blanc.

2007:

The Alpine Club celebrated its 150th anniversary in England's Lake District. 250 people attended.

2007:

Legendary Italian mountaineer Riccardo Cassin (1909 – 2009) had made over 2,500 climbs and is credited with 100 major first ascents around the world in his long climbing career. Among his most notable first ascents are:

1935: Cassin-Ratti Route on the Cima Ovest's north face. 60 hours.

1938: Walker Spur on the Grandes Jorasses. 82 hours.

1961: Cassin Ridge on Denali in Alaska.

2007: Technique – Frostbite Remedy

For many years, the accepted technique for treating frostbite was to rub the affected area with the bare hand or snow. Gently re-warming the affected area is now the most effective treatment. The frost-bitten area is inserted into warm water whose temperature should not fall below 42°C. Skin-on-skin rewarming is also recommended for early stages of frostbite (known as frostnip).

2008:

January 28. Swiss mountaineers Simon Anthamatten (1983 –) and Roger Schali achieved the fastest ascent time of the Eiger's north face (5,900 ft./1,798 m.) for a roped team: 6 hours 50 minutes. Schali had made nine previous ascents of this famous north face in Switzerland.

2008:

February 13. Swiss mountaineer Ueli Steck (1976 –) made a solo speed winter ascent of the Eiger's north face in 2 hours 47 minutes 33 seconds. Steck only carried eleven pounds of clothing and equipment up this 5,900 foot/1,798 meter rock face. He followed the original 1938 Heckmair route and climbed at the rate of 35 feet or 10.7 meters per minute. Steck has now made twenty-three ascents of the Eiger's north face via nine different routes.

2008: FIRST ASCENT

September 25 to October 5. French mountaineers Aymeric Clouet (1978 –) and Christophe Dumarest (1980 –) made the first north to south traverse of the eight north faces that comprise the Ecrins Massif in the Dauphine region of the French Alps. This eleven-day climb reached the summit of these eight peaks:

La Meije	13,068 ft./3,983 m.
La Roche Meane	
La Roche d'Alvau1	1,308 ft./3,538 m.
Le Dome des Ecrins	13,458 ft./4,102 m.
Ailefroide	12,973 ft./3,954 m.
Les Bans	12,038 ft./3,669 m.
Le Pic Bonvoisin	10,036 ft./3,059 m.
Le Sirac	11,286 ft./3,440 m.

2008:

The Piolet d'Or Award was cancelled this year for the first time in its 17-year history. This prestigious French mountaineering award had been presented annually since 1991 for the year's most outstanding achievement in world alpinism. The reason for the 2008 cancellation was that the award selection criteria was being re-evaluated.

2008: Film

The German documentary film *North Face* made its debut in theatres. This film about the 1936 attempt to climb the north face of the Eiger in Switzerland was directed by Phillip Stolzl and won the German film award for best cinematography and best sound.

2009:

January. Climber Ueli Steck (1976 –) made the fastest ascent of the Matterhorn (14,692 ft./4,478 m.) in Switzerland—1 hour 56 minutes from the Hornlihutte (10,696 ft./3,260 m.) to the summit via the Hornli Ridge.

2009:

July 26. Legendary Italian mountaineer Riccardo Cassin (1909 – 2009) died in his hometown village of Lecco at age 100. During his lifetime, Cassin achieved 100 major first ascents. At the age of 78 (1987), he climbed the Piz Badile (10,853 feet/3,308 meters) in the Italian Dolomites twice in one week. Among his most notable first ascents were:

1. 935. Sixty-hour climb of the Cassin-Ratti (1,600 feet/487 meters) route on the north face of the Cima Ovest in the Italian Dolomites.
2. 938. Cassin climbed the Walker Spur on the Grandes Jorasses (13,806 feet/4,208 meters) in 82 hours roundtrip. French Alps.
3. 1961. Cassin and his team (six climbers) climbed the Cassin Ridge on Denali (20,320 feet/6,193 meters) in Alaska.

2009:

August 5 to 23. Canadian mountaineer Maxime Turgeon (1981 –) enchained seven classic alpine routes in four countries in eighteen days. He bicycled from trailhead to trailhead for all seven climbs (742 miles/1,236 kilometers). These seven ascents were:

1. North face of the Petit Dru (12,248 feet/3,733 meters) in the French Alps. He climbed the Allain-Leininger Route (2,789 feet/850 meters).
2. Northeast face of the Piz Badile (10,853 feet/3,308 meters) in the Italian Dolomites. He followed the Cassin-Valsecchi Route (2,625 feet/800 meters).
3. The Vinatzer-Castiglioni route on the Marmolada (10,857 feet/3,309 meters) in the Italian Dolomites. This route is 2,723 feet/830 meters high.
4. Northeast face of La Civetta (10,565 feet/3,220 meters) in northern Italy. He climbed the Kees-Wiessner Route (2,461 feet/750 meters).
5. The Alvera-Pompanin Route (2,789 feet/850 meters) on the Tofana di Rozes (10,581 feet/3,225 meters) in northern Italy.
6. Dibona Route (1,640 feet/500 meters) on the Cima Grande (9,840 feet/2,999 meters) in the Italian Dolomites.
7. Turgeon's final ascent was the Skalaska Route (3,281 feet/1,000 meters) on the Triglav (9,397 feet/2,864 meters) in Slovenia.

2009:

Swiss mountaineers Ueli Steck (1976 –) and Simon Anthamatten (1983 –) were awarded the 2009 Piolet d' Or for their first ascent (alpine style) of the north face of Tengkampoche (21,326 feet/6,500 meters) in Nepal.

2009:

Famous Italian mountaineers Achille Compagnoni (1914 – 2009) and Lino Lacedelli (1925 – 2009) both died during this year. They were the first climbers to reach the summit of K2 (28,253 ft./8,611 m.) in Pakistan in 1954. Compagnoni made one hundred ascents of both the Matterhorn and Monte Rosa during his lifetime. He was a professional mountain guide and the owner of a hotel in Italy. Lacedelli was also a professional mountain guide.

2010:

March. The new Monte Rosa Hut (9,169 feet/2,795 meters) above Zermatt, Switzerland was officially opened replacing the 114-year-old original mountain hut (built in 1895). This new hut accommodates 120 climbers. Solar panels will produce 90 percent of the hut's power.

2010: Film

August. The adventure documentary film entitled *The Wildest Dream: Conquest of Everest* was released. This 90-minute film was directed by Anthony Geffen and replicates the ill-fated 1924 British expedition to Mount Everest.

2010: FIRST ASCENT

Norwegian big-wall climbers Sindre Saether and Ole Johan made a free ascent of the Arch Wall on Romsdal's Troll Wall in Norway. The Arch Wall route ascends the highest part of the Troll Wall (3,937 ft./1,200 m.).

2011:

January 19. Legendary British mountaineer Joe Brown (1930 –) was appointed Commander of the Order of the British Empire (CBE). Brown began climbing at age twelve and has many first ascents to his name. In 1955, he and George Band made the first ascent of Kangchen-Junga (28,171 ft./8,586 m.) on the Nepal – Sikkim border. Kangchen-Junga is the third highest mountain in the world.

2011:

April 20. Swiss mountain guide Dani Arnold (1984 –) set a new speed-climbing record on the north face of the Eiger (13,025 ft./3,970 m.) in Switzerland. Arnold climbed the 1938 Heckmair route reaching the summit in 2 hours 28 minutes. He passed twenty other climbing teams on the face, which is approximately 5,900 feet (1,798 m.) high. His record-setting ascent began at 9:05 a.m. and ended at 11:33 a.m. Swiss climber Ueli Steck (1976 –) set the previous speed record of 2 hours 47 minutes in 2008.

2011:

April 28. Well-known Swiss mountaineer Erhard Loretan (1959 – 2011) was accidentally killed in Switzerland when he and his client fell from the summit ridge of the Grunhorn (13,305 ft./4,043 m.) in the Bernese Alps. This tragic accident happened to occur on Loretan's 52nd birthday. In 1995, he completed the climbing of all fourteen 8,000-meter peaks in the world. Loretan was the third climber to achieve this goal. In 1996, he was awarded the King Albert Medal of Merit for his contributions to mountaineering.

2011:

July 12. Welsh mountaineer Richard Parks (1977 –) became the first person to complete the Explorers' Grand Slam challenge (see Appendix III) within one calendar year. Parks reached the North Pole, South Pole, and the Seven Summits in 6 months, 11 days, 7 hours, and 53 minutes. Here is Park's climbing schedule:

South Pole	December 27, 2010
Mount Vinson	January 8, 2011
Aconcagua	February 5, 2011
Kilimanjaro	February 27, 2011
Carstensz Pyramid	March 15, 2011
North Pole	April 11, 2011
Mount Everest	May 25, 2011
Denali	June 30, 2011
Elbruz	July 12, 2011

2011:

August 26. Well-known British mountaineer George C. Band (1929 – 2011) died at age 82. Band and Joe Brown (1930 –) were members of the 1955 British Kangchenjunga Expedition and were the first climbers to reach Kangchenjunga's summit (28,171 ft./8,586 m.) on the Nepal-Sikkim border.

2011:

September 10. Swiss mountain guide Micheal Lerjen (1985 –) became the youngest mountain guide (age 26) to climb all of the 4,000 meter peaks (82) in the European Alps. Lerjen was born and raised in Zermatt. His first 4,000 meter summit was the Matterhorn (age 11) and his 82nd summit was the Jungfrau.

2011:

September 14. One of the greatest mountaineers of all time Walter Bonatti (1930 – 2011) died in Rome, Italy at age 81. Bonatti was a member of the 1954 Italian expedition that first climbed K2 (28,253 ft./8,611 m.) on the Pakistan – China border. British mountaineer Sir Christian Bonington on learning of Bonatti's passing said: "He (Bonatti) was among the greatest of all time, without a shadow of a doubt." Among Bonatti's most noteworthy ascents are the following climbs:

1951 – East Face of the Grand Capucin (12,592 ft./3,838 m.). French Alps
1953 – First winter ascent. North face of Cima Ovest di Lavaredo (9,840 ft. /2,999 m.). Solo. Italian Dolomites.
1955 – Southwest Pillar of the Petit Dru (12,248 ft./3,733 m.). Solo. Now known as the Bonatti Pillar. French Alps.
1958 – First ascent of Gasherbrum IV (26,023 ft./7,932 m.) in the Karakoram Range. Pakistan – China border.
1959 – Route Major on the Brenva Face of Mont Blanc (15,782 ft./4,810 m.). Solo. French Alps.
1962 – Northeast face of the Grand Pilier d'Angle. French Alps.
1963 – First winter ascent of the Walker Spur on the Grandes Jorasses (13,806 ft. /4,208 m.). French Alps.
1964 – Whymper Spur on the Grandes Jorasses (13,806 ft./4,208 m.). French Alps.
1965 – New route on the Matterhorn's (14,692 ft./4,478 m.) north face in winter. Solo. Swiss Alps.

2011: FIRST ASCENT

American mountaineer Denise Wenger (1985 –) became the first woman to climb the Furggen Ridge (3,773 ft./1,150 m.) of the Matterhorn (14,692 ft./4,478 m.) in the winter. Swiss mountain guide Michael Lerjen (1985 –) was with Wenger on this ascent.

2011:

Since 1935, many climbers have died attempting to climb the 5,900 foot (1,798 meters) north face of the Eiger (13,025 ft./3,970 m.) above Grindelwald, Switzerland. As of the end of 2011, sixty-four deaths have occurred on this dangerous, vertical face.

2011:

Swiss mountain guide Kurt Lauber (1961 –) had made 350 ascents of the Matterhorn (14,692 ft./4,478 m.) above Zermatt, Switzerland. Lauber is also a ski instructor, helicopter pilot, and a trained rescuer. He began serving as Hutmaster for the Hornlihutte (10,700 ft./3,260 m.) at the base of the Matterhorn in 1997.

> **"The essence of the sport lies not in ascending a peak, but in struggling with and overcoming difficulties."**
>
> **Albert Frederick Mummery**
> **British mountaineer**
> **(1855 – 1895)**

Mont Blanc, France-Italy
15,782 ft./4,810 m.

Breithorn. Switzerland-Italy
13,665 ft./4,165 m.

Wetterhorn, Switzerland
12,143 ft./3,701 m.

Monte Rosa, Dufourspitze, Switzerland
15,204 ft./4,634 m

Eiger, Switzerland
13,025 ft./3,970 m

Weisshorn, Switzerland
14,804 ft./4,512 m.

Matterhorn, Switzerland-Italy
14,692 ft./4,478 m.

(L) Dom
14,912 ft./4,545 m.

(R) Taschhorn
14,732 ft./4,490 m.

Pennine Alps
Switzerland

Grandes Jorasses (L) and Dent Du Geant (R)
13,806 ft./4,208 m   13,166ft./4,013 m
Swiss Guide David Fasel (L) and Ian Wolfe (R)

Saussure and Balmat Monument.
First Ascent of Mont Blanc.
Chamonix, France

Alpine Club Monument
Zermatt, Switzerland

Edward Whymper Plaque
Monte Rosa Hotel
Zermatt, Switzerland

Ulrich Inderbinen, Zermatt, Switzerland
2000
F. Wolfe (L), K. Wolfe (R)

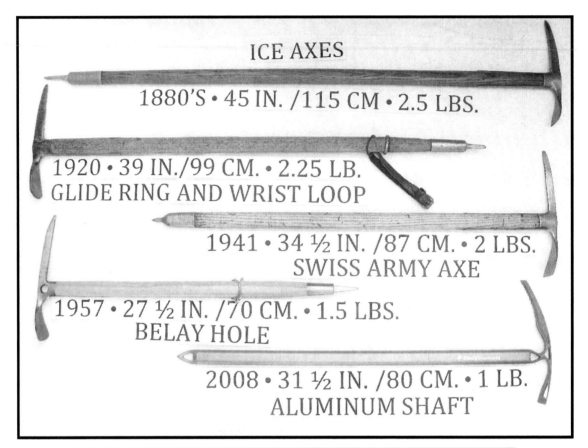

ICE AXES

1880'S • 45 IN. /115 CM • 2.5 LBS.

1920 • 39 IN./99 CM. • 2.25 LB.
GLIDE RING AND WRIST LOOP

1941 • 34 ½ IN. /87 CM. • 2 LBS.
SWISS ARMY AXE

1957 • 27 ½ IN. /70 CM. • 1.5 LBS.
BELAY HOLE

2008 • 31 ½ IN. /80 CM. • 1 LB.
ALUMINUM SHAFT

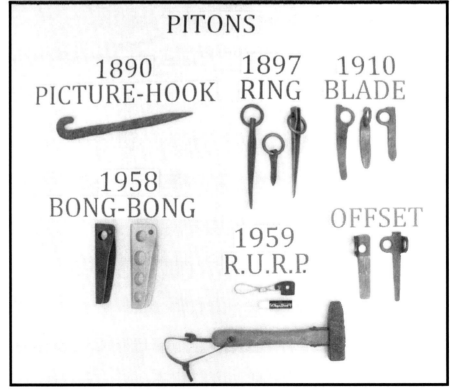

PITONS

1890
PICTURE-HOOK

1897
RING

1910
BLADE

1958
BONG-BONG

1959
R.U.R.P.

OFFSET

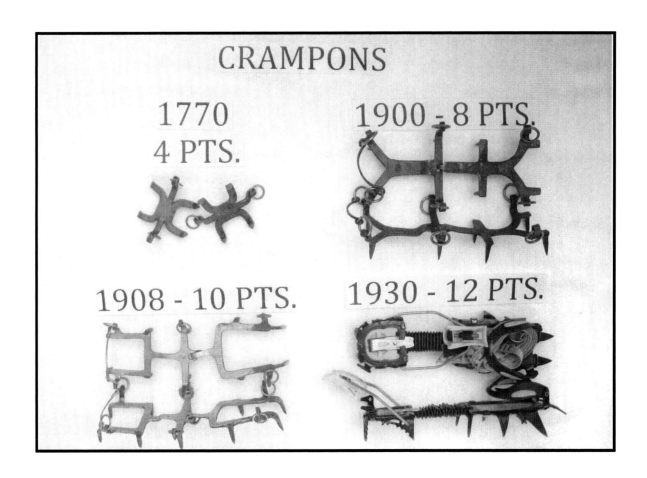

CRAMPONS

1770
4 PTS.

1900 - 8 PTS.

1908 - 10 PTS.

1930 - 12 PTS.

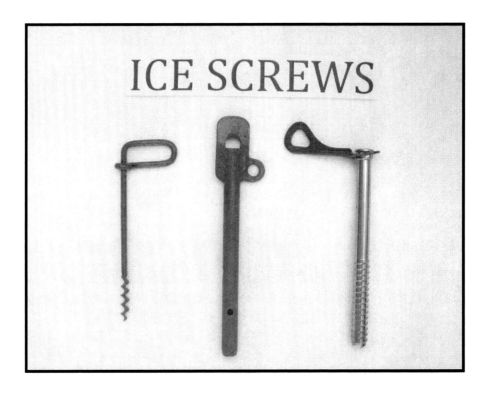

ICE SCREWS

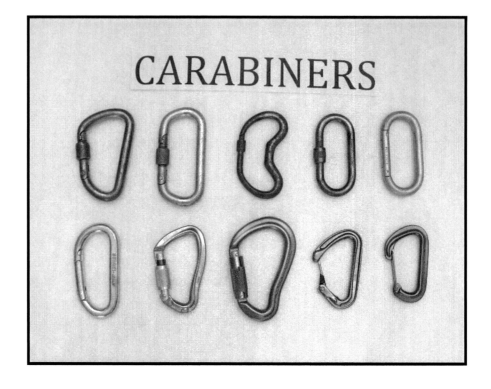

ROPES

RED THREAD

1885 • ALPINE CLUB • ½ IN. DIA.

1895 • MANILLA HEMP • 5/8 IN. DIA.

1942 • PLYMOUTH GOLDLINE • ½ IN. DIA.

1953 • KERNMANTEL • ½ IN. DIA.

CARABINERS

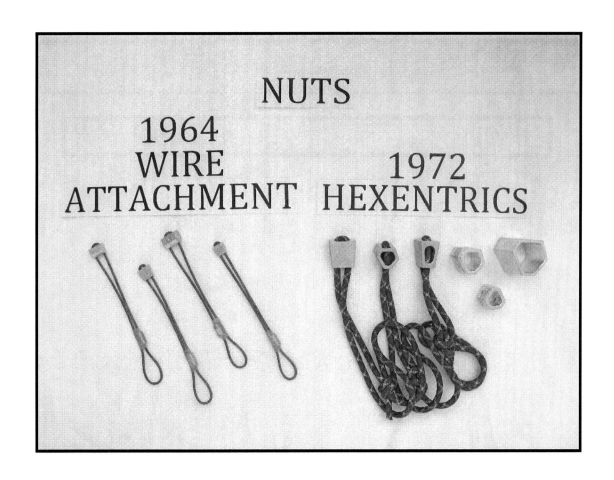

NUTS

1964
WIRE
ATTACHMENT

1972
HEXENTRICS

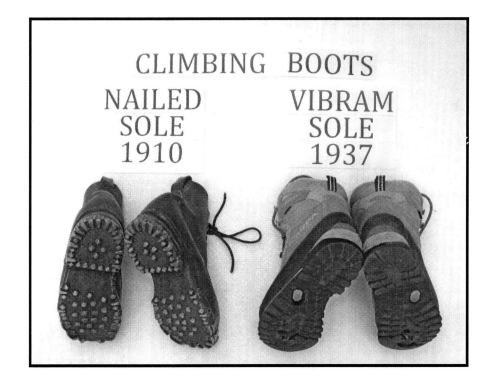

CLIMBING BOOTS

NAILED
SOLE
1910

VIBRAM
SOLE
1937

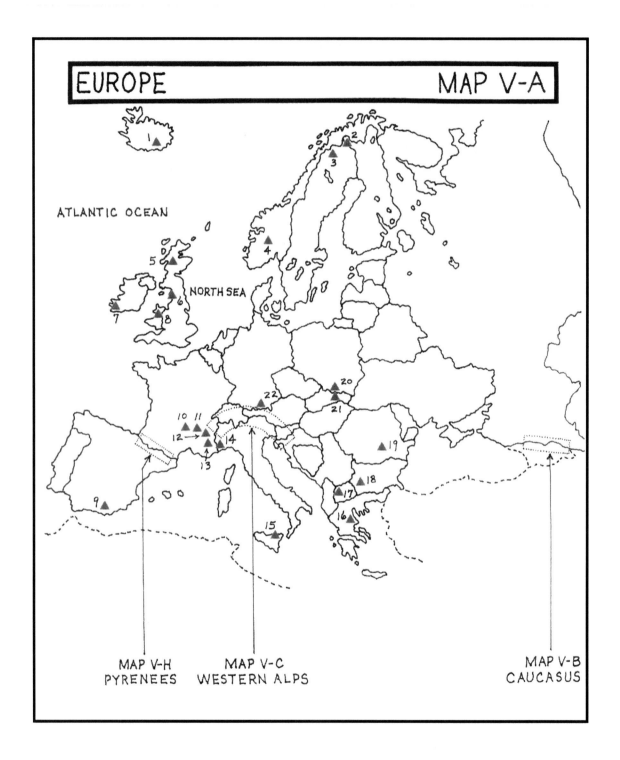

EUROPE   MAP V-A

ATLANTIC OCEAN

NORTH SEA

MAP V-H   MAP V-C   MAP V-B
PYRENEES   WESTERN ALPS   CAUCASUS

THE MAJOR MOUNTAINS OF EUROPE

#	PEAK NAME	LOCATION	FEET	METERS	FIRST ASCENT	MAP
1	HVANNADALSHNÚV	ICELAND	6,952	2,119	1963	V-A
2	HALTIATUNTURI	FINLAND	4,357	1,328	UNKN	V-A
3	KEBNEKAISE	SWEDEN	6,926	2,111	1883	V-A
4	GALDHØPPIGEN	NORWAY	8,101	2,469	1850	V-A
5	BEN NEVIS	SCOTLAND	4,406	1,343	1771	V-A
6	SCAFELL PIKE	ENGLAND	3,208	978	1802	V-A
7	CARRAUNTOOHIL	IRELAND	3,415	1,041	UNKN	V-A
8	SNOWDON	WALES	3,560	1,085	1639	V-A
9	MULHACEN	SPAIN	11,428	3,483	1840	V-A
10	MONT AIGUILLE	FRANCE	6,880	2,097	1492	V-A
11	LA MEIJE	FRANCE	13,068	3,983	1877	V-A
12	BARRE DES ECRINS	FRANCE	13,458	4,102	1864	V-A
13	MONT PELVOUX	FRANCE	12,842	3,914	1828	V-A
14	MONTE VISO	ITALY	12,602	3,841	1861	V-A
15	MT. ETNA	SICILY	10,903	3,323	450 B.C.	V-A
16	MT. OLYMPOS	GREECE	9,571	2,917	1913	V-A
17	MT. KORAB	MACEDONIA	9,069	2,764	UNKN	V-A
18	MUSALA	BULGARIA	9,596	2,925	UNKN	V-A
19	MOLDOVEANU	ROMANIA	8,346	2,544	UNKN	V-A
20	RYSY	POLAND	8,199	2,499	1840	V-A
21	GERLACHOVSKY	SLOVAKIA	8,711	2,655	1834	V-A
22	ZUGSPITZE	GERMANY	9,718	2,962	1820	V-A
23	PICO DE ANETO	SPAIN	11,168	3,404	1842	V-H
24	MONT BLANC	FRANCE – ITALY	15,782	4,810	1786	V-C/G
25	MATTERHORN	SWITZERLAND-ITALY	14,692	4,478	1865	V-C/F
26	MONTE ROSA-DUF.	SWITZERLAND	15,204	4,634	1855	V-C/F
27	EIGER	SWITZERLAND	13,025	3,970	1858	V-C/E
28	GROSSGLOCKNER	AUSTRIA	12,457	3,797	1799	V-C
29	MARMOLADA	ITALY	10,965	3,342	1864	V-C/D
30	TRIGLAV	SLOVENIA	9,396	2,863	1778	V-C

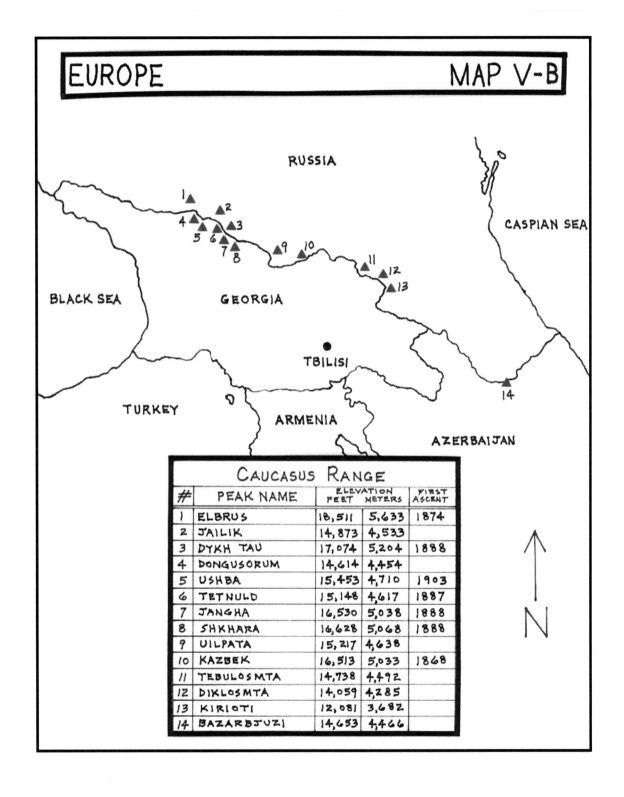

EUROPE   MAP V-B

RUSSIA

CASPIAN SEA

BLACK SEA

GEORGIA

TBILISI

TURKEY

ARMENIA

AZERBAIJAN

N

#	PEAK NAME	ELEVATION FEET	METERS	FIRST ASCENT
1	ELBRUS	18,511	5,633	1874
2	JAILIK	14,873	4,533	
3	DYKH TAU	17,074	5,204	1888
4	DONGUSORUM	14,614	4,454	
5	USHBA	15,453	4,710	1903
6	TETNULD	15,148	4,617	1887
7	JANGHA	16,530	5,038	1888
8	SHKHARA	16,628	5,068	1888
9	UILPATA	15,217	4,638	
10	KAZBEK	16,513	5,033	1868
11	TEBULOSMTA	14,738	4,492	
12	DIKLOSMTA	14,059	4,285	
13	KIRIOTI	12,081	3,682	
14	BAZARBJUZI	14,653	4,466	

CAUCASUS RANGE

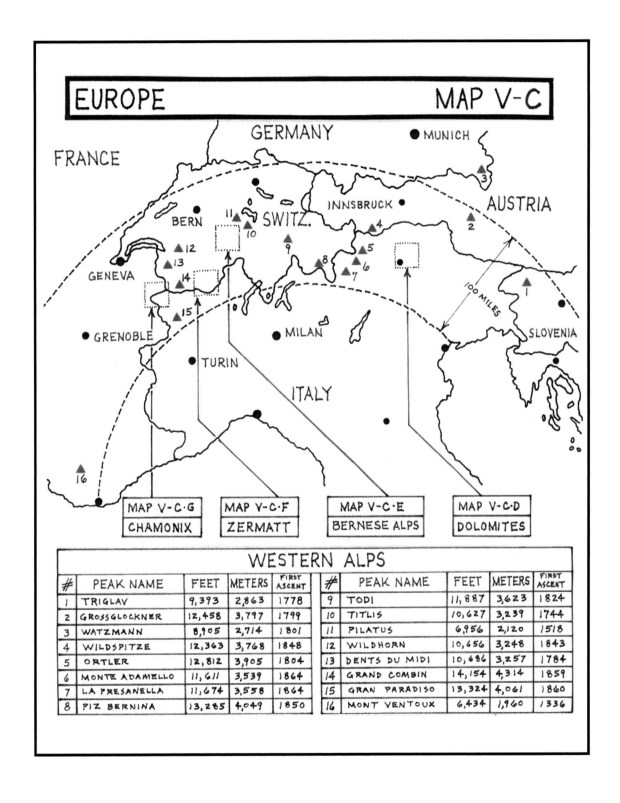

EUROPE — MAP V-C

WESTERN ALPS

#	PEAK NAME	FEET	METERS	FIRST ASCENT	#	PEAK NAME	FEET	METERS	FIRST ASCENT
1	TRIGLAV	9,393	2,863	1778	9	TODI	11,887	3,623	1824
2	GROSSGLOCKNER	12,458	3,797	1799	10	TITLIS	10,627	3,239	1744
3	WATZMANN	8,905	2,714	1801	11	PILATUS	6,956	2,120	1518
4	WILDSPITZE	12,363	3,768	1848	12	WILDHORN	10,456	3,248	1843
5	ORTLER	12,812	3,905	1804	13	DENTS DU MIDI	10,686	3,257	1784
6	MONTE ADAMELLO	11,611	3,539	1864	14	GRAND COMBIN	14,154	4,314	1859
7	LA PRESANELLA	11,674	3,558	1864	15	GRAN PARADISO	13,324	4,061	1860
8	PIZ BERNINA	13,285	4,049	1850	16	MONT VENTOUX	6,434	1,960	1336

MAP V-C-G CHAMONIX

MAP V-C-F ZERMATT

MAP V-C-E BERNESE ALPS

MAP V-C-D DOLOMITES

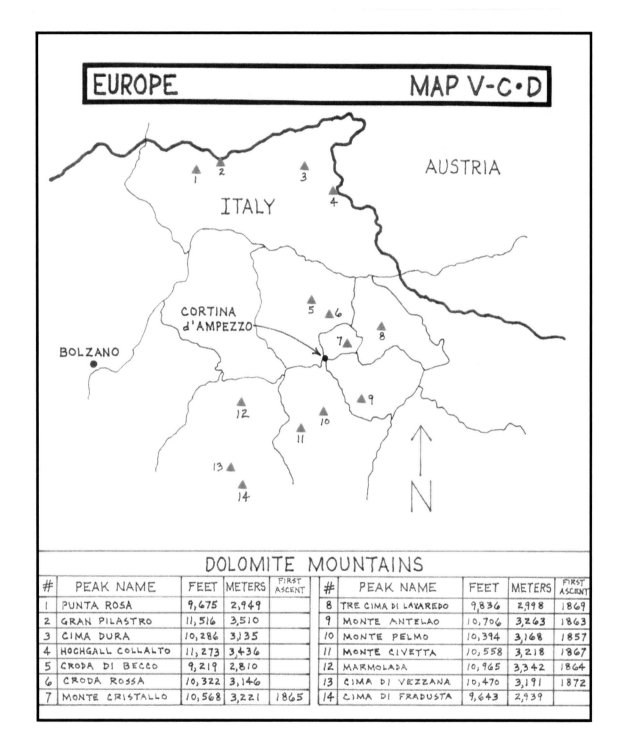

DOLOMITE MOUNTAINS

#	PEAK NAME	FEET	METERS	FIRST ASCENT	#	PEAK NAME	FEET	METERS	FIRST ASCENT
1	PUNTA ROSA	9,675	2,949		8	TRE CIMA DI LAVAREDO	9,836	2,998	1869
2	GRAN PILASTRO	11,516	3,510		9	MONTE ANTELAO	10,706	3,263	1863
3	CIMA DURA	10,286	3,135		10	MONTE PELMO	10,394	3,168	1857
4	HOCHGALL COLLALTO	11,273	3,436		11	MONTE CIVETTA	10,558	3,218	1867
5	CRODA DI BECCO	9,219	2,810		12	MARMOLADA	10,965	3,342	1864
6	CRODA ROSSA	10,322	3,146		13	CIMA DI VEZZANA	10,470	3,191	1872
7	MONTE CRISTALLO	10,568	3,221	1865	14	CIMA DI FRADUSTA	9,643	2,939	

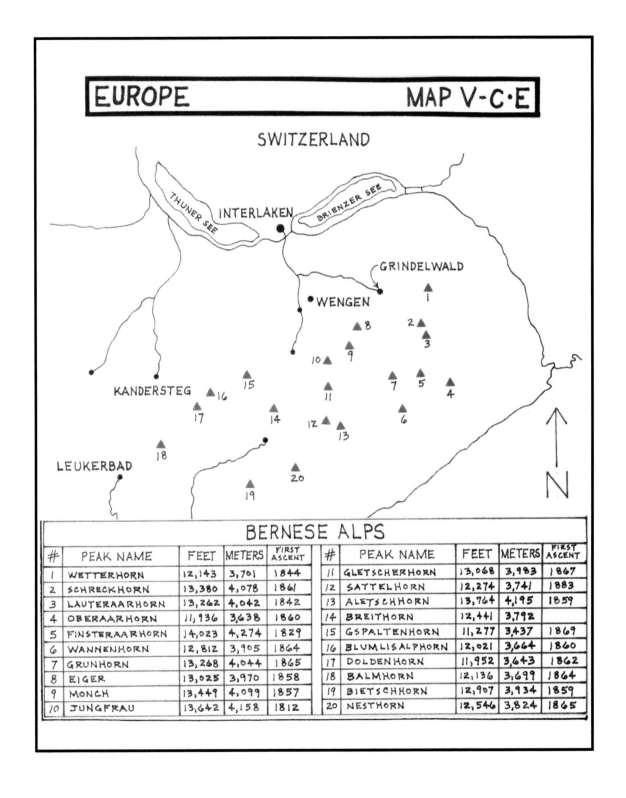

EUROPE   MAP V-C·E

SWITZERLAND

THUNER SEE   INTERLAKEN   BRIENZER SEE

GRINDELWALD

WENGEN

KANDERSTEG

LEUKERBAD

N

BERNESE ALPS

#	PEAK NAME	FEET	METERS	FIRST ASCENT	#	PEAK NAME	FEET	METERS	FIRST ASCENT
1	WETTERHORN	12,143	3,701	1844	11	GLETSCHERHORN	13,068	3,983	1867
2	SCHRECKHORN	13,380	4,078	1861	12	SATTELHORN	12,274	3,741	1883
3	LAUTERAARHORN	13,262	4,042	1842	13	ALETSCHHORN	13,764	4,195	1859
4	OBERAARHORN	11,936	3,638	1860	14	BREITHORN	12,441	3,792	
5	FINSTERAARHORN	14,023	4,274	1829	15	GSPALTENHORN	11,277	3,437	1869
6	WANNENHORN	12,812	3,905	1864	16	BLUMLISALPHORN	12,021	3,664	1860
7	GRUNHORN	13,268	4,044	1865	17	DOLDENHORN	11,952	3,643	1862
8	EIGER	13,025	3,970	1858	18	BALMHORN	12,136	3,699	1864
9	MONCH	13,449	4,099	1857	19	BIETSCHHORN	12,907	3,934	1859
10	JUNGFRAU	13,642	4,158	1812	20	NESTHORN	12,546	3,824	1865

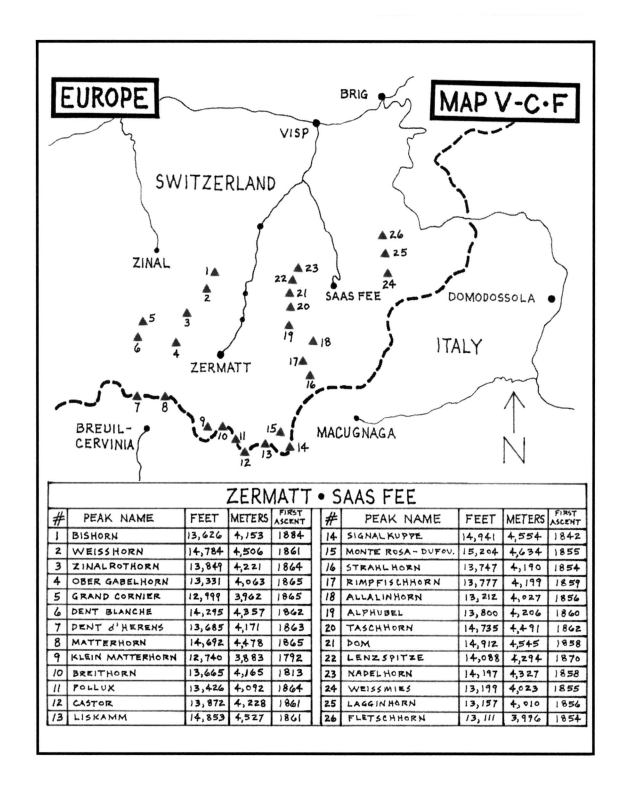

ZERMATT • SAAS FEE

#	PEAK NAME	FEET	METERS	FIRST ASCENT	#	PEAK NAME	FEET	METERS	FIRST ASCENT
1	BISHORN	13,626	4,153	1884	14	SIGNALKUPPE	14,941	4,554	1842
2	WEISSHORN	14,784	4,506	1861	15	MONTE ROSA – DUFOU.	15,204	4,634	1855
3	ZINALROTHORN	13,849	4,221	1864	16	STRAHLHORN	13,747	4,190	1854
4	OBER GABELHORN	13,331	4,063	1865	17	RIMPFISCHHORN	13,777	4,199	1859
5	GRAND CORNIER	12,999	3,962	1865	18	ALLALINHORN	13,212	4,027	1856
6	DENT BLANCHE	14,295	4,357	1862	19	ALPHUBEL	13,800	4,206	1860
7	DENT d'HERENS	13,685	4,171	1863	20	TASCHHORN	14,735	4,491	1862
8	MATTERHORN	14,692	4,478	1865	21	DOM	14,912	4,545	1858
9	KLEIN MATTERHORN	12,740	3,883	1792	22	LENZSPITZE	14,088	4,294	1870
10	BREITHORN	13,665	4,165	1813	23	NADELHORN	14,197	4,327	1858
11	POLLUX	13,426	4,092	1864	24	WEISSMIES	13,199	4,023	1855
12	CASTOR	13,872	4,228	1861	25	LAGGINHORN	13,157	4,010	1856
13	LISKAMM	14,853	4,527	1861	26	FLETSCHHORN	13,111	3,996	1854

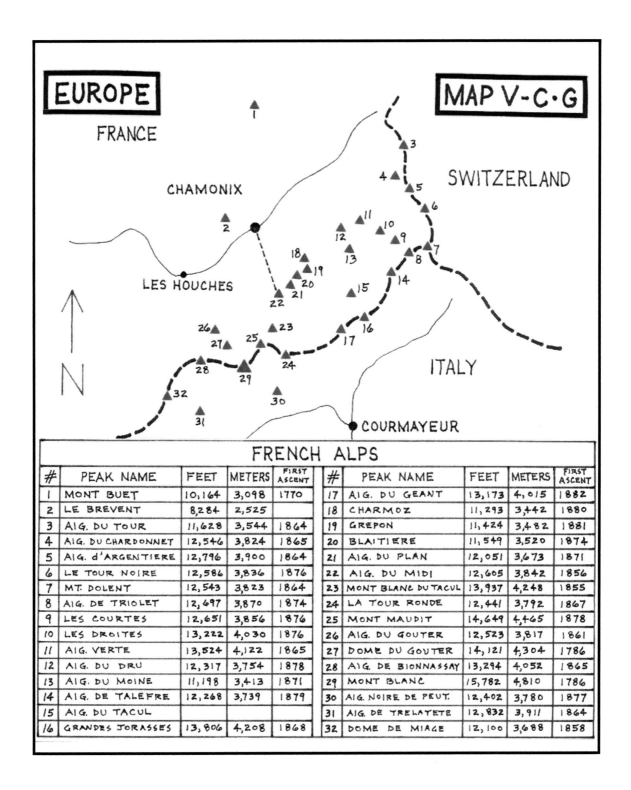

EUROPE

FRANCE

MAP V-C·G

CHAMONIX

SWITZERLAND

LES HOUCHES

N

ITALY

COURMAYEUR

FRENCH ALPS

#	PEAK NAME	FEET	METERS	FIRST ASCENT	#	PEAK NAME	FEET	METERS	FIRST ASCENT
1	MONT BUET	10,164	3,098	1770	17	AIG. DU GEANT	13,173	4,015	1882
2	LE BREVENT	8,284	2,525		18	CHARMOZ	11,293	3,442	1880
3	AIG. DU TOUR	11,628	3,544	1864	19	GREPON	11,424	3,482	1881
4	AIG. DU CHARDONNET	12,546	3,824	1865	20	BLAITIERE	11,549	3,520	1874
5	AIG. d'ARGENTIERE	12,796	3,900	1864	21	AIG. DU PLAN	12,051	3,673	1871
6	LE TOUR NOIRE	12,586	3,836	1876	22	AIG. DU MIDI	12,605	3,842	1856
7	MT. DOLENT	12,543	3,823	1864	23	MONT BLANC DU TACUL	13,937	4,248	1855
8	AIG. DE TRIOLET	12,697	3,870	1874	24	LA TOUR RONDE	12,441	3,792	1867
9	LES COURTES	12,651	3,856	1876	25	MONT MAUDIT	14,649	4,465	1878
10	LES DROITES	13,222	4,030	1876	26	AIG. DU GOUTER	12,523	3,817	1861
11	AIG. VERTE	13,524	4,122	1865	27	DOME DU GOUTER	14,121	4,304	1786
12	AIG. DU DRU	12,317	3,754	1878	28	AIG. DE BIONNASSAY	13,294	4,052	1865
13	AIG. DU MOINE	11,198	3,413	1871	29	MONT BLANC	15,782	4,810	1786
14	AIG. DE TALEFRE	12,268	3,739	1879	30	AIG. NOIRE DE PEUT.	12,402	3,780	1877
15	AIG. DU TACUL				31	AIG. DE TRELATETE	12,832	3,911	1864
16	GRANDES JORASSES	13,806	4,208	1868	32	DOME DE MIAGE	12,100	3,688	1858

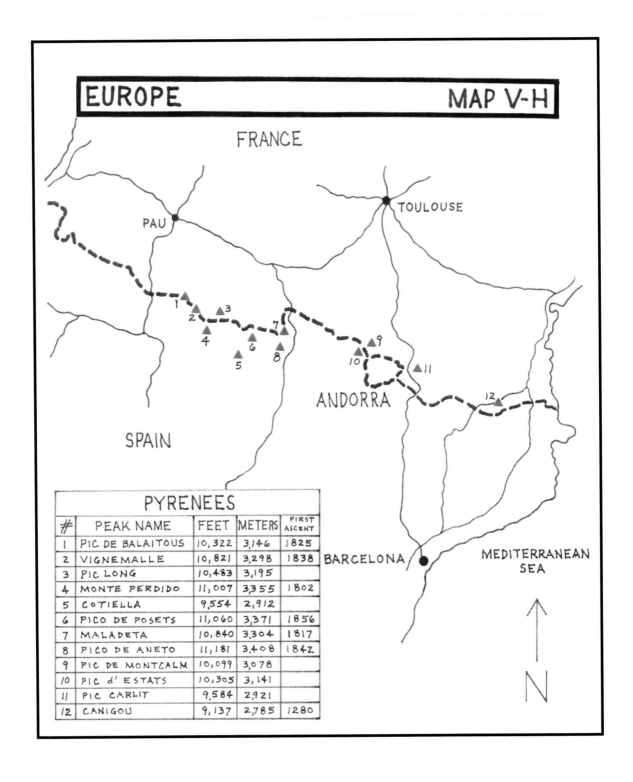

EUROPE   MAP V-H

FRANCE

TOULOUSE

PAU

SPAIN

ANDORRA

BARCELONA

MEDITERRANEAN
SEA

↑
N

PYRENEES

#	PEAK NAME	FEET	METERS	FIRST ASCENT
1	PIC DE BALAITOUS	10,322	3,146	1825
2	VIGNEMALLE	10,821	3,298	1838
3	PIC LONG	10,483	3,195	
4	MONTE PERDIDO	11,007	3,355	1802
5	COTIELLA	9,554	2,912	
6	PICO DE POSETS	11,060	3,371	1856
7	MALADETA	10,840	3,304	1817
8	PICO DE ANETO	11,181	3,408	1842
9	PIC DE MONTCALM	10,099	3,078	
10	PIC d' ESTATS	10,305	3,141	
11	PIC CARLIT	9,584	2,921	
12	CANIGOU	9,137	2,785	1280

EUROPE: The 25 Highest Peaks

RANK and PEAK NAME	ELEVATION FEET·METERS	LOCATION	FIRST ASCENT DATE	EXPEDITION	SUMMIT CLIMBERS
1 Mt. Elbrus – W	18,511·5,642	Caucasus Mtns.	July 28, 1874	British	F. Gardiner
2 Mt. Elbrus – E	18,442·5,621	Caucasus Mtns.	July 31, 1868	British	F. Devouassoud
3 Dych Tau	17,077·5,205	Caucasus Mtns.	July 24, 1888	British	A.F. Mummery
4 Shkhara	17,064·5,201	Caucasus Mtns.	Sept. 7, 1888	British	U. Almer J.G. Cockin C. Roth
5 Koshtan Tau	16,903·5,152	Caucasus Mtns.	Aug. 9, 1889	British	C. Jossi
6 Jangi Tau	16,598·5,059	Caucasus Mtns.	1888	British	U. Almer
7 Dzhangi Tau	16,565·5,049	Caucasus Mtns.	1888	British	U. Almer
8 Kazbek	16,559·5,047	Caucasus Mtns.	July 1, 1888	British	F. Devouassoud D.W. Freshfield A.W. Moore C.C. Tucker
9 Pushkin	16,513·5,033	Caucasus Mtns.			
10 Katyn Tau	16,356·4,985	Caucasus Mtns.	1888	British	U. Almer Holder C. Roth H. Woolley
11 Pik Rustaveli	16,274·4,960	Caucasus Mtns.			
12 Mishirgi	16,149·4,920	Caucasus Mtns.	1934		W. Frei H. Graf L. Saladin
13 Kunjum Mishirgi	16,011·4,880	Caucasus Mtns.			
14 Gestola	15,946·4,860	Caucasus Mtns.	1886	British	F. Andenmatten A. Burgener C.T. Dent W.F. Donkin

EUROPE The 25 Highest Peaks (continued)

RANK and PEAK NAME	ELEVATION FEET·METERS	LOCATION	FIRST ASCENT DATE	EXPEDITION	SUMMIT CLIMBERS
15 Tetnuld	15,923·4,853	Caucasus Mtns.	1887	British	Decky M. Devouassoud D.W. Freshfield
16 Mont Blanc	15,782·4,810	France-Italy	Aug. 8, 1786	French	Jacques Balmat Dr. M.G. Paccard
17 Gimaraikhokh	15,677·4,778	Caucasus Mtns.			
18 Mont Blanc de Courmayeur	15,577·4,748	Italy	1893	German	P. Gussfeldt et al
19 Ushba – S	15,454·4,710	Caucasus Mtns.	July 26, 1903		A. Schulze et al
20 Ushba – N	15,410·4,697	Caucasus Mtns.	1888	British	C. Almer
21 Uilpata	15,217·4,638	Caucasus Mtns.			
22 Monte Rosa-Dufourspitze	15,204·4,634	Switzerland	Aug. 1, 1855	British	V. Lauener J.G. Smyth A. Smyth E.J. Stephenson J. Zumtaugwald M. Zumtaugwald
23 Monte Rosa-Nordend	15,122·4,609	Switzerland	1861	British	Binder Edward Buxton T.F. Cowell Michel Payot
24 Monte Rosa-Zumsteinspitze	14,971·4,563	Italy	Aug. 1, 1820		Joseph Zumstein et al
25 Monte Rosa-Signalkuppe	14,948·4,556	Italy	1842		Giovanni Gnifetti 7 guides and porters

Selected Bibliography — Europe

Of the numerous books, journals, newspaper and magazine articles, and internet sites that have been used in the research for this book, the author is particularly indebted to the following sources:

Alexander, Henry. *The Cairngorms.* The Scottish Mountaineering Club, 1928.

Anker, Daniel – Editor. *Eiger – The Vertical Arena.* The Mountaineers, 2000.

Ardito, Stefano. *Mont Blanc – Discovery and Conquest of the Giant of the Alps.* The Mountaineers, 1996.

Ardito, Stefano. *Tales of Mountaineering.* White Star Publishers, 2000.

Band, George. *SUMMIT – 150 years of the Alpine Club.* Collins, 2006.

Barnes, Malcolm. *The Mountain World – 1956/57.* Harper & Brothers Publishers, 1957.

Barnes, Malcolm. *The Mountain World 1962/63.* George Allen and Unwin Ltd., 1964.

Barnes, Malcolm. *The Mountain World 1964/65.* George Allen and Unwin Ltd., 1966.

Barnes, Malcolm. *The Mountain World 1958/59.* George Allen & Unwin Ltd., 1958.

Bates, Robert H. *The Love of Mountains Is Best – Climbs and Travels From K2 To Kathmandu.* Peter E. Randall Publisher, 1994.

Beattie, Andrew. *The Alps – A Cultural History.* Oxford University Press, 2006.

Bell, J.H.B. *A Progress in Mountaineering – Scottish Hills to Alpine Peaks.* Oliver and Boyd, 1950.

Bender, Friedrich. *Classic Climbs in the Caucasus.* Diadem Books, 1992.

Bennet, Donald – Editor. *The Munros – Hillwalkers' Guide.* Volume One. The Scottish Mountaineering Trust, 1999.

Bensen, Joe. *Souvenirs From High Places – A History of Mountaineering Photography.* The Mountaineers, 1998.

Birkett, Bill. *Classic Rock Climbs in Great Britain.* The Oxford Illustrated Press, 1986.

Bonatti, Walter. *The Great Days.* Victor Gollancz Ltd., 1974.

Bonatti, Walter. *On The Heights.* Rupert Hart-Davis. 1964.

Bonatti, Walter. *The Mountains of My Life.* The Modern Library, 2001.

Bonington, Chris – General Editor. *Heroic Climbs – A Celebration of World Mountaineering.* The Mountaineers, 1994.

Bonington, Chris. *The Next Horizon.* Victor Gollancz Ltd., 1973.

Bonington, Chris. *Mountaineer – Thirty Years of Climbing on the World's Great Peaks.* Sierra Club Books, 1990.

Bonington, Chris. *Quest For Adventure – 21 Stories of the Men and Women Who Challenged Oceans, Mountains, Deserts, Snow and Space.* Clarkson N. Potter, Inc., 1981.

Bonington, Chris. *The Climbers – A History of Mountaineering.* Hodder & Stoughton, 1992.

Braham, Trevor. *When the Alps Cast Their Spell – Mountaineers of the Alpine Golden Age.* In Pinn, 2004.

Brett, David. *High Level – The Alps from End to End.* Victor Gollancz Ltd., 1983.

Brown, Rebecca A. *Women On High – Pioneers of Mountaineering.* Appalachian Mountain Club Books, 2002.

Brown, Joe. *The Hard Years.* Victor Gollancz Ltd., 1972.

Burlingham, Frederick. *How to Become An Alpinist.* T. Werner Laurie, Ltd., 1910.

Calvert, Harry. *Smythe's Mountains – The Climbs of F.S. Smythe.* Victor Gollancz Ltd., 1985.

Carter, H. Adams – Editor. *The American Alpine Journal 1964.* Volume 14, Number 1, Issue 38. The American Alpine Club, 1964.

Cassin, Riccardo. *50 Years of Alpinism.* Diadem Books Ltd., 1981.

Clark, Ronald. *The Early Alpine Guides.* Charles Scribner's Sons, 1950.

Clark, Ronald. *The Victorian Mountaineers.* Charles T. Branford Company, 1954.

Clark, Ronald W. *A Picture History of Mountaineering.* The MacMillan Company, 1956.

Clark, Ronald W. Pyatt, Edward C. *Mountaineering in Britian – A History From the Earliest Times to the Present Day.* Phoenix House Ltd., 1957.

Clark, Ronald W. *An Eccentric In The Alps – The Story of W.A.B. Coolidge, the Great Victorian Mountaineer.* Museum Press, 1959.

Clark, Ronald W. *The Day The Rope Broke – The Triumphant First Ascent of the Matterhorn – and Its Strange and Tragic Aftermath.* Harcourt, Brace & World, Inc., 1965.

Clark, Ronald W. *The Alps.* Alfred A. Knopf, 1973.

Clark, Ronald W. M*en, Myths & Mountains – The Life & Times of Mountaineering.* Thomas Y. Crowell Company, 1976.

Cleare, John. *Distant Mountains – Encounters With the World's Greatest Mountains.* Discovery Channel Books, 1998.

Cliff, Peter. *Ski Mountaineering.* Pacific Search Press, 1987.

Collie, Norman. *From the Himalayas to Skye.* Ripping Yarns, 2003.

Conefrey, Mick and Jordan, Tim. *Mountain Men – A History of the Remarkable Climbers and Determined Eccentrics Who First Scaled the World's Most Famous Peaks.* Da Capo Press, 2001.

Conway, Sir Martin. *The Alps.* Adam and Charles Black, 1910.

Coolidge, W.A.B. *Alpine Studies.* Longmans, Green and Co., 1912.

Corbett, Edmund V. *Great True Mountain Stories.* Arco Publications Limited, 1957.

Curran, Jim. *High Achiever – The Life and Climbs of Chris Bonington.* The Mountaineers, 1999.

Damilano, Francois. *Mont Blanc 4808m – 5 Routes to the Summit.* JM Editions, 2004.

Da Silva, Rachel – Editor. *LEADING OUT – Women Climbers Reaching For The Top.* Seal Press, 1992.

De Beer, Sir Gavin. *Early Travelers in the Alps.* October House, Inc., 1967.

Desmaison, Rene. *Total Alpinism.* Granada, 1982.

Diemberger, Kurt. *Spirits of the Air.* The Mountaineers, 1994.

Diemberger, Kurt. *Summits & Secrets.* George Allen & Unwin Ltd., 1971.

Douglas, John Scott. *Summits of Adventure – The Story of Famous Mountain Climbs and Mountain Climbers.* Dodd, Mead & Company, 1954.

Dumler, Helmut. Burkhardt, Willi P. *The High Mountain of the Alps.* Diadem Books, The Mountaineers, 1993.

Engel, Claire Eliane. *Mountaineering in the Alps – An Historical Survey.* George Allen & Unwin Ltd., 1971.

Engel, Claire Elaine. *Mont Blanc – An Anthology.* Rand McNally & Company, 1965.

Engel, Claire Eliane. *A History of Mountaineering in the Alps.* Greenwood Press, 1977.

Engel, Claire Eliane. *They Came to the Hills.* George Allen & Unwin Ltd., 1952.

Evans, Charles. *On Climbing.* The Countryman Press, 1955.

Faux, Ronald. *High Ambition – A Biography of Reinhold Messner.* Victor Gollancz Ltd., 1982.

Fleming, Fergus. *Killing Dragons – The Conquest of the Alps.* Atlantic Monthly Press, 2000.

Freshfield, Douglas W. *Below the Snow Line.* Constable and Company Limited, 1923.

Freshfield, Douglas W. *Italian Alps.* Basil Blackwell Oxford, 1937.

Frison-Roche, Roger. Tairraz, Pierre. *Mont Blanc and the Seven Valleys.* Arthaud, 1961.

Frison-Roche, Roger. Jouty, Sylvain. *A History of Mountain Climbing.* Flammarion, 1996.

Gervasutti, Giusto. *Gervasutti's Climbs.* The Mountaineers, 1979.
Gillman, Peter & Leni. *The Wildest Dream – The Biography of George Mallory.* The Mountaineers, 2000.

Girdlestone, Rev. A.G. *The High Alps Without Guides: Being A Narrative of Adventures in Switzerland.* Longmans, Green, and Co., 1870.

Goedeke, Richard. *The Alpine 4000m Peaks by the Classic Routes.* Diadem Books, 1991.

Gos, Francois. *Zermatt and its Valley.* Cassell and Company, Ltd., 1926.

Gos, Charles. *Alpine Tragedy.* Charles Scribner's Sons, 1948.

Green, Stewart M. *Rock Climbing Europe – More than 1,000 of Europe's Best Climbs.* Falcon Guide, 2006.

Green, Dudley. *Because It's There – The Life of George Mallory.* Tempus, 2005.

Hackett, June. Conrad, Ric. *Climb to Glory – The Adventures of Bill Hackett.* K2 Books, 2003.

Hankinson, Alan. *The Mountain Men – A History of Early Rock Climbing in North Wales – From Its Beginning to 1914.* Mara Books, 2004.

Hankinson, Alan. *Geoffrey Winthrop Young – Poet, Mountaineer, Educator.* Hodder & Stoughton, 1995.

Harlin, John III. *The Eiger Obsession – Facing the Mountain That Killed My Father.* Simon & Schuster, 2007.

Harrer, Heinrich. *The White Spider – The Story of the North Face of the Eiger.* Hart-Davis, MacGibbon, 1976.

Hattingh, Garth. *CLIMBING – The World's Best Sites.* Rizzoli, 1999.

Hiebeler, Toni. *North Face in Winter – The First Winter Climb of the Eiger's North Face.* J.B. Lippincott Company, 1963.

Hunt, John. *Life Is Meeting.* Hodder & Stoughton, 1978.

Huntford, Roland. *Two Planks and a Passion – The Dramatic History of Skiing.* Continuum, 2008.

Irving, R.L.G. *The Alps.* B.T. Batsford, 1939.

Irving, R.L.G. *A History of British Mountaineering.* B.T. Batsford Ltd., 1955.

Irving, R.L.G. *Ten Great Mountains.* J.M. Dent & Sons, 1947.

Irving, R.L.G. *The Romance of Mountaineering.* J.M. Dent and Sons, Ltd., 1935.

King, Tom. *In the Shadow of the Giants – Mountain Ascents, Past and Present.* A.S. Barnes & Company, 1981.

Klucker, Christian. *Adventures of an Alpine Guide.* John Murray, 1932.

Lanz, Heidi. De Meester, Liliane. *Ulrich Inderbinen – As Old As The Century.* Rotten Verlag, 1997.

Lee, Stephen. *The Alps.* B.T. Batsford Ltd., 1991.

Long, John – Editor. *The High Lonesome – Epic Solo Climbing Stories.* Falcon, 1999.

Longstaff, Tom. *This My Voyage.* Charles Scribner's Sons, 1950.

Lukan, Karl – Editor. *The Alps and Alpinism.* Coward-McCann, Inc., 1968

Lunn, Arnold. *Zermatt and the Valais.* Hollis & Carter, 1955.

Lunn, Sir Arnold. *Matterhorn Centenary.* Rand McNally & Company, 1965.

Lyall, Alan. *The First Descent of the Matterhorn – A Bibliographical Guide to the 1865 Accident & Its Aftermath.* Gomer, 1997.

MacInnes, Hamish. *The Price of Adventure.* The Mountaineers, 1987.

Madge, Tim. *The Last Hero – Bill Tilman: A Biography of the Explorer.* The Mountaineers, 1995.

McDonald, Bernadette. *Freedom Climbers.* Rocky Mountain Books, 2011.

McDonald, Bernadette and Amatt, John – Editors. *Voices From The Summit – The World's Great Mountaineers on the Future of Climbing.* Adventure Press, 2000.

McKeating, Carl. Crolla, Rachel. Europe's *High Points – Reaching the Summit of Every Country in Europe.* Cicerone, 2009.

McLewin, Will. *In Monte Viso's Horizon – Climbing All The Alpine 4000m Peaks.* Ernest Press, 1991.

Meade, C.F. *Approach to the Hills.* John Murray, 1940.

Messner, Reinhold. *The Big Walls – From the North Face of the Eiger to the South Face of Dhaulagiri.* The Mountaineers Books, 2001.

Messner, Reinhold. Hofler, Horst. *Hermann Buhl – Climbing Without Compromise.*
  The Mountaineers Books, 2000.

Milne, Malcolm – Editor. *The Book of Modern Mountaineering.* G.P. Putnam's Sons, 1968.

Milner, C. Douglas. *Mont Blanc and the Aiguilles.* Robert Hale Limited, 1955.

Moran, Martin. *The 4000m Peaks of the Alps.* Alpine Club, 2007.

Moran, Martin. *The Munros in Winter – 277 Summits in 83 Days.* David & Charles, 1988.

Moran, Martin. *Alps 4000 – 75 Peaks in 52 Days.* David & Charles, 1994.

Morin, Nea. *A Woman's Reach – Mountaineering Memoirs.* Dodd, Mead & Company, 1968.

Mummery, A.F. *My Climbs in the Alps and Caucasus.* Quarterman Publications, Inc., 1974.

Noyce, Wilfrid. *Scholar Mountaineers – Pioneers of Parnassus.* Roy Publishers, 1950.

Olsen, Jack. *The Climb Up to Hell.* Harper & Row, 1962.

Patey, Tom. *One Man's Mountains.* Victor Gollancz Ltd., 1975.

Paulcke, Wilhelm. Dumler, Helmut. *Hazards in Mountaineering.* Oxford University Press, 1973.

Perren, Beat H. *Faszination Matterhorn.* Stadler Verlagsgesellschaft Mbh, 1988.

Perrin, Jim. *The Villain – The Life of Don Whillans.* Hutchinson, 2005.

Poole, Michael Crawford. *The Love of Mountains.* Crescent Books, 1980.

Putnam, William Lowell. *The Mountaineer's Pontiff – Achille Ratti.* AuthorHouse, 2006.

Putnam, William L. *A Tale of Two Passes – An Inquiry into Certain Alpine Literature.*
  3 Light Technology, 2008.

Pyatt, Edward C. *Mountains of Britain.* B.T. Batsford Ltd., 1966.

Pyatt, Edward. *The Passage of the Alps.* Robert Hale, 1984.

Pye, David. *George Leigh Mallory – A Memoir By David Pye.* Orchid Press, 2002.

Rebuffat, Gaston. *Men and the Matterhorn.* Oxford University Press, 1973.

Rebuffat, Gaston. *On Ice and Snow and Rock.* Oxford University Press, 1971.

Rebuffat, Gaston. *On Snow and Rock.* Oxford University Press, 1965.

Rebuffat, Gaston. *The Mont Blanc Massif – The 100 Finest Routes.* The Mountaineers, 1996.

Rebuffat, Gaston. *Between Heaven and Earth.* Kaye & Ward, 1970.

Rebuffat, Gaston. *Starlight and Storm – The Ascent of Six Great North Faces of the Alps.* E.P. Dutton and Company, Inc., 1957.

Reinisch, Gertrude. *Wanda Rutkiewicz – A Caravan of Dreams.* Carreg, 2000.

Rey, Guido. Irving, R.L.G. – Editor. *The Matterhorn.* Basil Blackwell, 1949.

Reynolds, Kev. *Mountains of the Pyrenees.* Cicerone, 1982.

Ring, Jim. *How the English Made the Alps.* John Murray, 2000.

Roberts, Eric. *Welzenbach's Climbs.* The Mountaineers, 1980.

Robertson, David. *George Mallory.* Faber and Faber, 1969.

Roth, Arthur. *Eiger – Wall of Death.* W.W. Norton & Company, 1982.

Salkeld, Audrey. Bermudez, Jose Luis. *On the Edge of Europe – Mountaineering in the Caucasus.* The Mountaineers, 1993.

Salkeld, Audrey and Bermudez, Jose Luis. *On The Edge of Europe – Mountaineering in the Caucasus.* The Mountaineers, 1993.

Scott, Doug. *Big Wall Climbing – Development, Techniques and Aids.* Oxford University Press, 1974.

Sedeen, Margaret – Editor. *Mountain Worlds.* The National Geographic, 1988.

Sella, Vittorio. *Summit.* Aperture, 1999.

Shipton, Eric. *Mountain Conquest.* American Heritage Publishing Co., 1966.

Shipton, Eric. *Upon That Mountain*. Hodder & Stoughton, 1944.

Shoumatoff, Nicholas & Nina. *The Alps – Europe's Mountain Heart*. The University of
    Michigan Press, 2001.

Smith, George Alan. Smith, Carol D. *The Armchair Mountaineer*. Pitman Publishing Corporation, 1968.

Smythe, F.S. *The Spirit of the Hills*. Hodder & Stoughton, 1935.

Smythe, F.S. *Edward Whymper*. Hodder and Stoughton, 1940.

Smythe, F.S. *British Mountaineers*. Collins, 1946.

Stainforth, Gordon. *Eyes to the Hills – The Mountain Landscape of Britian*. Constable, 1991.

Steele, Peter. *Eric Shipton: Everest & Beyond*. The Mountaineers, 1998.

Stephen, Leslie. *The Playground of Europe*. Basil Blackwell Oxford, 1946.

Styles, Showell. *On Top of the World – An Illustrated History of Mountaineering and
    Mountaineers*. The Macmillan Company, 1967.

Styles, Showell. *Rock and Rope*. Faber and Faber, 1967.

Terray, Lionel. *The Borders of the Impossible – From the Alps to Annapurna*.
    Doubleday & Company, 1964.

Terray, Lionel. *Conquistadors of the Useless – From the Alps to Annapurna*. Victor Gollancz Ltd., 1963.

Tissot, Roger. *Mont Blanc*. The Medici Society Limited, 1924.

Thorington, J. Monroe. *A Survey of Early American Ascents In the Alps*. American
    Alpine Club, 1943.

Tyndall, John. *Hours of Exercise in the Alps*. D. Appleton and Company, 1897.

Ullman, James Ramsey. *Straight Up – John Harlin: The Life and Death of a
    Mountaineer*. Doubleday & Company, Inc., 1968.

Underhill, Miriam. *Give Me The Hills*. The Chatham Press, Inc., 1971.

Unsworth, Walter. *Because It Is There – Famous Mountaineers 1840 – 1940*. Victor Gollancz Ltd., 1968.

Unsworth, Walt. *Hold the Heights – The Foundations of Mountaineering*. The Mountaineers, 1994.

Unsworth, Walter. *Matterhorn Man – The Life and Adventures of Edward Whymper*. Victor Gollancz Ltd., 1965.

Unsworth, Walter. *Tiger in the Snow – The Life and Adventures of A.F. Mummery*. Victor Gollancz Ltd., 1967.

Unsworth, Walt. *Savage Snows – The Story of Mont Blanc*. Hodder & Stoughton, 1986.

Unsworth, Walt – Editor. *Peaks, Passes and Glaciers*. The Mountaineers, 1981.

Venables, Stephen. *First Ascent – Pioneering Mountain Climbs*. Firefly Books, 2008.

Vermeulen, James P. – Editor. *Mountain Journeys – Stories of Climbers and Their Climbs*. The Overlook Press, 1989.

Ward, Michael – Editor. *The Mountaineer's Companion*. Eyre & Spottiswoode, 1966.

Watson, Adam. *The Cairngorms*. The Scottish Mountaineering Trust, 1992.

Weir, Thomas. *Camps and Climbs in Arctic Norway*. Cassell and Company Ltd., 1953.

Wells, Colin. *A Brief History of British Mountaineering*. The Mountain Heritage Trust, 2001.

Whillans, Don and Ormerod, Alick. *Don Whillans – Portrait of a Mountaineer*. Heinemann, 1971.

Whymper, Edward. *Scrambles Amongst the Alps in the Years 1860 – 69*. John Murray, 1871.

Williams, Cicely. *Zermatt Saga*. George Allen and Unwin Ltd., 1964.

Willis, Clint. *The Boys of Everest – Chris Bonington and the Tragedy of Climbing's Greatest Generation*. Carroll & Graf Publishers, 2006.

Wills, Alfred. *Wanderings Among the High Alps*. Basil Blackwell Oxford, 1937.

Six

NORTH AMERICA

McKinley to Mexico

Years 1175 to 2011

"In justification, I would argue (and still do) that it is in the mountains that I have pursued dreams, grown confident, learned to survive, acquired a love out of the wilderness, and shared special moments with kindred spirits. My bond with high places has defined my professional and personal life. Mountains are my spiritual home; more than anything else, they have shaped who I am and how I relate to the world and those who share it with me. The rationalizations are not mine alone, of course; most climbers voice similar beliefs to justify our pastime."

2003
Dr Thomas F. Hornbein
American mountaineer
First ascent of Mount Everest's West Ridge in 1963
(1930 –)

NORTH AMERICA

O f the world's seven continents, North America has the widest range of mountaineering opportunities. Varied terrain, different climatic conditions, and easy accessibility to many mountain ranges and peaks provide all types of climbing experiences which include:

- High-altitude snow and ice climbs in Alaska and Canada.
- Ski mountaineering on over fifty 14,000 foot (4,267 meters) peaks in Colorado and on many of the 11,000 foot (3,353 meters) peaks in the Canadian Rockies.
- Spectacular big-wall technical rock climbs in Yosemite (California) and on Baffin Island (Canada).
- Rock monolith climbing in the desert mountains of Arizona, New Mexico, and Utah
- Multi-route cliff climbs near major metropolitan areas (i.e. the Schwangunks near New York City, NY, Seneca Rocks in West Virginia near Pittsburgh, PA and Washington, D.C. and Joshua Tree near Los Angeles, CA.
- High-altitude volcano climbing in Mexico.

There are approximately sixteen major mountain ranges in North America. The Rocky Mountain range of Canada and the United States is the second longest mountain chain on earth (the Andes of South America is the longest) extending from central New Mexico north to Alaska. The mountains of North America include 5 peaks over 18,000 feet (5,486 meters), 9 peaks over 17,000 feet (5,181 meters), and 114 peaks over 14,000 feet (4,267 meters). These 114 peaks are located are located in: Alaska (39), California (15), Colorado (54), Mexico (5), and Washington (1).

There are seventeen independent countries on the North American continent. The highest peak in seven of these countries exceeds 10,000 feet (3,048 meters) in height. In thirteen of the fifty United States, the highest summit exceeds 11,000 feet (3,353 meters). The highest peak in North America is Denali (20,320 feet/6,193 meters) in Alaska. As one of the world's Seven Summits, this high snow and ice peak receives over 1,000 climbers from America and many overseas countries each year. Approximately 50 percent of these mountaineers reach the summit. Altitude, high winds, sudden snow storms and below zero temperatures all contribute to making this climb difficult and dangerous. Denali (a.k.a. Mount McKinley) rises 18,000 feet (5,486 meters) from its level lowlands to its snowcapped summit which is about 5,000 feet (1,524 meters) more than a similar measurement on Mount Everest in Nepal-Tibet. Seventeen major glaciers surround Denali. This chapter includes numerous event entries involving this important peak.

This chapter identifies ninety-four (94) peak first ascents, one hundred and seventy-eight (178) first ascents, and five hundred and thirty-four (534) other mountaineering events in North America.

Ten Highest Peaks in North America

1. Denali – South	Alaska	20,320 ft./6,193 m.
2. Mount Logan	Canada	19,551 ft./5,959 m.
3. Citlaltepetl	Mexico	18,700 ft./5,700 m.
4. Mount St. Elias	Alaska	18,008 ft./5,489 m.
5. Popocatepetl	Mexico	17,887 ft./5,452 m.
6. Mount Foraker	Alaska	17,401 ft./5,304 m.
7. Iztaccihuatl	Mexico	17,343 ft./5,286 m.
8. Mount Lucania	Canada	17,147 ft./5,227 m.
9. King Peak	Canada	16,971 ft./5,172 m.
10. Mount Steele	Canada	16,645, ft./5,073 m.

Ten Highest Peaks in the Continental United States

1. Mount Whitney	California	14,505 ft./4,421 m.
2. Mount Elbert	Colorado	14,433 ft./4,399 m.
3. Mount Massive	Colorado	14,421 ft./4,395 m.
4. Mount Harvard	Colorado	14,420 ft./4,395 m.
5. Mount Rainier	Washington	14,411 ft./4,392 m.
6. Mount Williamson	California	14,384 ft./4,384 m.
7. Blanca Peak	Colorado	14,345 ft./4,372 m.
8. La Plata Peak	Colorado	14,336 ft./4,369 m.
9. Uncompahgre Peak	Colorado	14,309 ft./4,361 m.
10. Crestone Peak	Colorado	14,294 ft./4,357 m.

▲ Highest Mountain: Denali – 20,320 ft./6,193 m.
Location: Alaska
First Ascent Date: June 7, 1913
Expedition: American

"Climb the mountains and get their good tidings.
Nature's peace will flow into you as sunshine flows
into trees. The winds will blow their own freshness
into you and the storms their energy, while cares
will drop off like autumn leaves."

John Muir
American naturalist,
explorer, and mountaineer
(1838 – 1914)

North America Timeline

1175:

Local natives unofficially climbed to the summit of Citlaltepetl (also now known as Pico de Orizaba) in Mexico. This is the third highest peak in North America and is located east of Mexico City. There are several summit elevations in print for this extinct volcano but the most common elevations are 18,491 ft./5,636 m. or 18,702 ft./5,700 m.

1289: PEAK FIRST ASCENT *POPOCATEPETL*

A 17th century Spanish chronicle recorded the Aztec ascent of Popocatepetl (17,887 ft./5,451 m.) in Mexico. Popocatepetl means "smoking mountain" in the Aztec Language. It is the fifth highest mountain in North America and is located east of Mexico City. The first ascent date for this volcanic mountain varies.

1448:

Aztec Emperor Montezuma I sent ten men to climb Popocatepetl (17,887 ft./5,451 m.) in Mexico to find out why this mountain smoked (volcano). These men reached the crater rim but only two men survived.

1521: FIRST ASCENT

The first European ascent of the Mexican volcano Popocatepetl (17,887 ft./5,421 m.) occurred when Don Francisco Montaño led a group of Cortez's soldiers to the crater rim in search of sulfur for gun powder.

1524:

An Italian coastline navigator named Giovanni da Verrazzano (1485 – 1528) first reported sighting the high mountains of New England (i.e. Mount Washington — 6,288 ft./1,917 m. — in New Hampshire) which were then called "The Sheens of Precious Stones" referring to the rime ice and snow on these peaks.

1642: PEAK FIRST ASCENT WASHINGTON

June 22. Irishman Darby Field (1610–1649) of Exeter, New Hampshire made the first ascent of Mount Washington (6,288 ft./1,917 m.) in New Hampshire. Field was accompanied by two Native American Indians who stopped 8 miles short of the summit. Field continued this ascent solo. His journey and climb took 18 days. This was one of the earliest verifiable mountain climbs in North America. Mount Washington was then known as Christall Hill to the English and Agio-chook ("The mountain with the snow on its head") to the Native American Indians. Field also made the second ascent in October of 1642.

1741:

July 20. Danish explorer Captain Vitus Bering (1680–1741) of the Great Northern Expedition first sighted Mount Saint Elias (18,008 ft./5,489 m.) in Alaska. This high peak was named after Cape Saint

Elias (Alaska) by Captain James Cook in 1778. In 1786, the height of this peak was first calculated to be 12,672 ft./3,862 m. by French explorer Jean-Francois de La Pérouse (1741–1788) and later in 1791 as 17,851 ft./5,441 m. by Spanish explorer Alessandro Malaspina (1754–1810). The current elevation was determined in the mid 1890s.

1778:

British explorer Captain James Cook (1728–1779), on his third world voyage, first sights a high snow peak that he enters on his map as "Mount Fair Weather" (Alaska). The accepted summit elevation for this high peak is 15,325 ft./4,671 m. It was first climbed in 1931.

1784:

July. Manasseh Cutler and five other climbers were the first party to spend the night on the summit of Mount Washington (6,288 ft./1,916 m.) in New Hampshire. Until this year (1784), this peak was known as Agiocochook, Waumbekket-Methna, Christall Hill, and Trinity Height. This climbing party renamed this peak Mount Washington to honor the revolutionary war general George Washington (1732–1799).

1792:

May 7. Captain George Vancouver (1757–1798) of the British Royal Navy sailed his sloop Discovery through the Strait of Juan de Fuca (near Seattle, Washington) and saw a magnificent snow-capped mountain looming up in the East. Vancouver named this peak Mount Rainier after his friend Rear Admiral Peter Rainier. On October 29, Vancouver sighted and named Mount St. Helens (9,677 ft./2,949 m.) in Washington. He also sighted and named Mount Hood (11,239 ft./3,425 m.) in Oregon. He named this peak for Rear Admiral Samuel Hood (1724–1816) of the British Royal Navy. This is the most frequently climbed glaciated peak in North America.

1794:

English navigator Captain George Vancouver (1757–1798) made a reference in his daily log to a very high mountain while he was charting Cook Inlet off the coast of Alaska. This high peak was probably Mount McKinley or Denali (20,320 ft./6,193 m.) 130 miles/216 kilometers to the north.

1804: PEAK FIRST ASCENT KATAHDIN

Charles Turner and a survey team made the first ascent of Mount Katahdin (5,266 ft./1,605 m.) in Maine. This peak serves as the northern terminus for the 2,122-mile Appalachian Trail (Maine to Georgia). Katahdin's highest point is called Baxter Peak. Katahdin comes from the Abenaki Indian word "Kette Adene" meaning "greatest mountain."

1806:

November 27. Lt. Zebulon Montgomery Pike (1779–1813) first sighted the distant mountain he called "Grand Peak" on the Front Range of Colorado. He estimated the height of this peak, now known as Pikes Peak, to be 18,581 feet/5,663 meters. The actual summit elevation is 14,110 feet/4,301 meters. Pike attempted to climb this peak but was met by a blizzard and retreated 16 miles from the mountain. In 1819, Dr. John Robinson named this "Highest Peak" after Pike. Robinson was with Pike in 1806.

1811:

January. Canadian explorer, geographer, and cartographer David Thompson (1770–1857) and his men discovered the summit of Athabasca Pass (5,740 ft./1,750 m.) in the Canadian Rockies between British Columbia and Alberta. Upon reaching this pass in winter conditions, they struggled in snow up to six meters (nearly twenty feet) deep. Thompson initially measured the altitude of this pass at 11,000 feet/3,353 meters. In 1814, Thompson made the first detailed published map of the western Canadian Mountains. This map was the result of his field surveys from 1792 to 1812 (1.5 million square miles surveyed).

1820: PEAK FIRST ASCENT *PIKES*

July 14. Edwin James (1797–1861), a graduate of Middlebury College in Vermont where he studied botany and geology, a soldier named Wilson, and the civilian hunter named Verplank made the first ascent of Pikes Peak (14,110 ft./4,301 m.) in Colorado. This was the first "Fourteener" (a peak over 14,000 feet) that was climbed in America. James and Wilson were members of Major Stephen Long's expedition to explore the great plains of the United States. Long wrote the first description of a massive block-shaped mountain that eventually was known as Longs Peak (14,256 ft./4,345 m.) in Colorado.

1821: FIRST ASCENT

Two women named Austin (from Portsmouth, New Hampshire) became the first women to reach the summit of Mount Washington (6,288 ft./1,917 m.) in New Hampshire. Their guide was Ethan Crawford.

1827:

May 1. Young Scottish botanist David Douglas (1798–1834) made the first ascent of a Canadian Rockies peak above Athabasca Pass (5,740 ft./1,750 m.) between British Columbia and Alberta. Athabasca is the Cree Indian word for "place where there are reeds." After returning to England, Douglas named this peak Mount Brown (9,184 ft./2,799 m.) for the famous Scottish botanist Robert Brown (1773–1858). This was the first recorded ascent of a North American peak above the snowline. Douglas estimated the height of this peak to be between 16,000 and 17,000 feet/5,181 meters and claimed it was the highest peak in North America. Many consider Douglas to be the first North American mountaineer. The Douglas Fir tree was named for him.

1833:

Scottish botanist David Douglas (1798–1834) made the first serious attempt to climb Mount Hood (11,239 ft./3,425 m.) in Oregon. His journal of this climbing attempt was lost on the Fraser River in British Columbia, Canada.

1833:

Captain Benjamin Louis Eulalie Bonneville (1796–1878) claimed to have made the first ascent of Gannett Peak (13,804 ft./4,207 m.) in Wyoming. This ascent was doubted and not officially recognized. This peak was named in 1906 for Henry Gannett (1846 – 1914) of the Hayden Survey party.

1836: Book

American cartographer Henry Schenck Tanner (1786–1858) published his *Table of the Comparative Heights of the Principal Mountains in the World.* Dhaulagiri (measured at 26,462 feet at that time. Nepal.) is listed as the highest mountain in the world. Popocatepetl (17,710 feet) in Mexico is listed as the highest mountain in North America. Africa's Kilimanjaro is not mentioned at all.

1842: PEAK FIRST ASCENT *FREMONT*

August 15. American explorer John C. Fremont (1813–1890), Johnny Janisse, Basil Lajeunesse, De Coteau, Clement Lambert, and Charles Preuss made the first ascent of Fremont Peak (13,750 ft./4,191 m.) in Wyoming's Wind River Range.

1842:

Lt. Charles Wilkes and Lt. Case measured the height of Mount Rainier and arrived at a figure of 12,330 feet/3,758 meters. The next measurement, in 1870, by the United States Coast Survey, increased this figure to 14,444 feet/4,402 meters. This peak was thought to be the highest mountain in the United States.

1846:

September 8. American author Henry David Thoreau (1817–1862) climbed Maine's Mount Katahdin (5,266 ft./1,605 m.). Katahdin was first climbed in 1804. Thoreau and his friend McCauslin began their "Ktaadn" (peak's spelling at this time) climb fourteen miles from the summit.

1848: PEAK FIRST ASCENT ORIZABA

United States army soldiers F. Maynard and G. Reynolds are credited with making the first official (recorded) ascent of the high Mexican volcano known as Citlaltepetl or Pico de Orizaba. This is the third highest peak in North America. It is located sixty miles east of Puebla, Mexico. Citlaltepetl has been dormant since 1687. There are several summit elevations in print for this peak. The most common elevation is 18,702 ft./5,700 m. Citlaltepetl is the Aztec word meaning "star mountain."

1849: FIRST ASCENT

October. Englishman Fredrick Strickland (1820 – 1849) became the first person to climb Mount Washington (6,288 ft./1,917 m.) in New Hampshire in winter conditions (solo) and the first person to die on this mountain — he became lost in a storm. As of December 31, 2008, 136 people had died on the summit and slopes of Mount Washington.

1850:

October 19. American woman mountaineer Annie Smith Peck (1850–1935) was born in Rhode Island. She was a Professor of Latin at Purdue University and Smith College. She was the first woman in history to make high-altitude mountaineering her profession. Peck climbed her first major peak in 1888 — Mount Shasta (14,162 ft./4,316 m.) in northern California. She began her professional climbing career at age 45 (in 1895) and made the fifth ascent of the Matterhorn (14,692 ft./4,478 m.) by a woman (in 1895) and climbed both Pico de Orizaba and Popocatepetl in Mexico in 1897. Peck's greatest ascent occurred in 1908 when she climbed (at age 58) the south summit of Huascaran (22,205 ft./6,768 m.) in Peru on her sixth attempt. In 1909, she reached the summit of Coropuna (21,083 ft./6,426 m.) in Peru. Annie Peck's last ascent was of Mount Madison (5,366 ft./1,635 m.) in New Hampshire at age 82 in 1932.

1851:

March 27. United States Cavalry Major James D. Savage (with the Mariposa Battalion) and a physician named Dr. Lafayette H. Bunnell entered the seven-mile long Yosemite Valley in California and made the first recorded sighting of the massive rock wall now known as El Capitan. This granite wall rises over 3,500 feet/1,067 meters above the valley floor.

1852:

August 21. Sidney S. Ford, Jr., Robert S. Bailey, John Edgar, and Benjamin K. Shaw became the first white men to climb above timberline on Mount Rainier (14,411 ft./4,392 m.) in Washington.

1854: PEAK FIRST ASCENT *SHASTA*

August 14. U.S. Army Captain E.D. Pearce, a Eureka (California) sawmill foreman, and eight other men made the first ascent of Mount Shasta (14,162 ft./4,316 m.) in Northern California. This peak rises over 10,000 feet (3,048 m.) above its surroundings. Shasta is the second highest peak in the Cascade Range (Rainier is the highest). This was the only peak in this region to retain its Indian name Shasta which means "white mountain."

1854:

Thomas J. Dryer (editor of the Portland Oregonian newspaper) and his party made the first ascent of Mount Hood (11,239 ft./3,425 m.) in Oregon. Upon his return to Portland, Dryer (1808–1879) claimed that Mount Hood was 18,361 feet/5,596 meters high. This ascent has been disputed. Mount Hood is the second most frequently climbed mountain in the world behind Mount Fuji (12,389 ft./3,776 m.) in Japan. Over 10,000 climbers per year attempt to climb Mount Hood.

1855: FIRST ASCENT

October 11. Israel S. Diehl made the first solo ascent of Mount Shasta (14,162 ft./4,316 m.) in northern California.

1857: PEAK FIRST ASCENT *HOOD*

July 11. American mountaineers L.J. Powell, Lyman Chittenden, W.S. Buckley, James Deardorff, and H.L. Pittock made the first undisputed ascent of Mount Hood (11,239 ft./3,426 m.) in Oregon. This peak was named after Rear Admiral Samuel Hood (1724–1816) of the British Royal Navy.

1857:

July 15. Lt. August Valentine Kautz (1828–1895) led a private party to climb Mount Rainier (14,411 ft./4,392 m.) in Washington via the Kautz Glacier. Kautz, climbing solo, reached the crater rim (14,000 ft./4,267 m.) and then retreated due to time. This was not the peak's high point and, therefore, was not a complete first ascent. Kautz and his group were, however, the first non-natives in North America to set foot on a glacier. They were also the first climbers to use the metal-tipped alpenstock.

1857: Equipment – Alpenstocks

July 10. Mount Rainier (14,411 ft./4,392 m.) in Washington (United States). Lt. August Valentine Kautz and his companions were the first to use metal-spiked alpenstocks in North America. These alpenstocks were five feet long and made of dry ash wood.

1858: FIRST ASCENT

August 5. American pioneers John and Julia Archibald Holmes (1838–1887) traveled over 500 miles from eastern Kansas to the Front Range of Colorado in search of gold. They and two others made a five-day ascent of Pikes Peak (14,110 ft./4,301 m.) just west of Colorado Springs. Julia became the first woman to climb Pikes Peak.

1858: FIRST ASCENT

Lucius Hartshorn and guide Benjamin Osgood made the first winter ascent of Mount Washington (6,288 ft./1,917 m.) in New Hampshire.

1859:

Arapahoe Indian Gun Griswold (18) claimed to have climbed Longs Peak (14,256 ft./4,345 m.) in Colorado with other young Indian braves in 1859. Griswold made this ascent claim in a 1914 interview when he was 73 years old. He told of even earlier ascents of Longs Peak by his father Old Man Gun who trapped eagles there by baiting a summit trap.

1860:

James Kent Stone (1840–1921) became the first American member of England's Alpine Club (founded in 1857). Stone was from Brookline, Massachusetts. He was the first American climber to have ascents in more than one region in the European Alps.

1861: PEAK FIRST ASCENTS *GRAYS AND TORREYS*

July. Harvard University student Charles C. Parry made the first recorded ascents of Grays Peak (14,270 ft./4,349 m.) and Torreys Peak (14,267 ft./4,348 m.) in Colorado. Parry named Grays after the well-known Harvard botanist Asa Gray (1810–1888). Torreys Peak was later named for John Torrey (1796–1873) who visited nearby Georgetown, Colorado in 1872. Torreys Peak is located immediately north of Grays Peak.

1862:

Major John Wesley Powell (1834–1902) lost his right arm to a musket ball in the Civil War (April). On July 27, 1867 Powell climbed Pikes Peak (14,110 ft./4,301 m.) in Colorado. In August of 1867, he also climbed Mount Lincoln (14,286 ft./4,354 m.) in Colorado.

1863:

The Williamstown Alpine Club (Williamstown, Massachusetts) was founded by Professor Albert Hopkins. This was the earliest known alpine club in the United States.

1863: PEAK FIRST ASCENT *BIERSTADT*

German-born western landscape artist Albert Bierstadt (1830–1902) made the first ascent of Mount Bierstadt (14,060 ft./4,285 m.) in Colorado. This "fourteener" is located approximately 40 miles/66 kilometers west of Denver. Bierstadt's most famous painting, "The Rocky Mountains," was exhibited in 1863 and established his national (American) reputation. Mount Evans in Colorado was originally named Mount Rosalie for Bierstadt's wife.

1864: PEAK FIRST ASCENT *TYNDALL*

July 5. Mountaineering in the high Sierras of California began when surveyor and fanatical explorer Clarence King (1842–1901) and surveyor William Henry Brewer crossed the Kings-Kern Divide and made the first ascent of Mount Tyndall (14,020 ft./4,273 m.) in California. This peak was named for British mountaineer John Tyndall (1820–1893). King discovered a higher peak from Tyndall's summit. King would later name this distant peak Mount Whitney for his boss on the California Geological Survey—Josiah Dwight Whitney (1819–1896). King, known to many as the "Father of American Mountaineering," climbed to within 400 feet of Mount Whitney's summit (14,495 ft./4,418 m.) solo. Upon returning to his companions, he told them Mount Whitney was 14,740 feet/4,493 meters high. In 1871, King made a second attempt to climb Mount Whitney and failed. On September 19, 1873, King finally summited Mount Whitney only to find evidence of an earlier ascent which occurred a few weeks before King summited. King made over 100 first ascents in California's Sierra Nevada Mountains. On October 7th, King along with James T. Gardiner, and Richard Cotter made the first ascent of El Capitan (7,564 ft./2,305 m.). They placed a survey station on the summit of this Yosemite Valley mountain.

1865:

July. It has been recorded that John W. Goss and Robert L. Woodward made the first ascent of Longs Peak (14,256 ft./4,345 m.) in Colorado via the Keyhole Route. This ascent, however, is not recognized as the official first ascent (see 1868).

1867: FIRST ASCENT

August 26. Ms. Frances Case and Ms. Mary Robinson made the first women's ascent of Mount Hood (11,239 ft./3,425 m.) in Oregon via the south side with several men.

1868: PEAK FIRST ASCENTS *LONGS AND POWELL*

August 23. U.S. Army Major John Wesley Powell* (1834–1902), Walter Powell, Lewis Keplinger, Samuel Garman, William Byers, and local boys Jack Sumner and Ned Farrell made the first official ascent of Longs Peak (14,256 ft./4,345 m.) in Colorado. They approached the peak from the south side after hiking in from Grand Lake on the west and then climbing the Keplinger Couloir. Longs Peak was known as "Nestoaieux" (two guides) to the Arapahoe Indians because of the two peaks Longs and Meeker (13,911 ft./4,240 m.) beside each other. On September 26, Powell (1834–1902) and Ned E. Farrell made the first ascent of Mount Powell (13,504 ft./4,116 m.) in the Gore Range of Colorado. A newspaper reporter with Powell's party named this peak at this time. There are now over 100 named climbing routes to the summit of Longs Peak.

1868: PEAK FIRST ASCENT *BAKER*

British mountaineer and landscape painter Edmund Thomas Coleman (1823–1892) made the first ascent of Mount Baker (10,781 ft./3,286 m.) in Washington. Coleman's ice axe was the first to be used in the Pacific Northwest and perhaps in all of North America. He copied his ice axe from the ice axe Edward Whymper (first ascent of the Matterhorn in 1865) had made for himself from a British naval boarding axe. Coleman's axe was misplaced on an ascent of Mount Rainier in 1870 and now lies buried somewhere in the large snow and ice summit crater.

1868: Equipment – Crampons

On the first ascent of Mount Baker (10,781 ft./3,286 m.) in Washington, the climbing party wore "creepers" — iron spikes with chains and straps — on their boots. They were clumsy and heavy.

1869: PEAK FIRST ASCENTS *YALE AND HARVARD*

August 18. Josiah Dwight Whitney, William Brewer, William M. Davis, S.F. Sharpless, and Robert Moore made the first ascent of Mount Yale (14,196 ft./4,327 m.) in the Collegiate Range of Colorado. Whitney, a geology professor associated with both Harvard University (Cambridge, Massachusetts) and Yale University (New Haven, Connecticut), and his field survey students named both Mount Harvard and Mount Yale. On August 19, Davis and Sharpless made the first ascent of Mount Harvard (14,420 ft./4,395 m.) in Colorado. Ten days later on August 29, William Brewer was credited with making the first official sighting of the "snowy cross" on Mount of the Holy Cross (14,005 ft./4,269 m.) in Colorado. The rock formations and couloirs on the east face of this mountain formed this cross when filled with snow. Originally 1,400 feet/427 meters tall and 450 feet/137 meters wide, this snow cross has gradually changed its shape by falling rock and erosion. Brewer saw this peak from the summit of Grays Peak (14,270 ft./4,349 m.) in Colorado, a direct distance of approximately 40 miles/66 kilometers.

---

* Powell had his lower right arm amputated due to a Civil War injury he suffered in 1862. This physical condition did not prevent him from climbing.

1870: PEAK FIRST ASCENT *RAINIER*

August 17 and 18. Gold prospector Philemon Beecher Van Trump (1839–1916), U.S. Army General Hazard Stevens (1842–1918), British mountaineer Edmund T. Coleman (1823–1892), and Yakima Indian guide Sluiskin made the first ascent of Mount Rainier (14,411 ft./4,392 m.) in Washington. Coleman and Sluiskin did not actually reach the summit. This climbing party used primitive crampons that were called "snow-spikes" or "creepers." Stevens was the son of the first Governor of the Washington Territory and the youngest Brigadier General in the Union Army. He won the Congressional Medal of Honor. Van Trump and Stevens spent one night on Rainier's summit in the steam caves. This climbing party made the 250-mile roundtrip to Rainier from the town of Olympia, Washington. They reached the summit via the Gilbralter Ledges. On October 17, Samuel F. Emmons (1841–1911) and Allen Drew Wilson made the second ascent of Mount Rainier (14,411 ft./4,392 m.) in Washington. They were guided to the mountain by James Longmire and reached the summit via the Gilbralter route. The first scientific knowledge of this great volcanic peak resulted from the investigations of Emmons and Wilson. These scientists measured Mount Rainier's official elevation as 14,444 ft./4,402 m. The accepted elevation is 14,411 ft./4,392 m. There are now forty-two official routes to Rainier's summit.

1870: Equipment – Sunscreen

Mount Rainier (14,411 ft./4,392 m.) in Washington. Deer fat was applied to the face to protect the skin from sunburn.

1871: PEAK FIRST ASCENT *LANGLEY*

California mountaineers Clarence King (1842–1902) and Paul Pinson made the first ascent of Mount Langley (14,042 ft./4,274 m.) in California. They believed this peak to be Mount Whitney and enjoyed this accomplishment for two years before he (King) actually climbed Whitney in 1873.

1871:

Ms. Addie Alexander of St. Louis, Missouri became the first woman to climb Longs Peak (14,256 ft./4,345 m.) in Colorado. This was the first documented ascent by a woman. She had a guide with her.

1872:

July 29. Local Wyoming lore held that two members of Ferdinand Hayden's survey party — James Stevenson and Nathaniel Langford (Yellowstone Park superintendent) — reached the summit of the Grand Teton (13,766 ft./4,196 m.) first but this ascent was officially recognized for only twenty-six years or until 1898. In 1872, the Grand Teton was known as Mount Hayden. There are those historians that do believe that Langford's ascent was, in fact, the first ascent.

1873: PEAK FIRST ASCENT *WHITNEY*

August 18. Charles Begole, Albert Johnson, and John Lucas (collectively known as "the fishermen") made the first ascent of Mount Whitney (14,505 ft./4,421 m.) in California. William Crapo and Abe Leyda made the second ascent approximately two days later on August 20. Begole, Johnson, and Lucas named this high peak "Fishman's Peak" and built a summit stone monument. The name "Mount Whitney," however, was not officially recognized at this time. This name did become official in 1878 when the California governor vetoed the Fisherman's Peak name. Josiah Dwight Whitney (1819–1896) was appointed the state geologist of California in 1860 and later became a professor of geology at Harvard University in 1865.

1873: PEAK FIRST ASCENT *HOLY CROSS*

August 24. American surveyors James T. Gardner and William H. Holmes made the first ascent of Mount of the Holy Cross in Colorado. They were with the Hayden Survey party which established the first summit elevation — 14,170 feet (4,319 meters). On this same day, American pioneer photographer William Henry Jackson (1843–1942) stood on the summit of Colorado's Notch Mountain (13,237 ft./4,034 m.) and exposed his first glassplate negative of Mount of the Holy Cross. Jackson and his two assistants Coulter and Cooper also belonged to F.V. Hayden's Geological and Geographical Survey party. Jackson had heard about the legend of a snowy cross upon a mountain in Colorado. He took eight exposures with two cameras. This photograph of Mount of the Holy Cross was Jackson's most famous photograph. He took over 100,000 photographs during his lifetime.

In 1912, the first recorded spiritual pilgrimage was made to the summit of Notch Mountain to view the snowy cross on Mount of the Holy Cross. These pilgrimages reached their height in 1934 when 3,000 people climbed Notch Mountain to view the cross.

In the mid-1950s, a new survey adjusted the summit elevation to 13,996 ft. (4,266 m.). Then in 1964, this survey was once again corrected to 14,005 feet (4,268 m.).

1873: FIRST ASCENT

American naturalist John Muir (1838–1914) made the first ascent of the Mountaineer's Route on the east face of Mount Whitney (14,505 ft./4,421 m.) in California.

1873:

Lt. William L. Marshall and his assistants of the Wheeler Survey in Colorado climbed 36 peaks over 13,000 feet/3,962 m. in Colorado during this year.

1873: PEAK FIRST ASCENTS *CASTLE AND MASSIVE*

The Hayden Survey party made the first ascent of Castle Peak (14,265 ft./4,348 m.) in the Elk Range of Colorado. Henry Gannett (1846–1914) of the Hayden Survey party made the first ascent of Mount Massive (14,421 ft./4,395 m.) in the Sawatch Range of Colorado. Gannett climbed, named, and mapped this second highest peak in Colorado. He has been described as the "Father of Government Mapmaking." Gannett Peak (13,803 ft./4,207 m.) in Wyoming is named for him.

1873: Clothing

British woman climber Isabella Bird (1831–1904) climbed Longs Peak (14,256 ft./4,345 m.) in Colorado. She wore a wool jacket, an ankle-length skirt, and full Turkish trousers gathered into frills that fell over her nailed climbing boots. She called this outfit the "American Lady's Mountain Dress."

1874: PEAK FIRST ASCENTS *ELBERT, WILSON, AND UNCOMPAHGRE*

H.W. Stuckle of the Hayden Survey made the first documented ascent of Mount Elbert (14,433 ft./4,399 m.), the highest peak in Colorado. The Hayden Survey party climbed thirty-five mountains over 12,000 feet (3,657 meters) in Colorado in 1874. Most of these climbs were first ascents including the September 13th first ascent of Mount Wilson (14,246 feet/4,342 meters) by Allen D. Wilson (1844–1920) and Franklin Rhoda (1854–1929) via its southern ridge. These two surveyors/climbers also made the first ascent of Uncompahgre Peak (14,309 ft./4,361 m.). Both Mount Wilson and Uncompahgre Peak are located in southwestern Colorado. The Hayden Survey was the forerunner to the United States Geological Survey that was formally established five years later in 1879.

1874:

German-born American landscape artist Albert Bierstadt (1830–1902) created his painting of Longs Peak (14,256 ft./4,345 m.) in Colorado from a lake (Bierstadt Lake) in what is now known as Rocky Mountain National Park. This painting hung in the Rotunda of the U.S. Capital in Washington, D.C. for many years.

1875: PEAK FIRST ASCENT *HALF DOME*

October 12. Scottish carpenter George Anderson was the first climber to place a metal bolt in rock in the Yosemite Valley of California. He made the first ascent of Half Dome (8,836 feet/2,693 meters) via the northeast shoulder on October 12th. Anderson used large eye bolts. Standing on one eye bolt, he drilled in the next bolt and secured himself to it by using a short rope leash. He left a rope fixed to his high point each day so he could climb back up the next day and continue his ascent. Half Dome was originally known as South Dome. Cables were installed on the east face of Half Dome in 1919. This is the normal ascent route.

1876:

January. Massachusetts Institute of Technology Professor Edward Charles Pickering (1846 – 1919) and several of his friends created the Appalachian Mountain Club (AMC) to explore the high peaks of New Hampshire's White Mountain range. Charles Fay (1846 – 1931) became the first president and first editor of Appalachia, the club's official journal. The AMC would eventually construct eight mountain huts in this range to accommodate its members. As of 2005, the AMC's membership was over 90,000 and it conducted approximately 7,000 outing trips per year. This club admitted women immediately. The first excursion by the AMC was an ascent of Mount Katahdin (5,266 ft./1,605 m.) in Maine in 1887. Women members outnumbered the men on this climb.

1878: FIRST ASCENT

August 3. Mrs. Anna Mills became the first woman to climb Mount Whitney (14,495 ft./4,418 m.) in California. Three other women were with Mills on this ascent: Hope Broughton, Mary Martin, and Mrs. R.C. Reed. All were from Porterville, California. The total climbing party included thirty men and women.

1878:

Alaskan prospectors Arthur Harper and Alfred Mayo sighted a "great ice mountain off to the south" of Fairbanks, Alaska. This may have been the first written record of seeing Mount McKinley from the interior of Alaska. Thirty-five years later (1913), Harper's son Walter (1892–1918) would be the first person to reach McKinley's summit (20,320 feet/6,193 meters).

1881: PEAK FIRST ASCENT WILLIAMSON

An unknown party made the first ascent of Mount Williamson (14,375 ft./4,381 m.) in the California Sierra Mountains. The first recorded ascent was in 1884 by W.L. Hunter and C. Mulholland via the southeast ridge. Williamson is the second highest peak in California after Mount Whitney (14,495 ft./4,418 m.).

1883:

Conrad Kain (1883–1934) was born in Austria. Kain was credited with 60 first ascents in the Canadian Rockies including the highest peak Mount Robson (12,872 ft./3,923 m.) in 1913. Kain became a mountain guide at age 21 in 1904. He immigrated to Canada in 1910 and became Canada's most famous mountain guide.

1884:

September 23. Ms. Carrie Welton (1842–1884) of Waterbury, Connecticut became the first death on Longs Peak (14,256 ft./4,345 m.) in Colorado. She died of exhaustion and hypothermia near the Keyhole on her descent from the summit. Her guide was Carlyle Lamb.

1885: FIRST ASCENT

American naturalist, writer, and climber Enos Mills (1870–1922) made his first ascent of Longs Peak (14,256 ft./4,345 m.) in Colorado at age 15. Mills would eventually make 304 ascents of this peak, 257 of these ascents as a paid guide. He loved to climb Longs Peak in the moonlight. He built the Longs Peak Inn at the base of Longs Peak in 1903 and rebuilt it (after a fire) in 1907. Mills was the primary advocate for the creation of Rocky Mountain National Park in Colorado in 1915. He died of blood poisoning at age 52.

1885: Equipment – Eye Protection

Mount Rainier, Washington. To reduce sun glare, charcoal was rubbed on the skin around the eyes.

1886:

Mountaineer Frederick Schwatka organized the first attempt to climb Mount St. Elias (18,008 ft./5,489 m.) in Alaska. His party only reached 7,300 ft./2,225 m.

1886:

American volcanologist, geologist, and mountaineer Angelo Heilprin (1853–1907) climbed the two highest mountains in Mexico: Pico de Orizaba (18,700 ft./5,699 m.) and Popocatepetl (17,887 ft./5,452 m.).

1887: PEAK FIRST ASCENT *STEPHEN*

September 9. Canadian surveyor James Joseph McArthur (1856–1925) and his assistant Tom Riley made the first ascent of a peak over 10,000 ft./3,049 m. in Canada. They climbed Mount Stephen (10,496 ft./3,199 m.) in British Columbia's Selkirk Mountains. They did not use any ropes.

1887:

The Glacier House was constructed below Rogers Pass (4,364 ft./1,330 m.) in the Selkirk Mountains of British Columbia, Canada by the Canadian Pacific Railway. Initially built as a dining room with six small bedrooms, this gathering place for Canadian mountaineers eventually became a large 90-room hotel. The Glacier House was considered to be the "Birthplace of Canadian Mountaineering." The last official season for the Glacier House was 1925 and it remained until 1929.

1887:

New Jersey hiker/climber Lucia Cook Pychowska traversed the summits of Mount Washington (6,288 ft./1,917 m.), Mount Jefferson (5,716 ft./1,742 m.), Mount Adams (5,779 ft./1,768 m.), and Mount Madison (5,366 ft./1,636 m.), a rugged chain of peaks in the Presidential Range in New Hampshire.

1887: Technique – Step Cutting

Steps were carved in steep snow and ice of the Canadian Rockies of British Columbia and Alberta (Canada) with the iron tips of wooden alpenstocks. This use of the alpenstocks was during the pre-ice axe period for Canada.

1888:

January 19. The Appalachian Mountain Club announced its plans to build the Lake of the Clouds Hut in New Hampshire, the first above timberline mountain hut in North America. This hut on the southern shoulder of Mount Washington (6,288 ft./1,916 m.) is located at 5,050 ft./1,539 m. It can accommodate 90 climbers.

1888:

August 8. American naturalist John Muir (1838–1914) climbed Mount Rainier (14,411 ft./4,392 m.) in Washington with Edward Sturgis Ingraham (a Seattle teacher) and Arthur Warner (a photographer) who took the first photographs of the summit and its crater. They spent a night at what is now known as Camp Muir (10,000 ft./3,048 m.). Muir became known as "John of the Mountains."

1888: Equipment – Crampons

On an ascent of Mount Rainier (14,411 ft./4,392 m.) in Washington, a climbing party that included American naturalist John Muir (1838–1914) at one point took off their boots and drove steel caulks about a half an inch long into them having brought tools along for this purpose.

1888: Technique – Photography

American inventor George Eastman (1854–1932) introduced the Kodak hand-held camera. Climbers using this convenient camera could now take photographs throughout their climbs.

1889: PEAK FIRST ASCENT *IZTACCIHUATL*

November. Swiss mountaineer and resident of Mexico City James de Salis made the first recorded ascent of Iztaccihuatl (17,343 ft./5,286 m.) in Mexico. He left a note in a bottle on the summit (the highest of three summits) which he reached via the Ayaloco Glacier. Iztaccihuatl in the Aztec language means "White Woman." It is the seventh highest mountain in North America.

1889:

Prospector Frank Densmore was so enthusiastic about the huge white mountain in Alaska that fellow prospectors came to call it "Densmore's Mountain." This name was used for eight short years before William A. Dickey (prospector) proposed the name "McKinley" after William McKinley of Ohio. Although the name Mount McKinley has lasted for over 100 years, Alaskans and mountaineers prefer to use the Athabascan Indian name "Denali" (meaning The Great One) for this peak.

1889: Equipment – Tent

August 23 and 24. Mount Rainier (14,411 ft./4,392 m.) in Washington. Climbers Charles H. Gove and J. Nichols used a small tent on their ascent. This was the first "mountain tent" used on Mount Rainier.

1890: FIRST ASCENT

August 10. Yelm, Washington school teacher Ms. Fay Fuller (20) became the first woman to climb Mount Rainier (14,411 ft./4,392 m.) in Washington. With her on this ascent were the Reverend E.C. Smith and nine other climbers from Seattle and Yelm, Washington. Fay Peak in the Cascade Mountains is named for her. By the end of this year's climbing season, a total of 38 climbers had summited Mount Rainier (14,411 ft./4,392 m.) in Washington since its first ascent in 1870.

1890:

Professor Herschel Parker (electrical engineering at Columbia University—New York City) made the first of his eleven winter ascents of Mount Washington (6,288 ft./1,917 m.) in New Hampshire.

1890: PEAK FIRST ASCENT *SIR DONALD*

Emil Huber and Carl Sulzer of the Swiss Alpine Club made the first ascent of Mount Sir Donald (10,818 ft./3,297 m.) in the Selkirk Range of the Canadian Rockies (British Columbia, Canada). This was one of the first ascents of a major Canadian Peak in which mountaineering equipment (ropes, etc.) was used and a special climbing plan was developed before the ascent via the southwest face and southeast arête.

1892:

May 28. Two University of California at Berkeley professors gathered together a small group in a San Francisco office to form "a Sierra Club." The articles of incorporation were signed on June 4th by 27 people and American naturalist John Muir (1838–1914) was elected President. The Sierra Club now has over 1,400,000 members.

1892: FIRST ASCENT

August 20. A Dr. James G. Van Marter of Rome, Italy became the first foreign mountaineer to climb Mount Rainier (14,411 ft./4,392 m.) in Washington. A separate climbing party finally reached the North Summit (14,112 ft./4,301 m.) of Mount Rainier (14,411 ft./4,392 m.), known as Liberty Cap.

1892:

American explorer Joseph "Little Joe" LeConte (1870–1950) made the first of 44 extended trips into the high Sierra Mountains of California (from 1892 –1930). LeConte made the first accurate maps of the High Sierra. Mount LeConte (13,960 ft./4,255 m.) is named for him.

1892: Equipment – Sleeping Bags

The first sleeping bags to be used on Mount Rainier in Washington were introduced by Dr. James G. Van Marter of Rome, Italy. These sleeping bags were rubber-covered.

1893:

July 4. Wyoming ranchers William Rogers and Willard Ripley made the first ascent of Devils Tower (5,117 ft./1,560 m.) in Wyoming. They spent six weeks hammering precut 30" wooden pegs into one of the vertical cracks of this 865 foot/264 meter high volcanic plug (1,000 feet thick at its base and 200 feet thick at its top). The outside ends of these pegs were joined by 2x4 boards creating a 350-foot/107-meter long ladder. Climbers used this wooden ladder for the next 20 years. Over 1,000 July 4th onlookers and picnickers watched this climb. Rogers and Ripley unfurled an American flag on the summit. Devils Tower rises 1,280 feet/390 meters above the Belle Fourche River and became the first National Monument in the United States National Park system. Devils Tower is considered to be a sacred site for many Native Americans. (See 1937).

1893:

Summer. School teacher and author Katherine Lee Bates (1859–1929) reached the summit of Pikes Peak (14,110 ft./4,301 m.) in Colorado. While on the summit, Bates wrote the famous song "America the Beautiful."

1893:

Canadian mountaineer and surveyor James J. McArthur (1856–1925) completed six seasons of climbing in the Canadian Rockies. From 1887 to 1893, McArthur made 160 peak ascents including seven first ascents. During the 1889 season alone, he climbed 43 mountains.

1894:

July 19. A group of Oregon mountaineers (155 men and 38 women) climbed Mount Hood (11,239 ft./3,425 m.) in Oregon and decided on the summit to form a mountain club. They called their new club "The Mazamas Climbing Club" (Mazamas means "mountain goat" in Spanish) and elected Will G. Steel as their first president. The club's motto was "Nesika Klatawa Sahale" which in the Chinook Indian language meant "We Climb High." This was the first of the great alpine clubs in North America.

1894: PEAK FIRST ASCENT *TEMPLE*

August 17. American mountaineers Samuel Allen (1874–1945), Louis Fox Frissell, and Walter Dwight Wilcox (–1949) made the first ascent of Mount Temple (11,626 ft./3,543 m.) in Banff National Park, Alberta, Canada. This was the first ascent of a peak over 11,000 feet/3,353 meters in Canada. Mount Temple was the first of 54 Canadian Rockies peaks over 11,000 ft./3,353 m. to be climbed. It has been called the "Eiger of the Rockies."

1895: FIRST ASCENT

September 28. Mr. A.R. Hamilton and a Dr. Scheller became the first Englishmen to climb Citlaltepetl or Pico de Orizaba (18,702 ft./5,700 m.) in Mexico.

1895:

American mountaineer Charles E. Fay (1846–1931) began his period of first ascents in the Canadian Rockies. He made twelve first ascents between 1895 and 1903. Fay, Philip S. Abbot (1869–1896), and Charles S. Thompson made the first high ascent for Appalachian Mountain Club members. They climbed Mount Hector (11,205 ft./3,415 m.) in the Canadian Rockies. Fay was also the first president of the American Alpine Club (founded in 1902).

1895: Clothing

Each member of a climbing party on Mount Rainier (14,411 ft./4,392 m.) in Washington wore a canvas suit coated with linseed oil.

1895: Equipment – Rope

August 3. On an attempt to climb Mount Lefroy (11,115 ft./3,388 m.) in the Canadian Rockies, the climbing team used the English Alpine Club Rope that contained the identifying red thread in its braiding signifying its approval by the Alpine Club (of England).

1895: Technique – Rope As A Chockstone

While climbing Mount Clarence King (12,905 feet/3,933 meters) in the California Sierra Mountains, Stanford University (Palo Alto, California) Professor Bolton Brown first used a knotted rope as a chockstone (jamming a knotted rope into a rock crack as an anchor) and as an etrier — a French term for a short lightweight rope ladder composed of two or three steps ten to eighteen inches apart.

1896:

August 3. American climber Philip Stanley Abbot (1869–1896) became the first person to die in a fall while climbing in the history of North American mountaineering. This climbing fatality occurred on Mount LeFroy (11,230 ft./3,423 m.) above Lake Louise in the Canadian Rockies. Abbot fell from near the summit on this first ascent attempt. Abbot's death caused a Matterhorn-like furor with the public and the press. The legitimacy of mountaineering was once again being questioned. But all of the resulting news coverage only focused more attention on the Canadian Rockies. The accident caused the Canadian Pacific Railroad to import Swiss mountain guides to encourage tourism and safe climbing.

1897: PEAK FIRST ASCENT *ST. ELIAS*

July 31. Luigi Amedeo Di Savoia—Duke of the Abruzzi (1873-1933) and nephew of the King of Italy— led five fellow climbers, four alpine guides, and eleven porters on the first ascent of Mount St. Elias (18,008 ft./5,489 m.) in Alaska. This was the first great mountaineering expedition to Alaska. Mount St. Elias is located less than twelve miles from the Pacific Ocean and is the largest coastal mountain on earth. Well-known Italian mountaineer and photographer Vittorio Sella (1859–1943) was a member of this first ascent party. Other expedition members included Umberto Cagni, Francesco Gonella, Filippo de Filippi, Erminio Botta and four mountain guides: Joseph Petigax, Laurent Croux, Antoine Maquignaz, and Andrea Pellissier. Eleven Americans were hired to serve as porters. Mount St. Elias had seen four previous unsuccessful attempts by other parties (1886, 1888, 1890, and 1891). It is the fifth highest peak in North America. Although he has never been given the credit, the Duke of the Abruzzi was the first person to bring professional mountain guides to North America. After being assigned an elevation of 12,672 ft./3,862 m. in 1741, Mount St. Elias' current elevation was calculated in the 1890s. On August 1st, Sella and Botta re-climbed the peak from their high camp to take summit photographs. The third ascent occurred in 1946.

1897:

The Mazamas summer outing to Mount Rainier (14,411 ft./4.392 m.) in Washington introduced "the modern era of mountaineering clubs." Individual mountaineers could now climb the high peaks by joining a mountaineering club.

1897: PEAK FIRST ASCENT LEFROY

A prominent group of English mountaineers visited the Canadian Rockies. This group was led by George Percival Baker (1856–1951). British mountaineers Dr. John Norman Collie (1859–1942) and Harold Dixon invited Swiss mountain guide Peter Sarbach (1844–1930) to visit Canada's western mountains and be a member of a climbing party that was attempting a first ascent of Mount Lefroy (11,231 ft./3,423 m.). On August 3, a party of nine climbers reached the summit of Mount LeFroy exactly one year after the death of Philip Stanley Abbot. Sarbach was from the village of St. Niklaus just down valley from Zermatt, Switzerland. He was one of the first European mountain guides to visit the Canadian Rockies of North America. Mount Lefroy is located on the east side of Abbot Pass (8,450 ft./2,575 m.) which lies on the border between Alberta and British Columbia.

1897:

American woman mountaineer Annie Peck (1850–1935) climbed Pico de Orizaba (18,702 ft./5,700 m.) and Popcatépetl (17,883 ft./5,450 m.) in Mexico. The Orizaba ascent represented a new altitude record for women. This record, however, would remain for only two years. American mountaineer Ms. Fanny Bullock Workman (1850–1925) climbed above 19,000 ft./5,791 m. in the Himalayas in 1899.

1897:

British mountaineer John Norman Collie (1859–1942) made thirteen first ascents in the Canadian Rockies from 1897 to 1911. He also climbed more than 80 Scottish peaks and completed many rock climbs on Snowdon in North Wales and in England's Lake District.

1897:

The New York Sun newspaper published a letter declaring Mount McKinley or Denali (20,320 ft./6,193 m.) higher than Mount St. Elias (18,008 ft./5,489 m.).

1897:

Gold miner William A. Dickey performed a crude survey and estimated the height of a high Alaskan mountain (Mount McKinley or Denali) to be 20,000 feet/6,096 m. He suggested that this prominent mountain be named "McKinley" after the newly elected 25th president of the United States William McKinley (served from 1897 to 1901).

1897: Equipment – Sleeping Bag

The first ascent of Mount St. Elias (18,008 ft./5,489 m.) in Alaska was led by the Duke of the Abruzzi from Italy. This climbing party used a modular sleeping bag system comprised of camel's hair, eiderdown, goatskin, and waterproof canvas.

1897: Technique – Food Pre-Packaging

Well-known Italian mountaineer the Duke of the Abruzzi (1873–1933) led an Italian expedition to Mount Saint Elias (18,008 feet/5,489 meters) in Alaska. The expedition's food (crackers, soup cubes, chocolate, compressed beef, bacon, rum, condensed milk, etc.) was sealed in 53-pound cans. Each can would supply one day's rations for a ten-man team. All ten climbers reached the summit on July 31st at noon. This was the first large-scale mountaineering expedition to systematically pre-package its food supplies. This expedition lasted 57 days.

1898: PEAK FIRST ASCENT *GRAND TETON*

August 11. William O. Owen (Wyoming state auditor), the Reverend Franklin Spalding (1865–1914), Frank Petersen, and John Shive made the first undisputed ascent of the Grand Teton (13,766 ft./4,196 m.) in Wyoming. Their climbing route is now known as the Owen-Spalding Route. This first ascent was finally officially recognized by the Wyoming legislature in 1929. Owen had a Kodak camera with him to prove this ascent. Two days later these climbers returned to the summit to take photographs, build a huge summit cairn, and chisel their names into the summit rocks. There are now over sixty named climbing routes leading to the summit.

1898: PEAK FIRST ASCENT *ATHABASCA*

August 18. Mountaineers John Norman Collie (1859–1942) and Hermann Woolley (1846–1920) made the first ascent of Mount Athabasca (11,453 ft./3,491 m.) in the Canadian Rockies via its north ridge. Athabasca is located in the Columbia Icefield of Jasper National Park. This was the highest peak in the Canadian Rockies climbed to date. From the summit, Collie and Woolley first saw and discovered the Columbia Icefield. This icefield (largest in the Canadian Rockies) contains eleven 11,000 foot/3,352 meter peaks and measures 195 square miles or 325 square kilometers. Athabasca is a Cree Indian word meaning "place where there are reeds."

1898:

Surveyors George Eldridge and Robert Muldrow made the triangulated measurements of Mount McKinley (a.k.a. Denali) and concluded that its elevation was 20,464 feet/6,237 meters. They only miscalculated by 144 feet/44 meters. McKinley's official elevation is 20,320 feet/6,193 meters.

1898:

The Vaux (pronounced "Vox") brothers from Philadelphia, Pennsylvania (distinguished amateur scientists) after hearing about a successful climbing trip in Canada that included a Swiss mountain guide (Peter Sarbach from St. Niklaus), suggested that the Canadian Pacific Railway (CPR) should engage Swiss mountain guides to be available to CPR patrons who wished to climb peaks in the Canadian Rockies. During the winter of 1898–99, the CPR brought two Swiss guides to Canada to help promote tourism. They were Christian Hasler, Sr. (1857–1924) and Edward Feuz, Sr. (1859–1944). These two guides were headquartered at the Glacier House (the first of the Grand Railway Hotels) below Rogers Pass (4,364 ft./1,330 m.).

1898:

The high peak just southwest of Denali in Alaska was named Mount Foraker (17,401 ft./5,304 m.) after an Ohio politician. The local Indian name for this peak when translated was "Denali's Wife."

1899:

August 16. David Starr Jordan, President of Stanford University in California, made the second ascent of Mount Stanford (13,963 ft./4,256 m.) in the southern Sierra Nevada Range of California. Bolton Brown named this peak after making the first ascent in 1896.

1899:

The Canadian Pacific Railroad (C.P.R.) was completed through the Canadian Rockies in 1884. The CPR brought three Swiss mountain guides to the Glacier House at Roger's Pass (4,364 ft./1,330 m.) in 1899 to encourage tourist travel to the mountains. These three guides were: Charlie Clark, Edward Feuz Sr., and Christian Hasler Sr. European mountain guides were employed by the CPR until 1954 (55 years).

1900: FIRST ASCENT

July 21. American woman mountaineer Mary Vaux (1860–1940) from Philadelphia, Pennsylvania made the first ascent of Mount Stephen (10,523 ft./3,207 m.) in the Canadian Rockies by a woman. Her guides were Christian Hasler and Edward Feuz. This was the first time a woman climbed a peak over 10,000 ft./3,038 m. in Canada.

1900: PEAK FIRST ASCENT *NORTH ARAPAHOE*

September. Swiss-American climbers Arnold F. Emch, Sr. and his brother Herman made this first ascent of North Arapahoe Peak (13,502 ft./4,115 m.) in the Indian Peaks of Colorado. They climbed the east face. Eight peaks in this mountain group have been given tribal names.

1900:

British mountaineer James Outram (1864–1925) arrived in Canada and began a two year climbing period in which he made 19 first ascents of peaks between 10,100 ft./3,078 m. and 12,500 ft./3,810 m. Formerly the vicar of St. Peter's in Ipswich, England, Outram had many climbing partners in the Canadian Rockies but used mountain guide Christian Kaufmann (1873–1939) on 12 of his first ascents.

1900: Equipment – Sunscreen

Canadian Rockies. Lanoline was used for sunburn protection.

1901:

May 9. Noted Arctic authority and volcanologist Angelo Heilprin (1853–1907) called for a meeting to be held in Philadelphia, Pennsylvania "to consider the formation of an alpine society." Twelve men attended this meeting. This discussion eventually led to the founding of the American Alpine Club (AAC) in 1902. By 1911, the AAC had 80 members. The 2005 membership was over 6,800 members. In 1886, Heilprin climbed Pico de Orizaba, Popocatepetl, and Ixtacchihuatl in Mexico.

1901: PEAK FIRST ASCENT *HABEL*

August 15. British mountaineer Edward Whymper (1840–1911) of Matterhorn fame arrived in Canada with 28 pieces of luggage and soon led the first ascent of Mount Habel (10,600 ft./3,161 m.) in the Canadian Rockies. This peak was named for a German explorer. Whymper was invited to Canada on a publicity assignment for the Canadian Pacific Railway. He brought four Swiss mountain guides with him: Christian Klucker (1853–1928), Joseph Pollinger (1876–), Christian Kaufmann (1873–1939), and Joseph Bossoney (1869–). This group made a total of 22 ascents. Edward Whymper returned to the Canadian Rockies in 1903, 1904, 1905, and 1909.

1901: PEAK FIRST ASCENT *ASSINIBOINE*

September 3. British-Canadian mountaineer James Outram (1864–1925) and two Swiss mountain guides (Christian Häsler and Christian Bören) made the first ascent of Mount Assiniboine (11,871 ft./3,618 m.) in the Canadian Rockies via the southwest face and south ridge. Assiniboine is located near Banff, British Columbia. This was the highest peak in Canada climbed to date. In addition to making this first ascent, this climbing party also made the first traverse of Mount Assiniboine by descending the north face. This traverse was considered a significant mountaineering achievement. Mount Assiniboine had more failed climbing attempts than any other peak in the Canadian Rockies. The name "Assiniboine" in the local American Indian language means: "Assini" = stone and "boine" = broiled food. Dr. G.M. Dawson named this peak in 1884 after a local Indian tribe. Mount Assiniboine has been called the "Matterhorn of the Canadian Rockies." Outram made ten first ascents in a two-week period during the 1901 climbing season.

1902:

March 15. The American Alpine Club (AAC) was founded by zoologist and geographer Angelo Heilprin (1853 – 1907). The forty-five founding members were primarily from the east coast of the United States. The first president of the AAC was Charles Earnest Fay (1846 – 1931). The club headquarters remained in New York City until 1993 when a more centralized location was favored in light of the club's coast-to-coast membership. The AAC was moved to Golden, Colorado, in 1993. The club's headquarters now includes the Henry S. Hall Jr. America Alpine Club Library and the Bradford Washburn American Mountaineering Museum. The AAC has two annual publications: *The American Alpine Journal* (first published in 1929) and *Accidents in North American Mountaineering.* As of December of 2011, the AAC had just over 8,700 members.

1902: PEAK FIRST ASCENT *SPLIT*

July 23. California climber Helen Gompertz LeConte (–1924) made the first ascent of Split Mountain (14,058 ft./4,284 m.) in the Sierra Nevada mountains of California. This peak was formerly known as South Palisade Peak. LeConte became the first and only woman to make a first ascent of a California mountain over 14,000 feet (4,267 meters).

1902:

August 4. Harvard University (Boston, Massachusetts) geologist Alfred Brooks became the first person in recorded history to walk upon Mount McKinley's (a.k.a. Denali) slopes in Alaska. He then wrote an article in the January 1903 issue of the National Geographic entitled "Plans For Climbing Mount McKinley." This article recommended a northern approach. Brooks was only able to reach approximately 7,500 feet/2,286 meters on McKinley.

1902: PEAK FIRST ASCENTS *COLUMBIA, EDWARD, FORBES, BRYCE, AND ALEXANDRA*

British–Canadian mountaineer James Outram (1864–1925) and Swiss mountain guide Christian Kaufmann (1873–1939) made five first ascents of peaks over 11,000 feet/3,353 meters in the Canadian Rockies. These first ascents were:

Mount Columbia	12,293 ft./3,747 m.	July 19
Edward Peak	11,529 ft./3,514 m.	July 24
Mount Forbes	11,850 ft./3,612 m.	August 10
Mount Bryce	11,506 ft./3,507 m.	August 21
Mount Alexandra	11,115 ft./3,388 m.	August 23

1902: Equipment – Sleeping Air Mattress

British mountaineer James Outram (1864–1925) used a seven-foot long by two-and-a-half foot wide heavy India-rubber air mattress on his climbs in the Canadian Rockies. He found this mattress to be very successful and never climbed again without it.

1903:

July 20. Judge James Wickersham (1857–1939) made the first attempt to climb Mount McKinley (20,320 ft./6,193 m.) in Alaska from the north. He established his first camp at the terminus of the Peters Glacier. He and his party reached at elevation of 8,100 feet/2,469 meters on what is now known as the Wickersham Wall which was not successfully climbed until 1963. From 1903 to 1913, nine climbing groups attempted to summit Mount McKinley.

1903: PEAK FIRST ASCENT *NORTH PALISADE*

July 25. Joseph Le Conte (1870–1950), James Hutchinson, James Moffitt, and Robert Pike made the first ascent of North Palisade Peak (14,242 ft./4,341 m.) in California via the southwest couloir. LeConte (a.k.a. "Little Joe") spent sixteen years making the first comprehensive map of the Sierra Nevada mountain range from the Yosemite Valley south to Mount Whitney.

1903: FIRST ASCENT

July. Scottish mountaineer W. Douglas of Edinburgh with guides Christian Hasler and Christian Kaufmann made the first ascent of the 5,000 foot/1,524 meter north face of Mount Assiniboine (11,870 ft./3,618 m.) in the Canadian Rockies. This was the second overall ascent of the peak (first ascent September 3,1901).

1903:

American explorer, surgeon, and ethnologist Dr. Frederick A. Cook (1865–1940) organized the first mountaineering expedition to Mount McKinley/Denali (20,320 ft./6,193 m.) in Alaska. Six men with fourteen pack horses made two attempts to reach the summit. They were only able to reach 11,000 ft./3,353 m. but they did accomplish the first circumnavigation of both Mount McKinley and Mount Foraker — a 540-mile journey.

1903: FIRST ASCENT

Well-known Colorado naturalist and climber Enos Mills (1870–1922) made the following first ascents on Longs Peak (14,256 ft./4,345 m.) in Colorado:

February First winter ascent

July First ascent of the north face (later to be known as the Cables Route).

1904: FIRST ASCENT

February. The Reverend John Herdman and his young guide Edward Feuz, Jr. (1884–1981) made the first winter ascent of a Canadian Peak — Mount Abbot (8,091 ft./2,466 m.). They both carried alpenstocks and ice axes for balance on their snowshoes.

1904: PEAK FIRST ASCENT FAY

British woman mountaineer Gertrude Benham (1867–1938) visited the Canadian Rockies for her first and only climbing season. She began her climbing with an ascent of Mount Lefroy (11,231 ft./3,423 m.) on June 27th with guides Hans and Christian Kaufman. Benham then went on to climb 19 more peaks including the first ascent of Mount Fay on July 20. Mount Fay (10,611 ft./3,234 m.) is located in the Valley of the Ten Peaks in Banff National Park (Alberta, Canada). She also made the first female ascent of Mount Assiniboine (11,871 ft./3,618 m.). Benham made seventeen trips to the European Alps where she accomplished 160 climbs.

1904:

The Explorers Club was founded in New York City. This professional society is dedicated to the scientific exploration of the Earth. It currently has thirty chapters worldwide and has sponsored numerous mountaineering expeditions. Sir Edmund Hillary of Mount Everest fame was a member of the Explorers Club.

1905: FIRST ASCENT

Warren Hart, Herschel Parker, and George Whipple made the first ascent of Mount Washington's north face in New Hampshire.

1906:

March 27. The Alpine Club of Canada (ACC) was founded in Winnipeg, Manitoba, Canada. Ms. Elizabeth Parker and Arthur Oliver Wheeler (1860–1945) were the two primary advocates. There were 26 original delegates. Sandford Fleming was elected Honorary President twenty-three years after conceiving the alpine club idea in 1883. British mountaineer Edward Whymper was also elected as an Honorary Member. One quarter of the original members were women. Those members who had made an ascent of a peak of at least 10,000 feet (3,049 meters) in a recognized mountain range were considered to be active. Now headquartered in Banff, the ACC manages 20 alpine and backcountry huts and has 10,000 members.

1906:

September 16. Surveyor–cartographer Donald Bittinger climbed to the summit of the South Peak of Seneca Rocks in West Virginia. This 900 foot/274 meter limestone/quartzite rock fin towers over the North Fork of the South Branch of the Potomac River. Bittinger worked for the U.S. National Park Service at the time. He left this inscription carved into a summit rock: "DB Sept 16, 1906." This inscription was discovered in 1974. Bittinger's climbing route is now known as the Old Ladies Route (rated 5.2).

1906:

September 16. Dr. Frederick A. Cook (1865–1940) perpetrated the most audacious mountaineering hoax of all time — a claim that he and horse packer Edward Barrill had been the first men to reach the summit of Mount McKinley/Denali (20,320 ft./6,193 m.) in Alaska. Cook reported that this climb required 12 days total (8-day ascent and 4-day descent). Cook's ascent was immediately doubted. Cook's summit photograph was actually taken of the summit of a very minor peak now known as "Fake Peak." This 5,386 ft./1,642 m. sub-peak is located 19.42 air miles southeast of Mount McKinley. In 1995, well-known Alaskan mountaineer, explorer, and photographer Bradford Washburn (1910–2007) conducted an extensive photographic analysis of Cook's claims and proved that Cook's ascent was a hoax.

1906:

The Mountaineers Club was founded in Seattle, Washington. Of the 151 charter members, 77 were women. Its goals were to explore, preserve, and to make frequent expeditions into the mountains of the Pacific Northwest. As of 1998, The Mountaineers Club had over 15,000 members and branches in five other Washington cities. This club was conceived by W. Montelius Price and Asahel Curtis while climbing Mount Baker (10,781 ft./3,286 m.) in Washington. Edmond Stephen Meany (1862–1933) served as the first President (for the first 27 years).

1906: FIRST ASCENT

American climber Victoria Broughm became the first woman to climb a major Colorado peak solo — Longs Peak (14,256 ft./4,345 m.).

1906:

Longs Peak (14,256 ft./4,345 m.) mountain guide Enos Mills (1870–1922) climbed the peak 32 times during the 31 days in August including 6 ascents by moonlight as well as making a daily trip (16 miles roundtrip) to Estes Park, Colorado on horseback.

1906:

Swiss mountain guide Christian Kaufmann (1873–1939) from Grindelwald, Switzerland made thirty first ascents in the Canadian Rockies between 1900 and 1906 including Mounts Assiniboine, Columbia, Bryce, Lyell, Freshfield, Forbes, Hungabee, Huber, and Deltaform.

1906: Equipment – Rope

Dr. Frederick A. Cook and Ed Barrill carried a one-pound horsehair rope on their failed attempt to climb Mount McKinley in Alaska.

1906: Equipment – Sunscreen

Male climbing members of The Mountaineers (Seattle, Washington based mountain club) mostly used greasepaint for sun protection.

1907: PEAK FIRST ASCENTS OLYMPUS– WEST, OLYMPUS– MIDDLE, AND OLYMPUS– EAST

August 13. Lorenz A. Nelson led a mountaineering group of eleven people on the first ascent of the west summit (highest) of Mount Olympus (7,969 ft./2,430 m.) in the Olympic Mountains of Washington. This peak was named in 1788 by an English navigator who thought its height may be the home of the Gods. The middle summit (7,929 ft./2,418 m.) was first climbed in July of 1907 by

Belmore Brown, Walter G. Clarke, Will Humes, Herschel C. Parker, and Dewitt Sisson. The east summit (7,762 ft./2,367 m.) was first climbed in 1899 by Jack McGlone of the Dodwell-Rixon survey party.

1907: PEAK FIRST ASCENTS *CAPITOL AND PYRAMID*

Colorado mountaineers Percy Hagerman (38) and Harold Clark (45) explored and climbed two of the 14,000 foot/4,267 m. peaks in Colorado's Elk Range. They made the first ascents of Capitol Peak (14,130 ft./4,307 m.) on August 22nd and Pyramid Peak (14,018 ft./4,272 m.) on August 31st.

1908: PEAK FIRST ASCENTS *MAROON AND NORTH MAROON*

Percy Hagerman made the first documented ascent of Maroon Peak (14,156 ft./4,315 m.) in the Elk Range of Colorado. Hagerman climbed the south ridge solo. Three days earlier, Hagerman and Harold Clark made the first ascent of North Maroon Peak (14,014 ft./4,271 m.).

1909:

Austrian mountain guide Conrad Kain (1883–1934) immigrated to Canada (Calgary, Alberta) and the Canadian Rockies. Hired as a professional guide, he was paid $2.00 per day plus $2.00 for each climb that he made. Kain was the first official guide for the Alpine Club of Canada. From 1909 to 1929, Kain made sixty-nine first ascents in the Canadian Rockies.

1910: PEAK FIRST ASCENT *MCKINLEY-NORTH*

April 10. Gold prospectors Pete Anderson (43), Tom Lloyd (50+), Charles McGonagill (40), and William Taylor (23) made the first ascent of Mount McKinley's north peak (19,470 ft./5,934 m.) in Alaska. Known as the Sourdough Expedition, this party placed a 14-foot spruce tree flagpole on the summit after climbing the final 8,000 feet/2,438 meters in 18 hours. Anderson and Taylor actually reached the summit. They had no rope, no ice axes, no real crampons and cut no steps in the snow and ice.

1910:

Mountaineer Belmore Brown (1880–1954) led an expedition to climb Mount McKinley (20,320 ft./6,193 m.) in Alaska. This 8-member party attempted a route up the southwest ridge but only reached 10,300 ft./3,139 m. on July 19. This route proved to be impossible for them. This expedition did, however, gather evidence that Dr. Frederick A. Cook did not reach the actual summit of Mount McKinley. Belmore Brown and Hershel Parker were the first to explore the Ruth Gorge in Alaska. They named most of the peaks in this gorge which was named by Cook after his stepdaughter Ruth Hunt.

1911:

British scientist John Scott Haldane (1860 – 1936) of Oxford, England led the first medical expedition to high altitudes in the western hemisphere. This was the Anglo-American Expedition to Pikes Peak (14,110 ft./4,301 m.) in Colorado. Haldane and three colleagues spent one month on the summit conducting various experiments. This expedition laid the foundations for nearly all of our understanding of high-altitude acclimatization.

1912:

April 3. Seven Colorado hikers and climbers met to discuss the feasibility of starting a club. A second meeting was held on April 26 when 25 people signed on as charter members of the Colorado Mountain Club (CMC). In 1912, this new club conducted ten high-country outings. James Grafton Rogers (1883–1971), a Denver attorney, served as the first president. The total membership of the C.M.C. in 2005 was nearly 8,000.

1912: PEAK FIRST ASCENT *BLACKBURN*

May 19. American mountaineers Dora Keen (1871–1963) and George Handy (who later married Keen) made the first ascent of Mount Blackburn (16,390 ft./4,995 m.) in Alaska. Keen was the first woman to make an Alaskan ascent and a first ascent in Alaska. This climb represented several other firsts in Alaskan mountaineering:

1. First expedition to use dogs on a mountain
2. First expedition to have members live in snow caves.
3. First expedition to make a prolonged night ascent.

Dora Keen died in a Hong Kong hotel room January 31, 1963 at age 91. She had been a member of the American Alpine Club since 1907.

1912:

June 29. Mountaineer, author, and noted landscape painter, Belmore Brown (1880–1954) led an expedition to climb Mount McKinley (20,320 ft./6,193 m.) in Alaska. They climbed the northeast ridge and reached a point 300 feet/91 m. from the summit. They were forced to retreat due to a raging storm. Two days later, an earthquake destroyed the summit ridge. Herschel Parker was with Brown.

1912: FIRST ASCENT

A group of Dartmouth College (Hanover, New Hampshire) mountaineers made the first ski ascent of New Hampshire's Mount Washington (6,288 ft./1,917 m.).

1913: PEAK FIRST ASCENT *McKINLEY-SOUTH*

June 7. Alaskan mountaineer and Episcopal Archdeacon of the Yukon Hudson Stuck (1863–1920) led Harry Karstens, Robert Tatum, and Walter Harper (1892–1918) on the first ascent of the south summit of Mount McKinley or Denali (20,320 ft./6,193 m.) in Alaska. This party climbed the mountain's north side via the Muldrow Glacier. They began their ascent on April 18. Walter Harper was the first climber to reach the summit. Tatum's summit comment was: "The view from the top of Mount McKinley is like looking out the windows of heaven." No more climbing parties would visit this area until 1925. This group of climbers wore a moccasin type shoe with five pairs of socks.

"I remember no day in my life so full of toil, distress, and exhaustion, and yet so full of happiness and keen gratification."
Hudson Stuck
1863–1920
Reflecting on his successful ascent of Mount McKinley.

1913: PEAK FIRST ASCENT *ROBSON*

July 31. Mountaineers William W. Foster, Albert H. MacCarthy (1876–1956), and mountain guide Conrad Kain (1883–1934) made the first ascent of Mount Robson (12,972 ft./3,954 m.) in the Canadian Rockies via the east face. This ascent (30 hours roundtrip) of the highest peak in the Canadian Rockies was the most difficult climb in North America to date. This was the sixth attempt to reach Robson's summit. They climbed the Northeast Face (now known as the Kain Face) and the southeast ridge. This was the first long, difficult ice climb in North America. The local Indian name for Robson was "Yuh-Hai-Has-Kun" which meant "The Mountain of the Spiral Road." The second ascent of Robson was not until 1924 and also involved Conrad Kain.

1913: Technique – Step Cutting

Long-shafted ice axes were meant to be used with both hands when cutting steps in the Canadian Rockies of Alberta and British Columbia.

1914:

By this year American mountaineer Henry F. Montagnier (1877–1933) had climbed over 70 peaks in the Alps and became a well-known authority on the history of Mont Blanc (15,775 ft./4,808 m.). His personal mountaineering library exceeded 4,000 volumes. His donation of several hundred of these books in 1915 was the beginning of the American Alpine Club Library.

1914:

American mountaineer and explorer Norman Clyde (1885–1972) made his first first ascent in the High Sierras of California. From 1920 to 1946, Clyde made over 1,000 peak climbs of which approximately 120 were either first ascents or new routes on previously climbed peaks.

1914: Equipment – Pitons

American mountaineer Albert Ellingwood (1888–1934) brought pitons to the United States from Europe.

1914: Technique – Belaying

The mountaineering technique of belaying was introduced to the United States.

1915: FIRST ASCENT

March 7. The first winter ascent of Mount Hood (11,239 ft./3,425 m.) in Oregon was accomplished.

1915 to 1925:

Swiss guide Hans Fuhrer (from Grindelwald, Switzerland) led over 250 ascents of Mount Hood (11,239 ft./3,425 m.) in Oregon and Mount Rainier (14,411 ft./4,392 m.) in Washington during this ten-year period.

1915: PEAK FIRST ASCENTS *KIT CARSON, CRESTONE PEAK, AND CRESTONE NEEDLE*

American mountaineer Albert Ellingwood (1888–1934) led the first ascents of the last remaining unclimbed Colorado fourteen thousand foot peaks: Kit Carson Peak (14,165 ft./4,317 m.), Crestone Peak (14,294 ft./4,357 m.), and Crestone Needle (14,197 ft./4,327 m.). Ellingwood was accompanied by Eleanor Davis Ehrman, Joe Deutschbein, and Francis "Bee" Rogers. On July 24, Ellingwood and Davis made the first ridge traverse between Crestone Peak and Crestone Needle in the Sangre de Christo Range.

1916:

The Henry S. Hall, Jr. American Alpine Club Library was formerly established. This library of over 60,000 books (30 percent are considered to be rare), journals, letters, maps, films, and mountaineering artifacts is now located in Golden, Colorado, at the American Mountaineering Center. This library may be the largest mountaineering library in the world. Other significant mountaineering libraries include the Oxford Mountaineering Library of Oxford University in England and the British Alpine Club Library (over 40,000 items) in London, England.

1916:

Austrian-Canadian guide Conrad Kain (1883–1934) made twelve first ascents in the Canadian Rockies during this climbing season. Age 33.

1917:

February 24. Mount McKinley National Park (9,468 square miles) was created in Alaska. President Woodrow Wilson signed the official legislation in Washington, D.C. This park was renamed Denali National Park in 1980.

1917:

The guide service on Mount Rainier was established by noted Seattle-based photographer Asahel Curtis (1874–1941).

1918:

June 9. Ms. Alma Wagen (1878–1967) became the first woman mountain guide employed by the United States government. She worked in Mount Rainier National Park in Washington. Joseph Hazard was the Chief Climbing Guide at Mount Rainier at this time.

1919: FIRST ASCENT

March. Canadian mountain guide Conrad Kain (1883–1934) made a solo ascent of Jumbo Mountain (11,152 ft./3,399 m.) in the Purcell Range of the Canadian Rockies. This was the first winter ascent of any Canadian peak over 11,000 feet/ 3,353 meters.

1920:

July 4. The Barr Trail was officially opened on Pikes Peak (14,110 ft./4,300 m.) in Colorado. This

12-mile/20 kilometer trail begins at 6,600 ft./2,012 m. and leads to the summit — a 7,510 ft./2,289 m. vertical gain. This trail was named for Fred Barr who built the first three miles.

1920:

The idea of climbing all 47 peaks in Colorado over 14,000 feet/ 4,267 meters occurred to Colorado climbers Carl Blaurock (1894–1993) and William Ervin as they sat on the summit of Mount Eolus (14,083 ft./4,292 m.) in southwestern Colorado. In 1923, these two mountaineers did, in fact, complete the climbing of all 47 peaks. None of their ascents were first ascents. Colorado climber Albert R. Ellingwood (1888–1934) was the third person to complete all 47 peaks. At some point after 1920, there were seven additional summits added to this exclusive list making a total of fifty-four 14,000-foot peaks.

1920: Equipment – Ice Axe

The most widely used ice axe in North America was 41" long (104 ct.) and weighed three pounds. The wood shaft was hewn from either hickory or ash.

> *"For anchorage purposes the axe is very useful, and comes in handy at times in pulling one's self up as well as in descending. Its uses are innumerable on and off the ice. In glissading it acts as a support and brake simultaneously; it clears away debris, probes for hidden crevasses, cuts steps, serves as a balancing pole when crossing streams on fallen logs, or as a balustrade for timid folks, chops wood for fires and boughs for beds, is a distinct success as a can opener, and, on an emergency, comes in hand as a camera stand, two making a most effective substitute for the conventional tripod."*
>
> 1923
> James Outram (1864–1925)
> British/Canadian Mountaineer
> *In The Heart Of The Canadian Rockies*

1920: Technique – Belaying

American climbers Albert Ellingwood (1888–1934) and Barton Hoag made the first ascent of Lizard Head (13,113 feet/3,997 meters) in the San Juan Mountains of Colorado. The final 350 feet of Lizard Head is composed of loose and rotten rock. At this time, this climb was considered to be America's most difficult summit and its most difficult rock climb. This was the first widely known United States climb in which a conscious effort was made to belay each climber. PEAK FIRST ASCENT. LIZARD HEAD. August.

1921:

Eleven-year old Bradford Washburn (1910–2007) made his first ascent of Mount Washington (6,288 ft./1,917 m.) in New Hampshire. Washburn would become a well-known mountaineer, explorer, photographer, and cartographer.

1921:

As of this year, 17 members of The Mountaineers (Seattle, Washington-based mountain club) had summited the six prominent glaciated summits in Washington:

1. Mount Rainier 14,411 ft./4,392 m.
2. Mount Adams 12,307 ft./3,751 m.
3. Mount Baker 10,781 ft./3,286 m.
4. Glacier Peak 10,541 ft./3,213 m.
5. Mount St. Helens 8,366 ft./2,550 m.
6. Mount Olympus 7,965 ft./2,428 m.

1921:

Princeton University (Princeton, New Jersey) mathematics professor James Waddell Alexander III (32) first visited Longs Peak (14,256 ft./4,345 m.) in Colorado. From 1921 to 1924, he climbed Longs Peak 20 times — the only Colorado peak he would ever climb. He made ten ascents in 1922, including the first ascent of Alexander's Chimney on the East Face.

1921: Clothing – Climbing Suit

Rocky Mountain National Park (Colorado) Superintendent Roger W. Toll (1883 – 1936) wrote an article on clothing recommendations for climbing: "A suit of corduroy or other strong, heavy material… some men find knickerbocker breeches with knit leggings a good combination." On the feet, climbers wore high, hobnailed boots, which had been studded with soft-iron cleats for traction. The leather boots were waterproofed with special oils, if you could obtain them, or simply with bacon fat or axle grease.

1922: FIRST ASCENT

February 13. A trio of visiting French mountaineers (Jean and Jacques Landry and Jacques Bergues) and American mountaineer Charles Perryman made the first winter ascent of Mount Rainier (14,411 ft./4,392 m.) in Washington via the Gibralter Route.

1922:

March 26. The Club de Exploration de Mexico was founded by American climber Otis McAllister (1899–) and others on the summit of Ajusco (12,894 ft./3,930 m.), a volcano south of Mexico City. McAllister climbed many mountains in the United States and the European Alps.

1922:

September 20. American mountaineer and conservationist Enos A. Mills (1870–1922) died at age 52 from injuries he suffered in a New York City subway train collision in January of 1922. Mills made 257 ascents of Longs Peak (14,256 ft./4,345 m.) in Colorado as a mountain guide. He also wrote seventeen books.

1922:

December 22. Five mountaineers from Colorado Springs, Colorado decided to climb Pikes Peak (14,110 ft./4,301 m.) and reach the summit on New Year's Eve to set off fireworks to celebrate the new year. This initial winter ascent led to the founding of the AdAmAn Club. Each year a new member is added to this 85-year old-climbing club — "Add-a-man" or "AdAmAn." As of December 31, 2007, this club had 90 members. Each new member must have completed ten previous New Year's Eve climbs as a guest. A maximum of thirty climbers makes this annual two-day New Year's Eve climb.

1922: PEAK FIRST *ASCENT GANNETT*

Mountaineers Arthur Tate (45) and Floyd Stahlnaker made the first confirmed ascent of Wyoming's highest peak — Gannett Peak (13,803 ft./4,207 m.) via the route now known as the Gooseneck Route. Gannett is the highest of the 51 peaks in Wyoming over 13,000 feet/3,962 meters.

1923: PEAK FIRST ASCENT *GRANITE*

August 29. American climbers Elers Koch, R. Ferguson, and J. Whitam made the first ascent of Granite Peak (12,799 ft./3,901 m.), the highest mountain in Montana. This peak was the last of the state highpoints (in the United States) to be climbed.

1923:

W.S. Ladd, J.M. Thorington, and guide Conrad Kain made the first ascent of North Twin (12,237 ft./3,730 m.), the third highest peak in the Canadian Rockies via the east face. Only four peaks exceed 12,000 feet/3,658 meters in the Canadian Rockies.

1923:

American climber Norman Clyde (1885–1972) climbed 36 peaks in 36 days in Glacier National Park in Montana including ten first ascents. Most of Clyde's climbs were done solo.

1923: FIRST ASCENT/PEAK FIRST ASCENTS *MIDDLE TETON AND SOUTH TETON*

The year of 1923 was considered to be the most significant year in the history of mountaineering in the Teton Mountains of Wyoming. The following climbs occurred during this year:

1. August 25. Montana students Quin Blackburn, Andy DePirro, and David DeLap made the second ascent of the Grand Teton (13,766 ft./4,196 m.) 25 years after the official first ascent in 1898. This was also the first one-day ascent (Owen-Spaulding route).

2. American climber Eleanor Davis (Colorado Springs, Colorado) made the first female ascent of the Grand Teton on August 7th. With her was Albert R. Ellingwood (Lake Forest, Illinois). They climbed the Owen-Spaulding route. As a result of this ascent, Davis became the first Colorado woman to become a member of the American Alpine Club.

3. August 29. Albert R. Ellingwood (1888–1934) made the first ascent (solo) of Middle Teton (12,804 ft./3,903 m.). He and Eleanor Davis also made the first ascent of South Teton (12,505 ft./3,811 m.) on the same day.

1923:

As of this year, Canadian guide Conrad Kain (1883–1934) was the only person to have climbed the three highest peaks in the Canadian Rockies: Robson (12,972 ft./3,954 m.), Columbia (12,293 ft./3,747 m.), and North Twin (12,237 ft./3,730 m.).

1923: Technique – Climbing Rope

In the Canadian Rockies of British Columbia and Alberta, the rope distance between two climbers was recommended to be 15 to 18 feet (4.5 to 5.5 meters) when traveling across glaciers. A longer interval distance was recommended when rock climbing.

1924: PEAK FIRST ASCENT *WARREN*

August 10. On August 10, Blaurock and Ellingwood made the first ascent of Mount Warren (13,720 ft./4,182 m.) also via the East Ridge in the Wind River Mountains of Wyoming.

1924: FIRST ASCENT

August. American climbers Carl Blaurock (1894–1993) and Albert Ellingwood (1888–1934) made the first complete ascent of the northeast ridge of Mount Moran (12,605 ft./3,842 m.) in the Teton Mountains of Wyoming. Mount Moran was first climbed July 22, 1922, by LeGrand Hardy, Bennett McNulty, and Ben Rich of the Chicago Mountaineering Club via the Skillet Glacier Route.

1924: FIRST ASCENT

Canadian woman mountaineer Phyllis Munday (1894–1990) became the first woman to summit Mount Robson (12,972 ft./3,954 m.) in British Columbia, Canada with guide Conrad Kain (1883–1934).

1924: PEAK FIRST ASCENT HEAVENS

The Sierra Club held its annual summer outing in Glacier National Park (Montana). 210 club members, 50 employees, and 135 horses were involved with this outing. Club member Norman Clyde (1885–1972) climbed 21 peaks including the first ascent of Heavens Peak (8,987 ft./2,739 m.) during the outing.

1925: FIRST ASCENT

January 12. Colorado woman mountaineer Agnes Vaille (1890–1925) died of exposure on Longs Peak (14,256 ft./4,345 m.) in Colorado after completing the first winter ascent with Swiss mountain guide Walter Kiener. She was the sixth person to die on Longs Peak. Vaille had climbed nearly all of the peaks over 14,000 feet/4,267 meters in the continental United States. This was her fourth winter attempt to climb Longs Peak. One of her rescuers also died on this day — Herbert Sortland. The Agnes Vaille Shelter (stone-built) was constructed in 1927 just above the Boulderfield on Longs Peak at approximately 13,200 feet/4,023 meters.

1925: PEAK FIRST ASCENT LOGAN

June 23. A Canadian-American mountaineering team led by Howard F. Lambert and Albert H. MacCarthy (1876–1956) made the first ascent of Mount Logan (19,551 ft./5,959 m.) in Canada. Mount

Logan has five summits between 18,300 ft./5,578 m. and 19,551 ft./5,959 m. Other team members were Allen Carpé (1894–1932), William Foster, Henry Hall Jr., Hamilton Laing, Lennox Lindsay (British), Robert Morgan, Norman Read, and Andy Taylor. Their Camp VI at 18,500 ft./5,639 m. was the highest campsite established in North America up to that time. This ascent required 70 days and nearly 200 miles of travel through wild country. Six climbers reached the summit (MacCarthy, Lambert, Foster, Taylor, Read, and Carpé). Mount Logan was named for Sir William E. Logan, founder of the Geological Survey of Canada. Logan is the largest mountain massif in North America with a circumference of 90 miles/150 kilometers. Its summit plateau is eleven miles long and contains ten summits over 17,000 feet (5,181 meters).

1925: PEAK FIRST ASCENT *ALBERTA*

July 21. The first ascent of Mount Alberta (11,874 ft./3,619 m.) in the Canadian Rockies was made by Japanese mountaineer Yuko Maki (1894–1989) and five other members of the Japanese Alpine Club. Their Swiss guides were Heinrich Fuhrer, H. Kohler, and J. Weber. They climbed the east face. This was the first overseas mountaineering expedition for Japanese climbers and may be the earliest foreign climbing expedition to the Canadian Rockies. Mount Alberta is the sixth highest peak in the Canadian Rockies and was named for Louise Caroline Alberta, the fourth daughter of Queen Victoria of England. The second ascent of Mount Alberta was not until 1948. The ice axe that Yuko Maki left on the summit in 1925 as summit proof was retrieved by American climber John Cameron Oberlin (1914–2006) in 1948. Maki made the first ascent of the Eiger's Mittellegi Ridge (Switzerland) in 1921 and was the leader of the Japanese expedition in 1956 that made the first ascent of Manaslu (26,760 ft./8,156 m.) in the Nepal Himalaya.

1925:

Teenage brothers Bob (1901–1939) and George Marshall and Herb Clark completed the climbing of all forty-six 4,000 foot (1,219 meters) peaks in New York's Adirondack Mountains. They began this 46-peak journey in 1918. Eight of these climbs were first ascents and only fourteen of these peaks had trails.

1925:

American climber Norman Clyde (1885–1972) summited 48 Peaks in the California Sierra Mountains — half of them first ascents. He solo-climbed 42 of the 48 peaks.

1925: FIRST ASCENT

American mountaineers Albert Ellingwood (1888–1934), Eleanor Davis, Stephen Hart, and Marion Warner made the first ascent of the northeast buttress of Crestone Needle (14,197 ft./4,327 m.) in Colorado. This route is now known as the Ellingwood Arete (2,000 ft./609 m., rated 5.7). This was the highest rock climb in the United States at the time.

1925:

Canadian Mountaineers Don and Phyllis (1894–1990) Munday first sighted and then named an isolated high peak in the coastal range of British Columbia, Canada. This peak they named "Mystery

Mountain." Later on, this name would be officially changed to Mount Waddington (13,186 ft./4,019 m.) for Alfred Waddington who developed the first road across the Coastal Mountain Range in the 1860s.

1925: Equipment – Air Mattress

First ascent of Mount Logan (19,551 ft./5,959 m.) in Canada. Rubber air mattresses were used for the first time on a mountaineering expedition. Unfortunately, these mattresses had many leaks.

1925: Equipment – Sleeping Bag

An American expedition made the first ascent of Mount Logan (19,551 ft./5,959 m.) in Canada. This expedition used sleeping bags that were composed of two eiderdown quilts, one camel's hair blanket, one waterproof cover, and one ground cloth for a total weight of 18 pounds.

1925: Equipment – Tents

First ascent of Mount Logan (19,551 ft./5,959 m.) in Canada. Steel tent poles replaced wood poles for the first time.

1925: Equipment – Fixed Chains and Cables

Two ¾" steel cables were anchored to the rock on the north face of Longs Peak (14,256 feet/4,345 meters) in Colorado to assist climbers. These cables were eventually removed in 1973.

1925: Technique – Route Marking

On the first ascent of Mount Logan (19,551 feet/5,959 meters) in Canada, the climbing team used 36" willow branches to mark their climbing route. These willow "wands" were inserted into the snow at 40 to 50 foot (12 to 15 meters) intervals. These marking wands allowed the climbers to stay on-route in bad weather/low visibility conditions.

1926:

May. American mountaineers Allen Carpé (1894–1932), Dr. William S. Ladd (1887–1949), and Andrew S. Taylor made the first attempt to climb Mount Fairweather (15,318 ft./4,669 m.) in the Alaskan panhandle. This peak is located 13 miles/22 kilometers from the coast. Due to a lack of enough food supplies, this party turned around just above 9,000 feet/2,743 meters.

1926:

September 2. The Reverend William "Colonel Billy" Butler climbed Longs Peak (14,256 ft./4,345 m.) in Colorado on his 85th birthday. He is the oldest person to climb Longs.

1926:

Joseph W.A. Hickson (1873–) completed his seventeenth climbing season (1909 to 1926) in the Canadian Rockies. With his guide Edward Feuz, Sr. (1859–1944), Hickson made thirty-one first ascents. Two mountains in Canada have been named for him.

1926: PEAK FIRST ASCENT *ELLINGWOOD*

American mountaineer Albert Ellingwood (1888–1934) made the first ascent of Ellingwood Peak (13,052 ft./3,978 m.) in the Wind River Mountains of Wyoming. He made this ascent solo.

1927:

September 15. The Stettner brothers, Joe (26) and Paul (21), arrived at the base of Longs Peak (14,256 ft./4,345 m.) in Colorado after riding their motorcycles for 12 days from Chicago, Illinois. On the east face of Longs Peak, they discovered and climbed their now famous route — the Stettner Ledges. It took them five hours (approximately 1,000 ft./305 m.) to reach the Broadway Ledge and two more hours to reach the summit. This climb remained the most difficult climb in North America for the next 20 years. Paul Stettner led every pitch.

1927:

Harvard University student Alfred James Ostheimer III (19) and guide Hans Fuhrer (1897–1957) climbed 36 peaks in 63 days in the Canadian Rockies including 27 first ascents. These first ascents included 4 peaks over 11,000 feet/3,353 meters.

1927:

The official elevation of British Columbia's Mystery Mountain was established by J.T. Underhill's survey party — 13,186 feet/4,019 meters. Later that same year, the peak was renamed Mount Waddington after Alfred Waddington who advocated a major road through British Columbia.

1927: Technique – Climbing Communication

Wyoming mountaineer Paul Petzoldt (1908–1999) devised the climber's communication system while climbing in the Tetons (Wyoming). This voice system was universally accepted and used immediately. Petzoldt based his system on the number of syllables in each command message to reduce confusion when communication was difficult. For example:

      1st Command: Belayer to lead climber "On belay" (3 syllables)

      2nd Command: Lead climber back to belayer "Climbing" (2 syllables)

      3rd Command: Belayer to lead climber "Climb" (1 syllable)

1928: FIRST ASCENT

August 26. American climbers Arthur and Orville Emmons and their guide Mark Weygandt made the first ascent of Mount Hood's (11,239 ft./3,425 m.) north face in Oregon.

1928–1929:

Winter. Orland "Bart" Bartholomew (1899–1957) completed one of America's greatest ski mountaineering feats — a three-month solo traverse of the Sierra Mountain Range in California from Lone Pine to the Yosemite Valley (100 days, 250 miles, 140,000 feet of vertical ascents and descents). He finished this journey on April 3, 1929. This route was not repeated until 1970.

1929: FIRST ASCENT

January 10. Orland "Bart" Bartholomew (1899–1957) made the first winter ascent of Mount Whitney (14,495 ft./4,418 m.) in California via the western chutes.

1929: FIRST ASCENT

July 22. American climbers Robert Underhill (1889–1983) and Kenneth Henderson (1907–2001) made the first ascent of the East Ridge on the Grand Teton (13,766 ft./4,196 m.) in Wyoming. This was the first new route on the Grand Teton since 1896. This route is rated 5.7.

1929: FIRST ASCENT

August 14. American geologist Fritiof Fryxell (1900–1986) and Phil Smith (1905–1979) made the first ascent of Mount Teewinot (12,317 ft./3,754 m.) in the Teton Range of Wyoming. They climbed the east face. Fryxell became the first Park Naturalist in Grand Teton National Park.

1929:

Swiss-born Oregon mountaineer Joseph Leuthold (1906–1965) made the first of his 64 ascents of Mount Hood (11,239 ft./3,425 m.) in Oregon.

1929:

The American Alpine Club (AAC) began publishing the American Alpine Journal on an annual basis. The AAC was founded in 1902 to provide "knowledge and inspiration, conservation and advocacy, and logistical support to the climbing community."

1930: FIRST ASCENT

February. Canadian ski mountaineer Peter Parsons made the first ski ascent of a Canadian Rockies peak over 11,000 feet/3,353 meters—Resplendent Mountain: 11,240 ft./3,426 m.

1930: FIRST ASCENT

May 4. Ski mountaineers Ed Loness and Robert B. Sperlin made the first ski ascent of a major north-west peak when they climbed Mount Baker (10,778 ft./3,285 m.) in Washington.

1930: PEAK FIRST ASCENT *BONA*

July 2. American mountaineers Andy Taylor, Allen Carpé (1894–1932), and Terris Moore (1908–1993) made the first ascent of Mount Bona (16,421 ft./5,005 m.) in Alaska via the northwest ridge. This peak was named by the Duke of the Abruzzi in 1897 after his young girl cousin.

1930: PEAK FIRST ASCENT *STARLIGHT*

July 9. Well-known Sierra mountaineer Norman Clyde (1885–1972) made the first recorded ascent of Starlight Peak (14,200 ft./4,328 m.) near the eastern boundary of Kings Canyon National Park of California. Clyde made this ascent solo and self-belayed himself up the final section of this rock monolith summit.

1930: PEAK FIRST ASCENT OWEN

July 16. Kenneth Henderson (1907–2001), Robert Underhill (1889–1983), Fritiof Fryxell (1900–1986) and Phil Smith (1905–1979) made the first ascent of Mount Owen (12,922 ft./2,938 m.) in the Teton Range of Wyoming via the east ridge.

1930:

American climber David Brower (1912–2000) completed 16 first ascents in the Yosemite Valley of California including Cathedral Chimney, Yosemite Point Couloir, and Circular Staircase on Sentinel Rock. Brower would later become the executive director of the Sierra Club and the founder of the Friends of the Earth environmental group.

1930:

The Rev. Harry Pierce Nichols (1850–) made his 250th ascent of Mount Washington (6,288 ft./1,917 m.) in New Hampshire on his 80th birthday.

1930:

Swiss-Canadian mountain guide Edward Feuz, Jr. (1884–1981) made his 50th first ascent in the Canadian Rockies. All of these first ascents were of peaks exceeding 10,000 feet/3,048 meters.

1930:

American mountaineer Bradford Washburn (1910–2007) organized his first expedition to Alaska at age 20. This was a six-man expedition to Mount Fairweather (15,318 ft./4,669 m.). They were not able to reach the summit. By 2005, Washburn had made 70 trips to Alaska for climbing, photography, or cartography purposes.

1930: Technique – Climbing Rope

September 7. American climbers John Mendenhall and Max Von Patten climbed Laurel Mountain (11,812 feet/3,600 meters) in California via its northeast face. This climb was perhaps the first roped climb in the High Sierras of California.

1931:

January 25. Tufts University (Massachusetts) professor Charles Ernest Fay (1846–1931), the "Grand Old Man" of American alpinism, died at age 85. Fay was one of the founders of the Appalachia Mountain Club (AMC) and editor of Appalachia (the AMC magazine) for 40 years. He was also a three-term president of the American Alpine Club. Fay is credited with 16 first ascents in the Canadian Rockies from 1895 to 1913.

1931: PEAK FIRST ASCENT *FAIRWEATHER*

June 8. American mountaineers Allen Carpé (1894–1932) and Terris Moore (1908–1993) made the first ascent of Mount Fairweather (15,318 ft./4,669 m.) in Alaska. Other members of this expedition were Andrew M. Taylor, Dr. William Sargent, and William Ladd. This was the first technically demanding Alaskan ascent. Mount Fairweather was not climbed again for 27 years (1958).

1931: FIRST ASCENT

July 15. Glenn Exum (1911–2000), a 19-year-old climber from Idaho, first climbed (solo) the Grand Teton (13,766 ft./4,196 m.) in Wyoming via the south buttress now known as the Exum Ridge. He wore Paul Petzoldt's oversized leather football cleated shoes and used no rope. This is still the most popular climbing route in Grand Teton National Park.

1931: FIRST ASCENT

July. American mountaineer Robert Underhill (1889–1983) accomplished the following four first ascents in Wyoming's Teton mountains over an eight-day period:

1. July 12. East Ridge of Nez Perce (11,900 ft./3,637 m.) with Fritiof Fryxell (1900–1986).

2. July 15. Underhill Ridge (southeast ridge) of the Grand Teton (13,766 ft. /4,196 m.) with Phil Smith and Francis Truslow.

3. July 17. North ridge of Middle Teton (12,798 ft./3,901 m.) with Fritiof Fryxell (1900–1986).

4. July 19. North ridge of the Grand Teton (13,766 ft./4,196 m.) with Fritiof Fryxell (1900–1986).

1931: FIRST ASCENT

August 16. American climbers Norman Clyde (1885–1972), Robert Underhill (1889–1983), Glen Dawson (1912–), and Jules Eichorn (1912–2000) made the first ascent of the 2,000 foot/610 meter East Face of Mount Whitney (14,495 ft./4,418 m.) in California. They climbed mostly unroped and all wore tennis shoes.

1931: FIRST ASCENT

Colorado climbers Joe Merhar and Dave Norton completed the first traverse of the narrow ridge between Blanca Peak (14,345 ft./4,372 m.) and Little Bear Peak (14,037 ft./4,278 m.) in Colorado. Many climbers believed that this ridge traverse may be the most difficult connecting ridge between two 14,000 foot/4,267 meter peaks in Colorado.

1931: FIRST ASCENT

Swiss ski mountaineer Andre Roch (1906–2002) made the first ski ascent and descent of Mount Hood via the Eliot Glacier (11,239 ft./3,425 m.) in Oregon. In 1952, Roch (then 46 years old) reached Mount Everest's South Col (25,890 ft./7,891 m.) with Swiss mountaineer Raymond Lambert and Tenzing Norgay Sherpa.

1931: Technique – Shoulder Stand

American climber Robert L.M. Underhill (1889–1983) introduced various European climbing techniques to Sierra Club members in California. These techniques included rope management, belay positions, and the shoulder stand ("courte echelle" in French). During the first ascent of Thunderbolt Peak (14,003 ft./4,268 m.) in the Sierra Nevada mountains, Underhill demonstrated the shoulder stand. In order to reach higher hand or footholds on a rock face, one climber climbs up the back of another climber to stand on his or her shoulders and hopefully then reach useable rock holds. This climbing technique was also known as the "two-man stand." Thunderbolt Peak was the only 14,000 foot peak in California to have ropes used on its first ascent.

1931: Technique – Shoe/Boot Combination

During an ascent of Mount Temple (11,638 feet/3,547 meters) in the Canadian Rockies, the climbers alternated wearing rubber-soled shoes with hobnailed climbing boots depending upon the rock's steepness.

1932: FIRST ASCENT

May 7. Mountaineers Harry Liek, Alfred Lindley (1904–1951), Erling Strom, and Park Ranger Grant Pearson made the second ascent of Mount McKinley (20,320 ft./6,193 m.) in Alaska. This was the first successful expedition to use skis on Mount McKinley. They climbed Karstens Ridge. On May 9th, this group also climbed McKinley's north peak (19,470 ft./5,934 m.) becoming the first expedition to climb both peaks.

1932:

May 9. The first deaths occurred on Mount McKinley (20,320 ft./6,193 m.) in Alaska when Allen Carpé (1894–1932) and Theodore Koven fell on their descent. As of July 2002, there had been 92 fatalities on McKinley. Carpé and Koven were landed on the Muldrow Glacier at 5,700 feet (1,737 meters) in a small, ski-equipped plane by pilot Joe Crosson.

1932:

Colorado climber Clerin Zumwalt reached the summit of Longs Peak (14,256 ft./4,345 m.) in Colorado 53 times—still a one-year record.

1932: Equipment – Tents

The Lindley-Like expedition to Mount McKinley in Alaska used two 8 x 8 foot square tents made of Scotch sail silk. Each tent weighed 16 pounds.

1932: Equipment – Food Preparation

American mountaineer Bradford Washburn (1910–2007) used waxed canvas bags for packing food into one-day rations in Alaska.

1932: Technique – Air Support

April 25. Alaskan pilot Joe Crosson, flying a Fairchild 71 monoplane, became the first person to land an airplane on Mount McKinley. Crosson landed at the 5,700 foot/1,737 meter elevation on the Muldrow Glacier near McGonagall Pass. He was the first to supply a mountaineering expedition (Carpe-Koven Cosmic Ray Expedition) anywhere by air. This was the first glacier landing in Alaska.

1932: Technique – Mountain Radios

Early 1930s. American mountaineer Bradford Washburn (1910–2007) was the first to use small radio transceivers to maintain climber contact with other camps on a mountain.

1932: Technique – Ski Mountaineering

Ski promoter Erling Strom along with climbers Lindley, Liek, and Pearson were the first to use skis on Mount McKinley (20,320 feet/6,193 meters) in Alaska.

1932: Technique – Dynamic Belay

American climber Richard Leonard of the Cragmont Climbing Club in California discovered or devised the "dynamic belay." By letting the force of a fall pull the rope through the gloved hands of the belayer before stopping the falling climber, Leonard discovered that the force could be gradually reduced. In 1942, Leonard and Arnold Wexler continued to experiment with the dynamic belay. They tested different climbing ropes and climbing equipment at the National Bureau of Standards during World War II in Washington, D.C.

1933:

August 15 and 16. The first aerial search in the Sierra Nevada mountains of California (biplane) was conducted to find Walter A. "Peter" Starr, Jr. (1903–1933). Starr died in a fall on the northwest face of Michael Minaret (12,276 ft./3,742 m.) on August 3rd. His body was eventually located on August 27th and was buried on the mountain. California climber Clarence King (1842–1902) named these nineteen serrated peaks the "Minarets" in 1866.

1933: FIRST ASCENT

August. Well-known Colorado climber Dwight Lavender and T. Melvin Griffiths made the first winter ascent of Mount Sneffel's (14,158 ft./4,315 m.) north face in southwestern Colorado.

1933:

September 2. The first roped climb in California's Yosemite Valley was made by Jules Eichorn (1912–2000), Richard Leonard, Bestor Robinson (1898–1987), and Hervey Voge. All four of these climbers were members of the Cragmont Climbing Club (California). They climbed the Washington Column via the Lunch Ledge Route using ten-inch hardware nails as pitons. Eichorn was hired as Yosemite's first climbing ranger in 1940. He eventually made thirty-five first ascents in the Sierra Nevada Mountains of California.

1933:

American mountaineer James Monroe Thorington (1895–1989) completed fifteen consecutive climbing seasons (1914–1933) in the Canadian Rockies. During this period, he made fifty-two first ascents. Thorington was also known as the "mountaineering historian of the Rockies."

1933:

Oregon mountaineer Gary Denzel Leech made the first of his 116 ascents of Mount Hood (11,239 ft./3,425 m.) in Oregon. Leech always climbed with an alpenstock rather than an ice axe.

1933:

Washington climber and member of The Mountaineers, Amos Hand, was the first mountaineer to complete the climbing of all six of Washington's major peaks twice:

1.	Mount Rainier	14,411 ft./4,392 m.
2.	Mount Adams	12,307 ft./3,751 m.
3.	Mount Baker	10,781 ft./3,286 m.
4.	Glacier Peak	10,541 ft./3,213 m.
5.	Mount St. Helens	8,366 ft./2,550 m.
6.	Mount Olympus	7,965 ft./2,427 m.

1933: Technique – Double Roping

On ascent. American mountaineer Jules Eichorn (1912–2000) climbed the southwest face of Higher Spire in the Sierra mountains of California. He decided to climb with two ropes (one rope on his right side and one rope on his left side) because his single rope created too much friction zigzagging through different carabiners at protection points. Eichorn alternated the two ropes at carabiner clipping points. It has been reported that Eichorn learned of this two-rope climbing technique from a German climber.

1934:

February 2. Canadian mountain guide Conrad Kain (1883–1934) died at age 51 from encephalitis lethargica. Kain was born in Austria and came to Canada in 1909 as a guide for the Alpine Club of Canada. He made sixty-nine first ascents in the Canadian Rockies of peaks over 10,000 ft./3,048 m. (1909–1929). His greatest first ascent was of Mount Robson (12,872 ft./3,954 m.) in 1913. Mount Conrad (10,670 ft./3,252 m.) and Mount Kain (9,449 ft./2,880 m.) in the Canadian Rockies are named for him. He also made thirty first ascents in New Zealand. One New Zealand peak is named for Kain. He made over 1,000 separate climbs during his climbing career in Austria, Switzerland, Canada, and New Zealand.

1934: PEAK FIRST ASCENT *HIGHER CATHEDRAL SPIRE*

April. The first ascent of Higher Cathedral Spire (6,644 ft./2,025 m.) in Yosemite National Park (California) was made by three American climbers: Jules Eichorn (1912–2000), Richard Leonard, and Bestor Robinson (1898–1987). At this time, this was the most technical climb in North America. This was the first climbing team to use pitons in the United States for direct aid. They used 38 pitons during the climb of this six-hundred foot route.

1934:

July 13. A high peak in California's Sierra Mountains was officially named and dedicated to noted American photographer Ansel Adams (1902–1984). Adams was present for this dedication of Mount Ansel Adams (11,700 ft./3,566 m.)

1934: PEAK FIRST ASCENT *FORAKER*

August 6. American mountaineers Charles Houston (1913–2009), Charles Storey, Carl Anderson, Thomas Graham Brown (1882–1965), and Chychele Waterston made the first ascent of Mount Foraker (17,401 ft./5,303 m.) in Alaska. They climbed the north summit (the highest) via the northwest ridge. On August 10, they also reached the lower south summit (17,200 ft./5,242 m.). Oscar Houston (1883–1966) led this expedition.

1934: FIRST ASCENT

Colorado climber Mary Cronin became the first woman to climb all of the Colorado peaks over 14,000 feet/4,267 meters. There are 54 peaks that exceed this elevation. Cronin was the fourth overall climber to achieve this goal behind Carl Blaurock, William Ervin and Albert Ellingwood.

1934: FIRST ASCENT

Washington mountaineers Ome Daiber (1908–1989), Jim Borrow Jr., and E.A. "Arne" Campbell made the first ascent of the Liberty Ridge (8,400 ft./2,560 m.) in Washington. This ridge is located on the Willis Wall of Mount Rainier's north face.

1934: Equipment – Radios

The Harvard-Dartmouth Mount Crillon Expedition was led by American mountaineer and explorer Bradford Washburn (1910–2007). This was the first time that high-frequency 56-megacycle radios were used for inter-camp communications (walkie-talkies) on a mountaineering expedition. This climb of Mount Crillon (12,728 ft./3,879 m.) was Washburn's first first ascent in Alaska. **PEAK FIRST ASCENT. *CRILLON.***

1934: Technique – Air Support

American mountaineer and Alaskan explorer Bradford Washburn (1910–2007) was the first to parachute vital supplies to a climbing party. He air-dropped these supplies to an expedition on Mount Crillon (12,728 feet/3,879 meters) in Alaska.

1934: Technique – Pitons

American climber Bestor Robinson (1898–1987) introduced aid climbing to Yosemite's (California) granite walls by hammering iron pitons into rock cracks.

1934: Technique – Route Marking

Trail marking wands were improved for the first ascent of Mount Crillon (12,728 feet/3,879 meters) in Alaska. Rigid maplewood dowels 36" long and 3/8" in diameter with the top 12" painted black (for better visibility on snow) were now used. These wooden wands were easy to plant, easy to carry, and readily available. This type of marking wand was used again on Mount McKinley in Alaska in 1947.

1935: FIRST ASCENT

September 7 and 8. Washington mountaineers Wolf Bauer and Jack Hossack made the first ascent of Mount Rainier's (14,411 ft./4,392 m.) Ptarmigan Ridge. This 4,000 foot/1,219 meter ascent required 12 hours of step-cutting on ice and verglas.

1935: FIRST ASCENT

December 17 to 20. American mountaineers Paul Petzoldt (1908–1999), Eldon "Curly" Petzoldt, and Fred Brown made the first winter ascent of the Grand Teton (13,766 ft./4,196 m.) in Wyoming. Using skis and relaying loads up Garnet Canyon, they reached the summit on their fourth day. They followed the Owen-Spaulding route.

1935:

Technical rock climbers discovered the Shawangunk Cliffs (or "Gunks") on the west side of New York's Hudson River near New Paltz, New York. By 1939, this eight-mile long cliff band had been popularized mainly due to the efforts of German immigrant climber Fritz Wiessner (1900–1988), Lawrence G. Coveney, and Dr. Hans Kraus (1905–1996). This long ridge of white quartz cliffs (up to 230 feet high) now contains over 1,200 different routes. No new bolts or pitons may be placed here except to replace those installed prior to November of 1986. The 6,300 acres of the Shawangunk Ridge is now managed by a trust.

1935:

American mountaineer Bradford Washburn (1910–2007) first discovered an Alaskan peak that became known as East Hubbard Peak (13,869 ft./4,227 m.). This peak was renamed Mount Kennedy in 1965 after assassinated U.S. President John F. Kennedy. (See 1965)

1935: PEAK FIRST ASCENT *GUNNBJORNSFJELD*

British mountaineer Lawrence Wager (1904–1965) and his party (British East Expedition) made the first ascent of Gunnbjornsfjeld (12,139 ft./3,700 m.), the highest peak in Greenland (Watkins Range).

1935:

Tahquitz Rock in southern California was "discovered" by Sierra Club climbers. This climbing area is located on the shoulder of Mount San Jacinto. The first route was climbed here in 1936 (the Trough – rated 5.0).

1935: Equipment – Ice Axe
The European ice axe reached the average American climber.

1935: Equipment – Ice Axe
Seattle, Washington mountaineer Lloyd Anderson (1902–2000) mail ordered an Austrian made ice axe. The cost on arrival of this axe was $3.50. Anderson began a recreational equipment cooperative in his basement in 1938 that eventually became known as REI.

1936: FIRST ASCENT
January 17. Washington mountaineer Delmar Fadden (22) made the first winter ascent of the Emmons Glacier (solo) on Mount Rainier (14,411 ft./4,392 m.) in Washington and then died on his descent of a fall and hypothermia. Fadden's camera photos proved this ascent via the Emmons Glacier.

1936: PEAK FIRST ASCENT *WADDINGTON*
July 26. Fritz H.E. Wiessner (1900–1988) and William P. House (1914–1997) made the first ascent of Mount Waddington (13,186 ft./4,019 m.) in British Columbia, Canada via the southwest face. They used pitons and a rope on the final 13-hour climb. This was thought to be the most difficult climb in North America. Wiessner came to the United States in 1929. Waddington had seen sixteen previous climbing attempts.

1936: FIRST ASCENT
August 11. American climbers Paul (1908–1999) and Eldon Petzoldt and Jack Durrance (1912–2003) made the first ascent of the Grand Teton's (13,766 ft./4,196 m.) north face (3,000 foot/914 meter) in Wyoming. Their route was not considered to be a direct finish to the summit.

1936:
American mountaineer Arthur Harman Marshall became the first person to climb the highest point in all 48 states of the continental United States.

1936:
Canadian mountaineering couple Don and Phyllis Munday (1894–1990) ended their ten-year (1927–1936) exploration of the area surrounding Mount Waddington (13,186 ft./4,019 m.) in the Coastal Range of British Columbia, Canada. Over this ten-year period, they spent a total of 15 months exploring this area and attempted to climb Mount Waddington 16 times coming within 50 feet/15 meters of the actual summit. This peak was named for Alfred Waddington of the geological survey for this area of Canada and is located approximately 175 miles northwest of Vancouver, British Columbia.

1936: FIRST ASCENT
American climbers Jack Durrance (1912–2003) and Kenneth Henderson (1907–2001) made the first ascent of the complete Exum Ridge on the Grand Teton (13,766 ft./4,196 m.) in Wyoming.

1936:

American mountaineer Bradford Washburn (1910–2007) began a lifelong relationship with Mount McKinley (20,320 ft./6,193 m., a.k.a. Denali) in Alaska. Washburn (from Boston, Massachusetts) would eventually make 70 trips to Alaska for mountaineering, photography, cartography, and surveying purposes.

1936: Clothing – Down Parka

Eddie Bauer of Seattle, Washington, patented the first quilted down-filled jacket. It was known as the Skyliner down parka—the first in the United States. Eddie Bauer also first developed the goose down vest.

1936: Technique – Aerial Photography

July. American mountaineer Bradford Washburn (1910–2007) made the first large-scale aerial photographic flights over Mount McKinley (20,320 feet/6,193 meters) in Alaska for the National Geographic Society. Flying in a twin-engine Lockheed Electra airplane, Washburn made three separate flights over McKinley using a 53-pound/24-kilogram Fairchild F-6 camera. His photographs were published in the National Geographic magazine.

1937: PEAK FIRST ASCENT *LUCANIA*

July 9. American mountaineers Bradford Washburn (1910–2007) and Robert Bates (1911–2007) made the first ascent of Mount Lucania (17,150 ft./5,227 m.), the highest unclimbed peak in North America. This peak is located in the Yukon Territory of Canada and was named by the Duke of the Abruzzi (Italian mountaineer, 1873–1933) after the ship his climbing party sailed on from Liverpool, England to New York City. The second ascent of Mount Lucania did not occur until 1967. On this same climbing trip in 1937, Washburn and Bates made the second ascent of Mount Steele (16,644 ft./5,073 m.) in Canada's Centennial Range.

1937: PEAK FIRST ASCENT *DEVILS TOWER*

July 28. American climbers Fritz Wiessner (1900–1988), William P. House (1914–1997), and Lawrence P. Coveney made the first free ascent and the first "real" ascent of Devils Tower (5,371 ft./1,637 m.) in Wyoming. This 902 foot/275 meter columnar monolith was first climbed in 1893 by W. Ripley and W. Rogers who constructed a wooden ladder to the top. They were not credited with the first true climbing ascent. Devil's Tower is not climbed during the month of June due to respect for Native Americans who consider the site sacred. (Although this is voluntary.)

1937: FIRST ASCENT

September. The east Buttress of Mount Whitney (14,505 ft./4,421 m.) is considered to be the most classic climbing route to the summit. American mountaineers Bob Brinton, Glen Dawson, Muir Dawson, Richard Jones, and Howard Koster made the first ascent of this route. Mount Whitney is located in California.

1937:

Canadian mountaineers Rex Gibson and Sterling Hendricks became the first to climb all four 12,000 foot/3,657 meter peaks in Canadian Rockies. These four peaks were:

1. Mount Robson	12,972 ft. – 3,954 m.
2. Mount Columbia	12,293 ft. – 3,747 m.
3. North Twin	12,237 ft. – 3,730 m.
4. Mount Clemenceau	12,001 ft. – 3,658 m.

1937:

Colorado climbers Carl Melzer, Bob Melzer (9 year old son), and Junius Johnson climbed all fifty (now 54) 14,000 foot peaks in Colorado in 39 days.

1937: Equipment – Tents

Mountaineers in Alaska and the Yukon territory of Canada began using the nine-foot square, central pole Logan tent which was made of Egyptian cotton. This tent weighed 16 pounds.

1937: Equipment – Rope

February 16. Nylon (Fiber 66) was awarded U.S. Patent # 2,071,250. This patent eventually led to the development of Plymouth Goldline climbing rope.

1937: Equipment – Boots

Shoepacs were used on the glaciers of Alaska and the Yukon Territory of Canada. These heavy boots had rubber lowers, leather uppers, and felt inner soles. They were rigid enough to fit crampons but were not practical for steep climbing. The rubber insulation of these cold-weather boots slowed the onset of frostbite.

1937: Technique – Climb Classifications

The Sierra Club System of six rock climbing grades was introduced in the United States.

Grade

I	– Hiking: Hands never touch rock.
II	– Off-trail scrambling: Hands may be used to climb.
III	– Climbing with a rope for beginners.
IV	– Belayed climbing: Very steep terrain, but not vertical.
V	– Leader uses protection: Very steep to vertical.
VI	– Aid climbing.

1938: PEAK FIRST ASCENT *SANFORD*

July 21. American mountaineers Bradford Washburn (1910–2007) and Terris Moore (1908–1993) made the first ascent of Mount Sanford (16,237 ft./4,949 m.) in the Wrangell–St. Elias mountains of Alaska. Mount Sanford, until this ascent, was the highest unclimbed peak in North America. Washburn and Moore relied mainly on skis with sealskins to make this ascent.

1938: FIRST ASCENT

August. Washington mountaineers George Martin, Bob Scott, and Don Dooley made the first Olympus Traverse in the Olympic Mountains of Washington. This was a traverse of all three summits of Mount Olympus (West: 7,969 ft./2,429 m., Middle: 7,929 ft./2,417 m., and East: 7,762 ft./2,366 m.).

1938: Technique – Waterproofing

Seattle mountaineer Ome Daiber (1908–1989) invented Sno-Seal, a waterproofing for leather boots.

1939: FIRST ASCENT

July 1. Sigurd Hall made the first ski ascent of Mount Rainier (14,411 ft./4,392 m.) in Washington. Andy Hennig was with Hall but did not use skis.

1939:

July. Colorado climbers Carl Melzer and his 11-year-old son Bob were the first to complete the climbing of all 64 peaks in the continental United States over 14,000 feet (4,267 meters). California –13 peaks, Colorado –50, and Washington– 1. Two additional peaks in California and four in Colorado now brings the total to 70 peaks.

1939: PEAK FIRST ASCENT *SHIPROCK*

October 12. American rock climbers David Brower (1912–2000), Bestor Robinson (1898–1987), John Dyer, and Raffi Badayn (1915–1982) made the first ascent of the 1,700 ft./518 m. volcanic rhyolite plug known as Shiprock Peak in New Mexico. The summit stands 7,178 ft./2,188 m. above sea level. This first ascent took four days and 54 pitons. Twenty unsuccessful attempts preceded this first ascent. The second ascent occurred in 1952. Shiprock is considered to be a holy site by the Navajo Indians.

1939:

German born mountaineer Wolfgang Friedrich "Fred" Beckey (1923–) joined The Mountaineers climbing club at age 16 and made 35 ascents (including one first ascent—Mount Despair) in the Cascade Range of northern Washington. By the age of 19 (1942), Beckey had nearly 100 ascents to his credit.

1939: Equipment – Expansion Bolts

California climber Bestor Robinson adapted an eye bolt used in concrete construction into the expansion bolt for climbing. Robinson experimented with this new climbing aid on local rock areas in California before actually using them on the first ascent of Shiprock in New Mexico.

1939: Technique – Bolting

Sierra Club members Raffi Bedayn, David Brower, John Dyer, and Bestor Robinson made the first ascent of New Mexico's Shiprock. This desert volcanic plug is 1,800 feet/549 meters high. For the first time in climbing, expansion bolts were used for protection.

1939: Technique – Belaying

American climbers David Brower, Bestor Robinson, Raffi Bedayn, and Johnny Dyer were the first in American climbing history to place two expansion bolts for belaying and for protection. Shiprock is in western New Mexico.

1939: Technique – Man-Made Climbing Rock

The first man-made climbing rock was constructed at Camp Long (U.S. Army) in West Seattle, Washington by the Works Progress Administration. This artificial twenty-five foot concrete climbing rock was originally called Monitor Rock and was later renamed Schurman Rock in honor of Clark E. Schurman (1883–1955). Schurman was the Chief Mountain Guide at Mount Rainier National Park from 1939 to 1942. This rock allowed climbers to practice their open chimney, closed chimney, crack climb, and ridge walking techniques without having to travel to the Cascade mountains.

1940: FIRST ASCENT

March 17. American mountaineers David Brower (1912–2000) and Fred Kelly made the first winter ascent of North Palisade Peak (14,242 ft./4,341 m.) in California.

1940: FIRST ASCENT

American climbers Jack Durrance (1912–2003) and his future brother-in-law Henry Coulter made the first ascent of the Grand Teton's (13,766 ft./4,196 m.) three-thousand foot west face in Wyoming. This was considered to be the most demanding alpine climb in North America at the time.

1940:

American mountaineer William Hackett (1918–1999) from Portland, Oregon completed his 50th ascent of Mount Hood (11,239 ft./3,425 m.) in Oregon. Hackett climbed eleven different ascent routes on Mount Hood including three first ascents and two second ascents.

1940: Equipment – Food Preparation

Early 1940s. The U.S. Army's Tenth Mountain Division developed dehydrated meats and vegetables, instant oatmeal and powdered drinks.

1941: FIRST ASCENT

July 18. Colorado climbers Rit Burrows, Jim Patterson, and Werner Schnackenberg made the first ascent of Vestal Peak's (13,864 ft./4,225 m.) Wham Ridge in the Grenadier Range of southwestern Colorado. This beautiful ridge (or face) soars 1,300 feet (396 meters) up the north side of Vestal Peak. The Burrows team spent three hours climbing this ridge and used one piton near the summit for protection. Vestal Peak was first climbed in 1908.

1941: PEAK FIRST ASCENT *HAYES*

July. Mount Hayes (13,832 ft./4,216 m.) in Alaska was first climbed by Bradford (1910–2007) and Barbara Washburn (1914–), Benjamin Ferris, Henry Hall, Sterling Hendricks, and William Shand.

This team followed the north ridge to the summit. The elevation gain was approximately 6,410 feet (1,951 m.).

1941:

October 1. George Hopkins parachuted onto the summit of Devils Tower in Wyoming and was marooned there for five days. American climber Paul Petzoldt (1908–1999) led a rescue team that brought Hopkins down this 902 foot/275 meter rock tower.

1941:

American rock climbers Fritz Wiessner (1900–1988) and Dr. Hans Kraus (1905–1996) made the first ascent of High Exposure (now rated 5.6) on the Shawangunk Cliffs near New Paltz, New York. They used a hemp rope and three soft-iron pitons. This is the most popular climbing route in the "Gunks." By the end of the 1940s, the "Gunks" had 58 designated routes:

26	First ascents by Hans Kraus
23	First ascents by Fritz Wiessner
9	First ascents by Others

1941:

Members of the 3rd Division, 15th Regiment, 87th Mountain Infantry of the U.S. Army made the first circumnavigation of Mount Rainier (14,411 ft./4,392 m.) on skis.

1941: Equipment – Rope

November. The Plymouth Cordage Company (PCC) manufactured large diameter nylon ropes for rope-driven sawmills. The PCC was asked to produce smaller diameter nylon ropes that could be used for mountain climbing. These nylon ropes were field-tested by U.S. combat troops at Seneca Rocks, West Virginia. Unlike stiff, non-elastic hemp ropes, nylon ropes held up to 150 falls and could stretch 39 percent of their length before breaking (7/16" diameter). This nylon rope became known as Plymouth Goldline. It was cut into lengths of 120 feet (36.5 meters) which then became the standard length.

1942:

April. Construction was begun on developing Camp Hale (5,000 Acres) in Pando, Colorado, for the 15,000 mountain troops of the Tenth Mountain Division of the U.S. Army. This was the first division in the U.S. military to specialize in mountain warfare. Construction of the 400 buildings was completed on October 16. Located at 9,100 ft./2,774 m., Camp Hale trained army soldiers to become ski mountaineers. Approximately one half of the volunteers to this new division came from the National Ski Patrol system that was established by Charles Minot "Minnie" Dole (1899–1976) in 1938. Mountain training emphasized rock climbing, ice climbing, crampon techniques, rappelling, and winter camping. 14,000 troops trained at Camp Hale: 8,000 trained on skis and 6,000 trained on snowshoes. This army camp was deactivated in 1965.

1942:

May–June. The U.S. Army Alaskan Test Expedition made the third ascent of Mount McKinley/Denali (20,320 ft./6,193 m.) in Alaska. This team tested 30 new cold-weather clothing and equipment items for the newly formed U.S. Army mountain troops. Robert Bates, Einar Nilsson, Terris Moore, and Bradford Washburn reached the summit. On July 19th, Washburn and Nilsson reached Denali Pass (18,200 ft./5,547 m.) between Denali's two peaks. They looked down on the west buttress and Washburn predicted in his personal diary that this route would one day be climbed (first ascent in 1951).

1942:

Seattle, Washington mountaineering twin brothers Jim and Lou Whittaker (1929–) climbed their first mountain, Silver Peak, in the nearby Cascade Mountains. In 1963, Jim became the first American to reach the summit of Mount Everest (29,035 ft./8,839 m.) in Nepal. Lou led the following expeditions to the Himalayas:

> 1975 – K2
> 1982 – Mount Everest
> 1884 – Mount Everest. First American ascent of the North Col route.
> 1989 – Kanchenjunga

1942: Book

Kenneth Henderson. *Handbook of American Mountaineering.* Henderson published his book for the United States government to use as a manual to assist the U.S. Army in its plans for training mountain troops. The American Alpine Club published this book which is considered to be a classic.

1942: Equipment – Rope

May. The Plymouth Cordage Company delivered the world's first nylon climbing rope to the U.S. Army. U.S. Army Major Robert Bates (1911–2007) of the Quartermaster General's Office tested this new rope by rappelling out of his Pentagon office window in Washington, D.C. frightening office secretaries on lower floors.

1942: Equipment – Stoves

The U.S. Army's Tenth Mountain Division developed compact, portable stoves for its mountain troops to carry.

1942: Equipment – Tents

The U.S. Army's Tenth Mountain Division developed a lightweight nylon tent originally made from parachute fabric with small circular sleeve air vents to prevent moisture build-up. Two collapsible steel poles supported this tent.

1942: Equipment – Boots

Early 1940s. The U.S. Army's Tenth Mountain Division developed insulated, pac-style climbing boots with rubber bottoms and leather uppers to provide warmth and prevent trenchfoot.

1942: Equipment – Boots

The U.S. Army adopted vibram-soled boots for the use of its Tenth Mountain Division troops.

1942: Technique – Ice Climbing Wall

The first artificial ice climbing wall was developed by American climber and Tenth Mountain Division (U.S. Army) soldier Joe Stettner at Camp Hale, Colorado. Water was piped up a hill and over a rock cliff where it froze. Tenth Mountain Division troops could then practice crampon, ice axe, and rope handling techniques during winter conditions.

1942: Technique – Man-Made Climbing Walls

Spring. Captain John Woodward (U.S. Army) ordered the construction of three thirty-foot (9 meter) climbing walls for mountain troop training. These log walls were located in an abandoned gravel pit and were probably the first artificial climbing walls ever built.

1943:

January 1. The U.S. War Department approved the formation of a Mountain Division for the U.S. Army. In August, Tenth Mountain Division officers David Brower (1912–2000) and Peter Gabriel were sent to Seneca Rocks in West Virginia to establish the Assault Climbing School for infantry soldiers. This school operated until July of 1944. Army climbers pounded over 75,000 pitons into Seneca's sandstone rock.

1943:

December 25. Three Tenth Mountain Division soldiers from Camp Hale in Colorado made the first known winter ascent of Mount of the Holy Cross (14,005 ft./4,269 m.) in Colorado.

1943: Technique – Mountain Rescue

Early 1940s. The U.S. Army's Tenth Mountain Division developed modern avalanche control and mountain rescue techniques.

1944: FIRST ASCENT

January. Canadian Army mountain troops training for winter warfare, made the first winter ascents of Mounts Columbia (12,294 ft./3,747 m.), Kitchener (11,500 ft./3,505 m.), Andromeda (11,300 ft./3,444 m.), and Nigel Peak (10,535 ft./3,211 m.) in the Canadian Rockies.

1944:

February 21 to 24. Thirty-three U.S. Army/Tenth Mountain Division ski troopers skied fifty miles (83 kilometers) and crossed three 13,000 foot (3,962 meters) passes in Colorado's Sawatch mountain range between Leadville and Aspen. These soldiers carried 90-pound packs on this winter ski trek that was called the "Trooper Traverse."

1944:

Canadian mountain guide Edward Feuz, Jr. (1884–1981) made 78 first ascents in the Canadian Rockies during his guiding career: 1903 to 1944.

1945:

Only three mountaineering expeditions had reached the summit of Mount McKinley/Denali (20,320 ft./6,193 m.) in Alaska.

> 1913 The Stuck Expedition. First ascent.
> 1932 The Lindley–Like expedition.
> 1942 The U.S. Army test expedition.

1945:

The American Alpine Club had 302 members while the Alpine Club in England had 586 members.

1945: Equipment – Pitons

Yosemite National Park in California. Swiss-born John Salathé (1899–1992) began making stronger pitons using chrome-moly steel and an improved heat treatment. Salathé began climbing at age 45 (1944). His pitons could be driven into narrower cracks in Yosemite's hard granite. These pitons could also be removed and reused.

1946:

June. Americans Dr. Charles Houston (1913–2009) and Richard L. Riley began a project known as "Operation Everest I." The condition of hypoxia (inadequate oxygenation of the blood) was studied by simulating the ascent profile of Mount Everest (29,035 ft./8,849 m.) in a hyperbaric chamber. Four men were sealed in this chamber where the pressure was gradually decreased over a 34-day period. All four men reached 26,700 feet without using supplemental oxygen. Two men reached 29,030 feet without using supplemental oxygen. This experiment was approved by the U.S. Navy and took place at the Naval facility in Pensacola, Florida. Houston had been a flight surgeon in the U.S. Navy from 1941 to 1946 and had been on expeditions to Nanda Devi (1936) and K2 (1938).

1946: FIRST ASCENT

July 16. A Harvard (University) Mountaineering Club team led by Maynard M. Miller (1922–) made the first American ascent of Mount Saint Elias (18,008 ft./5,489 m.) on the Alaskan–Yukon territory border. Other team members included Benjamin Ferris, Andrew Kauffman, Elizabeth Kauffman, Bill Latady, Cornelius Molenaar, Dee Molenaar, and Bill Putnam. Seven of these eight climbers reached the summit. This expedition recorded four firsts which are:

1. First ascent of the southwest ridge
2. First ascent by a female
3. First successful civilian use of military air support on an expedition
4. First major American expedition after World War II.

This American team also summited on the 205th anniversary (1741) of the discovery of Mount St. Elias by Danish explorer Vitus Bering (1681–1741).

1946: FIRST ASCENT

October 13 and 14. American rock climbers John Salathe (1899–1993) and Anton "Ax" Nelson (1918–2001) made the first ascent of the southwest face of Half Dome (8,836 ft./2,693 m.) in Yosemite National Park in California. This ascent took 20 hours and 150 pitons. This was also the first time that an overnight bivouac was used on a Yosemite climb.

1946:

American mountaineers Glenn Exum (1911–2000) and Paul Petzoldt (1908–1999) founded the Petzoldt-Exum School of American Mountaineering in the Teton Mountains of Wyoming.

1946: Equipment – Carabiners

California climber Raffi Bedayn (1915–1982) hammered out the first American-made carabiners of steel.

1946: Equipment – Pitons

American rock climbers Anton ("Ax") Nelson (1918 –2001) and John Salathe (1899 – 1993) first used a new type of piton — a replaceable one: placed, removed, reused. They used this reusable piton on the southwest face (1,200 ft. route, 150 placements) of Half Dome in Yosemite National Park (California). Older "soft iron" carbon steel pitons are also removable but more often get stuck and/or wear out faster.

1947: FIRST ASCENT

June 6. American mountaineer Bradford Washburn (1910–2007) led the Operation White Tower Expedition to Mount McKinley/Denali (20,320 ft./6,193 m.) in Alaska. Washburn's wife Barbara (1914–) became the first woman to reach Mount McKinley's summit along with her husband, Bob Craig, Shorty Lange, Bill Hackett, Jim Gale, Bill Deeke, George Brown, and Grant Pearson. This was the fourth overall ascent. On this expedition Brad Washburn again sighted and recognized the West Buttress as being perhaps the safest route to the summit. The next day, June 7, Barbara Washburn became the first woman to summit both peaks of Mount McKinley/Denali when she summited the North Peak (19,470 ft./5,934 m.).

1947: PEAK FIRST ASCENT *LOST ARROW SPIRE*

September 3. Swiss born blacksmith John Salathé (1899–1993) and Anton "Ax" Nelson (1918–2001) made the first ascent of the 200 foot/61 meter Lost Arrow Spire in Yosemite National Park in California. This was the first "big-wall" climb in Yosemite. This technical ascent took five days, required 4 bivouacs, and used 18 pitons made by Salathé. They made use of the prusik knot and introduced "sixth class" climbing to Yosemite.

1947:

American climber Dr. William Sargent Ladd (1887–1949) gifted "the old firehouse" to the American Alpine Club (AAC) as their permanent headquarters. Formerly his own office, this property was located at 113 East 90th Street in New York City. AAC members Albert MacCarthy and Henry Hall each donated $15,000.00 to initiate an acquisition fund for this property. Ladd was also an Honorary Member of the Club Alpin Francais.

1947:

American mountaineers Joe Stettner (46), Jack Fralick, and John Speck made the first ascent of the 1,200 foot/366 meter east face of Monitor Peak (13,695 ft./4,174 m.) in the San Juan Mountains of Colorado. This 26-hour climb required 19 pitons, two shoulder stands, and one bivouac. This was the first recorded multi-day climb in Colorado. The final 300 feet/91 meters took 4 ½ hours to climb.

1947:

Thirteen-year-old American climber Ruth Ewald guided her first party (for pay) up Long's Peak (14,256 ft./4,345 m.) in Colorado. Ewald still holds the women's record for most ascents of Longs Peak — 72.

1947: Technique – Gear Hauling

American climbers John Salathe (47) and Anton "Ax" Nelson made the first ascent of Lost Arrow Spire in Yosemite National Park in California. This climbing team led on one rope and hauled their gear up in a burlap equipment sack on a second lighter rope.

1947: Technique – Igloo Building

American mountaineer and Alaskan explorer Bradford Washburn (1910–2007) decided to build snow igloos instead of pitching tents on Mount McKinley (20,320 feet/6,193 meters) in Alaska. Igloos did not flap in the wind, did not need to be carried from camp to camp, and usually maintained a constant temperature of 25°F to 30°F. In addition to its better thermal insulation, the outer skin of an igloo eventually becomes ice which serves as a windproof barrier. Igloo was originally spelled "iglu" which is the Eskimo language word for "snow-house."

1948: FIRST ASCENT

July 18. Washington ski mountaineers Kermit Bengston, David Roberts, Cliff Schmeidtke, and Charles E. Welsh made the first ski ascent and descent of Mount Rainier (14,411 ft./4,392 m.) in Washington.

1948: FIRST ASCENT

July. American mountaineers Bob Craig (1925–) and Dee Molenaar (1918–) made the first direct ascent of the Nisqually Icefall on Mount Rainier (14,411 ft./4,392 m.) in Washington.

1948:

Mr. and Mrs. J. Daniel McKenzie climbed all of the 4,000 foot (1,219 meters) peaks in Vermont (5), New Hampshire (48), and New York (46) for a total of 99 ascents.

1948: Equipment – Helmets

The Safety Committee of the American Alpine Club first urged the use of protective helmets for climbers. This may be the single most important piece of equipment for climbers.

1949: FIRST ASCENT

August 13. American climbers Dick Pownall (1928–), Art Gilkey (1926–1963), and Ray Garner made the first direct ascent of the Grand Teton's (13,766 ft./4,196 m.) north face in Wyoming. They reached the summit at 10:00 p.m. and bivouacked.

1949:

August. American climber Elizabeth Strong Cowles Partridge (1902–1974) completed the climbing of all 54 peaks in Colorado over 14,000 feet/ 4,267 meters. She was the fifth or sixth woman to accomplish this goal. Another woman climber, Dorothy Teague Swartz, reached the same goal on this same day completely independent of Partridge.

1949:

American mountaineer Bill Hackett first conceived the idea of reaching the world's seven summits (the highest summit on each of the world's seven continents). He had climbed Mount McKinley/Denali (20,320 ft./6,193 m.) in North America in 1947 and Aconcagua (22,835 ft./6,960 m.) in South America in 1949. It was not until 1985 that American mountaineer Dick Bass (1937–) did complete the climbing of all seven summits.

1949:

Swiss-Canadian mountain guide Edward Feuz, Jr. (1885–1981) retired after 44 years of guiding in the Canadian Rockies (1905–1949). Feuz made 100 first ascents of peaks exceeding 10,000 feet/3,049 meters and 15 first ascents of peaks exceeding 11,000 feet/3,353 meters. Feuz died in 1981 at age 96.

1949: Equipment – Carabiners

Lightweight aluminum carabiners were first introduced in the United States by Raffi Bedayn (1915–1982). These carabiners were also known as "safety snaps" or "snap links."

1949: Technique – Helicopter Support

Lt. Bill Weed landed his Sikorsky H5G helicopter on the Muldrow Glacier on Mount McKinley (20,320 feet/6,193 meters) in Alaska. American climbers Bradford Washburn (1910–2007) and Jim Gale were on-board. This was the first helicopter landing on a glacier.

1949: Technique – Bolting

Colorado climbers Tom Hornbein (1930–), Bob Riley, and Dick Sherman made the first ascent of the Northwest Passage route on the Third Flatiron above Boulder, Colorado. On one steep pitch, they made the first recorded attempt in Colorado to drill expansion bolts to pass a blank rock section (no cracks). Their drilling equipment failed. They finished their ascent which represented Boulder's first major artificial climb.

1950:

July. American climbers Mike Brewer and Dick Pownall (1928–) completed the "Grand Traverse" in the Tetons of Wyoming. They climbed these five major peaks in 14 ½ hours:

1st – Nez Perce	11,900 ft./3,627 m.
2nd – Cloudveil Dome	12,026 ft./3,665 m.
3rd – South Teton	12,505 ft./3,811 m.
4th – Middle Teton	12,798 ft./3,901 m.
5th – Grand Teton	13,766 ft./4,196 m.

1950:

October: A mass climbing party of 5,000 people attempted to climb the Mexican volcano Popocatepetl (17,887 ft./5,452 m.). 200 of the climbers (4 percent) died and over 1,000 (20 percent) were injured.

1950:

The two-man team of André Roch (Swiss, 44) and Norman Read (American, 60) made the second ascent of Mount Logan (19,525 ft./5,951 m.) in Canada. Read was a member of the first ascent team in 1925.

1950: Equipment – Helmets

Early 1950s. Climbing helmets were first introduced but only achieved popularity in the 1960s. These early helmets were made of fiberglass.

1950: Technique – Climb Classification

Grade 5 (leader uses protection) of the Sierra Club System was sub-divided into decimals according to the climb's difficulty — 5.0 to 5.12.

1951: FIRST ASCENT

July 10. American climbers Bradford Washburn (1910–2007), Bill Hackett (1918–1999), Jim Gale, Barry Bishop (1932–1994), Dr. Henry Buchtel, Dr. John Ambler, Melvin Griffiths, and Jerry Moore made the first ascent of the West Buttress route on Mount McKinley/Denali (20,320 ft./6,193 m.) in Alaska. This was Washburn's third ascent (1942, 1947, 1951) of Mount McKinley. He, Hackett, and Gale reached the summit. This was also the first expedition to use an aircraft to ferry supplies onto the mountain.

1951: Clothing – Insulation

The climbing team for the Mount McKinley West Buttress Expedition experimented with wearing paper socks under their regular heavy socks for additional insulation. The results of this experiment are unknown.

1951: Equipment – Boots

The climbing team for the Mount McKinley West Buttress Expedition wore felt boots (very light and warm) inside their shoepac rubber boots. Each pair of boots weighed 3.5 pounds. These boots were made by the Little Falls Felt Shoe Company of Little Falls, New York.

1951: Equipment – Cameras

American mountaineer and photographer Bradford Washburn (1910–2007) led the Mount McKinley West Buttress Expedition in Alaska. Washburn used the new instant Polaroid camera to photograph climbing route details that were then examined and discussed by the climbing team in their camps up the mountain. Inventor and businessman Edwin H. Land (1909–1991) began marketing his Polaroid camera in 1948.

1951: Equipment – Pitons

Early 1950s. Yosemite (California) climber Charles Wilts invented the "knife blade" piton which was made of chrome-molybdenum aircraft steel. This piton was made for very thin cracks.

1951: Equipment – Ski Planes

Summer in Alaska. American mountaineer and pilot Terris Moore (1908–1993) purchased a 125-horsepower Cessna Super Cub airplane that he then equipped with the first "ski-wheels" to ever fly in Alaska. Metal skis could be hydraulically lowered below the rubber landing wheels in preparation for glacier landings. This ski-equipped airplane made the first ascent of Mount McKinley/Denali's West Buttress climbing route possible in 1951. Terris Moore was a close friend and climbing partner of Bradford Washburn (1910–2007).

1951: Equipment – Snowshoes

Mount McKinley/Denali West Buttress expedition in Alaska. The climbing team used the "bear-paw" snowshoe model every day for climbing from the 7,650 foot (2,332 m.) base camp up to the 15,500 ft. (4,724 m.) bergschrund camp on the West Buttress. The bear-paw snowshoe became the most favored snowshoe by mountaineers.

1951: Equipment – Tents

An American designed a tent which could be zipped to an adjoining tent at the door making the two tents into one tent.

1951: Technique – Air Support

American pilot Terris Moore (1908–1994) made the highest airplane landing in Alaska when he landed at 10,000 feet/3,048 meters on the Kahiltna Glacier below Mount McKinley (20,320 feet/6,193 meters).

1952: FIRST ASCENT

Spring. American climbers Bill Dunmire, Will Siri, Allen Steck, and Bob Swift made the first rock climbing ascent of the first route (El Cap Tree) on El Capitan (7,564 ft./2,305 m.) in Yosemite National Park in California.

1952:

Canadian mountain guide Hans Gmoser (1932–2006) pioneered the first rock climbing routes up Yamnuska (7,850 ft./2,393 m.), a south-facing limestone cliff (one mile long) on Mount John Laurie in Canada. Located between Banff and Calgary in Alberta, some consider Yamnuska to be the birthplace of modern rock climbing in Canada.

1952: FIRST ASCENT

American rock climbers Royal Robbins (1935–) and Don Wilson (1932 – 1970) decided to add "decimals" to the climbing category fifth class to indicate the relative free-climbing challenge. Robbins made the first 5.9 rated free climb in the United States — Open Book (300 foot/91 meter right-angle corner) — at Tahquitz Rock near Idyllwild, California. Robbins used no direct aid or rope tension. This was the first "free" ascent in the United States.

1952: FIRST ASCENT

A Mexican expedition made the first ascent of Mount McKinley (20,320 ft./6,193 m.) in Alaska by a climbing party from outside the United States. This ascent took only thirteen days from Wonder Lake to the summit. These climbers did not use any horses, snowshoes, or airplanes.

1952: Equipment – Packs

American company Kelty manufactured the first aluminum external frame pack. There were wooden external frames (Trapper Nelson Packboard, for example) long before this year.

1952: Technique – Chimney Climbing

November 23. Canadian Rockies mountain guide Hans Gmoser (1932–2006) and his clients Leo Grillmair and Isabel Spreat climbed the south face of Yamnuska (7,850 feet/2,393 meters) in Canada by a system of chimneys (later known as the Grillmair Chimneys). This face climb represented the beginning of high angle rock climbing in Canada.

1953:

American mountaineer and Alaskan explorer Bradford Washburn (1910–2007) identified the so-called "Fake Peak" in Alaska that Dr. Frederick Cook (1865–1940) claimed was the summit of Mount

McKinley/Denali in 1906. This 5,386 ft./1,642 m. peak is actually located 19.4 air miles southeast of Mount McKinley. Cook just wanted the publicity that would get him the financial backing for a North Pole expedition which he also faked.

1954:

February 11th. U.S. President Dwight D. Eisenhower presented the National Geographic Society's Hubbard Medal to Sir Edmund Hillary (New Zealand) and Sir John Hunt (England) at the White House in Washington, D.C. for their successful Mount Everest ascent on May 29, 1953.

1954: FIRST ASCENT

May 15. American mountaineers Morton Wood, Elton Thayer (leader, died on descent), Leslie Viereck, and George Argus made the first ascent of Mount McKinley/Denali's South Buttress. This team hiked and climbed over 130 miles for this roundtrip climb. A 1,000 foot/305 meter fall on the descent by all four climbers resulted in the death of Elton Thayer. This climb also represented the first traverse of Mount McKinley.

1954: PEAK FIRST ASCENTS HUNTER, DEBORAH, AND DRUM

July 4. The first ascent of Mount Hunter (14,574 ft./4,442 m.) in Alaska was made by Fred Beckey (1923–), Heinrich Harrer (1912–2006), and Henry Meybohm via the west ridge (8,000 vertical feet/2,438 meters along a five-mile ridge of cornices). This same team on June 19 had made the first ascent of Mount Deborah (12,540 ft./3,822 m.), also in Alaska via the southwest ridge. This advanced ice climb took three days. Deborah was named in 1907 by James Wickersham after his wife. Prior to the Hunter and Deborah climbs, Harrer also made the first ascent of Mount Drum (12,010 ft./3,660 m.) on June 4th with Keith Hart and George Schaller via the north ridge.

1954:

Well-known mountaineer, author, and landscape painter Belmore Brown (1880–1954) died at age 74. Brown made three attempts (1906, 1910, and 1912) to climb Mount McKinley (20,320 ft./6,193 m.) in Alaska.

1954: Clothing – Down Suits

The Northwest Buttress Expedition to Mount McKinley (20,320 ft./6,193 m.) in Alaska tested the Walking Penguin down sleeping robes. American mountaineer Bill Hackett (1918–1999) tested these down suits for the U.S. Air Force. Hackett and his party reached the summit of McKinley's north peak (19,470 ft./5,934 m.) on May 27 at 6:45 p.m..

1955:

July 11. The worst mountaineering accident in Canadian Rockies history occurred on the north face of Mount Temple (11,624 ft./3,543 m.) when seven American teenagers were killed in a summer snow avalanche. They were climbing a snow bowl with no ropes, no guides, poor footwear, and one ice axe. They fell 650 feet/198 meters down to a snowfield.

1955:

November. North America's first mountaineering periodical, *Summit* magazine, was founded by two southern California women. It began its publication in Bishop, California and was for many years (1955 – 1996) the only mountaineering magazine in America.

1955:

North American mountaineers Sterling Hendricks, Arnold Wexler, Donald Hubbard, Ray D'Arcy, and David Bernays made 18 first ascents in the Northwest Territories of Canada. This team coined the name "Cirque of the Unclimbables" for this area.

1956:

As of this year, George R. Senner and J. Wendell Trosper had climbed 9 different routes to the summit of Mount Rainier (14,411 ft./4,392 m.) in Washington. Other climbers and their number of different routes to Rainier's summit include: Dee Molenaar— 8, Robert W. Craig— 7, Elvin R. Johnson— 7, and Cornelius Molenaar— 7.

1956:

American mountaineer Bill Hackett (1918–1999) from Portland, Oregon was the first person to have climbed the highest peak on five of the world's seven continents. Only Mount Everest in Asia and Mount Vinson in Antarctica eluded him. These five summits were:

> 1947: Mount McKinley. 20,320 ft./6,193 m.
>
> North America (Alaska)
>
> 1949: Aconcagua. 22,834 ft./6,959 m.
>
> South America (Argentina)
>
> 1950: Mount Kilimanjaro. 19,341 ft./5,895 m.
>
> Africa (Tanzania)
>
> 1956: Mount Kosciuszko. 7,310 ft./2,228 m.
>
> Australasia (Australia)
>
> 1956: Mont Blanc. 15,775 ft./4,808 m.
>
> Europe (France). Mount Elbrus is actually the highest peak in Europe but many
> people still consider Mont Blanc the highest which it is in the European Alps.

1956:

Rock climbers in Colorado "discover" the 700 foot/213 meter high Redgarden Wall in the mile-long Eldorado Canyon just south of Boulder, Colorado. This canyon was officially designated as Eldorado State Park in 1979. This climbing area (approximately 600 climbing routes) is regarded as one of the four top rock climbing locations in the continental United States. California's Yosemite National Park, New York's Shawangunk Cliffs, and West Virginia's Seneca Rocks are the other three areas.

1957: FIRST ASCENT

June 23. American mountaineers Fred Beckey (1923–), Don Gordon, Tom Hornbein (1930–), John Rupley, and Herb Staley made the first ascent of Mount Rainier's (14,411 ft./4,392 m.) west face (Mowich Face) in Mount Rainier National Park, Washington. This team climbed this 5,000 ft./1,524 m., 40° face and then descended this same route.

1957: FIRST ASCENT

June 24 to 28. The first Grade VI climb in North American was achieved when American climbers Royal Robbins (22), Jerry Gallwas (21), and Mike Sherrick (21) first climbed the Northwest Face of Half Dome in Yosemite National Park in California. Five days of continuous climbing completed this first ascent. This team used 45 pitons and 20 expansion bolts on this 2,000 foot/610 meter high face.

1957: FIRST ASCENT

July. The east ridge of Mount Logan (19,550 ft./5,959 m.) rises approximately 12,500 feet (3,810 m.) from the Hubbard Glacier to the summit. This ridge was first climbed by Dave Collins, Don Monk, Cecil Oulette, Gil Roberts, and Kermith Ross. This ascent lasted 24 days and required 9 camps to reach the East Peak (19,351 ft./5,898 m.).

1957:

Colorado mountaineer Carl Blaurock (1894–1993) became the first person to complete the climbing of all 69 peaks in the continental United States that exceeded 14,000 feet (4,267 meters).

1957:

19-year-old American climber Yvon Chouinard (1938–) borrowed $800.00 from his parents to buy a portable forge to make iron pitons. Chouinard traveled to various climbing centers in the western United States selling his climbing hardware. Chouinard also established Chouinard Equipment this year.

1957:

The American Alpine Club reported that there were fifty-three climbing fatalities in the United States in 1956 — the greatest number ever to date. The average number of fatalities per year was approximately twenty-five.

1957: Equipment – Chalk

American rock climber John Gill (1937–) first introduced gymnastic chalk to climbing in the Tetons of Wyoming. Gymnast's chalk was found to reduce the lubricating effects of perspiration on the hands and fingers of rock climbers. Chalk was carried in small open bags attached to the climber's belt.

1957: Technique – Hammerless Protection

British immigrant to Canada Brian Greenwood (23) climbed the Belfry Route (graded 5.8) on Yamnuska (7,850 feet/2,393 meters) in Canada. He placed wedge-shaped machine nuts in rock cracks to protect himself while he climbed. This was perhaps the first time that hammerless (no pitons) hardware was used in North America.

1958: FIRST ASCENT

November 12. The first climbing route (the Nose Route) up El Capitan (7,569 ft./2,307 m.) in Yosemite National Park (California) was completed by American climber Warren Harding (1924–2002) with partners George Whitmore, Wayne Merry, and Allen Steck. The completion of this 2,900 foot/885 meter route took 47 days of climbing over a 17-month period. They used 675 pitons and 125 expansion bolts. This route (rated 5.10) is perhaps the most famous rock climb in the world. El Capitan is the largest granite monolith in the world. There are now over ninety (90) different climbing routes to its summit. The second ascent in 1960 required seven days.

1958: FIRST ASCENT

The first international climbing team to Alaska summited Mount McKinley/Denali (20,320 ft./6,193 m.) via the West Buttress route (its third ascent).

1958: Equipment – Haulsacks

Rock climber Bill Feuerer, a climbing partner of Warren Harding (1924–2002) on El Capitan's Nose Route, designed a rubber-wheeled gear hauling cart known as the "Dolt Cart." This cart, however, proved not to be practical on uneven rock surfaces.

1958: Equipment – Overboots

To protect boots from deep snow, canvas lace-up overboots (also known as mukluks) were used by mountaineering expeditions. Crampons were then strapped over these nearly shapeless overboots.

1958: Equipment – Pitons

A wider-type piton called a "bong-bong" was first used on the first ascent of El Capitan's Nose Route in Yosemite National Park in California. Bong-bongs were first made from the nine inch metal legs of an abandoned wood-burning stove. These angle-iron legs were hammered into wider cracks. These angle-iron legs were later developed into cow-bell shaped pitons called bong-bongs because of the noise they made when hammered.

1959: FIRST ASCENT

June 19. The first ascent of Mount McKinley/Denali's (20,320 ft./6,193 m.) West Rib route was made by American mountaineers Jake Breitenbach (1935–1963), Bill Buckingham, Barry Corbet (1936–2004), and Pete Sinclair. The actual climb took eleven days after this team landed on the Kahiltna Glacier. This ascent was considered the most difficult route on McKinley to date.

1959:

June. American pilot Terris Moore (1908–1994) landed his Super Cub ski-plane on the summit of

Mount Sanford (16,237 ft./4,949 m.) in Alaska. Moore participated in a U.S. Army project that was investigating the uses of small aircraft in high mountain environments.

1959: FIRST ASCENT

December 23. American mountaineers Patrick Caywood, Eliot Goss, Walter Gove, Albert Nickerson, and Leif-Norman Patterson made the first winter ascent of Gannett Peak (13,803 ft./4,207 m.) in the Wind River Range of Wyoming.

1959: FIRST ASCENT

The Cathedral Traverse in Wyoming's Teton mountains was first accomplished by American mountaineers Richard Pownall (1928–), Pete Schoening (1927–2004), and Willi Unsoeld (1926–1979). This traverse linked the three peaks of Teewinot (12,324 ft./3,756 m.), Grand Teton (13,766 ft./4,196 m.), and Mount Owen (12,928 ft./3,940 m.).

1959:

The last of the great Swiss mountain guides in Canada — Hans Fuhrer — died at age 71 (1888–1959). From 1915 to 1917, Fuhrer led over 100 ascents of Mount Hood (11,239 ft./3,425 m.) in Oregon. From 1919 to 1925, he guided over 150 ascents of Mount Rainier (14,411 ft./4,392 m.) in Washington. Fuhrer arrived in Jasper, Alberta in 1926 and went on to make many climbs in the Canadian Rockies.

1959: FIRST ASCENT

The American Mount Logan Expedition made the first ascent of Logan's North Peak (18,239 ft./5,559 m.). During this ascent, the highest climbing camp in North America was established at 18,500 ft./5,639 m. (Camp VI). Expedition members included Bill Hackett, Smoke Blanchard, Dr. Norton Benner, David Bohm, Richard Kaufman, and Jules Eichorn.

1959:

Well-known America rock climber Warren Harding (1924–2002) had accomplished seventeen first ascents in Yosemite National Park (California) as of this year.

1959: Equipment – Ice Screw

American climbers Gary Rose and Dick McGowan first successfully used the newly developed ice screw on the second ascent of the Nisqually Icefall on Mount Rainier in Washington.

1959: Equipment – Pitons

American climbers Yvon Chouinard (1938–) and Tom Frost (1940–) attempted to climb the Kat Pinnacle in Yosemite National Park in California. They developed a new kind of piton to handle the climb's crux (the climb's most difficult section) — a hairline crack. This new thin-bladed piton could penetrate ¼" into a rock crack. Chouinard and Frost named this new piton the "rurp" for Realized Ultimate Reality Piton. Rurp's were also called "crack tacks." They were made of chrome-moly steel.

1959: Technique – Capsule Style Climbing

Another term for alpine style climbing is "capsule style" climbing. This style was first tried on Mount McKinley's west rib in 1959 and later on Mount Logan's Hummingbird Ridge in 1964. Using this capsule style, climbers progress up a mountain retrieving camps and fixed ropes as they ascend. No lifeline of camps or ropes leading back down to base camp are utilized.

1960: Book

April. The Mountaineers publishing company in Seattle, Washington introduced the first edition of *The Freedom of the Hills*. This mountaineering instruction manual was heavily illustrated and provided climbers with up-to-date climbing techniques, wilderness skills, and equipment recommendations. The 600-page eighth edition appeared in 2010. This classic book has been translated into ten languages.

1960:

May. The most massive mountaineering rescue in the history of Mount McKinley occurred when four climbers slipped and fell while descending from Denali Pass (18,200 feet/5,547 meters). After reaching the summit on May 17th, John Day (broken leg), Peter Schoening (concussion), Jim Whittaker (knocked out), and Lou Whittaker (also knocked out) fell 400 feet/122 meters. All were rescued and survived. Helicopter pilot Link Luckett made two landings at 17,400 feet/5,303 meters to remove two of these injured mountaineers.

1960: FIRST ASCENT

August 3. California climbers Robert Kamps (1931 – 2005) and David Rearick (1934 –) made the first ascent of the Diamond Face on Longs Peak (14,256 ft./4,345 m.) in Rocky National Park (Colorado). This ascent involved 52 hours on the face, 28 ½ hours of actual climbing. The Diamond Face is approximately 1,000 feet/305 m. high and 1,000 feet wide. Their ascent route is now known as D1.

1960: FIRST ASCENT

September 13. Four American rock climbers made the second ascent of the Nose route on El Capitan (7,569 ft./2,307 m.) in Yosemite National Park (California). Joe Fitschen, Tom Frost (1940–), Chuck Pratt (1939–2000), and Royal Robbins (1935–) spent seven days climbing this 2,900 foot/885 meter face. They used sixty-seven pitons. This was the first continuous climb of this route. There are now over seventy named climbing routes on El Capitan.

1960:

September. Dr. Charles Houston (1913–2009) published the first documented case (in English literature) of high-altitude pulmonary edema (H.A.P.E.) in the New England Journal of Medicine. Houston's article was entitled "Acute Pulmonary Edema of High Altitude." Prior to this article physicians in the United States considered only two possible causes of pulmonary edema: heart failure or pneumonia. Houston's article introduced a third cause — high altitude. The eventual term for this high altitude induced edema was "high-altitude pulmonary edema" or H.A.P.E. Houston is considered by many to be "the father of high-altitude physiology." He published four books between 1980 and 2005 on high altitude illnesses.

1960:

December 23. American climbers Miriam Underhill (1899–1976) and her husband Robert Underhill (1889–1983) became the first to complete the climbing of New Hampshire's 48 peaks above 4,000 feet/1,219 meters in the winter. Their final peak was Mount Jefferson at 5,716 ft./1,742 m.

1960:

The Swiss Foundation For Alpine Research published Bradford Washburn's (1910–2007) detailed, authoritative map of Mount McKinley/Denali (20,320 ft./6,193 m.) in Alaska. This map was the result of a 15-year mapping effort by Washburn (1945–1960). This was the first time that the Swiss had published a map on any location outside of Switzerland.

1960:

Alaskan pilot Don Sheldon (1920–1975) became the first man to land a plane at 14,300 ft./4,358 m. on the western flank of Mount McKinley/Denali (20,320 ft./6,193 m.) in Alaska.

1961: FIRST ASCENT

July 19. An Italian mountaineering team led by Riccardo Cassin (1909–2009) made the first ascent of the 9,000 ft./2,743 m. South Spur of Mount McKinley/Denali (20,320 ft./6,193 m.) in Alaska. This spur was later renamed the Cassin Ridge. Riccardo Cassin was 52 years old at this time. Six climbers reached the summit (Cassin, Giancarlo Canali, Luigi Alippi, Annibale Zucchi, Romano Perego, and Luigi Airoldi).

1961: FIRST ASCENT

July 21. American climbers Fred Beckey (1923–) Yvon Chouinard (1938–), and Dan Doody (1934–1965) made the first ascent of the 4,500 ft./1,372 m. north face of Mount Edith Cavell (11,033 ft./3,363 m.) in the Canadian Rockies. This was the first big north face to be climbed in the Canadian Rockies.

1961: FIRST ASCENT

July. Climbers Tom Spencer and Ron Perla made the first ascent of the Emperor Ridge on Mount Robson (12,972 ft./3,954 m.) in the Canadian Rockies. This was the biggest ridge climb in the Canadian Rockies.

1961: FIRST ASCENT

September 24. American rock climbers Royal Robbins (1935–), Tom Frost (1940–), and Chuck Pratt (1939–2000) made the first ascent of the Salathé Wall (southwest face of El Capitan) in Yosemite National Park in California. They used 13 expansion bolts and 484 pitons during this six-day ascent. Their route is rated 5.10.

1961: FIRST ASCENT

October. American rock climbers Glen Denny (1939–) and Warren Harding (1924–2002) took eighteen days and one hundred and eleven expansion bolts to complete the first ascent of the overhanging west face of the Leaning Tower in the Yosemite Valley of California. This ascent has always been very controversial due to Harding's excessive use of bolts. This 700 foot/213 meter climb was repeated in May of 1963 by American climber Royal Robbins (1935–) solo. Robbins took four days to finish this ascent.

1961:

American cardiologist Dr. Herbert Hultgren (1917–1997) of the Stanford University School of Medicine published an article on high altitude pulmonary edema. This may have been the first time that this term "high altitude pulmonary edema" was used. In June of 1997, Hultgren published his book High Altitude Medicine.

1961: FIRST ASCENT

American climber Royal Robbins (1935–) made the first one-day solo ascent of the 4,000 ft./1,219 m. north face of Mount Assiniboine (11,860 ft./3,615 m.) in the Canadian Rockies.

1961: FIRST ASCENT

American climber Charlie Bell made the first ascent of Mount Rainier's (14,411 ft./4,392 m.) true north face — The Willis Wall — solo. He returned in 1962 to repeat this ascent with a camera to prove his claim.

1962:

Six new routes were established on Mount Moran (12,596 ft./3,839 m.) in the Tetons of Wyoming. This peak was named for well-known American landscape artist Thomas Moran (1837–1926).

1962: FIRST ASCENT

American rock climbers Layton Kor, Huntley Ingalls, and George Hurley made the first ascent of the Titan (900 ft./274 m.) in the Fisher Towers of eastern Utah. The summit of this rock stack was reached after five days of difficult aid-climbing.

1962: FIRST ASCENT

Helmut Tschaffert and Willi Schmidt made the first complete ski ascent of Denali (20,320 ft./6,193 m.) in Alaska.

1962: Equipment – Ascenders

A Colorado team made the first ascent of the Titan in the Fisher Towers of eastern Utah. Layton Kor (1938–2013), Huntley Ingalls, and George Hurley reached the summit. American climber/photographer Barry Bishop (1932–1994) contributed a new rope ascending device from Switzerland to this team— the Jumar. This Utah climb introduced Jumars to American climbers.

1962: Technique – Bivouacking

The bivouac technique was improved with the development of the lightweight sleeping bag and the sheltering "tent-sack" (or bivi bag).

1963: FIRST ASCENT

May 11. American rock climber Royal Robbins (1935–) made a solo ascent of the west face of Leaning Tower in Yosemite National Park (California). This ascent took four days. This was the first ever solo ascent of a big wall in the Yosemite Valley.

1963: FIRST ASCENT

June 13. Canadian Rockies' guide Hans Gmoser (1932–2006), Gunther Prinz, and Hans Schwartz made the first ascent of Mount McKinley/Denali's Wickersham Wall (north face of north peak — 19,470 ft./5,934 m.) in Alaska.

One month later on July 16, members of the Harvard Mountaineering Club (Harvard Wickersham Wall Expedition) made the same ascent of this 14,000 ft./4,267 m. high Wickerhsam Wall via the Central Buttress. These climbers were David Roberts, Don Jensen, John Graham, Peter Carman, Rick Millikan, Hank Abrows, and Chris Goetze.

1963: FIRST ASCENT

Summer. American mountaineers John Evans (1938–), Dick Long, and Allen Steck (1927–) first accomplished the so-called "Grand Traverse of the Tetons" in Wyoming. In less than 21 hours, they climbed the following seven prominent peaks (south to north): Nez Perce (11,901 ft./3,627 m.), Cloud-veil Dome (12,026 ft./3,665 m.), South Teton (12,514 ft./3,814 m.), Middle Teton (12,804 ft./3,902 m.), the Grand Teton (13,766 ft./4,196 m.), Mount Owen (12,928 ft./3,940 m.), and Mount Teewinot (12,324 ft./3,756 m.).

1963: FIRST ASCENT

August 9. Patrick Callis and Dan Davis made the first ascent of Mount Robson's (12,972 ft./3,954 m.) north face (55° ice slope) in the Canadian Rockies.

1963: FIRST ASCENT

October 31. American climbers Yvon Chouinard (1938–), Tom Frost (1940–), Chuck Pratt (1939–2000), and Royal Robbins (1935–) made the first ascent of the North American Wall on the southeast face of El Capitan in Yosemite National Park in California. This was considered to be the hardest technical climbing route in the world at the time. This ascent took nine days.

1963:

American mountaineer Fred Beckey (1923–) made 26 North American first ascents in a single year (Canada and the United States). From 1940 to 1996, Beckey made over 1,000 first ascents in North America. He has also authored ten books about the mountains.

1963:

The National Geographical Society bestowed its highest honor—The Hubbard Medal—on the leader of the 1963 American Mount Everest Expedition, Norman Dyhrenfurth (1919–). Past recipients included Charles Lindberg and Admiral Peary.

1963:

The Denali-Hunter Traverse in Alaska was accomplished by Vincent Hoeman, Tom Choate, and Dave Johnston. They ascended the Muldrow Glacier to the North Summit (19,470 ft./5,934 m.) of Denali before crossing over to the South Summit (20,320 ft./6,193 m.). They descended the West Buttress route before ascending the west ridge of Mount Hunter (14,574 ft./4,442 m.) to the south and middle summits.

1963:

The National Climbing Classification System was first introduced in *Summit* magazine by American climber Leigh Ortenburger (1928–1991). This system was designed to grade the difficulty of a free-climbing pitch with a simple digit. It also included a five-level category A1-A5 for direct aid pitches.

1963: FIRST ASCENT

American technical rock climbers, Royal Robbins, Layton Kor, Jim McCarthy, and Dick McCracken made the first ascent of the southeast face of Mount Proboscis (8,563 ft./2,610 m.) in the Northwest Territories of Canada. Their climbing route is now known as the Original Route. This climbing team used 251 pitons and two expansion bolts during this three-day climb. This ascent represented the first time that Yosemite Big-Wall climbing techniques had been used on a remote Big Wall.

1964: PEAK FIRST ASCENT *HUNTINGTON*

May 26. A French mountaineering team led by well-known guide Lionel Terray (1921–1965) made the first ascent of Mount Huntington (12,240 ft./3,731 m.) in Alaska (via the northwest ridge). Jacques Batkin and Sylvain Sarthou first reached the summit followed a day later by Terray, Paul Gendre, Jacques Soubis, Marc Martinetti, Maurice Gicquel, and Jean-Louis Bernezat. Terray badly injured his arm on the ascent and was forced to temporarily stop his climbing. However, nine days after his accident, he stood on the summit. Huntington is located seven miles south of Mount McKinley/Denali. This was the last national expedition of the Federation Francaise de la Montagne. Their ascent route is now known as the Terray Ridge. Terray and Martinetti died in a climbing accident in France in 1965.

1964: FIRST ASCENT

July 22 to 25. American climbers Royal Robbins (1935–), Dick McCracken, and Charlie Raymond spent 3 ½ days in making the first ascent of the north face (1,800 ft./549 m.) of Mount Hooker (12,504 ft./3,811 m.) in the Wind River Range of Wyoming. This is the highest rock wall in the Wind Rivers. This climb represented the first remote Grade VI climb in the United States.

1964:

July. Mount Everest first ascender Tenzing Norgay Sherpa (1914–1986) and his wife Daku traveled to the World's Fair in New York City where they met United Nations Secretary General U Thant. In August, they were invited to Washington to climb Mount Rainier (14,411 ft./4,392 m.) with guide and Everest summiter (1963) Jim Whittaker (1929–). 1963 Everest summiters Lute Jerstad (1937–1998) and Tom Hornbein (1930–) also joined this Rainier climb.

1964: FIRST ASCENT

October 22 to 31. The southeast face of El Capitan contains the North American Wall route. The first ascent of this route was made by Yvon Chouinard (1938–), Tom Frost (1940–), Chuck Pratt (1939–2000), and Royal Robbins (1935–) over a period of ten days.

1964:

An expedition sponsored by The Mountaineers (Seattle, Washington) placed fifteen climbers on the summit of Mount McKinley/Denali (20,320 ft./6,193 m.) in Alaska. This was the second largest American climbing expedition on record at the time (18 members) and the largest single group ever to climb McKinley/Denali. Alvin Randall was the leader. Three women reached the summit (a record) and the first African-American also reached the summit (Charles Crenshaw).

1964:

The North Face company was founded by American businessman Doug Tompkins (1943–) and his wife Susie. This company specialized in the design and manufacture of rock climbing, mountaineering, and camping equipment.

1964: Clothing – Insulation

The ultra-lightweight, heat conserving thermal blanket known as the Space Blanket became available in the United States. When wrapped around an injured climber, this emergency blanket reflected and retained up to 80 percent of the body's natural radiated body heat.

1964: Equipment – Ice Dagger

American climber Don Jensen invented an ice dagger he called the "Icelite." Approximately two feet in length, this barbed, pointed section of L-bar aluminum was designed for better protection and anchorage in soft snow or ice. This ice dagger was invented specifically for the Mount Deborah (12,540 ft./3,822 m.) expedition in Alaska.

1965: PEAK FIRST ASCENT *KENNEDY*

March 24. American mountaineer Jim Whittaker (1929–), the first American to climb Mount Everest (1963), guided Senator Robert Kennedy (39, New York) up Mount Kennedy (13,905 ft./4,238 m.) in the Canadian Yukon. Formerly named East Hubbard Peak, this mountain was renamed in honor of slain U.S. President John F. Kennedy. At the time, this was the highest unclimbed peak in Canada. The

National Geographic Society sponsored this expedition that also included James Craig, William Allard, Barry Prather, Dee Molenaar, Barry Bishop (3rd American to climb Mount Everest–1963), and George Senner. Kennedy, Whittaker, Allard, and Molenaar reached the summit. Kennedy made the roundtrip from Washington, D.C. to the summit and back to D.C. in five days.

1965: FIRST ASCENT

March. The first winter ascent of Mount Robson's (12,972 ft./3,954 m.) north face in the Canadian Rockies was accomplished by American mountaineers Alex Bertulis and Leif-Norman Patterson (1934–1976). Their ascent route was on the Kain Face. This was the fourth attempt to climb this mountain in the winter.

1965: FIRST ASCENT

July 30. Four climbers from the Harvard Mountaineering Club made the first ascent of Mount Huntington's (12,240 ft./3,730 m.) west face in Alaska. Ed Bernd (killed on the descent), Matt Hale, Don Jensen, and David Roberts reached the summit. This was the second overall ascent of Mount Huntington.

1965: FIRST ASCENT

August 7. An American climbing team made the first ascent of the ten-mile long, 12,000 foot high Hummingbird Ridge on Mount Logan (19,551 ft./5,959 m.) in Canada's Yukon Territory. They established five camps prior to reaching this ridge and then located ten camps on the ridge itself between 10,000 feet (3,048 m.) and 17,000 feet (5,181 meters). They placed 24,000 feet of fixed ropes on this ridge. All six team members reached the summit and spent twenty minutes there. The summit temperature was 12° F. The team included Paul Bacon, Frank Coale, John Evans, Dick Long, Allen Steck, and Jim Wilson. This expedition lasted for thirty days.

1965: FIRST ASCENT

August. Irene Beardsley Ortenburger and Susan Chaplin Swedlund were the first all-woman team to climb the 2,500 foot/762 meter north face of the Grand Teton (13,766 feet/4,196 meters) in Wyoming. This was the most difficult all-woman ascent to date in North America.

1965:

Canadian mountaineers Charlie Locke and Don Gardner completed a Canadian peak traverse on the Continental Divide that ringed the Valley of Ten Peaks and the Lake Louise cirque. This 6 ½ day traverse reached 22 summits.

1965: Book

American mountaineer Dr. Tom Hornbein (1930–) published his book entitled *Everest: The West Ridge*. This large format book is a celebration in photographs of the successful ascent of Mount Everest in 1963 by an American expedition. Hornbein and Willi Unsoeld (1926–1979) reached the summit on May 22nd via the west ridge—a first ascent.

1966: FIRST ASCENT

August 4. Canadian mountaineers Brian Greenwood and Charlie Locke made the first ascent of the 4,500 foot/1,372 meter north face of Mount Temple (11,637 ft./3,547 m.) in the Canadian Rockies.

1966: FIRST ASCENT

August. American mountaineers Lito Tejada-Flores and Jim McCarthey (1933–) made the first "Grand Traverse of the Tetons" in the north to south direction. They climbed ten peaks in two days (14 miles).

1966: Equipment – Crampons

American climbers Tom Frost (1940–) and Yvon Chouinard (1938–) invented the rigid crampon for steep icewall climbing. This 12-point crampon was made from chrome-molybdenum steel and was fully adjustable. The Salewa-Chouinard rigid crampons became available in 1972.

1966: Equipment – Pitons

Wide-angled pitons that could be driven sideways into wide cracks were developed in the United States. These pitons were called "American bongs."

1967: FIRST ASCENT

February 28. The first winter ascent of Mount McKinley/Denali (20,320 ft./6,193 m.) in Alaska was achieved by an American expedition led by Gregg Blomberg. Other expedition members included Art Davidson, Dave Johnston, Shiro Nishimae, John Edwards, George Wichman, Ray "Pirate" Genet (1931–1979), and Jacques "Farine" Batkin (killed in a hidden crevasse fall). Following the West Buttress route, Davidson, Johnston, and Genet reached the summit at 7:00 p.m. on February 28. During the descent, these three mountaineers became trapped by bad weather at Denali Pass (18,200 ft./5,547 m.) for six days and seven nights. Winds of over 130 miles per hour and temperatures as low as -45°F produced a wind-chill factor of -148°F. Eventually, they were able to leave their tentless bivouac (ice cave) and descend to 10,200 ft./3,109 m. where helicopters safely rescued them (42 days after beginning their climb). Art Davidson authored the book Minus 148° (1969) that documented this epic ascent.

1967: FIRST ASCENT

May. American rock climbers Royal and Liz Robbins climbed the Nutcracker Sweet route on Ranger Rock in Yosemite National Park (California). They only used nuts on this 800 foot/244 meter climb. This was the first major first ascent in North America to be climbed with only using nuts. This ascent began the "clean-climbing" movement in the Yosemite Valley.

1967: FIRST ASCENT

July 23 and 24. Yvon Chouinard (1938–), Joe Faint, and Chris Jones made the first ascent of Mount Assiniboine's (11,860 ft./3,615 m.) North Face in the Canadian Rockies. This was a significant ice climb.

1967:

July. Two American mountaineering expeditions were combined to form one twelve-man team. The Colorado Mount McKinley Expedition (Howard Snyder: Leader, Jerry Lewis, and Paul Schlichter) joined the 1967 Joseph F. Wilcox Mount McKinley Expedition (Joe Wilcox: Leader, Jerry Clark, Hank Janes, Dennis Luchterhand, Mark McLaughlin, John Russell, Anshel Schiff, Steve Taylor, and Walt Taylor).

On July 15th, the first climbing group reached Mount McKinley's summit (20,320 ft./6,193 m.)— Lewis, Schlichter, Snyder, and Wilcox. This group made radio contact with National Park Climbing Ranger Wayne Merry at the Wonder Lake Ranger Station (north of Mount McKinley). This was the first time that an on-summit team had directly communicated with national park personnel. This four-man team plus Anshel Schiff began their descent from Camp VII (17,900 feet/5,456 meters) on July 16.

The second climbing group (Clark, Janes, Luchterhand, McLaughlin, and Walt Taylor) reached the summit on July 18th after bivouacking near Archdeacon's Tower (19,650 feet/5,989 meters). John Russell did not reach the summit and Steve Taylor remained at Camp VII. On July 19th, this second summit group was forced to dig two snow caves on their summit descent due to 100 m.p.h. winds. No further radio contact could be made with this group. These five climbers plus Russell and Steve Taylor eventually died in one of the worst storms (8 days) in Mount McKinley National Park history. All of these climbers still remain on the mountain in several locations between 17,900 feet (5,456 meters) and 19,400 feet (5,913 meters) just east of Denali Pass.

1967:

July. A high-altitude research laboratory known as "Logan High Camp" was constructed on a Mount Logan (19,551 ft./5,959 m.) glacier at 17,500 ft./5,334 m. in the Yukon Territory of Canada. This project was sponsored by the Arctic Institute of North America. From 1967 until 1979, this research facility was occupied by scientists who studied high altitude physiology. Retinal hemorrhages due to high altitude were first noted here in 1968.

1967: FIRST ASCENT

July. American climber Liz Robbins became the first woman to climb a Grade VI rated route. This was accomplished on the northwest face of Half Dome in Yosemite National Park in California. She climbed with her husband Royal Robbins (1935–).

1967:

In Canada's centennial year (1867–1967), the Alpine Club of Canada sponsored the Yukon Alpine Centennial Expedition. Teams of Canadian mountaineers ascended thirteen unclimbed and unnamed peaks north of Mount Logan (19,550 ft./5,958 m.). Each of these peaks was then named for one of Canada's provinces.

1967:

Canadian woman mountaineer Phyllis Munday (1894–1990) received an honorary membership in the American Alpine Club at age 73. She received the same honorary memberships in the Ladies Alpine

Club (England) in 1936 at age 42 and Alpine Club of Canada in 1938 at age 44. Munday is the only mountaineer to receive these three international memberships. She died in 1990 at the age of 96.

1967: Equipment – Alpine Hammer

American climbers and equipment designers Yvon Chouinard (1938–) and Tom Frost (1940–) introduced their "alpine hammer"—a piton hammer with an extended, curved, and toothed-pick for biting into ice.

1967: Equipment – Backpack

Colorado climber Greg Lowe developed the first internal frame backpack (Lowe Alpine).

1967: Equipment – Nuts

American climber Royal Robbins (1935–) brought climbing nuts to America. Robbins returned to California from climbing in Great Britain. He brought home a variety of anchor nuts—regular machined nuts threaded with cord and custom-made nuts specifically designed for crack wedging. Robbins actively promoted the use of nuts over pitons in Yosemite National Park in California. The use of nuts did not cause the rock to be scarred as the use of pitons did by both hammering the piton into the rock crack and then loosening and removing it later.

1967: Technique – Ultra-Lightweight Climbing

The ultra-lightweight alpine style climbing was beginning to be applied to peaks in Alaska and the Andes of South America that had previously only been attempted by expedition style climbing (fixed ropes, multiple camps, load porters). Only experienced mountaineers were experimenting with alpine style climbing which demanded more commitment than expedition style.

1968: FIRST ASCENT

March 2. American mountaineers George Lowe (1944–), Mike Lowe, Greg Lowe, and Rick Horn made the first winter ascent of the Grand Tetons (13,766 ft./4,196 m.) 2,500 foot North Face in Wyoming. This was the most advanced alpine ascent at the time in the lower 48 United States. They spent 3½ days on the face.

1968: FIRST ASCENT

April. American climber Royal Robbins (1935–) made a 9½ day solo ascent of the John Muir Wall on El Capitan (7,568 ft./2,307 m.) in California's Yosemite National Park. This was the first solo ascent of El Capitan.

1968:

Young Colorado climber Tyle Smith (age 8) completed the climbing of all 54 peaks in Colorado over 14,000 feet (4,267 meters). He climbed with his brothers and his father. As of the end of this year, 100 people had climbed all 54 fourteeners in Colorado.

1968:

Roger Brown's film entitled: *Sentinel – The West Face* was awarded first prize at the Trento (Italy) Film Festival. This film was about a rock climb in Yosemite National Park in California.

1968: Equipment – Bivouac Hammocks

American climber Warren Harding (1924–2002) designed his legendary "BAT" (Basically Absurd Technology) equipment. Harding's Bat Tents were semi-waterproof, fully enclosed, and suspended by a single point on a rock face. These tents were designed for one person.

1968: Equipment – Boots

American boot designer Bob Lange developed the first all-plastic ski boot which led to all-plastic climbing boots ten years later.

1969: FIRST ASCENT

February 21. The first winter ascent of Mount Waddington (13,186 ft./4,019 m.) in British Columbia, Canada was made by Dick Culbert, Barry Hagen, and Allen Steck. There were six climbers in the total party.

1969:

May 13. American mountaineer Oliver Perry-Smith (1884–1969) died at age 85. He made over 90 ascents in Switzerland that included 32 first ascents, 13 solo climbs, 33 climbs that were rated Grade VI +. He led 36 of these climbs.

1969:

May 25 to September 13. American climber F.T. Ashley took 109 days to climb the highest point in each of the 48 contiguous United States. The lowest summit was in Florida (345 ft./105 m.) while the highest was in California (Mount Whitney: 14,495 ft./4,418 m.). Ashley hiked and climbed over 600 miles/1,000 kilometers.

1969: FIRST ASCENT

American climber Tom Bauman made the first solo ascent of the Nose on El Capitan (7,568 ft./2,307 m.) in Yosemite National Park in California.

1969:

The Yosemite Mountaineering School was established. Wayne Merry was the school's first director.

1969:

Alaska Mountain Guides became the first guide service on Denali. This name was later changed to Genet Expeditions.

1969: Equipment – Swami Belt

Late 1960s. A swami belt was a piece of nylon webbing one to two inches in width and approximately seventeen feet in length that was looped three times around the climber's waist and tied tight. The climbing rope was then tied into this swami belt. The wide band created by these three webbing loops cushioned a fall more effectively than a single loop. The development of the seat harness replaced the swami belt which tended to ride-up and squeeze the chest.

1969: Technique – Clean Climbing

American rock climbers Liz and Royal Robbins (1935–) made two piton-less ascents in Yosemite National Park in California — Boulder Field Gorge and the Nutcracker. These two landmark climbs made a significant contribution to "clean climbing" in Yosemite.

1970: FIRST ASCENT

July 6. The first all-women ascent of Mount McKinley/Denali (20,320 ft./6,193 m.) in Alaska was led by American mountaineers Arlene Blum (1945–) and Dr. Grace Hoeman (1922–1971). Known as the "West Buttress Broads," this team of six women (Blum, Hoeman, Margaret Clark, Margaret Young, Faye Kerr, and Dana Isherwood) all reached the summit.

1970: FIRST ASCENT

August 26. Japanese mountaineer Naomi Uemura (1942–1984) made the first solo ascent of Mount McKinley/Denali (20,320 ft./6,193 m.) in Alaska. In 1984, he made the first solo winter ascent but disappeared on his descent.

1970: FIRST ASCENT

November. California rock climbers Warren Harding (1924–2002) and Dean Caldwell took 28 consecutive days to make the first ascent of the Wall Of The Early Morning Light on El Capitan (7,568 ft./2,307 m.) in Yosemite National Park (California). Harding and Caldwell slept in hammock-like "bat tents" on this face. Every one of the 333 expansion bolt holes that they drilled required several hundred hammer blows to drill out.

1970: FIRST ASCENT

American climber Bill Forrest (1939–2012) made the first solo ascent of the Diamond face on Longs Peak (14,256 ft./4,345 m.) in Colorado. This ascent took four days. Forrest was a gifted inventor of climbing gear. He is credited with first developing cam-able nuts, leg loops for seat harness and lightweight ice tools with interchangeable picks.

1970:

North America's first high-altitude rescue group was established in Yosemite National Park (California) by the National Park Service (NPS). American climber Jim Bridwell (1944–) was hired by the NPS to manage YOSAR (Yosemite Search and Rescue). In 2007, YOSAR had 25 to 30 full and part-time members.

1970:

American climbers James P. McCarthy (1933–), Yvon Chouinard (1938–), and Bill Putnam (1924–) made the first non-step-cutting ascent of Pinnacle Gully on Mount Washington (6,288 ft./1,916 m.) in New Hampshire. This climb represented the coming of age of eastern American ice climbing.

1970: Equipment – Ice Axe

The Chouinard-Frost (Yvon Chouinard and Tom Frost) ice axe with the "drooping pick" became available to climbers worldwide. The shorter ice axe (55 centimeters/21 ½ inches) aided climbers in ascending vertical and overhanging ice climbs.

1970: Technique – Expansion Bolts

American rock climber Warren Harding (1924–2002) spent twenty-six consecutive bivouacs and placed three hundred expansion bolts in making the first ascent of El Capitan's Wall of the Early Morning Light in Yosemite National Park (California). This massive use of expansion bolts caused significant revulsion against the use of such artificial aid techniques.

1971: FIRST ASCENT

May. American climber Johanna Marte became the first woman to climb El Capitan (7,568 ft./2,307 m.) in Yosemite National Park in California. Her husband Egon and Royal Robbins were with her.

1971: FIRST ASCENT

October 23 to November 18. American rock climbers Warren Harding (1924–2002) and Dean Caldwell spent 27 days making the first ascent of El Capitan's Dawn Wall. They used 330 expansion bolts on this 2,800 foot/853 meter ascent.

1971: FIRST ASCENT

Washington climber Peter Whittaker (1959–) became the youngest person at age 12 to reach the summit of Mount Rainier (14,411 ft./4,392 m.) in Washington. Peter is the son of well-known American mountaineer Lou Whittaker (1929–), founder of Rainier Mountaineering, Inc. in 1968.

1971:

Dr. Grace Hoeman (1922–1971) died at age 50 in an Alaskan avalanche. During her climbing career (approximately 1965 to 1971) she made over 120 ascents in Alaska including 20 first ascents (5 of them solo). In 1970, she led an all-female ascent of Denali (20,320 ft./6,193 m.) in Alaska. She also climbed both Chimborazo (20,702 ft./6,310 m.) and Illiniza (17,261 ft./5,261 m.) in Ecuador.

1971:

American mountaineer James Waddell Alexander III (1888–1971) died at age 83. He was a member of the Princeton University faculty from 1920 to 1951. He climbed Longs Peak in Colorado 20 times. He made the following ascents in the Alps:

1923	22 ascents in the Zermatt area
1925	25 ascents between Zermatt and Chamonix, France
1926	23 ascents
1927	23 ascents
1928	20 ascents
1929	15 ascents

1971:

American mountaineering author James Ramsey Ullman (1908–1971) died at age 63. Ullman wrote many books (fiction and non-fiction) about the mountains including:

High Conquest (1941)	*Tiger Of The Snows* (1955)
The White Tower (1945)	*The Age Of Mountaineering* (1956)
Kingdom of Adventure (1947)	*Americans On Everest* (1964)
River Of The Sun (1951)	*Straight Up* (1968)
The Sands Of The Karakorum (1953)	*And Not To Yield* (1970)
Banner In The Sky (1954)	

1971: Book

American rock climber Royal Robbins (1935–) published his book entitled *Basic Rockcraft*. This was the first good instructional book for rock climbing. In 1973, Robbins published a follow-up book entitled *Advanced Rockcraft*. He founded the Rockcraft Climbing School in Modesto, California, in 1968.

1971: Equipment – Nuts

Chouinard Equipment (Yvon Chouinard-Founder) developed and patented the metal Hexcentric chock for crack climbing. These chocks ranged in size from 7/16" to 2 ½." Ventura, California.

1971: Technique – Ice Climbing

American climber Greg Lowe became the first person to free-climb vertical ice using the front two crampon prongs.

1972: FIRST ASCENT

March 17. American mountaineers Pat McGrane, Charles Campbell, and John Rehmer made the first winter ascent of the Crestone Needle (14,197 ft./4,327 m.) and the traverse to Crestone Peak (14,294 ft./4,357 m.) in the Sangre de Cristo Range in Colorado. They were forced to bivouac at 13,300 ft./4,054 m. on Crestone Peak.

1972: FIRST ASCENT

May 3. American climbers Bill Forrest (1940–2012) and Kris Walker (1952–) made the first Grade VI climb in Colorado when they climbed the 2,200 foot/671 meter Painted Wall route in the Black Canyon of the Gunnison River. This nearly boltless (expansion bolts) ascent of twenty-six pitches took four days.

1972: FIRST ASCENT

August. The north face of Mount Alberta (11,873 ft./3,619 m.) in Canada is 3,300 feet (1,006 m.) high. This face was first climbed by George Lowe (1944–) and Jocelyn Glidden.

1972:

December 23. Well-known California mountaineer Norman Clyde (1885–1972) died at age 87. During his climbing career (1914 to 1972), Clyde made over 1,500 California ascents including 160 first ascents. Norman Clyde Peak (13,956 ft./4,254 m.) in California's Sierra Mountains is named for him. During the summer of 1923, he climbed thirty-six different peaks in thirty-six days.

1972: FIRST ASCENT

American mountaineer Helen I. Buck (1884–1972) died at age 88. She was the first American woman to climb the three peaks of Mont Blanc, the Matterhorn, and the Jungfrau in the Alps. Buck also climbed Popocatepetl and Iztaccihuatl in Mexico, Mount Robson in Canada, and was the first woman to climb Mount Edith Cavell in Canada.

1972: FIRST ASCENT

American climber Barbara Lilley reached the summit of Mount St. Elias (18,008 ft./5,489 m.) in Alaska. With this ascent, Lilley became the first person to summit the five highest peaks in North America (Denali, Logan, Orizaba, St. Elias, and Popocatepetl). She also summited all of the 14,000 foot/4,267 meter peaks in Colorado, California, and Washington.

1972:

Canadian Prime Minister (1968–1979, 1980–1984) Pierre Elliot Trudeau (1919–2000) climbed the Bugaboo Spire (10,420 ft./3,176 m.) in the Purcell Range of the Canadian Rockies with professional mountain guide Hans Gmoser (1932–2006).

1972:

The five summits of Mount Lyell in the Canadian Rockies were renamed to honor five Swiss guides who served their clients over a long period of time and settled in Golden, British Columbia, Canada. These five Lyell peaks are:

Lyell 1	Rudolph Peak	11,506 ft./3,507 m.
Lyell 2	Edward Peak	11,529 ft./3,514 m.
Lyell 3	Ernst Peak	11,519 ft./3,511 m.
Lyell 4	Walter Peak	11,155 ft./3,400 m.
Lyell 5	Christian Peak	11,122 ft./3,390 m.

1972: Fabric – Gore-Tex

Dupont Chemicals researcher Wilbert L. Gore (later W.L. Gore & Associates, Maryland) developed the revolutionary new fabric called "Gore-Tex." It was waterproof yet allowed body moisture to escape. The registered patent for Gore-Tex was filed in 1973 and eventually issued in 1976.

1972: Equipment – Nuts

Chouinard, Inc. introduces "Stoppers" and "Hexentrics." These wedge-shaped metal nuts were used for passive protection. Stoppers were available in a variety of sizes and weights.

1972: Equipment – Tents

American climber Greg Lowe designed the first portable or hanging tent. It was first used on the first winter ascent of the northwest face of Half Dome (2,000 ft./610 m. high) in Yosemite National Park in California by Lowe and Rob Kiesel.

1972: Equipment – Bivouac Hammock

Early 1970s. American climbers Bill Forrest (1939 – 2012) and Kris Walker (1952 –) developed the single-point suspension hammock for bivouacking on big wall climbs.

1973: FIRST ASCENT

July 10. The southwest ridge of Mount Fairweather (15,318 ft./4,669 m.) in Alaska was first climbed by four young American mountaineers: Peter Metcalf (17), Lincoln Stoller (17), Henry Florschutz (19), and Toby O'Brien (19). This team witnessed extensive avalanches caused by a 5.9 earthquake.

1973: FIRST ASCENT

September 25 to October 2. Beverly Johnson (–1994) and Sybille Hechtel made the first all-female ascent of El Capitan's 3,500 ft./1,067 m. face in Yosemite National Park (California). They climbed the Triple Direct route (Salathe Wall — first 1,000 ft., Muir Wall — second 1,000 ft., and the Nose Route — last 1,000 feet).

1973: FIRST ASCENT

American climbers Doug Robinson (1945–), Galen Rowell (1940–2002), and Dennis Hennek completed the historic first "clean" ascent (no pitons or expansion bolts used) of Half Dome (2,000 ft./610 meter high) in Yosemite National Park in California. Robinson later became the first president of the American Mountain Guides Association. In addition to being an excellent climber, Rowell was also a noted mountain photographer and writer. Unfortunately, he and his wife Barbara were killed in a plane crash near Bishop, California in 2002.

1973:

The two ¾" steel cables were removed from the north face of Longs Peak (14,256 ft./4,345 m.) in Rocky Mountain National Park (Colorado). These cables were fixed to the 55° north face rock in 1925.

1973:

Washington climber Bruce Carson climbed the Nose Route (3,500 ft./1,067 m.) on El Capitan in Yosemite National Park (California) using only chocks for protection— no pitons.

1973:

American mountaineer Gary Neptune (Mount Everest summit May 14, 1983) opened his Boulder, Colorado climbing shop — Neptune Mountaineering. In the late 1970s, Neptune (1945–) began to exhibit in his shop his collection of mountaineering artifacts, memorabilia, historic clothing and equipment. By the year 2000, the Neptune Mountaineering and Ski Museum represented the finest collection of historic mountaineering equipment and clothing in the United States. Included in this collection are over 200 antique ice axes from the European Alps and other mountain regions. Many of the most famous mountaineers in the world have also donated their personal equipment and clothing to Neptune's museum. Neptune has also climbed Makalu (1987), Gasherbrum II (1997), and Ama Dablam (1981) in the Himalayas. In addition, Neptune made the second winter ascent of the Diamond on Longs Peak and numerous ascents of Yosemite walls.

1973:

Oregon mountaineer Ole Lien (1898–1973) died at age 75. Lien made 444 ascents of Mount Hood (11,239 ft./3,425 m.).

1973: Equipment – Friend

American rock climber Ray Jardine (1944–) invented the modern spring-loaded camming device that would be known as the "Friend." This device was used to jam into rock cracks for protection while climbing. Friends began to be commercially manufactured in 1977 in England by Mark Vallance (a friend of Ray Jardine) who established the climbing equipment company known as Wild Country. The first "friends" prototypes were tested in Colorado's Front Range rock crags by Jardine, Kris Walker (1952 –), and Bill Forrest (1939 – 2012).

1973: Equipment – Ice Axe

American climbers Bill Forrest (1939 – 2012) and Kris Walker (1952 –) developed exchangeable pick ice tools.

1973: Equipment – Ice Axe

Newly designed drooped pick ice tools were produced by the Simond Company of Chamonix, France. The new technique of ice climbing was now fully underway.

1973: Technique – Clean Climbing

American climbers Yvon Chouinard (1938–) and Bruce Carson made the first ascent of the Nose on El Capitan (7,568 feet/2,307 meters) in Yosemite National Park (California) without using hammers and pitons. They did use existing fixed pitons and expansion bolts.

1974: FIRST ASCENT

January 2. American ice climbers Jeff Lowe (1950–) and Mike Weiss made the first ascent of the 350 foot/107 meter Bridalveil Falls near Telluride, Colorado. This sustained vertical and overhanging ice climb laid the groundwork for the water-ice climbing revolution. This first ascent took ten hours.

1974:

The Climbing Smiths (father and three sons) reached the summits of all 54 Colorado peaks over 14,000 feet/4,267 meters in 33 days. They first completed this 54-peak climbing journey in 1968.

1974:

The Chouinard-Frost Equipment Catalog (United States) first introduced the climbing community to "clean" climbing. In this catalog, American rock climber Doug Robinson (1945–) wrote an essay that defined clean climbing: "Climbing with only nuts and runners for protection is clean climbing. Clean because the rock is left unaltered by the passing climber. Clean because nothing is hammered into the rock and then hammered back out, leaving the rock scarred and the next climber's experience less natural. Clean because the climber's protection leaves little track of his ascension. Clean is climbing the rock without changing it; a step closer to organic climbing for the natural man." American climbers and equipment inventors Yvon Chouinard (1938–) and Tom Frost (1940–) also first introduced rigid crampons and the curved ice axe in this catalog (first published in 1972).

1974:

Colorado climber Glenn Porzak (1948–) completed the climbing of the 100 highest peaks in Rocky Mountain National Park (Colorado). Porzak began this climbing goal in 1961 at age 13 with ascents of both the lowest peak of the 100 — Estes Cone (11,006 ft./3,354 m.) — and the highest peak — Longs Peak (14,256 ft./4,345 m.). Porzak went on to climb the world's Seven Summits and four 8,000 meter peaks in the Himalayas including Mount Everest in 1990.

1974: FIRST ASCENT

American climbers George Lowe (1925–) and Chris Jones made the first ascent of the 4,500 ft./1,372 m. north face of North Twin (12,237 ft./3,730 m.) in the Canadian Rockies. This face climb was regarded as the most difficult alpine route in North America at the time. Since 1974, this route has seen fifteen serious repeat attempts with no successes.

1974: Equipment – L.U.R.P. Tent

American climber Greg Lowe developed this new type of collapsible portaledge that has a solid aluminum frame around the nylon decking bed that prevented the inhabitants from leaning against the rock face. This portaledge was hung from six nylon webbing straps. L.U.R.P. stood for Limited Use of Reasonable Placements. The L.U.R.P. tent was first used on the first winter ascent of the northwest face of Half Dome in Yosemite National Park (California).

1974: Equipment – Double-Wall Tent

The integrated double-wall mountaineering tent was developed by William S. Nicolai who founded the Early Winters Ltd. Outdoor equipment company.

1974: Equipment – Ice Tools

The first modular ice tools and the first tubular pick and adze were developed by Lowe Alpine in Colorado.

1975: FIRST ASCENT

May 26. American climbers Jim Bridwell (1944–), John Long, and Billy Westbay made the first one-day ascent of the 3,000 ft./914 m. Nose route on El Capitan in Yosemite National Park (California) in 15 hours. Most climbers today take 4 to 5 days to climb this route which has a 60 percent success rate.

1975: FIRST ASCENT

Molly Higgins Bruce, Stephanie Atwood, and Laurie Wood made the first all-female ascent of the Diamond Face on Longs Peak (14,256 ft./4,345 m.) in Colorado.

1975: FIRST ASCENT

California rock climbers John Bachar (1957–2009), Ron Kauk (1958–), and John Long made the first free-climb of Astroman — a 1,400 foot/427 meter overhanging face on Washington Column in the Yosemite Valley of California. This twelve-pitch climb as of this year was called "the most continuously difficult free-climb in the world."

1975: Equipment – Ice Axe

Ice axe shafts made of rexilon (18 laminates of wood) were first introduced by Yvon Chouinard and Tom Frost. These shafts came in 60, 70, and 80 centimeter lengths.

1976: FIRST ASCENT

May 2. British mountaineers Dougal Haston (1940–1977) and Doug Scott (1941–) made the first alpine-style ascent of Denali's South Face (8,500 ft./2,591 m.) in Alaska. This ascent took fourteen days.

1976:

June. American mountaineer Charlie Porter (1951 –) climbed the Cassin Ridge on Mount McKinley/Denali (20,320 ft./6,193 m.) in Alaska solo in 1 ½ days.

1976: FIRST ASCENT

Four American climbers made the first ascent of Reality Ridge on Denali (20,320 ft./6,193 m.) in Alaska. Henry Florschutz, Peter Metcalf, Lincoln Stoller, and Angus Thuermer.

1976: FIRST ASCENT

American rock climber John Bachar (1957–2009) made the first ropeless 5.11 route in Yosemite when he solo climbed New Dimensions.

1976:

American mountaineer William L. Putnam (1924–) completed thirty years of climbing (1946 to 1976) in Canada's Selkirk Mountains during which he made 78 first ascents of peaks over 3,000 meters (9,843 ft.).

1977: FIRST ASCENT

April. American climbers Molly Higgins and Barbara Eastman completed the first all-female ascent of the 3,000 ft./915 m. Nose route on El Capitan (Yosemite National Park, California) in 3 ½ days.

1977: FIRST ASCENT

Colorado climber Ray Jardine (1944–) made the first 5.13 graded climb in Yosemite National Park (California) by climbing The Phoenix. Jardine used his recently developed multiple cam unit known as the "Friend" which he patented in 1978.

1977: FIRST ASCENT

American mountaineers Michael Kennedy (1952–) and George Lowe (1944–) made the first ascent of the Infinite Spur route on Mount Foraker (17,401 feet/5,303 meters) in Alaska.

1977:

Colorado climber Steve Boyer climbed all 54 Colorado peaks over 14,000 feet/4,267 meters in 21 days — a new record.

1977: Fabric – Polyester Pile

Patagonia created one of the first polyester pile jackets. This new material repelled moisture and retained heat.

1977: Equipment – Packs

American company Lowe Alpine Systems began marketing Greg Lowe's design for an internal-frame backpack that carried larger loads closer to the body.

1977: Equipment – Tents

American climber Todd Bibler developed a tiny (4' x 7'), single-skin, two-person bivouac tent that weighed 4 pounds. This tent had two poles and required two minutes to erect. Constructed of ToddTex — a waterproof, windproof, and breathable fabric. Bibler designed this small tent for high-altitude, lightweight climbing.

1977: Equipment – Tents

American Bruce Hamilton of the North Face Company collaborated with American architect, engineer, and inventor Buckminster Fuller (1895–1983) to design and produce the first geodesic dome tent. This lightweight coated nylon tent used a new grade of aluminum support poles.

1977: Technique – Free Climbing

Late 1970s. The "free climbing" trend was born. Nothing but natural rock features were used as a means of progression.

1978:

May. Colorado ski mountaineer Chris Landry made the first ski descent of Pyramid Peak's (14,018 ft./4,272 m.) east face near Aspen, Colorado. This was regarded as the most difficult ski descent ever accomplished in North America. The second descent was in 2006 by Chris Davenport, Neil Beidleman, and Ted Makon.

1978:

July 2. American climber John Mallon Waterman (1952–1981) completed a 145-day solo ascent (his third attempt) of Mount Hunter (14,573 ft./4,442 m.) in Alaska. Hunter, the third highest peak in the Alaska range, has been called the hardest fourteen-thousand foot peak on the North American continent. Waterman climbed Mount Hunter expedition style (placing camps and fixed ropes) and reached the south summit on his 101st day. It took him 44 days to descend the northeast ridge. Waterman disappeared in 1981 while solo climbing the unclimbed East Buttress of Mount McKinley/Denali in Alaska.

1978: FIRST ASCENT

American climber Charlie Fowler (1954–2006) solo climbed the Diamond Face on Longs Peak (14,256 ft./4,345 m.) in Colorado without any ropes or protection. His route is now called the Casual Route.

1978: FIRST ASCENT

Jim Logan (1947–) and Mugs Stump (1949–1992) made the first ascent of the Emperor Face (8,000 ft./2,438 m.) of Mount Robson (12,872 ft./3,954 m.) in the Canadian Rockies. This face has been called "North America's Eiger."

1978:

The Mount McKinley Great Circle Expedition made a complete circumnavigation of Mount McKinley/ Denali (20,320 ft./6,193 m.) in Alaska on light-touring skis in nineteen days. Galen Rowell (1940–2002), Ned Gillette (1945–1997), Alan Bard, and Doug Weins skied entirely above tree-line while connecting five separate glaciers.

1978: FIRST ASCENT

American rock climber Bev Johnson became the first female to solo climb El Capitan in Yosemite National Park (California). Johnson climbed the Dihedral Wall route.

1978: Film

Fred Padula's film entitled *El Capitan* won the Grand Prize at the Banff (Alberta, Canada) Mountain Film Festival.

1978: Clothing – Insulation

Late 1970s. Malden Mills of Lawrence, Massachusetts, developed a new insulating material called "fleece." This velour material combined the warming qualities of pile with an attractive appearance and comfortable feel.

1978: Equipment – Boots

Kolflach, an Austrian boot company, produced the first successful rigid plastic climbing boot. Initially supplied with felt liners, these boots eventually adopted a closed-cell material for the inner boots. Reinhold Messner and Peter Habeler climbed Mount Everest (first ascent without using oxygen) in 1978 wearing plastic buckle boots. This was one of the first major mountain climbs to use plastic double boots rather than the traditional leather boot.

1978: Equipment – Crampons

The Lowe brothers (American) created the step-in "footfang" crampon which increased rigidity. Crampon design now became more functionally focused and less multi-purpose.

1978: Equipment – Nuts

A new type of nut was introduced. Called a "Copperhead," these blobs of soft copper were attached to the end of a thin wire cable. They were used in shallow cracks too small for a piton. This copper blob molded itself to the rock surface.

1979:

March 4. Well-known Mount Everest mountaineer Willi Unsoeld (1926–1979) died in an avalanche while descending Cadaver Gap on Mount Rainier (14,411 ft./4,392 m.) in Washington. One of Unsoeld's students, Janie Diepenbrock, was also buried in this avalanche. Unsoeld and Dr. Tom Hornbein (1930–) made the first ascent of Mount Everest's West Ridge in 1963.

1979:

American climber Philip Dodd Smith (1905–1979) died at age 74 after a 37-year climbing career. A pioneer of Teton (Wyoming) climbing, Smith made the first ascent of 13 major peaks in the Teton Range. He was a national park ranger for 11 years (1929 to 1940).

1979:

Canadian mountaineer Don Forest (1920–2003) completed the climbing of all 54 11,000 foot/3,353 m. peaks in the Canadian Rockies at age 59.

1979: FIRST ASCENT

American mountaineers Galen Rowell (1940–2002) and Ned Gillette (1945–1997) made a one-day ascent of Mount McKinley/Denali (20,320 ft./6,193 m.) in Alaska in 18 hours and 45 minutes. Their ascent distances and times were:

> 7,300 ft to 17,300 ft.   : 9 hours
> 17,300 ft. to 20,320 ft.   : 9 hours 45 minutes

1979:

The so-called Palisade Traverse in the California Sierra Mountains was first accomplished by John

Fisher and Jerry Adams. This eight-mile long traverse crossed over six 14,000 foot/4,267 meter peaks and many 13,000 foot/3,962 meter summits. Fisher and Adams spent one week making this traverse.

1979:

The American Mountain Guides Association (AMGA) was formed by twelve guides. The AMGA was established to support "the guiding profession by providing representation for land-use access, education, training, and examination based on international standards for guiding." In 1997, the AMGA became a member of the International Federation of Mountain Guides Associations. The AMGA is headquartered in Golden, Colorado. In 2005, there were 32 fully certified mountain guides in the AMGA and 248 partially certified guides.

1980:

May 18. Mount St. Helens (volcano) in Washington erupted altering its summit elevation from 9,677 ft./2,949 m. to 8,366 ft./2,550 m. — a loss in height of 1,311 ft./400 m. The previous eruption occurred in 1841 which involved only smoke. The 1980 ash plume extended to 60,000 feet and the volcanic flows reached up to 200 m.p.h. This volcanic disaster killed 58 people and impacted 230 square miles of forest. Seventy percent of the mountain's glacier ice was lost.

1980:

November 16. American mountaineer Otis McAllister (1889–1980) died at age 91. McAllister is regarded as the founder of mountaineering activity in Mexico. He moved there in 1917 and founded the Club de Exploraciones de Mexico in 1922. He was the first president of this club for the first 9 years.

1980: FIRST ASCENT

Jean Ruwitch Goresline (32) and Louise Shepherd (22) made the first all-female free ascent of Longs Peak's (14,256 ft./4,345 m.) Diamond Face in Colorado.

1980: Book

American internist and physiologist Dr. Charles S. Houston (1913–2009) published *Going High: The Story of Man and Altitude.* This book became the first publication to link medicine with high-altitude mountaineering for the layperson. Houston published three additional books about high altitude illnesses: *Going Higher: The Story of Man and Altitude* (1987), *High Altitude: Illness and Wellness* (1993), and *Going Higher: Oxygen, Man and Mountains* (2005).

1981:

June 21. The greatest mountaineering disaster in North American history killed eleven climbers (1 guide and 10 clients) on Mount Rainier (14,411 ft./4,392 m.) in Washington. A massive avalanche on the Ingraham Glacier was triggered and buried this ascending group in a crevasse. Eighteen in this climbing party survived.

1981:

August 4. American adventurers Dick Bass (1929–) and Frank Wells (1932–1994) met one another and agreed to pursue the Seven Summits together. They eventually climbed six summits together in 1983. Dick Bass climbed his seventh summit, Mount Everest, on April 30, 1985.

1981: FIRST ASCENT

American mountaineer Michael Kennedy (1952–) solo climbed the Cassin Ridge on Mount McKinley/ Denali (20,320 ft./6,193 m.) in Alaska.

1981:

Swiss mountain guide Edward Feuz, Jr. (1884–1981) died at age 97. Feuz immigrated to the Canadian Rockies in 1906 (age 22) and eventually made 78 first ascents and 102 new climbing routes.

1981: Equipment – Camming Devices

Greg Lowe introduced his Lowe Tri-Cam to the market. This lightweight, small camming device was first designed by Lowe in 1973. It was made for small crack placement.

1981: Technique – Layering

The first outdoor clothing company to "preach the virtues" of layering when dressing for cold-weather activities was the California based company known as Patagonia. This company recommended the following dressing system:

First layer next to the skin should be a lightweight synthetic material worn on the top (above the waist) and the bottom.

Second layer should be a wool or polyester pile (synchilla or polartec) garment.

Third layer (outer layer exposed to the weather) should be a nylon or polyester windproof shell, both top and bottom.

1982: FIRST ASCENT

March 7. Roger Mear, Jon Waterman, and Mike Young completed the first winter ascent of the Cassin Ridge on Mount McKinley/Denali (20,320 ft./6,193 m.) in Alaska.

1982:

May. The Denali Medical Research Project was established at the site of Camp IV (14,300 ft./4,358 m.) below the West Buttress of Mount McKinley/Denali (20,320 ft./6,193 m.) in Alaska. This medical/rescue clinic and research laboratory was organized by Dr. Peter Hackett (1947–) and Dr. Bill Mills. Rob Roach (1956–) served as a high-altitude research assistant. This project treated over 100 climbers by the end of its first year. Hackett and Roach maintained this research facility until 1989.

1982:

Mount Rainier (14,411 ft./4,392 m.) in Washington experienced a record number of climbing attempts (8,358) of which only 50 percent (4,179) were successful in reaching the summit.

1982: FIRST ASCENT

American mountaineer Mark Hesse solo climbed the 9,000 foot/2,743 meter South Face of Mount McKinley/Denali (20,320 ft./6,193 m.) in Alaska.

1983:

May. American ski mountaineer John Harlin III (1956–) made the first complete ski descent of the North Face of Longs Peak (14,256 ft./4,345 m.) in Colorado.

1983: FIRST ASCENT

June. American climbers Todd Bibler and Doug Klewin made the first ascent of the 6,300 foot/1,920 meter North Buttress of Mount Hunter (14,574 ft./4,442 m.) in Alaska.

1983:

American climber Dan Davis spent 24 years (1959 to 1983) climbing 429 different routes on 261 different peaks in Washington.

1983: Equipment – Rock Climbing Shoes

British climber Jonathan "Jonny" Woodward (1961–) first imported sticky rubber rock climbing shoes (Scarpa Crag Ratz) to the United States. American climber John Bachar (1957–2009) is also credited with introducing these sticky rubber shoes to American rock climbers during this same year.

1984: FIRST ASCENT

February 13. Well-known Japanese mountaineer Naomi Uemura (1941–1984) disappeared on Mount McKinley/Denali (20,320 ft./6,193 m.) in Alaska on his descent from the first solo winter ascent. It is believed that he fell into a crevasse somewhere between 14,300 ft./4,358 m. and 16,400 ft./4,998 m. Uemura accomplished several feats during his lifetime:

1. He was the first person to reach the highest summit on five continents including Mount Everest. Four of these ascents were solo.

2. He made the longest solo dogsled journey on record, more than 7,444 miles/12,407 kilometers in 313 days from Greenland to Alaska.

3. He was the first person to solo to the North Pole, covering 500 miles in 55 days by dogsled.

4. He rafted 3,782 miles/6,303 kilometers down the Amazon River in Brazil by himself.

5. He walked the length of Japan — 1,700 miles/2,833 kilometers — by himself. He made the first successful solo climb of Mount McKinley/Denali in Alaska.

1984:

American woman climber Arlene Blum (1945–) was presented a Gold Medal by the Society of

Women Geographers for leading the first women's climbs of Denali (20,320 ft./6,193 m.), Annapurna (26,547 ft./8,091 m.), and Bhrigupanth (22,217 ft./6,772 m.).

1984: FIRST ASCENT

American mountaineer Paul Petzoldt (1908–1999) made the 60th anniversary climb of the Grand Teton (13,766 ft./4,196 m.) in Wyoming at age 76. Petzoldt became the oldest person to have reached the summit.

1985: FIRST ASCENT

March 3. Dave Pahlke, Rich Burton, Paul Denkewalter, and Earl Redman made the first winter ascent of Mount Bona (16,421 ft./5,005 m.) via the northwest ridge in Alaska. It was -25°F on the summit.

1985:

July 26–30. Peter Croft, Greg Foweraker, and Don Serl completed the Waddington Traverse of nine summits in British Columbia, Canada. The climbing sequence was as follows:

1.	Mount Waddington	13,186 ft./4,019 m.
2.	Mount Combatant	12,323 ft./3,756 m.
3.	Mount Tiedemann	12,625 ft./3,848 m.
4.	Mount Asperity	12,192 ft./3,716 m.
5.	Serra V1	1,877 ft./3,620 m.
6.	Serra IV	12,008 ft./ 3,660 m.
7.	Serra III	11,949 ft./3,642 m.
8.	Serra II	11,614 ft./3,540 m.
9.	Serra I	11,286 ft./3,440 m.

1985:

October 1. American physician and noted mountaineer Dr. Charles Houston (1913–2009) directed the research project known as "Operation Everest II." Based in Natick, Massachusetts, this project placed eight volunteer subjects in a decompression chamber. Over a 40-day period, these men were gradually taken up to the summit of Mount Everest (29,000 feet/8,839 meters) while 25 scientists and 40 support personnel monitored their reactions to high-altitude.

1985:

Colorado mountaineer Gerry Roach (1943–) became the second person (behind Dick Bass) to climb the so-called "Seven Summits" of the world.

1985: Equipment – Packs

Dana Gleason (Dana Design of Bozeman, Montana) introduced the Terraplane pack. This internal frame design pack with a single aluminum strut came in four sizes. When fully extended, the largest size could hold 5,600 cubic inches.

1985: Fabric – Synchilla

Patagonia pioneered the use of fleece under the brand name "Synchilla." Synchilla fleece was the successor to pile and bunting and was used for layering.

1985: Technique – Sport Climbing

The sport climbing revolution began to grow in popularity. This climbing style is essentially a gymnastic pursuit based on pure athletic performance. Protection for the climber is pre–placed via rappels. Unlike alpine climbing, weather, rockfall, snow, and ice do not influence the sport climbing experience.

1986: FIRST ASCENT

March 16. Six American mountaineers (John Bauman, Todd Frankiewicz, Willy Hersman, Steve Koslow, George Rooney, and guide Vern Tejas) made the first winter ascent of Mount Logan (19,551 ft./5,959 m.) in Canada. They followed the King Trench route. This climb took 28 days and experienced temperatures as low as –50°.

1986: FIRST ASCENT

May. American rock climbers John Bachar (1957–2009) and Peter Croft (1958–) climbed the Nose route on El Capitan and the Northwest Face on Half Dome in a single day. Yosemite National Park, California. Bachar made numerous "first free ascents" in California, Colorado, and Nevada from 1975 to 1990.

1987:

December. The Colorado Mountain Club listed 389 climbers to date who had reached all 54 summits in Colorado that exceed 14,000 feet (4,267 meters).

1987: FIRST ASCENT

American mountaineers Alex Lowe (1958–1999) and Jack Tackle (1954–) made the first winter ascent of the Grand Teton's (13,766 ft./4,196 m.) north face. They climbed the "direct" route.

1988: FIRST ASCENT

February 15 to March 8. Alaskan mountaineer Vern Tejas (1953–) made the first solo winter ascent and descent of Mount McKinley/Denali (20,320 ft./6,193 m.) in Alaska. Tejas carried (standing between the rungs) a sixteen foot sectional aluminum ladder to his 14,300 foot/4,358 meter camp. This lightweight ladder would prevent him from accidentally falling into a hidden crevasse. He uncovered buried food caches from previous climbing expeditions to supplement his own food supply. He reached the summit on March 8. His book Dangerous Steps documents this climb. Tejas went on to complete the Seven Summits circuit five times.

1988:

February. South Tyrol mountaineer Reinhold Messner (1944–) and Polish mountaineer Jerzy Kukuczka (1948–1989) were presented Silver Medals of the Olympic Order at the 15th Winter Olympics in Calgary, Alberta, Canada. Messner was the first and Kukuczka the second mountaineer to climb all fourteen 8,000 meter peaks in the world.

1988:

August. American climber Alex Lowe (1958–1999) climbed eleven Teton peaks (Wyoming) in less than nine hours. Lowe was killed in a huge avalanche on Shishapangma (26,399 ft./8,046 m.) in China in 1999. This 14-mile traverse is called the "Grand Traverse" in the Tetons.

1988:

November. The National Geographic Society published Brad Washburn's (1910–2007) Mount Everest map which was circulated to 10.6 million Society members.

1988:

Colorado mountaineer Mike Garratt (1951–) completed the climbing of all 636 peaks in Colorado between 13,000 feet and 13,999 feet. This climbing goal required sixteen years (1972 to 1988).

1988: FIRST ASCENT

American mountaineer Don Henry (1917–) reached the summit of Denali (20,320 ft./6,193 m.) in Alaska at age 71. Henry is the oldest climber to summit Denali. He began climbing in 1963 at age 46.

1988: FIRST ASCENT

American climbers Todd Skinner (1958–2006) and Paul Piana made the first free-ascent of the difficult Salathé Wall route on El Capitan in Yosemite National Park (California). This climb involved 36 pitches of up to 5.13b difficulty.

1988: Equipment – Belay Device

Lowe Alpine in Colorado developed the first tubular belay device.

1988: Technique – Crevasse Crossing

March. American mountaineer Vern Tejas (1953–) made the first winter solo ascent and descent of Mount McKinley/Denali (20,320 ft./6,193 m.) in Alaska. To prevent himself from falling into hidden crevasses on the Kahiltna Glacier, Tejas wore a lightweight, (18 lb.), sixteen foot aluminum ladder (he stood between the middle rungs). If a crevasse fall did occur, the ladder would hit both edges of the crevasse and keep Tejas from plunging further. This ladder also served as the roof support for the snow trenches he dug to sleep in (he carried no tent). Tejas eventually abandoned his ladder at the 14,300 ft./4,358 m. camp on the West Buttress of Denali on his ascent.

1989:

April 2. American mountaineer Ome Daiber (1908–1989) — "The Father of American Mountain Rescue" — died at age 81 in Seattle, Washington.

1989:

American mountaineer Ruth Dyar Mendenhall (1912–1989) died at age 77 after a fifty year climbing career. She and her husband John made twenty-one first ascents in North America.

1989:

Dr. James Monroe Thorington of Philadelphia, Pennsylvania died at age 94 (1895–1989). Thorington was an ophthalmologist but was regarded by many as the "greatest scholar of alpinism in North America." Author of many mountaineering books about the Canadian Rockies, Thorington also served as the Editor of the American Alpine Club Journal for many years.

1989:

Canadian mountaineer Bill Corbett and several companions made a single-day traverse of all five Lyell Peaks in the Canadian Rockies.

Lyell Peak 1   Rudolph Peak   11,506 ft./3,507 m.
Lyell Peak 2   Edward Peak   11,529 ft./3,514 m.
Lyell Peak 3   Ernest Peak   11,519 ft./3,511 m.
Lyell Peak 4   Walter Peak   11,155 ft./3,400 m.
Lyell Peak 5   Christian Peak 11,122 ft./3,390 m.

1989: FIRST ASCENT

Mark Wellman (1966–) became the first paraplegic to climb the Nose route on El Capitan (7,569 ft./2,307 m.) in Yosemite National Park (California). His lead climbing partner was Mike Corbett who had climbed El Capitan more than fifty times. This climb took seven days.

1990:

May 23. Russian mountaineer Anatoli Boukreev (1958–1997) made a solo speed ascent of Mount McKinley/Denali (20,320 ft./6,193 m.) in Alaska. He climbed from the 7,000 ft./2,134 m. base camp (a.k.a. Kahiltna International Airport-K.I.A.) to the summit via the West Rib route in 10 ½ hours.

1990:

American guide Kathy Cosley Houston became the first mountain guide (male or female) to be both Alpine and Rock certified by the American Mountain Guide Association. In 1991, she received the Alpine Guide's certification.

1990:

British climber Adrian Crane (1956–) summited the highest point in all 50 United States in 101 days.

1990:

Colorado climbers Quade and Tyle Smith summited all 54 Colorado peaks over 14,000 feet (4,267 meters) in 16 days — a new record.

1990:

Dr. Charles S. Houston (1913–2009) founded the Colorado Altitude Research Institute (C.A.R.I.) in Keystone, Colorado. This organization was the first to develop the relationship between altitude investigation and educational/clinical activities. C.A.R.I. conducted the largest study to date of travelers to moderate altitude (3,300 meters or 10,827 feet) and described the effects of altitude on these visitors (Annals of Internal Medicine 1993). In March of 2004, the Colorado Center For Altitude Medicine and Physiology (CCAMP) was founded by Drs. Benjamin Honigman (1948–) and Robert Roach (1956–). CCAMP is based at the University of Colorado School of Medicine in Aurora, Colorado. In 2006, the name of this research facility was changed to the Altitude Research Center (A.R.C.) at the University of Colorado School of Medicine. ARC has a major mission of studying the effects of altitude (hypoxic) at moderate elevations on human health and disease.

1990: Equipment – High Altitude Pressure Chamber

Invented and patented by University of Colorado Professor of Chemical Engineering Rustem Igor Gamow (1936–), the Gamow Bag acts as a portable pressure chamber for climbers experiencing high-altitude sickness. After placing the patient inside, this bag is zipped closed and made airtight. A foot pump is attached to this huge, heavy plastic duffle bag. By using this foot pump a lower altitude can be simulated inside the bag. After the bag is fully expanded, each foot pump can produce an altitude drop of approximately 300 feet (depending upon the pump size) inside the bag. A clear plastic window allows the patient to maintain constant eye contact with the rescue staff. Many trekking and mountaineering groups now carry a Gamow Bag with them. A Gamow Bag weighs 14.5 pounds and is constructed of polyurethane-coated nylon.

1991: FIRST ASCENT

June 22 to July 1. American mountaineers Greg Collins, Phil Powers, and Tom Walters climbed a new route on the northwest face of Denali's (20,320 ft./6,193 m.) West Buttress in Alaska. They spent thirty-nine hours climbing this 9,200 foot (2,804 meters) face which they then named the Washburn Face.

1991: FIRST ASCENT

September 4. Former Yosemite National Park ranger Mark Wellman (1966–) became the first paraplegic to climb Half Dome (8,836 ft./2,693 m.) in Yosemite. Wellman was paralyzed in a mountain climbing accident in 1982. He and his partner Mike Corbett spent thirteen days climbing the 2,200 foot/670 meter Tis-sa-ack route on Half Dome.

1991:

Canadian mountaineer Roger Neave (1906–1991) died at age 85. Neave made 35 first ascents in the Canadian Rockies from 1929 to 1978 (49 years). He came to Canada from England in 1928. By profession, he was an engineer.

1991:

American mountaineer Mugs Stump (1949–1992) made a solo ascent of the 9,000 foot (2,743 meter) Cassin Ridge on Denali in Alaska in fifteen hours.

1991: FIRST ASCENT

Canadian mountaineer Don Forest (1920–2003) became the oldest climber to summit Mount Logan (19,551 ft./5,959 m.) in Canada. He actually reached the West Summit of Mount Logan. He was 71 years old. With Forest were Chic Scott (1945–), Bill Louie, Terry Duncan, and Bill Hawryschuk.

1991:

Colorado ski mountaineer Louis Dawson (1952–) became the first person to climb all 54 peaks in Colorado over 14,000 feet/4,267 meters and then make a ski descent. This quest took Dawson 14 years to complete (1978 to 1991). His first ascent/ski descent was on Castle Peak (14,265 ft./4,348 m.) and his final ascent/ski descent was on Kit Carson Peak (14,165 ft./4,317 m.).

1992:

March to July. This was the deadliest year on Mount McKinley/Denali (20,320 ft./6,193 m.) — 13 climbers died with 22 rescue efforts involving 28 people.

1992:

American climbers Peter Croft and Hans Florine made a speed ascent of the Nose route on El Capitan (7,568 ft./2,307 m.) in Yosemite National Park (California) — 4 hours and 22 minutes. American climbers Dean Potter and Tommy O'Neill lowered this time to 3 hours 24 minutes in 2001.

1992:

British mountaineer Adrian Crane (1956–) climbed Colorado's 54 peaks over 14,000 feet (4,267 meters) in just over 15 days. This was a new record by only several hours.

1992:

Colorado mountaineer Tom Mereness completed a 16 year quest (1976 to 1992) to summit all 54 Colorado peaks over 14,000 feet/4,267 meters in the winter. His partner on most of these climbs was Colorado climber Jim Bock.

1992:

The Company of Canadian Mountain Guides was founded by Canadian mountaineer Chic Scott (1945–).

1992:

American mountaineer, pediatrician, photographer, and writer Margaret Jo Prouty (1908–1992) died at age 84. Prouty traveled the world making 400 ascents of peaks above 10,000 feet (3,048 meters) in twenty-two countries.

1992: Technique – Dry Tooling

American climber Jeff Lowe (1950–) made the first ascent of the frozen waterfall in Vail, Colorado, known as Octopussy. Lowe's ascent advanced the concept of modern mixed climbing that adopted the use of leashless tools (ice axes). Dry tooling uses leashless (although not necessarily) ice axes and 12-point crampons on mixed climbs (rock and ice).

1993: FIRST ASCENT

September 12. American climbers Lynn Hill (1961–) and Brooke Sandahl made the first free ascent of the Nose route on El Capitan (7,569 feet/2,307 meters) in Yosemite National Park in California. This climb took 3 ½ days and involved 33 pitches over the 3,000 foot/914 meter vertical face. Hill led all of the pitches. This ascent was regarded as the hardest free climb in the world at the time.

1993:

The American Alpine Club (A.C.C.–founded in 1902) relocated its headquarters from New York City to Golden, Colorado (15 miles west of Denver) after it was determined that a more central location in the United States would better serve its membership. The former Golden Junior High School building was purchased for $100,000.00 and renovated by the American Alpine Club, the Colorado Mountain Club, and the Colorado Outward Bound School. This 37,000 square foot building was then renamed the American Mountaineering Center and included the offices of the three above named organizations, an extensive alpine library (over 60,000 volumes), a 350-seat auditorium, and a world mountaineering museum.

1993:

American mountaineer Walter Abbot Wood, Jr. (1907–1993) died at age 86. Wood was president of the American Alpine Club from 1947 to 1949. He made the following first ascents in the Yukon Territory of Canada:

Mount Steele	1935	16,645 ft./5,073 m.
Mount Wood	1941	15,887 ft./4,842 m.
Mount Walsh	1941	14,787 ft./4,507 m.
Mount Hubbard	1951	15,017 ft./4,577 m.
Mount Alverstone	1958	14,564 ft./4,439 m.

Wood also qualified as a mountain guide in Europe.

1993:

Well-known Colorado climber Carl Blaurock (1894–1993) died at age 98. He began climbing in Colorado in 1909 at age 15 with an ascent of Pikes Peak. In 1923, Blaurock and William Ervin (1884–) were the first people to climb all 47 Colorado peaks over 14,000 feet. Seven additional peaks were later recognized as being "fourteeners." Blaurock climbed the east face of Longs Peak (14,256 ft./4,345 m.) 18 times. He made his last climb (Notch Mountain – Colorado) in 1973 at age 79.

1993: Fabric – Synchilla Fleece

Patagonia introduced 100 percent recycled synchilla fleece made from recycled plastic bottles. This fleece material was a softer and finer version of the polyester pile jacket that Patagonia introduced in 1977.

1994: FIRST ASCENT

September 19. American rock climber Lynn Hill (1961–) made the first solo all-free ascent of the Nose route on El Capitan (7,569 ft./2,307 m.) in Yosemite National Park (California). Hill climbed this 3,000-foot (914 meters) high rock face in twenty-three hours.

1994:

Alaskan mountaineer Dolly Lefever (1947–) became the first American woman and the 26th person overall to climb all Seven Summits (the highest summit on each of the world's seven continents). Japanese woman mountaineer Junko Tabei was the first woman to climb the Seven Summits (completed in 1991 and 11th person overall) and French climber Christine Janin was the second woman completing the Seven Summits in 1992 (20th person overall). Lefever was the third woman overall.

1994:

American climbers Rick Trujillo (1946–) from Ouray, Colorado, and Ricky Denesik (1958–) from Telluride, Colorado, climbed all 54 Colorado peaks over 14,000 feet (4,267 meters) in 15 days, 9 hours, and 55 minutes breaking Adrian Crane's 1992 record.

1994:

The Colorado Fourteeners Initiative (C.F.I.) was established to protect and preserve the natural integrity of Colorado's fifty-four 14,000 foot (4,267 meters) peaks. The C.F.I. is based in Golden, Colorado and has been recognized as a partnership model of national importance. As of 2007, C.F.I. volunteers had carried-out trail and restoration projects on 19 of these 54 peaks.

1994: Book

Famous Colorado climber Robert Ormes (1904–1994) died. Ormes wrote the *Guide To The Colorado Mountains* in 1952. He climbed Pikes Peak (14,110 ft./4,301 m.) in Colorado 40 times.

1994: Technique – Free Soloing

September 19. American climber Lynn Hill (1961–) made the first all-free solo ascent of the 3,000 foot/914 meter Nose route on El Capitan (7,568 feet/2,307 meters) in Yosemite National Park in California in 23 hours of continuous climbing. Many climbers regard this ascent as the greatest rock climbing accomplishment ever.

1995:

April 1. American mountaineer, skier, teacher, and internationally acclaimed Editor of the American Alpine Journal for 36 years (1960 to 1995) H. Adams Carter (1914–1995) died at age 81. Carter climbed

Mount Washington (6,288 ft./1,916 m.) in New Hampshire at age five and the Matterhorn (14,692 ft./4,478 m.) at age fifteen. In 1934, he made two first ascents in Alaska: Mount Quincy Adams (13,616 ft./4,150 m.) and Mount Crillon (12,727 ft./3,879 m.). He was also a member of the 1936 British-American expedition that made the first ascent of the Nanda Devi (25,644 ft./7,816 m.) in northern India.

1995:

June 27. American blind mountaineer Erik Weihenmayer (1968–) climbed the first of his Seven Summits — Mount McKinley/Denali (20,320 ft./6,193 m.) in Alaska. He completed his Seven Summits in 2002 when he climbed Mount Elbrus (18,481 ft./5,633 m.) in western Russia and Mount Kosciuszko (7,310 ft./2,228 m.) in Australia. Weihenmayer has been blind since the age of 13.

1995:

Climbers Cindy DiSanto, Cathy Goodwin, and Steve Martin were the first to climb all forty-eight 4,000 foot/1,219 meter peaks in New Hampshire in one calendar winter.

1995:

American ski mountaineers Daryl Miller (51) and Mark Stasik (31) completed a 350 mile/583 kilometer winter ski trek around Mount McKinley/Denali (20,320 ft./6,193 m.) in Alaska. This circumnavigation took 45 days.

1995:

July. Well-known American mountaineer Dr. Tom Hornbein (1930–) and his American guide Jim Detterline (1956–) climbed the Diamond on the east face of Longs Peak (14,256 ft./4,345 m.) in Rocky Mountain National Park (Colorado). The vertical rock face known as the Diamond is approximately 1,000 feet (305 meters) high and 1,000 feet wide. The Diamond is located above 13,000 feet (3,962 m.). Hornbein was 64-years-old at this time. He is best known for his first ascent of the West Ridge of Mount Everest in 1963. Jim Detterline served as the Longs Peak Supervisory Climbing Ranger from 1987 to 2009. See 2010 for Detterline's Longs Peak ascent record.

1996:

From 1932 through 1996, 87 mountaineers had been killed on the slopes of Mount McKinley/Denali (20,320 ft./6,193 m.) in Alaska. 34 bodies still remain on the mountain.

1996: FIRST ASCENT

Gardner Heaton, Dave Briggs, and Joe Reichert made the first winter ascent of Mount St. Elias (18,008 ft./5,489 m.) in Canada via the southwest ridge.

1996:

American physician and mountaineer Charles Houston (1913 – 2009) was presented the King Albert Gold Medal in Switzerland for his pioneering research in high-altitude physiology.

1997:

November 22. The American Mountain Guide Association was accepted as a member of the International Federation of Mountain Guide Associations which was composed of 21 member nations in North America, South America, Europe, Asia, and New Zealand.

1997:

December 18. Well-known American mountaineer William P. House (1913–1997) died at age 84. House made the first ascent of Mount Waddington (13,186 ft./4,019 m.) in British Columbia, Canada with Fritz Wiessner (1900–1988) in 1936 and made the first climbing ascent of Devils Tower (5,112 ft./1,558 m.) in Wyoming in 1937 with Wiessner and Lawrence Coveney. During the 1938 American attempt to climb K2 (28,253 ft./8,611 m.) in Pakistan, House first climbed the crux chimney that is now named after him. By profession, House was a forester.

1997:

Ms. Hulda "Grandma Whitney" Crooks (1886–1997) died at age 111 in California. From 1951 to 1977 (ages 65 to 91), Crooks climbed Mount Whitney (14,505 feet/4,421 meters) in California 23 times. During this same 26-year period, she also climbed 97 other mountains. Crooks Peak, just east of Mount Whitney, was renamed in her honor.

1997: FIRST ASCENT

American mountaineer skier, photographer, and author Galen Rowell (1940–2002) became the oldest person (57) to climb El Capitan's Nose Route in a single day (16 hours). Rowell and his wife Barbara tragically were killed in 2002 when their small plane crashed in the California Sierras near Bishop. Rowell made over 1,000 separate climbs on four continents and was a member of 40 expeditions (10 to the Himalayas). He was the author of at least twenty books on mountaineering and photography.

1997:

Famed American climber Pete Schoening (1927–2004) completed the climbing of the high points of all 50 United States with his ascent of Gannett Peak (13,785 ft./4,201 m.) in Wyoming at age 70.

1998: PEAK FIRST ASCENT *GREAT SAIL*

June 25. An American expedition made the first ascent of Great Sail Peak (5,300 ft./1,615 m.) on Baffin Island directly north of Quebec Province in Canada. The expedition's base camp was located at 275 feet/84 meters above sea level making this extreme rock climb more than 5,000 feet/1,524 meters of vertical rock. Climbers Greg Child (41), Gordon Wiltsie (46), Alex Lowe (39), Jared Ogden (26), and Mark Synnott (27) all reached the summit after 23 days. John Catto (videographer) and David Hamlin (film producer) were also members of this expedition.

1998:

American climber Alison Osius (1958–) was elected as the first female president of the American Alpine Club and the first female president of any national climbing club.

1998:

Climbing Ranger Mike "Gator" Gauthier summited Mount Rainier (14,411 ft./4,392 m.) in Washington 36 times in one year.

1998:

Japanese mountaineer Masatoshi Kuriaki (1973–) solo climbed Denali (20,320 ft./6,193 m.) in Alaska in the winter. As of April of 2007, 16 people had climbed Denali in the winter.

1999: FIRST ASCENT

May 13. American rock climber Gerry Bloch (1918–2008) became the oldest person to climb El Capitan (7,564 ft./2,305 m.) in the Yosemite Valley of California. Bloch, age 81, and two climbing partners spent twelve days climbing the Aquarian Wall route on El Capitan. Bloch began to rock climb at age 16 (1934).

1999:

June. American climber Peter Croft (1958–) completed the "Evolution Traverse" in the central Sierra Nevada mountains of California. This 8 mile/13 kilometer nine-summit ridge traverse took Croft 15 hours to complete (solo). These nine peaks ranged from 13,117 ft./3,998 m. to 13,830 ft./4,215 m. in elevation.

1999:

October 30. The 128th person to die on Mount Washington (6,288 ft./1,916 m.) in New Hampshire was 68-year-old Douglas Thompson of Hanover, New Hampshire. He collapsed and died on the summit. The first fatality on Mount Washington was 29-year-old Frederick Strickland of England on October 19, 1849.

1999:

November 13. American climbers Tom Frost (1940–) and Dick Duane were awarded American Alpine Club Gold Medals for their efforts to preserve Camp 4 in Yosemite National Park (California).

1999: FIRST ASCENT

American mountaineer Edward Hommer (1955–) became the first double amputee to climb Mount McKinley/Denali (20,320 ft./6,193 m.) in Alaska.

1999:

Well-known American mountaineer Bill Hackett (1918–1999) died at age 81. Hackett made eighty-eight ascents of Mount Hood (11,239 ft./3,427 m.) in Oregon by eleven different routes. His other important ascents were:

1946	Mexico	Orizaba, Popocatepetl, Ixtacihuatl, and Toluca
1947	Alaska	Mount McKinley, 4th ascent

1949	Argentina	Aconcagua. 1st American ascent
1950	Tanzania	Kilimanjaro
	Kenya	Mount Kenya. 1st American ascent
1951	Alaska	Mount McKinley. First ascent of West Buttress
1952	Alaska	Mount McKinley. Muldrow Glacier. 7th ascent
1954	Alaska	Mount McKinley. First ascent of Northwest Buttress
1956	France	Mont Blanc
	Australia	Mount Kosciuszko
1958	Alaska	Mount McKinley. Northwest Buttress.

1999: Equipment – Crampon

An American company named Kahtoola began marketing a new, lightweight type of crampon called MICROspikes. This type of footwear traction can be used for general mountaineering where no technical ice and snow conditions are encountered. Each MICROspike (each foot) has ten 3/8" stainless steel spikes with an elastomer harness that stretches over a hiking or climbing boot. MICROspikes are available in eight sizes for men, women, and youth.

2000:

August. American climber Rolando Garibotti (1971–) established a new speed climbing record by completing the "Grand Traverse of the Tetons" in six hours forty-nine minutes. Nine of the ten summits Garibotti traversed were over 12,000 feet (3,657 meters). The previous best time of 8 hours 40 minutes was set by American climber Alex Lowe (1958–1999) in 1988.

2000:

Colorado climber Gerry Roach (1943–) became the first person to climb the ten highest summits in North America. His first of these summits was Mexico's Iztachihuatl (17,343 ft./5,286 m.) in 1959 at the age of 16:

Peak Name	Country	Feet	Meters
Denali South Summit	United States	20,320 ft.	6,193 m.
Mount Logan	Canada	19,551 ft.	5,959 m.
Pico de Orizaba	Mexico	18,700 ft.	5,699 m.
Mount St. Elias	Alaska	18,009 ft.	5,489 m.
Popocatepetl	Mexico	17,887 ft.	5,451 m.
Mount Foraker	Alaska	17,401 ft.	5,303 m.
Iztaccihuatl	Mexico	17,343 ft.	5,286 m.
Mount Lucania	Canada	17,147 ft.	5,226 m.
King Peak	Canada	16,971ft.	5,172 m.
Mount Steele	Canada	16,645 ft.	5,073 m.

2000:

Climber Teddy Keizer (29) reached the summits of Colorado's 55 peaks over 14,000 feet/4,267 meters in less than eleven days (10 days, 20 hours, 26 minutes). He frequently climbed in darkness with a headlamp. Keizer hiked and climbed a total of 315 miles/525 kilometers.

2000:

Lloyd A. Anderson, founder of Recreational Equipment Inc. (REI) in 1938 died at age 98 (1902–2000). A member of the American Alpine Club since 1942, Anderson made over 500 peak ascents in the Pacific Northwest including many first ascents.

2000:

American mountaineers Mark Twight, Scott Backes, and Steve House climbed the Czech Direct Route on the South Face of Mount McKinley/Denali (20,320 ft./6,193 m.) in Alaska in one continuous 60-hour climb (9,000 vertical feet/2,743 meters).

2000:

American mountaineer Peter Croft (1958–) made the first traverse of six peaks over 13,000 feet/3,962 meters in the Sierra mountains of California. These six peaks are: Mount Mendel (13,710 ft./4,179 m.), Mount Darwin (13,837 ft./4,218 m.), Mount Haeckel (13,435 ft./4,095 m.), Mount Fiske (13,503 ft./4,116 m.), Mount Warlow (13,508 ft./4,117 m.), and Mount Huxley (13,086 ft./3,989 m.).

2000:

American climber and environmentalist David Brower (1912–2000) died at age 88. Brower is credited with seventy first ascents. Between 1934 and 1940, Brower made sixteen first ascents in the Yosemite Valley — a record that would stand until 1957.

2000: Equipment – Gaiters

Waterproof, mid-calf to knee length gaiters with rollback vents for better ventilation, secure lace hooks, and reinforced inner panels for crampon snag protection were available from many companies.

2001:

August. Denver, Colorado, attorney Jim Gehres (1932–) completed his 12th full circuit of climbing all 54 peaks in Colorado over 14,000 feet/4,267 meters. This accomplishment represented a total of 648 summits and 1,944,000 vertical feet of hiking and climbing. Gehres began climbing the "fourteeners" in 1961 (40 years).

2001:

October 29. Bradford (1910–2007) and Barbara (1914–) Washburn received the Lowell Thomas Award for "Outstanding Careers In Mountaineering" from the Explorers Club of New York in New York City.

2001:

From 1903 through 2001, 25,023 climbers have attempted to climb Mount McKinley/Denali (20,320 ft./6,193 m.) in Alaska. 12,850 (51 percent) climbers have reached the summit. 91 climbers have died.

2001: FIRST ASCENT

The first high-country 5.13 graded rock climb in the lower 48 United States occurred when American climber Tommy Caldwell (1979–) free-climbed The Honeymoon Is Over route on Longs Peak (14,256 ft./4,345 m.) in Colorado's Rocky Mountain National Park.

2002:

June 17. Colorado climber Jack Eggleston completed the climbing of the 600 highest peaks in Colorado. His final peak was Lizard Head (13,113 ft./3,997 m.) on June 17.

2002:

August 11. American mountaineer, skier, photographer, and author Galen Rowell (1940–2002), his wife Barbara, their pilot, and a friend were killed when their small plane crashed upon landing near Bishop, California. Rowell made over 1,000 separate climbs on four continents including nineteen first ascents in the Yosemite Valley and one hundred first ascents in the Sierra Nevada mountains of California. He was a member of forty major expeditions (ten to the Himalayas) and authored at least twenty books.

2002:

August. American mountaineer Dick Pownall (1928–) at the age of 75 reached the summit of the Grand Teton (13,766 ft./4,196 m.) in Wyoming for the 150th time since 1947. Pownall, who lives in Vail, Colorado, has climbed the Grand Teton by 8 different routes. He was a member of the 1963 American Mount Everest Expedition. Pownall and Jake Breitenbach (killed in Everest's Khumbu Icefall) were to be the first team to make a Mount Everest summit attempt in 1963.

2002:

August. American climber Teddy Keizer (30) climbed all forty-eight 4,000-foot (1,219 meters) peaks in the White Mountains of New Hampshire in 3 days, 17 hours, and 21 minutes. In this same summer season, Keizer also climbed all forty-six 4,000 foot (1,219 meters) peaks in the Adirondack Mountains of New York.

2002:

Hans Florine (1964–) and Yuji Hirayama made a speed ascent of the Nose route (3,000 ft./914 m.) on El Capitan (7,569 ft./2,307 m.) in Yosemite in 2 hours 48 minutes 50 seconds.

2002:

22 Americans had climbed all Seven Summits including Carstensz Pyramid (16,023 ft./4,884 m.) in New Guinea while 28 Americans had climbed the Seven Summits using Mount Kosciuszko (7,310 ft./2,228 m.) in Australia.

2002:

American professional mountain guide Eric Simonson has guided 271 successful ascents of Washington's Mount Rainier (14,411 ft./4,392 m.) and over 85 expeditions including 16 expeditions on Mount McKinley/Denali (20,320 ft./6,193 m.) in Alaska.

2002: FIRST ASCENT

Eleven-year-old Galen Johnston (son of Dave Johnston — 1967 first winter ascent of Denali) became the youngest climber to summit Mount McKinley/Denali (20,320 ft./6,193 m.) in Alaska. He was with his father (60) and his mother Cari.

2002:

A mountain hut in Canada's Selkirk Mountains was renamed the Bill Putnam Hut. This two-story hut was built in 1973 and can accommodate 20 mountaineers or skiers. It is located at 6,700 feet/2,042 meters. American mountaineer Bill Putnam (1924–) is the only living person to have a hut named after him by the Alpine Club of Canada.

2003:

May 17. The National Park Service of the United States and the American Alpine Club placed a bronze plaque commemorating Camp 4 in Yosemite National Park (California) as a National Historic Place.

2003:

Spring. American rock climber Dean Potter free-climbed Yosemite's Half Dome (8,836 ft./2,693 m.) and El Capitan (7,568 ft./2,307 m.) in a single 24-hour period.

2003:

June 27. American mountaineer Chad Kellogg (1965–) made the fastest ascent of Mount McKinley (20,320 ft./6,193 m.) in Alaska– 14 hours and 22 minutes from the Kahiltna Glacier Base camp (7,800 ft./2,377 m.) to the summit via the West Buttress Route. He began this ascent at 2:15 a.m. and reached the summit at 4:37 p.m. His 9 hour and 33 minute descent resulted in a total roundtrip time of 23 hours and 55 minutes.

2003:

Colorado mountaineer Kenneth Nolan (1947–) completed the climbing of all 1,313 Colorado peaks over 12,000 feet (3,657 meters). Nolan began this climbing journey in 1978.

2003:

Climber Erden Eruc bicycled from Seattle, Washington to Talkeetna, Alaska. He then solo climbed Mount McKinley/Denali (20,320 ft./6,193 m.) and bicycled back to Seattle.

2003:

Irish-born Canadian mountaineer John Clarke (1945–2003) died of a brain tumor at age 58. From 1964 to 2003 (39 years), Clarke made 600 first ascents in British Columbia. In 2002, he was one of a few mountaineers to be inducted as a Member of the Order of Canada.

2003:

Mount McKinley/Denali (20,320 ft./6,193 m.) climbing activity:

United States	685 climbers
Great Britain	87 climbers
Canada	52 climbers
France	41 climbers
Spain	34 climbers

Success Rate: 58 percent. The summit on June 12 welcomed 115 climbers.

2004: FIRST ASCENT

January 17. Two independent American climbing teams made the first winter ascent (traverse) of the "Grand Traverse of the Tetons" in Wyoming. Stephen Koch and Mark Newcomb completed this 14-mile/10-peak traverse in three days (January 17 to 19) while Renny Jackson and Hans Johnstone took four days. The Grand Traverse of the Tetons is comprised of the following ten summits (north to south):

1.	Mount Teewinot	12,324 ft./3,756 m.
2.	Mount Owen	12,928 ft./3,940 m.
3.	Grand Teton	13,766 ft./4,196 m.
4.	Middle Teton	12,798 ft./3,900 m.
5.	South Teton	12,505 ft./3,811 m.
6.	Ice Cream Cone	12,300 ft./3,749 m.
7.	Spalding Peak	12,200 ft./3,718 m.
8.	Gilkey's Tower	12,350 ft./3,764 m.
9.	Cloudveil Dome	12,026 ft./3,665 m.
10.	Nez Perce	11,901 ft./3,627 m.

2004: FIRST ASCENT

May 22. Yosemite National Park, California. American climber Tommy Caldwell (1979–) became the first person to free-climb El Capitan's Dihedral Wall (2,500 ft./762 meters). Many believe this climb to be the hardest big-wall free-climb in the world. Caldwell encountered 15 pitches of 5.12 or harder during this four-day climb. He took two falls of 25 feet/8 meters each. He used no jumars (ascenders). One 70 ft./21 m. overhang had to be climbed.

2004: FIRST ASCENT

June 2. American mountaineers Karen McNeil (35) and Sue Nott (34) were the first women to summit Mount McKinley/Denali (20,320 ft./6,193 m.) via the Cassin Ridge in Alaska. This ascent took four days. They spent 20 hours on the summit in their tent in a bad windstorm.

2004:

December 18. American mountaineer James Barry Corbet (1936–2004) died at age 68. He made the first ascent of Denali's West Rib Route in 1959, the first ascent of Mount Vinson (16,050 ft./4,892 m.) in Antarctica in 1966, and was a member of the 1963 American Mount Everest Expedition.

2004:

Six mountaineers had climbed all 54 11,000 foot (3,353 meters) peaks in the Canadian Rockies.

2004:

Colorado high school physics teacher Roger Briggs (1951 –) climbed the Diamond Face on Longs Peak's (14,256 ft./4,345 m.) east face for the 100th time. This face is 945 feet/288 meters high and is above 13,100 feet/3,993 meters. Briggs has spent 36 years climbing on Longs Peak's east face.

2005:

March 7. Colorado climber Aron Ralston (1975–) reached the summit of Mount Eolus (14,083 ft./4,292 m.) thereby becoming the first climber to solo climb all 54 Colorado peaks over 14,000 feet (4,267 meters) in the winter. He began this winter quest in 1998.

2005: FIRST ASCENT

May 1 to 23. Polish climber Marek Klonowski (25) made the first solo ascent of Mount McKinley/Denali (20,320 ft./6,193 m.) in Alaska via the Muldrow Glacier. He descended the West Buttress route.

2005:

May 10. British woman mountaineer Annabelle Bond (36) reached the summit of Mount McKinley/Denali (20,320 ft./6,193 m.) in Alaska — her seventh summit (worldwide) — all within one year. She was the first female to climb all Seven Summits the fastest.

2005:

July 22 to August 18. British mountaineers David Swinburne and Stuart Howard made sixteen first ascents in the Kangerdlugssuaq South mountains of Greenland. These peaks ranged in height from 6,683 ft./2,037 m. to 8,262 ft./2,518 m.

2005:

The United States Board on Geographical Names approved the naming of Alex Lowe Peak (10,031 feet/3,057 meters) in the Gallatin National Forest of Montana. American mountaineer Alex Lowe (1958–

1999) was suddenly killed by an avalanche on the Himalayan peak Shishapangma (26,399 ft./8,046 m.) on October 5,1999. Lowe is thought to have made the first ski descent of this peak in Montana.

2005:

American climber Harvey T. Carter (1931–2011) of Colorado Springs, Colorado has made over 5,000 first ascents over the past sixty years (1945 to 2005). During one 17-year period, he accomplished 100 new climbing routes per year in Colorado, New Mexico, and Utah.

2005:

American climber Michael Reardon (1970–2007) accomplished the Palisades Traverse in the Eastern Sierra mountains of California. This traverse involved 160 pitches across 13 peaks in 22 hours.

2005:

American mountaineers Sue Nott (35) and John Varko climbed Mount Foraker (17,401 ft./5,304 m.), Denali (20,320 ft./6,193 m.), and Mount Hunter (14,574 ft./4,442 m.) in Alaska in one season. They were the fourth and fifth climbers to accomplish this feat. Nott disappeared while climbing the Infinite Spur route on Mount Foraker in May of 2006 along with Karen McNeil.

2005:

American woman climber Heather L. Paul (1970–2005) died in a fall on Cloudveil Dome (12,026 ft./3,665 m.) in Wyoming's Teton Range. Her first eleven climbs of the Grand Teton (13,766 ft./4,196 m.) were by ten different routes.

2005: Clothing – Composite Seam System

American mountaineer and clothing designer Yvon Chouinard (1938– , founder of Patagonia) believed that outdoor clothing will soon be made without sewing in order to save weight. Chouinard named this new process the "Composite Seam System." This system creates a threadless lap seam by using a strong adhesive. In addition to saving weight, these new clothing garments will reduce bulk, improve mobility, and provide warmth and wicking.

2005: Equipment – Boots

A new climbing boot liner was developed by Intuition Sports for high-altitude climbing. Known as "Denali Boot Liners," this liner was made of ultralon EVA foam (a closed-cell foam that can be custom-molded to the foot) which was more durable, comfortable, and warmer than other liners. One pair weighed approximately seven ounces.

2005: Equipment – Flashlights

Lightweight hands-free headlamps had now replaced hand-held flashlights. These headlamps feature focused beams, variable brightness settings, waterproof construction, and wide comfortable head bands. Headlamps actually were first used in the 1960s.

2005: Equipment – Sleeping Bag

Nearly twelve U.S. sleeping bag manufacturers now offered a 14–18 ounce sleeping bag that was rated from 30°F to 55°F. The cost of this bag ranged from $179.00 to $220.00.

2006:

February. The American Alpine Club awarded American mountaineer Nickolas B. Clinch (1930–) its Gold Medal for Lifetime Achievement in Mountaineering. Clinch led three American expeditions that made the first ascents of:

1958	Hidden Peak	Himalayas
1960	Masherbrum	Himalayas
1966	Mount Vinson	Antarctica

2006:

April. The American Alpine Club made the decision to name their mountaineering museum in Golden , Colorado, the Bradford Washburn American Mountaineering Museum. This 5,000 square foot museum is scheduled to open on February 16, 2008. This museum will contain maps, photographs, interactive games, historical climbing equipment and artifacts, a theater for short films, a mountaineering timeline, and a twelve-foot square scale model of Mount Everest.

2006: FIRST ASCENT

May 28–30. Canadian mountaineers (from Quebec) Max Turgeon and Louis-Philippe Ménard made a 58-hour alpine-style ascent of Denali's (20,320 ft./6,193 m.) 8,000 foot/2,438 meter South Face. Their new route is known at the Canadian Direct.

2006:

June 16. Slovenian mountaineer Marko Prezelj (1965–) made a one-day (21 hours) ascent of the Cassin Ridge (7,874 ft./2,400 m.) on Denali (20,320 ft./6,193 m.) in Alaska.

2006: FIRST ASCENT

September 2. American climber Peter Stabolepszy (39) became the first person under the age of 40 to climb all 741 peaks in Colorado higher than 13,000 feet/3,962 meters. Stabolepszy climbed all of these peaks during the summer (275 peaks — solo) from 1986 to 2006 (20 years).

2006:

American mountain guide Miles Smart (23) became the youngest guide in North America to earn the U.I.A.G.M. certification (International Federation of Mountain Guide Associations).

2006:

Well-known American mountaineer Nick Clinch (1930–) announced his intention to donate his personal mountaineering library of over 28,000 books and journals to the American Alpine Club

(A.A.C.) Library in Golden, Colorado. This generous library gift will more than double the existing AAC library of approximately 25,000 books, journals, videos, maps, and periodicals. This AAC library will be the largest alpine library in the Western Hemisphere and perhaps the world.

2006: Equipment – Belaying Devices

Two types of belay devices were available to climbers: tubes and mechanical assists. These devices could accommodate rope diameters from 7.5 to 11 millimeters. Over forty different belay devices were being sold to climbers.

2006: Equipment – Helmets

Three types of climbing helmets were now available to climbers:
1. Hard Shell: Plastic, Kevlar, or carbon fiber
2. Hybrid: Plastic shell and high density foam liner
3. Co-Molded: Lightweight, polycarbonate shell cover over a molded foam inner liner.

2006: Equipment – Carabiners

Many types of carabiners are now available to climbers. Ovals, pears, D-ring, and D-shaped asymmetrical Ds. Locking and non-locking. 28–68 grams in weight. Solid aluminum gate or steel wire gate.

2006: Equipment – Rock Climbing Shoes

There were three main categories of rock climbing shoes: slippers, velcros, and lace-ups. Each had its particular climbing advantages and this selection allowed the climber to choose the type of last, the composition of the upper, the midsole, and the shoe rubber.

2006: Equipment – Rope

Ropes could be divided into two basic categories — dynamic and static. Dynamic ropes will stretch more than 30 percent of their length and are used for almost all types of climbing. Static ropes have very little stretch and are used for rescue, hauling, and fixed rope placement.

> *"When men climb on a great mountain together, the rope between them is more than a mere physical aid to the ascent; it is a symbol of men banded together in a common effort of will and strength against their only true enemies:inertia, cowardice, greed, ignorance and all weakness of the spirit."*
> Charles Houston
> American mountaineer
> (1913–2009)

2006: Equipment – Seat Harness

Three types of seat harnesses were now available to climbers:
1. Lightweight diaper style
2. Fixed-leg models
3. Fully adjustable

Additional features included molded gear loops, quick-release leg loops, and padded waistbands. Over a 100 seat harness designs were now being sold by various climbing equipment companies.

2006: Equipment – Tents

Lightweight single-wall mountaineering tents weighing approximately three pounds (2-man tent) and made of highly breathable nylon with a special coating (snowproof, showerproof, but not 100 percent waterproof) became available. These tents were designed for high-altitude use. The narrow profile shed snow quickly and the two-pole design allowed for easy set-ups. Vestibules could be joined to the tent for additional space.

2007:

January 10. Well-known American mountaineer, photographer, author, and cartographer Bradford Washburn (1910–2007) died in Boston, Massachusetts at age 96½. Washburn was considered by many to be one of the finest mountain photographers of all time. He received twenty-nine different awards between 1938 and 2000. He created twenty-three maps and was presented with eleven honorary doctorate degrees. His mountain photographs were displayed at twelve different exhibitions. From 1934 to 1955, Washburn made the following ten first ascents in Alaska:

1.	1934	Mount Crillon	12,726 ft./3,879 m.
2.	1937	Mount Lucania	17,150 ft./5,227 m.
3.	1938	Mount Marcus Baker	13,176 ft./4,016 m.
4.	1938	Mount Sanford	16,237 ft./4,949 m.
5.	1940	Mount Bertha	10,182 ft./3,103 m.
6.	1941	Mount Hayes	13,832 ft./4,216 m.
7.	1945	Mount Silverthorne	13,220 ft./4,029 m.
8.	1945	Mount Deception	11,000 ft./3,353 m.
9.	1951	Mount McKinley West Buttress Route	20,320 ft./6,193 m.
10.	1955	Mount Dickey	9,545 ft./2,909 m.

Washburn made seventy trips to Alaska during his lifetime. He also made the European Alps ascents of the Matterhorn, Mont Blanc, Charmoz, Grepon, and the Aiguille Verte.

2007: FIRST ASCENT

January 19. Colorado ski mountaineer Chris Davenport (1970–) successfully climbed up and skied down (from the true summit) all 54 peaks in Colorado over 14,000 feet/4,267 meters within one year (January 22, 2006 to January 19, 2007) — 363 days.

2007: FIRST ASCENT

March 10. Japanese mountaineer Masatoshi Kuriaki (1973–) made the first solo winter ascent of Mount Foraker (17,401 feet/5,304 meters) in Alaska. Kuriaki spent 57 days alone on the mountain (39 days for the ascent).

2007:

September 13. Well-known American mountaineer Robert H. Bates (1911–2007) died at age 96 in Exeter, New Hampshire. Bates made three visits to K2 in the Karakoram including the 1938 and 1953 American expeditions. In 1937, he made the first ascent of Mount Lucania in Canada with Bradford Washburn and the second ascent of Mount Steele in Canada also with Washburn. Bates was a member of the 1942 summit (3rd ascent) team on Mount McKinley/Denali. He was also the first director of America's Peace Corps.

2007:

October 8. German mountaineers Alex (1968 –) and Thomas (1966 –) Huber made a record time ascent of the Nose Route on El Capitan in Yosemite (California) — 2 hours 45 minutes. The first ascent in 1958 took 45 days over an 18-month period.

2007:

October 30. Colorado climber Robert D. "Bob" Martin (1920–2008) reached his 1,500th summit in Colorado. Martin began climbing Colorado peaks in 1977. Over this thirty-year period, he climbed approximately 3,000 peaks in Colorado (every peak in Colorado over 10,750 feet), Arizona, and several other states. He also authored five hiking books.

2007:

American climbing guide Rod Newcomb (1934–) has made over 400 ascents of the Grand Teton (13,766 ft./4,196 m.) in Wyoming. Newcomb (age 73), with the Exum Mountain Guides, still continues to lead clients up this well-known American peak.

2007:

Paul Barry and David Hart completed a 13-year climbing journey (1994–2006) during which they ascended the highest twenty-two peaks in Alaska and Canada. These peaks ranged from Denali (20,320 feet/6,193 meters) to University Peak (14,470 feet/4,410 meters).

2007:

American mountaineer and Mount Rainier (14,411 ft./4,392 m.) guide Peter Whittaker (1958–) had made 217 ascents of Rainier over the past twenty-five years.

2007:

As of this year, American climber Ammon McNeely (1970–) had made 53 ascents of El Capitan (3,593 feet/1,095 meters above the Yosemite Valley floor) via 39 different climbing routes. He accomplished this ascent record from 1996 to 2006.

2007:

Denali climbing summary:

> 1,218 mountaineers on the mountain.
>
> 1,099 mountaineers on the West Buttress Route (90 percent).
>
> 572 climbers reach the summit (47 percent).

2007: Equipment – Bivouac Sack

Bivouac bags were now constructed with a heavy duty nylon floor, waterproof/breathable top, double-slider zipper, rollable hood, a tie-in point for security, and zip-out mesh screens. These bags now weigh one to two pounds.

2007: Equipment – Sleeping Pad

Outdoor Research developed a new type of sleeping pad called the "downmat." This pad used nocar-treated goose down (700 fill) combined with full-length baffle chambers. The shell is laminated polyester. Weighing between 20 and 44 ounces (4 sizes), this pad produced a buffer thickness of 2.75 to 3.5 inches. This pad compressed into a small stuffbag.

2008:

January. Three women from the United States had qualified for the IFMGA* certification:

> Kathy Cosley (1969–)
>
> Margaret Wheeler (1965–)
>
> Olivia Cussen (1979–)

2008:

February. The Bradford Washburn American Mountaineering Museum officially opened in Golden, Colorado. This museum contains a scale model of Mount Everest, historic climbing artifacts, expedition journals, heroic mountaineering stories, displays on climate change, high peaks, mountain cultures, and mountain survival. The museum is immediately adjacent to the Henry S. Hall, Jr. American Alpine Club Library. Founded in 1916, this library now contains over 60,000 books, journals, videos, historic maps, and rare photographs.

2008:

May 11 to 18. Japanese mountaineers Fumitaka Ichimura, Yusuke Sato, and Katsutaka Yokoyama (a.k.a. Giri – Giri Boys) completed the enchainment of two Alaska Grade 6 routes on Denali (20,320 ft./6,193 m.). They first climbed the 7,200 ft./2,194 m. Isis Face. After traversing the South Buttress, they descended to the base of the 9,000 ft./2,743 m. Slovak direct route which they then climbed to the summit.

2008: FIRST ASCENT

May 12 to 17. American rock climbers Tommy Caldwell (1978–) and Justin Sjong achieved the first free ascent of the Magic Mushroom route (rated 5.12 to 5.14) on El Capitan (7,569 ft./2,307 m.) in Yosemite National Park (California). Following this climb, Caldwell said that this was "the most continuously difficult free climb in the world."

2008:

June 5. Danish mountaineer Henrik Kristiansen (1964–) completed the climbing of all Seven Summits (he actually climbed eight summits) in 136 days, a new record. His final (eight) summit was Denali in Alaska. The previous record was 156 days which was set by Irish climber Ian McKeever. As of 2008, over two hundred climbers had reached all Seven Summits.

2008:

July. Denali climbing summary for 2008:

May 30th – 91 climbers reached the summit

51 nations were represented on the peak including:

United States	692 climbers
Canada	72 climbers
United Kingdom	69 climbers
Germany	47 climbers
Spain	42 climbers

1,272 climbers attempted the climb. Fifty percent reached the summit.

1,123 climbers followed the West Buttress route. Fifty-eight percent reached the summit.

2008:

July. Mount Foraker (17,401 ft./5,303 m.) in Alaska had sixteen climbers attempting to reach its summit with only one climber being successful.

2008:

September 6. Well-known American rock climber Alex Honnold (1985–) made the first free solo ascent of the Northwest Face (2,130 ft./649 m.) of Half Dome (8,836 ft./2,693 m.) in Yosemite National Park in California. Honnold took 2 hours and 50 minutes to climb the 23 pitches of the regular Northwest Face route. Free-soloing is the most dangerous form of climbing. The free soloist uses no rope, no nuts, no carabiners or slings and has no climbing partner.

2008:

October 8. Colorado mountaineer Teresa Gergen (1964–) had climbed the 800 highest peaks in Colorado.

2008:

November 1. American mountain guide Michael A. Hamill completed the climbing of all Seven Summits in 335 days (11 months). Hamill began this seven summit climb on December 1, 2007 with the ascent of Mount Vinson in Antarctica and finished with the ascent of Mount Elbrus in Europe.

2008:

American mountain guide Phil Ershler (1951–) reached the summit of Mount Rainier (14,411 ft./4,392 m.) in Washington for the 435th time. Ershler is the oldest (57) active guide on Rainier.

2009: PEAK FIRST ASCENT *ICE PYRAMID*

May 3. American climbers Clint Helander and Seth Holden made the first ascent of Ice Pyramid (9,250 ft./2,819 m.) via the southwest ridge. This peak is located in the Revelation mountains of Alaska.

2009:

July 5. Legendary Yosemite rock climber John Bachar (1957–2009) died after a fall from the Dike Wall in the Sierra mountains of California. Bachar focused on free climbing and made many difficult ascents in and around the Yosemite Valley in the 1970s and 1980s. In 1986, Bachar and Peter Croft (1958–) climbed the Nose route on El Capitan and the Northwest Face of Half Dome in a single day.

2009: FIRST ASCENT

July 22. Kurt Hicks and Forest McBrian established a new route on the northeast buttress of Mount Formidable (8,325 ft./2,537 m.) in the Glacier Park Wilderness of Washington's Cascade Range.

2009:

American ski mountaineer Andrew McLean climbed and then skied down the three major Alaskan peaks: Denali (20,320 feet/6,193 meters), Mount Hunter (14,574 feet/4,442 meters), and Mount Foraker (17,401 feet/5,303 meters).

2009:

Denali Climbing Summary:

    1,161 climbers attempt summit

    144 women – 12.4 percent of total

    59 percent reach the summit

    93 percent climb West Buttress route

2010: FIRST ASCENT

May 7. Japanese mountaineers Katsutaka Yokoyama (1979–) and Yasushi Okada (1973–) made the first ascent of Mount Logan's (19,551 ft./5,959 m.) huge southeast face (8,498 ft./2,590 m.) in Canada. This was the biggest unclimbed wall in North America. After three-days of climbing this face, they reached the summit of Mount Logan's East Peak (19,357 ft./5,900 m.). They named their climbing route I-To, which means "line-thread relationship."

2010:

April 10. The Bradford Washburn American Mountaineering Museum in Golden, Colorado, hosted its First Annual Hall of Mountaineering Excellence Awards ceremony. This award is presented by the American Alpine Club to those climbers that have made significant contributions to mountaineering, business, and to their community. The first class of award recipients included Robert Bates (1911–2007), Yvon Chouinard (1938–), Robert Craig (1925–), and Dr. Charlie Houston (1913–2009).

2010:

May 16. American ski mountaineer Christy Mahon (1976–) became the third person to climb and then ski down all 54 peaks in Colorado over 14,000 feet (4,267 meters). Mahon spent six years (2005 to 2010) pursuing this unique goal.

2010: FIRST ASCENT

May. American mountaineers Sam Johnson and Ryan Hokanson reached the summit of Mount Hayes (13,832 ft./4,216 m.) in Alaska via a new route they called the Direct West Face (6,500 ft./1,981 m.). Hayes was first climbed in 1941 by a party of seven climbers led by Bradford Washburn (1910–2007) via its north ridge.

2010:

June 3 to July 16. Boulder, Colorado climbers Mike Moniz and son Matt Moniz climbed all fifty U.S. highpoints (highest point in each state) in 43 days 3 hours 51 minutes. The lowest point was 345 feet/105 meters in Florida. The highest point was Denali (20,320 feet/6,193 meters) in Alaska. This father/son team rated Granite Peak (12,807 ft./3,903 m.) in Montana as the most difficult climb in the lower 48 states.

2010:

June 22. American rock climber Alex Honnold (1985–) took ½ day to complete a solo link-up of two well-known Yosemite big-wall climbs. Honnold climbed the regular route (2,200 feet/620 meters) on the Northwest Face of Half Dome in 2 hours 9 minutes. He then climbed the Nose route (2,900 feet/884 meters) on El Capitan in 5 hours 59 minutes.

2010:

Longtime Longs Peak (14,256 ft./4,345 m.) Climbing Ranger Jim Detterline (1956–) broke Shep Husted's 100-year-old record of 350 ascents of Longs Peak (Colorado). Detterline made his 351st ascent (1985 to 2010) and by September 26, 2010, had added eight additional ascents. He once climbed Longs Peak every month for thirty consecutive months. Detterline served as the Longs Peak Supervisory Climbing Ranger from 1987 to 2009. He has been involved in countless rescues on Longs.

2011:

April 9. The Bradford Washburn American Mountaineering Museum in Golden, Colorado, hosted its Second Annual Hall of Mountaineering Excellence Awards ceremony. This award is presented by the

American Alpine Club to those climbers that have made significant contributions to mountaineering, business, and to their community. The second group of award recipients included Fred Beckey (1923–), Dr. Thomas Hornbein (1930–), Royal Robbins (1935–), Miriam Underhill (1899–1976), and Willi Unsoeld (1926–1979).

2011: FIRST ASCENT

April 17. American mountaineers Kevin Ditzler and John Kelley made the first ascent of the south-west spur of University Peak (14,470 ft./4,410 m.) in Alaska's St. Elias Mountains. This 8,500 foot (2,590 m.) route took seven days to climb on 60° to 75° ice.

2011: PEAK FIRST ASCENT *AUGUSTINE COURTAULD*

May 28. A British mountaineering team led by Ian Barker and Mark Basey-Fisher made the first ascent of Mount Augustine Courtauld (10,335 ft./3,150 m.) in Greenland. This peak is located in the Gunnbjornsfjeld group of mountains on the east coast of Greenland. It is named after a member of the party that made the first ascent of Greenland's highest peak, Gunnbjornsfjeld, (12,120 ft./3,694 m.) in 1935.

2011:

September. American climbers Chantel Astorga (1985–) and Libby Sauter (1984–) established a new women's climbing speed time on the Nose route of El Capitan (7,564 ft./2,305 m.): 10 hours 40 minutes. This time was 1 hour 35 minutes faster than the previous time. Astorga and Sauter were both members of the Yosemite Search and Rescue (YOSAR) group.

2011:

June 23 to September 29 (95 days). Colorado mountaineers, Jon Kedrowski (1979 –) and Chris Tomer (1980 –), accomplished a very unique climbing goal. They climbed all 54 peaks in Colorado over 14,000 feet (4,267 meters) and Mount Rainier (14,411 ft./4,392 m.) in Washington. They then spent the night on these summits. They were the first climbers to endure these fifty-five bivouacs. Kedrowski and Tomer recorded their "summit sleeps" in (2012).

2011:

November. The Colorado Mountain Club (CMC) reported that 1,437 people had climbed all 54 peaks in Colorado over 14,000 feet. The CMC began keeping a record of this climbing achievement in 1923 when Carl Blaurock (1894–1993) and William Ervin became the first climbers to summit all of Colorado's "fourteeners" (47 designated peaks of that time).

2011:

December 8. American mountaineer Lisa Foster reached the summit of Longs Peak (14,256 ft./4,345 m.) for the forty-ninth time thereby becoming the first woman to climb this famous peak in every month of the year. Longs Peak is the highest mountain in Rocky Mountain National Park (Colorado).

Foster has climbed Longs by fifteen different routes including two technical routes up the Diamond (east) face. She made this forty-ninth ascent in winter conditions up the north face. Her two climbing partners were longtime Longs Peak guide Jim Detterline and Elliott Demos. Foster's first ascent of Longs Peak was on July 24, 1987. She has been forced to turn back on this climb twenty-three times due to unfavorable weather conditions. Lisa Foster has served as a National Park Service Biological Field Technician in Rocky Mountain National Park since 1991.

2011:

American mountain guide George Dunn (1953–) had climbed Mount Rainier (14,411 ft./4,392 m.) over 500 times.

2011:

The International Federation of Mountain Guide Associations (IFMGA) reported that there were 200 certified mountain guides in North America (60 in the United States and 140 in Canada).

> **"There is a wonderful fascination about mountains. Their massive grandeur, majesty of lofty height, splendour of striking outline—crag and pinnacle and precipice—seem to appeal both to the intellect and to the inmost soul of man, and to compel a mingled reverence and love."**
>
> **Sir James Outram**
> **Canadian mountaineer**
> **(1864 – 1925)**

Mount Hood, Oregon, United States
11,239 ft./3,425 m.

Grays Peak (L), Colorado , United States   Torreys Peak (R), Colorado, United States
14,270 ft./4,349 m.   14,267 ft./4,348 m.

Longs Peak
Colorado, United States
14,256 ft./4,345 m.

Mount Whitney
California, United States
14,505 ft./4,421 m

Mount Rainier
Washington, United States
14,411 ft./4,392 m.

El Capitan
California, United States
7,564 ft./2,305 m.

Half Dome, California, United States
8,836 ft./2,693 m.

Grand Teton, Wyoming, United States
13,766 ft./4,196 m.

Mount McKinley, Alaska, United States
20,320 ft./6,193 m.

Capitol Peak, Colorado, United States
14,130 ft./4,306 m.

Maroon Bells, Colorado, United States
14,156 ft./4,315 m.   14,014 ft./4,271 m.

Crestone Needle
Colorado, United States
14,197 ft./4,327 m.

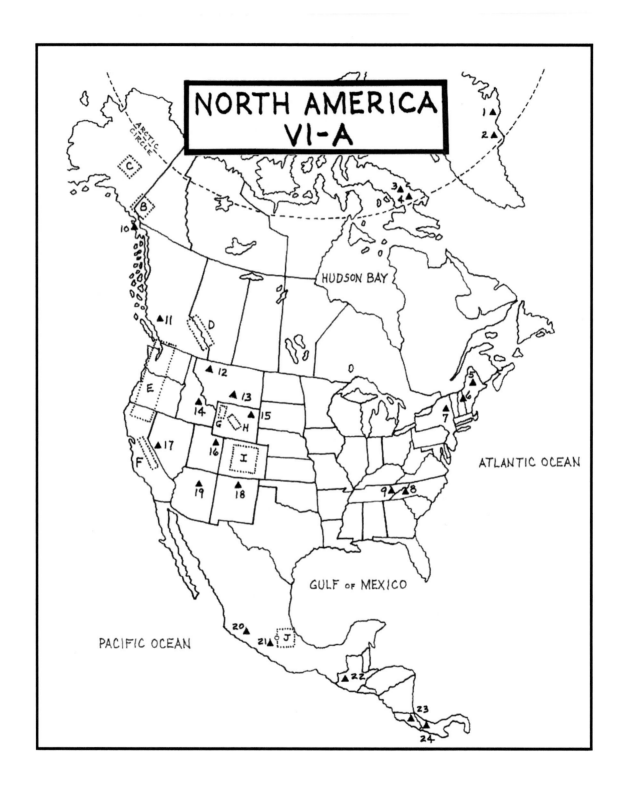

NORTH AMERICAN MOUNTAINS

#	PEAK NAME	LOCATION	FEET	METERS	FIRST ASCENT
1	GUNNBJORN FJELD	GREENLAND	12,139	3,700	1935
2	MONT FOREL	GREENLAND	11,024	3,360	1938
3	TETE BLANCHE	BAFFIN ISLAND	7,074	2,156	1953
4	MT. ASGARD	BAFFIN ISLAND	6,598	2,011	1953
5	MT. KATAHDIN	MAINE	5,266	1,605	1804
6	MT. WASHINGTON	NEW HAMPSHIRE	6,288	1,917	1642
7	MT. MARCY	NEW YORK	5,344	1,629	1837
8	MT. MITCHELL	NORTH CAROLINA	6,683	2,037	1835
9	CLINGMAN'S DOME	TENNESSEE	6,643	2,025	UNKN.
10	MT. FAIRWEATHER	ALASKA	15,300	4,663	1932
11	MT. WADDINGTON	BRITISH COLUMBIA	13,176	4,016	1936
12	MT. CLEVELAND	MONTANA	10,448	3,184	1920
13	GRANITE PEAK	MONTANA	12,799	3,901	1923
14	BORAH PEAK	IDAHO	12,662	3,859	1912
15	DEVILS TOWER	WYOMING	5,112	1,558	1937
16	KINGS PEAK	UTAH	13,528	4,123	UNKN.
17	BOUNDARY PEAK	NEVADA	13,140	4,005	UNKN.
18	WHEELER PEAK	NEW MEXICO	13,161	4,011	UNKN.
19	HUMPHREYS PEAK	ARIZONA	12,633	3,850	UNKN.
20	NEVADO DE COLIMA	MEXICO	14,236	4,339	UNKN.
21	NEVADO DE TOLUCA	MEXICO	15,017	4,577	1803
22	TAJUMULCO	GUATEMALA	13,846	4,220	UNKN.
23	CHIRRIPO GRANDE	COSTA RICA	12,530	3,819	UNKN.
24	VOLCAN BARU	PANAMA	11,401	3,475	UNKN.

REGIONAL MOUNTAIN MAPS

MAP #	MAP NAME
VI-B	ALASKAN MOUNTAINS
VI-C	MOUNT McKINLEY
VI-D	CANADIAN ROCKIES
VI-E	CASCADE RANGE
VI-F	HIGH SIERRA PEAKS
VI-G	TETON RANGE
VI-H	WIND RIVER RANGE
VI-I	COLORADO'S HIGH PEAKS
VI-J	VOLCANOES OF MEXICO

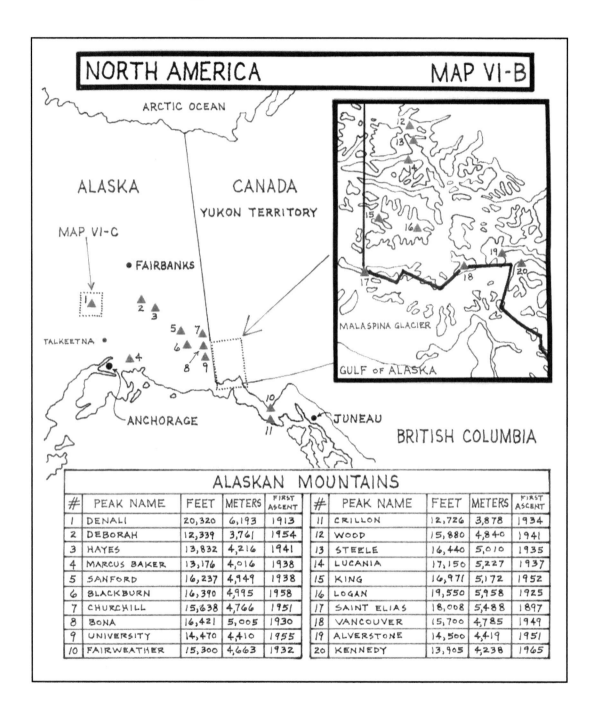

NORTH AMERICA   MAP VI-B

ARCTIC OCEAN

ALASKA   CANADA
                YUKON TERRITORY

MAP VI-C

• FAIRBANKS

TALKEETNA •

ANCHORAGE   JUNEAU

                   BRITISH COLUMBIA

MALASPINA GLACIER

GULF of ALASKA

ALASKAN MOUNTAINS

#	PEAK NAME	FEET	METERS	FIRST ASCENT	#	PEAK NAME	FEET	METERS	FIRST ASCENT
1	DENALI	20,320	6,193	1913	11	CRILLON	12,726	3,878	1934
2	DEBORAH	12,339	3,761	1954	12	WOOD	15,880	4,840	1941
3	HAYES	13,832	4,216	1941	13	STEELE	16,440	5,010	1935
4	MARCUS BAKER	13,176	4,016	1938	14	LUCANIA	17,150	5,227	1937
5	SANFORD	16,237	4,949	1938	15	KING	16,971	5,172	1952
6	BLACKBURN	16,390	4,995	1958	16	LOGAN	19,550	5,958	1925
7	CHURCHILL	15,638	4,766	1951	17	SAINT ELIAS	18,008	5,488	1897
8	BONA	16,421	5,005	1930	18	VANCOUVER	15,700	4,785	1949
9	UNIVERSITY	14,470	4,410	1955	19	ALVERSTONE	14,500	4,419	1951
10	FAIRWEATHER	15,300	4,663	1932	20	KENNEDY	13,905	4,238	1965

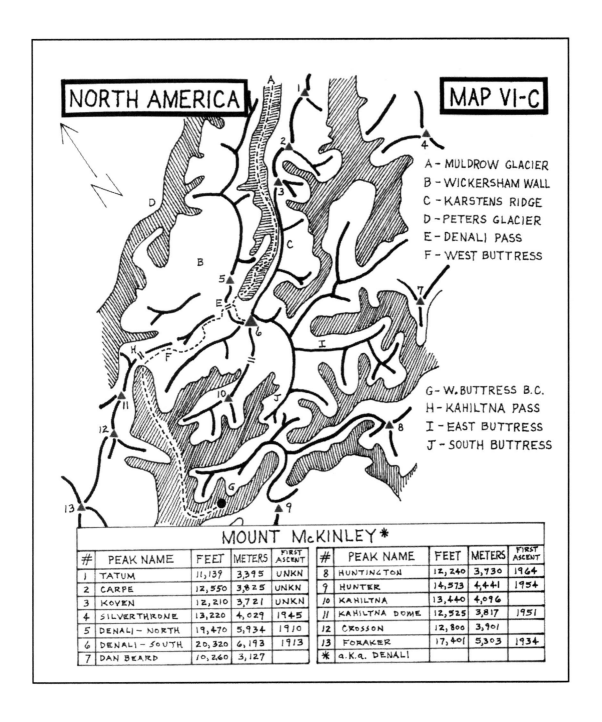

NORTH AMERICA

MAP VI-C

A – MULDROW GLACIER
B – WICKERSHAM WALL
C – KARSTENS RIDGE
D – PETERS GLACIER
E – DENALI PASS
F – WEST BUTTRESS

G – W. BUTTRESS B.C.
H – KAHILTNA PASS
I – EAST BUTTRESS
J – SOUTH BUTTRESS

MOUNT McKINLEY *

#	PEAK NAME	FEET	METERS	FIRST ASCENT	#	PEAK NAME	FEET	METERS	FIRST ASCENT
1	TATUM	11,139	3,395	UNKN	8	HUNTINGTON	12,240	3,730	1964
2	CARPE	12,550	3,825	UNKN	9	HUNTER	14,573	4,441	1954
3	KOVEN	12,210	3,721	UNKN	10	KAHILTNA	13,440	4,096	
4	SILVERTHRONE	13,220	4,029	1945	11	KAHILTNA DOME	12,525	3,817	1951
5	DENALI – NORTH	19,470	5,934	1910	12	CROSSON	12,800	3,901	
6	DENALI – SOUTH	20,320	6,193	1913	13	FORAKER	17,401	5,303	1934
7	DAN BEARD	10,260	3,127		*	a.k.a. DENALI			

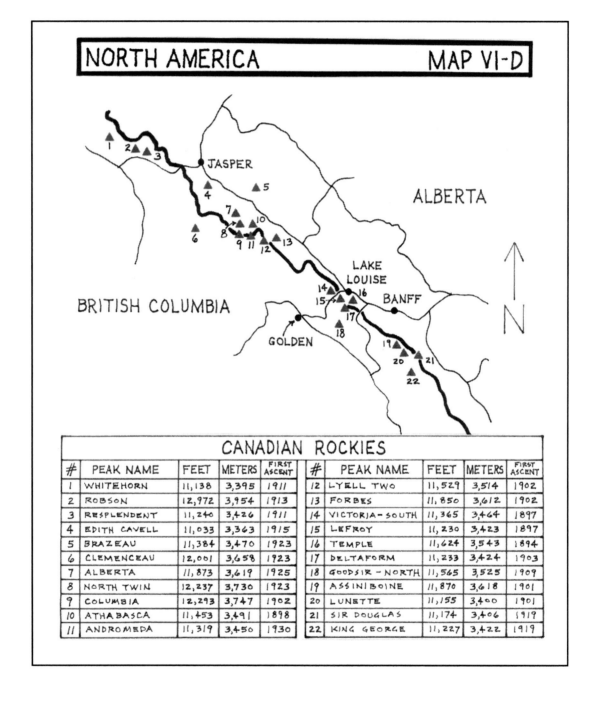

NORTH AMERICA

MAP VI-D

JASPER

ALBERTA

BRITISH COLUMBIA

LAKE LOUISE

BANFF

GOLDEN

N

CANADIAN ROCKIES

#	PEAK NAME	FEET	METERS	FIRST ASCENT	#	PEAK NAME	FEET	METERS	FIRST ASCENT
1	WHITEHORN	11,138	3,395	1911	12	LYELL TWO	11,529	3,514	1902
2	ROBSON	12,972	3,954	1913	13	FORBES	11,850	3,612	1902
3	RESPLENDENT	11,240	3,426	1911	14	VICTORIA-SOUTH	11,365	3,464	1897
4	EDITH CAVELL	11,033	3,363	1915	15	LEFROY	11,230	3,423	1897
5	BRAZEAU	11,384	3,470	1923	16	TEMPLE	11,624	3,543	1894
6	CLEMENCEAU	12,001	3,658	1923	17	DELTAFORM	11,233	3,424	1903
7	ALBERTA	11,873	3,619	1925	18	GOODSIR-NORTH	11,565	3,525	1909
8	NORTH TWIN	12,237	3,730	1923	19	ASSINIBOINE	11,870	3,618	1901
9	COLUMBIA	12,293	3,747	1902	20	LUNETTE	11,155	3,400	1901
10	ATHABASCA	11,453	3,491	1898	21	SIR DOUGLAS	11,174	3,406	1919
11	ANDROMEDA	11,319	3,450	1930	22	KING GEORGE	11,227	3,422	1919

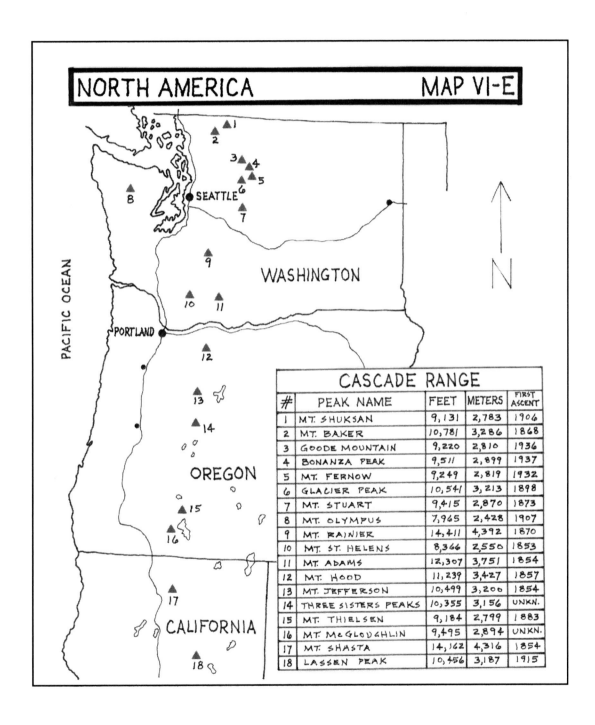

NORTH AMERICA　　MAP VI-E

PACIFIC OCEAN

SEATTLE

WASHINGTON

N

PORTLAND

OREGON

CALIFORNIA

#	PEAK NAME	FEET	METERS	FIRST ASCENT
CASCADE RANGE				
1	MT. SHUKSAN	9,131	2,783	1906
2	MT. BAKER	10,781	3,286	1868
3	GOODE MOUNTAIN	9,220	2,810	1936
4	BONANZA PEAK	9,511	2,899	1937
5	MT. FERNOW	9,249	2,819	1932
6	GLACIER PEAK	10,541	3,213	1898
7	MT. STUART	9,415	2,870	1873
8	MT. OLYMPUS	7,965	2,428	1907
9	MT. RAINIER	14,411	4,392	1870
10	MT. ST. HELENS	8,366	2,550	1853
11	MT. ADAMS	12,307	3,751	1854
12	MT. HOOD	11,239	3,427	1857
13	MT. JEFFERSON	10,499	3,200	1854
14	THREE SISTERS PEAKS	10,355	3,156	UNKN.
15	MT. THIELSEN	9,184	2,799	1883
16	MT. McGLOUGHLIN	9,495	2,894	UNKN.
17	MT. SHASTA	14,162	4,316	1854
18	LASSEN PEAK	10,456	3,187	1915

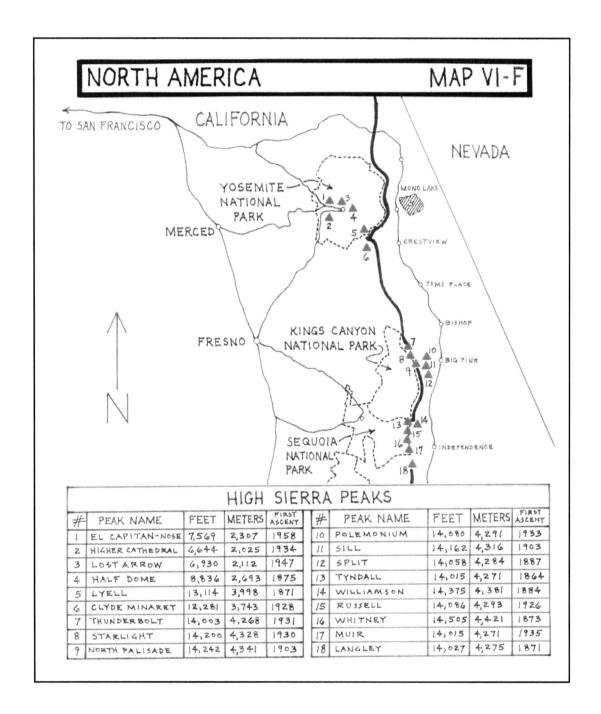

NORTH AMERICA   MAP VI-F

CALIFORNIA

TO SAN FRANCISCO

NEVADA

YOSEMITE
NATIONAL
PARK

MONO LAKE

MERCED

CRESTVIEW

TOMS PLACE

BISHOP

KINGS CANYON
NATIONAL PARK

FRESNO

BIG PINE

N

SEQUOIA
NATIONAL
PARK

INDEPENDENCE

HIGH SIERRA PEAKS

#	PEAK NAME	FEET	METERS	FIRST ASCENT	#	PEAK NAME	FEET	METERS	FIRST ASCENT
1	EL CAPITAN-NOSE	7,569	2,307	1958	10	POLEMONIUM	14,080	4,291	1933
2	HIGHER CATHEDRAL	6,644	2,025	1934	11	SILL	14,162	4,316	1903
3	LOST ARROW	6,930	2,112	1947	12	SPLIT	14,058	4,284	1887
4	HALF DOME	8,836	2,693	1875	13	TYNDALL	14,015	4,271	1864
5	LYELL	13,114	3,998	1871	14	WILLIAMSON	14,375	4,381	1884
6	CLYDE MINARET	12,281	3,743	1928	15	RUSSELL	14,086	4,293	1926
7	THUNDERBOLT	14,003	4,268	1931	16	WHITNEY	14,505	4,421	1873
8	STARLIGHT	14,200	4,328	1930	17	MUIR	14,015	4,271	1935
9	NORTH PALISADE	14,242	4,341	1903	18	LANGLEY	14,027	4,275	1871

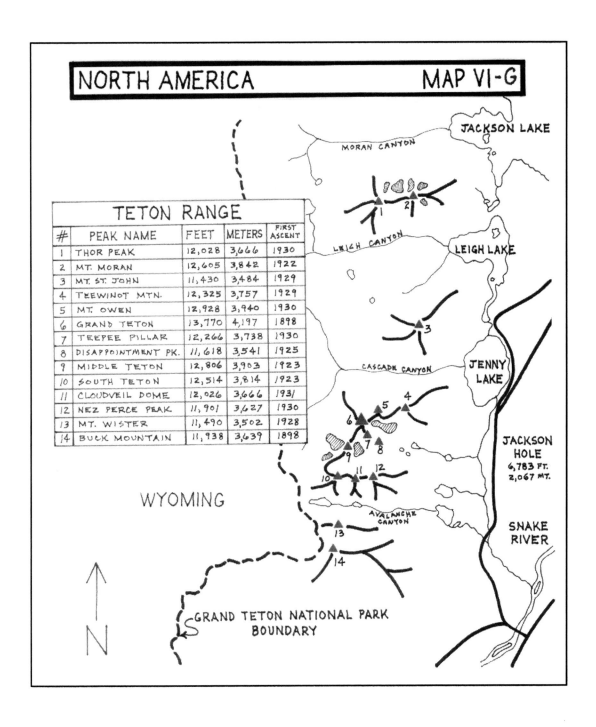

NORTH AMERICA   MAP VI-G

JACKSON LAKE

MORAN CANYON

LEIGH CANYON

LEIGH LAKE

TETON RANGE				
#	PEAK NAME	FEET	METERS	FIRST ASCENT
1	THOR PEAK	12,028	3,666	1930
2	MT. MORAN	12,605	3,842	1922
3	MT. ST. JOHN	11,430	3,484	1929
4	TEEWINOT MTN.	12,325	3,757	1929
5	MT. OWEN	12,928	3,940	1930
6	GRAND TETON	13,770	4,197	1898
7	TEEPEE PILLAR	12,266	3,738	1930
8	DISAPPOINTMENT PK.	11,618	3,541	1925
9	MIDDLE TETON	12,806	3,903	1923
10	SOUTH TETON	12,514	3,814	1923
11	CLOUDVEIL DOME	12,026	3,666	1931
12	NEZ PERCE PEAK	11,901	3,627	1930
13	MT. WISTER	11,490	3,502	1928
14	BUCK MOUNTAIN	11,938	3,639	1898

CASCADE CANYON

JENNY LAKE

JACKSON HOLE
6,783 FT.
2,067 MT.

WYOMING

AVALANCHE CANYON

SNAKE RIVER

N

GRAND TETON NATIONAL PARK BOUNDARY

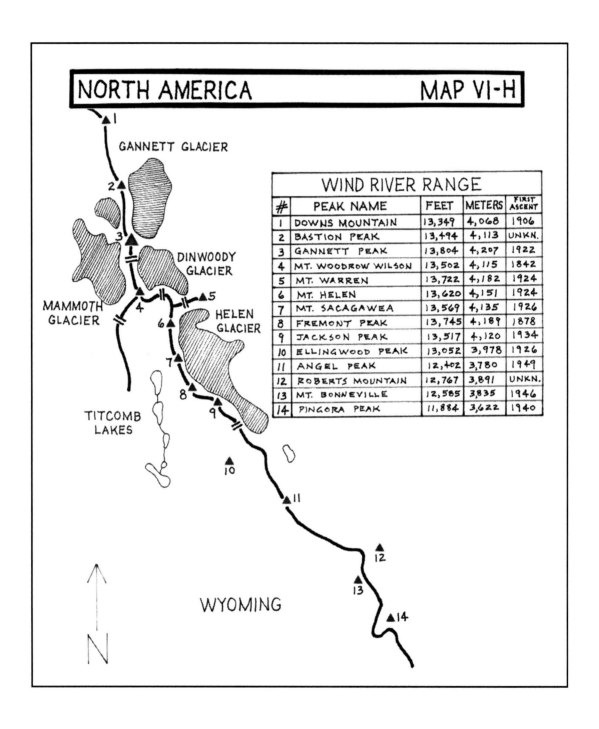

NORTH AMERICA   MAP VI-H

GANNETT GLACIER

DINWOODY GLACIER

MAMMOTH GLACIER

HELEN GLACIER

TITCOMB LAKES

WYOMING

N

WIND RIVER RANGE

#	PEAK NAME	FEET	METERS	FIRST ASCENT
1	DOWNS MOUNTAIN	13,349	4,068	1906
2	BASTION PEAK	13,494	4,113	UNKN.
3	GANNETT PEAK	13,804	4,207	1922
4	MT. WOODROW WILSON	13,502	4,115	1842
5	MT. WARREN	13,722	4,182	1924
6	MT. HELEN	13,620	4,151	1924
7	MT. SACAGAWEA	13,569	4,135	1926
8	FREMONT PEAK	13,745	4,189	1878
9	JACKSON PEAK	13,517	4,120	1934
10	ELLINGWOOD PEAK	13,052	3,978	1926
11	ANGEL PEAK	12,402	3,780	1949
12	ROBERTS MOUNTAIN	12,767	3,891	UNKN.
13	MT. BONNEVILLE	12,585	3,835	1946
14	PINGORA PEAK	11,884	3,622	1940

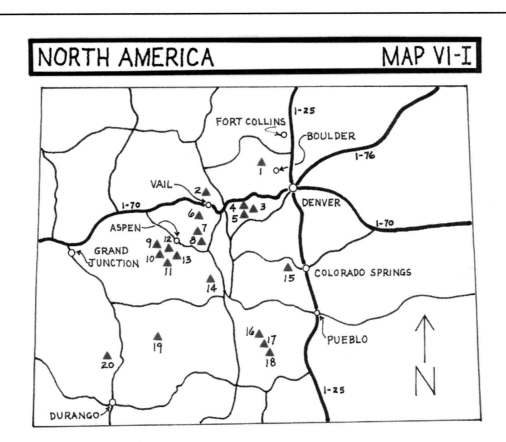

COLORADO'S HIGH PEAKS

#	PEAK NAME	FEET	METERS	FIRST ASCENT	#	PEAK NAME	FEET	METERS	FIRST ASCENT
1	LONGS	14,256	4,345	1868	11	PYRAMID	14,018	4,272	1907
2	POWELL	13,504	4,116	1868	12	NORTH MAROON	14,014	4,271	1908
3	BIERSTADT	14,060	4,285	1863	13	CASTLE	14,265	4,347	1873
4	TORREYS	14,267	4,348	1861	14	YALE	14,196	4,326	1869
5	GRAYS	14,270	4,349	1861	15	PIKES	14,110	4,300	1820
6	MT. OF THE HOLY CR.	14,005	4,268	1873	16	KIT CARSON	14,165	4,317	1915
7	MASSIVE	14,421	4,395	1873	17	CRESTONE PEAK	14,294	4,356	1915
8	ELBERT	14,433	4,399	1874	18	CRESTONE NEEDLE	14,197	4,327	1915
9	CAPITOL	14,130	4,306	1907	19	UNCOMPAHGRE	14,309	4,361	1874
10	MAROON	14,156	4,314	1908	20	WILSON	14,246	4,342	1874

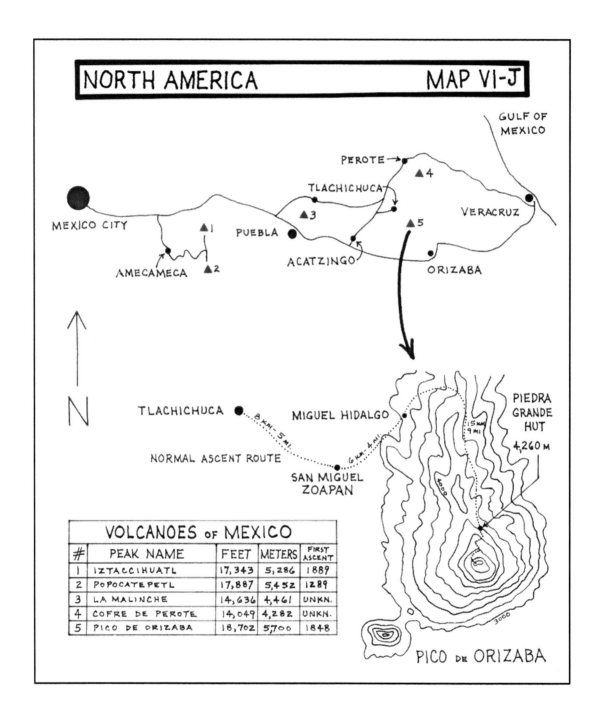

NORTH AMERICA   MAP VI-J

GULF OF MEXICO

PEROTE →
TLACHICHUCA
▲4
VERACRUZ
MEXICO CITY
▲1
▲3
PUEBLA
▲5
AMECAMECA
▲2
ACATZINGO
ORIZABA

N

TLACHICHUCA   8 KM - 5 MI.   MIGUEL HIDALGO   PIEDRA GRANDE HUT 4,260 M

15 KM 9 MI

NORMAL ASCENT ROUTE   6 KM. 4 MI.

SAN MIGUEL ZOAPAN

4000

3000

PICO DE ORIZABA

#	PEAK NAME	FEET	METERS	FIRST ASCENT
1	IZTACCIHUATL	17,343	5,286	1889
2	POPOCATEPETL	17,887	5,452	1289
3	LA MALINCHE	14,636	4,461	UNKN.
4	COFRE DE PEROTE	14,049	4,282	UNKN.
5	PICO DE ORIZABA	18,702	5,700	1848

VOLCANOES OF MEXICO

NORTH AMERICA: The 25 Highest Peaks

RANK and PEAK NAME	ELEVATION FEET·METERS	LOCATION	FIRST ASCENT DATE	EXPEDITION	SUMMIT CLIMBERS
1 Denali-South	20,320·6,193	Alaska	6-7-13	American	Walter Harper Harry Karstens Hudson Stuck Robert Tatum
2 Mount Logan	19,551·5,959	Canada	6-23-25	American	Allen Carpe William Foster H. Lambart L. Lindsay Albert MacCarthy Norman Read
3 Denali-North	19,470·5,934	Alaska	4-10-10	American	P. Anderson W. Taylor
4 Citlaltepetl	18,700·5,700	Mexico	1848	American	F. Raynolds G. Maynard
5 Mount St. Elias	18,008·5,489	Alaska-Canada	7-31-1897	Italian	Duke of the Abruzzi Five Fellow Climbers Four Alpine Guides
6 Popocatepetl	17,887·5,452	Mexico	1519	Spanish	Diego de Ordaz and Spanish soldiers
7 Mount Foraker	17,401·5,304	Alaska	8-6-34	American	T. Graham Brown Charles Houston C. Waterson
8 Iztaccihuatl	17,343·5,286	Mexico	11-3-1889	Swiss	James de Salis
9 Mount Lucania	17,147·5,227	Canada	7-9-37	American	Bradford Washburn Robert Bates
10 King Peak	16,972·5,173	Canada	1952		
11 Mount Steele	16,645·5,073	Canada	8-15-35	American	Walter Wood Hans Fuhrer 2 Other Climbers

NORTH AMERICA The 25 Highest Peaks (continued)

RANK and PEAK NAME	ELEVATION FEET•METERS	LOCATION	FIRST ASCENT DATE	EXPEDITION	SUMMIT CLIMBERS
12 Mount Bona	16,421•5,005	Alaska	7-2-30	American	Allen Carpe Terris Moore Andrew Taylor
13 Mt. Blackburn	16,390•4,995	Alaska	5-19-12	American	Dora Keen George Handy
14 Mount Sanford	16,237•4,949	Alaska	7-21-38	American	Terris Moore Bradford Washburn
15 Mount Wood	15,880•4,840	Canada	1941		
16 Mt. Vancouver	15,787•4,812	Alaska	7-5-49	American	William Hainsworth Robert McCarter Noel Odell A. Bruce Robertson
17 Mount Churchill	15,641•4,767	Alaska			
18 Mount Slaggard	15,575•4,747	Canada			
19 Mount McCauley	15,477•4,717	Canada	1959		
20 Mt. Fairweather	15,322•4,670	Alaska	6-8-31	American	Allen Carpe Terris Moore
21 Nevado de Toluca	15,017•4,577	Mexico	1799-1804		Humboldt
22 Mount Hubbard	14,952•4,557	Alaska	1951		
23 Mount Bear	14,830•4,520	Alaska	1951		
24 Mount Walsh	14,781•4,505	Canada	1941		
25 La Malinche	14,637•4,461	Mexico			

Selected Bibliography — North America

Of the numerous books, journals, newspaper and magazine articles, and internet sites that have been used in the research for this book, the author is particularly indebted to the following sources:

Achey, Jeff. Chelton, Dudley. Godfrey Bob. *Climb – The History of Rock Climbing in Colorado.* The Mountaineers Books, 2002.

Ament, Pat. *Royal Robbins – Spirit of the Age. The Biography of America's Most Distinguished Rock Climber.* Stackpole Books, 1998.

American Alpine Club. T*he American Alpine Journal.* Numerous issues.

Arnold, Daniel. *Early Days in the Range of Light – Encounters With Legendary Mountaineers.* Counterpoint, 2009.

Baars, Donald L. *The American Alps – The San Juan Mountains of Southwest Colorado.* University of New Mexico Press, 1992.

Baldwin, John. *Mountains of the Coast.* Harbour Publishing, 1999.

Bates, Robert H. *Mystery, Beauty, and Danger – The Literature of the Mountains and Mountain Climbing Published in English before 1946.* Peter E. Randall Publisher, 2000.

Beckey, Fred. *Range of Glaciers – The Exploration and Survey of the Northern Cascade Range.* Oregon Historical Society Press, 2003.

Beckey, Fred. *Cascade Alpine Guide – Climbing and High Routes. Second Edition.* The Mountaineers, 1987.

Beckey, Fred. MOUNT McKINLEY – Icy Crown of North America. The Mountaineers, 1993.

Beckey, Fred. *Mountains of North America – The Great Peaks and Ranges of the Continent.* Sierra Club Books, 1982.

Bonney, Orrin H. Bonney, Lorraine. *Guide to the Wyoming Mountains and Wilderness Areas.* Sage Books, 1960.

Bonney, Orrin H. Bonney, Lorraine G. *The Grand Controversy – The Pioneer Climbs in the Teton Range and the Controversial First Ascent of the Grand Teton.* The AAC Press, 1992.

Bornneman, Walter R. and Lampert, Lyndon J. *A Climbing Guide to Colorado's Fourteeners.* Pruett Publishing Company, 1978.

Brower, David – Editor. *Manual of Ski Mountaineering.* Sierra Club, 1962.

Bueler, William M. *Roof of the Rockies – A History of Mountaineering in Colorado.* Pruett Publishing Co., 1974.

Chouinard, Yvon. *Climbing Ice.* Sierra Club Books, 1978.

Coombs, Colby. *Denali's West Buttress – A Climber's Guide to Mount McKinley's Classic Route.* The Mountaineers Books, 1997.

Cooper, Ed. *Soul of the Rockies – Portraits of America's Largest Mountain Range.* Falcon Guides, 2009.

Corbett, Bill. *The 11,000ers of the Canadian Rockies.* Rocky Mountain Books, 2004.

Davidson, Art. *Minus 148° – The Winter Ascent of Mount McKinley.* W.W. Norton & Company, 1969.

Dawson, Louis W. *Wild Snow – A Historical Guide to North American Ski Mountaineering.* The American Alpine Club, 1997.

Dowling, Phil. *The Mountaineers – Famous Climbers in Canada.* Hurtig Publishers, 1979.

Duane, Daniel. *el capitan – historic feats and radical routes.* Chronicle Books, 2000.

DuMais, Richard. *Great American Rock Climbs.* High Peak Books, 1995.

Farquhar, Francis P. *History of the Sierra Nevada.* University of California Press, 1965.

Fay, Bent, Palmer, Thorington, Kauffman, & Putnam. *A Century of American Alpinism.* The American Alpine Club, 2002.

Fryxell, Fritiof. Smith, Phil D. *Mountaineering in the TETONS – The Pioneer Period 1898–1940.* The Teton Bookshop, 1978.

Glickman, Joe. Akerlund, Nels. *To The Top – Reaching for America's 50 State Summits.* NorthWord Press, 2003.

Gorby, John D. *The Stettner Way – The Life and Climbs of Joe and Paul Stettner.* Colorado Mountain Club Press, 2003.

Graydon, Don. Hanson, Kurt: Editors. *Mountaineering – The Freedom of the Hills. 6th Edition.* The Mountaineers, 1997.

Hackett, Peter H. *Mountain Sickness – Prevention, Recognition and Treatment.* The American Alpine Club, 1980.

Hartemann, Frederic V. Hauptman, Robert. *The Mountain Encyclopedia.* Taylor Trade Publishing, 2004.

Hempstead, Andrew. *Canadian Rockies Handbook.* Moon Travel Handbooks, 1999.

Herben, George. *Wrangell – St. Elias: America's Largest National Park.* Alaska Northwest Books, 1997.

Herron, Edward A. *Conqueror of Mount McKinley – Hudson Stuck.* Julian Messner, 1964.

Hill, Lynn. *Climbing Free – My Life In the Vertical World.* W.W. Norton & Company, 2002.

Hill, Pete. *The Complete Guide to Climbing and Mountaineering.* David & Charles, 2008.

Holmes, Don W. *Highpoints of the United States – A Guide To The Fifty State Summits.* Second Edition. The University of Utah Press, 2000.

Holmes, Richard. *A Climber's Guide to the St. Elias Mountains.* Volume 1. Icy Bay Press, 2005.

Houston, Charles S. *High Altitude – Illness and Wellness – The History and Prevention of a Killer.* ICS Books, Inc., 1993.

Houston, Charles S. Harris, David E. Zeman, Ellen J. *Going Higher – Oxygen, Man, and Mountains. Fifth Edition.* The Mountaineers Books, 2005.

Houston, Charles S. *Going Higher – The Story of Man and Altitude.* Little, Brown and Company, 1987.

Houston, Mark and Cosley Kathy. *Alpine Climbing: Techniques to Take You Higher.* The Mountaineers Books, 2004.

Howe, Nicholas. *Not Without Peril – 150 Years of Misadventure on the Presidential Range of New Hampshire.* Appalachian Mountain Club Books, 2000.

Jones, Chris. *Climbing in North America.* University of California Press, 1976.

Kauffman, Andrew J. Putnam, William L. *The Guiding Spirit.* Footprint, 1986.

Kearney, Alan. *Classic Climbs of the Northwest.* Alpen Books, 2002.

Kelsey, Joe. *Climbing and Hiking in the Wind River Mountains.* Falcon, 1994.

King, Clarence. *Mountaineering in the Sierra Nevada.* University of Nebraska Press, 1970.

Kingery, Hugh E. *The Colorado Mountain Club – The First Seventy – Five Years of a Highly Individual Corporation 1912–1987.* Cordillera Press Inc., 1988.

Kjeldsen, Jim. *The Mountaineers – A History.* The Mountaineers, 1998.

Kroese, Mark. *Fifty Favorite Climbs – The Ultimate North American Tick List.* The Mountaineers Books, 2001.

MacDonald, Dougald. *Longs Peak – The Story of Colorado's Favorite Fourteener.* Westcliffe Publishers, 2004.

Mazel, David. *Pioneering Ascents – the origins of climbing in America 1642–1873.* Stackpole Books, 1991.

Meany, Edmond S. *Mount Rainier – A Record of Exploration.* Binfords & Mort Publishers, 1916.

Mellor, Don. *American Rock – Region, Rock, and Culture in American Climbing.* The Countryman Press, 2001.

Miller, Tom. *The North Cascades.* The Mountaineers, 1964.

Molenaar, Dee. *The Challenge of Rainier.* The Mountaineers, 1971.

Molenaar, Dee. *Mountains Don't Care, But We Do – An Early History of Mountain Rescue in the Pacific Northwest and the Founding of the Mountain Rescue Association.* Mountain Rescue Association, 2009.

Morrisey, Thomas. *20 American Peaks & Crags.* Contemporary Books, Inc., 1978.

Neider, Susan M. Editor. *Wild Yosemite – Personal Accounts of Adventure, Discovery, and Nature.* Skyhorse Publishing, 2007.

Olympic Mountain Rescue. *Olympic Mountains – A Climbing Guide.* The Mountaineers, 2006.

Ortenburger, Leigh. *A Climber's Guide to the TETON RANGE.* The Sierra Club, 1956.

Outram, James. *In the Heart of the Canadian Rockies.* The Macmillan Company, 1923.

Porcella, Stephen F. Burns, Cameron M. *Climbing California's Fourteeners – 183 Routes to the Fifteen Highest Peaks.* The Mountaineers, 1998.

Putnam, William L. Boles, Glen W. Laurilla, Roger W. *Place Names of the Canadian Alps.* Footprint, 1990.

Randall, Glenn. *Mount McKinley – Climber's Handbook.* Chockstone Press, 1992.

Reeves, John T. and Grover, Robert F. *Attitudes on Altitude – Pioneers of Medical Research in Colorado's High Mountains.* University Press of Colorado, 2001.

Roach, Gerry. *Colorado's Fourteeners – From Hikes to Climbs.* Fulcrum Publishing, 1992.

Roberts, David. *The Last of His Kind – The Life and Adventures of Bradford Washburn, America's Boldest Mountaineer.* William Morrow, 2009.

Robertson, Janet. *The Magnificent Mountain Women – Adventure in the Colorado Rockies.* University of Nebraska Press, 1990.

Roper, Steve. *Above All – Mount Whitney and California's Highest Peaks.* Heyday Books, 2008.

Roper, Steve. Steck, Allen. *Fifty Classic Climbs of North America.* Sierra Club Books, 1979.

Rossiter, Richard. *Tetons Classics – Selected Climbs in Grand Teton National Park.* Chockstone Press, 1991.

Russell, Franklin. *The Mountains of America – From Alaska to the Great Smokies.* Bonanza Books, 1975.

Sandford, R.W. *The Canadian Alps – The History of Mountaineering in Canada, Volume 1.* Altitude Publishing, 1990.

Scott, Chic. *Pushing the Limits – The Story of Canadian Mountaineering.* Rocky Mountain Books, 2000.

Schneider, Paul. *The Adirondacks – A History of America's First Wilderness.* A John Macrae Book, 1997.

Secor, R.J. *The High Sierra – Peaks, Passes, and Trails.* The Mountaineers, 1992.

Secor, R.J. *Mexico's Volcanoes – A Climbing Guide.* The Mountaineers, 1981.

Secor, R.J. *Denali Climbing Guide.* Stackpole Books, 1998.

Selters, Andy. *Ways To The Sky – A Historical Guide to North American Mountaineering.* AAC Press, 2004.

Sfraga, Michael. *Bradford Washburn – A Life of Exploration.* Oregon State University Press, 2004.

Sherwonit, Bill – Editor. *Alaska Ascents – World-class Mountaineers Tell Their Stories.* Alaska Northwest Books, 1996.

Sherwonit, Bill. *To The Top Of Denali – Climbing Adventures on North America's Highest Peak.* Alaska Northwest Books, 1990.

Smith, Steven D. Dickerman, Mike. *The 4000-Footers of the White Mountains: A Guide and History.* Bondcliff Books, 2001.

Smoot, Jeff. Summit Guide to the Cascade Volcanoes. Chockstone Press, 1992.

Stuck, Hudson. *The Ascent of Denali (Mount McKinley).* Charles Scribner's Sons, 1914.

Washburn, Bradford. Freedman, Lew. *Bradford Washburn – An Extraordinary Life.* WestWinds Press, 2005.

Washburn, Bradford. Roberts, David. *MOUNT McKINLEY – The Conquest of Denali.* Harry N. Abrams, Inc., 1991.

Washburn, Brad. *Mount McKinley's West Buttress – The First Ascent.* Top of the World Press, LLC., 2003.

Washburn, Brad. *On High – The Adventures of Legendary Mountaineer, Photographer, and Scientist Brad Washburn.* National Geographic, 2002.

Waterman, Jonathan. *High Alaska – A Historical Guide to Denali, Mount Foraker & Mount Hunter.* The American Alpine Club, 1989.

Waterman, Jonathan – Editor. *Cloud Dancers – Portraits of North American Mountaineers.* The AAC Press, 1993.

Wilcox, Walter Dwight. *The Rockies of Canada.* G.P. Putnam's Sons, 1900.

Wilkerson, James A. – Editor. *Medicine for Mountaineering & Other Wilderness Activities. Fourth Edition.* The Mountaineers, 1992.

Wood, Michael and Coombs, Colby. *Alaska – A Climbing Guide.* The Mountaineers Books, 2001.

Worster, Donald. *A River Running West – The Life of John Wesley Powell.* Oxford University Press, 2001.

Zumwalt, Paul L. *Fifty State Summits.* Jack Grauer – Publisher, 1988.

"It's a round trip. Getting to the summit is optional, getting down is mandatory."

Ed Viesturs
American mountaineer
(1959 –)

SEVEN

SOUTH AMERICA

The High Andes

Years 1400 to 2011

"The true mountaineer, however much he may value the byproducts of the sports, such as the panorama from the summit, is primarily interested in the mountain as a problem to be solved. A peak does not cease to be a problem because it has been climbed. Every unclimbed ridge or face of a peak no longer virgin is a challenge to the mountaineer. Guideless climbing, winter mountaineering, ski-mountaineering all create new problems. Difficulties, artificial difficulties if you will, are introduced in order to maintain the reality of the conflict, for the essence of mountaineering is not mountain travel but the solution of mountain problems which present an exacting test not only of man's physical resources but also of his mental abilities."

1955
Sir Arnold Lunn
British climber and skier
(1888 – 1974)

South America

The Andes of South America is the longest mountain range in the world—4,500 miles/7,500 kilometers. This range stretches from the Sierra Nevada de Santa Marta mountains of Venezuela on the north to the Cordillera Darwin mountains of Chile on the south. Twenty-one separate mountain ranges comprise the Andes. There are 103 independent peaks over 6,000 meters (19,686 feet) in the Andes. The Cordillera Blanca (White Mountains) of Peru contains seventeen of these high summits and the Puna de Atacama of Chile and Argentina includes thirty-nine more high summits. Seven peaks in the Andes exceed 6,700 meters or 21,983 feet.

Although South America's highest mountain—Aconcagua (22,841 feet/6,962 meters)— was first climbed in 1897, organized expeditionary mountaineering did not begin until the 1930s. During this decade, many of the high 6,000 meter mountains were first climbed. These peak first ascents were recorded and are officially recognized. However, many of the high summits in South America were actually first reached during the Inca Empire which lasted from approximately 1400 to 1530. This early culture left primitive huts, pottery, clothing, and even corpses of sacrificial victims at or just below the summit of several very high peaks (e.g. Llullaillaco—22,111 feet/6,739 meters, Chile-Argentina border).

Due to their relative ease of access, mountaineers traveling to South America have a wide range of summit objectives. Isolated high volcanoes to steep ice-fluted peaks provide endless climbing challenges. This final chapter includes forty-eight (48) peak first ascents, sixty-four (64) first ascents, and sixty-one (61) other mountaineering events.

Ten Highest Peaks in South America

1.	Aconcagua	22,841 ft./6,962 m.
2.	Ojos del Salado	22,616 ft./6,893 m.
3.	Pissis	22,294 ft./6,795 m.
4.	Mercedario	22,209 ft./6,769 m.
5.	Huascaran Sur	22,205 ft./6,768 m.
6.	Bonete	22,176 ft./6,759 m.
7.	Tre Cruces Sur	22,140 ft./6,748 m.
8.	Llullaillaco	22,111 ft./6,739 m.
9.	Cachi	22,047 ft./6,719 m.
10.	El Libertador	22,047 ft./6,719 m

▲ Highest Mountain: Aconcagua – 22,841 ft./6,962 m.
Location: Argentina
First Ascent Date: January 14, 1897
Expedition: British

South America Timeline

1400 – 1499:

Inca Indians climbed Llullaillaco (22,111 ft./6,739 m.) on the Argentina-Chile border in South America. They left huts, sacrificial mummies, and other vestiges of their lives near the summit. The first recorded ascent of Llullaillaco was in 1952. Inca priests constructed shrines as high as 22,000 feet/6,705 meters on over fifty Andean volcanoes from southern Peru to central Chile.

1520:

Portuguese navigator Ferdinand Magellan (1480 – 1521) discovered the area at the southern tip of South America known as Patagonia. Magellan's men discovered large moccasin prints in the sand which they called "Patacones" (big foot).

1582: PEAK FIRST ASCENT *GUAGUA PICHINCHA*

July 29. A Spanish conquistador named José Toribio de Ortiguera and five other Spanish climbers made the first ascent of Guagua Pichincha (15,728 ft./4,794 m.) in Ecuador. This was the first recorded climb in Ecuador. Pichincha is an active volcano near Quito. This climb was repeated by Condamine in 1720, Bouguer in 1736, and Humboldt in 1802.

1590:

Father Joseph D'Acosta recorded the first important description of mountain sickness when he crossed a 14,000 ft./4,267 m. mountain pass in the Andes of South America. He wrote: "I was surprised with such pangs of straining and casting as though I thought to caste up fleugme and choller both yellow and greene. In the end I caste up blood with the straining of my stomach. To conclude, if this had continued I should undoubtedly have died."

1736:

The first major scientific mountaineering expedition to any high mountain range in the world was conducted by a Franco–Spanish expedition led by Frenchmen Bouguer and La Condamine and Spaniard Juan Jorge. As a result of their investigations, Peru's Chimborazo (20,702 ft./6,310 m.) was ranked as the highest mountain in the world for the next 84 years (until 1820).

1738: PEAK FIRST ASCENT *CORAZON*

July 20. Two French travelers, La Condamine and Bouguer, made the first ascent of Corazon (15,719 ft./4,791 m.) in Ecuador. This was one of the first recorded ascents in the South American Andes by mountain tourists.

1782:

Spanish explorer Antonio Viedma is credited with first sighting the Patagonian (southern tip of

South America) peak now known as Fitz Roy (11,290 ft./3,441 m.). This high peak was called "Chalten" by the local Tehuelche Indians.

1802:

June 23. German geographer Alexander von Humboldt (1769 – 1859) attempted to climb Ecuador's Chimborazo (20,702 ft./6,310 m.) via the southwest ridge but reached only 19,286 ft./5,878 m. He was stopped by a 400-foot deep ravine that was 65-feet wide. With him were guides Aimé Boupland and Carlos Montufar. Chimborazo was then thought to be the highest mountain in the world.

1818: Book

German geographer and explorer Alexander von Humboldt (1769 – 1859) took eleven years (1818 – 1829) to complete his book entitled *Personal Narrative of Travels to Equinoctial Regions of the New Continent*. This seven-volume set brought the Andean Mountains of South America international fame.

1831:

French mountaineer Joseph-Dieudonné Boussingault (29) and his British partner a Colonel Francis Hall made the first serious attempt to climb Chimborazo (20,702 ft./6,310m.) in Ecuador. They reached 16,781 ft./5,115 m. but were forced to retreat due to altitude and time constraints. A few days later, they made a second attempt and reached 19,698 ft./6,004 m. but were stopped due to altitude sickness.

1872: PEAK FIRST ASCENT COTOPAXI

November 28. German geologist Dr. Wilhelm Reiss and his Columbian partner Angel M. Escobar made the first ascent of the Ecuadorian volcano Cotopaxi (19,348 ft./5,897 m.). This was the highest active volcano in the world and the first great peak in South America to be climbed. Cotopaxi is the most popular mountain in Ecuador for climbing. The name Cotopaxi means "Necklace of the Moon." The last eruption of Cotopaxi was in 1904.

1880: PEAK FIRST ASCENTS CHIMBORAZO, SINCHOLAGNA, ANTISAMA, CAYAMBE, SARA-URCA, COTOCACHI

January 4. British mountaineer Edward Whymper (1840 – 1911) and Italian mountain guides Jean-Antoine (1829 – 1890) and Louis Carrel made the first ascent of Chimborazo (20,702 ft./6,310 m.) in Ecuador. They established three camps on this mountain (14,375 ft., 16,425 ft., and 17,285 ft.). The ascent/descent from their high camp took sixteen hours (the last three hours in the dark). They all suffered frostbite and altitude sickness. Whymper, in fact, compiled extensive notes on the symptoms of "mountain sickness" during his ascent of Chimborazo. The Indian word for Chimborazo was "Chimpu-raza" meaning "Mountain of Snow." In addition to Chimborazo which they climbed twice (2nd ascent on July 3rd), they made first ascents of these other peaks in Ecuador:

1. February 23	Sincholagna	16,053 ft./4,893 m.
2. March 10	Antisana	18,891 ft./5,758 m.
3. April 4	Cayambe*	18,993 ft./5,789 m.

| 4. April 17 | Sara-Urca | 15,341 ft./4,676 m. |
| 5. April 24 | Cotocachi | 16,204 ft./4,939 m. |

*Cayambe is the highest mountain in the world where snow is actually on the equator.

They spent a total of 36 nights above 14,000 feet/4,266 meters and 6 nights above 17,000 ft. while Whymper studied the effects of high altitude on the human body. Chimborazo was the first peak over 20,000 feet/6,095 meters to be climbed in the world and to be climbed by a European–British mountaineer: Edward Whymper (1840 – 1911).

1880:

February 18. Edward Whymper, Jean-Antoine and Louis Carrel reached the summit (crater rim) of Cotopaxi (19,348 ft./5,897 m.) in Ecuador. They spent one night in their tent 250 feet below the crater rim. Cotopaxi (a volcano) was in the midst of a fiery eruption at this time.

1883:

German mountaineer Paul Güssfeldt (1840 – 1920) made the first attempt to climb Aconcagua (22,841 ft./6,962 m.) in Argentina. He reached 21,522 ft./6,560 m. solo and then retreated. Aconcagua was first climbed in 1897. Güssfeldt continued his climbing and eventually made the first ascent of Mount Marpo (17,448 ft./5,318 m.), a lesser peak near Aconcagua.

1884:

The remains of habitation were discovered on the summit of the volcano Licancabur (19,410 ft./5,916 m.) in Bolivia.

1892: Book

British mountaineer Edward Whymper (1840 – 1911) completed and published his two-volume book entitled *Travels Amongst the Great Andes of the Equator*. Whymper spent ten years in England writing this book about his 1880 mountaineering expedition (six first ascents) to Ecuador. He included 138 drawings and wrote extensively on the physiological problems associated with high altitude. This book was published in the United States in 1987.

[7]▲1897: PEAK FIRST ASCENT ACONCAGUA

January 14. Swiss mountain guide Matthias Zurbriggen (1856 – 1917) made the first ascent of Aconcagua (22,841 ft./6,962 m.) in Argentina. Zurbriggen, climbing solo, reached the summit at 4:45 p.m. after ascending the west side via the Horcones Glacier. There had been five previous attempts to climb Aconcagua. Zurbriggen was part of an expedition that was led by British explorer Edmund A. Fitzgerald who stopped climbing at 6,700 meters (21,982 feet). On February 13, Zurbriggen made the second ascent of Aconcagua with British mountaineer Stuart Vines and Italian mountaineer Nicola Lanti.

---

7 One of the world's Seven Summits.

1897: PEAK FIRST ASCENT TUPUNGATO

April 12. Swiss mountain guide Matthias Zurbriggen (1856 – 1917) and British mountaineer Stuart Vines made the first ascent of Tupungato (21,490 ft./6,550 m.) in Chile. Their final bivouac camp was at 17,000 ft./5,181 m.

1897: Equipment – Sleeping Bags

First ascent of Aconcagua in Argentina. Special silk-covered eiderdown sleeping bags were used. These sleeping bags weighed less than four pounds and proved to be totally inadequate above 14,000 feet/4,267 meters.

1898:

September 9. British mountaineer William Martin Conway (1856 – 1937) and his two Swiss guides (A. Maquignaz and L. Pellissier) made the first ascent of Illimani (21,185 ft./6,457 m.) in Bolivia. This is the highest peak in the Cordillera Real.

1904:

British mountaineer C.R. Enoch made the first attempt to climb Huascarán (22,205 ft./6,768 m.) in Peru. He reached 16,733 feet/5,100 meters on the west slopes.

1908: PEAK FIRST ASCENT HUASCARAN-NORTH

September 2. American woman mountaineer Annie S. Peck (1850 – 1935) and Zermatt (Switzerland) guides Rudolf Taugwalder and Gabriel Zumtaugwald made the first ascent of Huascarán's north peak (21,835 ft./6,655 m.) in the Cordillera Blanca of Peru. Peck (age 58) was the only woman ever to achieve a first ascent of one of the world's major peaks. This climb was Peck's fifth attempt to climb Huascarán that she believed to be over 24,000 ft./7,315 m. high. The Lima (Peru) Geographical Society briefly renamed Huascaran after Peck's ascent Cumbra Ana Peck.

1911: PEAK FIRST ASCENT COROPUNA

October 15. Yale professor, explorer, senator, and aviator Hiram Bingham (1875 – 1956), Herman L. Tucker and two Peruvians made the first ascent of Nevado Coropuna (21,085 ft./6,427 m.) in Peru. This is the second highest peak in Peru and the ninth highest in South America. American mountaineer Annie S. Peck (1850 – 1935) also made an ascent of Coropuna in 1911.

1913:

The first good modern clinical description of other forms of mountain sickness was given by an English physician named Thomas Ravenhill who worked for a northern Chile (Ollague, Chile) mining company. This company had mining camps located between 13,000 ft./3,962 m. and 15,000 ft./4,572 m. He differentiated between a high-altitude cerebral oedemia and a cardiac form now regarded as being pulmonary oedema. Ravenhill was the first to identify the four types of mountain sickness.

1916: PEAK FIRST ASCENT HUEMUL

The first mountaineering expedition to FitzRoy (11,290 ft./3,441 m.) in Patagonia was sponsored by the German Scientific Society of Buenos Aires (Argentina). This climbing party reached the summit of a secondary peak—Cerro Huemul (9,023 ft./2,750 m.)—near FitzRoy. Argentine climbers Lutz Witte, Fritz Kuhn, and Alfredo Kolliker made the first ascent. This may have been the first ascent in the Patagonian Mountains.

1919: PEAK FIRST ASCENTS *ANCOHUMA, HUAYNA POTOSI*

German mountaineers Rudolf Dienst and Adolf Schulze made the first ascent of Ancohuma (21,087 ft./6,427 m.) in Bolivia. During this same climbing season, these two climbers also made the first ascent of Huayna Potosi (19,974 ft./6,066 m.) in Bolivia via its east face.

1926:

January. Austrian mountaineer Juan Stepanek became the first climber to die while climbing Aconcagua (22,841 ft./6,962 m.). Approximately three climbers per year die on this mountain.

1928: FIRST ASCENT

March 5. American novelist James Ramsey Ullman (1908 – 1971) and E. de la Motte (British) made the first American and fifth overall ascent of Aconcagua (22,841 ft./6,962 m.) in Argentina.

1928: PEAK FIRST ASCENT ILLAMPU

June 7. H. Pfann (German, 1872 – 1958), H. Hortnagel (Austrian, 1874 – 1957), H. Horeschowsky (Austrian, 1895 –), and E. Hein (Austrian, 1905 –) made the first ascent of Illampu (20,872 ft./6,362 m.) in Bolivia via the northwest ridge.

1929: PEAK FIRST ASCENT EL SANGAY

August 4. The first ascent of the Ecuadorian volcano El Sangay (17,160 ft./5,230 m.) was made by American climbers Waddell Austin, Robert Moore, Terris Moore, and Lewis Thorne. Sangay is believed to be the most continuously active volcano in the world. This team also made the fifth ascent of Chimborazo (20,702 ft./6,310 m.) on August 28.

1932: PEAK FIRST ASCENTS *HUASCARAN-SOUTH, HUANDOY, CHOPICALQUI, COPA SOUTH*

July 20. A German–Austrian expedition made the first ascent of Huascarán Sur (22,205 ft./6,768 m.) in the Cordillera Blanca of Peru. This is the highest peak in Peru. H. Bernard, P. Borchers, E. Hein, H. Hoerlin, and E. Schneider reached the summit. This same German expedition also recorded eight other first ascents including Huandoy (20,982 ft./6,395 m.), Chopicalqui (20,998 ft./6,400 m.), and Copa South (20,352 ft./6,203 m.) in Peru.

1934: PEAK FIRST ASCENT MERCEDARIO

January 18. Polish mountaineers Viktor Ostrowski, Adam Karpinski, S. Daszynski, and S. Osiecki made the first ascent of Mercedario (22,209 ft./6,769 m.) on the Argentina/Chile border via the west ridge. This is the highest peak in the Cordillera de la Ramada range. It is located approximately 60 miles/ 100 kilometers north of Aconcagua.

1934:

January 30. G. Clausen made the first ascent of Mount Tronador (11,385 ft./3,470 m.) in Patagonia. Other recorded accounts name Friedrich Reichert with this first ascent in 1942.

1934: FIRST ASCENT

March 8. Lieutenant Nicolas Plantamura made the first Argentine ascent of Aconcagua (22,841 ft./6,962 Mount) in Argentina. Five other mountaineers were with him. This was the eighth overall ascent.

1934: FIRST ASCENT

March. A Polish expedition climbed Aconcagua (22,841 ft./6,962 m.) in Argentina via its eastern aspect—The Polish Glacier. This ascent required 3 days and 1,800 ft./549 m. of technical ice climbing. Stefan Dasynski, Konstanty Narkiewicz-Jodko, Stefan Osiecki, and Viktor Ostrowski reached the summit.

1934:

The "father" of Ecuadorian climbing Nicolás Martínez (1874 – 1934) died at age 60. He made the following ascents:

1904	3rd ascent of Antisana: 18,892 ft./5,758 m.
1905	5th ascent of Tungurahua: 16,481 ft./5,023 m.
	7th ascent of Cotopaxi: 19,348 ft./5,897 m.
1911	4th ascent of Chimborazo: 20,702 ft./6,310 m.
1912	1st ascent of Iliniza Norte 16,817 ft./5,125 m.

1936: PEAK FIRST ASCENT QUITARAJU

June 17. German mountaineers A. Awerzger and E. Schneider made the first ascent of Quitaraju (19,817 ft./6,040 m.) in the Peruvian Andes via its west ridge.

1936: PEAK FIRST ASCENTS SIULA GRANDE

Austrian mountaineers Schneider and Awerzger made the first ascent of Siula Grande (20,841 ft./6,352 m.) in the Cordillera Huayhuash range of Peru. This peak later became famous as the location for the incredible climbing story as told in the book *Touching the Void* by Joe Simpson (1960 –).

1937: PEAK FIRST ASCENTS *NACIMIENTO, PISSIS, OJOS DEL SALADO*

February. Polish mountaineers made three significant first ascents in the Andes mountains of Argentina and Chile.

1. February 4. First ascent of Cerro Nacimiento. 21,302 ft./6,493 m. W. Pariski and J. Wojsznis.

2. February 6. First ascent of Nevado de Pissis. 22,294 ft./6,795 m. S. Osiecki and J. Szczepanski. Pissis was named after a French scientist and is the third highest summit in the Andes.

3. February 26. First ascent of Ojos del Salado. 22,616 ft./6,893 m. J. Wojsznis and J. Szczepanski. This is the highest active volcano in the world. This is the second highest mountain in South America. The name means "Eyes of the Salt."

1937:

A team of mountaineers from Italy reached a saddle or col between the peaks of Poincenot (9,961 ft./3,036 m.) and Fitz Roy (11,290 ft./3,441 m.) in Patagonia. This saddle is now known as the Italian Col (9,000 ft./2,743 m.) or Brecha de los Italianos. This was the first time that climbers had actually set foot on Fitz Roy.

1939: PEAK FIRST ASCENTS *SIMON BOLIVAR, CRISTOBAL COLON*

February 2. Mountaineers E. Kraus, E. Praolini, and G. Pilcher made the first ascent of Pico Simon Bolivar (18,948 ft./5,775 m.) in Columbia. On March 16, this same expedition made the first ascent of Pico Cristobal Colon (18,947 ft./5,775 m.). W. Wood, A. Bakewell, and E. Praolini reached the summit. These two peaks of nearly the same elevation in the Sierra Nevada de Santa Marta are the highest summits in Columbia.

1939: PEAK FIRST ASCENT *SAJAMA*

August 26. Austrian mountaineers Josef Prem, Wilfried Kuehm, and P. Ghiglione made the first ascent of Sajama (21,463 ft. 6,542 m.), the highest mountain (volcano) in Bolivia, via the eastern flank.

1940: FIRST ASCENT

Adriana Link became the first woman to climb Aconcagua (22,841 ft./6,962 m.) in Argentina, the highest peak in the western hemisphere.

1948:

A Swiss expedition made the first attempt to climb the fluted snow and ice peak known as Alpamayo (19,512 ft./5,947 m.) in Peru's Cordillera Blanca. These Swiss climbers followed the north ridge until a series of cornice collapses halted their progress. The Swiss called Alpamayo "the world's most beautiful mountain." In the local language, "Alpa" means land and "Mayo" means mountain.

1949:

February 19. Lt. William D. Hackett (1918 – 1999) from Fort Benning, Georgia became the second American to climb Aconcagua (22,841 ft./6,962 m.) in Argentina. Hackett became the first mountaineer to reach the highest summits in both North and South America. With Hackett on his Aconcagua ascent was Argentinian officer Lt. Jorge Mottet.

1950: PEAK FIRST ASCENT YERUPAJA

July 31. The Stanford (University) Alpine Club expedition made the first ascent of Yerupajà (21,758 ft./6,632 m.) in Peru via the south ridge. Dave Harrah and James Maxwell reached the summit. A bad fall on the descent forced these two climbers to bivouac. As a result of this cold bivouac, Harrah lost all his toes to frostbite and Maxwell lost parts of 3 toes. Yerupajà, when translated, means "the butcher." This is the third highest peak in Peru. The second ascent occurred in 1966 after 15 attempts.

1950: FIRST ASCENT

German mountaineer H. Ertl made the first solo ascent of Illimani (21,126 ft./6,439 m.) in Bolivia via the west ridge.

1951:

August 13. A Franco-Belgium expedition made the first ascent of Alpamayo's lower summit in the Cordillera Blanca of Peru. Georges Kogan, Raymond Leininger, Jacques Jongren, and Maurice Lenoir reached the summit. The highest summit of Alpamayo measures 19,512 feet/5,947 meters and was reached on June 20, 1957.

1951: FIRST ASCENT

Ms. Claude Kogan (1919 – 1959) and Nicole Leininger made the first all-woman ascent of Quitaraju (20,276 ft./6,180 m.) in the Peruvian Andes. This was the first all-woman team to climb a peak over 20,000 feet/6,096 meters.

1952: PEAK FIRST ASCENT *FITZ ROY*

February 2. French mountaineers Lionel Terray (1921 – 1965) and Guido Magnone (1917 –) made the first ascent of FitzRoy (11,290 ft./3,441 m.) in Patagonia (southern tip of South America). Five previous expeditions had failed. The native name for FitzRoy is Chalten which is the name of the village at the mountain's base.

Argentine geographer Francisco Moreno first saw this peak on March 2, 1877 and named it Fitz Roy for Robert Fitz Roy, a British ship captain who sailed the waters of Patagonia from 1826 to 1835. Terray and Magnone used 118 pitons and wedges during this ascent. They left a small Cassin carabiner on the summit buried under rocks to prove their ascent. This carabiner was found thirteen years later in 1965 by another summit team. Immediately following their FitzRoy ascent, this climbing team then climbed Aconcagua (22,841 ft./6,962 m.) in Argentina to assess its south face. Terray and Francisco Ibanez reached Aconcagua's summit.

After climbing Cerro Fitz Roy, Terray made the following comment: "Of all the ascents in my life, Fitz Roy was the one that took me closest to my limits of strength and endurance. Climbing it is mortally dangerous; its ascent more complex, risky, and difficult than anything in the Alps."

1952: PEAK FIRST ASCENT *SALCANTAY*

August 5. A Franco-American expedition led by American climber George Bell (1926 – 2000) made the first ascent of Salcantay (20,575 ft./6,271 m.) in the Cordillera Vilcabamba of Peru. French mountaineers

Bernard Pierre and Ms. Claude Kogan (1919 – 1959) joined American climbers Bell, Fred Ayers, Graham Matthews, John Oberlin, and David Michael in reaching the summit.

1952: PEAK FIRST ASCENT *LLULLAILLACO*

The first recorded ascent was made of Llullaillaco (22,111 ft./6,739 m.) on the Chile-Argentina border by Chilean mountaineers Bion Gonzalez and Juan Harseim. They discovered the highest archaeological site in the world with this ascent. Archaeological ruins were found at 21,650 ft./6,599 m. just below the summit. These remains prove that this peak had numerous earlier unrecorded ascents.

1953:

February 20. American mountaineer Richard Burdsall (1895 – 1953) reached the summit of Aconcagua (22,841 ft./6,962 m.) in Argentina and then died on the descent. Burdsall made the first ascent of Minya Konka (24,892 ft./7,587 m.) in China in 1933.

1953: PEAK FIRST ASCENT AUSANGATE

July 24. Heinrich Harrer (1912 – 2006), Jurgen Wellenkamp, Fritz März, and Heinz Steinmetz made the first ascent of Ausangate (20,946 ft./6,384 m.) in the Cordillera Vilcanota of Peru. This peak is considered to be the sacred home of Chief Apu or mountain god of the Cuzco region of Peru.

1953: FIRST ASCENT

September 11 to 15. The first winter ascent of Aconcagua (22,841 ft./6,962 m.) was made by E. Huerta, F. Godoy, and H. Vasalla.

1954: FIRST ASCENT

February 25. A French expedition led by R. Ferlet made the first ascent of Aconcagua's (22,841 ft./6,962 m.) 10,000 ft./3,049 m. south face in Argentina. This one-month expedition placed six (Lucien Bérardini, Edmond Denis, Adrien Dagory, Pierre Leseur, Robert Paragot, and Guy Poulet) of the seven mountaineers on the summit at night. Eight bivouacs were involved and these six climbers all suffered serious frostbite. This ascent represented one of the first big wall climbs in the world.

1956: PEAK FIRST ASCENT *SARMIENTO-EAST*

March 7. Italian mountaineers Clemente Maffei and Carlo Mauri (1930 – 1982) made the first ascent of the east summit of Monte Sarmiento (7,202 ft./2,195 m.) via the south face. This peak is located in the Tierra del Fuego region of Chile. This ice and snow peak was first discovered in 1913 by Padre Alberto Maria de Agostini who led this first ascent.

1956: PEAK FIRST ASCENT *CHACRARAJU-WEST*

July 31. A French expedition led by well-known French mountaineer Lionel Terray (1921 – 1965) made the first ascent of the west summit of Chacraraju (20,378 ft./6,211 m.) in Peru. Terray reached the summit via the northeast ridge and considered this peak to be his most difficult ice climb. Other expedition members were Maurice Davaille, Claude Gaudin, Raymond Jenny, Robert Sennelier, and Pierre Souriac. This was the last 6,000 meter peak in the Cordillera Blanca to be climbed.

1956: PEAK FIRST ASCENT *HUAGARUNCHO*

British mountaineers George Band (1929 – 2011) and Michael Westmacott (1925 – 2012) made the first ascent of Huagaruncho (18,797 ft./5,729 m.) in the Peruvian Andes. Both of these climbers were members of the 1953 British Mount Everest Expedition (first ascent). In 1955, Band and fellow British mountaineer Joe Brown (1930 –) made the first ascent of Kangchenjunga (3rd highest mountain in the world) in the Himalaya. In his later years, Westmacott developed the Himalayan Index—a computer index of 2,850 peaks over 6,000 m. (19,686 feet) in the Himalaya, Karakoram, Tibet, Hindu Kush, and China. Climbers use this index for mountain exploration and research.

1957: PEAK FIRST ASCENT *ALPAMAYO*

June 20. A small expedition of four German mountaineers arrived in the Cordillera Blanca of Peru and recorded ten first ascents including the fluted ice and snow peak Alpamayo (19,512 ft./5,947 m.). Gunter Hauser (29), Bernhard Huhn (23), Frieder Knauss (35), and Horst Weidmann (26) reached these summits.

1957:

Well-known Austrian mountaineer (first ascent of Eiger north face in 1938) Fritz Kasparek (1910 – 1957) died when a summit cornice collapsed on Salcantay (20,575 ft./6,271 m.) in Peru.

1957: FIRST ASCENT

French mountaineers Raymond (1914 – 1997) and Annette Lambert made the ascent of Cotopaxi (19,347 ft./5,897 m.) on March 9 and the ascent of Chimborazo (20,702 ft./6,310 m.) on March 17. This was the first time a woman had climbed either of these mountains.

1957:

The Harvard (University, Boston, Massachusetts) Andean Expedition of 1957 made nine first ascents in the Cordillera Vilcandta of Peru. These ascents ranged from 19,000 ft./5,791 m. to 20,050 ft./6,111 m.

1958: FIRST ASCENT

July 29. American mountaineer Irene Ortenburger made the first female ascent of Huascaran Sur (22,209 ft./6,769 m.) in Peru. This was the highest ascent made by a woman in the Western Hemisphere.

1958: FIRST ASCENT

The first traverse of all three peaks of Illimani in Bolivia was made by W. Karl, H. Richter, and H. Wimmer.

North Summit	: 6,380 m./20,933 ft.
Central Summit	: 6,362 m./20,874 ft.
South Summit	: 6,439 m./21,126 ft.

1959: PEAK FIRST ASCENT *CERRO TORRE*

January 31 – February 1. The first ascent of Cerro Torre (10,263 ft./3,128 m.) in Patagonia (tip of South America) was made by Italian Cesare Maestri (1929 –), Austrian Tony Egger (killed on the descent in an avalanche) and Cesarino Fava (stopped at the Col of Conquest). Their route was up the east face to the Col of Conquest and then onto the north and northwest faces. This ascent has been very controversial. Some climbers have argued that the real first ascent was actually accomplished in 1974 by Italian climbers Daniele Chiappa, Mario Conti, Casimiro Ferrari, and Guiseppe Negri via the West Face. On November 13, 2005, three Italian climbers—Rolando Garibotti (35), Alessandro Beltrami (24), and Ermanno Salvaterra (51)—made the ascent of the northeast face/north ridge and found no trace of Maestri's 1959 climb.

1961: FIRST ASCENT

A Spanish expedition made 38 first ascents in the unexplored Nudo de Ayacachi region of Peru. They also made the first ascent of the northeast ridge of Huascaran Sur (22,209 ft./6,769 m.) in the Cordillera Blanca of Peru.

1962:

January 10. An enormous avalanche from the north peak of Huascaran (21,835 ft./6,655 m.) killed 4,000 people in the Peruvian village of Ranrahirca in seven minutes.

1963: PEAK FIRST ASCENT *CENTRAL TOWER OF PAINE*

January 16. British mountaineers Don Whillans (1933 – 1985) and Chris Bonington (1934 –) made the first ascent of the Central Tower of Paine (8,071 ft./2,460 m.) in Patagonia via the north ridge.

1964: FIRST ASCENT

German mountaineer Anneliese Stobl made the first female ascent of Illimani (21,126 ft./6,439 m.) in Bolivia.

1965: FIRST ASCENT

January. Argentinean climbers Jose Luis Fonrouge and Carlos Comesana made the first ascent of Fitz Roy's (11,290 ft./3,441 m.) west face in Patagonia. This two and a half-day climb represented the second overall ascent of Fitz Roy.

1966: FIRST ASCENT

July 12. American climber Leif-Norman Patterson (1934 – 1976) and Jorge Peterek made the first ascent of the west face of Yerupaja (21,759 ft./6,632 m.) in Peru.

1966: FIRST ASCENT

An Austrian expedition led by Fritz Moravec (1922 – 1997) made the first ascent of the south face of Aconcagua's South Summit (19,778 ft./6,028 m.) in Argentina.

1968: PEAK FIRST ASCENT *CHIMBORAZO-NORTH*

August 10. Five American mountaineers made the first ascent of Chimborazo's north summit (20,275 ft./6,180 m.) in Ecuador. After making this ascent, this summit became officially known as "Pico Norteamericano."

1968:

An American climbing team known as the "Funhogs" made the ascent of the Southwest Ridge (The American Route) of Fitz Roy (11,290 ft./3,441 m.) in Patagonia. Yvon Chouinard, Doug Tompkins, Chris Jones (British), Dick Dorworth, and Lito Tejada-Flores became the third group to reach Fitz Roy's summit.

1969: FIRST ASCENT

July 6. An Italian team led by Riccardo Cassin (1909 – 2009) made the first ascent of Jirishanca's (20,099 ft./6,126 m.) west face in the Huayuash Cordillera of Peru.

1969: FIRST ASCENT

Tyrolean mountaineer Reinhold Messner (1944 –) and Austrian mountaineer Peter Habeler (1942 –) made their first international expedition together to Yerupajá (21,710 ft./6,617 m.) in Peru. They actually made the first ascent of the southwest face of Yerupaja Chico (20,083 ft./6,121 m.).

1970:

May 31. A massive earthquake that measured magnitude 7.8 on the Richter Scale released 100 million cubic meters of rock from the north face of Huascarán's north peak (21,819 ft./6,650 m.) in the Cordillera Blanca of Peru. This rock avalanche buried the town of Yungay killing nearly 20,000 people. Fourteen climbers from a Czech expedition were killed by this 40-second earth tremor as they were climbing Huascarán Norte.

1970:

Italian mountaineer Cesare Maestri (1929 –) returned to Cerro Torre (10,263 ft./3,128 m.) in Patagonia with five other climbers from Italy. With the aid of a gas-powered compressor drill that weighed over 300 pounds (136 kg), this team drilled 400 expansion bolts into the rock face of the Southeast Ridge. This team reached a location just below the summit ice mushroom. They left the compressor drill tied to the rock wall and began their descent. Their route on the Southeast Ridge is known as the Compressor Route. This climbing style was (and is today) very controversial. See 1959.

1971: FIRST ASCENT

June 17 to 21. New Zealand mountaineers Bruce Jenkinson, Murray Jones, and James Strang made a complete traverse of Huascaran Sur (22,209 ft./6,769 m.) in Peru. They ascended the southeast ridge and descended the northeast ridge.

1972:

October 13. A Fairchild FH-227 twin engine turboprop airplane flying from Montevideo, Uraguay to Santiago, Chile crash landed on a snowfield at 11,500 feet/3,505 meters in the Andes mountains of South America. Of the 45 passengers and crew (mostly members of the Old Christians Rugby Club and their relatives from Uruguay), 32 survived the crash but 16 later died at the crash site. The final 16 survivors were eventually rescued 72 days later on December 22, 1972. The media termed this rescue the "Christmas Miracle." In order to survive their ordeal, these young men chose to eat portions of the dead crash victims. The crash occurred near Cerro Sosneado in Argentina. On January 18, 1973, members of the Andean Rescue Corps flew back to the crash site in helicopters to gather the remains of the 29 dead bodies, which were then properly buried. *Alive – The Story of the Andes Survivors* (1974) by Piers Paul Read tells this amazing story of survival.

1973: PEAK FIRST ASCENT *CONDORIRI*

September. Italian mountaineers Angelo Gelmi, Jose Ferrari, and Alain Mesili made the first ascent of Condoriri (18,530 ft./5,648 m.) in Bolivia. This peak is also known as the "Matterhorn of South America."

1974: PEAK FIRST ASCENT *CERRO TORRE*

January 13. Italian climbing team (The Lecco Spiders) led by Casimiro Ferrari made the undisputed first ascent of Cerro Torre (10,263 ft./3,128 m.) in Patagonia. Daniele Chiappa, Mario Conti, Casimiro Ferrari, and Guiseppe Negri reached the summit via the west face (Ragni Route). This mountain has been called the most pointed peak in the world. Cerro means "mountain" and Torre means "tower."

1974: FIRST ASCENT

January 23. South Tyrol mountaineer Reinhold Messner (1944 –) made the first direct ascent of Aconcagua's (22,841 ft./6,962 m.) south face. He climbed solo from 20,998 ft./6,400 m.

1974: FIRST ASCENT

A South African climbing team led by Paul Fatti made the first ascent of the east face (3,937 ft./1,200 m.) of the Central Tower of Paine (10,007 ft./3,050 m.) in Patagonia. This is one of the world's highest rock walls. Michael Scott and Richard Smithers reached the summit.

1974: FIRST ASCENT

American mountaineer Vera Watson made the first female solo ascent of Aconcagua (22,841 ft./6,962 m.) in Argentina.

1976: PEAK FIRST ASCENT *TORRE EGGER*

February 22. American climbers Jim Donini, Jay Wilson, and John Bragg made the first ascent of Torre Egger (9,351 ft./2,850 m.) in Patagonia (tip of South America). This 4,000 foot/1,219 meter granite spire was considered to be the hardest summit in South America. A steel carabiner belonging to Austrian climber Toni Egger was left on the summit. Egger was killed on Cerro Torrre (10,263 ft./3,128 m.) in 1959.

1977:

November 13. Well-known British explorer and mountaineer, author, and sailor Harold William "Bill" Tilman (1898 – 1977) and his crew of six disappeared at sea while sailing his boat En Avant from Rio de Janeiro to the Falkland Islands. Tilman was headed for Smith Island to attempt climbing Mount Foster (6,700 ft./2,042 m.). He wrote fifteen books—seven on climbing and eight on sailing.

1977: FIRST ASCENT

Italian mountaineer Renato Casarotto (– 1986) climbed a new route solo (17-day climb) on the north face of Huascaran (21,835 ft./6,655 m.) in the Cordillera Blanch of Peru.

1978:

March 9. French ski mountaineer Thierry Renard made the first ski descent of Chimborazo (20,702 ft./6,310 m.) in Ecuador. With him on the ascent were Ecuadorians Rafael Gomez and Manuel Santamaria.

1979:

French mountaineer Dr. Nicolas Jaeger, a member of the 1978 French Mount Everest Expedition, lived for 66 days on the south summit of Huascaran (22,206 ft./6,768 m.) in Peru. He studied high-altitude physiology using himself as the study subject. This represented a new high-altitude endurance record.

1979: FIRST ASCENT

American climbers Steve Brewer and Jim Bridwell (1944 –) made the first complete ascent of the Southeast Ridge of Cerro Torre (10,263 ft./3,128 m.) in Patagonia. They found the last eighty feet (24 m.) of the route to be totally blank. There was no evidence of Maestri's 1970 disputed climb.

1979: FIRST ASCENT

Italian mountaineer Renato Casarotto made a solo ascent of the 4,921 ft./1,500 m. north pillar of Fitz Roy (11,290 ft./3,441 m.) in Patagonia. 43-day climb.

1981: FIRST ASCENT

American mountaineers Alan Kearney and Bobby Knight climbed the 2,953 ft./900 m. south face of the Central Tower of Paine in Patagonia.

1981: FIRST ASCENT

French mountaineer Ivan Girardini completed the first solo climb of Aconcagua's (22,841 ft./6,962 m.) south face.

1982:

Well-known American climber and ski mountaineer Ned Gillete (1944 – 1997) made the first telemark ski descent from the summit of Aconcagua (22,841 ft./6,962 m.) in Argentina.

1983: FIRST ASCENT

January 14. A Czech mountaineering team climbed the 7,874 ft./2,400 m. west face of Fitz Roy (11,290 ft./3,441 m.) in Patagonia (57 pitches). Robert Galfy, Michal Orolin, and Vladimir Petrick reached the summit.

1983: FIRST ASCENT

The first women's expedition to climb Aconcagua (22,841 ft./6,962 m.) in Argentina was led by Julia Mesa Ramirez. Of the ten total climbers on this expedition, five reached the summit.

1985: FIRST ASCENT

June 8. British mountaineers Joe Simpson (1960 –) and Simon Yates (1964 –) made the first ascent of Siulá Grandes (20,841 ft./6,352 m.) west face 250 miles/417 kilometers from Lima, Peru. On the descent at approximately 17,000 feet/5,181 m., Simpson slipped and fell breaking his right leg. Yates began lowering Simpson 300 ft./91 m. per stage. Simpson slipped again and fell over a snow and ice cliff. Yates could not haul Simpson back up and he too began to slip from his stance. Eventually, Yates made the decision to cut the rope to Simpson who fell into a crevasse. Yates made his own way off the mountain believing that Simpson was dead. Simpson crawled down the mountain and traveled eight miles back to his base camp. Yates discovered and rescued Simpson. This epic accident and self-rescue story resulted in the book *Touching The Void* (1988) by Joe Simpson.

1985: FIRST ASCENT

November. Swiss-Italian climber Marco Pedrini made the first solo ascent of Cerro Torre (10,263 ft./3,128 m.) in Patagonia via the north face.

1985:

Spaniard Fernando Garrido spent 62 days on the summit of Aconcagua (22,841 ft./6,962 m.) in Argentina. He did this only for the personal experience. Garrido lost all of his toenails and fingernails and forty pounds in the process.

1985: FIRST ASCENT

American ice climber Jeff Lowe (1949 –) made a solo ascent of the vertical wall of Trapecio (18,518 ft./5,644 m.) in Peru's Cordillera Huayhuash. Lowe rated this ascent as one of his most difficult climbs.

1985: FIRST ASCENT

Italian mountaineer Ermanno Salvaterra (1956 –) made a solo first winter ascent of Cerro Torre (10,263 ft./3,128 m.) in Patagonia.

1986: FIRST ASCENT

Argentinean mountaineers Sebastian de la Cruz, Gabriel Ruiz, and Eduardo Brenner made the first winter ascent of Fitz Roy (11,290 ft./3,441 m.).

1986: FIRST ASCENT

Michael Bearzi and Eric Winkelman made the first free ascent of Cerro Torre (10,263 ft./3,128 m.) in Patagonia. They climbed the Ragni di Lecco route on the west face.

1987: FIRST ASCENT

Rosanna Manfrini made the first female ascent of Cerro Torre (10,263 ft./3,128 m.) in the Patagonian region between Argentina and Chile.

1988:

Archeologist Johan Reinhard discovered the world's highest ritual archaeological site on the summit of Llullaillaco (22,111 ft./6,739 m.) in Chile. Reinhard found three small children buried near the summit along with the remains of an altar, fallen stone buildings, scraps of handicrafts, firewood, and ashes. The three preserved children are now at the Museum of High Altitude Archaeology in Salta, Argentina.

1988: Book

British mountaineer Joe Simpson (1960 –) published his book entitled *Touching the Void—The Harrowing First Person Account of One Man's Miraculous Survival.* This book is considered to be one of the best selling mountaineering books of all time.

1988:

Mountaineers discovered an old climbing boot on a glacier beneath Cerro Torre (10,263 ft./3,128 m.) in Patagonia. This boot contained part of a human leg and foot. These remains were determined to belong to Toni Egger (Austrian) who was killed in an avalanche on Cerro Torre in 1959.

1989: FIRST ASCENT

The first winter ascent was made of Ojos del Salado (22,570 ft./6,879 m.) near the Argentina–Chile border.

1991:

December. German mountaineer D. Porche made the fastest ascent of Aconcagua from the Plaza de Mulas (14,272 ft./4,350 m.) to the summit (22,841 ft./6,962 m.) in 5 hours 45 minutes.

1991:

Professor Lonnie Thompson of Ohio State University (Columbus, Ohio) established the world's two highest weather stations on the Peruvian peaks of Nevado Hualcan (20,086 ft./6,122 m.) and Pucajirca (19,836 ft./6,046 m.).

1991: FIRST ASCENT

Austrian mountaineer Thomas Bubendorfer climbed the South Face of Aconcagua (22,841 ft./6,962 m.) in Argentina in fifteen hours solo. He was supported by other climbers.

1992:

As of this year, there had been sixty-one separate archeological sites discovered on mountains in the Andes over 5,200 meters (17,061 feet). Mountains on the Chile – Argentina border contained eighteen sites while those peaks located entirely within Argentina had seventeen separate sites. Fourteen sites were located on the mountains along the Chile – Bolivia border. Peruvian peaks claimed eight sites.

1993:

A British military expedition re-calculated Chimborazo's (Ecuador) height. The new elevation was found to be 20,564 feet/6,268 meters.

1993:

Glaciologists Bruce Koci, Lonnie Thompson, and Vladimir Mikhalenko spent 53 consecutive days studying core samples drilled from the ice on the Garganth Col (19,500 feet/5,943 meters). This col is located between the north (21,835 ft./6,655 m.) and south (22,209 ft./6,769 m.) summits of Huascaran in Peru.

1995:

September 15 to October 5. Ecuadorian mountaineers Oswaldo Alcócer, Oswaldo Freire, Gabriel Llano, and Edison Oña climbed El Altar's nine peaks ranging from 16,570 ft./5,050 m. to 17,451 ft./5,319 m. in one continuous climb (seven days were lost to bad weather).

1995:

A 500-year-old frozen mummy of a young girl (12 years old) was discovered near the summit of Mount Ampato (20,631 ft./6,288 m.) in the Peruvian Andes by archaeologists Johann Reinhard and Miguel Zárate. This body was wrapped in wool and showed the existence of a severe blow to the head.

1995: FIRST ASCENT

Italian mountaineer Rolando Garibotti made an alpine-style first ascent of Fitz Roy's (11,290 ft./3,441 m.) north face in Patagonia.

1999:

March 16. Archaeologist and Anthropologist Constanza Ceruti summited Llullaillaco (22,111 ft./6,739 m.) in Chile and unearthed three preserved 500-year-old mummies on the summit.

1999: FIRST ASCENT

July. The first winter ascent of Cerro Torre's (10,263 ft./3,128 m.) west face was accomplished by American mountaineer Greg Crouch (1968 –) and Swiss climbers David Fasel (1973 –), Stephan Siegrist (1972 –), and Thomas Ulrich (1967 –). This ascent (1,969 ft/ 600 m.) involved the climbing of unstable snow and rime ice.

2000: FIRST ASCENT

July 9. American mountaineer Matt Wade made the first solo ascent of Cerro Sancayuni (17,717 ft./5,400 m.) in Bolivia via the West Face Hanging Glacier Route (first ascent in 1983).

2000:

July. A Dutch climbing team summited seventeen peaks above 5,000 meters (16,405 feet) in the northern Apolobamba region of Bolivia. These climbs included one first ascent and six possible new routes.

2002: FIRST ASCENT

January 17. American climber Dean Potter (1971 –) free-climbed (solo) FitzRoy (11,290 ft./3,441 m.) in Patagonia in 6 hours 49 minutes. He climbed the 6,000 ft./1,829 m. Super Couloir Route.

2002:

January 17. American climbers Zack Smith and Sean Leary summited the three towers (north, central, and south) of the Torres del Paine in Patagonia.

2002: FIRST ASCENT

January 22. American rock climber Dean Potter (1971 –) solo climbed the 5,000 ft./1,524 m. route that Cesare Maestri supposedly climbed in 1959 (a.k.a. the Compressor Route) on Cerro Torre (10,263 ft./3,128 m.) in Patagonia in eleven hours.

2002: FIRST ASCENT

February 16. American mountaineer Steve Schneider became the first climber to enchain the three towers of Torres del Paine in Patagonia (south—8,203 ft./2,500 m., central—8,071 ft./2,460 m., north—7,415 ft./2,260 m.) in a 51-hour continuous climb.

2002: FIRST ASCENT

February. American woman climber Steph Davis (1972 –) became the first woman to summit all seven major peaks in the FitzRoy Massif in Patagonia (southern tip of South America).

2002:

Argentine mountain guide Gabriel Cabrera made six ascents of Aconcagua (22,841 ft./6,962 m.) in one season.

2002: FIRST ASCENT

American climber Samantha Larson (13) became the youngest person to reach the summit of Aconcagua (22,841 ft./6,962 m.) in Argentina.

2002:

French mountaineer Bruno Sourzac climbed the south face of Aconcagua (22,841 ft./6,962 m.) in Argentina solo in 22 hours. This face is just over 8,000 feet (2,438 m.) high.

2003:

A 14-year-old girl reached the summit of Aconcagua (22,841 ft./6,962 m.) in Argentina becoming the second youngest mountaineer to climb this peak. On January 27, forty mountaineers summited Aconcagua.

2004: FIRST ASCENT

November 2 to 15. The Italian team of Alessandro Beltrami, Giacomo Rossetti, and Ermano Salvaterra made the first ascent of Cerro Torre's (10,263 ft./3,128 m.) east face direct in Patagonia.

2004: FIRST ASCENT

Monika Kambic-Mali (Argentina–Slovenia) and Tina di Batista (Slovenia) made the first all-female ascent of FitzRoy (11,290 ft./3,441 m.) in Patagonia.

2004:

The 1959 first ascent of Cerro Torre (10,263 ft./3,128 m.) in Patagonia was finally verified by a panel of Italian experts. Italian mountaineer Cesare Maestri (1929 –) was the climber who claimed Cerro Torre's first ascent. He was now 75 years old.

2005: FIRST ASCENT

January. Slovenian mountaineers Tanja Grmovsek and Monika Kambic made the first all-female ascent of Cerro Torre (10,263 ft./3,128 m.) in Patagonia.

2005: FIRST ASCENT

March 18 to April 5. The first all-free ascent of the Angel Falls Wall (3,773 ft./1,150 m.) in Venezuela was made by John Arran (British), Alex Klenov (Russian), Venezuelan climbers Ivan Calderon and Alfredo Rangel. British climbers Miles Gibson and Ben Heason were also with this team.

2005: FIRST ASCENT

November 11 to 14. Italian mountaineers Rolando Garibotti (1971 –), Ermanno Salvaterra (1954 –), and Alessandro Beltrami (1981 –) climbed a new route on the northern side of Cerro Torre (10,263 ft./3,128 m.) in Patagonia. They called their new route El Arca de Los Vientos ("Ark of the Winds"). This climb took 3 days (2 up and 1 down). They descended the so-called Compressor Route and found no evidence of Cesare Maestri and Toni Egger's 1959 ascent of the north face.

2005:

Archaeologist and anthropologist Constanza Ceruti had summited over 100 peaks exceeding 16,500 feet/5,029 meters while conducting her research and excavations in the Andes.

2006: FIRST ASCENT

February 22 – 24. American climbers Tommy Caldwell, Topher Donahue, and Erik Roed made the first free ascent of the northeast face (4,100 ft./1,250 m.) of FitzRoy (11,290 ft./3,441 m.) in Patagonia. They named their new route "Linea di Eleganza."

2006: FIRST ASCENT

July 31. Pablo Besser, Camilo Rada, Mauricio Rojas, Nicholas von Graevenitz made the first ascent and first winter ascent of Cerro Largo (9,187 ft./2,800 m.) via the northeast ridge in Patagonia.

2006: FIRST ASCENT

September 16. Mountaineers Guillermo Glass, Rolando Linzing, and Dario Bracali made the first winter ascent of Nevado De Pissis (22,580 ft./6,882 m.) in the Andes of Argentina. This is the second highest peak in the Andes. Southwest face.

2006: FIRST ASCENT

September 16. Argentinean climbers Guillermo Almaraz, Eduardo Namur, and Nicolas Pantaleon made the first winter ascent of Cerro Veladero (21,165 ft./6,436 m.) in Argentina's Andes.

2006:

Mountaineer Willie Benegas and members of the North Face athlete team climbed twenty-one 17,000 foot/5,181 meter plus peaks in twenty-one days in the Bolivian Andes.

2007:

November 26. Scott Lewis (1920 –) became the oldest mountaineer (age 87) to reach the summit of Aconcagua (22,841 ft./6,962 m.) in Argentina.

2007: FIRST ASCENT

September 13. Five Argentinean mountaineers (Diego de Angelis, Fernando Garmendia, Guillermo Glass, Rolando Linzing, and Dario Bracali) made the first winter ascent of Mount Tupungato (21,556 ft./6,570 m.) in Chile. This climb (roundtrip) lasted 18 days.

2007 – 2008:

Aconcagua climbing summary:

    7,658 climbers and trekkers registered

    4,548 had climbing permits

    1,400 climbers reached the summit (31 percent)

    278 climbers were evacuated

    1 death

2008: FIRST ASCENT

January 21 to 24. Rolando Garibotti (1971 –) and Colin Haley (1985 –) completed the first ascent of the Torre Traverse in Patagonia. This four-day climbing traverse reached the summits of Cerro Standhardt (8,957 ft./2,730 m.), Punta Herron (9,023 ft./2,750 m.), Torre Egger (9,351 ft./2,850 m.), and Cerro Torre (10,263 ft./3,128 m.).

2008:

December 16. American climber Matthew Moniz (1997 –) became the youngest person (age 11) to reach the summit of Aconcagua (22,841 ft./6,962 m.) in Argentina.

2009:

May 8. French mountaineers Jean Francois Fillot, Sylvain Mellet, and Nicolas Whirsching made the first ascent of the southwest face to the southeast face of Nevado Ticlla (19,348 ft./5,897 m.) in the Cordillera Yauyos of Peru.

2009: PEAK FIRST ASCENT *CONDOR*

September 27. Patagonia Alpine Guides Luis Troncoso, Pedro Binfa, and Christian Steidle made the first ascent of the Patagonian peak now known as Cerro Condor (5,751 ft./1,753 m.).

2009:

November. Anna Pfaff and Camilo Lopez took five days to climb and traverse six high summits in the Cocuy mountains of Columbia. This traverse is known as the Laguna Grande de la Sierra and is comprised of these six peaks (listed in the order that they were traversed): Pre-Concavo (16,733 ft./5,100 m.), Concavo (17,110 ft./5,215 m.), Concavito (16,782 ft./5,115 m.), Portales (16,142 ft./4,920 m.), El Toti (16,815 ft./5,125 m.), and Pan de Azucar (17,176 ft./5,235 m.).

2010: FIRST ASCENT

April 2. German climbers Ralf Gantzhorn, Jorn Heller, and Robert Jasper made the first ascent of a new route up the north face to the West summit of Monte Sarmiento (7,037 ft./2,145 m.) in Patagonia's Terra del Fuego. Over twenty-five expeditions have failed to climb this face. The Jasper team spent thirty-nine hours climbing this face and descending back to their boat.

2010: FIRST ASCENT

November 27. American mountaineer Colin Haley (1985 –) made the first solo ascent of Cerro Stanhardt (8,957 ft./2,730 m.) in Patagonia. Haley climbed the Exocet route (1,640 ft./500 m.) over two days. This peak was named after the German photographer Ernst Stanhardt (1888 – 1965).

2011: PEAK FIRST ASCENT *CHIMBOTE*

April 1. Cerro Chimbote is a rock peak just over 18,000 feet (5,486 m.) on the border of Chile and Argentina. The first attempt to climb it was in 1944. Many other attempts have been made since. Fernando Fainberg and Waldo Farias finally made the first ascent of Cerro Chimbote (18,022 ft./5,493 m.) via its north face. This peak contains three summits (17,717 ft./5,400 m.—18,022 ft./5,493 m.—17,520 ft./5,340 m.).

2011: FIRST ASCENT

August 14. Chilean mountaineers Maria Paz Ibarra and Camilo Rada made the first winter ascent of Cerro Paine Grande (9,462 ft./2,884 m.) in Patagonia. This is the highest summit in the Torres del Paine Group. This peak was first climbed in 1957 by an Italian team.

2011: FIRST ASCENT

August 22. Two British mountaineers made the first ascent of Chichicapac's (18,416 ft./5,613 m.) south face in Peru. Hamish Dunn and Tom Ripley of the Alpine Club took ten hours to climb this face. Chichicapac was first climbed in 1959 by Italian explorer Piero Ghiglione and his partner Forrunaro Mautino.

2011:

September 6 to October 5. Six alpinists from the Groupe Militaire de Haute Montagne (GMHM) made a 150 mile/250 kilometer traverse of the mountains in the Tierra del Fuego of Chile. Known as the Cordillera Darwin traverse, this expedition lasted for 30 days and involved over 57,000 feet/17,400 meters of ascent. Two peak first ascents were accomplished along the traverse. The GMHM was created in 1976 and serves as an adviser to the French Army.

2011: FIRST ASCENT

December 3. American climber Colin Haley (1985 –) and Jorge Ackermann established a new route (El Caracol) on the south face of Cerro Standhardt (8,957 ft./2,730 m.) in Patagonia.

2011: FIRST ASCENT

December 26. Bjorn-Eivind Artun and Ole Lied climbed a new route now known as Venas Azules on the south face of Torre Egger (9,351 ft./2,850 m.) in Patagonia.

"Mountaineering is a restless pursuit. One climbs further and further yet never reaches the destination. Perhaps that is what gives it its own particular charm. One is constantly searching for something never to be found."

Hermann Buhl
Austrian mountaineer
(1924 – 1957)

Cotopaxi, Ecuador
19,348 ft./5,897 m.

Chimborazo, Ecuador
20,702 ft./6,309 m

Aconcagua, Argentina
22,841 ft./6,962 m.

Huascaran, Peru
22,209 ft./6,769 m.

Fitzroy, Patagonia
11,073 ft./3,375 m.

Alpamayo, Peru
19,512 ft./5,947 m.

Cerro Torre, Patagonia
10,263 ft./3,128 m.

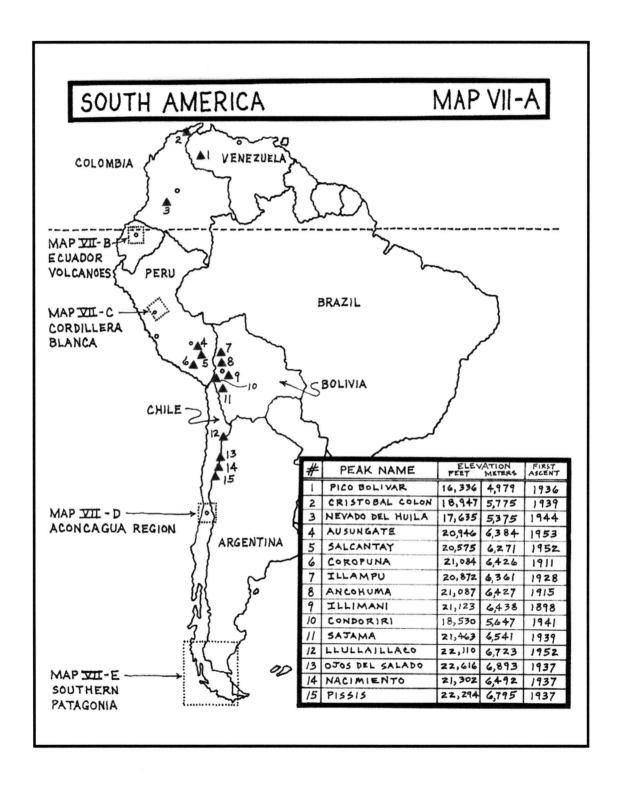

SOUTH AMERICA   MAP VII-A

COLOMBIA

VENEZUELA

MAP VII-B
ECUADOR
VOLCANOES

PERU

MAP VII-C
CORDILLERA
BLANCA

BRAZIL

BOLIVIA

CHILE

MAP VII-D
ACONCAGUA REGION

ARGENTINA

MAP VII-E
SOUTHERN
PATAGONIA

#	PEAK NAME	ELEVATION FEET	ELEVATION METERS	FIRST ASCENT
1	PICO BOLIVAR	16,336	4,979	1936
2	CRISTOBAL COLON	18,947	5,775	1939
3	NEVADO DEL HUILA	17,635	5,375	1944
4	AUSUNGATE	20,946	6,384	1953
5	SALCANTAY	20,575	6,271	1952
6	COROPUNA	21,084	6,426	1911
7	ILLAMPU	20,872	6,361	1928
8	ANCOHUMA	21,087	6,427	1915
9	ILLIMANI	21,123	6,438	1898
10	CONDORIRI	18,530	5,647	1941
11	SAJAMA	21,463	6,541	1939
12	LLULLAILLACO	22,110	6,723	1952
13	OJOS DEL SALADO	22,616	6,893	1937
14	NACIMIENTO	21,302	6,492	1937
15	PISSIS	22,294	6,795	1937

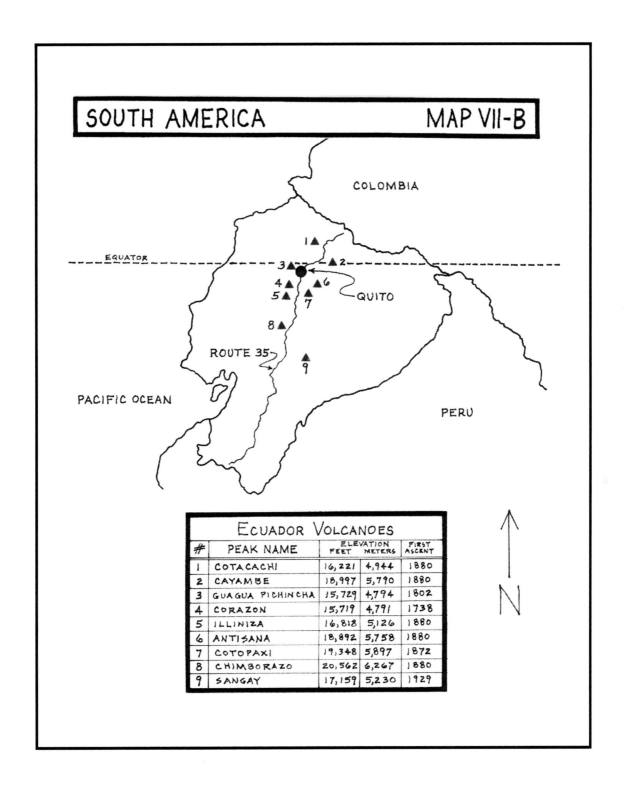

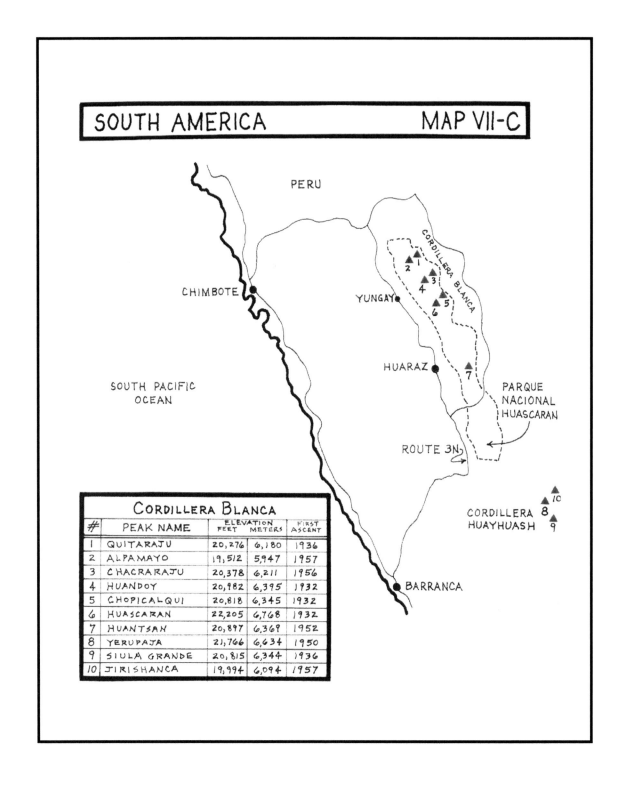

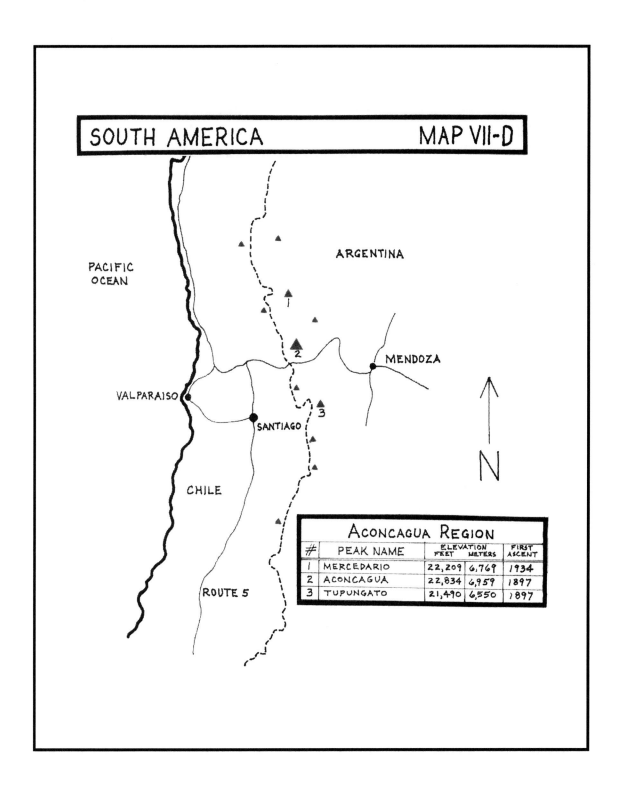

SOUTH AMERICA | MAP VII-D

PACIFIC OCEAN

ARGENTINA

MENDOZA

VALPARAISO

SANTIAGO

CHILE

ROUTE 5

N

#	PEAK NAME	ELEVATION FEET	METERS	FIRST ASCENT
1	MERCEDARIO	22,209	6,769	1934
2	ACONCAGUA	22,834	6,959	1897
3	TUPUNGATO	21,490	6,550	1897

ACONCAGUA REGION

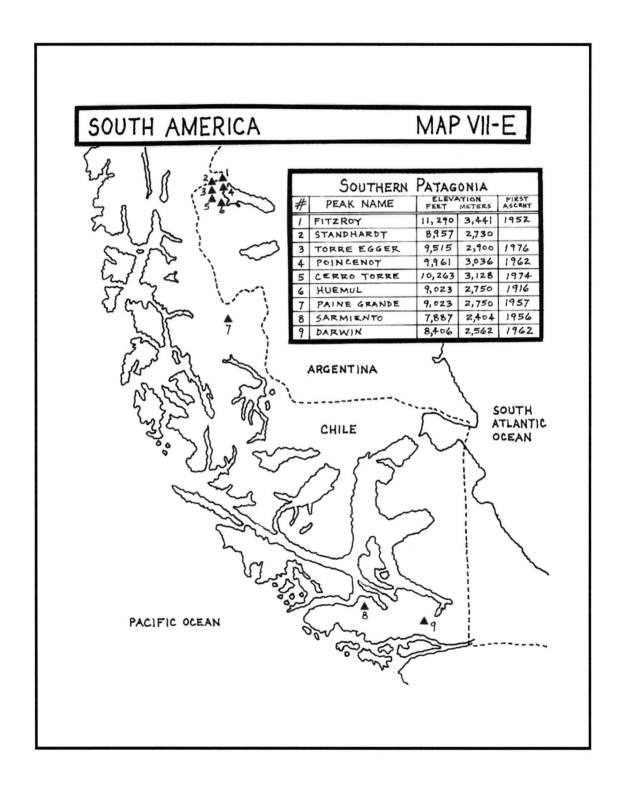

SOUTH AMERICA | MAP VII-E

Southern Patagonia

#	PEAK NAME	ELEVATION FEET	METERS	FIRST ASCENT
1	FITZROY	11,290	3,441	1952
2	STANDHARDT	8,957	2,730	
3	TORRE EGGER	9,515	2,900	1976
4	POINCENOT	9,961	3,036	1962
5	CERRO TORRE	10,263	3,128	1974
6	HUEMUL	9,023	2,750	1916
7	PAINE GRANDE	9,023	2,750	1957
8	SARMIENTO	7,887	2,404	1956
9	DARWIN	8,406	2,562	1962

ARGENTINA

SOUTH ATLANTIC OCEAN

CHILE

PACIFIC OCEAN

SOUTH AMERICA: The 25 Highest Peaks

RANK and PEAK NAME	ELEVATION FEET·METERS	LOCATION	FIRST ASCENT DATE	EXPEDITION	SUMMIT CLIMBERS
1 Aconcagua	22,841·6,962	Argentina	Jan. 14, 1897	British	M. Zurbriggen
2 Ojos del Salado	22,616·6,893	Chile	Feb. 26, 1937	Polish	J. Wojsznis J. Szczepanski
3 Monte Pissis	22,294·6,795	Argentina	Feb. 7, 1937	Polish	S. Osiecki J. Szczepanski
4 Mercedario	22,209·6,769	Argentina	Jan. 18, 1934	Polish	A. Karpinski V. Ostrowski
5 Huascaran-S	22,205·6,768	Peru	July 20, 1932	German	W. Bernhard P. Borchers E. Hein H. Hoerlin E. Schneider
6 Bonete	22,176·6,759	Argentina	1970		
7 Tres Cruces Sur	22,140·6,748		1937		
8 Llullaillaco	22,111·6,739	Argentina-Chile	Mar. 31, 1953	German-Argentinian	Dangl Morghen Rudel
9 Cachi	22,047·6,719	Argentina			
9 El Libertador	22,047·6,719	Argentina			
10 Cazadero	21,845·6,658		1970		
11 Huascaran-N	21,835·6,655	Peru	Sept. 1908	American	Annie S. Peck R. Taugwalder G. Zumtaugwald

SOUTH AMERICA The 25 Highest Peaks (continued)

RANK and PEAK NAME	ELEVATION FEET·METERS	LOCATION	FIRST ASCENT DATE	EXPEDITION	SUMMIT CLIMBERS
12 Cerro Sin Nombre	21,774·6,637	Argentina-Chile	1937	Polish	J. Wojsznis
13 Nevado Tres Cruces	21,753·6,630	Argentina-Chile	Feb. 26, 1937	Polish	S. Osiecki W. Paryski
14 Incahuasi	21,720·6,620	Argetina-Chile	Dec. 20, 1913		W. Penck
15 Yerupaja	21,709·6,616	Peru	July 31, 1950	American	D. Harrah J. Maxwell
16 Galan	21,654·6,600	Argentina			
17 Tupungato	21,490·6,550	Argentina-Chile	April 12, 1897	British	Stewart Vines M. Zurbriggen
18 Sajama	21,464·6,542	Bolivia	Aug. 26, 1939		J. Prem P. Ghiglione
19 El Muerto	21,457·6,540	Argentina-Chile	1950		
20 Puntas Negras	21,325·6,500	Argentina-Chile			
21 Nacimento	21,302·6,492	Argentina-Chile	1937		W. Pariski
22 Illimani	21,201·6,462	Bolivia	Sept. 9, 1898	British	William Martin Conway
23 Coropuna	21,083·6,425	Peru	1911	American	Hiram Bingham et al
24 Cerro Ramada	21,020·6,410	Argentina-Chile	1934		
25 Boneto Chico	20,997·6,400	Argentina-Chile			

Selected Bibliography — South America

Of the numerous books, journals, newspaper and magazine articles, and internet sites that have been used in the research for this book, the author is particularly indebted to the following sources:

Ardito, Stefano. *Tales of Mountaineering*. White Star Publishers, 2000.

Azema, M.A. *The Conquest of Fitz Roy*. Essential Books, Inc., 1957.

Barnes, Malcolm. *The Mountain World 1962/63*. George Allen and Unwin Ltd., 1964.

Barnes, Malcolm. *The Mountain World 1964/65*. George Allen and Unwin Ltd., 1966.

Barnes, Malcolm. *The Mountain World 1958/59*. George Allen and Unwin Ltd., 1958.

Barnes, Malcolm. *The Mountain World 1955*. Harper & Brothers Publishers, 1955.

Bates, Robert H. *The Love of Mountains Is Best – Climbs and Travels from K2 To Kathmandu*. Peter E. Randall Publisher, 1994.

Biggar, John. The Andes – A Guide for Climbers.

Bonatti, Walter. *The Mountains of My Life*. The Modern Library, 2001.

Bonatti, Walter. *On The Heights*. Rupert Hart-Davis. 1964.

Bonington, Chris. *Mountaineer – Thirty Years of Climbing on the World's Great Peaks*. Sierra Club Books, 1990.

Bonington, Chris – General Editor. *Heroic Climbs – A Celebration of World Mountaineering*. The Mountaineers, 1994.

Bonington, Chris. *The Next Horizon*. Victor Gollancz Ltd., 1973.

Brain, Yossi. *Ecuador – A Climbing Guide*. The Mountaineers Books, 2000.

Carter, H. Adams – Editor. *The American Alpine Journal 1964*. Volume 14, Number 1, Issue 38. The American Alpine Club, 1964.

Cassin, Riccardo. *50 Years of Alpinism*. Diadem Books Ltd., 1981.

Cleare, John. *Distant Mountains – Encounters with the World's Greatest Mountains.* Discovery Channel Books, 1998.

Corbett, Edmund V. *Great True Mountain Stories.* Arco Publications Limited, 1957.

Crouch, Gregory. *Enduring Patagonia.* Random House, 2001.

Curran, Jim. *High Achiever – The Life and Climbs of Chris Bonington.* The Mountaineers, 1999.

Darack, Ed. Wild Winds – Adventures in the Highest Andes. Alpenbooks, 2001.

Egeler, C.G., de Booy, T. *Challenge of the Andes – The Conquest of Mount Huantsan.* David McKay Company, Inc., 1955.

Egeler, C.G., de Booy, T. *The Untrodden Andes – Climbing Adventures in the Cordillera Blanca, Peru.* Faber and Faber Limited, 1954.

Frazier, Charles. Secreast, Donald. *Adventuring in the Andes.* Sierra Club Books, 1985.

Hattingh, Garth. *CLIMBING – The World's Best Sites.* Rizzoli, 1999.

Irving, R.L.G. *A History of British Mountaineering.* B.T. Batsford Ltd., 1955.

Johnson, Brad. *Classic Climbs of the Cordillera Blanch – Peru.* Alpenbooks/Cornice, Inc., 2003.

Kearney, Alan. *Mountaineering in Patagonia.* Cloudcap, 1993.

Kinzl, Hans. Schneider, Erwin. *Cordillera Blanca.* Universitats – Verlag Wagner, 1950.

Kurz, Marcel. *The Mountain World 1953.* Harper & Brothers, 1953.

LeBon, Leo. *Where Mountains Live – Twelve Great Treks of the World.* Aperture, 1987.

Long, John – Editor. *The High Lonesome – Epic Solo Climbing Stories.* Falcon, 1999.

Messner, Reinhold. *The Big Walls – From the North Face of the Eiger to the South Face of Dhavlagiri.* The Mountaineers Books, 2001.

Milne, Malcolm – Editor. *The Book of Modern Mountaineering.* G.P. Putnam's Sons, 1968.

Poole, Michael Crawford. *The Love of Mountains.* Crescent Books, 1980.

Reinisch, Gertrude. *Wanda Rutkiewicz – A Caravan of Dreams.* Carreg, 2000.

Sedeen, Margaret – Editor. *Mountain Worlds.* The National Geographic, 1988.

Slesser, Malcolm. *With Friends in High Places – An Anatomy of Those Who Take to the Hills.* Mainstream Publishing, 2004.

Tullis, Julie. *Clouds from Both Sides.* Sierra Club Books, 1987.

Venables, Stephen. *First Ascent – Pioneering Mountain Climbs.* Firefly Books, 2008.

Whillans, Don and Ormerod, Alick. *Don Whillans – Portrait of a Mountaineer.* Heinemann, 1971.

Whymper, Edward. *Travels amongst the Great Andes.* John Lehmann, 1949.

Whymper, Edward. *Travels amongst the Great Andes of the Equator.* Gibbs M. Smith, Inc., 1987.

Willis, Clint. *The Boys of Everest – Chris Bonington and the Tragedy of Climbing's Greatest Generation.* Carroll & Graf Publishers, 2006.

"I am happy on a hill, but I am happiest on a high hill. That is not to say I do not love low hills, but to love is not necessarily the same thing as to be happy. There is a bubbling, effervescent quality in the happiness inspired by the high hills. I feel as though I have been reborn. Care disappears. Worrying thoughts that loom large at lower elevations vanish like dew before the sun. I step lightly. My very body seems to weigh less than it does on the plain."

1935
Frank S. Smythe
British mountaineer
(1900 – 1949)

POSTSCRIPT

It has been 227 years since Mont Blanc was first climbed on August 8, 1786. This date is considered to be the "Birth of Alpinism." Since that August day, hundreds of other first ascents have been accomplished in mountain ranges all around the world and there are still many high summits that remain unclimbed in these same ranges. Many of these unclimbed summits, however, are sub-peaks of a main well-known summit that has already been climbed.

Even though few significantly high peaks remain to be climbed, the opportunity of accomplishing a peak first ascent continues to attract the interest of mountaineers. Many serious and professional climbers continue to scan remote mountain ridges and faces with an eager eye for these possible first ascents. A relatively small group of experienced, highly-technical, and well-conditioned mountaineers have redirected their focus from climbing virgin high peaks to making the first ascent of difficult big mountain walls or a new climbing route on a huge mountain face in the Himalayas, the European Alps, on Alaskan peaks, in the Andes of South America and in other remote mountain locations. For most mountaineers and rock climbers, however, just the opportunity to spend several hours, days, or even weeks on a previously climbed high mountain is enough to satisfy their desire or need for adventure and high altitude.

Since the early days of mountaineering, mountain climbing has evolved into a variety of specialties. Although tramping up a mountain trail to an isolated summit remains a popular activity for many hikers and climbers, a growing group of men and women now practice other more specialized forms or styles of climbing. These forms or styles include:

1. Alpine-style climbing
2. Big-wall climbing
3. Bouldering
4. Expedition mountaineering
5. Guideless climbing
6. Ice climbing
7. Ski mountaineering
8. Soloing
9. Speed climbing
10. Sport climbing
11. Winter mountaineering

The comfort, safety, and opportunity to experience the activity (or sport) of mountaineering has significantly changed since Paccard and Balmat reached the snow-covered summit of Mont Blanc high above the French village of Chamonix. Our knowledge of mountaineering has grown to include hundreds of improvements in what we wear to what we eat to how we climb. Here is a brief list of mountaineering considerations that have been improved upon over the years:

1. EQUIPMENT: Lighter, stronger, more functional.
2. CLOTHING: Warmer, lighter, more durable.
3. NUTRITION: Food preparation, packaging, variety.

4. HIGH-ALTITUDE PHYSIOLOGY: Understanding the prevention of high-altitude illnesses.
5. WEATHER FORECASTING: Accuracy.
6. PHYSICAL CONDITIONING: Year-round programs to increase stamina and endurance.
7. CLIMBING TECHNIQUES: Technical difficulties have been pushed to higher levels on snow, rock, and ice.
8. COMMUNICATION: Camp-to-camp on the mountain, country-to-country, rescue coordination, global positioning system (GPS) technology, use of helicopters.
9. EXPEDITION LOGISTICS: Approach planning, camp supply, personnel positioning.
10. ENVIRONMENTAL: Most climbers and expeditionary mountaineers throughout the world now take more responsibility in keeping their mountain campsites clean. Upon camp departure, all biodegradable trash and human waste is properly disposed of and all other trash is packed out to be disposed.
11. MOUNTAIN GUIDING: Availability of professional mountain guides and guiding organizations in all major mountain ranges.
12. EXPEDITION SPONSORSHIP: Opportunities are now available for individuals and climbing teams to be sponsored (financed).
13. ATTITUDE: Climbers have developed a high level of confidence and courage that allows them to assume more risk.

In conclusion, I would like all mountaineers and climbers to remember their days well spent in the mountains. Common memories may include:

- Approaching a wild and lonely peak in the early morning sunlight.
- Breathing the sweet-smelling fragrance of pine trees below the treeline.
- Crossing clear torrents of mountain water.
- Feeling the climbing rope in your hands—a physical bond to a friend, a partner. This has been termed the "brotherhood of the rope."
- Firmly grasping the ice axe in your gloved hand
- Listening to the quiet crunch of frozen snow beneath your crampons.
- Struggling upward, forever upward.
- Judging the climbing route difficulties ahead.
- Delighting in the grip of a good hand hold on a warm rock face.
- Finding a "bomb-proof" belay location.
- Enjoying the well-deserved unclouded views from the summit.
- Sensing the relief when the last rappel has been completed by the whole team.
- Smelling the fragrance of a flower-clad meadow on the descent from a high summit.
- Remembering and sharing the details of an ascent with your climbing partners once down.

Start early, be safe, have a great climb.

F.L.W.
July, 2013

APPENDICES

"Alpinism defines mountain climbing reduced to its purest essence. Carrying a minimum of equipment on their backs, climbers move quickly and autonomously in a single push. Alpinism means attempting to climb mountains on the most equitable footing possible, neither applying technology to overcome deficits in skill or courage, nor using permanently damaging tactics, and adhering to the ethos from beginning to end."

2000
Mark Twight
American alpinist
(1961 –)

APPENDIX I

WORLD'S HIGHEST SUMMITS* BY COUNTRY**

AFRICA

COUNTRY	HIGHEST MOUNTAIN	ELEVATION FEET	METERS	1ST ASCENT DATE	EXPEDITION
Algeria	Mt. Tahat	9,573	2,918	1931	Swiss
Angola	Mt. Moco	8,596	2,620		
Botswana	Tsodilo Hill	4,885	1,489		
Burundj	Mt. Heha	9,055	2,760		
Cameroon	Mt. Cameroon	13,435	4,095	1861	British
Cape Verde	Mt. Cano	9,281	2,829		
Cent. Afr. Rep.	Mt. Kayagangir	4,659	1,420		
Chad	Emi Koussi	11,204	3,415	1957	British
Comoros-Rep. of	Kartala	7,746	2,361		
Cote D'ivoire	Mt. Nimba	5,748	1,752		
Dem. Rep. of Congo	Mt. Stanley	16,765	5,110	1906	Italian
Djibouti	Mousa Alli	6,767	2,063		
Egypt	Jabal Katrina	8,649	2,637		
Equat. Guinea	Pico Basile	9,879	3,011		
Eritrea	Soira	9,899	3,018		
Ethiopia	Ras Dashen Terara	15,157	4,620	1841	French
Gabon	Mt. Iboundji	5,167	1,575		
Guinea	Mt. Nimba	5,748	1,752		
Kenya	Mt. Kenya	17,058	5,199	1899	British
Lesotho	Thabana Ntlenyana	11,424	3,482	1951	British
Liberia	Mt. Wuteve	4,528	1,380		
Libya	Bikubiti	7,497	2,285		
Madagascar	Maromokotro	9,436	2,876		

* Summits Over 1,000 Meters (3,281 Feet)

** Does not include Dependencies or Territories

WORLD'S HIGHEST SUMMITS* BY COUNTRY**

AFRICA

COUNTRY	HIGHEST MOUNTAIN	ELEVATION FEET	METERS	1ST ASCENT DATE	EXPEDITION
Malawi	Mt. Mulanje	9,846	3,001		
Mali	Hombori Tondo	3,789	1,155		
Morocco	Jebel Toubkal	13,665	4,165	1923	French
Mozambique	Monte Binga	7,992	2,436		
Namibia	Brandberg	8,439	2,573		
Niger	Mt. Greboun	6,540	1,994		
Nigeria	Chappal Waddi	7,936	2,419		
Rwanda	Karisimbi	14,783	4,507	1903	Berthelmy
Sao Tome and Prin.	Sao Tome Peak	6,640	2,024		
Sierra Leone	Loma Mansa	6,391	1,948		
Somalia	Mt. Shimbiris	7,927	2,416		
South Afr., Rep. of	Thabana Ntlenyana	11,424	3,482	1951	
Sudan	Mt. Kinyeti	10,456	3,187		
Swaziland	Emlembe	6,109	1,862		
Tanzania	Mt. Kilimanjaro	19,341	5,895	1889	German
Tunisia	Jabalash Sha Nabi	5,065	1,544		
Uganda	Mt. Stanley	16,765	5,110	1906	Italian
Zambia	Mafinga Hills	7,549	2,301		
Zimbabwe	Inyangani	8,504	2,592		

* Summits Over 1,000 Meters (3,281 Feet) ** Does not include Dependencies or Territories

WORLD'S HIGHEST SUMMITS* BY COUNTRY**

ANTARCTICA

COUNTRY	HIGHEST MOUNTAIN	ELEVATION		1ST ASCENT DATE	EXPEDITION
		FEET	METERS		
Argentine Claim	Mt. Coman	11,992	3,655		
Australian Antarctic Territory	Mt. McClintock	11,457	3,492		
Chilean Claim	Mount Vinson	16,050	4,892	1966	American
Norwegian Claim	Mt. Victor	8,491	2,588		
Ross Dependency (New Zealand)	Mt. Kirkpatrick	14,856	4,528	2005	Chinese

ASIA

COUNTRY	HIGHEST MOUNTAIN	ELEVATION		1ST ASCENT DATE	EXPEDITION
		FEET	METERS		
Afghanistan	Nowshak	24,557	7,485	1960	Japanese
Armenia	Aragats Lerr	13,419	4,090		
Azerbaijan	Bazarduzu Dag	14,652	4,466		
Bangladesh	Mt. Keokradong	4,035	1,230		
Bhutan	Kula Kangri	24,783	7,554	1986	Japanese
Brunei	Gunong Pagon	6,070	1,850		
Cambodia	Phnum Adral	5,810	1,771		
China	Mt. Everest	29,035	8,849	1953	British
Cyprus	Olympos	6,404	1,951		
Georgia	Gora Kazbek	16,558	5,047	1868	British
India	Nanda Devi	25,644	7,816	1936	British
Indonesia	Puncak Jaya	16,023	4,883	1962	Austrian-N.Z.
Iran	Mt. Damavand	18,605	5,671	1837	British
Iraq	Kuh-e Haji Ebrah Im	11,811	3,600		
Israel	Har Meron	3,963	1,208		

* Summits Over 1,000 Meters (3,281 Feet) ** Does not include Dependencies or Territories

World's Highest Summits* By Country**

ASIA

COUNTRY	HIGHEST MOUNTAIN	ELEVATION FEET	ELEVATION METERS	1ST ASCENT DATE	EXPEDITION
Japan	Mt. Fujisan	12,388	3,776	633	Japanese
Jordan	Jabal Ramm	5,755	1,754		
Kazakhstan	Khan Tengri	23,000	7,010	1929	Russian
Kyrgyzstan	Pik Pobedy	24,406	7,439	1956	Russian
Laos	Phou Bia	9,245	2,818		
Lebanon	Qurnat As Sanda	10,131	3,088		
Malaysia	Gunung Kinabalu	13,453	4,101	1858	British
Mongolia	Tavan Bogd Uul	14,350	4,374	1956	Russian
Myanmar	Hkakabo Razi	19,294	5,881	1996	Japanese
Nepal	Mt. Everest	29,035	8,849	1953	British
North Korea	Mt. Paektu	9,003	2,744	1886	British
Oman	Jabal Ash Sham	10,199	3,019		
Pakistan	K2	28,253	8,611	1954	Italian
Philippines	Mt. Apo	9,692	2,954		
Saudia Arabia	Jabal Sawda	10,279	3,133		
South Korea	Halla-San	6,398	1,950		
Sri Lanka	Mt. Pidurutalagala	8,281	2,524		
Syria	Jabal Ash Shaykh	9,232	2,814		
Taiwan	Yu Shan	13,114	3,997	1896	Chinese
Tajikistan	Pik Imeni Ismail Samani		7,495	1933	Russian
Thailand	Doi Inthanon	8,497	2,590		
Turkey	Mt. Ararat	16,949	5,166	1829	German
Turkmenistan	Ayrybaba	10,298	3,139		
United Arab Emir.	Jabal Yibir	5,010	1,527		
Uzbekistan	Adelunga Toghi	14,105	4,299		
Vietnam	Fan Si Pan	10,312	3,143		
Yemen	Jabal An-Nabi Shuayb	12,336	3,760		

* Summits Over 1,000 Meters (3,281 Feet) ** Does not include Dependencies or Territories

WORLD'S HIGHEST SUMMITS* BY COUNTRY**

AUSTRALIA – OCEANIA

COUNTRY	HIGHEST MOUNTAIN	ELEVATION FEET	METERS	1ST ASCENT DATE	EXPEDITION
Australia	Mt. Kosciuszko	7,313	2,229	1834	Polish
Fiji	Mt. Tomanivi	4,341	1,323		
New Zealand	Mt. Cook	12,319	3,755	1894	New Zealand
Papua New Guinea	Mt. Wilhelm	14,793	4,509	1938	New Guinean
Samoa	Mauga Silisili	6,092	1,858		
Solomon Islands	Mt. Makarakomburu	8,126	2,447		
Tonga	Mt. Kao	3,389	1,033		
Vanuatu	Mt. Tabwemasana	6,158	1,879		

EUROPE

COUNTRY	HIGHEST MOUNTAIN	ELEVATION FEET	METERS	1ST ASCENT DATE	EXPEDITION
Albania	Maja E Korabit	9,032	2,753		
Andorra	Coma Pedrosa	9,665	2,946		
Austria	Grossglockner	12,457	3,797	1800	Austrian
Bosnia-Herzegov.	Mt. Maglic	7,828	2,386		
Bulgaria	Mt. Musala	9,596	2,925		
Croatia	Dinara	6,004	1,830		
Czech Rep.	Mt. Snezka	5,256	1,602		
Finland	Haltiatunturi	4,357	1,328		
France	Mont Blanc	15,782	4,810	1786	French
Germany	Zugspitze	9,718	2,962	1820	German
Greece	Mt. Olympus	9,570	2,917	1913	Greek
Hungary	Mt. Kekes	3,327	1,014		
Iceland	Hvannadal Shnuvkur	6,952	2,119	1963	Italian
Ireland, Rep.	Carrauntoohil	3,415	1,041		

* Summits Over 1,000 Meters (3,281 Feet) ** Does not include Dependencies or Territories

WORLD'S HIGHEST SUMMITS* BY COUNTRY**

EUROPE

COUNTRY	HIGHEST MOUNTAIN	ELEVATION FEET	METERS	1ST ASCENT DATE	EXPEDITION
Italy	Mont Blanc	15,782	4,810	1786	French
Liechtenstein	Grauspitz	8,527	2,599		
Macedonia	Mt. Korab	9,032	2,753		
Norway	Glittertind	8,110	2,472	1850	Norwegian
Poland	Rysy	8,199	2,499	1840	
Portugal	Serra de Estrela	6,539	1,993		
Romania	Moldoveanu	8,346	2,544		
Russian Fed.	Mt. Elbrus	18,510	5,642	1874	British
Scotland	Ben Nevis	4,406	1,343	1771	Scottish
Serbia-Mont.	Daravica	8,714	2,656		
Slovakia	Gerlachovka	8,711	2,655	1834	
Slovenia	Mt. Triglav	9,396	2,864	1778	
Spain	Mulhacen	11,411	3,478	1840	
Sweden	Kebnekaise	6,926	2,111	1883	
Switzerland	Monte Rosa-Dufourspitze	15,204	4,634	1855	British
Ukraine	Hora Hoverla	6,762	2,061		
Wales	Snowdon	3,560	1,085	1798	Welsh

NORTH AMERICA

COUNTRY	HIGHEST MOUNTAIN	ELEVATION FEET	METERS	1ST ASCENT DATE	EXPEDITION
Belize	Victoria Peak	3,806	1,160		
Canada	Mt. Logan	19,550	5,957	1925	American
Costa Rica	Cerro Chirripo	12,530	3,819		
Cuba	Pico Turquino	6,476	1,974		

* Summits Over 1,000 Meters (3,281 Feet) ** Does not include Dependencies or Territories

World's Highest Summits* By Country**

NORTH AMERICA

COUNTRY	HIGHEST MOUNTAIN	ELEVATION FEET	METERS	1ST ASCENT DATE	EXPEDITION
Dominica	Morne Diablatins	4,747	1,447		
Dominican Republic	Pico Duarte	10,416	3,175	1851	British
El Salvador	Cerro El Pittal	8,957	2,730		
Guatemala	Volcan Tajumulco	13,845	4,220		
Haiti	Pic de la Selle	8,792	2,680		
Honduras	Cerro Las Minas	9,347	2,849		
Jamaica	Blue Mtn. Peak	7,402	2,256		
Mexico	Pico de Orizaba	18,701	5,700	1848	American
Nicaragua	Pico Mogoton	6,913	2,107		
Panama	Volcan Baru	11,401	3,475		
St. Kitts and Nevis	Mt. Misery	3,793	1,156		
St. Vincent and the Grenadines	Mt. Soufriere	4,048	1,234		
United States	Denali	20,320	6,193	1913	American

SOUTH AMERICA

COUNTRY	HIGHEST MOUNTAIN	ELEVATION FEET	METERS	1ST ASCENT DATE	EXPEDITION
Argentina	Aconcagua	22,834	6,960	1897	Swiss
Bolivia	Nevado Sajama	21,391	6,520	1939	Italian
Brazil	Pico da Neblina	9,888	3,014	1965	
Chile	Ojos del Salado	22,572	6,880	1937	Polish
Columbia	Nevado del Huila	18,865	5,750	1939	American
Ecuador	Chimborazo	20,702	6,310	1880	British
Guyana	Mt. Roraima	9,219	2,810	1973	British
Peru	Nevado Huascaran	22,204	6,768	1932	German

* Summits Over 1,000 Meters (3,281 Feet) ** Does not include Dependencies or Territories

WORLD'S HIGHEST SUMMITS* BY COUNTRY**

SOUTH AMERICA

COUNTRY	HIGHEST MOUNTAIN	ELEVATION FEET	METERS	1ST ASCENT DATE	EXPEDITION
Suriname	Julianatop	4,035	1,230		
Venezuela	Pico Bolivar	16,427	5,007	1936	German

* Summits Over 1,000 Meters (3,281 Feet) ** Does not include Dependencies or Territories

APPENDIX II
WORLD SUMMIT ALTITUDE RECORDS

WORLD SUMMIT ALTITUDE RECORDS—MEN

450 B.C.: 10,854 feet/3,308 meters. Greek philosopher and statesman Empedocles (490 – 430 B.C.) may have made the first ascent of Mount Etna in eastern Sicily. This was the earliest recorded ascent of any peak over 10,000 feet (3,048 meters).

633: 12,389 feet/3,776 meters. The first ascent of Mt. Fujiyama or Mt. Fuji (12,389ft./3,776 m.) in Japan by a Japanese monk named Enno Shokaku.

636: 19,686 feet/6,000 meters. Chinese Buddhist explorer Xuan Zang (602 – 664)traveled from China to India over the Pamir mountain range to obtain Buddhist scriptures from India. During this journey, Zang climbed Mount Lingshan (19,686 ft./6,000 m.) which is now known as Mount Musur in the Tengri range of the Tien Shan mountains of western China.

1400: 22,111 feet/6,739 meters. Inca Indians climbed Llullaillaco (22,111 ft./6,739 m.) on the Argentina-Chile border in South America.

1897: 22,831 feet/6,959 meters. Swiss mountain guide Matthias Zurbriggen (1856 – 1917) reached the summit of Aconcagua (22,831 ft./6,959 m.) in Argentina solo.

1907: 23,361 feet/7,120 meters. British mountaineer Thomas George Longstaff (1875 –1964) and Swiss guides Alexis and Henri Brocherel and a porter named Kabir made the first ascent of Trisul (23,361 ft./7,120 m.) in the Garhwal Himalaya of India.

1928: 23,407 feet/7,134 meters. German mountaineer Willi Rickmer Rickmers (1873 – 1965) led a Soviet-German expedition to the first ascent of Pik Lenin (23,407 ft./7,134 m.) in the Pamir Range of Kyrgyzstan (formerly southern Russia).

1930: 24,344 feet/7,420 meters. Swiss mountaineer Gunter Oscar Dyhrenfurth (1886 – 1975) led a four-nation climbing party to the first ascent of Jongsong Peak (24,344 ft./7,420 m.) on June 3. This peak is located in the Sikkim Haimalaya near Kangchenjunga.

1931: 25,447 feet/7,756 meters. British mountaineers Frank S. Smythe (1900 – 1949), Eric E. Shipton (1907 – 1977), Robert L. Holdsworth, and Lewa Sherpa made the first ascent of Kamet (25,447 ft./7,756 m.) in the Garhwal Himalaya of India. No supplemental oxygen was used.

1936: 25,644 feet/7,816 meters. British mountaineers H.W. "Bill" Tilman (1898 – 1977) and Noel E. Odell (1890 – 1987) reached the summit of Nanda Devi (25,644 ft./7,816 m.) in northern India. No supplemental oxygen was used.

1950: 26,545 feet/8,091 meters. French mountaineers Maurice Herzog (1919 – 2012) and Louis Lachenal (1921 – 1955) reached the summit of Annapurna (26,545 ft./8,091 m.) in Nepal. This was the first ascent of an 8,000 meter peak. No supplemental oxygen was used.

1953: 28,702 feet/8,748 meters. May 26. British mountaineers Tom Bourdillon (1924 – 1956) and Charles Evans (1912 – 1996) reached the South Summit of Mount Everest in Nepal. They were members of the successful 1953 British Mount Everest Expedition.

1953: 29,028 feet/8,847 meters. May 29. New Zealand mountaineer Edmund P. Hillary (1919 – 2008) and Tenzing Norgay Sherpa (1914 – 1986) reached the summit of Mount Everest (29,028 ft./8,847 m.) in Nepal using supplemental oxygen. They were members of the 1953 British Mount Everest Expedition.

WORLD SUMMIT ALTITUDE RECORDS—WOMEN

385: 7,497 feet/2,285 meters. An Aquitaine nun named Aetheria reached the summit of Mount Sinai in Egypt.

1786: 10,164 feet/3,098 meters. British sisters Elizabeth, Jane, and Mary Parminter made the first women's ascent of Mount Buet seven miles north of Chamonix, France.

1808: 15,775 feet/4,808 meters. French woman Maria Paradis (1778 – 1839) made the ascent of Mont Blanc from Chamonix, France.

1897: 18,700 feet/5,699 meters. American mountaineer Annie S. Peck (1850 – 1935) summited Pico de Orizaba or Citlalteptl in Mexico.

1899: 19,450 feet/5,928 meters. American mountaineer Fanny Bullock Workman (1859 – 1925) first climbed (by a woman) Mount Bullock Workman in Pakistan and then climbed Mount Koser Gunge (20,997 feet/6,400 meters) on August 25 in the same region.

1908: 21,819 feet/6,650 meters. American mountaineer Annie S. Peck (1850 – 1935) climbed the north peak of Huascaran in Peru on September 2.

1934: 24,000 feet/7,315 meters. German climber Hettie Dyhrenfurth reached the summit of Sia Kangri West (a.k.a. Queen Mary Peak) in the Kashmir region of Pakistan on August 3. G.O. Dyhrenfurth, H. Ertl, A. Hocht, and high-altitude porters Hakim Beg and Roji were with Hettie.

1959: 24,463 feet/7,456 meters. Eight Chinese women made the ascent of Mustagh Ata in China.

1961: 24,919 feet/7,595 meters. Two Chinese women, Panduo and Xirad, climbed Kongur Tiubie in China.

1974: 26,783 feet/8,163 meters. A Japanese expedition placed three women—Masako Uchida, Miyeko Mori, and Naoko Nakaseko—on the summit of Manaslu on May 4.

1975: 29,035 feet/8,849 meters. Japanese woman climber Junko Tabei (1939 –) became the first woman to climb Mount Everest. May 16.

"There have been joys too great to be described in words, and their have been griefs upon which I have not dared to dwell; and with these in mind, I say climb if you will, but remember that courage and strength are nought without prudence, and that a momentary negligence may destroy the happiness of a lifetime. Do nothing in haste; look well to each step; and from the beginning think what may be the end."

1871
Edward Whymper
British mountaineer
(1840 – 1911)

APPENDIX III
UNIQUE MOUNTAIN SUMMIT COLLECTIONS

The following seventeen (17) unique mountain summit collections share a particular similarity. This similarity can be divided into two major categories: elevation and geography. For example, the 8,000 Meter Peak collection is unique because of elevation—all fourteen peaks exceed the 8,000 meter (26,248 feet) elevation. The Seven Summits collection, however, is unique due to geography—the highest summit on each of the world's seven continents. The remaining fifteen (15) mountain summit collections are unique due to both elevation and geographical location.

1.	8,000 Meter Peaks	Asia	III-1
2.	Seven Summits	World	III-
3.	Second Seven Summits	World	III-
4.	Order of the Snow Leopard Award	Asia	III-
5.	The Munros of Scotland	Europe	III-
6.	The Alpine 4,000 Meter Peaks	Europe	III-
7.	The Six Great North Faces of the Alps	Europe	III-
8.	50 Highpoints of the United States	N. America	III-
9.	Colorado's Fourteeners	N. America	III-
10.	California's Fourteeners	N. America	III-
11.	The White Mountain 4,000 Footers	N. America	III-
12.	Adirondack Forty-Sixers	N. America	III-
13.	The Washington Six	N. America	III-
14.	16-Peak Award	N. America	III-
15.	The Canadian Rockies 11,000 Footers	N. America	III-
16.	China's Nine Sacred Mountains	Asia	III-
17.	The Explorers Grand Slam	World	III-

1. 8,000 METER PEAKS

The most difficult mountain summit collection to achieve is the 8,000 meter peak collection. Only twenty-seven mountaineers in the world have climbed all fourteen (14) peaks over 8,000 meters (26,248 feet) as of December 31, 2011. This unique mountaineering goal is dangerous, difficult, time-consuming, and expensive.

All fourteen 8,000 meter peaks are located in the Himalayan mountain range of Asia. This range is approximately 1,500 miles/2,500 kilometers long and approximately 150 miles/250 kilometers wide. The Himalaya ("Abode of the Snow") straddles the countries of Afghanistan, Bhutan, Burma, India, Nepal, Pakistan, and Tibet. Himalayan glaciers cover approximately 6,000 square miles/10,000 square kilometers. There are approximately 420 mountains in the Himalayas that exceed 7,000 meters (22,967 feet) and over 30 mountains that exceed 7,620 meters (25,000 feet). The most famous and most important Himalayan summits, however, are those that exceed 8,000 meters (26,248 feet). There are fourteen of these mountains not including their eight sub-peaks.

The first mountaineer to climb all fourteen official 8,000 meter peaks was South Tyrolean (northern Italy) Reinhold Messner (1944 –). Messner reached his 14th and final summit (Lhotse) in 1986. He climbed his first 8,000 meter summit (Nanga Parbat) in 1970. Since Messner completed all fourteen summits, twenty-six more mountaineers have achieved this unique goal. They are:

Rank	Name	Nationality	Climbing Period	Finish Age
2.	Jerzy Kukuczka (1948 – 1989)	Polish	9 yrs: 1979 – 1987	39
3.	Erhard Loretan (1959 – 2011)	Swiss	14 yrs: 1982 – 1995	36
4.	Carlos Carsolio (1962 –)	Mexican	12 yrs: 1985 – 1996	33
5.	Krzysztof Wielicki (1950 –)	Polish	17 yrs: 1980 – 1996	46
6.	Juanito Oiarzabel (1956 –)	Spanish	15 yrs: 1985 – 1999	43
7.	Sergio Martini (1949 –)	Italian	18 yrs: 1983 – 2000	51
8.	Park Young Seok (1963 – 2011)	Korean	9 yrs: 1993 – 2001	38
9.	Hong-Gil Um (1960–)	Korean	13 yrs: 1988 – 2001	40
10.	Alberto Inurrategui (1960 –)	Basque	11yrs: 1991 – 2002	33
11.	Han Wang Yong (1966 –)	Korean	10 yrs: 1994 – 2003	37
12.	Ed Viesturs (1959 –)	American	19 yrs: 1987 – 2005	46
13.	Silvio Mondinelli (1958 –)	Italian	15 yrs: 1993 – 2007	49
14.	Ivan Vallejo (1959 –)	Ecuadorian	12 yrs: 1997 – 2008	49
15.	Denis Urubko (1973 –)	Kazakhstan	10 yrs: 2000 – 2009	35
16.	Ralf Dujmovits (1961 –)	German	20 yrs: 1990 – 2009	47
17.	Veikka Gustafsson (1968 –)	Finnish	17 yrs: 1993 – 2009	41
18.	Andrew Lock (1961 –)	Australian	17 yrs: 1993 – 2009	48
19.	Joao Garcia (1967 –)	Portuguese	18 yrs: 1993 – 2010	43
20.	Piotr Pustelnik (1951 –)	Polish	1990 – 2010	58
21.	Edurne Pasaban* (1973 –)	Spanish	10 yrs: 2001 – 2010	36
22.	Abele Blanc (1954 –)	Italian	20 yrs: 1992 – 2011	56
23.	Mingma Sherpa (1978 –)	Nepalese	12 yrs: 2000 – 2011	33
24.	Gerlinde Kaltenbrunner** (1970 –)	Austrian	14 yrs: 1998 – 2011	40
25.	Vassily Pivtsov (1975 –)	Kazakhstan	11 yrs: 2001 – 2011	36
26.	Maxut Zhumayev (1977 –)	Kazakhstan	11yrs: 2001 – 2011	34
27.	Kim Jae-Soo (1951 –)	Korean	12 yrs: 2000 – 2011	50

* First woman to reach all fourteen summits.

** Second woman to reach all fourteen summits and the first woman to climb all fourteen peaks without the use of supplemental oxygen.

SPECIFIC 8,000 METER PEAK ACHIEVEMENTS

1. Reinhold Messner. (1944 –) He was the first to reach all fourteen 8,000 meter summits and he accomplished these ascents without using supplemental oxygen.

2. Jerzy Kukuczka, (1948 – 1989) was the second climber to reach all fourteen summits. On twelve of these ascents, he completed either a new route or did the first winter ascent. Kukuczka climbed all fourteen peaks in nine years, the shortest time period to date.

3. Mexican mountaineer Carlos Carsolio (1962–) was the fourth climber to reach all fourteen summits and he accomplished this goal at age 33 to become the youngest 8,000 meter peak climber.

4. Ed Viesturs (1959–) was the first American to climb all fourteen 8,000 meter peaks. Viesturs has twenty 8,000 meter summits to his credit including seven ascents of Mount Everest.

5. Basque Spanish woman Edurne Pasaban (1973–) became the first woman to reach all fourteen summits (2010).

6. Austrian mountaineer Gerlinde Kaltenbrunner (1970 –) became the first woman to climb all fourteen 8,000 peaks without the use of supplemental oxygen.

8,000 METER PEAK ASCENT SUMMARY

Rank	Peak Name and Location	Feet/ Meters	First Ascent Nationality	Total Ascents Individual Climbers	Total Deaths Descent Fatalities	Information Date
1st	Mount Everest Nepal-Tibet	29,035 8,849	May 29, 1953 British	5,104 3,684	231 56 (25 percent)	12-2011
2nd	K2 Pakistan-China	28,253 8,611	July 31, 1954 Italian	302	80 24 (30 percent)	2011
3rd	Kangchenjunga Nepal-India	28,171 8,586	May 25, 1955 British	209	40 8 (20 percent)	2011
4th	Lhotse Nepal-Tibet	27,941 8,516	May 18, 1956 Swiss	373+	20 3 (15 percent)	12-2011
5th	Makalu Nepal-Tibet	27,826 8,481	May 15, 1955 French	234	26 11 (42 percent)	6-2008

8,000 METER PEAK ASCENT SUMMARY *continued*

Rank	Peak Name and Location	Feet/ Meters	First Ascent Nationality	Total Ascents Individual Climbers	Total Deaths Descent Fatalities	Information Date
6th	Cho Oyu Nepal-Tibet	26,906 8,201	October 19, 1954 Austrian	2,668	47 8 (18 percent)	2011
7th	Dhaulagiri Nepal	26,795 8,167	May 13, 1960 Swiss/Austrian	358	58 5 (9 percent)	12-2007
8th	Manaslu Nepal	26,783 8,163	May 9, 1956 Japanese	297	53 4 (7 percent)	6-2008
9th	Nanga Parbat Pakistan	26,661 8,126	July 3, 1953 German/Austrian	287	64 5 (8 percent)	6-2008
10th	Annapurna Nepal	26,545 8,091	June 3, 1950 French	153	67 8 (14 percent)	2011
11th	Gasherbrum I Pakistan-China	26,471 8,068	July 5, 1958 American	265	25 7 (28 percent)	6-2008
12th	Broad Peak Pakistan-China	26,402 8,047	June 9, 1957 Austrian	359	19 5 (26 percent)	6-2008
13th	Gasherbrum II Pakistan-China	26,363 8,035	July 7, 1956 Austrian	836	19 4 (21 percent)	6-2008
14th	Shishapangma Tibet	26,291 8,013	May 2, 1964 Chinese	274	23+ 3 (12 percent)	10-2009

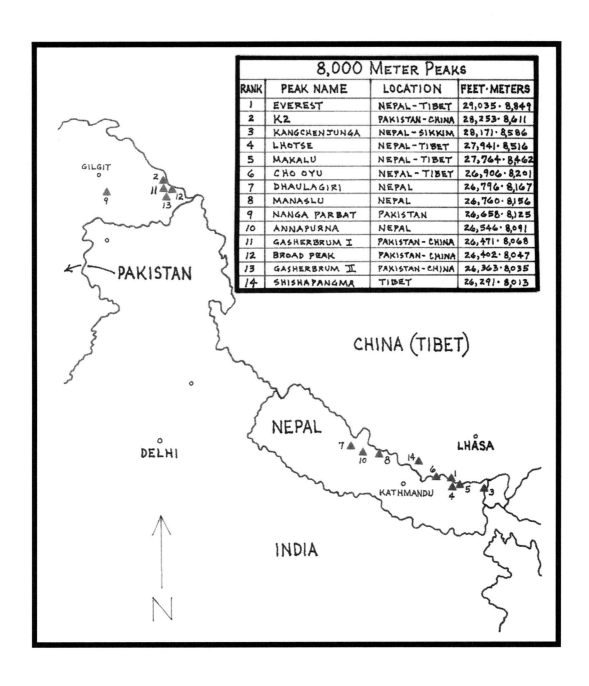

RANK	PEAK NAME	LOCATION	FEET·METERS
1	EVEREST	NEPAL – TIBET	29,035 · 8,849
2	K2	PAKISTAN – CHINA	28,253 · 8,611
3	KANGCHENJUNGA	NEPAL – SIKKIM	28,171 · 8,586
4	LHOTSE	NEPAL – TIBET	27,941 · 8,516
5	MAKALU	NEPAL – TIBET	27,764 · 8,462
6	CHO OYU	NEPAL – TIBET	26,906 · 8,201
7	DHAULAGIRI	NEPAL	26,796 · 8,167
8	MANASLU	NEPAL	26,760 · 8,156
9	NANGA PARBAT	PAKISTAN	26,658 · 8,125
10	ANNAPURNA	NEPAL	26,546 · 8,091
11	GASHERBRUM I	PAKISTAN – CHINA	26,471 · 8,068
12	BROAD PEAK	PAKISTAN – CHINA	26,402 · 8,047
13	GASHERBRUM II	PAKISTAN – CHINA	26,363 · 8,035
14	SHISHAPANGMA	TIBET	26,291 · 8,013

8,000 Meter Peaks

GILGIT

PAKISTAN

CHINA (TIBET)

NEPAL

DELHI

LHASA

KATHMANDU

INDIA

N

2. SEVEN SUMMITS

The most famous worldwide mountain summit collection is the Seven Summits. This collection is within the abilities of many mountaineers if the climber has the time, money (travel, permit fees), contacts within the mountaineering community, and persistence to stay focused on this goal.

There is no dispute about six of the seven continental summits in the world. These six summits are:

CONTINENT/ LOCATION	PEAK NAME	ELEVATION FEET / METERS	FIRST ASCENT DATE	EXPEDITION	SUMMIT CLIMBERS
Asia Nepal/Tibet	Everest	29,025 / 8,849	May 29, 1953	British	E. Hillary T. Norgay
S. America/ Argentina	Aconcagua	22,834 / 6,960	Jan. 14, 1897	British	M. Zurbriggen
N. America/Alaska	Denali	20,320 / 6,193	June 7, 1913	American	H. Stuck H. Karstens R. Tatum W. Harper
Africa/Tanzania	Kilimanjaro	19,341 / 5,895	Oct. 6, 1889	German	H. Meyer L. Purtscheller
Europe/Georgia	Mount Elbrus (West)	18,511 / 5,642	July 28, 1874	British	F. Gardiner H. Walker F. C. Grove
Antarctica	Mount Vinson	16,050 / 4,892	Dec. 18, 1966	American	W. Long P. Schoening B. Corbet J. Evans

However, there is widespread disagreement in the mountaineering community over the location of Australasia's highest summit. Some believe this seventh summit is Mount Kosciuszko (7,310 ft./2,228 m.) in Australia (approximately 70 miles southwest of Sydney) while others claim that Carstensz Pyramid (16,024 ft./4,884 m.) in New Guinea is the highest peak in Australasia.

CONTINENT/ LOCATION	PEAK NAME	ELEVATION FEET / METERS	FIRST ASCENT DATE	EXPEDITION	SUMMIT CLIMBERS
Australasia/ New Guinea	Carstensz Pyramid	16,024 ft. / 4,884 m.	Feb. 13, 1962	N. Zealand	German/ H. Harrer P. Temple
Australia	Kosciuszko	7,310 ft. / 2,228 m.	1834	Polish	L. Hotsky

Over half (57 percent) of those mountaineers claiming all Seven Summits used Carstensz Pyramid as part of their Seven Summits. Several recently published world atlas books, however, do not include New Guinea (the location of Carstensz Pyramid) in the Australasia continent. These world atlases include the western half of New Guinea in the Asian continent. To be safe, many mountaineers have climbed both Mount Kosciuszko and Carstensz Pyramid in order to eliminate any doubt as to their Seven Summit achievement. The debate continues. In any event, Carstensz Pyramid is the highest peak on any island in the world.

The idea of climbing the highest mountain on each of the world's seven continents was first conceived by American mountaineer William Hackett (1918 – 1999) in 1949 after he had reached the summit of Aconcagua (22,834 ft./6,960 m.) in South America (Argentina). Hackett had previously climbed Mount McKinley/Denali (20,320 ft./6,193 m.) in North America (Alaska) in 1947. After reaching the summits of Aconcagua and Denali, he went on to climb Mount Kilimanjaro (19,341 ft./5,895 m.) in Africa (Tanzania) in 1950 and then both Mount Kosciuszko (7,310 ft./2,228 m.) in Australia and Mont Blanc (15,775 ft./4,808 m.) in Europe (France) in 1956. The officially recognized highest summit in Europe—Mount Elbrus (18,511 ft./5,642 m.) in western Russia (Georgia)—was not open to climbing at this time. Therefore, Hackett climbed Mont Blanc, the highest summit in the European Alps. These climbs from 1947 – 1956 gave Hackett five of the seven continental summits. Only Mount Everest (Asia:Nepal) and Mount Vinson (Antarctica) eluded him and he had a permit to climb Everest in the early 1960s prior to the successful 1963 American expedition. For a number of reasons, Hackett could not keep this permit.

In 1981, American ski resort owner and adventurer Dick Bass (1929 –) reached the summit of Mount McKinley/Denali in Alaska. This experience prompted Bass to begin thinking about climbing the other six continental summits. A friend of Bass introduced him to Frank Wells (1932 – 1994), President of Warner Brothers Studio in California. Wells had also been thinking about this Seven Summits climbing goal ever since he summited Mount Kilimanjaro in Tanzania in 1954. Bass and Wells decided to pursue this climbing goal together.

They attempted to climb Mount Elbrus later that same year (1981). Bass reached the summit but Wells did not due to his lack of proper physical conditioning. In 1982, they traveled to Argentina to climb Aconcagua. Again, Bass summited but Wells did not. In late 1982, they were able to join an American expedition attempting to climb the north side of Mount Everest in Tibet. Due to many circumstances, neither Bass nor Wells was in a position to attempt the actual summit.

All of these mountain experiences prepared Bass and Wells for 1983. Frank Wells had worked very hard to get himself in shape for this year. Beginning with a successful ascent of Aconcagua, they went on together to climb Denali, Kilimanjaro, Elbrus, Mount Vinson, and Kosciuszko all in 1983. The only peak left for Bass and Wells to climb was Mount Everest. However, at this point, Frank Wells decided not to continue his Seven Summit quest for personal reasons. On April 30, 1985, Dick Bass reached the summit of Mount Everest at age 55 (the oldest person to summit of that date) to become the first person to climb all Seven Summits. Frank Wells was tragically killed in a heli-ski accident in Nevada in 1994.

The statistics that now describe the Seven Summits list of successful climbers is organized into two groups: the Mount Kosciuszko list (a.k.a. Bass List) and the Carstensz Pyramid list (a.k.a. Messner List).

Over one-hundred people have climbed both peaks to complete their Seven Summits. Here are the lists of the first twenty-five mountaineers to climb the Seven Summits (Kosciuszko and Carstensz Pyramid).

Kosciuszko

Rank	Name	Country	Birth Date	Total Climbing Time	Finish Year
1.	Dick Bass	American	(1929 –)	2 yr. 100 days	1985
*2.	Gerry Roach	American	(1943 –)	22 yr. 163 days	1985
*3.	Patrick Morrow	Canada	(1952 –)	14 yr. 182 days	1986
*4.	Gerhard Schmatz	Ger.	(1929 –)	14 yr. 301 days	1986
*5.	Reinhold Messner	Italy	(1944 –)	15 yr. 67 days	1986
*6.	Oswald Oelz	Austria	(1943 –)	12 yr. 312 days	1989
7.	Phil Ershler	U.S.	(1956 –)	13 yr. 207 days	1989
*8.	Geoff Tabin	U.S.	(1956 –)	9 yr. 323 days	1990
*9.	Rob Hall	N.Z.	(1961 –)	214 days	1990
10.	Gary Ball	N.Z.	(1953 –)	214 days	1990
*11.	Chris Kopczynski	U.S.	(1948 –)	14 yr. 329 days	1991
*12.	Glenn Porzak	U.S.	(1948 –)	18 yr. 220 days	1992
13.	Vernon Tejas	U.S.	(1953 –)	187 days	1992
*14.	Junko Tabei	Japan	(1939 –)	17 yr. 74 days	1992
*15.	Doug Mantle	U.S.	(1950 –)	18 yr. 225 days	1994
*16.	Mary Lefever	U.S.	(1946 –)	7 yr. 315 days	1994
*17.	Hall Wendel	U.S.	(1943 –)	6 yr. 110 days	1994
*18.	Ekkert Gundelach	Ger.	(1942 –)	25 yr. 165 days	1994
19.	Mark Rabold	U.S.	(1956 –)	9 yr. 255 days	1995
*20.	David Keaton	U.S.	(1965 –)	2 yr. 248 days	1995
*21.	John Dufficy	U.S.	(1953 –)	5 yr. 88 days	1995
*22.	Ginette Harrison	U.K.	(1958 –1999)	12 yr. 168 days	1995
*23.	Rebecca Stephens	U.K.	(1961 –)	4 yr. 161 days	1996
24.	David Hempleman-Adams	U.K.	(1956 –)	15 yr. 182 days	1996
25.	Vladas Vitkauskas	Lithuania	(1953 –)	2 yr. 291 days	1996

*Summited both Kosciuszko and Carstensz Pyramid

Carstensz Pyramid

Rank	Name	Country	Birth Date	Total Climbing Time	Finish Year
*1.	Patrick Morrow	Canada	(1952 –)	14 yr. 182 days	1986
*2.	Reinhold Messner	Italy	(1944 –)	15 yr. 67 days	1986
*3.	Oswald Oelz	Austria	(1943 –)	13 yr. 277 days	1990
* 4.	Geoff Tabin	U.S.	(1956 –)	9 yr. 323 days	1990
5.	Jean-Pierre Franchow	Fr	(1947 –)	3 yr. 62 days	1991
*6.	Gerhard Schmatz	Ger.	(1929 –)	20 yr. 18 days	1992
7.	Rowald Naar	Netherlands	(1955 –)	8 yr. 37 days	1992
8.	Skip Horner	U.S.	(1947 –)	3 yr. 161 days	1992
9.	Keith Kerr	U.K.	(1952 –)	7 yr. 259 days	1992
10.	Ralph Holbakk	Norway	(1937 –)	7 yr. 344 days	1992
*11.	Junko Tabei	Japan	(1939 –)	17 yr. 74 days	1992
12.	Christine Janin	Fr	(1957 –)	2 yr. 82 days	1992
13.	Pascal Tournaire	Fr	(1956 –)	2 yr. 82 days	1992
14.	Mauricio Purto	Chile	(1961 –)	9 yr. 258 days	1993
15.	Arne Naess	Norway	(1937 –)	11 yr. 62 days	1994
16.	Todd Burleson	U.S.	(1960 –)	4 yr. 63 days	1994
17.	Ramon Portilla	Spain	(1958 –)	8 yr. 79 days	1994
*18.	Gerry Roach	U.S.	(1943 –)	30 yr. 304 days	1994
*19.	Chris Kopczynski	U.S.	(1948 –)	17 yr. 322 days	1994
*20.	Glenn Porzak	U.S.	(1948 –)	20 yr. 260 days	1994
*21.	Ekkert Gundelach	Ger	(1942 –)	25 yr. 165 days	1994
*22.	Rob Hall	NZ	(1961 –)	4 yr. 345 days	1994
*23.	Hall Wendel	U.S.	(1943 –)	6 yr. 297 days	1994
*24.	Doug Mantle	U.S.	(1950 –)	19 yr. 129 days	1994
*25.	Rebecca Stephens	U.K.	(1961 –)	3 yr. 89 days	1994
26.	Jose Ramon Agirre	Spain	(1959 –)	1 yr. 223 days	1994

*Summited both Kosciuszko and Carstensz Pyramid

As of December of 2011, 357 mountaineers from 54 countries had climbed all Seven Summits. Fifty-four (15 percent) of the total number of seven summiters (348) were women. Those countries having the most seven summiters (as of December, 2011) were:

1.	United States	116 Climbers	32 percent
2.	United Kingdom	32 Climbers	9 percent
3.	Canada	18 Climbers	5 percent
4.	Spain	15 Climbers	4 percent
5.	Japan	15 Climbers	4 percent
6.	Germany	13 Climbers	3 percent
7.	France	9 Climbers	2 percent
8.	Russian	9 Climbers	2 percent
9.	Italy	8 Climbers	2 percent
10.	S. African	8 Climbers	2 percent

The following events are significant in the history of the Seven Summits.

1949: American mountaineer Bill Hackett (1918 – 1999) first conceives the idea of climbing the highest peak on each of the world's seven continents.

1954: After climbing Mount Kilimanjaro in Tanzania, American adventurer Frank Wells (1932 – 1994) begins thinking about the possibility of climbing all seven continental summits.

1956: By the end of this year American mountaineer Bill Hackett had climbed five of the seven world continental summits.

1981: After summiting Mount McKinley/Denali in Alaska, American adventurer and ski resort (Snowbird, Utah) owner Dick Bass (1929 –) began to think about climbing the remaining six continental summits. Mutual friends introduced Bass to Frank Wells in California.

1983: American adventurers/climbers Dick Bass and Frank Wells climbed six of the Seven Summits in one calendar year in this order:

1.	January 21, 1983	Aconcagua
2.	July 6, 1983	Denali
3.	September 1, 1983	Kilimanjaro
4.	September 13, 1983	Elbrus
5.	November 30, 1983	Mount Vinson
6.	December , 1983	Kosciuszko

Only Mount Everest remained.

1985: Richard Daniel "Dick" Bass (1929 –) reached the summit of Mount Everest on April 30,1985.

1991: Japanese woman mountaineer Junko Tabei (1939 –) became both the first woman and the oldest woman (age 52) to date to complete the Seven Summits. She was the 12th climber overall.

1992: New Zealand mountaineers Gary Ball (1953 – 1991) and Rob Hall (1961 – 1996) climbed all Seven Summits in seven months to the day (May 10 – December 10, 1990). They were the 9th and 10th seven summiters. Kosciuszko list.

1992: German mountaineer Gerhard Schmatz (1929 –) and Norwegian mountaineer Arne Naess (1937 –) tied for being the oldest climber to complete the Seven Summits (age 57).

1994: American woman mountaineer Dolly Lefever (1946 –) became the first American woman (age 48) to reach all Seven Summits. She was the 26th seven summiter. Kosciuszko list.

2001: British mountaineer Andrew Salter completed the climbing of all Seven Summit in 288 days. Carstensz Pyramid List.

2002: American mountaineer Erik Weihenmayer (1968 –) became the first blind climber to reach all Seven Summits. Overall, he was the 104th person. Kosciuszko list.

2002: American climbers Phil (1951 –) and Susan Ershler became the first married couple to climb the Seven Summits.

2003: Spanish mountaineer Ramon Blanco (1933 –) became the oldest person to climb all Seven Summits when he reached the summit of Kosciuszko in Australia on December 29 at age 70 years 242 days. Blanco took twenty-eight years to accomplish this mountaineering goal.

2005: American mountaineer Marshall Ulrich (1952 –) became the 134th person to climb the Seven Summits. Ulrich accomplished this goal in 2 years 267 days at age 53. Kosciuszko list.

2005: British mountaineer Annabelle Bond (1969 –) climbed the Seven Summits in 360 days—a new women's record and the fourth fastest overall time. Kosciuszko list.

2006: December. Slovenian ski mountaineer Davorin Karnicar (1962 –) became the first person to ski down all seven peaks (Kosciuszko list).

2007: Austrian mountaineer Christian Stangl (1966 –) completed the Seven Summits in a record total ascent time of 58 hours 45 minutes (base camp to summit). Stangl took 4 years 286 days to climb all Seven Summits (Carstensz Pyramid list).

2010: Japanese mountaineer Takao Arayama (1935 –) at age 74 years 138 days became the oldest person to climb the Seven Summits (Carstensz Pyramid list). Arayama took 10 years 228 days to achieve this goal.

2010: American mountaineer Vernon Tejas (1953 –) set the record for the shortest time to climb all Seven Summits: 134 days (January 18 – May 31). This was the ninth time that Tejas had climbed all Seven Summits.

2011: December 24. American climber Jordan Romero (1996 –) reached the summit of Mount Vinson (16,077 ft./4,900 m.) in Antarctica to become the youngest person (15 years, 5 months, 12 days) to complete the Seven Summits.

2011: December 31. As of this date:
- 357 mountaineers had climbed the Seven Summits since 1985.
- 54 women (15 percent) had climbed the Seven Summits.
- 122 mountaineers have reached the summits of both Mount Kosciuszko and Carstensz Pyramid.

3. SEVEN SECOND SUMMITS

On January 14, 2012, Italian mountaineer Hans Kammerlander (1956 –) became the first person to climb the Seven Second Summits. These seven peaks represent the second highest mountains on each of the world's seven continents. Kammerlander's final climb was up Mount Tyree (15,919 ft./4,852 m.) in Antarctica. Many mountaineers believe that the Seven Second Summits are more technically difficult to climb than the original Seven Summits.

Seven Second Summits of the World

Africa:	Mount Kenya	17,058 ft./5,199 m.
Antarctica:	Mount Tyree	15,919 ft./4,852 m.
Asia:	K2	28,251 ft./8,610 m.
Australia:	Mount Townsend	7,247 ft./2,209 m.
Europe:	Dych Tau	17,073 ft./5,203 m.
North America:	Mount Logan	19,550 ft./5,958 m.
South America:	Ojos del Salado	22,614 ft./6,892 m.
(Australasia:	Puncak Trikora	15,518 ft./4,729 m.)

Kammerlander's climbing sequence was as follows: K2 (2001), Mount Kenya (2009), Ojos del Salado (2009), Mount Logan (2010), Dych Tau (2010), Puncak Trikora (2011), and Mount Tyree (2012).

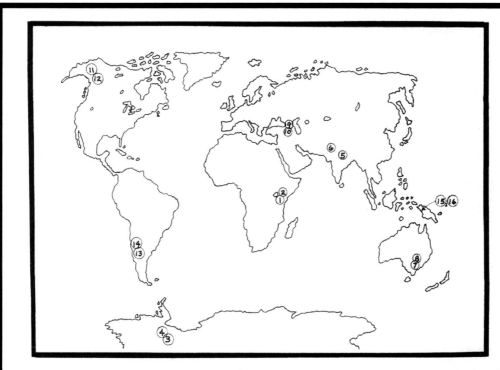

SEVEN SUMMITS					SEVEN 2ND SUMMITS			
CONTINENT	#	PEAK NAME	FEET	METERS	#	PEAK NAME	FEET	METERS
AFRICA	1	KILIMANJARO	19,341	5,895	2	KENYA	17,058	5,199
ANTARCTICA	3	VINSON MASSIF	16,077	4,900	4	TYREE	15,919	4,852
ASIA	5	EVEREST	29,035	8,849	6	K2	28,251	8,610
AUSTRALIA	7	KOSCIUSKO	7,310	2,228	8	TOWNSEND	7,247	2,209
EUROPE	9	ELBRUS	18,510	5,642	10	DYCH TAU	17,074	5,204
NORTH AMERICA	11	DENALI	20,320	6,193	12	LOGAN	19,550	5,958
SOUTH AMERICA	13	ACONCAGUA	22,834	6,959	14	OJOS DEL SALADO	22,614	6,892
AUSTRALASIA	15	CARSTENSZ PYR.	16,024	4,884	16	PUNCAK TRIKORA	15,518	4,729

4. ORDER OF THE SNOW LEOPARD AWARD

This award is presented to those mountaineers who have climbed the five 7,000 meter peaks in the former Soviet Union. These five peaks are located in the Pamir Range of Uzbekistan and Kyrgyzstan, and the Tien Shan Range ("Celestial Mountains" in Chinese) of Kazakhstan and Kyrgyzstan.

1970: Russian mountaineer Dr. Anatoly Outchinnikov (1927 –) was the first climber to earn the Snow Leopard Award by climbing four peaks (#1 – #4). Khan Tengri was added at a later date.

1985: July. American mountaineers William Garner and Randall Starrett became the first non-Soviet climbers to earn the Order of the Snow Leopard with their ascent of Pik Pobeda.

1994: Turkish mountaineer Nasuh Mahruki (1968 –) earned the award. He climbed all five peaks between 1992 – 1994.

1996: American mountaineer Andy Evans became a member of a very small group of non-Russian (formerly the Soviet Union) mountaineers to earn the Order of the Snow Leopard. Evans reached the summit of Pik Pobeda on August 22 with Australian climber Paul Walters.

1999: Russian mountaineer Denis Urubko reached all five summits within the span of 4 days (Summer).

2001: Russian mountaineer Evgueni Vinogradsky had climbed all five peaks four times.

2010: Russian mountaineer Boris Korshunov (1941 –) completed his ninth circuit of climbing all five Snow Leopard peaks (1981 – 2010). He completed this ninth circuit at age 69.

2011: As of this year, 611 climbers (including 29 women) had received the Snow Leopard Award (1970 – 2011).

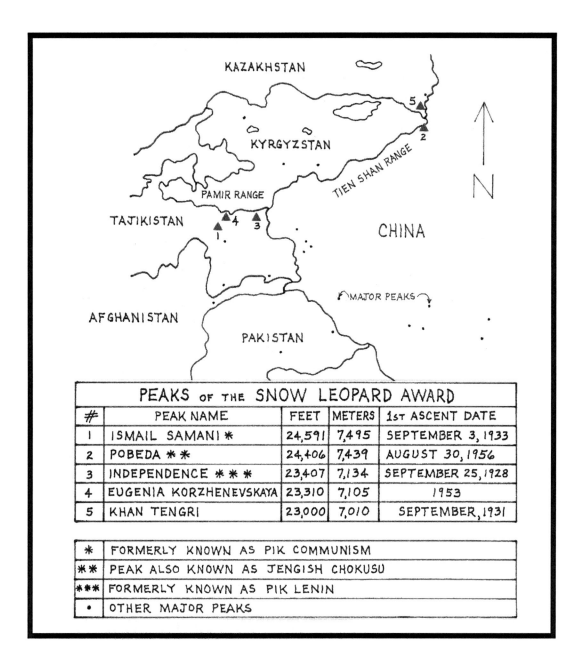

KAZAKHSTAN

KYRGYZSTAN

PAMIR RANGE

TIEN SHAN RANGE

TAJIKISTAN

CHINA

AFGHANISTAN

MAJOR PEAKS

PAKISTAN

PEAKS OF THE SNOW LEOPARD AWARD

#	PEAK NAME	FEET	METERS	1ST ASCENT DATE
1	ISMAIL SAMANI *	24,591	7,495	SEPTEMBER 3, 1933
2	POBEDA **	24,406	7,439	AUGUST 30, 1956
3	INDEPENDENCE ***	23,407	7,134	SEPTEMBER 25, 1928
4	EUGENIA KORZHENEVSKAYA	23,310	7,105	1953
5	KHAN TENGRI	23,000	7,010	SEPTEMBER, 1931

*	FORMERLY KNOWN AS PIK COMMUNISM
**	PEAK ALSO KNOWN AS JENGISH CHOKUSU
***	FORMERLY KNOWN AS PIK LENIN
•	OTHER MAJOR PEAKS

5. THE MUNROS OF SCOTLAND

1884: 236 mountains in Scotland were known to exceed 3,000 feet (914 meters).

1891: Sir Hugh Munro (1856 – 1919), a founding member and first president of the Scottish Mountaineering Club, first published his list of 3,000 foot mountains in Scotland. These 236 summits became known as "Munros." Munro eventually climbed all but two of these summits. The number of recognized "Munros" has increased several times since 1891. As of 2007, this number stood at 297.
1901: The first "Munroist," the Reverend A.E. Robertson, was the first person to climb all 236 identified summits over a ten-year period (1891 – 1901).

1923: The Rev. A.R.G. Burn became the second "Munroist" to complete the climbing of all 236 summits.

1947: A Mrs. Hurst became the first woman to climb all of the Munros. She and her husband became the first husband and wife team to climb all of the summits.

1974: Forty-one additional mountain tops were recognized as being "Munros" bringing the total to 277 summits.

1984: 381 climbers had now climbed all of the Munros.

1985: Scottish climber Martin Moran made the first non-stop winter traverse of the Munros in 81 days (December 23, 1984 – March 13, 1985). Moran hiked, climbed, and skied to 283 summits.

1990: Over 600 climbers had claimed to have climbed all 283 Munros.

1999: Fourteen additional new summits joined the Munros for a total of 297 summits inScotland exceeding 3,000 feet (914 meters). Forty six percent (137) of all Munro summits exceed 1,000 meters (3,281 feet).

Note: Scotland contains several other mountain summit categories. Here are two of them:
    Corbetts – Peak Summits between 2,500 feet (762 m.) – 2,999 feet (914 m.). There are 221 of these summits which as a group were named after John Rooke Corbett (1876 – 1949) who first published the official list.
    Grahams – These peaks range from 2,000 feet (610 m.) – 2,499 feet (762 m.). This group of 224 summits were named after Fiona Torbet Graham who first published this list in the early 1990s.

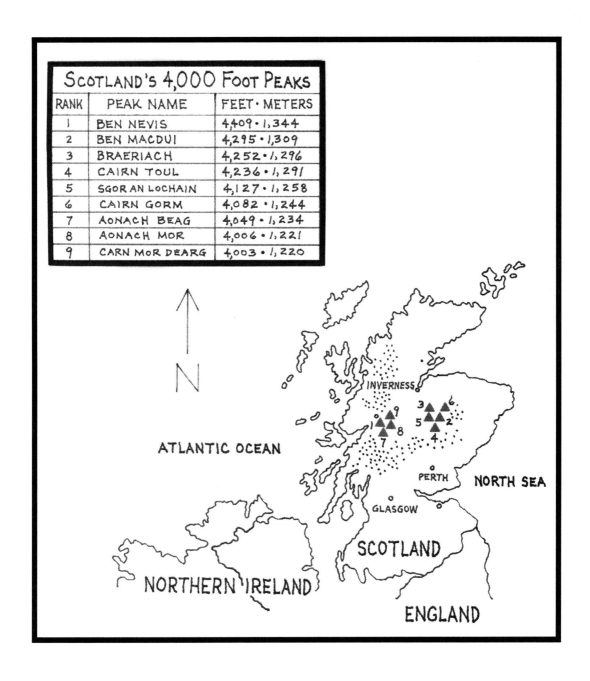

RANK	PEAK NAME	FEET · METERS
1	BEN NEVIS	4,409 · 1,344
2	BEN MACDUI	4,295 · 1,309
3	BRAERIACH	4,252 · 1,296
4	CAIRN TOUL	4,236 · 1,291
5	SGOR AN LOCHAIN	4,127 · 1,258
6	CAIRN GORM	4,082 · 1,244
7	AONACH BEAG	4,049 · 1,234
8	AONACH MOR	4,006 · 1,221
9	CARN MOR DEARG	4,003 · 1,220

SCOTLAND'S 4,000 FOOT PEAKS

6. THE ALPINE 4,000-METER PEAKS

The European Alps include approximately 700 peaks over 10,000 feet/3,048 meters, 120 peaks over 12,000 feet/3,657 meters, 23 main peaks over 14,000 feet/4,267 meters, and 4 main peaks over 15,000 feet/4,572 meters. Since the early 1900s mountaineers have been fascinated with climbing all of those peaks over 4,000 meters (or 13,124 feet). As measurement techniques improved, the list of 4,000-meter peaks expanded. The U.I.A.A. (Union Internationale Des Associations d'Alpinisme) added 21 new summits to the official list of 61 peaks over 4,000 meters in 1994 bringing the new official list up to 82 summits.

1911: The first mountaineer to climb all of the sixty-one 4,000 meter peaks (pre-1994) in the Alps was Austrian climber Karl Blodig (1859 – 1956). Blodig was 52 years old when he completed his 61st ascent. He climbed his 75th and 76th 4,000 meter peaks (his own list) in 1932 at age 73.

1932: British mountaineer Eustace Thomas (1869 – 1960) became the first Englishman to climb all 61 peaks (1924 – 1932). Thomas hired the well-known mountain guide Joseph Knubel (1881 – 1961) for most of his climbs.

1968: German mountaineer and alpine historian Helmut Dumler (1940 –) completed the 4,000 meter peak list (61 peaks).

1981: British mountaineer Will McLewin completed the 61 peaks plus 39 insignificant ridge points for a total of 100 summits in the Alps.

1993: British mountaineers Martin Moran and Simon Jenkins achieved the first continuous traverse of seventy-five 4,000 meter peaks in the Alps.

2011: September 10. Swiss mountaineer Michi Lerjen (1985 –) became the youngest mountain guide (age 25, eleven days from his 26th birthday) to climb all of the 4,000 meter peaks in the European Alps (82 summits). Lerjen climbed his first 4,000 meter summit—the Matterhorn—at age 11 with his father. His 82nd summit was the Jungfrau.

The Alpine 4,000 Meter Peaks

Rank	Peak Name	Location	Elevation Feet / Meters	First Ascent Date
1	Mont Blanc	Mont Blanc Massif	15,782 / 4,810	1786
2	Mont Blanc de Courmayeur	Mont Blanc Massif	15,578 / 4,748	1878

Rank	Peak Name	Location	Elevation Feet / Meters	First Ascent Date
3	Dufourspitze-Monte Rosa	Pennine Alps	15,204 / 4,634	1855
4	Nordend-Monte Rosa	Pennine Alps	15,121 / 4,609	1861
5	Zumsteinspitze-Monte Rosa	Pennine Alps	14,971 / 4,563	1820
6	Signalkuppe-Monte Rosa	Pennine Alps	14,948 / 4,556	1842
7	Dom	N. Pennine Alps	14,911 / 4,545	1858
8	Liskamm West	Pennine Alps	14,853 / 4,527	1861
9	Weisshorn	NW Pennine Alps	14,781 / 4,505	1861
10	Taschhorn	N. Pennine Alps	14,731 / 4,490	1862
11	Liskamm West	Pennine Alps	14,695 / 4,479	1864
12	Matterhorn	Pennine Alps	14,692 / 4,478	1865
13	Mont Blanc-Pic Luigi Amedeo	Mont Blanc Massif	14,663 / 4,469	1901
14	Mont Maudit	Mont Blanc Massif	14,650 / 4,465	1878
15	Parrotspitze-Mont Blanc	Mont Blanc Massif	14,555 / 4,436	1863
16	Dent Blanche	NW Pennine Alps	14,292 / 4,356	1862
17	Ludwigshohe	Pennine Alps	14,243 / 4,341	1822
18	Nadelhorn	N. Pennine Alps	14,197 / 4,327	1858
19	Schwarzhorn	Pennine Alps	14,177 / 4,321	1873

Rank	Peak Name	Location	Elevation Feet / Meters	First Ascent Date
20	Grand Combin de Grafeniere	Pennine Alps West	14,154 / 4,314	1857
21	Mont Blanc- Dome du Gouter	Mont Blanc Massif	14,121 / 4,304	1784
22	Lenzspitze	N. Pennine Alps	14,089 / 4,294	1870
23	Finsteraarhorn	E. Bernese Alps	14,020 / 4,273	1812
24	Mont Blanc du Tacul	Mont Blanc Massif	13,934 / 4,247	1855
25	Mont Blanc- Grand Pilier d' Angle	Mont Blanc Massif	13,921 / 4,243	1959
26	Stecknadelhorn	N. Pennine Alps	13,915 / 4,241	1887
27	Castor	Pennine Alps	13,872 / 4,228	1861
28	Zinalrothorn	NW Pennine Alps	13,849 / 4,221	1864
29	Hohberghorn	N. Pennine Alps	13,843 / 4,219	1869
30	Piramide Vincent	Pennine Alps	13,829 / 4,215	1819
31	Grandes Jorasses- Pt. Walker	Mont Blanc Mass. East	13,806 / 4,208	1865
32	Alphubel	Pennine Alps	13,800 / 4,206	1860
33	Rimpfischhorn	Pennine Alps	13,777 / 4,199	1859
34	Aletschhorn	Central Bernese Alps	13,764 / 4,195	1859
35	Strahlhorn	Pennine Alps	13,747 / 4,190	1854
36	Grand Combin de Valsorey	Pennine Alps West	13,728 / 4,184	unknown

Rank	Peak Name	Location	Elevation Feet / Meters	First Ascent Date
37	Grandes Jorasses-Pt. Whymper	Mont Blanc Massif East	13,728 / 4,184	1868
38	Dent d' Herens	Pennine Alps	13,685 / 4,171	1863
39	Breithorn-West	Pennine Alps	13,662 / 4,164	1813
40	Breithorn-Central	Pennine Alps	13,646 / 4,159	1884
41	Jungfrau	Cent. Bernese Alps	13,642 / 4,158	1811
42	Bishorn	NW Pennine Alps	13,626 / 4,153	1884
43	Combin de Tsessette	Pennine Alps West	13,587 / 4,141	unknown
44	Breithorn Twin West	Pennine Alps	13,580 / 4,139	1884
45	Aiguille Verte	Mont Blanc Mass. East	13,524 / 4,122	1865
46	Mont Blanc du Tacul-L'Isolee	Mont Blanc Massif	13,498 / 4,114	
47	Aiguille Blanche-Pt. Gussfeldt	Mont Blanc Massif	13,491 / 4,112	1885
48	Grandes Jorasses-Pt. Croz	Mont Blanc Mass. East	13,485 / 4,110	1909
49	Mont Blanc du Tacul-Pt. Carmen	Mont Blanc Massif	13,482 / 4,109	
50	Mönch	Cent. Bernese Alps	13,475 / 4,107	1857
51	Breithorn Twin East	Pennine Alps	13,472 / 4,106	1884
52	Grande Rocheuse	Mont Blanc Massif East	13,459 / 4,102	1865
53	Barre des Écrins	Haut Dauphiné	13,455 / 4,101	1864

Rank	Peak Name	Location	Elevation Feet / Meters	First Ascent Date
54	Mont Blanc du Tacul-Pt. Mediane	Mont Blanc Massif	13,442 / 4,097	
55	Pollux	Pennine Alps	13,426 / 4,092	1864
56	Schreckhorn	East Bernese Alps	13,379 / 4,078	1861
57	Breithorn-Schwarzfluh/ Roccis Nera	Pennine Alps	13,370 / 4,075	unknown
58	Mont Blanc du Tacul-Pt. Chaubert	Mont Blanc Massif	13,367 / 4,074	unknown
59	Grandes Jorasses-Pt. Marguérite	Mont Blanc Massif East	13,341 / 4,066	1898
60	Mont Blanc du Tacul-Corne du Diable	Mont Blanc Massif	13,334 / 4,064	
61	Obergabelhorn	NW Pennine Alps	13,331 / 4,063	1865
62	Gran Paradiso-Summit Towers	Graian Alps	13,323 / 4,061	1860
63	Mont Brouillard	Mont Blanc Massif	13,298 / 4,053	1906
64	Aiguille de Bionnassay	Mont Blanc Massif	13,295 / 4,052	1865
65	Piz Bernina	Bernina Alps	13,284 / 4,049	1850
66	Gross-Fiescherhorn	Cent. Bernese Alps	13,284 / 4,049	1862
67	Punta Giordani	Pennine Alps	13,275 / 4,046	unknown
68	Grandes Jorasses-Pt. Helene	Mont Blanc Massif East	13,272 / 4,045	1898

Rank	Peak Name	Location	Elevation Feet / Meters	First Ascent Date
69	Gross-Grünhorn	Cent. Bernese Alps	13,268 / 4,044	1885
70	Lauteraarhorn	East Bernese Alps	13,261 / 4,042	1842
71	Aiguille du Jardin	Mont Blanc Massif East	13,239 / 4,035	1904
72	Durrenhorn	N. Pennine Alps	13,238 / 4,035	1879
73	Allalinhorn	Pennine Alps	13,213 / 4,027	1856
74	Hinter-Fiescherhorn	Cent. Bernese Alps	13,206 / 4,025	unknown
75	Weissmies	E. Pennine Alps	13,199 / 4,023	1856
76	Dome de Rochefort	Mont Blanc Mass. East	13,173 / 4,015	1881
77	Dome de Neige	Haut Dauphine	13,173 / 4,015	unknown
78	Dent du Géant	Mont Blanc Mass. East	13,166 / 4,013	1882
79	Punta Baretti	Mont Blanc Massif	13,166 / 4,013	1880
80	Lagginhorn	E. Pennine Alps	13,156 / 4,010	1856
81	Aiguille de Rochefort	Mont Blanc Mass. East	13,127 / 4,001	1873
82	Les Droites	Mont Blanc Mass. East	13,124 / 4,000	1876

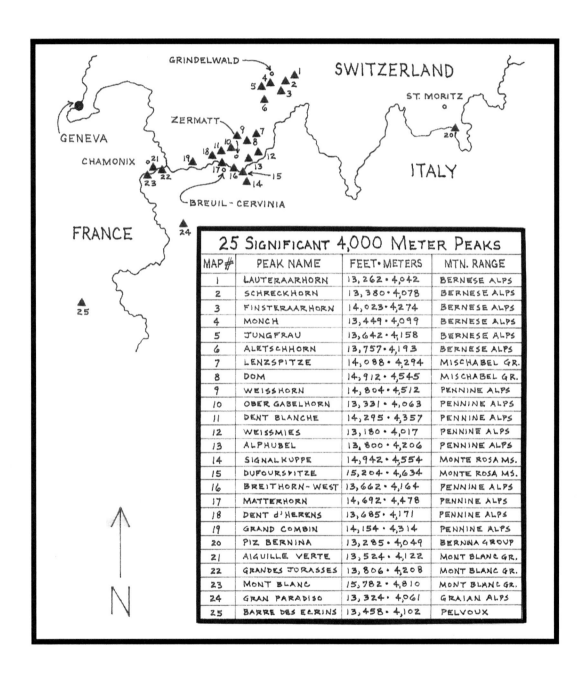

MAP #	PEAK NAME	FEET • METERS	MTN. RANGE
1	LAUTERAARHORN	13,262 • 4,042	BERNESE ALPS
2	SCHRECKHORN	13,380 • 4,078	BERNESE ALPS
3	FINSTERAARHORN	14,023 • 4,274	BERNESE ALPS
4	MONCH	13,449 • 4,099	BERNESE ALPS
5	JUNGFRAU	13,642 • 4,158	BERNESE ALPS
6	ALETSCHHORN	13,757 • 4,193	BERNESE ALPS
7	LENZSPITZE	14,088 • 4,294	MISCHABEL GR.
8	DOM	14,912 • 4,545	MISCHABEL GR.
9	WEISSHORN	14,804 • 4,512	PENNINE ALPS
10	OBER GABELHORN	13,331 • 4,063	PENNINE ALPS
11	DENT BLANCHE	14,295 • 4,357	PENNINE ALPS
12	WEISSMIES	13,180 • 4,017	PENNINE ALPS
13	ALPHUBEL	13,800 • 4,206	PENNINE ALPS
14	SIGNALKUPPE	14,942 • 4,554	MONTE ROSA MS.
15	DUFOURSPITZE	15,204 • 4,634	MONTE ROSA MS.
16	BREITHORN-WEST	13,662 • 4,164	PENNINE ALPS
17	MATTERHORN	14,692 • 4,478	PENNINE ALPS
18	DENT d'HERENS	13,685 • 4,171	PENNINE ALPS
19	GRAND COMBIN	14,154 • 4,314	PENNINE ALPS
20	PIZ BERNINA	13,285 • 4,049	BERNINA GROUP
21	AIGUILLE VERTE	13,524 • 4,122	MONT BLANC GR.
22	GRANDES JORASSES	13,806 • 4,208	MONT BLANC GR.
23	MONT BLANC	15,782 • 4,810	MONT BLANC GR.
24	GRAN PARADISO	13,324 • 4,061	GRAIAN ALPS
25	BARRE DES ECRINS	13,458 • 4,102	PELVOUX

7. SIX GREAT NORTH FACES IN THE ALPS

1952	French mountaineer Gaston Rebuffat (1921 – 1985) became the first person to climb all six north faces.
1945	Walker Spur of the Grandes Jorasses
	Petit Dru
	Piz Badile
1949	Matterhorn
	Cima Grande di Lavaredo
1952	Eiger

1969—New Zealand mountaineers Murray Jones and Graeme Dingle completed the climbing of all six north faces in one climbing season.

1993—British mountaineer Alison Hargreaves (1962 – 1995) climbed all six north faces in a combined climbing time of 23 hours and 45 minutes.

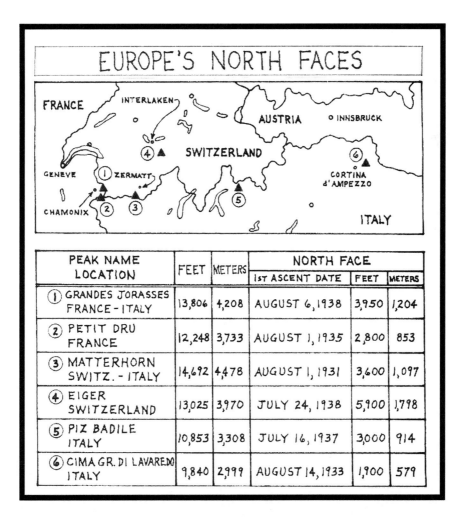

PEAK NAME LOCATION	FEET	METERS	NORTH FACE		
			1ST ASCENT DATE	FEET	METERS
① GRANDES JORASSES FRANCE - ITALY	13,806	4,208	AUGUST 6, 1938	3,950	1,204
② PETIT DRU FRANCE	12,248	3,733	AUGUST 1, 1935	2,800	853
③ MATTERHORN SWITZ. - ITALY	14,692	4,478	AUGUST 1, 1931	3,600	1,097
④ EIGER SWITZERLAND	13,025	3,970	JULY 24, 1938	5,900	1,798
⑤ PIZ BADILE ITALY	10,853	3,308	JULY 16, 1937	3,000	914
⑥ CIMA GR. DI LAVAREDO ITALY	9,840	2,999	AUGUST 14, 1933	1,900	579

8. 50 HIGHPOINTS OF THE UNITED STATES

1923: August 29. Montana's Granite Peak (12,799 ft./3,901 m.) was the last of the fifty state highpoints to be climbed (first ascent).

1936: American Arthur Marshall (1886 – 1951) was the first person to climb the highest point in the 48 United States. Marshall spent eighteen years (1919 to 1936) climbing to these 48 summits. During his lifetime, he made 622 total ascents (281 ascents were solo).

1950: Michigan climber C. Rowland Stebbins became the second person to climb the highest summit in the "lower" 48 states. His three sons became the 5th, 6th, and 7th climbers to achieve the same goal in the early 1960s.

1969: American John Vincent "Vin" Hoeman was the first to climb all 50 highpoints. After completing his 50th ascent, Hoeman traveled to Nepal where he was unfortunately killed in an avalanche on Dhaulagiri (26,794 ft./8,167 m.) on April 28, 1969.

1969: American climber F.T. Ashley climbed 48 state highpoints in 109 days (May 25 – September 13).

1990: British climber Adrian Crane climbed all 50 highpoints in 101 days.

1997: American mountaineer Pete Schoening (1927 – 2004) reached his 50th state highpoint Gannett Peak (13,785 ft./4,201 m.) in Wyoming at age 70.

1999: As of this year, 75 people had climbed all 50 state highpoints.
Lowest highpoint   Florida   345 ft./105 m.
Highest highpoint   Alaska   20,320 ft./6,193 m.

Highpoints over 10,000 feet/3,038 meters: 13
Highpoints over 12,000 feet/3,657 meters: 12
Highpoints over 14,000 feet/4,267 meters: 4
Highpoints over 15,000 feet/4,572 meters: 1

50 Highpoints of the United States

State	Highpoint Name	Elevation Feet / Meters	First Ascent Date	*	Trailhead To Summit Distance In Miles
Alabama 1	Cheaha Mountain	2,405 / 733	**	1	
Alaska 2	Denali	20,320 / 6,193	1913	3	16
Arizona 3	Humphreys Peak	12,633 / 3,850	**	2	9
Arkansas 4	Magazine Mtn.	2,753 / 839	**	2	1
California 5	Mount Whitney	14,505 / 4,421	1873	3	21
Colorado 6	Mount Elbert	14,433 / 4,399	1874	2	9
Connecticut 7	Mount Frissell	2,380 / 725	**	2	3.6
Delaware 8	Ebright Azimuth	448 / 136	**	1	
Florida 9	Lakewood Park	345 / 105	**	1	
Georgia 10	Brasstown Bald	4,784 /1,458	**	2	1
Hawaii 11	Mauna Kea	13,796 / 4,205		2	.4
Idaho 12	Borah Peak	12,662 /3,859	**	3	3.4
Illinois 13	Charles Mound	1,235 / 376	**	2	.4
Indiana 14	Hoosier High Point	1,257 / 383	**	2	.1
Iowa 15	Hawkeye Point	1,670 / 509	**	2	.1
Kansas 16	Mount Sunflower	4,039 / 1,231	**	1	
Kentucky 17	Black Mountain	4,139 / 1,261	**	2	.1
Louisiana 18	Driskill Mountain	535 / 163	**	2	1.8
Maine 19	Mount Katahdin	5,267 / 1,605	1804	2	10.4
Maryland 20	Backbone Mtn.	3,360 / 1,024	**	2	2.2
Massachusetts 21	Mount Greylock	3,487 / 1,063	**	2	.1
Michigan 22	Mount Arvon	1,979 / 603	**	2	2
Minnesota 23	Eagle mountain	2,301 701	**	2	7
Mississippi 24	Woodall Mountain	806 / 246	**	1	
Missouri 25	Taum Sauk Mtn.	1,772 / 540	**	2	.4
Montana 26	Granite Peak	12,799 / 3,901	1923	3	11.1

* 1-Drive To Actual Summit   ** First Ascent Date Unknown
  2-Hike to Summit: Miles
  3-Climb to Summit: Miles

State	Highpoint Name	Elevation Feet / Meters	First Ascent Date	*	Trailhead To Summit Distance In Miles
Nebraska 27	Panorama Point	5,424 / 1,653	**	1	
Nevada 28	Boundary Peak	13,140 / 4,005	**	2	7.4
New Hampshire 29	Mount Washington	6,288 / 1,916	1642	2	.1
New Jersey 30	High Point	1,803 / 549	**	2	.2
New Mexico 31	Wheeler Peak	13,161 / 4,011	**	2	6.2
New York 32	Mount Marcy	5,344 / 1,629	1837	2	14.8
North Carolina 33	Mount Mitchell	6,684 / 2,037	1835	2	.2
North Dakota 34	White Butte	3,506 / 1,068	**	2	2
Ohio 35	Campbell Hill	1,549 / 472	**	1	
Oklahoma 36	Black Mesa	4,973 / 1,516	**	2	8.6
Oregon 37	Mount Hood	11,239 / 3,425	1857	3	4
Pennsylvania 38	Mount Davis	3,213 / 979	**	1	
Rhode Island 39	Jerimoth Hill	812 / 247	**	1	
South Carolina 40	Sassafras Mtn.	3,560 / 1,085	**	2	.2
South Dakota 41	Harney Peak	7,242 / 2,207	**	2	5.8
Tennessee 42	Clingmans Dome	6,643 / 2,025	**	2	1
Texas 43	Guadalupe Peak	8,749 / 2,667	**	2	8.4
Utah 44	Kings Peak	13,528 / 4,123	**	2	
Vermont 45	Mount Mansfield	4,393 / 1,339	**	2	2.8
Virginia 46	Mount Rogers	5,729 / 1,746	**	2	
Washington 47	Mount Rainier	14,411 / 4,392	1870	3	8
West Virginia 48	Spruce Knob	4,861 / 1,482	**	2	.4
Wisconsin 49	Timms Hill	1,951 / 595	**	2	.4
Wyoming 50	Gannett Peak	13,804 / 4,207	1922	3	20.2

* 1-Drive To Actual Summit   ** First Ascent Date Unknown
   2-Hike to Summit: Miles
   3-Climb to Summit: Miles

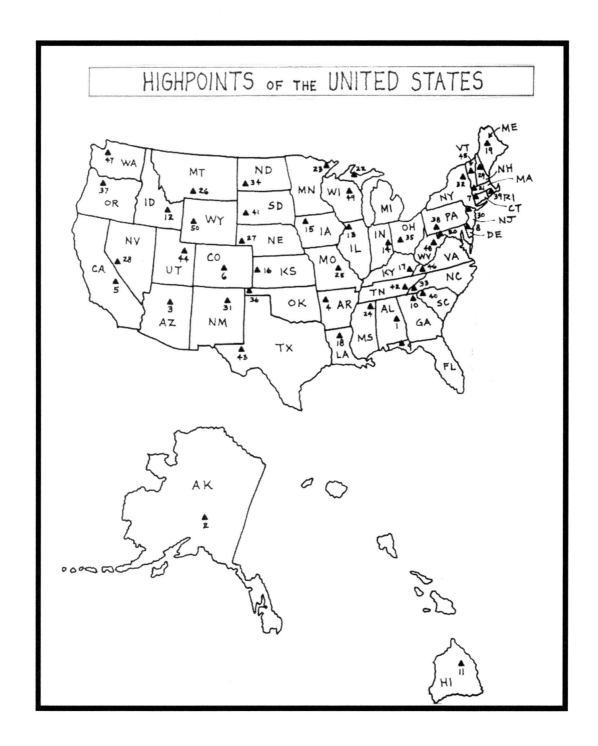

9. COLORADO'S FOURTEENERS

There are 54 peaks in Colorado that are officially recognized as being separate mountains over 14,000 feet (4,267 meters). All of these peaks were climbed (documented ascents) between 1820 (Pikes Peak) and 1916 (Crestone Peak, Crestone Needle, and Kit Carson Peak). To qualify as a separate "fourteener," a peak must rise at least 300 feet above a saddle connecting to other high summits.

1923: Colorado mountaineers Carl Blaurock (1894 – 1993) and William Ervin were the first to climb all of those known peaks in Colorado that exceeded 14,000 feet (4,267 meters) in height. Known as the "fourteeners," there were 47 peaks in this mountain group at this time. At some later date, five additional summits were added to the official list (52) and then two more summits were identified to reach the current accepted list of 54 peaks.

1934: Albert R. Ellingwood (1888 – 1934) became the third person to climb all of the fourteeners. Mary Cronin became the fourth climber and the first woman to climb all of these high peaks.

1937: Carl Melzer, Bob Melzer (9 year old son), and Junius Johnson climbed all 50 14,000 peaks in 39 days.

1940: By this year, eleven (11) mountaineers had climbed all of the fourteeners.

1949: American climber Elizabeth Strong Partridge (1902 – 1974) completed the climbing of all 52 fourteeners. She was the fifth of six women to reach this goal by 1949. Dorothy Teague Swartz reached her 54th summit on the same day as Partridge.

1957: Colorado mountaineer Carl Blaurock (1894 – 1993), at age 63, became the first person to climb all 70 peaks over 14,000 feet (4,267 meters) in the continental United States (California – 15, Colorado – 54, Washington – 1).

1960: Colorado mountaineer Cleve McCarty climbed the official 52 peaks in 52 days.

1968: Climbing with his father and three older brothers, eight-year-old Tyle Smith became the youngest person to climb all 54 peaks in Colorado over 14,000 feet (4,267 meters).

1972: Barbara Lilley completed the climbing of all those peaks over 14,000 feet (4,267 meters) in California (15), Colorado (54), and Washington (1).

1974: The Climbing Smith's of Colorado (father and four sons) climbed all 54 fourteeners in 33 days.

1980: Colorado climber Steve Boyer established a new 54 peak climbing time of 18 days.

1990: 534 mountaineers had climbed all 54 peaks.

1990: Quade and Tyle Smith (of the climbing Smith's) lowered the 54 peak climbing time to 16 days, 21 hours, and 25 minutes.

1991: Colorado ski mountaineer Louis Dawson (1952 –) took thirteen years (1978 – 1991) to make the first ski descent of all 54 peaks.

1992: Colorado mountaineer Tom Mereness spent sixteen years (1976 – 1992) to become the first person to climb all 54 peaks in the winter. Jim Bock was Mereness' partner on most of these ascents.

1994: Colorado mountaineers Rick Trujillo (1946 –) and Ricky Denesik (1958 –) lowered the 54 peak climbing time to 15 days, 9 hours, and 55 minutes.

1997: Seven-year old Megan Emmons climbed all 54 peaks becoming the youngest person to accomplish this goal. She broke Tyle Smith's age record (8 years old) that had lasted since 1968 (29 years).

2000: Mountaineer Teddy Keizer (29) climbed 55 Colorado peaks over 14,000 feet (4,267 meters) in 10 days, 20 hours and 26 minutes. Keizer frequently climbed in the dark with a headlamp.

2001: Denver attorney Jim Gehres completed his 12th full cycle of climbing all 54 peaks in Colorado over 14,000 feet (4,267 meters) for a total of 648 summits (1961 – 2001).

2005: Colorado mountaineer Aron Ralston (1975 –) spent eight years (1998 – 2005) to become the first person to climb all 54 peaks in the winter solo.

2011: As of November 30, 1,437 mountaineers had climbed all 54 peaks over 14,000 feet (4,267 meters) in Colorado. (Source: Colorado Mountain Club).

Colorado's Fourteeners

RANK	PEAK NAME	FEET	METERS	1ST ASCENT DATE
1	Mount Elbert	14,433	4,399	1874
2	Mount Massive	14,421	4,395	1873
3	Mount Harvard	14,420	4,395	1869
4	Blanca Peak	14,345	4,372	1874
5	La Plata Peak	14,336	4,369	1873
6	Uncompahgre Peak	14,309	4,361	1874
7	Crestone Peak	14,294	4,357	1915
8	Mount Lincoln	14,286	4,354	1861
9	Grays Peak	14,270	4,349	1861

Colorado's Fourteeners

RANK	PEAK NAME	FEET	METERS	1ST ASCENT DATE
10	Mount Antero	14,269	4,349	unknown
11	Torreys Peak	14,267	4,348	1861
12	Castle Peak	14,265	4,347	1873
13	Quandary Peak	14,265	4,347	unknown
14	Mount Evans	14,264	4,347	1863
15	Longs Peak	14,256	4,345	1865/1868
16	Mount Wilson	14,246	4,342	1874
17	Mount Shavano	14,229	4,337	unknown
18	Crestone Needle	14,197	4,327	1915
19	Mount Belford	14,197	4,327	unknown
20	Mount Princeton	14,197	4,327	1877
21	Mount Yale	14,196	4,327	1869
22	Mount Bross	14,172	4,319	unknown
23	Kit Carson Peak	14,165	4,317	1915
24	El Diente	14,159	4,315	1890
25	Maroon Peak	14,156	4,314	1908
26	Tabeguache Peak	14,155	4,314	unknown
27	Mount Oxford	14,153	4,313	1873
28	Mount Sneffels	14,150	4,312	1874
29	Mount Democrat	14,148	4,312	unknown
30	Capitol Peak	14,130	4,307	1907
31	Pikes Peak	14,110	4,301	1820
32	Snowmass Mountain	14,092	4,295	1907
33	Mount Eolus	14,083	4,292	unknown
34	Windom Peak	14,082	4,292	unknown
35	Mount Columbia	14,073	4,289	unknown
36	Mount Missouri	14,067	4,287	unknown
37	Humboldt Peak	14,064	4,286	1883
38	Mount Bierstadt	14,060	4,285	1863
39	Sunlight Peak	14,059	4,285	unknown
40	Handies Peak	14,048	4,282	1875
41	Culebra Peak	14,047	4,281	1875
42	Ellingwood Point	14,042	4,280	unknown
43	Mount Lindsey	14,042	4,280	1875
44	Little Bear Peak	14,037	4,278	1888
45	Mount Sherman	14,036	4,278	unknown
46	Redcloud Peak	14,034	4,277	1875

Colorado's Fourteeners

RANK	PEAK NAME	FEET	METERS	1ST ASCENT DATE
47	Pyramid Peak	14,018	4,272	1907
48	Wilson Peak	14,017	4,272	unknown
49	Wetterhorn Peak	14,015	4,271	1906
50	North Maroon Peak	14,014	4,271	1908
51	San Luis Peak	14,014	4,271	unknown
52	Mount of the Holy Cross	14,005	4,268	1873
53	Huron Peak	14,003	4,268	unknown
54	Sunshine Peak	14,001	4,267	1875

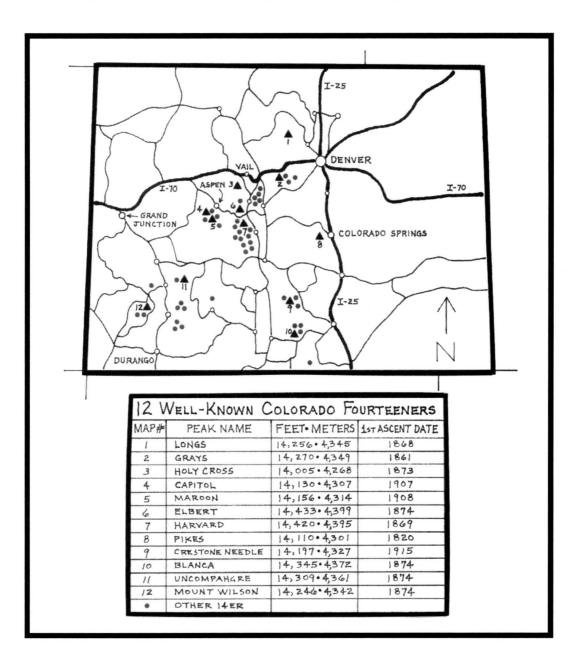

12 WELL-KNOWN COLORADO FOURTEENERS			
MAP#	PEAK NAME	FEET·METERS	1ST ASCENT DATE
1	LONGS	14,256·4,345	1868
2	GRAYS	14,270·4,349	1861
3	HOLY CROSS	14,005·4,268	1873
4	CAPITOL	14,130·4,307	1907
5	MAROON	14,156·4,314	1908
6	ELBERT	14,433·4,399	1874
7	HARVARD	14,420·4,395	1869
8	PIKES	14,110·4,301	1820
9	CRESTONE NEEDLE	14,197·4,327	1915
10	BLANCA	14,345·4,372	1874
11	UNCOMPAHGRE	14,309·4,361	1874
12	MOUNT WILSON	14,246·4,342	1874
•	OTHER 14ER		

10. CALIFORNIA'S 14,000 FOOTERS

RANK	PEAK NAME	FEET	METERS	1ST ASCENT DATE
1	Mount Whitney	14,505	4,421	1873
2	Mount Williamson	14,375	4,381	1884
3	White Mountain	14,246	4,342	unknown
4	North Palisade	14,242	4,341	1903
5	Polemonium Peak *	14,200	4,328	1903
6	Starlight Peak *	14,200	4,328	1930
7	Mount Shasta	14,162	4,316	1854
8	Mount Sill	14,162	4,316	1903
9	Mount Russell	14,086	4,293	1926
10	Split Mountain	14,058	4,285	1887
11	Middle Palisade	14,040	4,279	1922
12	Mount Langley	14,027	4,275	1864
13	Mount Muir	14,015	4,272	1935
14	Mount Tyndall	14,015	4,272	1864
15	Thunderbolt Peak	14,003	4,268	1931

* This peak has not been officially accepted by the U.S. Geological Survey as an independent 14,000 foot peak. This peak is considered to be a sub-peak of a nearer high peak.

1920 – 1931: Well-known California mountaineer Norman Clyde (1885 – 1972) climbed ten of California's fifteen peaks over 14,000 feet (4,267 meters). Other active climbers during this same time period included Glen Dawson (1912 –), Jules Eichorn (1912 – 2000), Frances Farquhar (1887 – 1974), Clifton Hildebrand, and Walter Huber.

1930: August 22. California mountaineer Walter A. Starr, Jr. (1903 – 1933) reached the summit of Middle Palisade Peak (14,040 ft./4,279 m.) in the Sierra mountains. Starr now claimed to have climbed all Sierran 14,000 foot peaks except Mount Langley (14,027 ft./4,275 m.). This peak total would, therefore, equal twelve. He did not climb either Mount Shasta (14,162 ft./4,316 m.) or White Mountain (14,246 ft./4,342 m.). Unfortunately, Starr fell while climbing Michael Minaret (12,280 ft./3,743 m.) in the Sierras on August 3, 1933 and was killed.

1931 – 1936: California climber Lewis F. Clark reached the summits of eight 14,000 foot (4,267 m.) peaks in the Sierras.

1990: American mountaineer Stephen F. Porcella completed the climbing of all fifteen California fourteeners.

1994: August. Thirteen-year-old Sierra Richins completed the climbing of all fifteen peaks in California over 14,000 feet (4,267 meters). She began this climbing journey in September of 1991 (age 10) with an ascent of Mount Whitney.

2007: Colorado climber Cameron M. Burns had now reached the summits of all fifteen peaks.

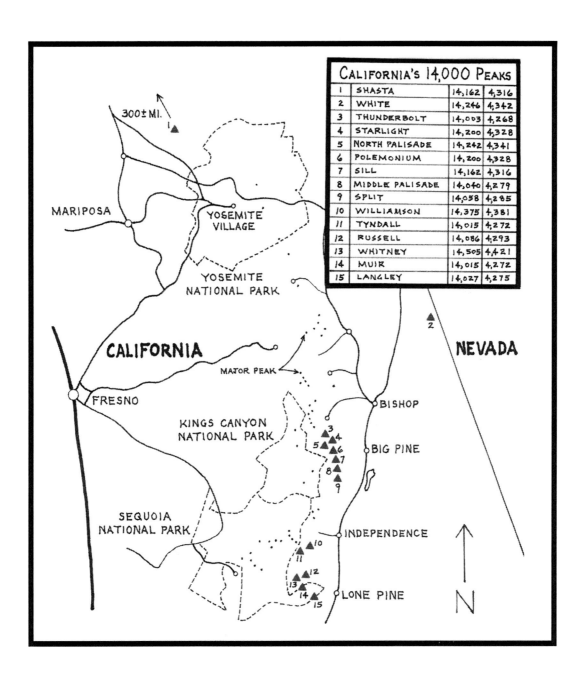

	CALIFORNIA'S 14,000 PEAKS		
1	SHASTA	14,162	4,316
2	WHITE	14,246	4,342
3	THUNDERBOLT	14,003	4,268
4	STARLIGHT	14,200	4,328
5	NORTH PALISADE	14,242	4,341
6	POLEMONIUM	14,200	4,328
7	SILL	14,162	4,316
8	MIDDLE PALISADE	14,040	4,279
9	SPLIT	14,058	4,285
10	WILLIAMSON	14,375	4,381
11	TYNDALL	14,015	4,272
12	RUSSELL	14,086	4,293
13	WHITNEY	14,505	4,421
14	MUIR	14,015	4,272
15	LANGLEY	14,027	4,275

11. WHITE MOUNTAIN 4,000 FOOTERS (NEW HAMPSHIRE)

1931: Dartmouth College librarian Nathaniel L. Goodrich first suggested a list of 36 White Mountain (New Hampshire) 4,000 foot peaks.

1948: Mr. and Mrs. J. Daniel McKenzie climbed all of the recognized 4,000 foot peaks in New Hampshire, New York, and Vermont.

1956: Appalachian Mountain Club member Roderick Gould was the first person to climb Goodrich's 36 peaks in the White Mountains plus two additional peaks—Willey and West Bond. These two peaks would soon be added to the official list of 4,000 footers.

1957: May 26. Roderick Gould became the first person to climb the new official list of 46 peaks in the White Mountains over 4,000 feet. On September 2, Thomas S. Lamb became the second person to complete all 46. On September 14, Miriam (1899 – 1976) and Robert (1889 – 1983) Underhill were the third and fourth people to climb all 46.

1957: The Four Thousand Footer Club was established. By the year 2000, this club had 6,851 members.

1960: December 23. Miriam (62) and Robert (71) Underhill became the first to climb all 46 peaks during the winter season (December 22 – March 20).

1962: 129 climbers had completed all 46 peaks.

1970: The Reverend Henry Folsom from Old Saybrook, Connecticut climbed all 48 (new total) White Mountain peaks during a 19-day journey (not consecutive days).

1991: Three strong hikers climbed all 48 peaks in 8 days during the summer.

2002: American climber Teddy Keizer (30) climbed all 48 peaks in 3 days, 17 hours, and 21 minutes. Keizer also climbed all 46 peaks over 4,000 feet in New York's Adirondack Mountains during the same season.

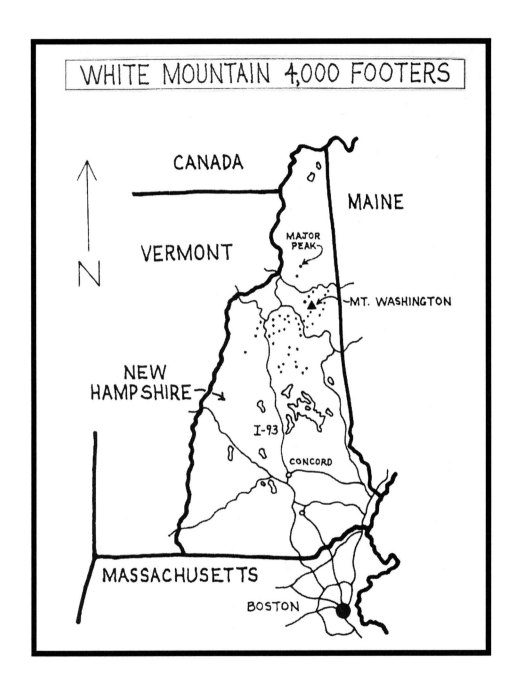

12. ADIRONDACK FORTY-SIXERS

The Adirondack State Park in upstate New York contains approximately 6,000,000 acres. There are 43 mountains in the Adirondacks that exceed 4,000 feet (1,219 meters) in elevation and 3 other mountains that are just shy of this elevation but are included in the official list of 46 peaks.

1925: Brothers Bob and George Marshall and Herb Clark were the first people to climb all 46 peaks (1918 – 1925). Eight of these climbs were considered first ascents and only fourteen peaks had trails to the summit area.

1937: The Forty-Sixers Club was established.

1948: Mr. and Mrs. J. Daniel McKenzie climbed all of the 4,000 foot peaks in New Hampshire, New York, and Vermont.

1948: The Adirondack Forty-Sixers Club was established to succeed the Forty-Sixers Club.

1999: 4,600 people had climbed all 46 peaks.

2002: American climber Teddy Keizer (30) climbed all 46 peaks during the summer.

The Adirondack Forty-Sixers

RANK	PEAK NAME	FEET	METERS	1ST ASCENT DATE
1	Mount Marcy	5,344	1,629	1837*
2	Mount Algonquin	5,114	1,559	1837
3	Mount Haystack	4,960	1,512	1849
4	Mount Skylight	4,926	1,501	
5	Mount Whiteface	4,867	1,483	
6	Mount Dix	4,857	1,480	1807
7	Mount Gray	4,840	1,475	
8	Mount Iroquois	4,840	1,475	
9	Mount Basin	4,827	1,471	
10	Mount Gothics	4,736	1,443	
11	Mount Colden	4,714	1,437	
12	Mount Giant	4,627	1,410	1797**
13	Nippletop	4,620	1,408	
14	Mount Santanoni	4,607	1,404	
15	Mount Redfield	4,606	1,404	
16	Mount Wright	4,580	1,396	

The Adirondack Forty-Sixers

RANK	PEAK NAME	FEET	METERS	1ST ASCENT DATE
17	Saddleback	4,515	1,376	
18	Mount Panther	4,442	1,354	
19	Table Top	4,427	1,349	
20	Rocky Peak Ridge	4,420	1,347	
21	Mount Macomb	4,405	1,343	
22	Mount Armstrong	4,400	1,341	
23	Mount Hough	4,400	1,341	
24	Mount Seward	4,361	1,329	
25	Mount Marshall	4,360	1,329	
26	Mount Allen	4,340	1,323	
27	Big Slide Mountain	4,240	1,292	
28	Mount Esther	4,240	1,292	1839
29	Upper Wolf Jaw	4,185	1,276	
30	Lower Wolf Jaw	4,175	1,272	
31	Mount Street	4,166	1,270	
32	Mount Phelps	4,161	1,268	
33	Mount Donaldson	4,140	1,262	
34	Mount Seymour	4,120	1,256	
35	Mount Sawteeth	4,100	1,250	
36	Mount Cascade	4,098	1,249	
37	South Dix	4,060	1,237	
38	Mount Porter	4,059	1,237	1875
39	Mount Colvin	4,057	1,236	1875
40	Mount Emmons	4,040	1,231	
41	Mount Dial	4,020	1,225	
42	East Dix	4,012	1,223	
43	MacNaughton Mtn.	4,000	1,219	
44	Green Mountain	3,980	1,213	***
45	Blake Peak	3,960	1,207	***
46	Cliff Mountain	3,960	1,207	***

* State geologist Ebenezer Emmons made the first ascent of Mount Marcy and gave the name Adirondacks to this mountain region. The term "Adirondack" refers to a member of the Algonquin people who lived mainly north of the St. Lawrence River (in Canada).

** First ascent of any Adirondack 4,000 foot peak.

*** These three peaks must be climbed in order to have membership in the Adirondack Forty-Sixers Club.

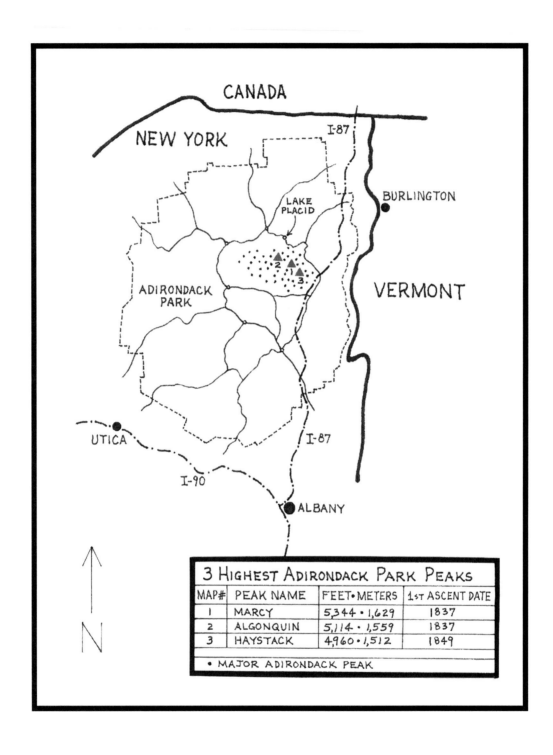

3 Highest Adirondack Park Peaks

MAP#	PEAK NAME	FEET•METERS	1st ASCENT DATE
1	MARCY	5,344 • 1,629	1837
2	ALGONQUIN	5,114 • 1,559	1837
3	HAYSTACK	4,960 • 1,512	1849

• MAJOR ADIRONDACK PEAK

13. THE WASHINGTON SIX

1921: As of this year, seventeen members of The Mountaineers, a northwest United States climbing club, had summited all six significant peaks in Washington.

1933: Washington mountaineer Amos Hand was the first person to climb all six peaks twice.

WASHINGTON'S SIX PEAKS

#	PEAK NAME	FEET · METERS	1st ASCENT DATE
1	MOUNT OLYMPUS	7,965 · 2,428	1907
2	MOUNT BAKER	10,781 · 3,286	1868
3	GLACIER PEAK	10,541 · 3,213	1898
4	MOUNT RAINIER	14,411 · 4,392	1870
5	MOUNT ST. HELENS	8,366 · 2,550	1853
6	MOUNT ADAMS	12,276 · 3,742	1854

14. 16-PEAK AWARD

The Mazamas climbing club was founded in 1894 on the summit of Mount Hood (11,239 ft./3,427 m.) in Oregon. In 1935, the Mazamas established the 16-Peak Award that is resented to those mountaineers that successfully climb sixteen specifically designated peaks in California, Oregon, and Washington. These peaks range in height from 7,794 feet (2,376 m.) – 14,411 feet (4,392 m.). The first 16-Peak Award was presented on October 14, 1935 to Edward J. Hughes. As of December 31, 2007, 447 mountaineers had received this award.

These sixteen peaks are:

Washington:	#1 Mount Shuksan	9,131 ft./2,783 m.
	#2 Mount Baker	10,781 ft./3,286 m.
	#3 Glacier Peak	10,541 ft./3,213 m.
	#4 Mount Stuart	9,415 ft./2,870 m.
	#5 Mount Olympus	7,965 ft./2,428 m.
	#6 Mount Rainier	14,411 ft./4,392 m.
	#7 Mount St. Helens	8,365 ft./2,550 m.
	#8 Mount Adams	12,307 ft./3,751 m.
Oregon:	#9 Mount Hood	11,239 ft./3,427 m.
	#10 Mount Jefferson	10,497 ft./3,199 m.
	#11 Three-Fingered Jack	7,841 ft./2,390 m.
	#12 Mount Washington	7,794 ft./2,376 m.
	#13 South Sister	10,358 ft./3,157 m.
	#14 North Sister	10,085 ft./3,074 m.
	#15 Middle Sister	10,047 ft./3,062 m.
California:	#16 Mount Shasta	14,162 ft./4,316 m.

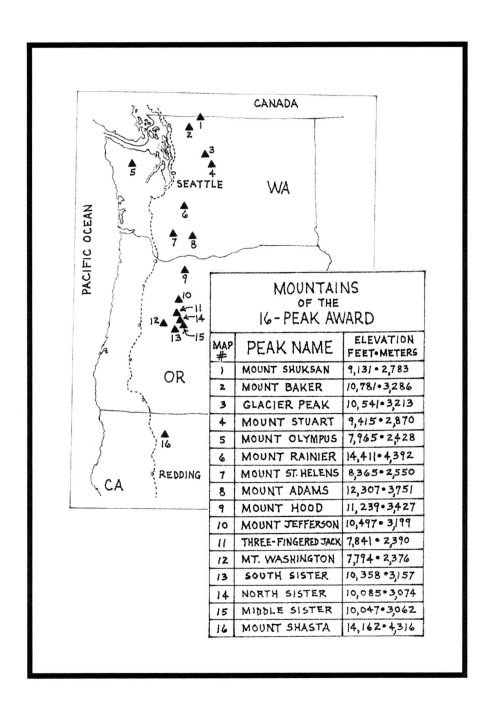

MOUNTAINS
OF THE
16-PEAK AWARD

MAP #	PEAK NAME	ELEVATION FEET•METERS
1	MOUNT SHUKSAN	9,131 • 2,783
2	MOUNT BAKER	10,781 • 3,286
3	GLACIER PEAK	10,541 • 3,213
4	MOUNT STUART	9,415 • 2,870
5	MOUNT OLYMPUS	7,965 • 2,428
6	MOUNT RAINIER	14,411 • 4,392
7	MOUNT ST. HELENS	8,365 • 2,550
8	MOUNT ADAMS	12,307 • 3,751
9	MOUNT HOOD	11,239 • 3,427
10	MOUNT JEFFERSON	10,497 • 3,199
11	THREE-FINGERED JACK	7,841 • 2,390
12	MT. WASHINGTON	7,794 • 2,376
13	SOUTH SISTER	10,358 • 3,157
14	NORTH SISTER	10,085 • 3,074
15	MIDDLE SISTER	10,047 • 3,062
16	MOUNT SHASTA	14,162 • 4,316

15. THE CANADIAN ROCKIES 11,000 FOOTERS

All 54 peaks were first climbed between 1894 and 1979.

1937: Canadian mountaineers Rex Gibson and Sterling Hendricks were the first to climb all four 12,000 ft. peaks in the Canadian Rockies.

1903: Canadian mountain guide Christian Kaufmann (1873 – 1939) made his ninth first ascent of a Canadian 11,000 foot peak—Mount Huber (11,050 ft./3,368 m.). His other first ascents were Columbia, Edward Peak, Forbes, Bryce (SW Peak), Alexandra, Goodsir (South Tower), Hungabee, and Deltaform.

2003: As of this year, the following six mountaineers had climbed all 54 Canadian Rockies peaks over 11,000 feet.

	Climber	Finish Date	Final Peak
1st	Don Forest (1920 – 2003)	1979	Lunette
2nd	Rick Collier	1994	
3rd	Bill Corbett	2002	
4th	Forbes MacDonald	2003	Alberta
5th	Roman Pachovsky	2003	Alberta
6th	Nancy Hansen*	2003	Forbes

* The first and only woman to climb all 54 peaks.

The Canadian Rockies 11,000 Footers

RANK and MAP #	PEAK NAME	ELEVATION FEET / METERS	1ST ASCENT DATE
1	Mount Robson	12,972 / 3,954	July 31, 1913
2	Mount Columbia	12,293 / 3,747	July 19,1902
3	North Twin	12,237 / 3,730	July 10, 1923
4	Mount Clemenceau	12,001 / 3,658	Aug. 9, 1923
5	Twins Tower	11,942 / 3,640	July 29, 1938
6	Mount Alberta	11,873 / 3,619	July 21,1925
7	Mount Assiniboine	11,870 / 3,618	Sept. 3, 1901
8	Mount Forbes	11,850 / 3,612	Aug. 10, 1902
9	South Twin	11,745 / 3,580	July 8, 1924
10	Mount Goodsir-South Tower	11,686 /3,562	July 16, 1903
11	Mount Temple	11,624 / 3,543	Aug. 17, 1894
12	Mount Goodsir-North Tower	11,565 / 3,525	Aug. 16, 1909

The Canadian Rockies 11,000 Footers

RANK and MAP #	PEAK NAME	ELEVATION FEET / METERS	1ST ASCENT DATE
13	Edward Peak-Lyell 2	11,529 / 3,514	July 24, 1902
14	Ernest Peak-Lyell 3	11,519 / 3,511	July 9, 1926
15	Mount Bryce-SW Peak	11,506 / 3,507	Aug 20, 1902
16	Rudolph Peak-Lyell 1	11,506 / 3,507	July 5, 1926
17	Hungabee Mountain	11,457 / 3,492	July 21, 1903
18	Mount Athabasca	11,453 / 3,491	Aug. 17, 1898
19	Mount King Edward	11,450 / 3,490	Aug. 11,1924
20	Mount Kitchener	11,417 / 3,480	July 3, 1927
21	Mount Brazeau	11,384 / 3,470	July 9, 1923
22	Mount Victoria-S. Summit	11,365 / 3,464	Aug. 5, 1897
23	Snow Dome	11,322 / 3,451	Aug. 20, 1898
24	Mount Andromeda	11,319 / 3,450	July 21, 1930
25	Stutfield-West Peak	11,319 / 3,450	July 2, 1927
26	Mount Joffre	11,319 / 3,450	Aug. 18, 1919
27	Resplendent Mountain	11,240 / 3,426	August, 1911
28	Tsar Mountain	11,233 / 3,424	Aug. 8, 1927
29	Deltaform Mountain	11,233 / 3,424	Sept. 1, 1903
30	Mount Lefroy	11,230 / 3,423	Aug. 3, 1897
31	Mount King George	11,227 / 3,422	Aug. 10, 1919
32	The Helmet	11,220 / 3,420	July, 1928
33	Mount Sir Douglas	11,174 / 3,406	Aug. 11, 1919
34	Mount Woolley	11,171 / 3,405	July 26, 1925
35	Walter Peak-Lyell 4	11,155 / 3,400	July 8, 1927
36	Lunette Peak	11,155 / 3,400	Sept. 2, 1901
37	Whitehorn Mountain	11,138 / 3,395	Aug. 12, 1911
38	Mount Hector	11,135 / 3,394	July 30, 1895
39	Christian Peak-Lyell 5	11,122 / 3,390	July 9, 1926
40	Stutfield-East Peak	11,122 / 3,390	Aug. 15, 1962
41	Mount Victoria-N. Summit	11,115 / 3,388	August, 1900
42	Mount Alexandra	11,115 / 3,388	Aug. 23, 1902

The Canadian Rockies 11,000 Footers

RANK and MAP #	PEAK NAME	ELEVATION FEET / METERS	1ST ASCENT DATE
43	Mount Goodsir-Centre Peak	11,102 / 3,384	Aug. 17, 1979
44	Mount Willingdon	11,066 / 3,373	1919
45	Diadem Peak	11,060 / 3,371	Aug. 25, 1898
46	Mount Bryce-Centre Peak	11,056 / 3,370	July 27, 1961
47	Mount Huber	11,050 / 3,368	1903
48	Mount Edith Cavell	11,033 / 3,363	Aug. 5, 1915
49	Mount Fryatt	11,027 / 3,361	July 10, 1926
50	Mount Cline	11,027 / 3,361	July, 1927
51	Tusk Peak	11,023 / 3,360	July 31, 1927
52	West Twin	11,023 / 3,360	July, 1975
53	Mount Harrison	11,020 / 3,359	Aug. 11, 1964
54	Recondite Peak	11,010 / 3,356	Aug. 26, 1927

CANADIAN ROCKIES

MAP #	PEAK NAME	ELEVATION FEET • METERS	1st ASCENT DATE
1	MOUNT ROBSON	12,972 • 3,954	JULY 31, 1913
2	MOUNT COLUMBIA	12,293 • 3,747	JULY 19, 1902
4	MOUNT CLEMENCEAU	12,001 • 3,658	AUGUST 9, 1923
6	MOUNT ALBERTA	11,873 • 3,619	JULY 21, 1925
7	MOUNT ASSINIBOINE	11,870 • 3,618	SEPTEMBER 3, 1901
8	MOUNT FORBES	11,850 • 3,612	AUGUST 10, 1902
11	MOUNT TEMPLE	11,624 • 3,543	AUGUST 17, 1894
16	RUDOLPH PEAK	11,506 • 3,507	JULY 5, 1926
21	MOUNT BRAZEAU	11,384 • 3,470	JULY 9, 1923
22	MOUNT VICTORIA	11,365 • 3,464	AUGUST 5, 1897
30	MOUNT LEFROY	11,230 • 3,423	AUGUST 3, 1897
31	MOUNT KING GEORGE	11,227 • 3,422	AUGUST 10, 1919
33	MOUNT SIR DOUGLAS	11,174 • 3,406	AUGUST 11, 1919
44	MOUNT WILLINGDON	11,066 • 3,373	1919
48	MOUNT EDITH CAVELL	11,033 • 3,363	AUGUST 5, 1915

16. CHINA'S NINE SACRED MOUNTAINS

Nine mountains in China are considered sacred by those who believe in Taoism (five of the nine mountains) or Buddhism (four of the nine). These nine mountains range in height from 932 feet/ 284 meters to 10,168 feet/3,099 meters. Thousands of Chinese people have made yearly pilgrimages to climb these peaks over many, many years. To my knowledge, there is no actual record of those people who have climbed to the summits of all nine mountains. No technical climbing experience is required for any of these ascents. Small hotels provide accommodations for hikers on all nine mountains.

Map No.	Peak Name	Province	Religion	Feet / Meters	Elevation Gain
1	Emei Shan*	Sichuan	Buddhist	10,168 / 3,099	8,363 F/2,549 M
2	Wu Tai Shan	Shanxi	Buddhist	10,033 / 3,058	7,162 F/2,183 M
3	Heng Shan Bei	Shanxi	Taoist	6,618 / 2,017	1,368 F/417 M
4	Hua Shan	Shanxi	Taoist	6,552 / 1,997	4,912 F/1,497 M
5	Tai Shan**	Shandong	Taoist	5,000 / 1,524	4,262 F/1,299 M
6	SongShan	Henan	Taoist	4,902 / 1,494	3,540 F/1,079 M
7	Jiu Hua Shan	Anhui	Buddhist	4,400 / 1,341	2,431 F/741 M
8	Heng Shan Nan	Hunan	Taoist	4,233 / 1,290	3,904 F/1,190 M
9	Putuo Shan	Zhejiang	Buddhist	932 / 284	866 F/264 M

*This mountain is also known as Omei Shan and has 35 monasteries and 56 pagodas on its slopes.

**Tai Shan was reportedly climbed by Chinese philosopher and teacher Confucius (551 – 478 B.C.) sometime prior to 500 B.C. This is the most popular climb of all nine mountains.

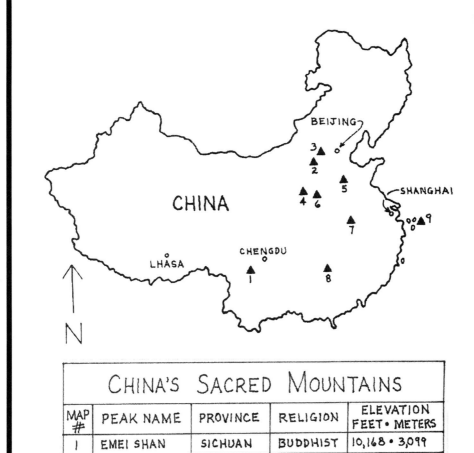

CHINA'S SACRED MOUNTAINS

MAP #	PEAK NAME	PROVINCE	RELIGION	ELEVATION FEET • METERS
1	EMEI SHAN	SICHUAN	BUDDHIST	10,168 • 3,099
2	WU TAI SHAN	SHANXI	BUDDHIST	10,033 • 3,058
3	HENG SHAN BEI	SHANXI	TAOIST	6,618 • 2,017
4	HUA SHAN	SHANXI	TAOIST	6,552 • 1,997
5	TAI SHAN	SHANDONG	TAOIST	5,000 • 1,524
6	SONG SHAN	HENAN	TAOIST	4,902 • 1,494
7	JIU HUA SHAN	ANHUI	BUDDHIST	4,400 • 1,341
8	HENG SHAN NAN	HUNAN	TAOIST	4,233 • 1,290
9	PUTUO SHAN	ZHEJIANG	BUDDHIST	932 • 284

17. THE EXPLORERS GRAND SLAM*

This challenge recognizes those people who have:

1. Reached the North Pole
2. Reached the South Pole
3. Climbed the Seven Summits which included Mount Everest that has been called the "Third Pole."

Twenty-six adventurers have completed the Explorers' Grand Slam as of December, 2011 including these six Americans:

William H. Cross (1968 –)
Lei Wang (1st woman)
Alison Levine (1966 –)
Randall Peeters
Stuart Smith
Suzanne K. Nance

In 2011, former Wales rugby player Richard Parks (1977 –) became the first person to complete the Explorers Grand Slam within a single calendar year. Parks actually accomplished this goal within seven months (December 27, 2010 – July 12, 2011).

---

* Also known as The Adventurers' Grand Slam

APPENDIX IV

THE TEN MOST SIGNIFICANT EVENTS IN MOUNTAINEERING HISTORY

Ever since Dr. Michel-Gabriel Paccard (1757 – 1827) and mountain guide Jacques Balmat (1762 – 1834) first climbed Mont Blanc in 1786, there have been many significant mountaineering achievements throughout the world. In addition to first ascents, there have been many difficult climbing routes accomplished on previously climbed peaks. Mountaineers from many different countries have made difficult winter ascents, traverses of high peaks, and enchainments of multiple summits. To rank the most important or significant mountaineering achievements is, therefore, impossible. The following summary of ten events in mountaineering history is obviously subjective. However, I believe most knowledgeable climbers would agree with most, if not all, of my selections. I am certain that my ten events could be expanded to include other climbs.

However, if one specific event could be singled out as the most significant mountaineering event, it certainly would be the first ascent of Mount Everest in 1953. This ascent represented the culmination of climbing efforts over the previous 31 years (1921 – 1952). Beyond the Mount Everest first ascent, here are nine other events I believe represent significant achievements in mountaineering history around the world.

The events listed are in order of the date of achievement:

1. Mont Blanc – 1786
2. Matterhorn – 1865
3. Eiger: North Face – 1938
4. Annapurna – 1950
5. Mount Everest – 1953
6. Mount Everest: West Ridge – 1963
7. Mount Everest: First Ascent Without Using Supplemental Oxygen – 1978
8. Mount Everest: First Solo Ascent – 1980
9. Seven Summits: First Person to Climb All Seven Mountains – 1985
10. Fourteen 8,000 Meter Peaks: First Person To Climb All Fourteen – 1986

Additional information about each of these events can be found within Chapters Three and Five.

1. MONT BLANC

Location: French – Italian border (French Alps)
Elevation: 15,782 feet/4,810 meters
First Ascent Date: August 8, 1786
Summit Climbers: Dr. Michel-Gabriel Paccard (1757 – 1827)
             Jacques Balmat – Guide (1762 – 1834)

Significance: After many exploration climbs and several summit attempts (beginning in 1762), this highest peak in Europe's Western Alps was finally climbed. Many believe this ascent represented the "Birth of Mountaineering."

2. MATTERHORN

Location: Swiss – Italian border (Pennine Alps)
Elevation: 14,692 feet/4,478 meters
First Ascent Date: July 14, 1865
Summit Climbers:

Lord Francis Douglas*	(1847 – 1865)
Douglas Hadow*	(1846 – 1865)
Charles Hudson*	(1828 – 1865)
Edward Whymper	(1840 – 1911)
Michel Croz – Guide*	(1830 – 1865)
Peter Taugwalder, Sr. – Guide	(1820 – 1888)
Peter Taugwalder, Jr. – Guide	(1843 – 1923)

Significance: This was the last of the major 4,000 meter (13,124 feet) peaks in the Alps to be climbed. For many years, this peak was thought to be unclimbable and that evil spirits dwelled on the summit. This was Edward Whymper's eighth attempt (1st attempt: 1861) to climb the Matterhorn (age: 25). This ascent and the subsequent accident on the descent (four climbers fell to their deaths – *) ended the so-called "Golden Age of Mountaineering" (1854 – 1865) that included the first ascents of 180 peaks in the Alps.

3. EIGER – NORTH FACE

Location: Switzerland (Bernese Oberland Alps)
Elevation: 13,025 feet/3,970 meters
  North Face: 5,900 feet/1,798 meters
First Ascent Date: July 24, 1938
Summit Climbers:

Heinrich Harrer	Austrian	(1912 – 2006)
Fritz Kasparek	Austrian	(1910 – 1954)
Anderl Heckmair	German	(1906 – 2005)
Ludvig Vorg	German	(1911 – 1941)

Significance: This ascent was the fifth of the six great north faces in the Alps (see Appendix II, number 7) to be climbed. Prior to this successful ascent, eight mountaineers from Austria, Germany, and Italy had died while attempting to climb this vertical face. Even today, an ascent of the Eiger's north face is still considered a major mountaineering achievement.

4. ANNAPURNA

Location: Nepal (Himalayas)
Elevation: 26,545 feet/8,091 meters
First Ascent Date: June 3, 1950
Summit Climbers:
>Maurice Herzog (1919 – 2012) Leader
>Louis Lachenal (1921 – 1955) French Expedition

Significance: This was the first 8,000 meter peak in the world to be climbed and it was climbed on its first attempt. Very little geographical knowledge was known about Annapurna at this time. The French expedition had intended to climb Dhaulagiri (26,796 ft./8,167 m.) but could not locate the right approach route. They then decided to turn their attention to Annapurna. No supplemental oxygen was used. Expedition leader Maurice Herzog authored the classic mountaineering book *Annapurna* immediately after this climb. I believe that this ascent was more difficult and challenging than the Mount Everest first ascent three years later in 1953.

5. MOUNT EVEREST

Location: Nepal-Tibet border (Himalayas)
Elevation: 29,035 feet/8,849 meters
First Ascent Date: May 29, 1953
Summit Climbers:
>Edmund Hillary / New Zealand (1919 – 2008) New Zealand
>Tenzing Norgay Sherpa / Nepal and India (1914 – 1986) British Expedition

Significance: This was the first ascent of the highest peak in the world. The British Mount Everest Expedition of 1953 was the ninth serious expedition to attempt this ascent. Supplemental oxygen was used. As of December, 2011, there had been 3,684 mountaineers that had reached the summit of Mount Everest.

6. MOUNT EVEREST: WEST RIDGE

Location: Nepal-Tibet border (Himalayas)
Elevation: 29,035 feet/8,849 meters
First Ascent Date: May 22, 1963
Summit Climbers:
>Thomas Hornbein (1930 –)
>William Unsoeld (1926 – 1979) American Expedition

Significance: The West Ridge ascent represented both a new climbing route up Mount Everest and the first traverse of an 8,000 meter peak (Ascent: West Ridge. Descent: Southeast Ridge). Up until 1963, no one seriously considered that a traverse of Mount Everest was possible given the altitude, weather, and difficult climbing considerations.

7. MOUNT EVEREST: FIRST ASCENT WITHOUT USING SUPPLEMENTAL OXYGEN

Location: Nepal – Tibet border (Himalayas)
Elevation: 29,035 feet/8,849 meters
First Ascent Date: May 8, 1978
Summit Climbers:
    Peter Habeler (1942 –) Austria
    Reinhold Messner (1944 –) South Tyrol

Significance: Mountaineers had been warned for years not to venture above 26,000 feet without using oxygen. Many physiologists and experienced mountaineers thought that it was impossible to climb Mount Everest without using supplemental oxygen. Habeler and Messner had specifically trained and acclimatized themselves prior to this climb. Neither one suffered any lasting ill-effects from this ascent. They proved that the 8,000 meter peaks could be climbed without using supplemental oxygen if the proper preparations were made. Messner termed this approach "climbing by fair means."

8. MOUNT EVEREST: FIRST SOLO ASCENT

Location: Tibet (Himalayas)
Elevation: 29,035 feet/8,849 meters
First Solo Ascent Date: August 20, 1980
Summit Climber:
    Reinhold Messner (1944 –) South Tyrol

Significance: To climb Mount Everest alone, without using supplemental oxygen and by a new route (North Face and Great Couloir) in the post-monsoon season was thought to be impossible. In fact, the thought of this type of climb up the highest peak in the world did not even occur to most mountaineers. Messner very carefully prepared himself and his equipment (a 33 lb. pack, a camera, and an ice axe) to accomplish this three-day roundtrip climb from his Rongbuk Glacier base camp. Many mountaineers regard this ascent as the single greatest climb in mountaineering history.

9. SEVEN SUMMITS: FIRST PERSON TO CLIMB ALL SEVEN MOUNTAINS

Location: The highest peak on each of the world's seven continents.
Elevations: See below.
Ascent Dates (By Bass): See below.

Peak	Continent	Elevation Feet / Meters	Ascent Date
Mount Kilimanjaro	Africa	19,341 / 5,895	September 1, 1983
Mount Vinson	Antarctica	16,050 / 4,892	November 30, 1983
Mount Everest	Asia	29,035 / 8,849	April 30, 1985
Mount Kosciuszko*	Australasia	7,317 / 2,230	December 1983
Mount Elbrus	Europe	18,811 / 5,642	September 13, 1983
Mount McKinley**	N. America	20,320 / 6,193	July 6, 1983
Aconcagua	S. America	22,834 / 6,959	January 21, 1983

Significance: American mountaineer Richard Bass (1929 –) was the first person to climb all Seven Summits. This goal, however, had occurred to other climbers before Bass actually achieved it. A group of climbers had, in fact, reached four or five of the seven summits before Bass climbed Mount Everest (his final summit) on April 30, 1985. As of December, 2006 over 150 mountaineers from 40 countries had climbed all Seven Summits.

* Some believe the peak known as Carstensz Pyramid (16,023 F/4,883 M) in New Guinea is the highest peak in Australasia. Geographers and mountaineers continue to debate this controversy.

** Also known as Denali.

10. FOURTEEN 8,000 METER PEAKS: FIRST PERSON TO CLIMB ALL FOURTEEN PEAKS

Location: China – Nepal – Pakistan
Elevation Range: 26,286 ft./8,012 m. to 29,035 ft./8,849 m.
Time Period: 1970 – 1986 (15 years)
Summit Climber:
    Reinhold Messner (1944 –) South Tyrol
Final Summit:
    Lhotse 27,941 ft./8,516 m.
    October 16, 1986

Significance: After New Zealand mountaineer Edmund Hillary (1919 – 2008) and Tenzing Norgay Sherpa (1914 – 1986) reached the summit of Mount Everest on May 29, 1953, they were celebrated and presented many awards by numerous countries. They had just climbed the highest mountain in the world. These two men and the other climbers on this British Expedition were exhausted by their efforts over the past several months on the mountain. The thought of climbing another 8,000 meter peak did not occur to them. On June 27, 1970 mountaineer Reinhold Messner climbed Nanga Parbat (26,661 ft./8,126 m.) in Pakistan—his first 8,000 meter peak. After his 1980 solo ascent of Mount Everest, Messner's ambition was now to climb all fourteen 8,000 meter peaks and to do all of these climbs without using supplemental oxygen. As of 1980, he had summited five different 8,000 meter peaks. From 1981 – 1986, Messner climbed the remaining nine peaks.

As of 2011, twenty-seven mountaineers from fifteen countries had summited all fourteen 8,000 meter peaks.

INDEXES

"When my old body is finished, and dies, my soul will come to a place like this… It will travel all over the glaciers, which I love so dearly, and the sparkling snow fields, the deep blue crevasses and shining seracs—and the steep snow ridges and rock faces—and finally, with all the world at my feet, to sit exalted on my summit and just look, and look, and love it, deep, deep down in my soul."

Late 1940s
Phyllis Munday
Canadian mountaineer
(1894 – 1990)

GENERAL INDEX

Clothing & Equipment Index

T

W

Climbing Techniques Index

LIST OF MAPS

LIST OF MAPS IN THE APPENDIX

ABOUT THE AUTHOR

Fred Wolfe has been climbing mountains for over fifty years. He has climbed in Alaska, Arizona, California, Colorado, France, New Hampshire, Washington, West Virginia, Wyoming, Ireland, Italy, Mexico, Nepal, and Switzerland. He has reached the summit of over 400 peaks including all 54 peaks in Colorado over 14,000 feet. In addition to being a member of the American Alpine Club since 1989, Fred has served on the Board of Trustees for the Colorado Outward Bound School (1995 – 2005). He is currently on the Board of Directors for the Altitude Research Center Foundation within the Division of Emergency Medicine at the University of Colorado School of Medicine. He and his family have lived in Denver since 1971.

www.High-Summits.com

CPSIA information can be obtained at www.ICGtesting.com
Printed in the USA
LVOW09*0703210914

405068LV00007B/73/P